COMMON MARKET AND
AMERICAN ANTITRUST

THE EUROPEAN COMMON MARKET ANTITRUST PROJECT
OF THE
SPECIAL COMMITTEE ON THE
EUROPEAN COMMON MARKET
ASSOCIATION OF THE BAR OF THE CITY OF NEW YORK

———————●———————

Vols. I, II and III

*BUSINESS REGULATION IN THE COMMON
MARKET NATIONS*
Belgium, The Netherlands, Luxembourg
France and Italy
Germany

General Editor, HARLAN MORSE BLAKE

Vol. IV

COMMON MARKET AND AMERICAN ANTITRUST
Overlap and Conflict

Editor, JAMES A. RAHL

COMMON MARKET AND
AMERICAN ANTITRUST

Overlap and Conflict

JAMES A. RAHL, Editor

McGRAW-HILL BOOK COMPANY

New York   St. Louis   San Francisco   Düsseldorf   London
Mexico   Panama   Sydney   Toronto

COMMON MARKET AND AMERICAN ANTITRUST

Foreword

This is the fourth and last volume of the series sponsored and developed in the European Common Market Antitrust Project of our Special Committee. It describes and analyzes comprehensively instances of business conduct in foreign trade and investment that may encounter inconsistencies, and even collisions, between United States antitrust law and the growing body of foreign restrictive practice laws and related laws and policies of foreign nations. The foreign laws selected for primary attention for this purpose are those of the European Economic Community, the European Coal and Steel Community and the six member nations which have formed these Communities. The antitrust and other regulatory laws of the six member nations have been exhaustively analyzed in the first three volumes of this series.

This concluding volume contains an extensive analysis of the extraterritorial substantive and procedural scope of the antitrust laws of the United States. It also contains a substantial discussion of the antitrust laws of the European Communities and the Member States, including not only analysis of their extraterritorial features, but also a large amount of general discussion of key regulations, doctrines, policies and cases under the European laws as a necessary step in identifying the types of overlap and conflict which may arise. The book also examines various methods heretofore attempted internationally to accommodate the problems created by collisions of the kind which seem likely to occur between these systems of law. It should be added that in thus seeming to stress areas of collision we do not mean to minimize, and indeed we wish to draw attention to, possibilities of collaboration in reducing or eliminating the kind of stormy clashes that have sometimes occurred in the past between American antitrust enforcement and some other nations.

When we consider collision, it may grow directly out of the extraterritorial reach of any one or more of these systems of law. Difficulty is added when we note and examine basic national differences of approach towards business and the control of restrictive business practices. Despite these difficulties and differences, international trade and investment must pursue their activities as best they can. Their capacity to accommodate to whatever may be found as they cross national boundaries is impressive evidence of ability to adapt and conform and, perhaps too, of restraint on the part of governments in dealing with them. However, often there comes a point when conformity with one system of law and governmental policy may produce non-conformity with another and when penalty and burden may no longer be measured only under one or the other, but must be measured under both.

It is the view of the Special Committee that the problems created by potential and actual conflicts between systems of law in the field of trade regulation as applied to international trade are of sufficient importance to warrant attention now by government officials and legislatures as well as by private practitioners.

This volume represents the first major step in that direction in the statement and identification of the great number of legal, economic, political, social and diplomatic problems involved. This is a necessary prelude to what the Special Committee regards as an urgent task confronting the international community, national antitrust enforcement authorities and the legal and other specialists, professional and lay, in the area. That task is to devise ways and means of avoiding or at least minimizing predictable conflicts and difficulties before they happen.

We submit that the first task is to state and recognize the problems in this area. We further submit that when this has been done, enforcement authorities, courts and diplomats ought to be able to devise ways and means to avoid controversy or, at least, to hold it to a minimum with only whatever minimal sacrifice of the proper objectives of the applicable laws may be necessary. These objectives, no matter how they may differ between nations, are the objectives of nations whose respective systems of law stand as equals in the world.

The first five chapters of this book examine the development of American and Common Market antitrust laws and analyze the extent to which they overlap in scope and may conflict in their application. We introduce this first part with a chapter on the building of the European Economic and Coal and Steel Communities and their restrictive practice laws in the setting of other far-reaching objectives (Chapter 1). We continue with two chapters that state the extraterritorial reach of the antitrust laws of the United States, the general nature and extraterritorial scope of the laws of the European Communities and the extraterritorial scope of laws of the Member States, including discussion of procedural and enforcement problems that are involved (Chapters 2 and 3). We then turn to identification and analysis of the overlap, conflict and collision that may grow out of the extraterritorial situations presented. This is done in Chapter 4 in a detailed examination of a series of selected problem areas, including horizontal agreements with competitors, acquisitions and joint ventures, distribution arrangements, various types of patent license restrictions and governmentally-imposed restraints. This first part ends with a special chapter devoted exclusively to problems of territorial restrictions arising out of the existence of separate systems of industrial property law in the different nations involved (Chapter 5).

The last four chapters of the book go beyond the specific focus of relationships between Common Market and American law to identify broadly different approaches on the international level to the avoidance of antitrust-engendered conflict. This group begins with a chapter on the *Swiss Watch* case (Chapter 6), which is probably the most extreme example of collision between governmental policies in the antitrust field, and of the deep irritations which can be created by efforts of the United States to apply its antitrust law to an industry which is indispensable to the economy of a foreign country. The story of the case not only details the conflict itself, but also illustrates the difficulties which attend primary reliance upon a national court as the means of resolving international conflict. Remaining chapters review international ways and means that have been, and may be, employed to attempt to minimize and resolve antitrust conflicts. We here consider relevant principles of international law (Chapter 7); past efforts through treaties and international organizations (Chapter 8); and methods of international consultation, notification and cooperation that have been developed and practiced in recent years (Chapter 9).

Professor James A. Rahl of the Northwestern University School of Law was retained by the Special Committee as editor of this volume. He is also primary author of over a third of the book. His work has been outstanding. It is fair to say that this volume would never have been completed nor its quality achieved without his diligence, patience and thoughtful work as editor.

Below we acknowledge the diligence of the named Committee members and of Professor Rahl and Professor Peter Hay as to specific chapters. We do not mean to attribute all of the views expressed in these chapters to the named authors or to the editor, however. This book stands as a whole and it is one to which many expert minds have contributed. In the process, individual matters of opinion, sometimes strongly held, have necessarily been modified.

Professor Hay of the University of Illinois was retained for the specific purpose of writing the first chapter and the Special Committee acknowledges his contribution with gratitude.

Chapter 1	Peter Hay
Chapter 2	James A. Rahl
Chapter 3	James G. Johnson, Jr., André W. G. Newburg, Donald T. Fox, and James A Rahl
Chapter 4	James A. Rahl
Chapter 5	Lawrence F. Ebb
Chapter 6	G. Winthrop Haight
Chapter 7	Carlyle E. Maw, Isaac N. P. Stokes, and G. Winthrop Haight
Chapter 8	John D. Garrison
Chapter 9	Sigmund Timberg, Robert L. Werner, and John D. Garrison

We acknowledge again, as we did in the Foreword to the first volume of this series, our deep appreciation to The Ford Foundation for the grants that made this book possible.

Special Committee on the European
Common Market of The Association
of the Bar of the City of New York

Breck P. McAllister, Chairman

The Right Honorable Lord Devlin
Professor Henry P. de Vries
Lawrence F. Ebb
Donald T. Fox

John D. Garrison
G. Winthrop Haight
James G. Johnson, Jr.
Carlyle E. Maw

André W. G. Newburg
Isaac N. P. Stokes
Sigmund Timberg
Robert L. Werner

Preface

As this book goes to press, European Common Market authorities are engaged in a case involving the first major test of their power to enforce the Rome Treaty's antitrust provisions directly against foreign corporations with subsidiaries operating within the Common Market.[1] At the same time, American antitrust enforcement once again is increasing the tempo of its application to foreign firms and to American business operations abroad.[2]

Such proceedings are the stuff of which international antitrust conflict is made. For such enforcement activities often encounter two factors, either of which alone would be enough to give rise to the kinds of conflict with which this book is concerned. The most frequent is the presence of inconsistent laws of different jurisdictions which are applicable to the same parties or transactions. With one or both laws being of the public antitrust type, the rules of private conflict of laws do not apply and a choice of law by the courts or other authorities

---

[1] The *Dyestuffs* cartel case, pending on appeal to the Court of Justice of the European Communities from a decision of the EC Commission; see *infra*, 135-38.

[2] *E.g.*, the complaint filed by the United States in April, 1970 (too late for mention in the text of this book) against Westinghouse Corp., Mitsubishi Electric Corp. and Mitsubishi Heavy Industries, Ltd., alleging international patent licensing restraints and seeking compulsory licensing of both U.S. and Japanese patents (N.D. Cal.); see also the merger and joint venture cases involving foreign companies mentioned *infra* at 170, 175-78 and 183-85.

concerned is rarely possible; both sets of laws persist. A second factor sometimes present is a seeming infringement of the sovereignty of one of the nations concerned. Even if both have very similar laws, this factor can still produce trouble, as the history of antitrust relations between Canada and the United States vividly shows.

The United States was long the sole originator of this kind of conflict—not surprisingly, since it was long the only nation with a vigorous antitrust enforcement policy. Now it appears that it may have a companion in the Common Market. Eventually, others are also likely to join this company. Germany is the most probable, with its explicit statutory coverage of acts outside the country; and one or more other Common Market nations, as well as some nations whose antitrust laws are not dealt with in this book, are also possibilities. All nations are under increasing pressure to extend their laws to deal more effectively with the great expansion of international trade and investment, and with the rapid growth of "multi-national" enterprises.

While it is impossible for any existing sovereignty in this politically divided world to match its antitrust system fully to the dimensions of international business, it is possible for a given antitrust law to have a major impact upon some kinds of international restrictive or monopolistic practices which injure a nation's domestic or foreign trade interests. Such enforcement efforts may benefit other nations as well—American attacks upon international cartels have undoubtedly diminished the effectiveness of some of these cartels throughout the world. In the past, however, other nations have not wished to make such unilateral efforts. Many will doubtless continue a benign policy, expecting the same of others and preserving their full right to complain if another sovereignty's antitrust law seems to intrude. But the greater the importance attached to antitrust by a given sovereignty, the greater is the likelihood that it will consider applying its laws extraterritorially to international restraints. As the dimensions of business expand, these restraints may tend to increase in number and severity. Then the impulse to practice mutual sovereign territorial forbearance may yield to a stronger urge to expand the force of one's antitrust laws to the boundaries of relevant international markets. Concurrently, such a nation is likely to change its views as to what limitations are placed by principles of international law upon extraterritorial antitrust enforcement. This seems to have occurred in the United States, and it may be occurring in the Common Market.

With more and more nations adopting antitrust-type laws, the potentiality of international conflict thus seems definitely to be rising. There are, however, different levels of such conflict. Only occasionally does open dispute between nations break out. Far more often, the conflict of laws is on the less visible level of the day-to-day operations of firms which are subject to inconsistent rules. Such firms may suffer substantial or even prohibitive disadvantages from given types of conflict. On the other hand, some apparent conflicts at the working level may be of little significance, as there may be readily available alternatives which will avoid the problems entirely.

This book is an attempt to respond to the need stated by Mr. McAllister in his Foreword for a definition of the sources, types and seriousness of international antitrust conflict, with the United States and the Common Market as specific objects of study, and for an examination of past and present methods of dealing with these problems. The foreground focus of the book is on the outlines and principal features of conflict problems themselves. But the book also involves a second and longer focus upon the national and international law, history and governmental policies which constitute the background of the problems.

It is thus hoped that the book will have two kinds of utility: one for those whose concern is specifically that of solution of the international problems, and another for those who wish to learn more broadly about the operative antitrust laws and enforcement machinery of the United States and the Common Market and about international antitrust generally. At various points, directions for improvement are indicated. The book does not, however, seek to offer full blueprints either for the solution of conflict problems, or for the practical handling of the numerous other kinds of antitrust situations which arise in foreign transactions. This task must be pursued by those who follow.

About four-fifths of the book is devoted to European Common Market and American antitrust law, history and policy, and the remainder to discussion of general international approaches to antitrust issues. In the American portions, found primarily as parts of Chapters 2 through 6, the book carries on and extends work on issues of extraterritoriality done by Professor Brewster, Mr. Fugate, the Report of the Attorney General's National Committee to Study the Antitrust Laws, the American Bar Association's Antitrust Section Supplement to that Report, and the many other writers who have contributed much to this area.[3] It should probably be added that the book has not benefited a great deal from expressions of American judicial and administrative thought; for a field which has witnessed so much litigation, this one unfortunately has been relatively unenlightened by expositions in the formal opinions themselves, with a few exceptions. The American law treatment attempts more than a restatement of the work of others, and seeks to offer a more definitive statement and illustration of American foreign commerce doctrines, procedural and enforcement rules and practices, and substantive law principles in this area than appears to have been previously available. It is hoped that this will prove useful to Americans and non-Americans alike.

On the Common Market side, a still broader treatment has been sought. Chapter 1 is designed to give readers—especially Americans, but others as well—an overall view of the post-World War II setting in which the Common Market antitrust rules have developed. Chapters 2 through 5, in their European portions, seek not only to present a counterpart to American extraterritoriality doctrines (a very difficult task at this juncture because of the relatively small amount of case law available), but also to provide a more complete exposition of the general substantive and procedural antitrust law of the Common Market than was believed necessary for American law. Since this work on European laws has been done by Americans, it may be expected to suffer from some of the infirmities usually to be found in any work by foreigners. Efforts have been made to hold such errors to a minimum by resort to much of the rather substantial literature happily being generated in the English language by European writers, and by exposure of drafts of portions of the work to European experts in the United States and abroad. Insofar as the laws of the Member States of the European Communities are concerned, heavy reliance has been placed upon the first three volumes of this series, developed under the general direction of Professor Blake.

The conflict focus of the first six chapters is primarily upon the laws of the United States and the Common Market. While this largely involves a study of possible areas of conflict *between* these two sets of laws, as well as identifying the many areas in which there appears to be no likelihood of any conflict at all, the study is not limited to the American-and-Common Market relationship. Much of what is said is

[3] For bibliography, see *infra* at 54, note 13.

transferrable to relations of either of the latter with third countries. Indeed, the example of high conflict which is given the most detailed treatment, the *Swiss Watch* case (Chapter 6), does not involve Common Market law.

At the level of international approaches to conflict solution discussed in Chapters 7 through 9, the American-and-Common Market relationship is only incidentally involved, although of course the approaches dealt with there have relevance to that relation. These chapters, like the first six, rely much upon the scholarship and experience of others. At the same time, they represent what is believed to be the first instance of the drawing together into a unified discussion of a description and analysis of all of the chief types of international approaches to antitrust conflict solution and harmonization. While they do not offer comprehensive plans for change, it is hoped that they will supply a foundation for the needed innovations.

As the Foreword indicates, the authorship of this book is the joint and several work of a number of writers, all of whom are members of the Special Committee, except for the two outside academics retained by it. The list has a serious omission, however, in that it fails even to hint at the decisive role played by the Chairman of the Committee, Breck P. McAllister. The overall plan and scope of this work are mainly his doing—the product of his remarkably wide grasp of the entire area, and of his enlightened perception of the great need for improvement in the approaches used in the international antitrust field. The book simply would not have come into being without him. Moreover, he has been the indispensable leader and a vital participant at every stage of the writing, editorial and technical processes. Several of the chapter-drafts underwent substantial revision under his pen, and every paragraph was reviewed by him at both the draft and the proof stage. It has been a most rewarding experience to work with him, and with the outstanding committee which he heads.

One in my position might nevertheless be understandably apprehensive about serving as editor for such a relatively large and distinguished group of lawyers and writers, not to mention the further problem of coordinating my own written contributions with their work. But such fears quickly turned into admiration for the quality of their research and writing, and for their great patience and cooperation in accepting changes in both substance and style. Quite a few changes were urged by me in the interests of achieving a reasonably uniform level of argument, and it should be recorded that unquestionably these changes resulted in sacrifices by some of the contributors in the strength of statement of their views. Such modifications were always settled with good grace on their part, but none of them should be stopped from hereafter asserting a personally different position.

All concerned have also exhibited great patience with the time gap between completion of basic drafts of chapters and final publication, a problem largely due to my other commitments. If any of the data or citations are not the latest, it is I who must be held responsible.

Many persons have given valuable ideas and other forms of assistance at different times to each of the authors of the various chapters, and it is regrettable that it has not been possible to produce here a list of acknowledgments of such contributions. For their assistance to me in the overall production of the book, I do want to record here my great gratitude to the following: William G. Kelly, Jr. and George P. Sullivan, Jr. of the Northwestern Law Classes of 1970 and 1969, respectively, who checked the entire manuscript and contributed important research on a number of the problems; Bernice Le Beau, my secretary at Northwestern, and Niki Dimitrelias, my secretary at Michigan Law School during my visit there in 1970, both of whom contributed valuable secretarial assistance; and Eleanor B. Williams, Mildred Mitchell and Mary L. Donahue of the Northwestern staff, who typed and retyped portions of the manuscript.

Also, I wish to record my indebtedness to The Ford Foundation's grant for International and Comparative Legal Studies at Northwestern, which has heretofore supported general research by me in the area of antitrust and American business abroad, some of which has contributed to my work on this book; and to the General Electric Foundation, which also has contributed to my research, as well as supporting several graduate students working with me at various times in this area.

James A. Rahl

Contents

COMMON MARKET AND
AMERICAN ANTITRUST

CHAPTER 1 *The Building of the European Communities and Their Restrictive Practice Laws*

It is striking to contrast the condition of war-shattered Europe in 1945 with the assessment of its strength made in 1967 by Jean Rey, President of the European Commission,[1] in the context of the conclusion of the Geneva Kennedy Round negotiations in GATT:

> [T]he mere fact that we were united in the commercial field allowed us to speak as an equal with the United States. This is remarkable. Militarily, financially, industrially, we are less powerful, but the value and the volume of the European Economic Community's trade is greater than that of the United States. When I negotiated with my opposite number in Geneva, Ambassador William M. Roth, I spoke to him as an equal, and he knew it. We were absolutely comparable in power, this was one thing that gave us enough strength to make ourselves understood and to conclude with the Americans an agreement that both they and we consider balanced. The Kennedy Round has been an important lesson for Europe on how to conduct its relations amicably, but firmly, with the United States.[2]

The Common Market countries' political and economic come-back may indeed be the result of "one of the most important undertakings of the

[1]The European Commission is the common executive arm of all three Communities (EEC, ECSC, Euratom) since the ratification of the Treaty Establishing a Single Council and a Single Commission of the European Communities (Merger Treaty); an unofficial translation of the Treaty is reprinted in 1 CCH COMM. MKT. REP. ¶5115 (1967) and in STEIN & HAY, LAW AND INSTITUTIONS IN THE ATLANTIC AREA, 2: Documents 194 (1967).

[2]From An Interview with Jean Rey, European Community No. 109 (Feb. 1968) 4.

1

Twentieth Century," as a group of American businessmen had predicted in 1959.[3]

To provide a framework for the evaluation of current problems, this chapter traces the circumstances which led to the formation of the "Europe of the Six," recalls the objectives which the Common Market Treaty was designed to achieve, and sketches the progress of Treaty implementation and the course of the integration idea. Against this background, it may be possible to identify more easily the areas of actual and potential conflict between Common Market and American antitrust policies, as well as the possibilities of accommodation or, at least, the priorities which may be assigned to economic and political policy considerations.

I. THE FORMATION OF THE "EUROPE OF THE SIX"

A. Europe 1945-1947

In 1938, the countries which today form the European Communities had a combined gross national product of about $51 billion, compared with over $85 billion for the United States. Two years after the conclusion of World War II (1947), the European level had reached almost $80 billion, while the United States had skyrocketed to almost $235 billion.[4] The relatively small European increase, of course, reflected the ravages of war; in the case of Germany, in fact, the gross national product had decreased by over $11 billion from its 1938 level. The setback suffered by the German economy also appears from other comparative figures: assuming an index of 100 for the year 1958, German industrial production had reached 53 in 1938, compared with 33 for the United States, but fell to 27 by 1948 as against 73 for the United States in that year.[5] The physical destruction alone was enormous: 24% of all West-German dwellings were destroyed or heavily damaged; for Berlin, the estimate ranged up to 40%.[6]

---

[3] The European Common Market and Its Meaning to the United States, A Statement on National Policy by the Research and Policy Committee for Economic Development 19 (1959).

[4] U.N. 1966 YEARBOOK OF NATIONAL ACCOUNTS STATISTICS 681 (1967).

[5] U.N. 1966 STATISTICAL YEARBOOK 154 (1967).

[6] 10 ENCYCLOPAEDIA BRITANNICA 306 (1960).

Trade figures as well demonstrate the extent of economic distress. In the last full pre-war year—1938—the countries which today form the Common Market imported $5 billion and exported over $4 billion, incurring an imbalance of $760 million. In 1948, imports had doubled, but exports had not, and the imbalance was now almost $4 billion.[7] On the other hand, the strength of the American trade position was demonstrated by the fact that, while exports exceeded imports by only $901 million in 1938, post-war export surpluses fluctuated between $4 and $5 billion annually, with a highpoint of $9.5 billion in 1947,[8] much of this outflow no doubt reflecting increasing foreign aid.

In Europe, the immediate post-war years were years of great continuing problems resulting from the physical destruction; of unemployment—in some countries made more severe by the problems of refugees and displaced persons;[9] of black markets, trade deficits, and monetary instability;[10] and of the outflow of the last treasures of the national economies—in the form of relief projects, other holding actions, and reparations—without a point in sight where the corner would be turned.

B. Post-War Attitudes and the Beginning of International Cooperation

1. RECONSTRUCTION: MARSHALL PLAN AND OEEC

It was against this background of economic need, and the helplessness of those caught up in it, that then Secretary of State George C. Marshall in 1947 proposed the American economic aid program which was to become a lasting monument to his name. A far-sighted condition of the proffered help was that the Europeans themselves agree on the establishment of some cooperative mechanism. This led to the creation

[7]U.N. 1965 YEARBOOK OF INTERNATIONAL TRADE STATISTICS 14-15 (1967). These comparisons exclude exports and imports of gold.

[8]*Id.* at 814.

[9]For instance, in Germany the total population had decreased from 68,578,000 in 1938 to 65,899,000 in 1946. In West Germany, however, there had been an increase from 43,008,000 in 1939 to 46,190,000 in 1946, without counting refugees of foreign nationality in camps maintained by the IRO; U.N. Monthly Bulletin of Statistics (Dec. 1948); 1967 STATISTISCHES JAHRBUCH FÜR DIE BUNDES-REPUBLIK DEUTSCHLAND 27.

[10]For instance, the far-reaching devaluation (10:1) of the German Mark in 1948.

in 1948 of the Organization for European Economic Cooperation (OEEC),[11] buttressed on the American side by the adoption of the aid program known as the "Marshall Plan." Eighteen European countries participated in OEEC.[12] The Soviet Union declined the invitation to participate, wishing rather to make up its own "shopping list of imports to be bought with United States aid,"[13] as did the other Eastern-bloc states. One of them, Czechoslovakia, first accepted but subsequently yielded to Soviet pressure to withdraw.[14]

Although it was active in many fields,[15] three achievements of OEEC stand out as lasting contributions. In the area of trade, the most serious post-war impediment was the existence of quantitative restrictions or quotas. Their removal was difficult because of a second problem, *i.e.,* the then existing payment system which required bilateral clearing of accounts and, therefore, balanced terms of trade of every country with every other country.[16] The establishment of the European Payments Union (EPU)[17] within the OEEC in 1950 provided a multilateral clearing system to solve this second problem. Financed by a United States contribution of $350 million, EPU cleared its members' accounts monthly and on a multilateral basis. Settlements required of members amounted to an average of 40% of debits (in gold), with credits available for the financing of the remainder. The regional solution of the payments problem also facilitated removal of trade barriers. A "Code of Liberalization" was adopted by OEEC, providing for staged quota increases by members from a common base year (1948).[18] Both EPU

[11] Great Britain, Foreign Office, 1949 Treaty Series No. 59, Cmnd. 7796. For a history of this organization see OEEC, A DECADE OF COOPERATION, 9th REPORT OF THE OEEC 19 (1958).

[12] Austria, Belgium, Denmark, France, Germany, Greece, Iceland, Ireland, Italy, Luxembourg, Netherlands, Norway, Portugal, Spain, Sweden, Switzerland, Turkey, United Kingdom. Canada and the United States were associate members.

[13] OEEC, *supra* note 11, at 21.

[14] STEIN & HAY, LAW AND INSTITUTIONS IN THE ATLANTIC AREA 322 (1967).

[15] See Elkin, *The Organisation for European Economic Cooperation: Its Structure and Powers,* 4 EUROPEAN Y.B. 96 (1958).

[16] The General Agreement on Tariffs and Trade (GATT), adopted in 1947, permits quotas to safeguard the balance of payments (Article XII), and hence provided no help for the solution of this problem.

[17] 1951 BUNDESGESETZBLATT II, 31. See also STEIN & HAY, *supra* note 14, at 321-22.

[18] A later reference year was adopted for Austria and Germany whose 1948 trade was still too small to serve as a meaningful reference.

and the Code were every effective and contributed significantly to the restoration of international trade in Western Europe. By the end of 1958 all Common Market countries had reached or exceeded the quota liberalization target of 90%.[19]

The advent of free currency convertibility in 1958 permitted the replacement of EPU with the European Monetary Agreement (EMA),[20] which provides for monthly clearing in U.S. dollars, and under which credit financing is no longer automatic but requires special application and payment within two years. By 1958 also, the trade imbalance of the EEC countries had been reduced to only $180 million.[21] Both EPU and the Code thus provided much of the base on which the Common Market could build. Indeed, the EEC Treaty adopted the Code level of liberalization as the starting point in its Article 31, thus "freezing" the members' ability to introduce new quotas at that level, and provided for a staged removal of all remaining quota barriers in Articles 33 and 34. And Article 106 could provide, quite simply, that members shall make foreign exchange available for all liberalized trade.

OEEC's third achievement was institutional and procedural. It consisted of the OEEC practice of conducting an annual "confrontation" at which each Member State had to justify its economic policies to the group, particularly with respect to its use of Marshall Plan aid. Even if the organization lacked power to issue binding decisions and recommendations as a result of such confrontations, the procedure was nevertheless very useful. It provided states with the incentive to review their policies, with the need in some cases of persuading others of a policy's value or necessity, and with the opportunity to have their key officials develop close working relations.[22] It attests to the value of this procedure that it was retained when the OEEC was reconstituted as the Organization for Economic Cooperation and Development (OECD) in 1960, in which Canada, the United States, and Japan (since 1964) are full members.[23]

Cooperation in this period also took other forms, all of them,

[19] Ouin, *The Establishment of the Customs Union,* in 1 AMERICAN ENTERPRISE IN THE EUROPEAN COMMON MARKET: A LEGAL PROFILE 101, 113-14 (Stein & Nicholson eds. 1960).

[20] 1959 BUNDESGESETZBLATT II, 1016. See also note 17 *supra.*

[21] U.N. 1965 YEARBOOK OF INTERNATIONAL TRADE STATISTICS 14-15 (1967).

[22] See CURTIS, WESTERN EUROPEAN INTEGRATION 68-70 (1965).

[23] STEIN & HAY, *supra* note 14, at 931. The OECD Convention may be found in T.I.A.S. 4891 (effective Sept. 30, 1961).

however, still mainly relating to immediate problems. In the military field, the Brussels Treaty Organization in 1948 translated war-time alliances and the post-war (1947) Franco-British Dunkirk Treaty into institutional form—the Western Union[24] —comprising the Benelux countries, France, and the United Kingdom. Communist expansion in Eastern Europe prompted the further enlargement of the defense shield through the establishment of NATO in 1949,[25] and the Western European Union in 1955.[26] In the economic field, the emphasis was on reconstruction under OEEC and consultation through the UN Economic Commission for Europe.[27] Only minimal attention was given to attempts to build closer unions; indeed the only concrete integration effort was that of the Benelux Economic Union, begun in 1944 and consolidated through further agreements in 1949 and 1960.[28]

2. THE EARLY BASES OF FUTURE INTEGRATION

In addition to the great technical achievements of OEEC, the immediate post-war years provided the legal and political bases for the integration efforts of the Fifties. The idea of European unity, of course, is not new. Indeed, since medieval times the division of Europe produced intermittent proposals and plans for unification—to recreate the unity of the Church,[29] express the humanism of the Renaissance, or secure to all the enlightenment of the French Revolution. Rousseau,[30] Kant,[31] and Bentham[32] were its early advocates, followed by Briand and

[24] BALL, NATO AND THE EUROPEAN UNION MOVEMENT 9-12 (1959).

[25] T.I.A.S. 1964 (effective Aug. 24, 1949). For discussion of the origins of NATO, see MOORE, NATO AND THE FUTURE OF EUROPE 24 (1958); for the Vandenberg Resolution, S. Res. 239, 80th Cong., 2d Sess., 94 CONG. REC. 7791, 7846 (1948).

[26] The Western European Union was formed to permit German membership in NATO. It is in fact the former Brussels Treaty Organization (Western Union)—reconstituted and enlarged by the addition of Germany and Italy, and given the power to control the maximum armaments of its members in Europe. See BALL, *supra* note 24.

[27] See generally, United Nations Department of Economic and Social Affairs, Five-Year Prospective: 1960-1964, E/3347/Rev. 1-2 (1960).

[28] STEINBERGER, GATT UND REGIONALE WIRTSCHAFTSZUSAMMENSCHLÜSSE 26-27 (1963).

[29] DUBOIS, DE RECUPERATIONE TERRAE SANCTAE (1305-7).

[30] ROUSSEAU, PROJET POUR LA PAIX PERPETUELLE (1760).

[31] KANT, VOM EWIGEN FRIEDEN (1795).

[32] BENTHAM, PLAN FOR AN UNIVERSAL AND PERPETUAL PEACE (1843).

Coudenhove-Kalergi[33] during the period between the Great Wars. Yet despite common cultural traditions and romanticized views of historic unity, the facts of political reality were otherwise. The assumption of the continued existence of the Holy Roman Empire, until its destruction by Napoleon,[34] did not prevent the Austro-Prussian War of 1749. The building of great national states in Germany and Italy, as well as the competition for colonial empires, were but few of the counter-forces.

By the end of World War I, the state system had become rigid, with victor and vanquished confronting each other in continued animosity. Common economic needs and the depression were insufficient to overcome these factors, not to mention the social upheavals (*e.g.,* in Germany), which sought the maintenance of the traditional state, but one oriented toward a new philosophy. World War II showed the limitations inherent in the traditional concept of the European state and provided the impetus which permitted the cultural and historic notions of European unity to find political expression. However, many contemporary signs (*e.g.,* the 1965 Common Market crisis, the French attitudes toward supranationalism) point again to a more traditional conception.

Three post-war constitutions of European nations provided for limitation of state sovereignty in favor of a collective international entity, or for particular limited purposes. The statements were vague, but no concrete institutions existed which might have served as models. The Preamble of the French Constitution of 1946 provided that "[on] condition of reciprocity, France accepts the limitations of sovereignty necessary to the organization and defense of peace." The Preamble of the 1958 Constitution incorporated this statement by reference. Article 11 of the Italian Constitution of 1947 provides that Italy "agrees, on condition of equality with other states, to the limitations of her sovereignty necessary for an order which is to assure peace and justice

[33] COUDENHOVE-KALERGI, PANEUROPA (1923). For discussion of the history of European unity movements and ideas see Albonetti, *Vorgeschichte der Vereinigten Staaten von Europa,* 22 SCHRIFTENREIHE ZUM HANDBUCH FÜR EUROPÄISCHE WIRTSCHAFT (1961); v. Puttkamer, *Historische Pläne europäischer Verfassungsbildung,* in FESTGABE FÜR CARL BILFINGER 345 (1954); Meyer-Cording, *Die europäische Integration als geistiger Entwicklungsprozess,* 10 ARCHIV DES VÖLKERRECHTS 42 (1962).

[34] In 1806, when Francis II renounced the Roman imperial title and took the title of Emperor of Austria.

among nations. . . ." And the 1949 German Constitution states in Article 24(1): "The Federation may, by statute, transfer sovereign powers to international institutions."[35] In addition, both the Netherlands and the Luxembourg Constitutions, dating from 1815 and 1868 respectively, were amended in 1953-56 and 1956 to assure conformity of constitutional law with the then existing European Coal and Steel Community and with contemplated further integration.[36]

3. THE COUNCIL OF EUROPE

The first political expression of the new "supranational idea" was the call of the "Congress of Europe" (held in the Hague in 1948 and attended by over 700 participants from 16 countries) that "[t]he nations of Europe must create an economic and political union . . . and for this purpose they must agree to merge certain of their sovereign rights."[37] The Congress called for a European Consultative Assembly, a Charter of Human Rights, and a Court of Justice, all of which were realized in the Statute of the Council of Europe which was signed in 1949 and in the human rights conventions subsequently sponsored by the Council.[38] In the history of European international organizations, the Council of Europe represents a significant development. The Brussels Treaty took the form of an alliance, with scant provision for institutions, and OEEC placed major emphasis on governmental obligations. The Council of Europe, however, for the first time provides comprehensive international machinery for international cooperation in Europe (consultations, draft treaties for harmonization of laws, and the like).[39] The forward-looking call of the Congress of Europe—almost revolutionary when judged by the state-orientation of traditional law—had borne fruit.

The greatest achievement of the Council was its quick implementation, in 1950, of the Hague Congress' call for a Human Rights Convention and a Human Rights Court, a call which had also been expressly adopted as one of the Council's aims in its Statute. The Convention has been ratified by all members of the Council, except

[35] For interpretation of this provision see HAY, FEDERALISM AND SUPRANATIONAL ORGANIZATION 273-89 (1966).

[36] See text following note 181 *infra.*

[37] Quoted after ROBERTSON, THE LAW OF INTERNATIONAL INSTITUTIONS IN EUROPE 11 (1961).

[38] *Id.* at 87.

[39] *Id.* at 23.

France, Malta, and Switzerland.[40] It is treated as domestic law in several states,[41] and it imposes international obligations on all the states. Further, it provides remedies to many nationals—even as against their own governments—before international tribunals,[42] a monumental achievement for international law.[43]

Beyond the human rights field, however, actual accomplishments of the Council of Europe have in some cases fallen short of expectations. The lack of decision-making power in the Committee of Ministers and the purely advisory role of the Assembly deprive the Council of effectiveness in many areas. While it has been very active in collecting and making available data and studies, and has sponsored a variety of conventions, with respect to both public and private law subjects,[44] relatively few of these efforts have produced changes in the domestic law of the members.[45] In these fields, the great value of the Council has been in providing a forum for consultation, sometimes for cooperative action. But integration in the sense of a central decision-making body has not been achieved, owing not only to the initial structure of the organization but also to the diversity and number of states it embraces (eighteen as of 1968). The evolution of that kind of a "supranational" institution was left to the more homogeneous Six of the European Coal and Steel Community of 1951 (ECSC) and the European Economic, and Atomic Energy, Communities of 1958 (EEC and Euratom).

---

[40] 213 U.N.T.S. 221 (1955). Late in 1969, Greece withdrew from the Council because of a question of its compliance with the Convention. The Council also sponsored the European Social Charter (European Treaty Series No. 35 [1961]) which took effect in 1965 upon ratification by Denmark, Germany, Ireland, Italy, Norway, Sweden, and the United Kingdom.

[41] Buergenthal, *The Effect of the European Convention on Human Rights on the Internal Law of Member States,* INT'L & COMP. L.Q. SUPP. No. 11, 79 (1965).

[42] The Convention establishes a Commission and a European Court before which private parties have standing if the defendant state has accepted Article 25 (right of individual petition to the Commission) and Article 46 (compulsory jurisdiction of the Court). Eleven states have accepted Article 25 and ten have accepted Article 46.

[43] For a collection of cases and further references to literature see STEIN & HAY, *supra* note 14, ch. VIII.

[44] Baade, *The Council of Europe: Its Activities Relating to Law,* 15 AM. J. COMP. L. 639 (1967); Krüger, *The Council of Europe and Unification of Private Law,* 16 AM. J. COMP. L. 127 (1968).

[45] See Hay, *The United States and International Unification of Law: The Tenth Session of the Hague Conference,* 1965 U. ILL. L.F. 820, 822 n. 11.

**C. From International Cooperation to Supranational Institutions:
The Building of the European Communities**

1. THE CONCEPT OF SUPRANATIONALISM

Institutions set up by treaties traditionally do not possess law-making powers because such powers would be difficult to fit into traditional notions of international law, whose only subjects are sovereign states. States conclude treaties, to which they may or may not give the force of domestic law,[46] and thereby define the extent of their obligations. Institutions created by treaty, even in the rare cases in which they possess independent decision-making power,[47] do not have domestic law-making power. Their decisions create international obligations, but do not achieve effectiveness in a member's internal law without implementing action by that member state. Hence, when domestic legislation differs or is lacking, a breach of the international obligation may occur, but no way exists for injured individuals to seek redress.

Thus, from the viewpoint of international law theory as well as from that of efficiency in the practical realization of an organization's goals, the "supranational" form of institutional organization developed in the Europe of the Fifties represents a revolutionary advance. Probably only two previous organizations had displayed "supranational" characteristics—the German Zollverein,[48] and the Danube Commission.[49] But both had been mere technical organizations, and neither possessed functions so comprehensive as those ultimately conferred upon the European Communities. Yet, the Zollverein especially has often been recalled in discussions of the ECSC and of the Common Market, both to explain their origin and as an argument for their expansion.[50]

In the modern context, the "supranational idea" was first expressed in the summer of 1949.[51] A proposal in the Consultative Assembly of the

[46]Compare U.S. CONST., art. VI, with English law, WADE & PHILLIPS, CONSTITUTIONAL LAW 39, 212-14 (5th ed. 1955).

[47]HAY, *supra* note 35, at 31.

[48]*Id.* at 4 n.25.

[49]*Id.* at 4 n.26.

[50]Keeton, *The Zollverein and the Common Market,* in ENGLISH LAW AND THE COMMON MARKET (16 CURRENT LEGAL PROBLEMS) 1, particularly at 14-16 (Keeton & Schwarzenberger eds. 1963); Schwarzenberger, *Federalism and Supranationalism in the European Communities, id.* 17, 22.

[51]The following is based on Robertson, *Legal Problems of European Integration,* 91 HAGUE ACADEMY RECUEIL DES COURS 105, 143-48 (1957).

Council of Europe called for "the creation of a coordinated administration of economic and technical organizations on a supranational plane. . . ." But the debate on this proposal showed how little concrete legal meaning this term held for many delegates. One referred to the Committee of Ministers of the proposed organization as a "European Cabinet in embryo," while another envisioned "a supranational functional organization which would be subordinated to all governments." The first time the concept was used in today's sense was by the great proponent of the ECSC, Robert Schuman, when he outlined to the Consultative Assembly of the Council of Europe the plan which was later to bear his name. Of the proposed High Authority, he said that it would "be the first example of an independent supranational organization." The final text of Article 9, paragraphs 5 and 6 of the ECSC Treaty, reflects this view. It provides:

> The members of the High Authority shall exercise their functions in complete independence, in the general interest of the Community. In the fulfillment of their duties, they shall neither solicit nor accept instructions from any government or from any organization. They will abstain from all conduct incompatible with the supranational character of their functions.
>
> Each member State undertakes to respect this supranational character and not to seek to influence the members of the High Authority in the execution of their duties.

A "supranational" organization is a combination of several attributes,[52] including: (1) independence of the organization and of its institutions from the member states, as illustrated by the ECSC provision quoted above; (2) the ability of the organization to bind its members by majority vote; and (3) the direct binding effect of law enacted by the organization on natural and legal persons in the member states, *i.e.,* without implementation by national legislative organs. The direct binding effect of the organization's law especially distinguishes such an organization from the traditional form of international organization described earlier. Illustratively, Article 189 of the EEC Treaty provides that "[r]egulations shall have general application. They shall be binding in every respect and directly applicable in each Member State. . . ." The ECSC and Euratom Treaties contain similar provisions.[53]

Direct law-making power alone, however, while a novel feature in an

---

[52] HAY, *supra* note 35, at 30-31 with references.
[53] ECSC Treaty arts. 14-15, Euratom Treaty art. 161.

international organization, perhaps does not distinguish supranational from traditional international organizations because member states may still be free to supersede the treaty or organization law by subsequent and inconsistent domestic legislation. In the Communities, the supremacy of Community law (consisting of the Treaty and actions of the Community institutions) is ensured in some countries as a matter of constitutional law.[54] For others, supremacy over national law is evolving as a constitutional principle, reinforced by the landmark decisions of the Court of Justice of the Community which claims such supremacy as a matter of Community constitutional law.[55] Hence, as a matter of law in some cases, and of fact in others, the establishment of the Communities does indeed represent a *transfer* of national sovereign powers and the creation of a new legal entity:

> The contribution of the Communities to legal science is the breaking-up of the rigid dichotomy of national and international law. The Treaties and the Communities' experience demonstrate that an alternative to the creation of treaty-based obligations for the solution of common problems is the constituting of a *lawmaker* with authority to prescribe norms which bind their addressees. Thus the focus is neither on the specific substantive provisions nor on the completed federal edifice. The central point is that, *while forming*, the Communities fashion intermediate forms of law which are neither national nor international law. It is municipal law in effect, federal in structure, but not national in origin.[56]

Once the planned integration and the accompanying legal structure are complete (perhaps even expanded to include other sectors of cooperation), the Communities may appear to the outside world, with respect to the areas subject to their jurisdiction, like any other federated nation-state.

[54] See text following note 171 *infra*.

[55] N.V. Algemene Transport- en Expeditie Onderneming van Gend & Loos v. The Netherlands Fiscal Administration, 9 Recueil de la Jurisprudence de la Cour 1 (1963); Costa v. ENEL, 10 *id.* 1141 (1964). For comment see HAY, *supra* note 35, at 165-75; Stein, *Toward Supremacy of Treaty-Constitution by Judicial Fiat in the European Economic Community*, 48 RIVISTA DI DIRITTO INTERNAZIONALE 3 (1965).

[56] Hay, *The Contribution of the European Communities to International Law*, 59 PROC. AM. SOC. INT'L L. 195, 199 (1965).

2. FROM ECSC TO EEC

It is no accident that this far-reaching concept for the structuring of international cooperation was first employed in the Coal and Steel Community. Coal and steel pose special economic problems in Europe.[57] In addition, the desire of the United States, as NATO's chief paymaster, to resolve the question of a German contribution to the alliance made an international solution for control of the Ruhr complex particularly urgent. The establishment of the ECSC was therefore desirable for a variety of reasons: it would serve as an effective control of an important part of the German war potential; it could help to eliminate Franco-German friction and historic jealousies in the area of heavy industry; and it was desirable on the German side, because agreement on the ECSC would permit the termination of the International Agreement on the Ruhr which Germany regarded as unduly burdensome. The immediate objective of Franco-German cooperation and the long-term goal of European integration envisioned by Adenauer, de Gasperi, Monnet, and Schuman therefore were equally important.[58]

The pressure from the Allies for German rearmament also resulted in other proposals. Almost simultaneously with its proposal of ECSC, the French Government also advanced the idea of a European Defense Community (EDC). While ratification of that Treaty was pending, the Six also began work on a Draft Treaty for a European Political Community (EPC). The latter was to assume the functions of the institutions under the ECSC and EDC Treaties, but would gradually expand until complete federation would result. Both treaties contained references to the "supranational" character of the Communities.[59] But the projects proved too ambitious, and what had worked for the limited sector of coal and steel could not as yet be duplicated in the more sensitive areas of defense and political policy. Between 1950 and 1954, only Germany had ratified the EDC Treaty, after protracted internal controversy over the desirability and constitutional legality of

[57]See DIEBOLD, THE SCHUMAN PLAN 380-90 (1959). See generally SCHEIN-GOLD, THE RULE OF LAW IN EUROPEAN INTEGRATION: THE PATH OF THE SCHUMAN PLAN (1965).

[58]DIEBOLD, *supra* note 57, at 383; Steindorff, *Europäische Gemeinschaft für Kohle und Stahl,* in 1 STRUPP & SCHLOCHAUER, WÖRTERBUCH DES VÖLKERRECHTS 458, 459 (2d ed. 1960).

[59]MATHIJSEN, LE DROIT DE LA COMMUNAUTE EUROPEENNE DU CHARBON ET DE L'ACIER 147 n. 8, 148 (1958).

rearmament.[60] On August 30, 1954, the French Assembly defeated the proposal and thereby rendered the EPC project obsolete. The immediate issue—German rearmament—had to be resolved in other ways: enlargement of the Brussels Treaty Organization to include Germany and Italy; its renaming to "Western European Union"; giving it power to supervise German armaments; and, thereupon permitting German and Italian membership in NATO. The long-range objective—European integration—had become stalemated.

New efforts began in 1955 with the calling of the Messina Conference of the six foreign ministers. The new initiative was due in part to continued pressure by such "pro-European" forces as Jean Monnet, who had also served as first President of the ECSC High Authority, and his "Action Committee." It was also due to the realization that the development of nuclear energy in Europe could only be achieved through a pooling of resources, and to the Suez crisis which had once more emphasized Europe's lack of economic independence.[61] The Messina Conference led to the creation of an inter-governmental committee under the chairmanship of Paul Henri Spaak. The "Spaak Report," approved in 1956 in Venice, became the basis for the drafting of the EEC and Euratom Treaties, both of which were ratified by the six states in less than a five-month period in 1957.[62] Neither treaty, however, contains a reference to "supranationalism." The omission was deliberate and sought to assure adoption of the treaties at a time when the rejection of EDC and EPC was still a painful reminder of political sensitivities on "supranationalism."[63] One government, Germany, nevertheless explained the EEC Treaty Proposal to its Parliament as establishing a "supranational Community equipped with sovereign powers."[64]

---

[60]See Smend, *Gutachten zum Wehrbeitrag,* 2 KAMPF UM DEN WEHRBEITRAG 561 (1953); Menzel, *Die Geltung internationaler Verträge im innerstaatlichen Recht,* 1962 Sonderveröffentlichung von RABELS ZEITSCHRIFT FÜR AUSLÄNDISCHES UND INTERNATIONALES PRIVATRECHT 401, 406.

[61]Stein, *An American Lawyer Views European Integration: An Introduction,* in 1 AMERICAN ENTERPRISE IN THE EUROPEAN COMMON MARKET: A LEGAL PROFILE, *supra* note 19, 1 at 3.

[62]For references to national ratification statutes, see Stein, *supra* note 61, at 3 n. 4.

[63]Jaenicke, *Supranationale Organisation,* in 3 STRUPP & SCHLOCHAUER, WÖRTERBUCH DES VÖLKERRECHTS 423, 424 (1962).

[64]Germany, Erläuterungen der Bundesregierung, Bundestags-Drucksache No. 3440 (2. Legislaturperiode) 108 (1957).

The extent of EEC "supranationalism" has continued to be a matter of political dispute, and the sharp differences of opinion between the Community under President Hallstein and French President de Gaulle in part precipitated the crisis of 1965. Yet, the polemic smokescreen cannot hide nor reverse the fact that the Community possesses and has exercised very far-reaching powers of economic legislation, that its action has fundamentally affected, and often changed, the economic posture and the law of the Member States, and that this position of power and influence, in the wide sector of activity subject to its intervention and action, had made it into a supranational force which eclipses the earlier ECSC effort. The "Merger Treaty" of 1965,[65] under which the functions of the hitherto separate EEC, ECSC, and Euratom Councils and executive bodies (Commission, High Authority, and Commission, respectively) have been merged into a single European Council and European Commission, does not increase the powers of the institutions; the single Commission continues to administer three separate treaties. Yet, inevitably a unified policy will result. The merged institutions are a first step toward a merger of the substance of the treaties. And pending treaty projects which relate only peripherally to the existing treaties (*e.g.,* on recognition of judgments, bankruptcy, and a "European" company law) will all further enhance the relative position of the "Community." An evolutionary trend is thus clearly discernible, even if formal and explicit work toward political integration has not been resumed since the days of EPC and seems as remote today.[66]

II. THE COMMUNITIES IN OPERATION: ORIGINAL OBJECTIVES AND THEIR MODERN IMPLEMENTATION

A. Introduction: Customs Union, Common Market, Community

All three European organizations are called "Communities," rather than "customs unions," "free trade areas" (in the case of the ECSC), or "common markets," although the Treaties also use these terms. There is little doubt that their use was intended to convey differences in meaning

---

[65] *Supra* note 1. For detailed discussion of the Merger Treaty see Houben, *The Merger of the Executives of the European Communities,* 3 C.M.L. REV. 37 (1965); Thompson, *The Leiden Meeting,* 15 INT'L & COMP. L.Q. 276 (1966).

[66] See STEIN & HAY, *supra* note 14, at 1108-16.

and scope. The history of the EEC Draft Treaty shows this. Its original title was "Common Market," but during subsequent negotiations this term was moved to Article 2 and subordinated to the term "Community" which became the final designation of the organization.[67]

How do these concepts interrelate? On the lowest level of the EEC structure, to put the terms in some hierarchical order, is the "customs union."[68] It is designed to merge the four customs territories into one,[69] so that trade within the union will no longer face barriers (tariffs, quotas and other restrictions with like effect), and so that the new union will be protected against the outside world by a common external tariff and a common commercial policy. On a higher, still technical level, is the concept of the "common market." Beyond free trade it contemplates integration of the economies by providing conditions for the optimal use of the benefits of free trade. This category includes the Treaty provisions dealing with the right of establishment of companies, with the free movement of labor and capital, with the free supply of services across national frontiers, and with the maintenance of competition.

The terms, "customs union" and "common market," describe operational functions of the EEC. The "community" concept indicates the direction of development of the structure. The EEC was created to promote "a harmonious development of economic activities, a continuous and balanced expansion, an increased stability, an accelerated raising of the standard of living and closer relations between its Member States" (Article 2). This purpose is realized through a variety of common policies with respect to agriculture, transport, business cycles, and fiscal problems. Provision is made for the "harmonization," "approximation," or "coordination" of national law,[70] for the advance commitment to

[67]WOHLFARTH, EVERLING, GLÄSSNER & SPRUNG, DIE EUROPÄISCHE WIRTSCHAFTSGEMEINSCHAFT, KOMMENTAR ZUM VERTRAG, n.1 to art. 1 at 3 (1960).

[68]EEC Treaty arts. 12-29. For a discussion of the economics of customs unions see VINER, THE CUSTOMS UNION ISSUE (1950); on customs unions and GATT, see STEINBERGER, *supra* note 28; on the history of customs unions, Pescatore, *Les relations extérieures des Communautés européennes,* 103 HAGUE ACADEMY RECUEIL DES COURS 1, 74-80 (1961).

[69]Benelux, France, Germany, Italy.

[70]See Stein, *Assimilation of National Laws as a Function of European Integration,* 58 AM. J. INT'L L. 1 (1964).

engage in additional unification-of-law projects,[71] and—perhaps most important—for the creation of supranational institutions with law-making power, as previously discussed.

This view of the EEC emphasizes the significant difference between it and typical customs unions and free trade areas (for instance, the European Free Trade Area) not only in extent of coverage but also in orientation and institutional structure. Though at present limited by its basic economic purpose, it bears out the Preamble's statement that the contracting states sought "to establish the foundations of an ever closer union among the European peoples."

B. Translating Objectives into Reality

1. THE TRADE PROVISIONS

a. In General

In economic theory, the customs union established by the EEC Treaty means simply that internal barriers to trade are removed, a common external tariff wall is established as against the outside world, and within the area economic benefits may therefore be realized from "optimization of trade" and "maximization of production" as a result of increased economies of scale.[72] But the theoretical desirability of free trade is one thing, its achievement in practice quite another. Opening national frontiers to foreign production will cause serious injury to certain long-protected domestic industries and consequently to employment. And free trade is not even indicated for certain sectors of the economy by reason of social, defense, or other key considerations (*e.g.,* agriculture and transport). Free trade in practice must therefore be selective with respect to the sectors of the economy included, subject to escape provisions, and combined with domestic measures for relief from the effects of dislocation.

The EEC Treaty guards in a variety of ways against potential dislocations and injury. Trade barriers were dismantled only gradually

---

[71] EEC Treaty art. 220: non-discriminatory treatment of EEC nationals, elimination of double taxation, mutual recognition of companies, recognition and enforcement of judgments and arbitral awards.

[72] MEADE, PROBLEMS OF ECONOMIC UNION 9-13 (1953). See also JOHNSON, THE WORLD ECONOMY AT THE CROSSROADS 8-19, 37-45 (1965).

over a flexible transitional period which could be extended for a total of fifteen years from the entry into force of the Treaty in 1958. In fact, economic conditions permitted faster progress for industrial goods and the transitional period terminated as to them on July 1, 1968. During the transitional period, additional relief was available to countries in the form of special tariff quotas,[73] temporary escape from Treaty obligations in the case of domestic economic difficulty,[74] "mutual aid" for balance-of-payments difficulties,[75] and for the effects of trade diversion.[76] Some of these, such as the trade-diversion section, were used frequently; others, rarely (for instance, the balance-of-payments relief[76a]).

b. Agriculture

Agricultural products were another matter. European agricultural production is structurally different from that in North America in that small-scale farming still predominates, and automation and economic returns consequently are lagging. The social problems which abrupt change would create appear from the demographic figures: the farm population in the Six still represents 14.5% of the population, compared with 6% in the United States (in 1965). The present EEC level compares more closely with the United States in 1950, when farm population still represented 16% of the population.[77] The difference in *kind* of

[73] EEC Treaty art. 25. See EEC COMMISSION, TENTH GENERAL REPORT ON THE ACTIVITIES OF THE COMMUNITY 67 (1967).

[74] EEC Treaty art. 226. For brief comparison of EEC, EFTA and GATT safeguard clauses see Hay, Cooley & Moorhead, *Problems of United States Participation in the European Common Market,* 23 U. PITT. L. REV. 595, 626-27 (1962).

[75] EEC Treaty arts. 104-09. For discussion see Millet, *The Economic Policy,* in INTERNATIONAL MANUAL ON THE EEC 117, 118-19 (Junckerstorff ed. 1963); Everling, *Die Koordinierung der Wirtschaftspolitik in der Europäischen Wirtschaftsgemeinschaft als Rechtsproblem,* RECHT UND STAAT 296/297, 19-22, 24-26 (1964).

[76] EEC Treaty art. 115. For discussion, in the context of East-West trade, see Hay, *Some Aspects of East-West Trade in Britain, Germany and the Common Market,* 1 STUDIES IN LAW AND ECONOMIC DEVELOPMENT 122, 135-37 *passim* (1966). See also EEC COMMISSION, *supra* note 73, at 306.

[76a] For a notable exception in the setting of the 1968 French economic crisis, see 1968 E.C.J.O. Aug. 1 at 13; July 25 at 15; Dec. 7 at 10.

[77] See FOOD AND AGRICULTURAL ORGANIZATION OF THE UNITED NATIONS [U.N. FAO], 1966 PRODUCTION YEARBOOK 15, 18 (1967). "Agricultural population is generally defined as all persons who depend upon agriculture for a livelihood, that is to say persons actively engaged in agricultural occupations and their non-working dependents;" U.N. FAO YEARBOOK OF FOOD AND AGRICULTURAL STATISTICS 245 (1952).

agricultural activity—large scale versus relatively small scale family farming—is also demonstrated by the figures. In 1959, the United States had 457,500,000 acres under permanent crops, and in 1965 had a farm population of 11,700,000. In the EEC, the farm population in 1965 was still 25,900,000, but acres under permanent crops amounted to only 114,500,000.[78] As a result, agriculture in Europe historically has required a planned economy with heavy reliance on subsidies, price support systems, and other means in addition to traditional trade-regulation devices such as tariffs and quotas.

The EEC Treaty therefore does not subject agricultural trade to the general customs union provisions. Instead, it calls for a "common agricultural policy" which provides special temporary rules for agriculture within the customs-union framework,[79] and which will bring about "common organizations" for certain sectors of the agricultural economy. Several such "market organizations" now exist—for example, that for grain.[80] All involve a levy and pricing system. In the case of grain, domestic target prices determine the "threshold price" of a product upon entry. Variable levies, plus or minus a *montant forfaitaire* to benefit EEC-Member trade and discourage non-Member trade, assure that imported grain meets the threshold price, and a system of governmental intervention avoids fluctuations of more than 10% from the target price.[81] The goal of a single market is to be achieved by a gradual approximation of national target prices and subsequent elimination of intra-EEC levies.[81a]

c. Adjustment Assistance

The gradual adjustment to the single market, both in the industrial and agricultural sectors, softens the blow but does not prevent all

[78] U.N. FAO 1966 PRODUCTION YEARBOOK 3 (1967).

[79] See Hjorth, *The Common Agricultural Policy: Crisis in the Common Market,* 40 WASH. L. REV. 685 (1965); Riesenfeld, *Common Market for Agricultural Products and Common Agricultural Policy in the European Economic Community,* 1965 U. ILL. L.F. 658; Dam, *The European Common Market in Agriculture,* 67 COLUM. L. REV. 209 (1967).

[80] Regulation 19, 1962 Journal Officiel des Communautés Européennes 936 [hereinafter cited E.C.J.O.]; see 1 CCH COMM. MKT. REP. ¶438, amended by Regulation 50/66, 1966 E.C.J.O. 1282. For discussion see references in note 79 *supra.*

[81] For details see Hjorth, *supra* note 79.

[81a] Late in 1969, the Six reached important agreement on the financing of EEC farm policy and budgetary powers of the Commission; CCH EUROMARKET NEWS, Dec. 22, 1969.

dislocations. The cost of these falls largely on the individual countries, with some help from the Community. As with the ECSC before it, the EEC undertakes to share some of the burden, mainly through the creation of the European Social Fund.[82] With funds provided by the Member States, the Fund reimburses a Member State for 50% of its expenses in providing retraining, resettlement, and unemployment compensation during the period of an enterprise's conversion to other production. The European Investment Bank,[83] with a capital of $1 billion, also plays a role in the adjustment process. Its financing authority extends to "projects for developing less developed regions, . . . projects for modernizing or converting enterprises or for creating new activities which are called for by the gradual establishment of the Common Market . . . , [and to] projects of common interest to several Member States. . . ."

Adjustment problems, as well as subsequent spill-overs of economic problems, are alleviated by means of "common policies." The "mutual aid" provision for balance-of-payments problems was mentioned earlier; the "policy relating to economic trends" (Article 103) is another example. Article 103 is far less specific than comparable ECSC provisions which permit the Community to intervene by means of production quotas, price floors and ceilings, and other such regulatory devices.[84] Instead, the provision calls rather generally for "consultation" regarding economic trend policy, but also empowers the Community to take "appropriate measures" by directive.[85] As a result, the provision is a potentially far broader, and perhaps more effective, instrument in the case of cyclical problems than exists for the ECSC.

2. SECURING THE BENEFITS OF FREE TRADE: FREE MOVEMENT OF WORKERS, COMPANIES, AND CAPITAL

The benefits of free trade are maximized if it is accompanied by freedom of movement for the factors and instruments of production. If

---

[82] EEC Treaty arts. 123-28.

[83] EEC Treaty arts. 129-30.

[84] Millet, *supra* note 75, at 118.

[85] "Directives," as distinguished from "regulations," do not have direct and immediate effect in the national law of the Member States; they are addressed to a Member State and bind it to implement the objective prescribed in the directive. EEC Treaty art. 189.

companies are able to move to the sources of labor and materials, if workers can move to areas of high employment opportunity, and if capital can take advantage of investment opportunities as well as serve as the necessary concomitant for the movement of companies, then free trade can mean more than national specialization within the limits of national resources. Instead, the resources of the entire area will support the optimization of production.

Yet mobility of these economic factors has been singularly limited since World War I. Various economic problems led to a closing of national labor markets,[86] and by the 1950's all six EEC countries utilized a wide variety of regulatory devices and administrative practices to control and protect domestic employment.[87] Similarly, the movement of capital was restricted by means of exchange control and licensing requirements in response to economic problems. Even today, obligations of Members under the Articles of Agreement of the International Monetary Fund extend only to "payments for current transactions," and not, as a rule, to capital transfers.[88] The movement of companies, finally, has been impeded by a variety of factors, including exchange restrictions on direct investments or on the repatriation of profits or of investment capital, restrictions on foreign ownership of local companies (either by controls relating to the percentage of ownership or to the sector of the economy or both), and by the widespread company-law concept of "seat" which, for practical purposes, precludes transnational transfers and mergers of companies.[89]

Against this background, the EEC Treaty's objective of a single market in goods, labor, companies, services, and capital is ambitious, and progress has also been impressive. Two major regulations[90] have

---

[86] See Lewin, *The Free Movement of Workers,* 2 C.M.L. REV. 300 (1964).

[87] See Reisner, *National Regulation of the Movement of Workers in the European Community,* 13 AM. J. COMP. L. 360 (1964).

[88] See GOLD, THE INTERNATIONAL MONETARY FUND AND PRIVATE BUSINESS TRANSACTIONS: SOME LEGAL EFFECTS OF THE ARTICLES OF AGREEMENT 9-14, 16-20 (1965) for a discussion of Articles VIII and XIV.

[89] Hay, *Four Lectures on the Common Market: Trade Provisions—German and French Company Law—Establishment,* 24 U. PITT. L. REV. 685, 754-57 (1963). However, on February 29, 1968, the Member States signed a new Convention Relating to the Mutual Recognition of Companies and Legal Persons which, in the meantime, has been ratified by France. The text of the Convention may be found in CCH COMM. MKT. REP. ¶6083 (1968).

[90] Regulation 15, 1961 E.C.J.O. 1073, superseded by Regulation 38/64, 1964 E.C.J.O. 965, 1 CCH COMM. MKT. REP. ¶1031.

substantially removed preferences in favor of a Member's own labor market; major steps have been taken for the removal of capital controls;[91] and the establishment of companies (including subsidiaries) and the rendition of services across frontiers has been facilitated.[92] And even the thorny "seat" problem and the related problems of corporate transfer and merger now seem closer to solution.[93]

3. PROTECTING COMPETITION

The Communities have been extraordinarily innovative in dealing with restrictive practices and problems of economic power, *i.e.,* in antitrust law. Until the ECSC Treaty in 1951, such laws were rare among the Six and in Europe generally. At the war's end, France and the Netherlands had laws governing certain forms of cartels and restrictive practices, but these provisions were not used to enforce a general regime of competition.[94] The occupation of Germany brought with it decartelization measures, but the modern German law itself was not enacted until 1958.[95] Belgium adopted a law in 1960 which is limited to control over

[91] Summarized in STEIN & HAY, *supra* note 14, at 792-96.

[92] General Program for Removal of Restrictions on the Right of Establishment, 1962 E.C.J.O. 36, 1 CCH COMM. MKT. REP. ¶1335, and the Council's First Implementing Directives, 1964 E.C.J.O. No. 117, 1 CCH COMM. MKT. REP. ¶1349.51-.671; General Program for the Removal of Restrictions on the Free Supply of Services, 1962 E.C.J.O. 32, 1 CCH COMM. MKT. REP. ¶1545. See also STEIN & HAY, *supra* note 14, at 772-88; Hay, *supra* note 89, at 751-66; EEC COMMISSION, *supra* note 73, at 75-79.

[93] *Cf.* Convention Relating to the Mutual Recognition of Companies and Legal Persons, 2 CCH COMM. MKT. REP. ¶6083 (1968). Additional proposals are also still under consideration; see Memorandum from the French Government to the EEC Council for the creation of a "European-type Commercial Company," 2 CCH COMM. MKT. REP. ¶9025 (1965). See also Conard, *Corporate Fusion in the Common Market,* 14 AM. J. COMP. L. 573 (1966); Storm, *Statute of a Societas Europea,* 5 C.M.L. REV. 265 (1967); Thompson, *The Creation of a European Company,* 17 INT'L & COMP. L.Q. 183 (1968); Albrecht and Schulze-Brechmann, *Die nationale und internationale Unternehmenskonzentration, unter besonderer Berücksichtigung einer Europäischen Handelsgesellschaft,* 1968 AUSSENWIRT-SCHAFTSDIENST DES BETRIEBS-BERATERS 81.

[94] See Reboul, *Horizontal Restraints under the French Antitrust Laws: Competition and Economic Progress,* 19 VAND. L. REV. 303 (1966).

[95] For comprehensive treatment of the antitrust laws of each Member State, see BUSINESS REGULATION IN THE COMMON MARKET NATIONS (Blake ed. 1969): vol. 1 (Benelux nations); vol. 2 (France and Italy); and vol. 3 (Germany). See also Riesenfeld, *Protection of Competition,* in 2 AMERICAN ENTERPRISE IN THE

abuse of economic power, and Italy and Luxembourg still have no anti-trust laws.

In this light it seems at first surprising that the ECSC Treaty should contain such strong antitrust provisions, and indeed their exact origins have never been revealed. But at least a partial cause was doubtless the cartelization of the Ruhr, which worried the French and also concerned the occupation authorities who had pursued decartelization and decon-centration policies.[96] In fact, High Authority President Jean Monnet flatly stated in his opening speech to the Common Assembly in May of 1954 that GEORG—the German coal market cartel[97]—could not be authorized in its then existing form.

The reason for the inclusion of strong antitrust provisions in the EEC Treaty is more obvious: a general industrial common market requires for its success that private parties be prevented from reestablishing barriers to free trade—by agreements or by the exercise of monopoly power—which the trade provisions of the Treaty are designed to dismantle. In the United States, the need for legislation protecting competition became clear only after the Industrial Revolution had occurred, and long after free interstate commerce was established. In the EEC, where the task is to join countries with an existing high level of industrial development, such legislation was a necessary element at the outset of the creation of free interstate commerce.

The need for antitrust legislation as a part of free trade was emphasized as early as 1953 in a report of an advisory committee of the German Ministry of Economic Affairs.[98] Also, the "Spaak Report" of 1956, which contained the original recommendations for the establish-ment of the EEC, dealt extensively with this problem. It recommended that anticompetitive and monopolistic practices be curbed if they contravened the objectives of the common market by dividing markets, for example, or by limiting production, or by market domination.[99]

EUROPEAN COMMON MARKET: A LEGAL PROFILE, *supra* note 19, at 197, 207-94.

[96] RACINE, VERS UNE EUROPE NOUVELLE PAR LE PLAN SCHUMAN 94 (1954); Riesenfeld, *supra* note 95, at 299.

[97] DIEBOLD, *supra* note 57, at 380 *et seq.*

[98] Gutachten des Wissenschaftlichen Beirats des Bundesministers für Wirtschaft vom 1. Mai 1953, MINISTERIALBLATT DES BUNDESMINISTERIUMS FÜR WIRTSCHAFT 143 No. 45.

[99] COMITE INTERGOUVERNEMENTAL CREE PAR LA CONFERENCE DE MESSINE, RAPPORT DES CHEFS DE DELEGATION AUX MINISTRES DES

The conception of the role of antitrust laws as essential to, and supportive of, the free trade objective of the customs union provisions has remained a central theme in the pronouncements of the EEC Commission and of the Court. Examples are the statements of Commissioner von der Groeben, and the Court's view of the problem in the *Grundig-Consten* case, both discussed below.

As the next chapter indicates more fully, the ECSC and EEC treaties (Articles 65 and 85 respectively) prohibit agreements which prevent, restrict, or distort competition in the Common Market, provided effect on trade between Member States is also shown. These prohibitions would be very similar to those of American law but for the fact that they are modified by allowance for administrative exemptions under standards of public interest, efficiency and competition. Also prohibited, without possibility of exemption, is the abuse of dominant power (Articles 66 and 86).

The ECSC Treaty differs from the EEC Treaty in its approach to the problem of price discrimination. The EEC reaches this practice only if it occurs as a result of collective action or a dominant position, whereas Article 60 of the ECSC Treaty, like American law, applies to single-firm price discrimination, and also establishes a rigid system for price publication and price "alignment." One commentator remarked on this: "Monnet's specific proposals on market rules . . . were accepted in essence in the final version of the Treaty, including the rigorous interpretation of Article 60 which made 'non-discrimination' almost the equivalent of 'no price competition,' a deliberate device to limit the flow of German steel to the French market."[100] In practice, however, the rigidity of price publication was softened by the producers' ability to reduce their prices to match lower prices quoted at any one of forty-one basing points. It has been argued that this "right of alignment serves a vital Community purpose, for it promotes inter-market penetration, thus advancing the cause of a common market. . . ."[101] While secret rebating obviously violates the non-discrimination principle of Article 60, alignment of prices, especially as to "semi-fictitious" foreign offers, has

AFFAIRES ETRANGERES 16, 17, 23, 53 (1956). See also the official commentary of the German Government submitted to the German Parliament during the course of the ratification debates in *Gemeinsamer Markt,* 1 SCHRIFTENREIHE ZUM HANDBUCH FÜR EUROPÄISCHE WIRTSCHAFT 223 (1957).

[100] HAAS, THE UNITING OF EUROPE 245 (1958).

[101] SCHEINGOLD, *supra* note 57, at 57.

the same effect. Yet, alignment does introduce some flexibility and thereby also somewhat reduces the great differences in approach between the Treaties.[102]

The other basic difference between the EEC and the ECSC approaches is as to their treatment of mergers. Without attempting to restructure the existing market, Article 66(1) of the ECSC Treaty undertakes to control and check the rise of concentration by subjecting the acquisition of "control" by one enterprise over another to prior approval of the High Authority. In this fashion, the deconcentration policies of the Allied authorities in West Germany could be secured and maintained for the future.[103] In contrast, neither Article 85 nor Article 86 of the Rome Treaty expressly undertakes to deal with mergers, although a small amount of room may remain for such application.[104]

The limited control of mergers has been emphasized as a good thing in policy statements of EEC officials. For example, EEC Commissioner von der Groeben said in 1965 that the Commission, as part of its policy for industrial growth, "must remove artificial obstacles to mergers that are economically desirable within the Common Market and thus ensure that Common Market firms can compete on world markets."[105] He left the door open a little for use of Articles 85 and 86, "when the merger really amounts to a cartel, that is, when there is no irreversible change in the ownership situation but . . . merely a case of market understanding between independent business concerns,"[106] or when "an enterprise in a dominant position approaches monopoly by merging with another enterprise and consequently endangers the freedom of action and choice

---

[102]*Id.* at 57-58. The ECSC publication requirement nevertheless makes for a more rigid system, and early attempts of the High Authority to permit limited departures from the published price lists—the 2.5% "Monnet Margin"—were held by the Court of Justice to violate the Treaty. SCHEINGOLD, *supra* note 57, at 58-70. For purposes of a workable system of competition, Article 60 demonstrates the pitfalls of the adoption of highly specific models and preconceptions in statutory form.

[103] Riesenfeld, *supra* note 95, at 314.

[104] See Chapter 2 *infra*; EEC Commission, Memorandum to the Governments of the Member States, Dec. 1, 1965, CCH COMM. MKT. REP. No. 26 (separate print) 52-66; Von der Groeben, *Competition Policy as Part of Economic Policy in the Common Market,* 1965 BULLETIN OF THE EUROPEAN ECONOMIC COMMUNITY No. 8, at 5.

[105] Von der Groeben, *supra,* at 5 *et seq.*

[106]*Id.*

of suppliers, buyers and consumers," thus perhaps committing an abuse.[107]

In the ECSC, which started with a seemingly opposite statutory policy, the actual development has been somewhat similar to the EEC situation, resulting in supervision but not in prohibition of mergers. The contrast here with American policy is probably due to differences in market structure and in economic attitude. While 10 firms accounted for 80% of U.S. steel production in 1961, 35 firms made up this percentage in the ECSC.[108] Additionally, the original post-war objectives with regard to deconcentration in Germany began to fade as integration proved successful. Statistics show this development quite strikingly: as of December 31, 1967, the High Authority had taken up 328 merger cases under Article 66, of which 255 came to it as part of an application for authorization and 73 were examined by it on its own initiative. Authorization was granted in 146 cases; one case was "examined" under Article 66; in 13 cases the concentration was found to have been effected before the signing of the Treaty; 24 cases were exempt under implementing regulations to Article 66(3); in 80 cases Article 66 was found "inapplicable"; 12 cases were withdrawn, the project dropped, or "otherwise handled"; and 52 were still pending.[109]

Some of the concentrations authorized were quite significant, such as the acquisition of a 60% interest in Hadir by Arbed which gave these companies a 23% share of the ECSC market in wide-flanged beams,[110] and the steady expansion of the German firm of August Thyssen Hütte.[111] The High Authority publicly acknowledged this development in 1967:

> As can be seen from the particulars of the cases in which authorization was given, enterprises were out even more than in the previous year to face up to

[107]*Id.* See also Hefermehl, *Unternehmenszusammenschlüsse im Lichte der Artikel 85 und 86 des Vertrages über die Europäische Wirtschaftsgemeinschaft,* in RECHTS-VERGLEICHUNG UND RECHTSVEREINHEITLICHUNG 329 (1967).

[108]Buxbaum, *Antitrust Regulation Within the European Economic Community,* 61 COLUM. L. REV. 402, 415-16 (1961).

[109]Commission of the European Communities, ERSTER GESAMTBERICHT ÜBER DIE TÄTIGKEIT DER GEMEINSCHAFTEN 56 (1968).

[110]ECSC HIGH AUTHORITY, FIFTEENTH GENERAL REPORT ON THE ACTIVITIES OF THE COMMUNITY 157 (1967).

[111]*Id.* at 161; see also extracts from prior reports in STEIN & HAY, *supra* note 14, at 558-59.

the stiffening competition by organizing link-ups and cooperation agreements for purposes of rationalization; as a result, the size of the operators in the already oligopolistic steel market further increased, and their number further diminished.

One or two general observations should be made in this connection on the subject of competition as such, which is becoming a matter of some concern, quite apart from the particular cases dealt with by the High Authority in the course of the year. More specifically, the trend towards industrial concentration has been the subject of much debate in business and political circles of all kinds, as well as in the academic world. . . .

It is no part of the purpose of the present section to go into details of the conclusions reached in this debate insofar as there have been any. There appears on the face of it to be pretty general agreement that concentrations can be a help in coping with tougher economic conditions, that they are usually preferable to cartels, that they are not the universal remedy for all possible ills, and that while they tend to reduce the number of market operators they can result in more active competition among those that are left. . . .

The High Authority's policy with regard to cartels and concentrations is based on passages in the Treaty which are often considered unduly constricting and no longer appropriate to present circumstances. This is not the place to discuss this question in detail: the point to be borne in mind is that the High Authority has continued to construe and apply the Treaty's provisions on cartels and concentrations—in full conformity, incidentally, with the basic provisions, and in particular with Articles 2-5—in a manner which has enabled the economy to move with the times.

With this end in view, the High Authority some time ago worked out and submitted to the Council of Ministers a new set of arrangements with regard to exemption from prior authorization for certain types of concentration.[112]

Despite original differences, then, the administration of EEC and ECSC antitrust law has moved closer together and, in the ECSC case, further away from the American concept of competition. Coal and steel, however, is a special case, and the permitted oligopolistic trend of that market has little predictive value for sectors subject to the EEC Treaty. But in any event, neither the ECSC nor the EEC has shown much concern about mergers (in the latter, this is subject to future developments, including the degree of foreign domination—of which there is hardly any in the ECSC[113]). The control and supervisory mechanisms of the Treaties are more often utilized and perhaps more effective than the prohibitory approach, and market growth and expansion with "reason-

[112] ECSC HIGH AUTHORITY, *supra* note 110, at 151.
[113] *Id.* at 164.

able" competition has taken the place of earlier post-war notions of American origin, particularly as introduced in Germany.

The evolution of new and more functional control and supervisory mechanisms is shown most clearly by EEC practice under Article 85. The first implementing legislation for that provision--Regulation 17/62[114] – provided for notification to the EEC Commission of most agreements falling within the prohibition of Article 85(1). Exemption under Article 85(3) could be granted only upon application,[115] and a flood of notifications ensued. By March 31, 1967 there had been 37,014 cases before the Commission, a net increase of 127 over the prior year.[116]

Given a small enforcement staff and the fact that the Commission necessarily must accord priority to actual complaints,[117] and to investigations which it deems particularly crucial,[118] the effectiveness of the notification system is open to serious question, as it brought in a large number of unimportant cases. On the other hand, experience has shown that certain kinds of cases arise with great frequency and may be susceptible to "group treatment." This is true, for instance, of exclusive dealing agreements—indeed, over 31,000 of the notifications received by the Commission concerned such agreements[119] —and of patent licenses. The Commission's first attempt to sort out the good from the bad took the form of two "Official Notices" published late in 1962,[120] in which it outlined its view as to the applicability of Article 85(1) to contracts concluded with commercial agents and to certain patent licenses.[121]

---

[114] 1962 E.C.J.O. 204, 1 CCH COMM. MKT. REP. ¶2411, as amended by Council Regulation 59/62, 1962 E.C.J.O. 1655, 1 CCH COMM. MKT. REP. ¶2441.

[115] Reg. 17, arts. 4(1), 5(1).

[116] EEC COMMISSION, *supra* note 73, at 85.

[117] *Id.* at 87.

[118] *Id.* at 88.

[119] *Id.* at 84.

[120] Official Notice Concerning Contracts for Exclusive Representation Concluded with Commercial Agents, 1962 E.C.J.O. 2921, 1 CCH COMM. MKT. REP. ¶2697; Official Notice Concerning Patent Licensing Agreements, 1962 E.C.J.O. 2922, 1 CCH COMM. MKT. REP. ¶2698. For other policy statements of the Commission, see Chapter 2 *infra*.

[121] The Court of Justice endorsed the Commission's view that contracts concluded with commercial agents do not fall within the prohibition of Article 85(1). Italy v. EEC Council and EEC Comm'n, 12-4 Receuil de la Jurisprudence de la Cour 563. CCH COMM. MKT. REP. ¶8048, 5 Comm. Mkt. L.R. 97 (1966): EEC COMMISSION, *supra* note 73, at 84.

A more far-reaching innovation was Council Regulation 19/65,[122] authorizing the Commission to grant exemption under Article 85(3) to certain types of exclusive dealing agreements and license restrictions as a group. The great usefulness of this device, compared with the Commission's Official Notices and negative clearance practice,[123] of course, lies in the fact that the Commission may now deal in wholesale fashion with many agreements technically falling within the prohibition of Article 85 but which nevertheless are economically harmless or even desirable. In its Regulation 67/67,[124] the Commission exercised the new authority and exempted as a group exclusive dealing agreements which satisfy certain conditions. These conditions codify the result of the *Grundig-Consten* litigation,[125] that such agreements must not bring about a new isolation of national markets through restrictions on re-exports or parallel imports.[126] The power to grant group exemptions enabled the Commission to reduce its backlog of cases by 13,037 in 1967.[127]

The evolution of the Community antitrust law is surely one of the most fascinating and significant developments in the process of European integration—both substantively and institutionally. Substantively, this process demonstrates the search for new socio-economic concepts for the building of a modern industrial market economy, unfettered by the philosophic and economic biases of another century.[128] Institutionally, the development of antitrust law has contributed significantly to the building and definition of the "federal" relation between Community law and the national law of the Member States. Regulation 17 allocates antitrust jurisdiction between national and Community authorities, sometimes providing for exclusive Community jurisdiction,[129] sometimes for concurrent jurisdiction with a power of preemption in the

---

[122] 1965 E.C.J.O. 533, 1 CCH COMM. MKT. REP. ¶2717.

[123] The negative clearance procedure is provided by Reg. 17, art. 2.

[124] 1967 E.C.J.O. 849, 1 CCH COMM. MKT. REP. ¶2727.

[125] Ets. Consten S.A. and Grundig-Verkaufs-GmbH v. EEC Comm'n, 12-4 Recueil de la Jurisprudence de la Cour 429, CCH COMM. MKT. REP. ¶8046, 5 Comm. Mkt. L.R. 418 (1966).

[126] See Fulda, *The Exclusive Distributor and the Antitrust Laws of the Common Market of Europe and the United States*, 3 TEXAS INT'L L.F. 209-33 (1967).

[127] Commission of the European Communities, *supra* note 109, at 59. See Chapter 2 *infra* for discussion of Commission decisions in individual exemption and negative clearance cases, and in extraterritorial application of the law.

[128] See Buxbaum, *Antitrust Policy,* in STEIN & HAY, *supra* note 14, at 517.

[129] *E.g.,* for exemption under Article 85(3); Reg. 17, art. 9(1).

Community.[130] When national jurisdiction is exercised, the interest of the Community in uniform solutions may be realized either through exercise of the preemptive power,[131] or through ultimate review of national action by the Community Court of Justice.[132] This allocation and balancing of jurisdiction is the mainspring of the supranational organization of the Community and will undoubtedly be an important factor in such an active field as antitrust administration.

C. Along with Development and Achievement–Some Reaction and Uncertainty

1. PROBLEMS OF ECONOMIC POLICY

In terms of internal economic direction, there is the question of proper direction and orientation now that the free trade market has been achieved. Should the Community be a free or planned (*dirigiste*) market economy, and should it be inward and protectionist-oriented, or press for free trade on an expanded regional or international level? The first problem was the subject of a celebrated exchange between the then German Minister of Economic Affairs Erhard and then EEC Commission President Hallstein on the occasion of the Commission's submission of its "Action Programme for the Second Stage." Mr. Erhard criticized the Program as representing undesirable economic planning: "It seems to me important to recognize . . . that two different systems cannot exist side by side. It is impossible to pursue, on the one side, competition and, on the other, planning, planification or programmization." President Hallstein replied—and this has become a consistent position of Commission members[133]—that Community intervention does not amount to "restrictions affecting the participants in the market place but operate[s] against the public authorities which so far have restricted the activity of the individual. Their sole purpose is to safeguard the freedoms which the

[130] Reg. 17, art. 9(3).

[131] See *id.* and generally STEIN & HAY, *supra* note 14, at 600-01 n.76.

[132] By means of the procedure of EEC Treaty art. 177, considered in text following note 184 *infra.* For summary of Court of Justice decisions in antitrust cases, see Chapter 2 *infra,* note 94.

[133] See Von der Groeben, *Policy on Competition in the European Economic Community,* Supplement to the 1961 BULLETIN OF THE EUROPEAN ECONOMIC COMMUNITY Nos. 7-8; Von der Groeben, *supra* note 104.

Treaty accords."[134] The Commission's position, however, is only partially responsive. The diversity and extent of national restrictions on trade and economic activity require action by the Community to *create* the free market which may then be responsive to the forces of competition alone. The question is rather how far, beyond this, the Community should influence the direction and kind of economic development. This question faces all economies.[135]

In the United States, economic growth and development are influenced through indirect governmental measures—*e.g.,* fiscal and tax policies, and governmental promotion of science, research and development through use of budgetary resources in such areas as defense, space, and health—but direct planning is lacking. In fact, it has been suggested that the structure of the economy does not require it, indeed that the economy performs better without it.[136]

In Europe, attitudes and practices are more disparate. To the Germans, the free market economy became an article of faith when it produced the post-war economic miracle, even though the original boom slowed down appreciably in the early 1960's.[137] In contrast, France has

[134] European Parliament, VERHANDLUNGEN, AUSFÜHRLICHE SITZUNGS-BERICHTE 872, 892, 894 (1962).

[135] The Community, it will be remembered, has now emerged from the position of economic weakness and dependence in which it found itself after World War II to become a highly advanced economy in which many factors and influences must achieve a proper balance. The achievements in trade ($52.6 billion in exports in 1966, compared with $30.0 billion for the United States, U.N 1966 YEARBOOK OF INTERNATIONAL TRADE STATISTICS 13 [1968]), and the increases in per capita income (from $780 in 1958 to $1,350 in 1966, compared with $2,115 and $3,153 for the United States) and in gross national product (from $166.4 billion in 1958 to $322 million in 1966, compared with $455.0 billion and $756.5 billion for the United States)—all demonstrate the rapid growth of a very complex economic system. Comparisons with 1947 of course are even more impressive, when Community gross national product stood at $79.7 billion and that for the United States at $234.78 billion. See OEEC, STATISTICS OF NATIONAL PRODUCT AND EXPENDITURE 304 (1954); U.N. 1967 YEARBOOK OF NATIONAL ACCOUNTS STATISTICS 825/832 (1968).

[136] See "Advances in Economic Policy-Making in the United States," Remarks by Otto Eckstein, Member, Council of Economic Advisers, mimeographed release by the Executive Office of the President, Council of Economic Advisers (1965), reprinted in STEIN & HAY, *supra* note 14, at 839-41.

[137] The slowdown led to the introduction of some planning measures in 1967: 15. Gesetz zur Änderung des Grundgesetzes vom 8.6. 1967, BUNDESGESETZ-

long pioneered "indicative" planning,[138] analyzing the market, establishing targets, and securing adherence through limited governmental controls, various incentives and occasional intervention (such as particular investment prohibitions). To her, the benefits of planning consist in stimulating growth consciousness, coordinating and balancing investment, and permitting "society to set detailed economic goals in a systematic and quantitative way."[139]

To what extent the Community will follow at least "indicative" planning is not clear from the Commission's statements, yet the record does indicate some influence of the French model. Its assumption of "major responsibilities for long-term policies in a number of sectors— such as agriculture, energy, and transportation— . . . will require the same perspective of the overall economic development of the Community as the national administrations require within their spheres of interest."[140] The 1962 Action Program for the Second Stage (*i.e.,* for the subsequent four years), for instance, provided (par. 95) for the creation of a "Community short-term economic policy, into which the national policies will merge. . . . The scope and content of national policies will be examined and consideration given to their expected results and the advisability of adjustments."[141] Further, "the object should be to devise ways in which [the national economic and financial policies] can be improved, aiming at the fullest possible utilization of the Community's productive resources without inflationary pressure. Such a general view could be termed a programme. . . . If economic activity for some substantive period gets too far out of line with the programme, going ahead too fast or too slowly while the bases of the initial forecast remain unchanged, it would be for the economic and financial authorities to take general measures to stimulate or put a brake on activity as the case may be."[142]

BLATT I, 581 (1967); Gesetz zur Förderung der Stabilität und des Wachstums der Wirtschaft vom 8.6. 1967, BUNDESGESETZBLATT I, 582 (1967).

[138] Hirsch, *French Planning and Its European Application,* 1 J. COMM. MKT. STUDIES 117 (1963).

[139] Eckstein, *supra* note 136.

[140] Summary of lecture by Prof. C. J. Oort, in STEIN & HAY, *supra* note 14, 893 at 897. On transport policy see Wägenbaur, *Grünes Licht für die gemeinsame Verkehrspolitik der EWG,* 1968 AUSSENWIRTSCHAFTSDIENST 41.

[141] EEC Doc. COM(62)300, Oct. 24, 1962.

[142] *Id.* at ¶96.

In April 1964, the Council issued a decision creating a "Medium-Term Economic Policy Committee"[143] to draft a medium-term economic policy for a five-year period, to be adopted by the Council and the Member States and to have the effect of showing their "intention to act in the area covered by the program in accordance with the directions provided for in such program." The Commission reexamines the program annually and may make adjustments. Finally, both in 1967[144] and in 1968,[145] the Council addressed Recommendations to the Member States containing guidelines for short-term business cycle policy. In the last of these, the Community also specifically dealt with internal inflationary pressures, British and French devaluation, German revaluation, and United States balance-of-payments difficulties. It recommended a variety of measures—from restraint in investments to stabilization of interest rates in the face of expected increases in demand for capital, avoidance of increased public expenditures, and stepped-up tax collections.

2. POLICIES TOWARD THIRD COUNTRIES

Will "indicative" planning (or more) make for a more protectionist attitude toward third country trade? The "chicken war" between the EEC and the United States of 1962-63[146] is sometimes cited in support of the expectation that it will. In response to the removal of German restrictions on poultry imports in 1959-61, American chicken exports to Germany increased substantially (from $2.5 million in 1958 to $35.5 million in 1961). The creation of the EEC and the adoption of a common agricultural policy, however, foreshadowed eventual preferences for Belgian and French producers. Regulation 22 of 1962 translated the policy into law,[147] creating a variable feed grain compensatory duty and a preferential EEC duty, among other provisions, all with the effect that American poultry imports into Germany faced a duty increase from 4.8 cents per pound in 1961 to 13.4 cents in August 1963. After negotiations became stalemated and a GATT arbitration panel had

---

[143] 1964 E.C.J.O. 1031, 1 CCH COMM. MKT. REP. ¶3665. See also Maier, *Das Programm für die mittelfristige Wirtschaftspolitik der EWG,* 1967 EUROPARECHT 320.

[144] 1967 E.C.J.O. No. 159, 2 CCH COMM. MKT. REP. ¶9185.

[145] 1968 E.C.J.O. No. 63, 2 CCH COMM. MKT. REP. ¶9222.

[146] Clubb, *Dismantling Trade Barriers: Implementation of the Trade Expansion Act,* 1965 U. ILL. L.F. 366, 368-75.

[147] 1962 E.C.J.O. 959.

determined the amount of American trade affected, the United States withdrew concessions to the EEC in the amount of $26 million,[148] in accordance with its rights under GATT Articles XXIV(6) and XXVIII(3). Subsequent statistics show (as of 1964) that the settlement cost the EEC about $13 million and the United States about $17 million in trade with each other.

Still, there may be argument that the chicken war lends only insufficient proof to an assessment of the EEC as "protectionist." All trade restrictions are protectionist, yet as a practical matter all countries must make some choices. The practical limits to obligations which a free trade orientation would impose are recognized in GATT. They extend to certain agricultural regulations, to defense products, certain types of government procurement, various types of emergency relief, and the formation of customs unions. The last favors, or at least accepts, the formation of new economic units. Or differently, if faced with the choice between greatly expanding regional trade and more limited general free trade, it is willing to accept the former.[149] As a result, the EEC and United States face each other as two economic units within the GATT framework. Each makes its choices within that framework. By these standards, the EEC action did not promote free trade, nor was it an unusually protectionist measure. It was, perhaps, an unwise exercise of a GATT right,[150] not essentially different from United States recourse to such provisions in cases before or after the chicken war (including, in 1962, an increase of tariffs on carpets and certain categories of glass which brought about EEC retaliation[151]).

Perhaps a more telling barometer of protectionism is the openness of the economy to economic activity by outsiders. The share of American business in Europe is extensive: its freedom to invest and to operate within the Common Market on terms equivalent to those enjoyed by local participants is therefore of great importance. In the period from 1960 to 1966, American direct investments in Western Europe increased from $6.7 billion to $16.2 billion. While American investments totalled

---

[148] Pres. Procl. No. 3564, Dec. 4, 1963, 28 Fed. Reg. 13247 (1963).

[149] For discussion of the customs union exception in GATT, see Dam, *Regional Economic Arrangements and the GATT: The Legacy of a Misconception*, 30 U. CHI. L. REV. 615 (1963).

[150] Clubb, *supra* note 146, at 375.

[151] 1962 E.C.J.O. 1518.

only \$0.6 billion in the six Community countries in 1950,[152] they increased to \$7.6 billion in 1966 and \$8.4 billion in 1967.[153] This investment produced a net profit (after European taxes) of about \$448 million in 1967, of which \$407 million was repatriated and the remainder reinvested.[154]

These figures document the extraordinary importance, and potential, of the EEC for American business. To many Europeans, however, they are an increasing cause for concern: "From the moment an English baby is weaned on American-owned baby food until he is carted away in an American-owned funeral car he is, to that extent, American-oriented from the cradle to the grave."[155] Economic dependence, loss of the initiative to develop one's own national market because of the presence of large and efficient and well-funded American companies, and the concomitant feeling of social and cultural dependence, all are very disturbing to Europeans. For Britain,

> Up against the reality of a struggle for primacy on the Continent, Britain may rediscover her lost nationalism. She will never do so as long as she sits crooning idiot ballads to herself in the shadow of the American Eagle.
> The threat of Russian aggression brought military unity to Western Europe. American commercial pressure is forcing some degree of economic unity. Just as the Europeans reacted against Soviet strength by arming themselves with military weapons, so they may well react to U.S. economic strength by arming themselves with economic weapons.
> The Common Market is either an all-out economic rival to the U.S.—or it is nothing.
> By a strange quirk it may be England, the reluctant, rejected, suitor, who will give leadership and purpose to the market.[156]

Many Continental voices are similar.[157]

[152] EDWARDS, INVESTMENTS IN THE EUROPEAN ECONOMIC COMMUNITY 1 (1964).
[153] U.S. Dep't of Commerce, Office of Business Economics, 48 SURVEY OF CURRENT BUSINESS No. 10, 24 (1968).
[154] *Id.* at 24.
[155] McMILLAN & HARRIS, THE AMERICAN TAKE-OVER OF BRITAIN 6 (1968).
[156] *Id.* at 224.
[157] *E.g.,* SERVAN-SCHREIBER, THE AMERICAN CHALLENGE (English ed. 1968).

Several problems are in issue: Will United States business continue to be able to enter the market freely? Will there be restrictions on the form of its economic activity? And will the internal market benefits of the EEC Treaty accrue to it as they do to locally-owned business? Freedom of entry is secured by bilateral commercial treaties between EEC countries and the United States, generally providing for entry on a national-treatment basis, although some specified activities (such as banking, transport, and exploitation of natural resources) may be excluded or limited. The main, remaining obstacle to establishment— restrictions on capital transfers—has been substantially lifted within the Community as a result of the Council's First and Second Directives,[158] and will be further reduced when the Proposed Third Directive is adopted.[159] Some countries still maintain controls on third-country capital transfers but may be expected to liberalize these soon as well. France, for instance, in 1967 substantially eased controls on direct foreign investments as well as on the sale of foreign issues on the French market.[160] While national law therefore presently poses decreasing obstacles to new foreign investments, the concerns and pressures described above do not rule out the possibility that "foreign overinvestment" in a particular country or a particular branch of the economy may produce some national or even Community restrictions or controls. The Commission stated as early as 1958 that it favored third-country investments but that it was "conscious of the problems which may result from an excessive concentration of such investment in any one country or in any given industry."[161] And France reportedly asked for Council consideration of this problem in 1963.

The second problem, relating to the manner of business activity, raises such questions as what legal form for company establishment should be selected, whether control should be shared with local investors, and to what extent the management structure shall be American. All EEC countries, except the Netherlands, provide two forms for corporate

[158] 1960 E.C.J.O. 921, 1 CCH COMM. MKT. REP. ¶1651 and 1963 E.C.J.O. 62, see 1 CCH COMM. MKT. REP. ¶1667.25.

[159] CCH COMM. MKT. REP. ¶1671 (1967).

[160] Law of December 28, 1966, implemented by Decree of January 27, 1967, both summarized in STEIN & HAY, *supra* note 14 at 794. However, the Commission filed suit against France for some restrictions, 1969 Amtsblatt C 129/1; CCH EURO-MARKET NEWS, Dec. 16, 1969, 2.

[161] 1958 E.C.J.O. 25, translation in Stein, *supra* note 61, at 29. See also Chapter 4, *infra* at 179.

organization: the "limited liability company," or close corporation, which requires few incorporators, a minimum of administrative structure and of publicity (but has only limited access to the capital market), and the "stock company," or publicly held corporation, which is subject to more formal requirements relating to organization, management, and publicity. The temptation is great to select the limited liability company as the formal structure because it permits maximum control and minimum disclosure. Indeed, in Germany there were only 2,420 stock corporations (publicly held corporations) in 1966 compared with 58,000 limited liability companies (although the total stated capital of the former was greater).[162] Yet American firms in Germany do not seem to have followed the European preference for the close corporation.[163] This, no doubt, is the wiser approach, especially if it is combined with local participation in the capital and in the management.[164] To the extent that the "foreign investment" in this fashion becomes part of the local economy it loses much of its "foreign-ness," and the question of "over-investment" can revert to the area of business cycle policy.

For interstate economic activity, the EEC Treaty's provisions on establishment, free movement of services, and capital become applicable. The former two apply to all companies established in a Member State—thus presupposing subsidiary organization for an American company—while the latter extends to "residents" generally. Implementing acts of the Council, however, contain a limited restriction against use of the establishment and services provisions by companies which, for instance, attempt to gain access to State B after a pro forma organization in State A. They define a beneficiary company as one which has an "effective and continuous link" with the economy of a Member State.[165] A manufacturing subsidiary of an American enterprise would surely qualify under this test, however.

At present, therefore, American and other third-country firms have not faced serious difficulties in engaging in economic activity in the

[162] 1967 BUNDESANZEIGER, April 7, 1967, at 3.

[163] Conard, *Organizing for Business,* in 2 AMERICAN ENTERPRISE IN THE EUROPEAN COMMON MARKET: A LEGAL PROFILE, *supra* note 19, 1 at 51.

[164] McMILLAN & HARRIS, *supra* note 155, at 106-07: "Just as irritating to British executives is the insistence of some American firms . . . in having 100 per cent US ownership of a subsidiary. . . . [Without British shareholders] these companies lack a spur and the American chiefs are denied the benefit of home-brewed criticism. In the long-term that is quite a price to pay for hogging all the capital—and the dividends—of the subsidiaries."

[165] General Program on Establishment, *supra* note 92, Title I(d).

Common Market. The expanding economy of the EEC so far has not drawn significant distinctions between Community nationals and foreigners, and the EEC's international trade posture perhaps has been less restrictive than others in terms of its willingness to grant concessions (*e.g.,* the numerous association agreements with other states, all of which involve free trade area structures). There are, however, proponents of greater restrictiveness. In addition to the overinvestment issue, there is the recent French proposal that the "European Company Statute," which France proposed in 1965 to facilitate Common Market-wide corporate organization,[166] should be available only to European-controlled companies.[167] One of the two proposed versions of Article 5 of the Draft Convention for a European Patent[168] would restrict the availability of the patent to nationals and companies of a Member State; and, while Article 211 so far is open-ended, some members of the study group would restrict accession to the Convention to European countries.

Conclusion. Clearly, the Community is in an uncertain stage. The difficult transition from single markets to a common market has been largely achieved, but the problems of dealing with economic questions on a Community-wide basis are just beginning—in antitrust, monetary policy, business cycle policy, and concomitantly external trade policy (how much free trade, with whom, and at what price?). At the same time, there is uncertainty about the proper role of the Community and its institutions, as to whether it should be a market administrator or catalyst for further integration through geographic expansion and through the internal addition of powers and responsibilities which were originally outside the scope of the Treaty—*e.g.,* limited private law unification.

III. SUPREMACY OF COMMUNITY LAW

A. The View of the Court of Justice

The possibility of conflict between national and Community law was mentioned earlier. The Treaty contains no special provision for this problem. How such a conflict is resolved, therefore, says much about

[166] CCH COMM. MKT. REP. ¶9025 (1965).
[167] *Id.* ¶9205 (1967).
[168] *Id.* ¶5503 (1965).

attitudes toward integration and national willingness to surrender domestic legislative freedom for the benefit of a larger community.

The Court of Justice has had occasion in several cases to express the concept that national law and Community law represent "separate legal orders." The context usually has been litigation concerning the validity of a Community act, in the course of which a party has relied on arguments drawn from national law. The "separation" idea has protected the Community against national law intrusion and permitted consideration of the contested Community act on Community-law grounds alone.

It was not until the celebrated case of *Costa v. ENEL* that the Court had an opportunity to state its view on the reverse problem—to what extent a national court should disregard national law in case of a substantive conflict and yield to Community law.[169] This is the classic supremacy problem of any two-tiered or federal legal system. The *Costa* case came to the Court on reference from an Italian Justice of the Peace under Article 177 of the Treaty, which requires national courts of final resort to refer Community law questions to the Court for "preliminary decision," and permits inferior courts to do so as well. The issue was the effect of Italian legislation nationalizing the production of electricity in conflict with the Treaty; immediately in issue was a consumer's refusal to pay his bill, in the amount of $3.08. Prior to the reference to the Court of Justice, there had been a reference to the Italian Constitutional Court which had held that the law ratifying the EEC Treaty was like any other law, and hence could be superseded by inconsistent subsequent legislation. In the Court's view, Article 11 of the Constitution, which permits limitations of Italian sovereignty, did not change this effect. Upon reference, the principal function of the Court of Justice was to interpret the Treaty provisions in question as to whether they were directly applicable in the Member States to begin with. In arriving at such an interpretation, however, the Court seized the opportunity to state quite bluntly that

> by creating a Community of unlimited duration, having its own institutions, its own personality and its own capacity in law, apart from having international standing and more particularly, real powers resulting from a limitation of competence or a transfer of powers from the States to the Community, the

[169] 10 Recueil de la Jurisprudence de la Cour 1141, CCH COMM. MKT. REP. ¶8023, 3 Comm. Mkt. L.R. 425 (1964); see also Wilhelm v. Bundeskartellamt, 15 Recueil de la Jurisprudence de la Cour 1969-1, CCH COMM. MKT. REP. ¶8056 (1969), discussed in text *infra*.

member-States, albeit within limited spheres, have restricted their sovereign rights and created a body of law applicable both to their nationals and to themselves. The reception, within the laws of each member-State, of provisions having a Community source, and more particularly of the terms and of the spirit of the Treaty, has as a corollary the impossibility, for the member-State, to give preference to a unilateral and subsequent measure against a legal order accepted by it on a basis of reciprocity. . . .

The supremacy of Community law is confirmed by Article 189 which prescribes that Community regulations have an "obligatory" value and are "directly applicable within each member-State." Such a provision which, it will be noticed, admits of no reservation, would be wholly ineffective if a member-State could unilaterally nullify its purpose by means of a Law contrary to Community dictates. It follows from all these observations that the rights created by the Treaty, by virtue of their specific original nature, cannot be judicially contradicted by an internal law, whatever it might be, without losing their Community character and without undermining the legal basis of the Community.

By transferring to the Community legal order [functions] which hitherto were part of their internal legal orders, the member-States have thus brought about a final limitation of their sovereign rights which cannot be revoked by means of subsequent unilateral measures which are incompatible with the concept of the Community. As a consequence, Article 177 should be applied regardless of any national law in those cases where a question of interpretation of the Treaty arises.[170]

This statement is clear and forceful. It asserts supremacy both on the basis of the legal concept that sovereignty has been limited, powers transferred, and a new superordinated entity created, and as a matter of policy and political necessity. The latter invokes the "federal fidelity" of the Community's Members, and the former, issues of national constitutional law.[171] In both cases the question is how responsive are the national legal systems to the need for Community law supremacy?

B. The View from the National Legal Systems[172]

1. ITALY

The *Costa* litigation itself came to a conclusion in keeping with the Community Court's view. On May 1, 1966, the Italian Justice of the

---

[170] Translation in STEIN & HAY, *supra* note 14, 200 at 204-05.

[171] HAY, *supra* note 35, ch. 7.

[172] See Hay, *Supremacy of Community Law in National Courts,* 16 AM. J. COMP. L. 524, 543 (1968).

Peace held the Italian legislation "inapplicable" to the litigation, thus finding that the consumer was not indebted to ENEL.[173] In keeping with European practice, ENEL as the losing party was ordered to pay the costs of the Italian, as well as Community Court proceedings, in the amount of about $1,000.

The Italian Constitutional Court had an opportunity to reexamine its position in 1965, in *Acciaierie San Michele v. High Authority.*[174] Here the conflict was not between Community treaty and national legislation but between the former and the national constitution. The question was: do the provisions of the ECSC Treaty conferring exclusive jurisdiction on the Community Court to judge the validity of Community law violate the Constitutional provisions that judicial functions must be exercised by regularly appointed judges and that there must be recourse to the ordinary and administrative courts? The Court responded by construing the Constitution strictly to provide protection of individual rights only within the national legal system. It thus embraced the Community Court's concept of the "separate legal orders," and as a result freed the Community system from the restraints of the national system. The Italian Court was careful to note that the Community system is also subject to restraints—its own, as well as possibly those of Article 6 of the European Human Rights Convention assuring individuals an inviolable right to judicial redress. This suggests, perhaps, that the establishment of, and grant of powers to, the Communities is constitutional in Italy only if the new system shares certain basic democratic and human rights, but that equivalence of rights, structures, and procedures is beyond the national constitution to control. The decision, of course, does not address itself to the *Costa* problem; it merely establishes the compatibility of the Communities with Italian Constitutional law but stops short of saying that the grant of powers was complete rather than concurrent, permanent rather than revocable.

2. GERMANY

Germany is the only other Community country which provides review of legislative acts by a Federal Constitutional Court, usually upon reference from other courts. The first such reference reached the Constitutional Court in 1963. The Fiscal Court of the Rhineland-

[173] EEC Doc. JUR/S/1944/66.
[174] Judgment No. 98, 118 Giurisprudenza Italiana I, 193 (1966).

Palatinate had reached the conclusion that a Community regulation was defective because based upon an unconstitutional delegation of power by Germany to the Community.[175] Several other courts soon faced similar issues, but all reached conclusions different from the Fiscal Court.[176] The Constitutional Court took four years to reach its decision—a dismissal on the ground (provided in the meantime by a decision of the Community Court[177]) that the issue in the case at bar is governed by the EEC Treaty directly, not by the contested regulation.[178] This inconclusive decision was followed, within three and a half months, by a case in which several German enterprises attacked EEC Council and Commission regulations as violative of their German constitutional rights.[179] It will be remembered that the Community Court had in a much earlier case declined to consider the validity of Community acts on the basis of national constitutional grounds. The German Court, in effect joining the Italian Court in *Acciaierie San Michele,* declined to review the Community acts, holding that they are not law emanating from *German* governmental authority, which is a prerequisite of the Court's jurisdiction. Again, the "separateness" of the legal systems, and with it their compatibility, is assured. Procedurally, the only—not very likely—remaining avenue for constitutional review in Germany is an attack on a German legislative act promulgated in accordance with a Community directive. However, to the extent that the Community Treaties deal with subject matter within the enumerated powers of the German federal government, such German implementing legislation would merely be an exercise of federal legislative power; what prompted the exercise would be irrelevant.

As do the Italian decisions, the German case law to date leaves unanswered what the result would be if German legislative power were

[175] 1964 ENTSCHEIDUNGEN DER FINANZGERICHTE 22, 1 C.M.L. REV. 463 (1964).

[176] *E.g.,* Administrative Court of Frankfurt, 1964 AUSSENWIRTSCHAFTS-DIENST 60; 2 C.M.L. REV. 102 (1964).

[177] Firma Alfons Lütticke GmbH v. Hauptzollamt Saarlouis, 12 Recueil de la Jurisprudence de la Cour 27, CCH COMM. MKT. REP. ¶ 8045 (1966).

[178] 1967 AUSSENWIRTSCHAFTSDIENST 364; 1967 NEUE JURISTISCHE WOCHENSCHRIFT 1707.

[179] 1967 AUSSENWIRTSCHAFTSDIENST 477. For analysis of German and other national case law on the supremacy problem see Hay, *supra* note 172.

exercised in contradiction to Community law and if German courts were asked to invalidate the former for the sake of the latter. However, persuasive German doctrine has suggested a variety of analyses leading to Community law supremacy in such cases.[180] Both the place of *doctrine* in European legal systems,[181] and the attitude of the German and Italian courts on the essentially equally fundamental question of constitutional review, lead to the conclusion that Community law supremacy—at least as a theoretical postulate—is assured in both countries.

3. OTHER EEC COUNTRIES

As mentioned in an earlier section, the Dutch Constitution contains the clearest statement in favor of Community law supremacy. Revised during the early years of the ECSC (in 1953 and 1956), the Constitution now provides: (1) that legislative, administrative, and judicial powers may be transferred to an international organization (Article 67); (2) that the agreement establishing such an organization may deviate from the Constitution (Article 63); and (3) that international agreements, as well as decisions of international institutions established by them, shall have priority over prior or subsequent national law (Articles 66 and 67).

Constitutional law or practice in France, Belgium, and Luxembourg precludes constitutional review of legislation, including treaties, by the courts.[182] The French Constitution (Article 55) also provides for supremacy of treaties over legislation, and a substantial body of opinion in Belgium and Luxembourg points to the same result in those countries.[183] It is interesting to note in passing that the solution of the supremacy problem would be a great deal more difficult in the case of

---

[180] See HAY, *supra* note 35, ch. 7.

[181] SCHLESINGER, COMPARATIVE LAW 312-13 (2d ed. 1959).

[182] See STEIN & HAY, *supra* note 14, at 27-37, 57-63.

[183] *Id.* at 61-63. However, notwithstanding the clear mandate of Article 55, the Conseil d'Etat refused in 1968 to accord EEC law supremacy over inconsistent French legislation. 1968 D.S. Jur. 285. In contrast, the Court of Appeal of Colmar concluded in 1967 that both the EEC Treaty and decisions of Treaty-interpretation by the Court of Justice take precedence over French law (88 Gazette du Palais 3-4. Nos. 115-17 (April 24-26, 1968)), and the Cour de Cassation made its first reference under Article 177 in the same year. 1967 D.S. Jur. 541. For discussion see Hay, *supra* note 179.

British membership in view of the traditional concept of Parliamentary supremacy.[184]

4. COMMUNITY LAW SUPREMACY IN ANTITRUST LAW

The theoretical supremacy of Community law may often be difficult to apply in practice, and some difficulties may be anticipated in the antitrust area. In *Wilhelm v. Bundeskartellamt,*[185] the Court of Justice in a reference under Article 177 began a process of accommodating national and Treaty antitrust laws by laying a strong foundation for assertion of Community law supremacy, while at the same time taking pains to preserve some scope for the national laws as long as Treaty objectives are not interfered with. The case arose because the German authorities had levied fines against several German firms and individuals who were found to have participated in an international cartel in the dyestuffs industry, which had fixed prices in violation of Section 1 of the German Law Against Restraints of Competition. At the time the German authorities acted, the Commission had also begun an investigation of the cartel members, including the German participants.[186] After the German proceeding reached the Berlin Commercial Court for review, the latter referred several questions to the Court of Justice. The principal questions pertained to whether it is compatible with the Treaty for national authorities to apply national law to facts which are also the subject of a Commission proceeding, especially where the result might be a different legal conclusion or a distortion of competition as to persons subject to the law.

The Court of Justice responded that Article 87, para. 2(e) of the Treaty gives the Council the authority to define the relationship between national and Community competition laws. As long as the Council has not provided otherwise, it said, the same cartel may be the subject of parallel Community and national proceedings, provided the national law

[184] *Id.* at 64-69. See particularly, Legal Implications of the Accession of the United Kingdom to the European Economic Community on the British Constitution, Report of the General Affairs Committee, Explanatory Memorandum, Assembly of Western European Union, Doc. 249 (1962).

[185] 15 Recueil de la Jurisprudence de la Cour 1969-1, CCH COMM. MKT. REP. ¶8056 (1969).

[186] Subsequently, the Commission levied fines against various participants, including four German firms which were involved in the national proceeding; see Chapter 2 *infra*, text and note 110.

is not applied in such a way as to "jeopardize the uniform application throughout the Common Market of the Community cartel rules or the full effect of the measures taken under such rules."[187] The Court mentioned the power of the Commission both to issue prohibitions under Article 85(1), and to grant exemptions under Article 85(3) for cartels which improve production or distribution or promote economic or technical progress. The "separate legal order" established by the Treaty is "to be incorporated into the legal systems of the Member States," and it would be inconsistent with this system to allow variant national approaches to jeopardize the benefits of the Treaty. Accordingly, any conflicts "must be resolved by applying the principle of preeminence of the Community rule."[188] Where national decisions prove incompatible with a Commission decision, or where it appears in a national proceeding that a Commission decision may interfere, the national authorities must respect Commission authority and take appropriate measures.

Ruling on other questions submitted, the Court added that it would not be improper for both authorities to levy penalties on the same persons; and that the prohibition in Article 7 of the Treaty against discrimination on grounds of nationality does not prevent a Member State from levying penalties against its nationals under these circumstances.

Under these principles, it is clear that Community law will apply even if the conduct would be lawful under national law. It is equally clear that national antitrust laws may be enforced against conduct which also falls within Article 85(1), as long as the question of a possible exemption under Article 85(3) has not arisen. If an exemption has been granted— either by Commission decision or under a group exemption regulation— the national authorities will obviously have to stand aside. The situation is less clear where an exemption has been applied for, but has not been acted upon by the Commission. Since subsequent granting of the exemption would presumably legalize the conduct as against national law, however, it would appear to be quite risky for national authorities to proceed in such cases, and the *Wilhelm* decision may have the effect of suspending national laws wherever there is a pending notification.

Perhaps the most difficult problem is what will be done where given

---

[187]CCH COMM. MKT. REP. ¶ 8056, at 7866.
[188]*Id.*

conduct violates national law and is also possibly within the scope of Article 85(1), but is given a negative clearance by the Commission under Regulation 17, or falls within the scope of permissible activity outlined in a Commission policy statement. It might be argued in the case of a negative clearance that the Community's interest in the matter is neutral and that national law may therefore prohibit the conduct without jeopardizing Treaty objectives. However, a Commission determination that given conduct does not fall within the Article 85 prohibition may be influenced by important considerations of policy, as witness the recent statement on permissible cooperation among small and medium-size enterprises.[189] It cannot be assumed automatically, therefore, that the inapplicability of Treaty law will guarantee the right of national law to apply. Instead, under the *Wilhelm* decision, the underlying reasons for Treaty inapplicability may have to be examined in each case, which can make for a quite complicated future picture in this area.

C. Article 177 of the EEC Treaty

The effectiveness of Community law as an integrating, "federal" force requires its uniform application. All three Treaties therefore contain provisions requiring national courts to refer Community-law questions to the Community Court of Justice. Article 41 of the ECSC Treaty is the most restrictive of these, requiring a reference only if the validity of ECSC acts is in question. Articles 177 of the EEC Treaty and 150 of the Euratom Treaty are broader, requiring national courts of last resort (inferior courts at their discretion) to refer all questions of interpretation and validity of Community law when such questions are necessary for the decision of the case pending before them.

Numerous difficulties, of which two stand out, have arisen in the application of this provision, which is pivotal to the development of the Community legal system. First, when does a reference become "necessary"—when the national court cannot dispose of the case on state-law grounds alone, or beyond this, only when the national court itself is unable to arrive at an interpretation of the Community law question? The former limitation seems quite proper; indeed a state court in the United States also need not reach the federal question if it can dispose of

[189] See Chapter 2 *infra,* text at note 105.

the case on the basis of state law.[190] Use of the second limitation, however, would seriously erode the purpose and effectiveness of Article 177, since uniformity would again be left to local discretion and good will. Yet a great many of the earlier cases turned on this narrow view. Taking a concept from their own administrative law, some French courts declined to make a reference when a Community act appeared to them as "clear," a view which some German courts adopted as well.[191] Since then, however, there have been references from France, and German courts have been effecting referrals quite frequently.

A second problem concerns the proper role of the Court of Justice in the referral process. Perhaps as a consequence of its "separateness of legal systems" concept, the Court has stated repeatedly that it cannot decide the issue before the national court but can only give an "abstract" interpretation of the applicable Community law. This restraint seems unrealistic, unnecessary, and even hard to follow for a variety of reasons which need not be repeated here.[192] The fact is, however, that despite the repeated statements of restraint and caution, many of the Court's opinions in referral cases are quite "concrete," as the earlier excerpt from the *Costa* opinion demonstrates.[193] With respect to both problems, therefore, initial difficulties seem to become resolved. For the development of the Community legal system, this means that an effective reference procedure will ensure, in practice as well as in theory, that the new "federal" law is applied and observed in a uniform fashion.

CONCLUSION

In its first ten years the EEC has succeeded in achieving its first goal—the creation of a common market for industrial goods and

[190] NAACP v. Alabama, 357 U.S. 449, 455 (1958). See also Fay v. Noia, 372 U.S. 391 (1963).

[191] The leading example is *Société des Pétroles Shell-Berre,* French Conseil d'Etat, 3 Comm. Mkt. L.R. 462 (1964). See also Cass. crim., 92 Journal du droit international 90 (1965) and Cour d'Appel, Paris, 1964 Dalloz Jurisp. 419. German cases are collected in DUMON, LE ROLE DES JURISDICTIONS NATIONALES— LE RENVOI PREJUDICIEL 42 (1965). See also note 183, *supra*.

[192] For further discussion see HAY, *supra* note 35, at 138-44, and Hay, *supra* note 172, at 526-43.

[193] See also the Court's opinion in Humblet v. Belgium, 6 Recueil de la Jurisprudence de la Cour 1125 (1960) and in Fohrmann, 10 *id.* 381 (1964).

significant progress toward a common agricultural policy. However, many difficult problems still await solution in the years ahead.

In its external relations, the Community maintains ties, in the form of association agreements, with most of the former colonial territories of its Members and with Greece, Turkey, and Nigeria, and has held trade negotiations with many other countries, including India, Iran, and Israel. In GATT, it now negotiates on behalf of the Six. But the far-reaching problem of relations with the EFTA, and particularly with Britain, still remains unsolved, even though opinion polls in 1966 showed over-whelming popular support for British entry.[194]

In the development of the internal market, equally difficult decisions still lie ahead, in particular those relating to agricultural, social, monetary, and antitrust (merger) policy. The future role of the institutions, especially the single Commission and the Court, will be an important factor for the question whether the Communities will remain essentially economic organisms or hold the potential for political integration.

The development and current trends in the European Communities also point to difficulties which lie ahead for U.S.–EEC relations: expanding the EEC's membership may, at least temporarily, bring about an inward-looking orientation which would favor the building of internal stability over freer trade and which may result in the Community's being less willing to share internal economic benefits with outsiders. Even without such expansion, the seemingly increasing attractiveness of at least "indicative planning" possibly points in the same direction, especially at a time when adverse economic conditions exist within the EEC or elsewhere in the world economy. On the other hand, to the extent that the EEC seeks trade expansion, traditional patterns may not remain the same, with a disproportionate share–at least of the increase–being assumed by trade with the East bloc.

For third countries, particularly the United States, new questions and difficult choices arise. American policy has long supported European integration; this policy received new expression in 1968 with the call of

---

[194] This poll showed that 98% of the "elite" in Germany and 84% in France favored British entry in the fall of 1966. When the Wilson Government renewed the British application for membership in 1967, 60% of Britons supported the idea. Durant, *Public Opinion and EEC,* 6 J. COMM. MKT. STUDIES 231, 232, 243 (1968).

the then United States Ambassador to the United Nations, George W. Ball, that Europe should assume the position of a third force.[195] At least in the economic sector, the EEC arguably has already achieved that position. The economic cost which this may involve for third countries is justified for some by the political objective of furthering European integration, but for others it is not.[196] To solve these problems it may be that traditional bilateral or multilateral forms of cooperation will no longer be adequate. Instead, new policies and approaches may be needed which will prevent new economic isolation (on both sides) and realize the fact and the benefits of economic interdependence.

[195] *Three and a Half Superpowers,* LIFE (Mar. 29, 1968).

[196] See, *e.g.,* the opposition to the Trade Expansion Act of 1962: Additional Views of Messrs. Mason, Knox, Betts, and Alger in Opposition to H.R. 11970, Report of the Committee on Ways and Means to Accompany H.R. 11970 (Trade Expansion Act of 1962), H.R. Rep. No. 1818, 87th Cong., 2d Sess., 102-04 (1962). See also the "Minority Views" expressed by Senators Ribicoff, Hartke, and Gore with respect to the U.S.–Canada Automotive Products Agreement of 1965, S. Rep. No. 782, 89th Cong., 1st Sess. (1965). Europeans have recently voiced increasing concern that the United States may be turning toward renewed protectionism in trade, for instance with respect to European steel. See *Uncle Sam's eiserner Vorhang,* DIE ZEIT, Feb. 18, 1969, at 13-14. See also text at note 151 *supra.*

CHAPTER 2 *Extraterritorial Substantive Scope of the Antitrust Laws of the United States and of the Communities and Member States*

The antitrust laws of the United States, of the European Communities, and of those Member States which have such laws, are all capable of some kind of extraterritorial application. In this chapter, the substantive provisions of these laws are analyzed and compared for the purpose of determining their extraterritorial scope and the extent to which they overlap. A discussion of domestic Common Market antitrust policies and cases is also included in Part II of the chapter as important background. Chapter 3 deals with the extraterritorial scope of enforcement and procedural rules of the different jurisdictions, and succeeding chapters seek to identify and evaluate particular types of conflict which may arise as a consequence of the overlapping.

I. AMERICAN LAW

A. Applicable American Statutes

Most of the American cases which have involved some kind of extraterritorial or foreign application have arisen under the Sherman Act,[1] and this Act will undoubtedly continue to be the leading source of extraterritorial American antitrust action. Section 1 reaches "[e]very contract, combination . . . or conspiracy, in restraint of trade or commerce among the several states, or with foreign nations," and Section 2

---

[1] Act of July 2, 1890, 15 U.S.C. §1 (1964).

covers monopolizing, attempting to monopolize or combining or conspiring to monopolize "any part of the trade or commerce among the several states, or with foreign nations." This language has been applied in several ways to reach a variety of different kinds of activity abroad or involving foreign commerce. Further discussion of the manner in which the Act may be applied follows after reference is made to the other principal antitrust statutes.

The chief antitrust provisions of the Clayton Act are of narrower applicability.[2] The price discrimination prohibition of Section 2(a) applies only where the goods involved are sold "for use, consumption, or resale" in the United States or somewhere within its jurisdiction. This provision would apply to discriminatory prices charged by foreign sellers in American import transactions, but would reach export situations in only a limited number of complex cases. One such case would be the completion within the United States of discriminatory sales transactions, followed by resale in the United States for export, coupled with a prohibited competitive effect on export competition among those who bought at resale, where the effect is attributable to the discrimination. Another might be price discrimination between a seller's domestic and export sales, with some kind of adverse effect on export competition at the seller's level. No decided cases in point have been found.

In contrast to Section 2(a), the brokerage allowances and services subsections of Section 2 (subsections c, d and e) contain no limitation as to territory of application and evidently may apply directly to export transactions. The treatment of exclusive dealing arrangements in Section 3 of the Clayton Act, however, contains the same limiting language as Section 2(a).

Section 7 of the Clayton Act has a different kind of limitation, in that the acquisition concerned may occur anywhere, but the required adverse effect on competition must be found "in any line of commerce in any section of the country." This language has not been fully tested by cases as yet insofar as foreign acquisitions are concerned. Assuming that the words, "the country," refer to the United States, it appears that the adverse effect on competition must occur within some part of the United States; if the effect is confined to a foreign market, the section would be inapplicable.

[2] Act of Oct. 15, 1914, *as amended,* 15 U.S.C. §12 (1964).

It is not clear, however, to what extent Section 7 would apply to mergers whose impact on competition is felt in American export or import trade, but not to a substantial extent in a discrete domestic market. Export and import transactions, of course, begin and end in the United States. The question, however, is whether the locus of the effect on competition in such transactions, as distinguished from mere contact points, may fairly be said to be "in" the country. The answer may be affirmative if the courts give the language a merely technical construction, as has been done domestically by the *Pabst* case.[3] On the other hand, if the language is given substantive significance so that the "section of the country" must be a "relevant geographic market," it will be necessary to have satisfactory economic proof that the requisite diminution of competition occurs in an identified domestic market. This would be possible in some cases, but not in others depending on particular facts.

The Sherman Act also applies to mergers, and is available for use in the event the Clayton Act's language requirements prove to be too limiting. In general, however, the Sherman Act requires a greater impact on competition than the Clayton Act.[4]

---

[3] United States v. Pabst Brewing Co., 384 U.S. 546 (1966). The Court reversed the district court's conclusion that the Government had failed to prove that certain areas of the country within which the merger was alleged to lessen competition were "relevant geographic markets." The Supreme Court stated that all that is required is that there be anti-competitive effect "somewhere in the United States;" that the "section of the country" need not be delineated by "metes and bounds" or proved by an "army of expert witnesses;" and that the issue is "entirely subsidiary" to the crucial question of substantial lessening of competition "anywhere" in the United States; *id*. at 549-50.

For further discussion of the application of Section 7 to mergers abroad or in foreign commerce, see Scott and Yablonski, *Transnational Mergers and Joint Ventures Affecting American Exports,* 14 ANTITRUST BULL. 1, 7 (1969); Donovan, *Antitrust Considerations in the Organization and Operation of American Business Abroad,* 9 B.C. IND. & COM. L. REV. 239, 278 (1968); Donovan, *The Legality of Acquisitions and Mergers Involving American and Foreign Corporations Under the United States Antitrust Laws—Part II,* 40 S. CAL. L. REV. 38, 41 (1967); BREWSTER, ANTITRUST AND AMERICAN BUSINESS ABROAD 192 (1958); FUGATE, FOREIGN COMMERCE AND THE ANTITRUST LAWS 249 (1958).

[4] See Donovan, *The Legality of Acquisitions and Mergers Involving American and Foreign Corporations under the United States Antitrust Laws—Part I,* 39 S. CAL. L. REV. 526, 535 (1966).

A further Clayton Act provision, Section 8, deals with interlocking directorates, and contains no limiting language other than that the corporations involved must be "engaged in commerce."

The above limitations on the scope of the Clayton Act control actions by the Justice Department and private litigants, but do not necessarily prevent the Federal Trade Commission from proceeding against similar types of activities under Section 5 of the Federal Trade Commission Act.[5] Section 5 applies to unfair methods of competition "in commerce," which is defined in Section 4 to mean "commerce among the several states or with foreign nations." The Supreme Court has held in domestic cases that the Commission may treat conduct of the type prohibited by either the Sherman or the Clayton Act as a violation of Section 5 of the Federal Trade Commission Act, and may also use Section 5 to reach "incipient" violations of either Act.[6] Moreover, it has recently been held that Section 5 may be used to fill gaps in the language of Clayton Act sections, and also to widen their scope to include transactions not quite fitting the particular Clayton Act descriptions, where to extend coverage would comport with the overall purpose and scheme of the Act.[7] While no case has been found in which Section 5 was used to supply foreign commerce coverage for types of conduct reached only domestically by the Clayton Act, this would seem to be a relatively simple step.

The qualification should be added, however, that in a proceeding under Section 5, it is probably necessary to show that the practice under attack was committed "in" foreign commerce; mere proof of effect on commerce may be insufficient. In the *Bunte Bros.* case,[8] the Supreme Court held Section 5 inapplicable to an unfair practice committed wholly within one state although its impact was felt by competitors selling in interstate commerce, stating that the Act is limited to unfair methods "in" and not merely "affecting" commerce. The same rationale would presumably apply to a foreign commerce case.[9] Lately, however,

---

[5] Act of Sept. 26, 1914, *as amended,* 15 U.S.C. §45 (1964).

[6] FTC v. Motion Picture Advertising Serv. Co., 344 U.S. 392 (1953); FTC v. Brown Shoe Co., 384 U.S. 316 (1966); FTC v. Texaco, Inc. 393 U.S. 223 (1968).

[7] Atlantic Refining Co. v. FTC, 381 U.S. 357 (1965); Grand Union Co. v. FTC, 300 F.2d 92 (2d Cir. 1962).

[8] FTC v. Bunte Bros., 312 U.S. 349 (1941).

[9] Section 4 of the Webb-Pomerene Act, enacted in 1918, 15 U.S.C. §64 (1964), provides that Section 5 of the FTC Act shall apply to acts "done without the

the courts have manifested some liberality in finding activities to be "in" interstate commerce under the Federal Trade Commission Act or under other statutes where a similar issue has been presented.[10]

In addition to the above statutes of generally applicability, the Wilson Tariff Act was designed explicitly to apply to restraints of trade in import transactions.[11] It is often used in addition to the Sherman Act in enforcement proceedings, but seems to add little, if anything, to the latter Act's substantive coverage. The Webb-Pomerene Act, which provides an exemption from the antitrust laws for certain American export associations,[12] will be discussed later.

B. American Law Commerce Tests

The broad substantive extraterritorial reach of the American antitrust laws has been the subject of much discussion in the literature.[13]

territorial jurisdiction of the United States," where such acts constitute unfair methods "in export trade against competitors engaged in export trade." This language, which seems to have been judicially construed only once, was not really needed to give to Section 5 an extraterritorial reach; see Branch v. FTC, 141 F.2d 31, 35 (7th Cir. 1944). It does not affect the *Bunte* case requirement that the illegal practice under attack must be carried out "in" commerce.

[10] *E.g.,* Holland Furnace Co. v. FTC, 269 F.2d 203 (7th Cir. 1959) (Section 5); Standard Oil Co. v. FTC, 340 U.S. 231 (1951) (Robinson-Patman Act); United States v. Utah Pharmaceutical Ass'n, 201 F. Supp. 29 (D. Utah 1962), *aff'd per curiam,* 371 U.S. 24 (1962) (Sherman Act applied to retail restraints on theory that goods were still in commerce); see also note 36 *infra.*

[11] Act of Aug. 27, 1894, § §73-77; 15 U.S.C. § §8-11 (1964).

[12] Act of April 10, 1918, 15 U.S.C. §61 (1964).

[13] See BREWSTER, ANTITRUST AND AMERICAN BUSINESS ABROAD (1958); FUGATE, FOREIGN COMMERCE AND THE ANTITRUST LAWS (1958); REPORT OF THE ATTORNEY GENERAL'S NATIONAL COMMITTEE TO STUDY THE ANTITRUST LAWS, ch. II (1955) [hereinafter cited ATTY. GEN. NAT. COMM. ANTITRUST REP.] ; ABA ANTITRUST SECTION SUPP. TO ATTY. GEN. NAT. COMM. ANTITRUST REP.: ANTITRUST DEVELOPMENTS 1955-1968, ch. II (1968); *Panel Discussion: Trade or Commerce with Foreign Nations* (Barnard, Kelleher, Rahl and Timberg), 37 ANTITRUST L. J. 716 (1968); *Panel Discussion: Conflicts Between, and the Extra-territorial Application of, the Antitrust Laws of the United States, the Common Market and Member States* (Günther, Jennings, Minoli, Rahl and Schwartz), PROCEEDINGS, ABA ANTITRUST SECTION CONFERENCE ON ANTITRUST AND THE EUROPEAN COMMUNITIES (Brussels and Luxembourg, Sept. 23-26, 1963) 180; Brewster. *Extraterritorial Effects of the U.S. Antitrust Laws: An Appraisal,* 11 ABA

The "commerce" provisions of the laws are the principal source of

ANTITRUST SECTION REP. 65 (1957); BURNS, A STUDY OF THE ANTITRUST LAWS ch. 5 (1958); Carlston, *Antitrust Policy Abroad,* 49 NW.U.L. REV. 569 (1954); Cooper, *Antitrust Aspects of Foreign Trade,* 35 U. MO. K.C.L. REV. 16 (1967); Dean, *Extraterritorial Effects of the U.S. Antitrust Laws,* 11 ABA ANTITRUST SECTION REP. 88 (1957); Devine, *Foreign Establishment and the Antitrust Law,* 57 NW. U.L. REV. 400 (1962); Haight, *Some Aspects of United States Antitrust Laws and Foreign Commerce,* in 1 DOING BUSINESS ABROAD 266 (Landau ed. 1962); Haight, *International Law and Extraterritorial Application of the Antitrust Laws,* 63 YALE L. J. 639 (1954); Haight, *The Sherman Act, Foreign Operations and International Law,* in LEGAL PROBLEMS IN INTERNATIONAL TRADE AND INVESTMENT 89 (Shaw ed. 1962); R. & G. Hale, *Monopoly Abroad: The Antitrust Laws and Commerce in Foreign Areas,* 31 TEX. L. REV. 493 (1953); Hansen, *The Enforcement of the United States Antitrust Laws by the Department of Justice to Protect Freedom of United States Foreign Trade,* 11 ABA ANTITRUST SECTION REP. 75 (1957); Jennings, *Extraterritorial Jurisdiction and the United States Antitrust Laws,* 33 BRIT. Y.B. INT'L L. 146 (1957); Kahn-Freund, *Extraterritorial Application of Antitrust Laws,* ABA SECTION OF INT'L & COMP. L., 1957 PROCEEDINGS 33; Kramer, *The Application of the Sherman Act to Foreign Commerce,* 3 ANTITRUST BULL. 387 (1958); Kronstein, *Extraterritorial Application of American Antitrust Legislation,* 1959 J. BUS. L. 205; Miller, *Extraterritorial Effects of Trade Regulation,* 111 U. PA. L. REV. 1092 (1963); Haight and Ellis (Comments), *id.* at 1117 and 1129; Raymond, *A New Look at the Jurisdiction in Alcoa,* 61 AM. J. INT'L L. 558 (1967); Snyder, *Foreign Investment and Trade: Extraterritorial Impact of United States Antitrust Law* 6 VA. J. INT'L L. 1 (1965); Timberg, *Antitrust and Foreign Trade,* 48 NW. U.L. REV. 411 (1953); Timberg, *Extraterritorial Jurisdiction under the Sherman Act,* 11 RECORD 101 (1956); Timberg, *United States and Foreign Antitrust Laws Governing International Business Transactions,* in A LAWYER'S GUIDE TO INTERNATIONAL BUSINESS TRANSACTIONS 619 (Surrey & Shaw eds. 1963); Verzijl, *The Controversy Regarding the So-Called Extraterritorial Effect of the American Antitrust Laws,* 8 NETHERLANDS INT'L L. REV. 3 (1961); Whitney, *Sources of Conflict between International Law and the Antitrust Laws,* 63 YALE L.J. 655 (1954); Whitney, *Anti-trust Law and Foreign Commerce,* 11 RECORD 134 (1956); Report of Special Committee on Antitrust Laws of the Association of the Bar of the City of New York (1954); REPORT OF SPECIAL COMMITTEE ON ANTITRUST LAWS AND FOREIGN TRADE OF THE ASSOCIATION OF THE BAR OF THE CITY OF NEW YORK, NATIONAL SECURITY AND FOREIGN POLICY IN THE APPLICATION OF AMERICAN ANTITRUST LAWS TO COMMERCE WITH FOREIGN NATIONS (1957); *Int'l Law Ass'n, Extra-territorial Application of Restrictive Trade Legislation,* in INT'L LAW ASS'N, REPORT OF THE FIFTY-FIRST CONFERENCE (TOKYO) 304 (1964); INT'L LAW ASS'N, REPORT OF THE FIFTY-SECOND CONFERENCE (HELSINKI) 26 (1966); Report of the Legal Committee to the Consultative Assembly of the Council of Europe on the Extra-territorial Application

their extensive territorial scope, and at the same time they impose certain limits on it. The purpose of this part of the discussion is to try to locate as clearly as possible the lines of demarcation drawn by American case law in the application of the commerce tests. It should be emphasized, however, that these tests do not provide the only limitation upon the reach of American antitrust law in foreign transactions. In other chapters, consideration is given to limits imposed by rules concerning the obtaining of personal jurisdiction over necessary parties and the discovery of documents and other evidence located abroad (Chapter 3); doctrines of sovereign and other immunities (Chapter 4); relevant principles of international law (Chapter 7); and international consultation procedures and practices (Chapter 9).

Considerable difficulty is encountered in using the commerce concept to map the outer lines of the statutes. Concrete meaning depends upon a pattern of cases, and while there have been a substantial number of decisions, they do not by any means add up to a complete jurisprudence. In the great majority of past decided cases, the presence of an adequate commerce foundation has apparently been sufficiently obvious that the problem has not been given exhaustive attention in the opinions. Also, no cases have been brought concerning several types of activities to which the law might, but does not necessarily, apply. The number of true test cases has been small.

Probably nothing does as well to mark a legal boundary as does a negative holding. But it appears that in the entire course of American antitrust history to date, only one reported litigated case, *i.e., American Banana*,[14] has gone to final judgment for the defendant on the ground that the facts were too remote territorially from the statute's substantive reach. That decision itself did not rest upon the ground that the commerce language of the Sherman Act did not reach the conduct concerned, but rather on the ground that the Sherman Act would not prohibit conduct abroad which was lawful under the laws of the nation in which it occurred. This strict territorial and conflicts construction has been replaced by later opinions which interpret the

---

of Anti-Trust Legislation (Jan. 25, 1966) (deGrailly, Rapporteur), COUNCIL OF EUR. CONSULT. ASS. DOC. No. 2023.

[14] American Banana Co. v. United Fruit Co., 213 U.S. 347 (1909), involving alleged acts of defendant in excluding plaintiff from business in Central America.

Act as applying even if all the conduct occurs abroad and is lawful in the place where it occurs,[15] provided American commerce is affected.

Support which the territorial view in *American Banana* may have received from American ideas of international law seems also to be greatly weakened by developments in this field of law, in particular the position adopted by Section 18 of the Restatement (Second) of Foreign Relations Law of the United States. Section 18 asserts that a nation has jurisdiction over acts of both nationals and aliens abroad which cause effects "within" the nation's territory, subject to certain qualifications.[16] The Restatement thus lends additional support to application of the Sherman Act to acts abroad which affect domestic commerce, but its position has been the subject of considerable controversy and, as indicated more fully in Chapter 7, does not appear to be accepted by more than a rather small number of nations.

[15] ATTY. GEN. NAT. COMM. ANTITRUST REP. 70; ABA ANTITRUST SECTION SUPP., *supra* note 13, at 45; Sabre Shipping Corp. v. American President Lines, Ltd., 285 F.Supp. 949, 953 (S.D.N.Y. 1968).

[16] Section 18 is quoted in note 83, *infra*. See discussion in text there, and in Chapter 7, *infra*. Section 18 requires effects "within" the nation's territory which are "constituent elements" in the offense. It thus may not go as far as the Sherman Act coverage of restraint of foreign commerce. Would an effect on American exports qualify as an effect "within" the territory of the United States? Presumably persons "within" the United States would feel the impact of such an effect; but if it is necessary to prove such an impact in addition to showing the export restraint itself, something more than effect on foreign commerce would be required. Proof that the domestic effect is a "constituent element" in the offense is a further complication.

The Reporters' Notes to Section 18 state that "[t]he effect in the territory may be of a type that affects the interests of the state as a whole rather than just the interest of one or more persons." Since an effect on foreign commerce would affect the national economy, perhaps such an effect would be considered to be "within" the territory.

Insofar as the Restatement is concerned, the issue is decisive only as to jurisdiction over conduct of aliens abroad; jurisdiction over American nationals for acts abroad may be based alternatively, according to Section 30, on nationality alone. See Chapter 7 *infra*. This alternative is not necessarily of great importance to the American antitrust laws, however, because they limit their claim of jurisdiction to acts of nationals and foreigners alike which are "in" or which "affect" American commerce. But the nationality basis may provide some support from international law for jurisdiction over acts of Americans which occur abroad where similar jurisdiction over aliens would be hotly contested; *cf.* discussion of the *Alcoa* doctrine on the substantive test applied to aliens for conduct abroad, text *infra*.

Most of the cases to date have involved large horizontal combinations with seemingly important economic implications and substantial impact on the American economy. Failure of the government and of private litigants to initiate other kinds of cases, however, is not a reliable indication that the law cannot or will not be extended well beyond the scope of past cases. Specifically, there has been little application of the law to vertical marketing restrictions or to mergers and joint ventures abroad,[17] but as will be shown later in this chapter and in Chapter 4, the theoretical dimensions of the law reach well into these areas. Relative inactivity by the government in some areas may only mean that officials have chosen to allocate limited enforcement resources to other seemingly more pressing domestic problems. Also, difficulty in obtaining evidence and enforcing decrees abroad, coupled with adverse foreign reaction to a few of the American extraterritorial cases (see Chapters 3 and 6), may have brought about some forbearance where the practical difficulties might seem to outweigh prospective enforcement gains.

Government action may easily change if a different appraisal of American national interests arises. The increasing amount of American investment abroad amid rising foreign concern about its implications,[18] coupled with growing foreign government sympathy for antitrust policy, may be expected to encourage greater use of the American laws. In fact, the Justice Department has recently filed some foreign commerce cases involving distribution or vertical restraints, and has stated that it routinely reviews major American acquisitions of foreign companies.[19]

Lack of private suits in some of the relatively untested areas of the law may be due in part to the fact that many of the potential plaintiffs would be foreign firms who might be unaware of a right of action, or who would find suit in an American court inconvenient. There have been a few important antitrust decisions, however, in private cases brought by

[17]*Cf.* United States v. Minnesota Mining & Mfg. Co., 92 F. Supp. 947 (D. Mass. 1950), discussed in text *infra*; (illegal arrangements concerning foreign joint manufacturing ventures of competing American companies).

[18]*E.g.,* SERVAN-SCHREIBER, THE AMERICAN CHALLENGE (English version, 1968); McMILLAN & HARRIS, THE AMERICAN TAKE-OVER OF BRITAIN (1968).

[19]Zimmerman, in *Hearings on International Aspects of Antitrust Before the Subcomm. on Antitrust and Monopoly of the Sen. Comm. on the Judiciary,* 89th Cong., 2d Sess. 488-91, 496-511 (1966).

American firms for alleged injuries abroad caused by other Americans. As exposure to the risk of such injuries increases with the mounting volume of American trade and investment in foreign countries, more private suits are to be anticipated.

1. COMMERCE TESTS APPLICABLE TO FOREIGN ACTIVITIES, IN GENERAL

Extraterritorial applicability of the American antitrust laws may arise in a given case either because the activity involved affects domestic interstate commerce of the United States, or because it affects some aspect of the foreign trade of the nation. Often an activity abroad affects both kinds of commerce, because effects on export-import trade usually have some kind of domestic consequence. In much of the following discussion, attention is concentrated upon definition and application of the foreign commerce concept because of its rather unique importance to this subject, but the potential availability in many foreign cases of effect on interstate commerce as a ground for antitrust action should not be overlooked.

Using commerce concepts to map the outer lines of the extraterritorial scope of the antitrust laws requires working with three different questions: (1) What kinds of activity comprise the subject matter of "commerce"? (2) When is the commerce "with foreign nations"? (3) And what sort of relationship must exist between this commerce and the restraint of trade or other conduct substantively proscribed by the law? These questions in the first instance are jurisdictional, *i.e.*, they must be answered in order to determine whether the activity in question comes within the scope of the regulatory power of Congress over commerce as exercised in the statute.[20] They should be distinguished from additional substantive issues relating to legality of the particular restraint or other activity involved.

While the first two questions are not without difficulty, answers to them have developed which seem to satisfy most, though certainly not all, needs. "Commerce" for antitrust purposes comprehends all industrial, commercial and business activities with which the policy of the law is concerned, including: transactions in commodities; furnishing of

[20]The term, "legislative jurisdiction," is used as descriptive of these issues in BREWSTER, ANTITRUST AND AMERICAN BUSINESS ABROAD, ch. 4 *et seq.* (1958).

services such as transportation and communications; financial dealings, including banking, insurance, investment and credit transactions; transactions concerning industrial property rights; and "indeed the entire range of economic activity."[21]

The second question, of what is meant by commerce "with foreign nations," has not received discussion in many cases. It is clear enough, however, that the phrase at least comprehends all commerce conducted between any point in the territory of the United States and any point in any other nation's territory. Thus, it reaches any American export or import transaction, as well as commercial transportation or communication between the United States and a foreign country. It would not ordinarily reach commerce between two points both of which are outside the United States, but special additional American contacts may bring even such commerce within the Act, as in *Pacific Seafarers, Inc. v. Pacific Far East Line, Inc.*[22] A transaction between two foreign geographical points may also, of course, affect some other transaction which is in American foreign commerce and thereby be drawn within the statute's reach.[23]

The third question is the most difficult, *i.e.,* what kind of relationship must exist between the element of foreign commerce found to be present and the restraint or other prohibited activity? The Sherman Act speaks of "restraint of trade or commerce . . . with foreign nations" and thus requires a causal or functional relationship; the restraint must be applied to, or be connected with, the commerce in some way. It is not enough to tack some element of foreign commerce in one phase of a firm's business to some wholly unconnected restraint of trade in a different phase of its business.[24] Further, as in any field, the antitrust

---

[21]ATTY. GEN. NAT. COMM. ANTITRUST REP. 77-80; Gibbons v. Ogden, 22 U.S. (9 Wheat.) 1, 189-90 (1824), Congress may regulate "commercial intercourse between nations . . . in all its branches."

[22]404 F.2d 804 (D.C. Cir. 1968), *cert. denied,* 393 U.S. 1093 (1969); ocean shipping between foreign ports was held to be in American foreign commerce, where the cargo was financed by the American government under foreign aid programs and was limited by regulation and Congressional policy to American-owned vessels.

[23]This theory apparently underlies the provision in some consent decrees in the oil industry that a combination acting abroad shall be "presumed" to affect American commerce if its activities occur in three or more foreign nations; United States v. Standard Oil Co. (N.J.) (S.D.N.Y. 1968) 1968 Trade Cas. ¶72,742 (para. V[B]); *id.* (Gulf Oil Corp.) 1968 Trade Cas. ¶72,743 (para. V [B]).

[24]Differences between the language of the Sherman Act and of the FTC and Clayton Act sections have been discussed above. The statement here in the text

law is presumably not intended to concern itself with merely trifling contact between restraint and commerce; being enacted to protect commerce from restraint, it requires a showing that the restraint has at least enough relation to the commerce to make federal intervention something the lawmakers can reasonably have intended.

Where Section 1 of the Sherman Act is concerned, these considerations often find expression in a formula that the restraint must be shown to have a "direct and substantial effect" on either foreign or interstate commerce.[25] The meaning of this formula is far from clear. "Directness" as a standard has both the flexibility and the ambiguity of the "proximate cause" formula of tort law, which it closely resembles. As such, it is more a delegation of discretion to the judge or jury than it is a self-contained test or measure—a tool with which the court can catch cases obviously falling within the ambit of the law's policy while throwing out those which seem too far afield.

As a legal test, "substantiality" is more familiar in the antitrust field, but familiarity does not necessarily inspire confidence on the part of lawyers who recall the elusive usages of the word in the Clayton Act and in exclusive dealing, tying and other cases under both the Sherman and Clayton Acts.[26] In the presence of this word, one is sometimes

certainly applies also to cases under the FTC Act and Sections 2(a) and 3 of the Clayton Act, where the unfair method of competition, discrimination, or exclusive contract must be found to be "in" or "in the course of" commerce. Sections 7 and 8, however, appear to permit tacking of the fact that a corporation engages in commerce to the fact of a prohibited type of transaction to achieve statutory coverage; there appears to be no necessity of a functional relationship between the two facts.

[25] "Our courts have assumed jurisdiction under the antitrust laws over acts and contracts substantially and directly affecting, or interfering with, United States foreign trade . . . ," FUGATE, FOREIGN COMMERCE AND THE ANTITRUST LAWS 20 (1958); ". . . there must be some direct and substantial effect," *id.* at 255. "The vital question in all cases is the same: is the condition to so operate in this country as to directly and materially affect our foreign commerce?" United States v. Hamburg-Amerikanische P.F.A. Gesellschaft, 200 Fed. 806, 807 (S.D.N.Y. 1911), 216 Fed. 971 (S.D.N.Y. 1914), *rev'd as moot,* 239 U.S. 466 (1916); see other cases discussed in FUGATE, *supra,* 34 *et seq.* On interstate commerce, see Eiger, *The Commerce Element in Federal Antitrust Litigation,* 25 FED. B.J. 282 (1965).

[26] *E.g.,* the test of where the effect may be "substantially" to lessen competition as found in Sections 2(a), 3 and 7 of the Clayton Act; the short-lived doctrine of "quantitative substantiality" of Standard Oil Co. of California v. United States, 337 U.S. 293 (1949) (Section 3 of the Clayton Act applied to requirements contracts);

tempted to launch into an evaluation of the economic or business importance of the restraint's impact. In most foreign commerce cases, however, when the word "substantial" is used, it seems to mean merely that the effect of the restraint must not be too slight or *de minimis*; the courts do not really try to measure the volume of effect.[27] There are, however, significant possible borderline cases where it may be sensible to require a showing that the restraint has a very serious kind of effect, as will be pointed out later.

As for the type of effect which is relevant, the argument is sometimes made that *adverse* impact on the volume of the trade affected must be shown, an argument resulting from a literal reading of the words, "restraint of trade or commerce." But these words are terms of art which mean "restraint of competition in or affecting commerce," rather than merely interruption or restriction of the flow of commerce.[28] Of course, where a restriction of the flow results from a restraint of competition, the two concepts coalesce. But restraint of competition can occur in commerce without causing provable changes in volume; such restraint is nonetheless subject to Congressional regulation, and it is clear that the Sherman Act constitutes such regulation. Proof of adverse effect in the sense of a diminution of American exports or imports would be persuasive of violation as will be illustrated presently, but restraints which increase the volume of commerce as well as those which do not

the test of "not insubstantial amount of interstate commerce" of International Salt Co. v. United States, 332 U.S. 392 (1947) (tying under the Sherman Act).

[27] Responding to the question of how much effect is necessary, Mr. Fugate has answered, "any *substantial* effect," adding in a footnote that the courts have not asserted jurisdiction where the effects have been "only incidental." FUGATE, FOREIGN COMMERCE AND THE ANTITRUST LAWS 55 & n.20 (1958).

[28] The term, "restraint of trade," originally referred to contractual restriction of the freedom of a trader to pursue his trade, Mitchel v. Reynolds, 24 Eng. Rep. 347 (K.B. 1711); later common law cases applied it also to cover non-ancillary agreements among competitors to restrict competition, and this became its primary Sherman Act meaning, Standard Oil Co. of New Jersey v. United States, 221 U.S. 1 (1911). When the Act's draftsmen connected the phrase to the constitutional language giving power to Congress to regulate commerce, they created an awkward combination of two quite distinct concepts; to avoid error, these must be analytically separated. Draftsmen of Article 85(1) of the Rome Treaty avoided this kind of confusion by covering "agreements . . . likely to affect trade between Member States and which have the object or effect of preventing, restraining or distorting competition within the Common Market."

alter it at all may be equally within the jurisdictional scope of the law.[29]

It is here that it is particularly important to remember that the commerce issue is a jurisdictional issue which is separable from other questions of substantive violation. The latter questions also involve inquiry into effect, but of a different kind, *i.e.,* effect on competition, which must be shown to be unreasonable for Sherman Act purposes, or to amount to a substantial lessening for most Clayton Act purposes. As to those questions, the effect must indeed be "adverse," but it is an *adverse effect on competition* (in or affecting commerce), not an adverse effect on the volume of commerce, which must be shown.[30]

As a matter of fact, the cases not only do not require proof that the effect on commerce be adverse, but they seldom have insisted on very much strict proof of effect of any kind. Usually all that has seemed to be required has been a persuasive theory that commerce will be affected; attention has been concentrated upon the substantive issues.[31]

The phrase in the conjunctive, "direct *and* substantial" effect, does not appear to be an accurate generalization as to what most courts say

[29]In Ets. Consten S.A. and Grundig-Verkaufs-GmbH v. EEC Comm'n, CCH COMM. MKT. REP. ¶8046 at 7652, 5 Comm. Mkt. L.R. 418, 472 (1966), the Court of Justice stated that an agreement which increases the volume of interstate trade nonetheless "affects" trade within the meaning of Article 85(1).

[30]This may be illustrated by the *Timken* case, where the defendants argued that ordinary export-import trade was extremely difficult and that the restraints in issue were necessary to enable business to be conducted abroad. This was really an argument that the restraints favorably affected American commerce, but it was rejected as inconsistent with the purpose of Congress to foster *competition* in American foreign trade. Timken Roller Bearing Co. v. United States, 341 U.S. 593 (1951).

In Mandeville Island Farms, Inc. v. American Crystal Sugar Co., 334 U.S. 219 (1948), one of the leading modern Supreme Court antitrust decisions on effect on interstate commerce, the Court held that the Act would apply to a local California combination of beet sugar refiners which was fixing purchase prices paid to sugar beet producers; the Court stated that the effect of this local restraint among the refiners would inevitably be felt in the competition among them in subsequent interstate commerce in beet sugar. The effect which was relevant to the Court was effect on competition, not effect on the volume of beet sugar in interstate commerce, which might well have been increased by the defendants' control over the cost of the beets.

[31]See cases collected in Eiger, *supra* note 25.

they look for.[32] Since no foreign commerce cases have failed on commerce grounds, the opinions have not indulged in much critical examination of the problem. In the domestic commerce cases, however, some cases, though not many in recent years, have failed the commerce test. These almost invariably have been situations which the courts considered to be too "local" for the Act to apply to them, and hence too "indirect," "remote," or "incidental." Most such "local" restraints are also relatively small, and where they are both small and tangential to the stream of interstate commerce, their effects tend to be "insubstantial" as well as "indirect," thus failing both parts of the formula. But where a restraint is regarded as sufficiently "direct," the courts appear never to disqualify the case for failure to meet a "substantiality" test.[33] On the other hand, even if a restraint is indirect, demonstration that it will have a substantial impact on commerce may suffice.[34]

It would therefore probably be more accurate to say that the restraint must have either a "direct" *or* a "substantial effect."[35] The elements of directness and substantiality may be viewed as expressing different ways

[32]The following extracts by Mr. Fugate from leading foreign commerce cases suggest that the majority have not considered it necessary to find both a "direct" and a "substantial" effect: " 'the contract directly and materially affects foreign commerce'; 'the combination affected the foreign commerce of this country'; 'intended to affect imports and exports [and] . . . is shown actually to have had some effect on them'; 'though there is no showing as to the extent of commerce restrained it [the contract] deleteriously affected [United States] commerce'; 'with the effect of suppressing imports into and exports from the United States'; 'a conspiracy . . . affecting American commerce'; 'a direct and influencing effect on trade . . . between the United States and foreign countries'; 'a conspiracy . . . which affects American commerce.' " (citations omitted) FUGATE, FOREIGN COMMERCE AND THE ANTITRUST LAWS 52-53 (1958).

[33]See note 36 *infra.*

[34]As in Mandeville Island Farms, Inc. v. American Crystal Sugar Co.. 334 U.S. 219 (1948), see note 30 *supra*; Lieberthal v. North Country Lanes, Inc., 332 F.2d 269, 272 (2d Cir. 1964): "[T] he Sherman Act condemns wholly local restraints that affect interstate commerce as well as restraints in interstate commerce."

[35]See Timberg, *United States and Foreign Antitrust Laws Governing International Business Transactions,* in A LAWYER'S GUIDE TO INTERNATIONAL BUSINESS TRANSACTIONS 622 (Surrey & Shaw eds. 1963): "[T] he Sherman Act does not apply to agreements which do not directly or substantially affect United States imports, exports or interstate commerce."

In a quite different approach, the Attorney General's National Committee Report stated a substantiality requirement whose content was mixed with the law's

of asking whether the facts rise to the level of Congressional concern. The relative importance of either would thus vary inversely with changes in the strength of the showing on the other. The less "direct" the restraint is, the more important it would become to make a convincing showing that it produces a substantial effect. For example, a particular restraint carried out in a foreign market without being a part of an American export or import transaction may be in an "indirect" relation to American commerce; it might nevertheless be brought within the law, but only if a strong case of effect on American exports or imports is made. Conversely, if a restraint is so much a part of a foreign commerce transaction that it is easily seen to have a quite "direct" relation to that commerce, it becomes unimportant to ask how "substantial" it is.

The "direct-or-substantial effect on commerce" test is similar to the classification which is being made on a functional basis with increasing frequency in interstate commerce cases. This approach distinguishes between restraints which occur "in" commerce (or "in the course of," or "in the stream of" commerce), and restraints which cannot readily be said to be "in" commerce, but which nevertheless have an effect on it.[36] For cases in the first class, no

substantive standards of unreasonableness: "[T]he Sherman Act applies only to those arrangements . . . which have such substantial anti-competitive effects on this country's 'trade or commerce with foreign nations' as to constitute unreasonable restraints," ATTY. GEN. NAT. COMM. ANTITRUST REP. 76 (1955); *accord,* Haight, *The Sherman Act, Foreign Operations, and International Law,* in LEGAL PROBLEMS IN INTERNATIONAL TRADE AND INVESTMENT 89-90 (Shaw ed. 1962). This formula does not appear to have met with judicial approval.

After quoting the 1955 Report as above, the ABA ANTITRUST SECTION SUPP. TO ATTY. GEN. NAT. COMM. ANTITRUST REP., ANTITRUST DEVELOPMENTS: 1955-1968, at 47 (1968), summarized the rule, in light of the Restatement, as being that the scope of the antitrust laws "includes the conduct of American nationals, wherever it occurs, if the conduct has substantial anti-competitive effects on the commerce of the United States with foreign nations."

[36]The distinction was recognized in a Sherman Act case by the Supreme Court in Burke v. Ford, 389 U.S. 320 (1967), involving an agreement of liquor wholesalers in one state to divide the market in sales to retailers; the lower courts held that the restraint was not in interstate commerce, although the wholesalers purchased their supplies from out-of-state distillers, the liquor having "come to rest" in the wholesalers' warehouses; the Supreme Court reversed, *per curiam.* stating: "[W]hatever the validity of that conclusion, it does not end the matter. For it is well established that an activity which does not itself occur *in* interstate commerce comes within the scope of the Sherman Act if it substantially *affects* interstate commerce,"

effect need be shown, but for cases in the second class, effect must be demonstrated in order to establish jurisdiction. A case qualifying as "in" commerce meets the "directness" test. A restraint which is not "in" commerce is indirect and must meet a "substantial effect" test.

While no mere formula will supplant the need for making difficult judgments in this area, "in-or-substantial effect on commerce" appears to be preferable to "direct-or-substantial effect" for two reasons: (1) it may eliminate some confusion and wasted effort by removing the search for effect entirely, except in cases where it is clearly needed to justify an assertion of jurisdiction; and (2) it focuses on a somewhat more visible element than does the other formula—*i.e.,* the operative relationship between the restraint and the line of commerce.

It may be objected with some force that doctrine is not completely transferable from interstate to foreign commerce cases, and it must readily be conceded that great care should be exercised here. The interstate commerce clause expresses a relation between superior federal power and inferior state jurisdiction, while the foreign commerce clause concerns relations with foreign nations which acknowledge no subservience to the United States. Accordingly, doubts which are resolved in favor of federal jurisdiction as against the states might well be resolved in the opposite way when the question is the exercise of American power

id. at 321. The Court held that the restraint "inevitably affected" interstate commerce, (1) by causing an increase in prices and thereby a decrease in sales, with consequent reduced purchases in interstate commerce, and (2) by reducing the number of outlets available to out-of-state distillers.

The "in" and "substantially affecting" commerce tests were stated in Las Vegas Merchant Plumbers Ass'n v. United States, 210 F.2d 732, 739 n.3 (9th Cir. 1954), holding that a local combination of plumbing contractors to eliminate competition in local sales was a restraint "in" the course of interstate commerce in plumbing and heating equipment from manufacturer to consumer, the contractor being a "conduit" in the flow of this commerce; see also discussion and citation of cases in Lieberthal v. North Country Lanes, Inc., 332 F.2d 269 (2d Cir. 1964); see also Mandeville Island Farms, Inc. v. American Crystal Sugar Co., 334 U.S. 219, 234 (1948); United States v. Yellow Cab Co., 332 U.S. 218, 233 (1947).

In FTC v. Bunte Bros., 312 U.S. 349 (1941), the Court expressly distinguished FTC Act cases, in which it must be shown that the unfair practice is "in" commerce, from Sherman Act cases in which a showing of "effect" is enough. This distinction has also been applied to Section 2 of the Clayton Act and Section 3 of the Robinson-Patman Act, Myers v. Shell Oil Co., 96 F. Supp. 670, 676 (S.D.Cal. 1951).

abroad. This distinction could support stricter requirements of proof in foreign commerce cases, and it could also support the use of different substantive antitrust rules. But neither the statutory language nor the cases support the proposition that the relevant *elements* of the commerce analysis are themselves different.[37] On the contrary, the foreign commerce cases actually seem to fit the "in-or-substantial effect on commerce" formula quite well.

In the following discussion, this test is mainly relied upon in classifying different groups of cases involving foreign activity. In order to sharpen the analysis, the cases are delineated further into five categories: (1) cases involving foreign activities, but which can rest upon effect on domestic interstate commerce; (2) direct interference with, or restriction of export, import or other foreign commerce; (3) restraint of competition in transportation in foreign commerce; (4) restraint of competition in the course of business activity in foreign commerce; and (5) restraint of competition in foreign markets. Insofar as the "in-or-substantial effect on commerce" test is concerned, the first category contains cases of both types. Cases in the next three all fit the "in" commerce test. Some cases in the last category may fit an "in" commerce analysis, but in most cases, proof of substantial effect is likely to be critical to jurisdiction. The citation of cases, while extensive, does not purport to be exhaustive.

2. SPECIFIC TYPES OF RELATIONSHIP TO COMMERCE

a. *Effect on Domestic Commerce*

The great majority of situations in American antitrust cases which have involved foreign activities have also involved restraint of competition in American domestic, interstate commerce, so that the law probably could have reached them without a "foreign commerce" clause.

---

[37] It may be argued that this is not consistent with the approach taken in the *Alcoa* case as to acts of foreign firms abroad, requiring proof of both intent to restrain American commerce and effect (although proof of intent was held to make a prima facie case of effect), United States v. Aluminum Co. of America, 148 F.2d 416, 444 (2d Cir. 1945). If Judge Hand had also pointed out that the restraint was "in" commerce or was "direct" (it was an agreement to refrain from exporting to the United States), he would perhaps have been imposing a double requirement. But he did not discuss the "directness" question, and spoke only in terms of requiring both "*intent* and effect." Intent is not a jurisdictional factor; rather, it is an element of substantive violation; see text *infra*.

In this category could be placed all of the cases which have involved outright exclusion of one or more competitors from American national or multi-state domestic markets. Examples of such cases would be those involving division of world markets accompanied by exclusion of competitors from importing into or manufacturing in the United States.[38]

These cases include *Alcoa, Timken, I.C.I., Holophane,* and *Swiss Watch,* which have been the subject of the greatest controversies concerning application of the American law to foreign activities, and all of which included interstate commerce allegations. It is interesting to note that these controversies were not actually concerned with whether enough connection with American commerce had been shown to satisfy Sherman Act tests.[39] Rather, the disputes centered on such issues as whether the Act should be applied at all to conduct abroad, particularly on the part of foreign firms; to what extent it is limited by principles of international law; whether more lenient substantive rules should be used because of different conditions in foreign markets; what kind of relief is appropriate for activities abroad; and what recognition should be given to the public policy and interests of foreign governments.

In addition to the classic problem of market division, some of the cases involving international problems have dealt with other kinds of

[38] United States v. American Tobacco Co., 221 U.S. 106 (1911); United States v. General Dyestuff Corp., 57 F. Supp. 642 (S.D.N.Y. 1944); United States v. Aluminum Co. of America, 148 F.2d 416 (2d Cir. 1945); United States v. National Lead Co., 63 F. Supp. 513 (S.D.N.Y. 1945), *aff'd,* 332 U.S. 319 (1947); United States v. General Electric Co., 80 F. Supp. 989 (S.D.N.Y. 1948) (Carboloy); United States v. General Electric Co., 82 F. Supp. 753 (D.N.J. 1949) (incandescent lamp); Timken Roller Bearing Co. v. United States, 341 U.S. 593 (1951); United States v. Imperial Chem. Indus. Ltd., 100 F. Supp. 504 (S.D.N.Y. 1951); United States v. Holophane Co., 119 F. Supp. 114 (S.D. Ohio 1954), *aff'd,* 352 U.S. 903 (1956); United States v. Bayer Co., 135 F. Supp. 65 (S.D.N.Y. 1955); United States v. The Watchmakers of Switzerland Information Center, Inc. (S.D.N.Y. 1962), 1963 Trade Cas. ¶ 70,600, *order modified,* 1965 Trade Cas. ¶ 71,352.

[39] This is not to say that no issues at all on commerce were involved in these cases; see note 37 *supra* for mention of the "intent and effect" test of *Alcoa*; also, in the *Swiss Watch* case, United States v. The Watchmakers of Switzerland Information Center, Inc. (S.D.N.Y. 1962), 1963 Trade Cas. ¶ 70,600 at 77,454, an issue existed as to whether cartel agreements between Swiss producers and manufacturers in England, France and Germany restricting the latters' operations affected American commerce sufficiently; the court held that they were "intended" to and "did impose unreasonable restrictions" on American domestic and foreign commerce in watches.

restraint on domestic commerce. In *United States v. Singer Mfg. Co.,*[40] the American defendant combined with foreign firms to arrange patent rights so as to give the American firm the power to exclude Japanese competition from the domestic market. In the *Swiss Watch* case, defendants combined to restrain American manufacture of watches and parts and to exclude American imports of other than Swiss watches. *United States v. Sisal Sales Corp.*[41] involved monopolization abroad of the supply of a product imported into the United States.

As previously pointed out, attacks under Section 7 of the Clayton Act must rest on a theory of elimination of competition in a "section of the country." In *United States v. Jos. Schlitz Brewing Co.,*[42] the acquisition of stock in a Canadian beer company was found to affect actual domestic competition between the acquiring company and an American competitor controlled by the Canadian company. It was also believed that the merger would affect competition in the American market by excluding potential imports of the Canadian company's beer. The case illustrates how Section 7's narrow test of effect in a "section of the country" may easily be met in some foreign acquisition cases. A Justice Department official has pointed out that even a merger of two foreign firms could have adverse effects in the domestic market if the firms were competing in the United States directly or through subsidiaries.[43]

As will be noted later, effect on the domestic economy is the kind of effect upon which Common Market and national authorities in Europe must rely if they seek to deal with extraterritorial conduct, since the European laws contain no express "foreign commerce" provisions.

b. *Interference with or Restriction of Foreign Commerce*

Some of the cases involve anti-competitive interference with freedom to export or import and thus represent restraint of foreign commerce in

[40] 374 U.S. 174 (1963).

[41] 274 U.S. 268 (1927).

[42] 253 F. Supp. 129 (N.D. Cal. 1966), *aff'd per curiam,* 385 U.S. 37 (1966).

[43] Zimmerman, in *Hearings, supra* note 19, at 489.

Recently, the Justice Department filed suit challenging the acquisition of a German manufacturer of electric razors, Braun A.G., by an American manufacturer of safety razors, Gillette Co., alleging among other things that the acquisition would eliminate Braun as a potential independent competitor in the American market. No allegation was made concerning Gillette-Braun competition in foreign markets; United States v. Gillette Co. (D. Mass. 1968), CCH TRADE REG. REP. ¶45,068 (case 1988).

both the literal and the legal sense. Whenever competition in the domestic market is restrained through a restriction on imports, there is an effect on interstate commerce which merges with the effect on foreign commerce, as with most of the cases in the first category above. It is theoretically possible, however, to have an illegal restraint on imports which does not at the same time illegally restrain interstate commerce. Such a case could exist, for example, where the domestic effect of an import restraint is confined to one state. No reported case of this kind has been found.

Problems of outright interference with foreign commerce are more clearly isolated from interstate commerce when they occur in export transactions. There are very few decided cases of this kind, however, reflecting not only the Webb-Pomerene exemption for some export combinations, but also the bias of a nation in favor of competition in imports where it is in a buyer position, as against a lack of desire for competition when it is in a seller position.

A case of major interest in the export restraint category is *United States v. Minnesota Mining & Mfg. Co.*[44] Competing American firms, who had formed a Webb-Pomerene export association, entered into joint manufacturing ventures abroad. The court found that the parties had combined to reduce or eliminate exports to some parts of the world in favor of sales in those foreign markets from their foreign manufacturing plants. This choice was made because of the greater profitability of the latter sales, and not because exports were impossible under world trade conditions. On this basis, an illegal restraint in export trade was found. The Webb-Pomerene Act was held not to exempt the restraint because the Act, the court said, was designed to encourage exports. It did not exempt agreements to reduce exports on the part of participants in the export association, nor did it exempt concerted activity having the effect of restraining the competition of other American exporters who were not members of the association and whose sales were hurt by the success of the joint foreign manufacturing plants.

The opinion is important to our analysis for three reasons: (1) It refused to allow a reduction of exports of finished goods by the parties to be balanced by a finding that the combination had at the same time increased the export of raw materials to the foreign plants, stating:

[44]92 F. Supp. 947 (D. Mass. 1950).

". . . Congress has not said you may choke commerce here if you nourish it there."[45] It would seem to follow that when a given type of restraint reduces exports to some markets or customers, it is no defense that the net amount of exports by the parties has been kept level by increasing exports of the same goods to some other markets or customers. In other words, the Sherman Act's prohibitions against interference with free market forces are not put aside by showing that the restraint has not adversely affected the nation's balance of trade.

(2) The opinion in *Minnesota Mining* impliedly recognized the applicability of the Sherman Act to some kinds of vertical arrangements by stating that even the action of a single individual in refraining from exporting (in favor of manufacturing abroad) "would be a restraint upon American commerce with foreign nations," although it would not violate the statute because of the absence of a combination. If this kind of effect were coupled with a vertical contract, presumably the statute would apply. For example, an agreement by an American firm operating abroad to buy exclusively from a foreign firm in a foreign market could be analyzed, under this approach, as a restraint of American export if the buyer would otherwise patronize American exporters. Whether this would violate the American law, of course, would depend upon further substantive analysis.

(3) The case also explicitly recognizes two distinct kinds of relation between restraint and foreign commerce, either of which will suffice for a violation: (a) restraint of competition as to the defendants' own exports (subjective restraint), and (b) restraint of the export competition of competitors (objective restraint) through defendants' program of promoting their joint foreign manufacturing operations. This analysis is applicable to vertical as well as to horizontal cases. In some vertical cases, such as an agreement to export exclusively to a given buyer abroad in a defined market, the first kind of effect would exist. The second kind would be more important as to such things as requirements contracts obtained by American exporters from foreign buyers, the effect of which is to exclude the seller's export competitors. A contract by an American firm restraining its American distributor from exporting would seem to have the first kind of relation to foreign commerce; such a theory was apparently involved in a recent case filed by the Department of

---

[45] *Id.* at 962.

Justice.[46] Similar kinds of restraints of commerce may arise in connection with foreign joint ventures, as the *Minnesota Mining* case shows.

The recent case of *Continental Ore Co. v. Union Carbide & Carbon Corp.*[47] seems to show that a restraint on the competition represented by one American firm's exports which is achieved through agreement with a foreign purchaser sufficiently involves American foreign commerce for jurisdictional purposes. In that case, the Supreme Court held that there was sufficient evidence to go to the jury on the existence of a conspiracy among certain American producers in the vanadium industry. The facts allegedly included an understanding with the Canadian subsidiary of one of the defendants that the latter would prevent Canadians from purchasing from plaintiff, who was seeking to export to Canada. The Canadian subsidiary had the opportunity to do this, it was alleged, because it was acting as exclusive agent for the Canadian government for allocation of purchases of this commodity, then a strategic material, and it allegedly refused to authorize any purchases from plaintiff. The restraint evidently had no effect on the overall volume of exports, as plaintiff alleged that its former share of the Canadian market had been divided between the two defendant American producers. While the case involved a horizontal combination in domestic as well as foreign commerce, the foreign commerce analysis, as distinguished from possible questions of substantive law, would not be different if all that were present were a simple agreement between one American seller and one Canadian buyer that the latter will not buy from a competitor of the seller.

Many of the territorial division cases listed under the first category above involved not only restraints upon domestic and import competition, but also reciprocal restraint of exports. In some of the opinions, reference is made not only to the fact of restraint on exports, but to the amount or substantiality of the effect shown; in others, there is no discussion of the question. But no case has been found holding that proof of substantiality is *required* where the restraint operates directly to interfere with a line of export commerce by cutting it off, or by

---

[46]United States v. Dymo Indus., Inc. (Civ. No. 42672, N.D. Cal.), CCH TRADE REG. REP. ¶45,064 (case 1817), settled by consent decree, 1967 Trade Cas. ¶72,102.

[47]370 U.S. 690 (1962).

rechanneling it to different markets or customers, or into different products. As Judge Weinfeld said, in a foreign commerce case, quoting Justice Douglas' famous dictum, "the amount of interstate or foreign commerce restrained is not material * * * since § 1 of the Act brands as illegal the character of the restraint not the amount of commerce affected."[48]

The inference has been drawn from the cartel cases that restraints which explicitly govern United States foreign trade have been "vulnerable even if imports or domestic production were not proved to be seriously curbed or extortionately priced."[49] There seems to have been no reason for the author's not also saying that an explicit restraint on *exports* is equally vulnerable without showing that exports have been seriously curbed. Any distinction between imports and exports would have to rest upon the idea that the Sherman Act is more concerned with competition in the former than in the latter. But no court seems to have articulated such an idea, and it was really rejected in *Timken, Continental Ore* and *Minnesota Mining*—cases applying to exports the same substantive doctrines that are used in domestic cases, including per se doctrines. In *United States v. General Dyestuff Corp.*,[50] the defendant argued that the only effect of the restraint on exports by General Aniline in the facts at hand was to deprive the people of foreign nations of the benefit of the latter's competition, but the court replied: ". . . that is no answer to the policy of the Sherman Act which forbids conspiratorial restraints on foreign commerce, as well as on domestic interstate commerce."[51]

In summary, a restrictive agreement which interferes with the movement of either imports or exports is likely to be regarded as falling within the "foreign commerce" jurisdiction of the Sherman Act without regard to how much actual effect there has been, either upon the parties, or upon trade generally. The question of "how much effect" could play an important role in determining the legality of the agreement under the rule of reason, if the restraint present is not of the per se variety, but this

---

[48]United States v. Bayer Co., 135 F. Supp. 65, 70 (S.D.N.Y. 1955), quoting from United States v. Socony-Vacuum Oil Co., 310 U.S. 150, 225 n.59 (1940).

[49]BREWSTER, ANTITRUST AND AMERICAN BUSINESS ABROAD 28 (1958); also 81; see also discussion of exports in ch. 6, where treatment of the issues of commerce and of substantive questions is interwoven.

[50]57 F. Supp. 642 (S.D.N.Y. 1944).

[51]*Id.* at 647.

question would not seem to have much bearing upon the applicability of the Act insofar as commerce tests are concerned. The same rationale would apply to restraints upon exports or imports under Section 5 of the Federal Trade Commission Act.

c. Restraint of Competition in Transportation in Foreign Commerce

Some Sherman Act cases have involved restraints of competition committed in transportation in foreign commerce. Application of the American law to such activities would probably not often overlap with foreign antitrust law where the restraints are confined to international waters or airspace, because of the narrower extraterritorial scope of the foreign laws. But the cases are nonetheless of possible interest because of their similarity to the category discussed next, *i.e.,* restraint of competition "in the course of" transactions in foreign commerce.

The leading foreign commerce shipping cases are *United States v. Pacific & Arctic Co.*[52] and *Thomsen v. Cayser.*[53] In the *Pacific & Arctic* case, the Court sustained the sufficiency of an indictment under the Sherman Act which alleged a combination of American and Canadian ocean, rail and river boat corporations to monopolize ocean shipping between United States and Alaskan ports. This was accomplished by causing the participating railroads in Canada and Alaska to discriminate against or to refuse to serve shippers who used competing ocean carriers. Although the Court's language stresses that some acts occurred "in" the United States, the gist of the case was a combination to restrain competition in ocean shipping. There was no indication that any proof of reduction or alteration in the volume or kind of such foreign commerce was at all necessary.

This point was perhaps made clearer in *Thomsen v. Cayser,* which involved a combination of ocean carriers to monopolize transporation

[52] 228 U.S. 87 (1913).

[53] 243 U.S. 66 (1917). Other overseas transportation cases under the antitrust laws, which have not involved discussion of the commerce issue, include: Far East Conference v. United States, 342 U.S. 570 (1952) (primary jurisdiction in Federal Maritime Board); United States Navigation Co. v. Cunard Steamship Co., 284 U.S. 474 (1932) (similar issues); United States v. Hamburgh-American S.S. Line, 216 Fed. 971 (S.D.N.Y. 1914) (issues of reasonableness of practices used); Pan American World Airways, Inc. v. United States, 371 U.S. 296 (1963) (primary jurisdiction in Civil Aeronautics Board); see also note 55, *infra.*

between the United States and South Africa. Sherman Act jurisdiction was sustained, despite alleged formation of the combination abroad, on the ground that "the combination affected the foreign commerce of this country and was put into operation here."[54] The effect on foreign commerce was as to shipping itself, and consisted, not of preventing or reducing the amount of shipping, but of restraining competition in the conduct of such shipping.

While these cases offer almost nothing in the way of exposition on the point, they do stand implicitly for a theory that—in the language of the Act—there is "restraint of trade or commerce . . . with foreign nations" not only when such commerce is stopped or restricted, but also when competition in it is restrained with respect to rates, service and other aspects of trade, regardless of the effect thereof on volume.

It would ordinarily be a different matter where restraints of competition are alleged only as to transportation between foreign ports. Such restraints would not normally be "in" American foreign commerce itself.[55] As indicated in *In re Grand Jury Investigation of the Shipping Industry*,[56] Sherman Act application in such a situation would have to rest on a showing of consequential effect on shipping from American ports, or on American trade in the goods shipped.

d. Restraint of Competition in the Course of Foreign Commerce

It is only a short distance between the shipping cases and cases involving restraints of competition carried out in the process of engaging in business transactions in foreign commerce. The distinction between the latter and the "interference" cases discussed in the second category

[54] 243 U.S. at 88.

[55] *Cf.* Pacific Seafarers, Inc. v. Pacific Far East Line, Inc., 404 F.2d 804 (D.C. Cir. 1968), *cert. denied,* 393 U.S. 1093 (1969), where the Sherman Act was applied to a combination of ocean carriers operating between foreign ports which allegedly sought to destroy plaintiff's business between those ports; this commerce was held to be American foreign commerce because of certain special facts, see note 22 *supra.* The court stated, however, that "[i] t may be assumed that . . . the Sherman Act has no application where the market involved consists of shipping services between two foreign ports . . . and the only American aspect is that one or some of the persons competing in the transportation market is offering American flag ships;" *id.* at 816.

[56] 186 F. Supp. 298, 311-14 (D.D.C. 1960).

above is the difference between literal restraint of export or import, and other forms of restriction of competition which occur in foreign transactions without interfering physically with the trade itself. It is the difference, in other words, between prevention or redirection of a line of foreign commerce, on the one hand, and regulation of the prices, terms, customers, sales territories or other business aspects in a line of foreign commerce on the other hand. In terms of substantive antitrust law, such a distinction has no great significance. If it is true that when foreign trade is literally restrained, the Sherman Act applies without the need for any special showing about the amount or quality of the effect, there is no good reason for the commerce test to be more demanding if the restraint is simply a more sophisticated type of restriction of competition. It is, in fact, the latter category of restraints with which the law is most often concerned.

The notion seems to persist, however, that such restraints do not meet the foreign commerce test unless they stop or reduce the movement of trade. Although Professor Brewster stated that "[l]oose agreements governing price, output, or territories for export would seem to fall under the Sherman Act ban," he gave as his rationale for this the probable limitation of the "business potential" of the exporter which the restraint would cause, thus resting on an economic judgment that the volume of exports would be lessened.[57] Mr. Fugate apparently classifies the problem as one of illegality of price fixing "in foreign markets," concluding that application of the law to such situations is conjectural, except where there is "direct and substantial effect on United States trade."[58]

[57] BREWSTER, *supra* note 49, at 105.

[58] FUGATE, *supra* note 27, at 102-04 (1958). These views gain occasional support from judicial repetition of the "direct and substantial" test in cases which include a problem of non-exclusionary restraint. For example, in United States v. R.P. Oldham Co., 152 F. Supp. 818, 822 (N.D. Cal. 1957), the court held both the Wilson Tariff Act and the Sherman Act applicable to a conspiracy among American and Japanese wire nail firms to control American imports through controlling supply in Japan, allocating import purchases among American buyers, and controlling resale prices and territories in the United States. Although these restraints were quite "direct" and seemingly "in" American import and domestic commerce, the court justified its jurisdiction on the ground that the conspiracy was alleged "to operate as a direct and substantial restraint on interstate and foreign commerce."

As previously pointed out, developments in the doctrines applicable to interstate commerce make it enough to find that such restraints on competition in sales in commerce are being carried out "in" commerce, without requiring an additional special showing of effect on that commerce. The argument should be mentioned again, however, that interstate commerce doctrines do not necessarily carry over to the kinds of restrictive agreements in foreign commerce under discussion here because of different trade conditions, and because of problems of possible conflict with foreign law and sovereignty. Is the interpretation of the foreign commerce clause an appropriate place for trying to adapt to these considerations? It has been suggested that it is, on the theory that problems of the conflict of laws genre are better dealt with jurisdictionally than substantively.[59] But the idea does not seem fully to withstand analysis. Assuming that American "foreign commerce" must be held to be present if exports are actually shut off by a world territorial allocation, it would make little sense to say that "foreign commerce" is not involved if the same exports were not shut off but were subjected to price controls. The commerce clause is an awkward tool with which to manipulate solutions for the problems of conflict; such problems are better faced under the substantive law.

The conclusion of this chapter is that the concept of attaching antitrust jurisdiction to restraints of competition "in" foreign commerce applies to make any restraint of trade carried out in the course of an export or import transaction subject to the American law, regardless of how much effect on trade, if any, can be shown and regardless of the degree of overlap or conflict with foreign law. The extent of the effect may have a bearing on substantive legality, but it has none on jurisdiction.[60] *United States v. Learner Co.*[61] is a possible illustration, although the court used language of effect. The indictment charged a combination of steel scrap exporters to fix prices in export sales, exclude outsiders from the business through exclusive agreements,

[59]Comment, *Extraterritorial Application of the Antitrust Laws: A Conflict of Laws Approach,* 70 YALE L. J. 259, 282-83 (1960); see also, Trautman, *The Role of Conflicts Thinking in Defining the International Reach of American Regulatory Legislation,* 22 OHIO ST. L. J. 586 (1961).

[60]See Kramer, *The Application of the Sherman Act to Foreign Commerce.* 3 ANTITRUST BULL. 387, 397 (1958) ("[T]here is no doubt" that a horizontal price-fixing agreement in export sales would be per se illegal.)

[61]215 F. Supp. 603, 605 (D. Hawaii 1963).

and allocate the business among themselves territorially. While to some extent this was an exclusionary restraint case which would probably satisfy any test, the court commented separately on the price fixing charge with the observation that the amount of interstate or foreign trade involved is "immaterial."

Three cases filed by the Justice Department testing the Webb-Pomerene exemption, one of which—the *Concentrated Phosphate Export Association* case—resulted in a Supreme Court opinion, are founded upon the theory that price fixing and allocation of export sales violate the Sherman Act if the transactions (sales abroad to the United States Government or to foreign purchasers under United States foreign aid programs) are outside the exemption.[62]

The question remains whether a similar analysis would be applicable to vertical restrictions placed astride import or export transactions. Most vertical import restrictions—*e.g.,* resale price controls established by a foreign manufacturer on goods shipped to and sold in the United States[63]—would usually have a domestic commerce impact and therefore

[62] In United States v. Concentrated Phosphate Export Ass'n, 393 U.S. 199 (1968), the Court reversed the trial court and held that the sales were not in "export trade" within the meaning of the Webb-Pomerene exemption because the "transactions involved here were American, not Korean," and Congress did not intend American taxpayers to be "deprived of the main benefits of competition among American firms," *id.* at 209. See Kilcarr, *United States v. Concentrated Phosphate Export Association: A Small Case in the Big Court,* 14 ANTITRUST BULL. 37 (1969). The other cases are United States v. International Ore & Fertilizer Corp. United States v. International Minerals & Chem. Corp. (S.D.N.Y. 1966), CCH TRADE REG. REP. ¶45,063 (cases 1768, 1769) (pleas of *nolo contendere* on sales to A.I.D. purchasers); and United States v. Anthracite Export Ass'n (Civ. No. 9171, D. Penn.), CCH TRADE REG. REP. ¶45,065 (case 1879) (pending on charges of price fixing, allocation and joint bidding on sales to U.S. Army in Europe).

[63] In the following cases of this type, an American distributing subsidiary of a foreign manufacturer was the alleged source of resale price, exclusive dealing and territorial restraints allegedly violating Section 1 of the Sherman Act and Section 3 of the Clayton Act: United States v. Volkswagen of America, Inc. (D.N.J. 1962), CCH TRADE REG. REP. ¶45,003 (case 1368) (consent decree, 1962 Trade Cas. ¶70,256); United States v. Renault, Inc. (S.D.N.Y. 1962), CCH TRADE REG. REP. ¶45,059 (case 1488) (consent decree, 1962 Trade Cas. ¶70,386); United States v. American Honda Motor Co. (S.D. Cal. 1966), CCH TRADE REG. REP. ¶45,066 (case 1889) (*nolo contendere*). The presence of an American subsidiary in these cases facilitated taking personal jurisdiction, but there would appear to be no question that the antitrust laws would substantively apply to such restraints in the domestic

would seldom present a problem about the law's applicability. The more difficult question arises as to vertical price and similar non-exclusionary restrictions in export transactions. In these cases, the final direct impact of the restraint would normally be in a foreign market, and some of the writers have balked at the idea that the law extends this far.[64]

A solitary Federal Trade Commission case, however, represents some authority for use of the "in" commerce theory for such vertical restraints. In *Branch v. FTC,*[65] the court upheld an FTC order under Section 5 against a Chicago correspondence course firm which, in advertising to prospective students in Latin America, was misrepresenting itself as a "university" qualified to give various degrees. Troubled by the argument that the FTC was set up to protect United States interests, not residents of foreign countries, the court responded that the Commission was acting to protect the respondent's competitors against injury by respondent's unfair methods. This finding of motive may have been relevant to the question of whether the Commission was acting in the "public interest," but it had nothing to do with whether the unfair method itself was committed "in" foreign commerce, as required in FTC Act cases.[66] The affirmative finding on the latter issue necessarily rested simply upon the fact that respondent engaged in acts of misrepresentation in the course of selling its services in export transactions.

Clearly within range, therefore, would be unilateral predatory conduct in export sales challenged under either Section 5 or the "attempt" provision of Section 2 of the Sherman Act. Vertical restrictive agreements carried out in export sales would also, by analogy, be equally subject to FTC and court jurisdiction.[67] What would be the situation as

market irrespective of whether an American subsidiary, branch or agent of the foreign manufacturer existed.

[64]BREWSTER, *supra* note 49, at 134 (saying that explicit vertical restrictions against re-export to the United States would be covered, but not ordinary export resale price and territorial controls); FUGATE, *supra* note 27, at 106 (observing that there is no case holding resale price control illegal and suggesting that Alfred Bell & Co. v. Catalda Fine Arts, Inc., 191 F.2d 99 (2d Cir. 1951) is some authority against such a holding).

[65]141 F.2d 31 (7th Cir. 1944).

[66]See text at note 8 *supra.*

[67]Export sales pursuant to agreement with foreign distributors to buy exclusively from the American exporter, or to refrain from re-exporting to the United States

to an agreement for vertical resale price control over sales by an American exporter's customers in foreign markets? If the goods are purchased by the foreign distributor and are subject to an agreement governing resale prices in the foreign market, the impact of the restraint will be regarded as too remote by some observers.[68] But normally the goods would move in foreign commerce on the understanding that the restrictive agreement is to govern their resale, and the restraint would therefore be part of the transaction in commerce. Comparable domestic situations are routinely treated as meeting interstate commerce tests, and it is the necessary outgrowth of the analysis set forth in the present study that such cases are within the scope of the foreign commerce clause of the American laws, regardless of whether any particular effect on commerce is shown.

e. Restraint of Competition in Foreign Markets

The extraterritorial scope of American antitrust law is, of course, most doubtful when the restraints concerned are carried out solely in foreign market transactions. Where goods are sold and delivered to buyers abroad from plants or distribution facilities located abroad, such transactions often are not thought of as being "in" American commerce. American law may still apply if a sufficient "effect" on American commerce is shown, but this also often appears to be remote.

Goods Still "In" Commerce. The "in" commerce theory may be satisfied, however, in some situations in which the goods have been imported from the United States prior to their involvement in a particular restraint abroad. The question of whether the goods are still "in" commerce may be broken down into cases in which the goods—since their export from the United States and prior to imposition of a restraint—(a) have been sold, (b) have been altered by manufacturing or processing, or (c) have been stored in warehouse facilities. No foreign commerce antitrust cases directly in point appear to have been decided. Interstate commerce decisions, however, are fairly numerous and provide possible guidance. Although they are not necessarily controlling, they may be influential and should be noted.

would not only be restraints of competition carried out "in" American commerce, but they would also qualify as direct "interference" with commerce and therefore within the second category discussed in the text *supra*.

[68] See note 64 *supra*.

In interstate commerce situations, sale of the goods before they become involved in a restraint imposed by the buyer ordinarily terminates the interstate commerce, in the absence of additional facts.[69] This doctrine is subject to certain important qualifications, however. If the interstate seller ships particular goods to a buyer to fill a specific prior order received by the buyer from a local customer, the Supreme Court has held that interstate commerce survives the first sale and the goods remain "in" commerce until the final delivery to the person who ordered them.[70] More recently, some lower court decisions have held that, even in the absence of prior orders, goods from an interstate source remain in commerce after sale to a distributor or dealer until resale to a local customer. In these cases, the courts have stressed that the manufacturer and distributors have contemplated a continuing movement of the goods from plant to consumer. Sometimes they have referred to this as a "practical continuity of movement" of the goods,[71] an extension of a phrase used in the *Walling* case.[72] Other cases have said that the distributor or dealer who resells the goods locally is merely a "conduit" for their passage from interstate seller to ultimate con-

[69]Hiram Walker, Inc. v. A & S Tropical, Inc., 407 F.2d 4 (5th Cir. 1969) (local sales by wholesalers of liquor purchased in interstate commerce); Burke v. Ford, 337 F.2d 901, 904-06 (10th Cir. 1967), *rev'd on other grounds,* 389 U.S. 320 (1967) (similar); Lawson v. Woodmere, 217 F.2d 148, 150-51 (4th Cir. 1954). See also Walling v. Jacksonville Paper Co., 317 U.S. 564, 568-71 (1943), holding that a wholesaler's sales of goods purchased in interstate commerce were not themselves "in commerce" for purposes of the Fair Labor Standards Act, except in situations where particular goods had been purchased in interstate commerce pursuant to a prior order from a customer.

[70]FTC v. Pacific States Paper Trade Ass'n, 273 U.S. 52 (1927) (paper products); Plymouth Dealers' Ass'n v. United States, 279 F.2d 128, 135 (9th Cir. 1960) (automobiles); Walling v. Jacksonville Paper Co., 317 U.S. 564 (1943) (Fair Labor Standards Act).

[71]Food Basket, Inc. v. Albertson's, Inc., 383 F.2d 785, 788 (10th Cir. 1967) (Sherman Act applied to alleged predatory local sales of groceries processed in other states; Robinson-Patman Act, however, not applied); Northern California Pharmaceutical Ass'n v. United States, 306 F.2d 379 (9th Cir. 1962) (Sherman Act applied to local price fixing by retail pharmacies on theory that there was "practical continuity of movement" of packaged prescription drugs from out-of-state manufacturers to consumers, a high percentage of the drugs being sold in their original form; regulation of pharmacies by state does not interrupt commerce).

[72]Walling v. Jacksonville Paper Co., 317 U.S. 564, 568 (1943); see note 69 *supra.*

sumer.[73] If this approach becomes well-established, it will put most local distribution of out-of-state goods into interstate commerce. It has not as yet been examined by the Supreme Court, however, or even very carefully analyzed in lower court opinions.

In the absence of a sale, it now appears to be well-established that mere temporary local storage by the interstate seller in facilities controlled by him will not end interstate commerce for antitrust purposes, where the interstate shipment into temporary storage is in anticipation of sale of the goods.[74]

Even if the goods are subjected to a certain amount of processing by the interstate seller after they have arrived in the particular state, their subsequent sale there may still be held to be in interstate commerce.[75] On the other hand, conversion of the goods as raw materials into a different manufactured product ordinarily terminates the commerce.[76]

[73] Las Vegas Merchant Plumbers Ass'n v. United States, 210 F.2d 732 (9th Cir. 1954) (plumbing contractors "conduits" in stream of commerce of plumbing equipment from manufacturers to consumers); United States v. Utah Pharmaceutical Ass'n, 201 F.Supp. 29 (D. Utah, 1962), *aff'd per curiam,* 371 U.S. 24 (1962) (pharmacists "conduits").

[74] Standard Oil Co. (Indiana) v. FTC, 340 U.S. 231, 237 (1951) (temporary storage of gasoline after interstate movement and before sale to local distributors); Foremost Dairies, Inc. v. FTC, 348 F.2d 674, 678 (5th Cir. 1965) (temporary halt of milk for processing); Hardrives Co. v. East Coast Asphalt Corp., 329 F.2d 868 (5th Cir. 1964), *cert. denied,* 379 U.S. 903 (1964) (temporary storage of bitumen after shipment from Venezuela and other points to Florida).

[75] Dean Milk Co. v. FTC, 395 F.2d 696, 715 & n.37 (7th Cir. 1968) (milk processed by pasteurization, homogenization, and blending to standardize); Foremost Dairies, Inc. v. FTC, 348 F.2d 674, 676-77 (5th Cir. 1965) (same); Plymouth Dealers' Ass'n of No. Cal. v. United States, 279 F.2d 128, 135 (9th Cir. 1960) (assembly of automobile parts and equipment shipped from out-of-state does not terminate interstate commerce).

[76] *Held* not in interstate commerce: fish food made from imported whey, yeast, and fish meal, Rangen, Inc. v. Sterling Nelson & Sons, Inc., 351 F.2d 851 (9th Cir. 1965); burial boxes and vaults made from imported raw materials, Lawson v. Woodmere, Inc., 217 F.2d 148 (4th Cir. 1954); wallboard incorporating imported gypsum, Baldwin Hills Building Materials Co. v. Fibreboard Paper Products Co., 283 F.Supp. 202 (C.D. Cal. 1968); petroleum products refined from crude oil purchased from out of state, Myers v. Shell Oil Co., 96 F.Supp. 670, 676 (S.D. Cal. 1951); electrical systems assembled by contractors from components purchased from out of state, United States v. San Francisco Elec. Contractors Ass'n, 57 F.Supp. 57, 65 (C.D. Cal. 1944); see also Central Ice Cream Co. v. Golden Rod Ice Cream Co., 287

If these interstate commerce concepts were applied to foreign commerce, what would the practical consequences be? First, it should be observed that the "prior order" doctrine is well-established, and may therefore be readily transferable to American export situations. Many sales by American firms abroad undoubtedly would fit the description. The "prior order" doctrine, however, is designed to enable antitrust law to reach local restraints of competition carried out by buyers; the interstate seller is not subjected to liability by this doctrine; he is culpable only if he is a participant in the buyer's restraint. Accordingly, it would seem that not very many exporters would be affected, and that the impact of the doctrine would be mainly upon foreign buyers in foreign markets. This major difference from the domestic interstate commerce context in which the doctrine has developed may very well be enough to prevent its acceptance by the courts in foreign commerce cases. Further, if the "prior order" doctrine is not extended to foreign commerce, it would follow *a fortiori* that the more extended concepts based on "conduit" and "practical continuity" ideas will not be used.

The situation is otherwise as to shipments from the United States to foreign markets of goods which are involved in restraints there prior to sale. The American exporter who ships to facilities controlled by him abroad, warehouses the goods in anticipation of sales and then sells them would appear to be as subject to American antitrust law with respect to restraints applied to those sales as is the participant in a simple export sale without warehousing. If the law reaches the latter, there appears to be no reason why temporary warehousing will prevent its application to the former. At the same time, American manufacturers operating abroad presumably will have full benefit of the doctrine that substantial alteration of exported raw materials will remove them from commerce.

Effect on Commerce. Although a restraint of competition in a foreign market is not carried out "in" commerce, it must still be analyzed to determine whether it "substantially affects" American commerce in some way. The obvious restraints which directly exclude a line of American exports or imports have been discussed as restraints "in"

F.2d 265 (7th Cir. 1961) (ice cream); Brosious v. Pepsi-Cola Co., 155 F.2d 99 (3d Cir. 1946) (soft drinks); Ewing-Von Allmen Dairy Co. v. C and C Ice Cream Co., 109 F.2d 898 (6th Cir. 1940) (ice cream).

commerce under other headings above. Here, attention is focused upon restraints which are not plainly aimed at export or import trade, and which appear to be essentially connected only with activity in foreign markets.

There are almost no decided cases which fit this description, but *Sanib Corp. v. United Fruit Co.* is a possible example.[77] The defendant, United Fruit, which operated banana plantations in Honduras, had recently entered the banana dehydrating business there. Accordingly, it allegedly cut off the plaintiff's supply, which it had previously furnished, of reject bananas needed for plaintiff's competing dehydrating plant in Honduras. A Sherman Act violation was alleged on the basis of an intra-enterprise conspiracy between related United Fruit corporations. This complaint was held to state a cause of action, though based on acts abroad which were not carried out in American commerce, the court saying that the restraint "was intended to, and in fact did affect the interstate and foreign commerce of the United States." (It does not appear that the court's reference to intent meant that this was essential to the action.)

By analogy, an agreement between two firms abroad to boycott a third firm abroad as to raw materials, which prevents sales of finished goods which the third firm would otherwise make in export to the United States, would be illegal. Other types of agreement or conduct abroad producing the same effect, such as exclusive dealing agreements, tying arrangements, and monopolistic unilateral conduct, would similarly be within reach of the law.

According to a Justice Department spokesman, an acquisition by an American of a foreign firm, or even a merger of two foreign firms, could come within American law if there is a "substantial restraint of U.S. trade resulting from the merger."[78] A merger abroad could cut off a third firm's supplies—*e.g.,* by vertical integration—thereby in turn reducing its ability to export to the United States. Another kind of merger could redirect purchasing by the firms involved so as to affect American export commerce.

What would be the impact of American law on less complete restraints in foreign markets, such as price fixing, territorial division, etc.? Such restraints do not as obviously interfere with commerce

[77] 135 F.Supp. 764 (S.D.N.Y. 1955).
[78] Zimmerman, in *Hearings, supra* note 19, at 491.

anterior or posterior to the point of their application, as do boycotts and other exclusionary arrangements. But economic analysis demonstrates that they may still be expected to affect the movement of goods because of their impact on demand. Thus, in a recent interstate commerce decision, *Burke v. Ford*,[79] the Supreme Court held that the Sherman Act would reach a division of territory among wholesale liquor dealers in one state in their sales to local retailers of liquor purchased from out of the state. The Court simply reasoned that with the reduction in local competition, prices would increase, unit sales would decrease, and fewer purchases from out-of-state distillers would result. The Court disposed of the issue purely on the basis of economic theory, requiring no factual demonstration of effect. At the other end of commerce, it was similarly held years ago in the *Mandeville Island Farms* case that price fixing by competing manufacturers in purchases of raw materials from suppliers in a single state could be reached by the Sherman Act on the theory that this local restraint of buying competition would inevitably affect the interstate selling competition of the defendants.[80]

If the interstate commerce cases are any indication, American law could thus reach restraints of competition in foreign markets involving goods emanating from the United States, or destined for the United States, even though they are not "in" a line of American commerce. As with the "in" commerce theories discussed above, however, there may be good reasons not to give "effect" theories as extended an application abroad as they have received in interstate commerce. To do so—to carry the law as far as the logic of the *Burke* and *Mandeville Island Farms* cases—would push American law deeply into the functioning of foreign markets in some commodities, and would lay at least a claim to jurisdiction over many foreign firms in their home activities. It seems unlikely that the Supreme Court, when it eventually gets the question, will push the effect doctrine to its limits. On the other hand, the doctrine is integral to American antitrust law and is not likely to be entirely abandoned either. A line will have to be drawn.

One line could be drawn in terms of the quality and quantity of proof of effect which is demanded for an application of the law to foreign market restraints. In the domestic cases, as well as in the direct

[79]389 U.S. 320 (1967).
[80]Mandeville Island Farms, Inc. v. American Crystal Sugar Co., 334 U.S. 219 (1948).

export and import decisions, the courts have not required much proof of the fact of actual or probable effect; a plausible theory normally is enough. Moreover, there has not been much attention paid to the quantitative dimension of effect; the question, being jurisdictional, is satisfied with anything that can be called "substantial." In foreign market cases, however, the courts could very well call for convincing proof of the fact of effect and also for a demonstration that the effect is, or will be, really quantitatively significant.[81]

Intent Rule for Foreign Firms. An additional limitation upon the application of American law in foreign markets is the special rule developed in *Alcoa* for foreign firms acting abroad. Reacting to the sensitive question of whether American law should be applied to foreign firms for restrictive activities carried on outside the United States, Judge Learned Hand suggested what seems to have become accepted American doctrine, *viz.,* that the foreign firm should not be culpable unless both an intent to restrain American commerce and an effect on such commerce are shown.[82] The burden of showing no effect, however, shifts to the defendant, he said, where the requisite intent is shown.

This approach is very similar to the principles stated in Section 18 of the Restatement (Second) of Foreign Relations Law of the United States.[83] It differs, however, in two potentially significant respects.

---

[81] In United States v. Minnesota Mining & Mfg. Co., 92 F.Supp. 947, 958 (D.Mass. 1950), Judge Wyzanski pointed out that before it is concluded that commerce has been restrained, it should be shown that the commerce in question could have been conducted in the absence of the restraint.

[82] United States v. Aluminum Co. of America, 148 F.2d 416, 444 (2d Cir. 1945). This doctrine was followed in United States v. General Electric Co., 82 F.Supp. 753, 890 (D.N.J. 1949) (incandescent lamp case); and in United States v. Watchmakers of Switzerland Information Center, Inc., 1963 Cas. ¶ 70,600 (S.D.N.Y. 1962), *order modified,* 1965 Trade Cas. ¶ 71,352. Controversy over the doctrine is discussed in Chapter 7 *infra.*

[83] Section 18 reads, in part:

"A state has jurisdiction to prescribe a rule of law attaching legal consequences to conduct that occurs outside its territory and causes an effect within its territory, if . . .

. . . .

(b) (i) the conduct and its effect are constituent elements of activity to which the rule applies; (ii) the effect within the territory is substantial; (iii) it occurs as a *direct and foreseeable result* of the conduct outside the territory;

First, the Restatement speaks of an "effect within [the] territory" of the nation as the initial condition which gives jurisdiction, while in the *Alcoa* opinion, Judge Hand, with the foreign commerce clause of the Sherman Act before him, and in light of the facts at hand, spoke of effect on imports. There may appear to be little difference between these two kinds of effect. But if the effect "within" the nation's territory must be of the amount and kind necessary to satisfy the substantive requirements of the Sherman Act—as seems intended by the Restatement's condition that the effect be a "constituent" element of the activity to which the legal rule in question applies—a mere theory of effect on export or import sufficient to satisfy Sherman Act commerce tests, as summarized above, would not automatically qualify.

A second difference between *Alcoa* and the Restatement is that the latter specifies no "intent" requirement, although it has been suggested that the Restatement's requirement that the effect be a "direct and foreseeable result" of the activity abroad amounts to such a requirement.[84] If by "intent," Judge Hand meant a specific, conscious purpose to bring about the effect, as distinguished from a mere purpose to do the act which caused the effect, however, there would be an important difference. He did not explain, but in reviewing the evidence, he stated that the restriction in question "was deliberate and was expressly made to accomplish" an effect on imports into the United States, a statement which certainly sounds more like language of specific intent than of mere foreseeability. A strict intent requirement would comport with Judge Hand's concern that the American law be not too loosely applied to the conduct of foreigners abroad, and may be preferable to a lesser standard as a matter of policy so as to avoid the most extreme kinds of extraterritorial jurisdiction.

and (iv) the rule is not inconsistent with the principles of justice generally recognized by states that have reasonably developed legal systems." (emphasis added)

[84] The ABA ANTITRUST SECTION SUPP. TO ATTY. GEN. NAT. COMM. ANTITRUST REP.: ANTITRUST DEVELOPMENTS 1955-1968, ch. II, at 49 (1968), concludes that the "intent" requirement of *Alcoa* and the "direct and foreseeable" effect test of para. iii, *supra* note 83, are "essentially identical." because of the customary antitrust doctrine that a general intent (as distinguished from specific intent) requirement is satisfied if the defendant engages in deliberate conduct which he "should have known" would have the "forbidden effects."

Judge Hand did not say that this double requirement of intent and effect would apply to American firms for conduct abroad, and it seems clear that such firms, when operating through agents or branches, can be held liable purely on an intent *or* effect basis. If, for example, an American firm's foreign branch enters into a contract abroad which restricts exports to the United States, the agreement can be brought within the Sherman Act without a special showing of intent on the American's part. Awkwardness may result here from applying different rules to the conduct of parties to the same agreement depending upon their nationality, but this is not fatal to having such a differentiation.

Professor Brewster was apparently concerned about the potentially wide sweep of a mere "effect" rule for American firms abroad and concluded that there would be liability on an American firm for restraints arranged in foreign markets only if the agreement "explicitly" prohibits export to the United States.[85] But an explicit restriction on export to the United States would surely be an intentional restriction, and to require it would amount to reading in the "intent" requirement as to Americans as well as foreigners.

A question remains as to what rule will be applied to foreign subsidiaries of American firms—the *Alcoa* test of intent plus effect, or the rule applicable to American firms. Foreign subsidiary corporations cannot simply be assumed to possess the nationality of the parent since they possess foreign nationality under the laws of the jurisdiction of their incorporation. Treating the subsidiaries as foreign for corporate law purposes does not necessarily give them the benefit of the *Alcoa* rule, however, as the rule was designed to protect truly foreign business interests; to extend it to the subsidiaries of American firms would seem to pervert its purpose. On the other hand, foreign joint venture corporations owned by American and foreign interests would probably not be subjected to the American rule unless the American partner has control.

---

[85] "However, it is our judgment that conditions attached to exports designed to prevent their reentry in processed form into the United States would be illegal. Short of such conditions aimed explicitly at preventing American imports, there would seem to be no legal risk attached to foreign resale controls standing alone. Of course if such restraints are imposed in exchange for foreigners' agreements to stay out of the United States, then they would fall within the ban of the naked agreement not to export freely." BREWSTER, *supra* note 49, at 134.

In summary, the American law can reach some transactions in foreign markets, but only where the goods concerned are still "in" American commerce, or where there is a clear effect upon commerce. Concrete illustrations will be found in Chapter 4, where conflicts with foreign law which may be produced by this wide scope are analyzed.

The American law may be applied not only to American firms operating abroad, but also to foreign firms, provided intent is also demonstrated as to the foreign firms. This is an especially controversial doctrine, and the Government is not always inclined to push its apparent powers to the limit, as made clear recently by the then head of the Antitrust Division.[86] But on occasion, the Government has asserted an interest in activities abroad which have seemed at the edge of any connection with American trade,[87] and it can always move to the edge again. Also, there is no doctrine to prevent private litigants, whose limitations are generally practical ones, from pushing the scope of the law to its outer limits when the case calls for it.

In gauging the extent to which American law overlaps and potentially conflicts with foreign law, therefore, it is not wise to take a narrow view of the law's scope.

II. EUROPEAN COMMUNITY LAW

The antitrust principles of the European Communities of principal interest in this study are those contained in Articles 85 and 86 of the

[86]Turner, in *Hearings on Prices of Quinine and Quinidine Before the Subcomm. on Antitrust and Monopoly of the Sen. Comm. on the Judiciary,* 90th Cong., 1st Sess. 235 (1967).

[87]Remarks of American officials have guarded against conceding that the American law is limited by any fixed line. For example, Mr. Orrick, when head of the Antitrust Division, stated: "Our antitrust laws would not ordinarily cover activities of American companies relating solely to local activities and the internal commerce of a foreign country." PROCEEDINGS, ABA ANTITRUST SECTION CONFERENCE ON ANTITRUST AND THE EUROPEAN COMMUNITIES (Brussels and Luxembourg, Sept. 23-26, 1963) 204. The disclaimer as to "a foreign country" in the singular perhaps had in mind the rule of thumb used in some oil industry consent decrees that a combination within three or more foreign nations shall be "presumed," subject to rebuttal, to affect American foreign commerce; see note 23 *supra.*

Rome Treaty of 1957, and Articles 65 and 66 of the Treaty of Paris of 1951, governing coal and steel.[88]

A. European Economic Community

1. IN GENERAL

Article 85(1) of the Rome Treaty closely resembles Section 1 of the Sherman Act and prohibits agreements and other kinds of concerted practices which have the "object or effect of preventing, restraining or distorting competition within the Common Market," provided they also are "likely to affect trade between Member States."[89] Article 85(2)

---

[88]The Councils of Ministers and the executive bodies of the three Communities—the European Economic Community, the European Coal and Steel Community and the European Atomic Energy Community—were merged on July 1, 1967. The Communities themselves and their relevant treaty provisions are still legally separate, although it is ultimately planned to integrate the three under one set of laws. The merger treaty and discussion will be found at 1 CCH COMM. MKT. REP. ¶¶5111, 5115 *et seq.*

[89]For background, see Chapter 1 *supra,* text at note 94 *et seq.* Selected recent English language writings of general scope on EEC antitrust law, published since 1964, include: *(Books and treatises)*—DERINGER, THE COMPETITION LAW OF THE EUROPEAN ECONOMIC COMMUNITY (1968); EDWARDS, CONTROL OF CARTELS AND MONOPOLIES: AN INTERNATIONAL COMPARISON, ch. 15 (1967); GRAUPNER, THE RULES OF COMPETITION IN THE EUROPEAN ECONOMIC COMMUNITY (1965); JOLIET, THE RULE OF REASON IN ANTI-TRUST LAW: AMERICAN, GERMAN AND COMMON MARKET LAWS IN COMPARATIVE PERSPECTIVE (1967); JOLIET, MONOPOLIZATION AND ABUSE OF DOMINANT POSITION: A COMPARATIVE STUDY OF THE AMERI-CAN AND EUROPEAN APPROACHES TO THE CONTROL OF ECONOMIC POWER (1970); LANG, THE COMMON MARKET AND THE COMMON LAW, pt. VI (1966); see also CCH COMM. MKT. REP. (looseleaf); *(Articles and papers)*—*American Business and the Common Market—A Symposium,* 6 B.C. IND. & COM. L. REV. 391 (1965); *The Common Market—A Symposium,* 41 WASH. L. REV. 383 (1966); Comment, *The Substantive Rules of Antitrust in the Common Market: Anal-ysis and Approach,* 17 STAN. L. REV. 257 (1965); Fulda, *The First Antitrust Decisions of the Commission of the European Economic Community,* 65 COLUM. L. REV. 625 (1965); Kellcher, *The Common Market Antitrust Laws: The First Ten Years,* 12 ANTITRUST BULL. 1219 (1967); Mok, *The Cartel Policy of the EEC Commission,* 1962-1967, 6 C. M. L. REV. 67 (1968); H. Schwartz, *Common Market Antitrust Laws and American Business,* 1965 U. ILL. L. F. 617; Spier, *Restrictive Business Practices and Competition in the European Economic Community,* 53 CALIF. L. REV. 1337 (1965); van den Heuvel, *Some Unresolved Problems in Com-*

makes such agreements null and void. Article 85(3) establishes a basis for a declaration of inapplicability or exemption from the prohibitions of Article 85(1), if: (a) the agreement contributes to improved production or distribution, or to technical or economic progress; (b) the public receives a "fair share" of the resulting gains; (c) the restriction does not exceed what is "essential" to achieve these benefits; and (d) it does not "eliminate competition in respect of a substantial portion of the products in question."

Article 86 prohibits "abuse of a dominant position in the Common Market or any substantial part thereof" where also trade between Member States "may be affected." This abuse of power provision differs from Section 2 of the Sherman Act in that a monopoly or dominant position is not itself subject to attack; rather, provision is made for elimination of "abuse" of such economic power. Article 86 does not provide for an exemption.

EEC Council Regulation 17, which took effect on March 13, 1962, establishes a general scheme of enforcement for these substantive provisions. Under it, the Treaty prohibitions are self-executing. The Commission is given power to enforce them by conducting investigations and hearings, by the issuance of cease and desist orders, and by the levying of fines, which can be extremely high in amount. The Commission has exclusive power to administer the exemption provision of Article 85(3), and the regulation also provides that the Commission may give so-called "negative clearance" to interested parties who apply for a declaration that a given arrangement does not come within the Treaty prohibitions. As long as the Commission has not initiated a proceeding for enforcement or for the granting of negative clearance or exemption, the national authorities of the Member States are also competent to give effect to the Treaty prohibitions in cases arising before them.[90]

Application for negative clearance is in the form of a "request" to the Commission. To obtain exemption, a party must "notify" the Commission of the agreement. In both cases, parties must furnish required information. "Notification" is not actually compulsory except for

munity Law Concerning Restrictive Trade Practices, 4 C. M. L. REV. 180 (1966); von der Groeben, *Competition Policy in the Common Market and in the Atlantic Partnership*, 10 ANTITRUST BULL. 125 (1965); Statements of Fulda and Rahl on developments in EEC antitrust law, in *Hearings, supra* note 19, at 343-87.

[90]See DERINGER, *supra* note 89, at ¶ 2154.

purposes of seeking an exemption, but it has the advantage of staying the running of penalties pending a decision by the Commission,[91] and the Court of Justice has held in the *Portelange* case that it gives the agreement "provisional validity," *i.e.,* renders it valid contractually until the Commission acts on the exemption question.[92]

Certain classes of agreements need not be notified in order to obtain these advantages, including, subject to certain qualifications: (1) agreements which are solely between residents of one Member State and which do not restrict exports or imports as to any other Member State; (2) vertical resale price maintenance agreements; (3) restrictive assignment or licensing of industrial property rights, including patents, trademarks and know-how; and (4) agreements for standardization or joint research.

The Commission has been flooded with negative clearance requests and notifications, the great majority of which have been in the distribution and licensing areas.[93] To meet this problem, it sought and

[91] Regulation 17 (art. 15, ¶6) provides that the Commission may set aside the immunity from penalties for a notified agreement by conducting a preliminary examination and concluding that Article 85(1) is violated and that an exemption under Article 85(3) is not warranted. In S.A. Cimenteries C.B.R. Cementsbedrijven N.V. v. EEC Comm'n, CCH COMM. MKT. REP. ¶8052, 6 Comm. Mkt. L.R. 77 (1967), the Court of Justice held that such action by the Commission is a decision, for which reasons must be given of a sufficient nature to permit judicial review.

[92] S. A. Portelange v. Smith Corona Marchant International, 15 Recueil de la Jurisprudence de la Cour 1969-4, 309 (1969).

[93] By Dec. 31, 1968, well over 37,000 applications for negative clearance or notifications seeking exemption had been filed. Of these, about 31,400 concerned exclusive dealing agreements of various kinds, and about 4,700 concerned license agreements; see FIRST GENERAL REPORT ON THE ACTIVITY OF THE COMMUNITIES IN 1967, 59-61 (1968); SECOND GENERAL REPORT ON THE ACTIVITY OF THE COMMUNITIES IN 1968, 43-44 (1969).

In 1968, the number of requests and notifications diminished appreciably in comparison with earlier years, because of, according to the Commission, the group exemption, certain decisions of the Commission in individual cases, and policy announcements indicating approval of some kinds of agreements. At the same time, the number of complaints filed with the Commission and of proceedings instituted on its own motion increased during 1968; *id.* at 44. By the end of 1968 the Commission had found ways of disposing of about 25,000 files in the exclusivity area, relieving it of much of the problem created by the mass of files and freeing it for the first time since Regulation 17 was adopted to concentrate on "really important cases," *id.*

received authorization from the Council to promulgate blanket exemptions for certain types of exclusive arrangements, and licenses of industrial property rights. Pursuant to this, it issued Commission Regulation 67/67 on exclusive distribution arrangements, and is working on a licensing regulation.

Actions of the Commission are reviewable by the Court of Justice of the European Communities, which may also receive on reference from the national courts, under Article 177 of the Treaty, questions concerning interpretation of the Treaty provisions. To date, the Court has given opinions in ten antitrust cases, all involving Article 85.[94]

[94] deGeus v. Bosch GmbH, CCH COMM. MKT. REP. ¶8003, 1 Comm. Mkt. L.R. 1 (1962) (holding that Article 85 was in force from the time the Treaty became effective and interpreting Regulation 17); Ets. Consten S.A. and Grundig-Verkaufs-GmbH v. EEC Comm'n, CCH COMM. MKT. REP. ¶8046, 5 Comm. Mkt. L.R. 418 (1966) (sustaining the Commission's order against a territorial confinement plan of distribution, and reversing for lack of adequate findings as to other restrictions); Société Technique Minière v. Maschinenbau Ulm GmbH, CCH COMM. MKT. REP. ¶8047, 5 Comm. Mkt. L.R. 357 (1966) (on reference from a French court, stating that an exclusive selling agreement is not necessarily illegal under Article 85(1) and that issue turns on the market circumstances); Italy v. EEC Council and Comm'n, CCH COMM. MKT. REP. ¶8048, 5 Comm. Mkt. L.R. 97 (1966) (sustaining validity of Council Reg. 19/65 giving EEC Commission authority to grant group exemptions for certain classes of agreements); S.A. Cimenteries C.B.R. Cementsbedrijven N.V. v. EEC Comm'n, CCH COMM. MKT. REP. ¶8052, 6 Comm. Mkt. L.R. 77 (1967) (holding that Commission must render decision based on facts and give reasons when it acts to start the running of fines); S.A. Brasserie de Haecht v. Consorts Wilkin-Janssen, CCH COMM. MKT. REP. ¶8053, 7 Comm. Mkt. L.R. 26 (1967) (on reference from a Belgian court, holding that requirements contracts are not in and of themselves violative of Article 85(1), but that legality may turn upon facts placing them in their market context, including information on contracts of other sellers in same market); Parke, Davis and Co. v. Probel Co., CCH COMM. MKT. REP. ¶8054, 7 Comm. Mkt. L.R. 47 (1968) (on reference from a Dutch court, holding that Articles 85(1) and 86 do not prevent a patentee in one Member State from exercising his patent rights to exclude from that state, by infringement suit, products made in another Member State where no patent exists, even where selling price of product is higher in first state than in second); Wilhelm v. Bundeskartellamt, CCH COMM. MKT. REP. ¶8056, 8 Comm. Mkt. L.R. 100 (1969) (on reference from a German court, stating that national authorities may proceed against a cartel under national law even though the Commission is also proceeding against the same parties on the same facts, provided that national law must not prejudice the uniform application of Community law, as manifested in prohibitions under Articles 85 and 86, or exemptions under Article 85(3), Community law being preeminent; both authorities may levy penalties on the same persons, although prior sanctions should

The Court has approached basic questions of interpretation of Article 85 in a manner which has created great flexibility in the law and has established a basis for substantial administrative and judicial discretion in its future case-by-case development. Thus, in application of the interstate commerce requirement the Court has avoided a purely technical jurisdictional approach, and has said that the question is whether the restriction will have effects which are inconsistent with realization of the goal of a single common market among the Member States.[95] In the

be taken into account as a matter of equity; Article 7 of the Treaty does not prevent national authorities from imposing penal sanctions against their own nationals when the Commission at the same time is proceeding against the same nationals as well as persons from other countries; these principles can be altered by regulation of the Council under Article 87(2)(e) of the Treaty); Völk v. Ets. J. Vervaecke S.P.R.L., 8 Comm. Mkt. L. R. 273 (1969) (on reference from a German Court, stating that a territorial protection provision in an exclusive distribution contract would escape the prohibition of Article 85(1) where the market share of the parties was so weak that there could be no effect on interstate commerce of the kind which could jeopardize the objective of forming a single common market, and where there would be only an insignificant effect on competition in the relevant market; according to a mimeo. report of the decision, the washing machines concerned accounted for only 0.08% of Common Market production, 0.2% of production in Germany, and 0.6% of sales in the assigned territory, *i.e.,* Belgium and Luxembourg); S.A. Portelange v. Smith Corona Marchant International, 15 Recueil de la Jurisprudence de la Cour 1969-4, 309 (1969) (on reference from a Belgian court in a suit in which the validity of an exclusive dealing contract under Article 85(1) was in issue, holding that agreements which have been properly notified to the Commission are valid and enforceable as long as the Commission has not ruled on the question of exemption under Article 85(3)).

[95] The Court has stated the test in various ways: whether the agreement may jeopardize "freedom of trade between the Member States" so as to "prejudice the realization of the objectives of a single market between States," *Grundig-Consten,* CCH COMM. MKT. REP. ¶8046 at 7652, 5 Comm. Mkt. L. R. 418, 472 (1966); "may have some influence, direct or indirect, actual or potential, on the flow of trade between Member States," making it "necessary to know whether it is capable of partitioning the market in certain products between Member States and of thus rendering the economic interpenetration sought by the Treaty more difficult," *Technique Minière,* CCH COMM. MKT. REP. ¶8047 at 7696, 5 Comm. Mkt. L. R. 357, 375 (1966); "may exercise a direct or indirect influence on the flow of trade between Member States, contribute to a partitioning of the market, and make it more difficult to achieve the economic interpenetration intended by the Treaty," *de Haecht,* CCH COMM. MKT. REP. ¶8053 at 7804, 7 Comm. Mkt. L. R. 26, 41 (1967); see also Völk v. Ets. J. Vervaecke, S.P.R.L. 8 Comm. Mkt. L. R. 273 (1969).

In *Grundig-Consten, supra,* the Court said that proof that the agreement actually

Völk case,[96] the Court stated that an exclusive distribution agreement, under which the manufacturer agreed to sell exclusively to the distributor in Belgium and Luxembourg and to protect him against sales in his territory by distributors in Germany, could be held not to affect trade among Member States in the required sense where the market share of the particular brand was so small that it could not exert an influence on interstate trade sufficient to "jeopardize the realization of the objectives of a single market among the States."[97]

It is not clear whether this "Common Market objectives" test is intended only to create a quantitative, or *de minimis,* exception, or whether it will permit broader considerations of Common Market policy to enter into a determination of whether the interstate commerce requirement is met. Even the quantitative approach is perhaps surprising as applied to territorial division along national lines, for it is difficult to imagine a type of restrictive agreement which is more clearly inconsistent with the Common Market than one which erects sales barriers on national boundaries. The *Völk* decision changes the impression created by the earlier *Grundig-Consten* case that agreements of this type may be per se illegal; instead, very small ones may escape (in *Völk,* the particular brand accounted for less than 1% of sales of washing machines in the distributor's assigned territory, and much less than 1% of production of such machines in the Common Market and in Germany).[98]

A similarly flexible approach is evolving on the question of what kinds of restrictive agreements will be held to prevent, restrain or distort competition. At first, the Commission seemed to adopt the position that Article 85(1) prohibits all appreciable restrictions of competition regardless of their market significance.[99] In a series of decisions, however, the Court has held that restraints must be examined in their

increased the volume of interstate trade would not necessarily mean that it did not "affect" trade in the Treaty sense. It went on to hold that the restriction, which prevented all but Consten from importing the goods into France and prohibited Consten from re-exporting from France, "unquestionably" impaired interstate trade.

[96] Author's translation from mimeo. text of decision; 8 Comm. Mkt. L. R. 273 (1969).

[97] *Id.*

[98] From summary of submission of EC Commission, *id.*

[99] See JOLIET, THE RULE OF REASON IN ANTITRUST LAW, *supra* note 89, 'at 116 *et seq.*

actual market context and to be prohibited must be shown to have a significant adverse effect on competition in the relevant market.[100] This approach is by no means necessarily the same as that of the American Rule of Reason, but it moves in the same general direction, *i.e.*, of confining the prohibition to restrictions of competition which would have some demonstrably serious effect on market competition. Now the Commission has not only acceded to the Court's approach in this regard, but has begun to turn it into a matter of affirmative policy-making, as manifested in its liberal approach to permissible cooperation among competitors, discussed below.

In seeking to clarify the law, the Commission has issued several statements concerning arrangements which do not, in its opinion, fall within the prohibitions of Article 85(1). In 1962, it indicated that the prohibitions do not extend to certain restrictions in unilateral patent licenses of a type which it regards as within the scope of the patent grant, including: limitations as to field, quantity or territory of use; specification of standards or restriction of sources of supply if "indispensible for a technically proper utilization of the patent;" grant-back of licenses on improvement patents and know-how, provided the grant-back licenses are non-exclusive and the licensor is mutually obligated; exclusive license agreements; and other provisions.[101] Also in

---

[100] In the *Technique Minière, Italy, de Haecht* and *Völk* cases, the Court stated in various ways that a realistic inquiry into the market setting of a particular restraint is necessary to see whether it transgresses Article 85's prohibitions. In *Völk*, following a similar argument by the Commission, the Court held that "an agreement escapes the prohibition of Article 85 when it only affects the market in an insignificant manner taking account of the weak position occupied by the parties in the market for the products in question." (Author's translation from mimeo. text of decision.)

See generally JOLIET, THE RULE OF REASON IN ANTITRUST LAW: AMERICAN, GERMAN AND COMMON MARKET LAWS IN COMPARATIVE PERSPECTIVE (1967); Cohen, *The Application of Article 85(3) of the Treaty Establishing the European Economic Community to Exclusive Dealing Agreements*, 54 CORN. L. REV. 379 (1969); Ebb, *The* Grundig-Consten *Case Revisited: Judicial Harmonization of National Law and Treaty Law in the Common Market*, 115 U. PA. L. REV. 855 (1967); Fulda, *The First Antitrust Decisions of the Commission of the EEC*, 65 COLUM. L. REV. 625 (1965); Fulda, *The Exclusive Distributor and the Antitrust Laws of the Common Market of Europe and the United States*, 3 TEX. INT'L L. F. 209 (1967); de Keyser, *Territorial Restrictions and Export Prohibitions under the United States and the Common Market Antitrust Laws*, 2 C. M. L. REV. 271 (1964-65).

[101] EEC Commission, Official Notice on Patent Licensing Agreements, Dec. 24, 1962, 1 CCH COMM. MKT. REP. ¶ 2698. The Notice states that it is not possible to

1962, the Commission expressed the view that Article 85(1) does not apply to exclusive arrangements with commercial representatives who are true agents, as distinguished from independent merchants.[102]

The Commission has adopted a policy of encouraging small nationally-confined enterprises to achieve greater scale so as to take advantage of the larger Common Market and to compete more effectively with foreign firms.[103] In accordance with this policy, it has adopted a legal interpretation that Article 85 as a rule does not reach corporate mergers and acquisitions, nor the formation of joint venture companies,[104]

give a general opinion as to "joint patents, reciprocal licenses or multiple parallel licenses."

Council Regulation 19/65 (art. 1 [1] [b]) authorizes the Commission to devise a group exemption for restrictive two-party agreements on patents, designs, trademarks and know-how, 1 CCH COMM. MKT. REP. ¶ 2718. See Deringer, *EEC Antitrust Laws and Industrial Property Rights–Latest Developments,* 13 ANTI-TRUST BULL. 341 (1968).

[102] EEC Commission, Official Notice on Contracts for Exclusive Representation Concluded with Commercial Agents, Dec. 24, 1962, 1 CCH COMM. MKT. REP. ¶ 2697. The Court of Justice agreed with this interpretation in Italy v. EEC Council and Comm'n, CCH COMM. MKT. REP. ¶ 8048 at 7719, 5 Comm. Mkt. L.R. 97 (1966).

[103] This policy has been summarized by the Commission as follows: "It has . . . been found that in a number of industries many firms are not big enough to make full use of the possibilities offered them by the Common Market and to compete effectively. The Commission has drawn two conclusions: obstacles to the external growth of firms caused by company and fiscal law must be removed as soon as possible; and co-operation agreements concluded between two or more firms for purposes of specialization, joint research or rationalization should be approved on condition that they still permit effective competition on the markets in question. Over the next few years the Commission will have to specify the conditions on which these classes of agreement may be considered permissible.

"Regarding external growth and combination, work on company and fiscal law is advancing satisfactorily, as has been shown above. However, in this sphere too, care should be taken to ensure that the combination process does not impair effective competition or lead to monopoly situations." EEC COMMISSION, TENTH GENERAL REPORT, JUNE 1967, 38.

[104] EEC Commission, Memorandum to the Governments of the Member States, Dec. 1, 1965, CCH Comm. Mkt. Rep. No. 26 (separate print) ¶ 53. In this, the Commission rejected the view of a majority of a working party of professors appointed by it that Article 85 should be applied to corporate mergers where the enterprises concerned remain legally distinct from each other. See DERINGER, *supra* note 89, ¶ 169; JOLIET, MONOPOLIZATION AND ABUSE OF DOMINANT POSITION, *supra* note 89; statement of de Jong, in *Hearings on Economic Concentration: Concentration Outside the United States Before the Subcomm. on*

although it will apply to restrictive agreements, if any, which continue after the merger or joint venture is consummated. In general, the Commission has indicated that mergers and joint ventures are to be dealt with only under Article 86 to the extent that they involve abuse of a dominant market position. This "hands-off" policy, at a time when American anti-merger law is becoming increasingly severe, is a potential source of substantial conflict in the application of the two sets of laws to multi-national firms.

The Commission has issued some potentially far-reaching guides for lawful cooperation among enterprises in the Common Market. In its view, and subject to certain qualifications, agreements having the following activities as their sole purpose do not fall within the prohibitions of Article 85(1): (1) preparation and exchange of information and joint market research; (2) cooperation as to accounting, credit guarantees, debt collection and business and tax consultant service; (3) joint research and development; (4) joint use of production, storage and transportation facilities; (5) joint ventures to carry out projects among non-competitors or among competitors who are unable to execute a project by themselves; (6) joint selling, service and repair arrangements by non-competitors; (7) joint advertising; and (8) use of a common label to designate quality, where the label is available to all competitors under the same conditions.[105]

Antitrust and Monopoly of the Sen. Comm. on the Judiciary, 90th Cong., 2d Sess., pt. 7, at 3612, 3628 (1968); Markert, *Antitrust Aspects of Mergers in the EEC,* 5 TEX. INT'L L. F. 32 (1969); Swann, *Concentration and Competition in the European Community,* 13 ANTITRUST BULL. 1473 (1968).

[105] EEC Commission, Notice Concerning Agreements, Decisions and Concerted Practices in the Field of Co-operation Between Enterprises, July 23, 1968, CCH COMM. MKT. REP. ¶9248. The Notice seeks to enable firms to work more "rationally and increase their productivity and competitiveness." Other forms of cooperation may also be permissible if the parties' market position is too weak to lead "to an appreciable restraint of competition in the common market and—for Article 85 of the EEC Treaty—impair trade between the Member States." *Id.* at 8519-20; see Société Commerciale et d'Etudes des Maisons d'Alimentation et d'Approvisionnement à Succursales (Socémas), July 27, 1968, CCH COMM. MKT. REP. ¶9250, at 8530. The Commission intends to develop the "appreciable" test into a general means of limiting Article 85(1); OECD, ANNUAL REPORTS ON DEVELOPMENTS IN THE FIELD OF RESTRICTIVE BUSINESS PRACTICES (August, 1969) 88. See Joliet, *La Coopération entre Entreprises selon la Jurisprudence de la Commission des Communautés Européenes,* 1969 CAHIERS DE DROIT EUROPEEN No. 2, at 127.

In addition to these broad categories of activities considered to be outside the scope of the prohibitions, the Commission has shown liberality in the granting of exemptions in individual cases under Article 85(3) for various forms of cooperation among small and medium-sized firms. For example, relying primarily upon the existence of major outside competition, the Commission found the efficiencies produced by an arrangement to be adequate for an exemption for a group of eighteen medium-sized marine paint manufacturers, each of which was located in a different country (five Common Market and thirteen other nations). The firms cooperate with respect to research and agree to make a line of paints of the same quality which they sell under a common trademark. The parties may not make other paints of the same quality, but do make others of higher and lower quality which are sold under their own marks. The exemption was denied until the parties eliminated a division-of-territory provision on sales of paint bearing the cooperative brands, but the Commission somewhat surprisingly permitted them to continue to require a payment to be made to the home firm on such sales in its territory by another member firm, apparently on the ground that this is necessary to encourage each firm to intensify its efforts in its home territory, thereby enabling the group to compete more effectively with the larger firms.[106]

The Commission has approved a joint development agreement between a transmission manufacturer and a motor coach manufacturer because of technical and economic advantages despite restrictions on selling, including a provision allowing the transmission manufacturer to sell to only one coach manufacturer in each Common Market country except Belgium.[107] It has also approved some "specialization," or

---

[106]Transocean Marine Paint Ass'n, June 27, 1967, CCH COMM. MKT. REP. ¶9188, 6 Comm. Mkt. L.R. Supp. D9; see Waelbroeck, *Cooperation Agreements and Competition Policy in the E.E.C.,* 1 N.Y.U. J. INT'L L. & POL. 5, 12, 16 (1968); *cf.* V.V.V.F., June 25, 1969, CCH. COMM. MKT. REP. ¶9312 (negative clearance granted to association of Dutch paint manufacturers, who established quality standards for paints sold within the Common Market under specified names; the Commission had previously denied an exemption for price fixing and other restrictions, which were then removed from the agreement insofar as sales within the Common Market are concerned).

[107]S.A. Ateliers de Contructions Electriques de Charleroi and Société des Automobiles Berliet, July 17, 1968, CCH COMM. MKT. REP. ¶9251, 7 Comm. Mkt. L.R. Supp. D35.

division-of-fields, agreements between small manufacturers, coupled with exclusive buying and selling provisions.[108] Some of these interpretations of the Common Market antitrust law, if they become permanent, will result in more lenient rules than are followed in the American law applicable to similar arrangements, thus laying a foundation for fairly substantial conflicts in this area.

With respect to horizontal restraints of the most serious variety, however, Rome Treaty law is evolving along lines which are not discernibly different from those of American law. In 1969, the Commission found violations of Article 85(1) on the part of a quinine cartel and a dyestuffs cartel, and utilized for the first time its power to impose fines upon the offending enterprises. In the quinine case, six Common Market firms were found to have engaged in price fixing, territorial market allocation, establishment of sales quotas and limitation of production.[109] Fines totalling $500,000 were imposed, with one firm

---

[108]JAZ S.A. and Peter-Uhren GmbH, July 22, 1969, CCH COMM. MKT. REP. ¶9317 (agreement between French and German clockmakers under which one will specialize in electric, and the other in mechanical clocks, with each to buy and sell exclusively in its own territory the product specialized in by the other); Clima Chappée and Buderus'sche Eisenwerke Co., July 22, 1969, CCH COMM. MKT. REP. ¶9316 (similar agreement in air conditioning and heating equipment).

[109]N.V. Nederlandse Combinatie voor Chemische Industrie, July 16, 1969, CCH COMM. MKT. REP. ¶9313; one Dutch company, two German companies and three French companies were found to have violated Article 85(1); in a press conference, Commissioner Sassen explained that two British companies involved in the case, one of which was a subsidiary of an American company, were not found guilty because the evidence against them was not sufficient, rather than because they were from non-Member countries, Agence Europe, No. 380 (new series), July 24, 1969, at 3; N.Y. Times, July 25, 1969.

The activities of the quinine cartel came to light in U.S. Senate committee hearings, *Hearings on Prices of Quinine and Quinidine Before the Subcomm. on Antitrust and Monopoly of the Sen. Comm. on the Judiciary,* 90th Cong., 1st Sess. pt. 2 (1967). On October 25, 1968, a federal grand jury returned an indictment against participants in the cartel under the Sherman and Wilson Tariff Acts and under 18 U.S.C. §371 (conspiracy to defraud the United States), United States v. N.V. Nederlandse Combinatie voor Chemische Industrie, No. 68-CR 870 (S.D.N.Y. 1968); the initial defendants in the American proceeding included six Dutch, three German, one French, one British and three American companies, as well as eight officers and directors of certain of the European and American firms. In the summer of 1969, pleas of *nolo contendere* were entered as to certain counts by: an American firm, Mead Johnson and Co., and by its French subsidiary, Société Nogentaise de Produits

being fined $210,000 and another, $190,000. In the dyestuffs case, the offense was price fixing on the part of six Common Market firms, three Swiss firms and one British firm, each of which was fined $50,000, except for the Italian company, which was fined $40,000.[110]

Such restraints as these on the part of combinations controlling a major portion of the supply in the Common Market are unlikely to qualify for exemption under Article 85(3) because of the requirement of that provision that they not "eliminate competition in respect of a substantial portion of the products in question." It remains to be seen whether combinations having only a small share of the market will be able to obtain authorization for restraints of competition of the "hard-core" variety.

2. EXTRATERRITORIAL SCOPE

The principal difference between the antitrust provisions of the Rome Treaty and of American law as to extraterritoriality is that the former has no "foreign commerce" clause. Jurisdiction therefore cannot be based simply upon a showing of effect upon the foreign trade of the Community. Domestic effect must be shown, and under Articles 85 and 86, two types of effect are required: effect on trade between Member

Chimiques S.A. (each fined $40,000); a German firm, C.F. Boehringer & Soehne GmbH (fined $80,000); and Vantorex, Ltd., a British subsidiary of the American firm, Rexall Drug and Chemical Co. (fined $100,000). A *nolle prosequi* was entered as to Rexall Drug and Chemical Co., and charges were dismissed as to a German firm, Vereinigte Chininfabriken Zimmer & Co. GmbH. See CCH TRADE REG. REP. ¶45,068 (Case 2023).

[110]Badische-Anilin- und Soda-Fabrik AG, July 24, 1969, CCH COMM. MKT. REP. ¶9314. The Common Market participants included four German companies, one French company and one Italian company. Previously, the German Bundeskartellamt had found violations of German law on the part of German participants in the cartel and had levied fines. This led to the contention on appeal from that action in the *Wilhelm* case, note 94 *supra*, that national authorities should not be allowed to proceed under national law when the Commission is proceeding against the same parties on the same facts under the Rome Treaty; the Court of Justice, however, held that both may proceed.

In other horizontal restraint cases, the Commission has found violations as to an exclusive dealing cartel of producers and dealers in ceramic tile, CCH COMM. MKT. REP. ¶2412.35, at 2741; and in wood, *id.* ¶9223; and as to several price fixing and market-sharing cartels, *id.* ¶¶9201, 9182, 9085, 9066, 9024, 9018, 9012, 9287, 9292 and 9299. See Mok, *The Cartel Policy of the EEC Commission, 1962-1967,* 6 C. M. L. REV. 67, 81 (1968).

States, and a restraint of competition or an abuse of dominant power within the Common Market.[111] As a consequence, it appears that the extraterritorial scope of Common Market antitrust law, insofar as the language of the Treaty provisions is concerned, is that: (1) conduct occurring outside the Common Market which causes the prohibited internal effects can be reached; and (2) conduct inside the Common Market which causes only external effects cannot be reached.

There have been no decided cases as yet basing jurisdiction purely upon a finding of internal effects caused by acts of a firm entirely outside the Common Market. The Commission has stated, however, that it is entitled to assert jurisdiction on the basis of "effects within the Common Market."[112] And in the dyestuffs cartel case, it found violations on the part of three Swiss firms and one British firm which participated in the international price-fixing arrangements, as well as on the part of several Common Market firms, and undertook to levy fines against them. The decision stated that it was binding on all enterprises that took part in the concerted practices regardless of whether they were "domiciled within or outside the Common Market," or of where they had their "head office." The Treaty rules of competition apply to all restrictions "that produce within the Common Market effects to which Article 85(1) applies," it said.[113]

Taken literally, these statements claim no lesser jurisdiction over foreign firms for acts abroad than that described by Section 18 of the Restatement or by *Alcoa*. Although each of the non-Common Market

[111] Article 85(1) prohibits agreements and concerted practices which are "likely to affect trade between Member States and which have the object or effect of preventing, restraining or distorting competition within the Common Market." Article 86 prohibits abuse of a dominant position "in the Common Market or any substantial part thereof," where "trade between Member States may be thereby affected." The interstate trade test, of course, is like that of the Sherman Act; *cf.* note 95 *supra* and text; the additional requirement of effect on competition within the Common Market appears to be similar to the requirement of Section 7 of the Clayton Act that the merger must threaten substantially to lessen competition "in any section of the country;" see text at note 3 *supra*.

[112] EEC Commission Answer to Written Question No. 29 (on the international quinine cartel), June 7, 1967, CCH COMM. MKT. REP. ¶9180; see note 109 *supra*.

[113] Badische Anilin- und Soda-Fabrik AG, CCH COMM. MKT. REP. ¶9314, at 8593-94. The British defendant, I.C.I., and the two Swiss defendants, Geigy and Sandoz, appealed the decision; Financial Times, Aug. 2, 1969; N.Y. Times, Nov. 28, 1969, 63; see also Chapter 3, *infra,* note 76.

firms had subsidiaries in the Common Market, the foreign parent companies, rather than the subsidiaries, were made responsible for the violations, leaving open the possible interpretation that they were held on a purely "effects" basis. On the other hand, the subsidiaries did engage in conduct within the Common Market, and notice of the decision and fines was served on them, on the theory that they were part of the "sphere of influence" of the foreign parents.[114]

In a succession of negative clearance cases, the Commission has held agreements among Common Market firms to be outside the scope of Article 85(1), though made within the Common Market, where they were to be carried out in export trade or in foreign markets, in the absence of proof that there would also be the necessary internal effects. In 1964, clearance was given to the *Dutch Engineers and Contractors Association* for an arrangement to pool bids and share jobs with respect to construction projects to be carried out outside the EEC because the agreement, on its face, would not affect competition within the Common Market.[115] Recognizing that there would be a possibility of jurisdiction nevertheless if the restraints outside the Common Market produced secondary effects within the Market, the Commission added that there was no evidence of any such effects.

In *Grosfillex Co.,*[116] the Commission granted negative clearance to an agreement of a French exporter of plastic articles giving a Swiss distributor an exclusive arrangement for Switzerland. The Commission went so far as to approve provisions which had the effect of prohibiting the distributor from re-exporting from Switzerland back to the Common Market, and also from making or selling any competing goods. As in the *Dutch Engineers and Contractors Association* case, the Commission again looked first to the face of the agreement, noting this time that it expressly prohibited sales by the distributor in the Common Market. It went on, however, to apply a practical test of whether this theoretical prohibition would really "prevent, restrain or distort" competition within the Common Market. It found that it would not, because the goods, to be resold back into the Common Market, would have to pass through a second tariff barrier, which would make such re-export unlikely in the absence of "exceptional circumstances." The Commission

[114] CCH COMM. MKT. REP. ¶ 9314 at 8694.
[115] CCH COMM. MKT. REP. ¶ 2412.31, 4 Comm. Mkt. L.R. 50 (1965).
[116] CCH COMM. MKT. REP. ¶ 2412.37, 3 Comm. Mkt. L.R. 237 (1964).

added that there are a large number of competing manufacturers in the product operating inside the Common Market.

In the *Rieckermann* case, it took still another step by holding Article 85 inapplicable to a provision prohibiting the exporter himself from making sales in the internal market. Again it relied on practical conclusions that competition within the Common Market would not be affected,[117] partly because of the existence of strong competition in the domestic market.[118]

In several cases the Commission has given negative clearance to associations of fertilizer manufacturers who are all located in one Member State. The associations operate a joint selling agency for sales

[117]Johs. Rieckermann Kg., CCH COMM. MKT. REP. ¶9267, 7 Comm. Mkt. L.R. Supp. D78 (1968). A German manufacturer of electrical heating, melting and tempering equipment gave Rieckermann, a German exporter, an exclusive contract for the sale of the manufacturer's equipment to Japan, with provisions (1) prohibiting sales of this equipment by Rieckermann elsewhere than in Japan; (2) prohibiting Rieckermann from selling competitive products in Japan; and (3) providing that the manufacturer would not sell to others for export to Japan and would impose restrictions on purchasers against resale in Japan. Although the first restriction explicitly prohibited Rieckermann from competing in the Common Market, the Commission concluded that this had no "practical significance" because Rieckermann was not "equipped to make sales in the Common Market," and because sales were made there directly by manufacturers whose costs were lower than Rieckermann's. The other restrictions were viewed as unlikely to affect, or "perceptibly impair," the "relationship between supply and demand" within the Common Market because of characteristics of the market structure which convinced the Commission that at most there would be only "minor alterations" of competition. By implication, the Commission's definition of "competition within the Common Market" seems to be limited to competition for sales for use of the product in the Common Market; *i.e.,* it does not seem to regard competition among exporters located in the Common Market as being competition "within the Common Market." The decision's emphasis on practical effects on market competition as the test of whether the prohibitions of Article 85(1) apply is consistent with the trend of Court of Justice decisions; see note 100 *supra.*

[118]A similar ground was given as one reason for a negative clearance in S.A. Nicholas Frères, CCH COMM. MKT. REP. ¶2412.46, 3 Comm. Mkt. L.R. 505 (1964), and in V.V.V.F., CCH COMM. MKT. REP. ¶9312 (1969); in the latter case, the Commission decided that there would be no adverse effect on competition within the Common Market from an agreement of Dutch paint manufacturers to fix minimum prices and to use a single exclusive agent or representative in sales outside the Common Market, on the ground that the minimum prices were "rather low compared to prices actually applied," and that there is "lively competition" in paint products in the Common Market.

within the single Common Market nation ar.d for sales to nations outside the Market, but leave sales to other Member States to the individual firms.[119] The rationale of the decisions is that, although competition is restrained within the Common Market because of restraints occurring in a single Member State, trade among Member States is not likely to be affected. In each case, the agreements were amended to eliminate factors which the Commission believed would have interstate effects. No independent discussion of the extraterritorial problem was given.

Writers have largely agreed that the Rome Treaty provisions may be applied to conduct outside the Common Market which produces effects within the Market.[120] Thus, an American export association selling to Common Market buyers, but not "established" in the Common Market, might violate Article 85 despite a Webb-Pomerene exemption under

---

[119] Cobelaz-Synthetic Products Mfrs., CCH COMM. MKT. REP. ¶9265, 7 Comm. Mkt. L.R. Supp. D45 (1968); Cobelaz-Cokeries, CCH COMM. MKT. REP. ¶9266, 7 Comm. Mkt. L.R. Supp. D68 (1968); Comptoir français de l'azote, CCH COMM. MKT. REP. ¶9268, 7 Comm. Mkt. L.R. Supp. D57 (1968); S.E.I.F.A., CCH COMM. MKT. REP. ¶9282 (1969).

[120] See DERINGER, *supra* note 89, ¶127; Hug, *The Applicability of the European Community Treaties against Restraints of Competition to Restraints of Competition Caused in Non-Member States, But Affecting the Common Market*, in 2 CARTEL AND MONOPOLY IN MODERN LAW 639, 653 (1960); GRAUPNER, THE RULES OF COMPETITION IN THE EUROPEAN ECONOMIC COMMUNITY 38 (1965). Kruithof, *The Application of the Common Market Anti-trust Provisions to International Restraints of Trade*, 2 C. M. L. REV. 69, 74 (1964); Mok, *supra* note 110, at 67, 86; OBERDORFER, GLEISS & HIRSCH, COMMON MARKET CARTEL LAW 23 (1963); Thiesing, Remarks on the Problems of the Extra-Territorial Effect of "Anti-Turst" Law, Concerning the European Economic Community, before the Ass'n of the Bar of the City of N.Y., May 8, 1969 (to be published in the RECORD).

It has been stated as to EEC law that: "[T]he place of conclusion or performance of an agreement, or the law or venue agreed upon by the parties, or the seat of the court of arbitration in cartel matters is of no importance as points of contact. The same is true as to the nationality of the party concerned, the domicile of natural, and the seat of legal corporate personalities." I. Schwartz, Remarks, Panel on Conflicts Between, and the Extra-Territorial Application of, the Antitrust Laws of the United States, the Common Market and Member States, in PROCEEDINGS, ABA ANTITRUST SECTION CONFERENCE ON ANTITRUST AND THE EUROPEAN COMMUNITIES (Brussels and Luxembourg, Sept. 23-26, 1963) 205-06. *Cf. Extra-Territorial Application of Restrictive Trade Legislation—Jurisdiction and International Law* (Riedweg, Rapporteur), Annex A, European Economic Community, in INT'L LAW ASS'N, REPORT OF THE FIFTY-FIRST CONFERENCE (TOKYO) 478 (1964).

American law.[121] The Treaty provisions might reach vertical arrangements with distributors in the EEC made by American firms shipping to the Common Market. For example, it has been pointed out that agreements by an American firm giving an exclusive franchise to a given distributor in each Member Nation and confining the distributor to sales in that nation would come within EEC jurisdiction;[122] under the *Grundig-Consten* case such restrictions would probably be illegal.

In these cases, it would be possible to find that some act in pursuance of the illegal agreement has been carried out inside the Common Market. The question arises, assuming that the Treaty will be given the broad extraterritorial reach described, whether it will be applied to foreign firms for conduct occurring entirely outside the Common Market, but producing effects within it, in the manner of the *Alcoa* case. It has been suggested that, because of limitations imposed by international law, the scope of Common Market law may not go this far.[123]

In practice, the Commission has been quite conservative in its approach to extraterritorial situations, as the cases discussed above show. Adverse secondary effects on competition within the Common Market from such restraints are not readily presumed, and small effects will evidently be tolerated.[124] Even where the arrangement on its face explicitly bars sales in, or re-export to the Common Market it may escape in the absence of positive proof that it will produce significant adverse effects. In contrast, a comparable restriction would clearly be subject to American law. To what extent these differences result from a different philosophy on extraterritoriality, or from the absence in the Rome Treaty provisions of a foreign commerce clause has not become clear.

As for the territorial scope of Article 86, there have as yet been no reported cases to elucidate any of the questions concerning application

[121] See Orrick, Remarks, in PROCEEDINGS, *supra* note 120, at 204.

[122] I. Schwartz, *supra* note 120, at 207. Dr. Schwartz raised, but did not answer the interesting question of whether a single such agreement with one distributor for the entire EEC would come within the Treaty provisions; presumably it could if it were coupled with a parallel restraint upon distributors outside the EEC.

[123] Thiesing, *supra* note 120; see I. Schwartz, *Applicability of National Law on Restraints of Competition to International Restraints of Competition,* in 2 CARTEL AND MONOPOLY IN MODERN LAW 701, 715-16 (1961). See discussion in Chapter 7 *infra.*

[124] See notes 117 and 118 *supra.*

of this provision. The Commission's Memorandum on Concentration makes one observation relevant to firms outside the EEC, however, which may have extraterritorial significance. In determining whether a firm has a dominant position in the Common Market, the Commission has said that account must be taken not merely of the firm's market share in that market, but of its entire "economic potency."[125] This means that the firm's power abroad will be appraised, and perhaps its behavior and performance outside the EEC also will be studied. In that sense the activities of a firm in other parts of the world might be given effect in determining culpability under the Rome Treaty.

B. European Coal and Steel Community Law

Article 65 of the treaty establishing the European Coal and Steel Community is similar to Article 85, of which it was the immediate forerunner. It covers agreements "tending . . . to prevent, restrict or distort the normal operation of competition within the common market," but does not contain an interstate trade requirement. Under the treaty, the High Authority (now the Commission of the European Communities as a result of the merger) has exclusive enforcement jurisdiction and may impose penalties for violations. It may also grant—and it has granted—exemptions for "specialization" agreements and for joint buying and selling arrangements on grounds similar to those specified in Article 85(3) of the Rome Treaty.[126]

Article 66 requires that approval from the High Authority be obtained for any "concentration" or merger involving at least one enterprise

[125] EEC Commission, Memorandum, *supra* note 104, at 40.

[126] See generally Hamburger, *Inter-Relationship of the Cartel, Monopoly and Merger Provisions of the European Coal and Steel Community Treaty,* in 1 CARTEL AND MONOPOLY IN MODERN LAW 243 (1961); Kronstein, *The Significance of the Provisions Concerning Restraints of Competition within the Total Perspective of the European Coal and Steel Community Treaty and the European Economic Community Treaty, id.* at 131; Lang, *Trade Regulations in the Treaty Establishing the European Coal and Steel Community,* 52 NW. U.L. REV. 761 (1958); Matthies, *Law on Cartels and Concentrations in the European Coal and Steel Community,* 6 INT'L & COMP. L. Q. SUPP. 146 (1963); Riesenfeld, *The Protection of Competition,* in 2 AMERICAN ENTERPRISE IN THE EUROPEAN COMMON MARKET: A LEGAL PROFILE 197, 294-319 (Stein & Nicholson eds. 1960); STEIN & HAY, LAW AND INSTITUTIONS IN THE ATLANTIC AREA 535-60 (1967).

which engages in coal or steel production or wholesale distribution in the Community. Exemption from this prior authorization requirement may be made for mergers below a certain size. A merger is to be approved if it will not give the parties the power to control prices, production or distribution, or to prevent effective competition "in a substantial part of the market for the products." Under these provisions, the High Authority has authorized a large number of mergers, and has disapproved none.[127] Article 66 also provides for controls over prices, conditions of sale, and production and delivery programs of firms having a dominant position.[128]

With respect to extraterritoriality, these provisions are limited in application to enterprises engaged in production or distribution of coal or steel in the Community (Article 89). Article 65 applies only to agreements and concerted practices of *such* firms having the proscribed effect *within* the ECSC. This led the High Authority in 1953 to refrain from opposing the export price agreement of the "Brussels Convention" of steel producers.[129] Recently, however, the Commission indicated that it could deal with arrangements of the ECSC steel producers to curtail exports to the United States, if effects on competition within the Common Market result.[130]

[127]Pursuant to Section 3 of Article 66, the High Authority issued a regulation exempting from the prior authorization requirement mergers of various kinds falling below a certain size; see Markert, *Antitrust Aspects of Mergers in the EEC,* 5 TEX. INT'L L. FOR. 32, 37 (1969). Authorizations of mergers not falling within the exemption have been numerous, and no requests have been formally refused; mergers are permitted even though they result in increased concentration in existing oligopolistic structures, *id.* at 44. For statistical summary, see Chapter 1 *supra,* text at note 109.

[128]In addition, Article 60 of the Treaty contains price discrimination provisions, including prohibitions of temporary or local price cuts for the purpose of acquiring a monopoly, and discrimination between different buyers in comparable transactions. Both prohibitions pertain only to sales "within the Common Market." See Mestmäcker, *The Prohibition Against Discrimination in the European Coal and Steel Community Treaty,* in 1 CARTEL AND MONOPOLY IN MODERN LAW 323 (1961); Mueller, *The Prohibition of Price Discrimination in the European Coal and Steel Community,* 11 ANTITRUST BULL. 733 (1966); Chapter 1 *supra,* text at note 100.

[129]ECSC High Authority Answer to Written Question No. 11, E.C.S.C.J.O. No. 13, Dec. 15, 1953, at 202.

[130]EC Commission Answer to Written Question, E.C.J.O. No. C42, April 2, 1969, at 4; Thiesing, *supra* note 120; *cf.* Riedweg, *supra* note 120, at 481.

Article 66 could have an impact upon mergers between Community and foreign-based firms; *e.g.,* a merger between an American and an ECSC steel firm would require approval, and could be frustrated by the Commission.

III. NATIONAL ANTITRUST LAWS IN THE EUROPEAN COMMUNITY

The background and provisions of the antitrust and related laws of nations which are members of the European Community have received detailed treatment in the first three volumes of this series.[131] Discussion of national laws at this point will therefore be quite brief and will be confined to the question of the extraterritorial substantive scope of the four national antitrust laws presently found within the Common Market, *i.e.,* the laws of Belgium, France, Germany and the Netherlands.

A. Belgium

The Belgian Law of 1960 is a very narrow statute substantively, applying only to abuse of economic power. Its application is limited to exercise—"within the territory of the Kingdom"—of a prohibited degree of dominance over supply, price or quality. Accordingly, the authorities are agreed that effect must be felt within the nation, as with the Rome Treaty provisions.[132]

Subject to this limitation, the law will reach any person causing the proscribed effect regardless of nationality or domicile,[133] and apparently

[131] BUSINESS REGULATION IN THE COMMON MARKET NATIONS (Blake ed. 1969): vol. 1 (Benelux nations); vol. 2 (France and Italy); vol. 3 (West Germany). These volumes, like the present book, were sponsored by the Special Committee on the European Common Market of the Association of the Bar of the City of New York.

[132] BUSINESS REGULATION IN THE COMMON MARKET NATIONS (Blake ed. 1969), vol. 1 (Ginsburg ed.), pt. 1, BELGIUM (by de Keyser & Suetens) 69, 160; del Marmol & Fontaine, *Protection Against the Abuse of Economic Power in Belgium: The Law of May 27, 1960,* 109 U. PA. L. REV. 922 (1961); Smit, Belgian and Dutch Antitrust Law, in *Hearings, supra* note 19, at 389, 403; Suetens, *Belgian Antitrust Law "in action,"* 2 C. M. L. REV. 325 (1964).

[133] BUSINESS REGULATION IN THE COMMON MARKET NATIONS, *supra* note 132, at 69.

also regardless of where the actions bringing about the effect are committed. It has been noted that this broad scope is "academic if the headquarters of an economic power and all of its property are situated in another country," because enforcement of Belgian law would then be completely "ineffectual."[134] It is perhaps unlikely that such a remotely-situated business would be able to exert dominant power in Belgium anyway.

Import cartels and other import restrictions exercising dominant influence inside Belgium could be reached. Export cartels, however, would apparently be generally beyond the scope of the law.

B. France

The modern French law contained in the Price Ordinance of June 30, 1945, as amended, deals explicitly with territorial coverage in certain respects. Article 61 provides that the antitrust provisions, Articles 37 and 59, are applicable to transactions carried out in metropolitan France and its territorial waters, to CIF prices of imported goods, and to imports from all locations.[135] Article 62 specifically exempts exports. Restrictions on imports applied by persons operating within France are thus covered by the law, while export restraints are not.

It is not clear, however, to what extent the French antitrust laws reach conduct outside of France having effects within the nation. In the only case applying Article 419 of the Penal Code (an older antitrust provision) to foreign business activities, the *Secrétan* case of 1890 involving monopolization of the world copper supply, the decision was based both upon activities carried on in France and upon effect on the French market.[136] As to the Price Ordinance provisions, there are no judicial decisions in point. Some writers have concluded that effects within France are all that is required;[137] and that the law would reach a seller

---

[134] del Marmol and Fontaine, *supra* note 132, at 931.

[135] Ordonnance No. 45-1483, June 30, 1945, C. PEN. 628, 644 (1966).

[136] BUSINESS REGULATION IN THE COMMON MARKET NATIONS (Blake ed. 1969), vol. 2 (Perillo & B. Blake eds.), pt. 1, FRANCE (by Bergsten) 306.

[137] Plaisant, *Restrictive Trade Practice in France,* in INT'L LAW ASS'N, REPORT OF THE FIFTY-SECOND CONFERENCE (HELSINKI) 89 (1966); PLAISANT, FRANCESCHELLI & LASSIER, DROIT EUROPEEN DE LA CONCURRENCE 39 (1966); BUSINESS REGULATION IN THE COMMON MARKET NATIONS, *supra* note 136, at 310.

located outside France who, contrary to Article 37, refuses to sell to a French buyer. Similarly, foreign export groups, including Webb-Pomerene associations, might come within the law if their activities affect prices within France. The contrary has also been stated, however, *i.e.*, that the law is limited to application to conduct in France.[138]

Insofar as criminal prosecution is concerned, as distinguished from civil and administrative application, evidently the scope of the law is narrowly limited. Criminal prosecution of a French national located outside France and exporting to France would apparently depend not only upon whether his activities had an effect in the French market, but also whether they were unlawful under the law of the nation whence he made the sale. Apparently foreign nationals could not be prosecuted criminally for acts abroad merely having effects in France, but some civil consequences are possible, and of course they may be prosecuted for conduct in France.[139]

C. Germany

The German Act Against Restraints of Competition contains express provisions defining its scope as to foreign activities. Section 98(2) states that the Act "shall apply to all restraints of competition which have effect in the area in which this Act applies, even if they result from acts done outside such area." The area referred to is the domestic area of the nation. As to that area, the Act apparently relies upon substantially the same objective territorial principle as is embodied in Section 18 of the Restatement (Second) of Foreign Relations Law of the United States.[140]

Accordingly, the Act reaches cartels and other restrictive arrangements formed and carried on outside Germany if they have the necessary "effect" in Germany. What kind of effect is required has not been settled by decisions. Leading commentators have concluded that there must be a

[138] Statement of Professor Riesenfeld on French antitrust law, in *Hearings, supra* note 19, at 403, 406.

[139] BUSINESS REGULATION IN THE COMMON MARKET NATIONS, *supra* note 136, at 306-07.

[140] See BUSINESS REGULATION IN THE COMMON MARKET NATIONS (Blake ed. 1969), vol. 3 (K. Ebb ed.), WEST GERMANY (by Juenger, Markert, Pfeifer & Steckhan) ch. 6; Market, *The Application of German Antitrust Law to International Restraints on Trade,* 7:2 VA. J. INT'L L. 47 (1967); Günther, Remarks, Panel on Conflicts, *supra* note 120, at 189. Günther, in *Hearings, supra* note 104, at 3484.

direct negative effect on the competitive process or on the economic freedom of individual enterprises in a domestic market.[141]

Under the German approach, a horizontal price fixing arrangement on American exports shipped to Germany would probably fall under Section 1 of the Act, regardless of whether the agreement were exempted under American law by the Webb-Pomerene Act.[142] Section 7 also permits an exemption for a German import cartel if the importers are confronted with a monopoly or a controlling cartel on the seller's side. Thus, an American Webb-Pomerene association may precipitate a lawful retaliatory German import cartel.

Vertical restrictions upon resale in the German market imposed by foreign sellers would be treated the same, insofar as extraterritoriality is concerned, although the substantive rules for vertical price control (Sections 15-17) and for exclusive distribution arrangements (Section 18) are quite different from those of Section 1.[143]

Court and administrative jurisdiction to apply the substantive rules to acts occurring outside Germany is evidently as extensive as the rules themselves. On the other hand, the German government's view of its investigatory and enforcement powers is rather strictly territorial.[144]

Insofar as restrictions upon competition in German export trade are concerned, the legal situation is similar to that of American law. Export cartels having no domestic effects are exempt under Section 6, if notified to the government cartel authority, where they remain under the latter's control as to "abuse." Export cartels having domestic effect are subject

[141]Markert, *supra,* 53. Dr. Markert cites the following for this view: REHBINDER, EXTRATERRITORIALE WIRKUNGEN DES DEUTSCHEN KARTELL-RECHTS 112-13 (1965); I. SCHWARTZ, DEUTSCHES INTERNATIONALES KARTELLRECHT 32 (1962); Würdinger, *Exportkartell und EWG,* 10 WUW 313, 315 (1960). The additional argument that the effect must be "substantial" as well as "direct" is made by REHBINDER, *supra,* 130, 149.

    Dr. Markert adds that a broader view, "that any effect on the domestic economy is sufficient," is set forth in articles by Hoppman in: *Die Anwendung des Territorialprinzips auf reine Exportkartelle im GWB als volkswirtschaftliches Problem,* in FESTSCHRIFT FÜR HERMANN NOTTARP 300 (1961); and *Exportkartelle und Gesetz gegen Wettbewerbsbeschränkungen,* in EICHLER, HOPPMAN & SCHAFER, EXPORTKARTELLE UND WETTBEWERB 106 (1964).

[142]BUSINESS REGULATION IN THE COMMON MARKET NATIONS, *supra* note 140, at 357; Günther, Remarks, Panel on Conflicts, *supra* note 120, at 186.

[143]Markert, *supra* note 140, at 58-60.

[144]*Id.* at 63-66.

to the Section 1 prohibition, but may be exempted under Section 6(2) and (3), if necessary to carry out "desired regulation of competition in the markets outside" Germany,[145] and if they do not violate German treaty obligations or lead to a substantial restraint of domestic competition where "there is a predominating interest in preserving competition."

Patent license restrictions applicable only in foreign markets are given a statutory exemption from the provision in Section 20 invalidating restrictions which exceed the scope of the patent. This exemption, however, has been narrowly construed by the Federal Cartel Office to the effect that it does not cover foreign market restrictions imposed as part of a domestic license. Licenses relating solely to foreign countries, on the other hand, may contain restrictions exceeding the scope of the patent, provided there is no accompanying domestic effect under Section 98(2).[146]

In sum, though not containing an explicit "foreign commerce" clause, the German law theoretically can have a very substantial extraterritorial scope. In practice, however, it has been applied cautiously insofar as restraints occurring outside Germany are concerned, its actual extraterritorial operation being largely confined to an administrative practice of narrowly construing the export and international license exemptions.[147]

D. The Netherlands

The Dutch Economic Competition Act, though a very mild law substantively, potentially has a quite substantial extraterritorial scope. Its description in Section 1 of the "agreements governing competition" which are to be registered and subjected to administrative authority has no territorial limitation. The definition of "dominant position," like the Belgian law, is confined to a predominant influence in some market in the Netherlands.

[145] Unlike the Webb-Pomerene Act, the German law has been interpreted as allowing, insofar as the exemption is concerned, German exporters to combine with foreign firms in restricting competition in foreign markets. *Id.* at 58.

[146] Markert, *supra* note 140, at 60-63.

[147] *Id.* at 66. As of 1966, no enforcement cases had been brought against foreign firms for acts done in a foreign country; Jaenicke, Annex E, *Germany,* in INT'L LAW ASS'N, REPORT OF THE FIFTY-SECOND CONFERENCE (HELSINKI) 93 (1966).

Procedural requirements of the law, however, establish some important limits. Agreements relating entirely to competition outside the Netherlands are exempt from the registration requirement, by virtue of Section 4(1) and a ministerial order.[148] Administrative proceedings to invalidate an agreement under Section 19 may be taken only if the agreement is contrary to the "public interest;" this phase has been interpreted as precluding application to a cartel in a foreign market merely because it raises prices in that market.[149] Further, the enforcement sanctions, which are primarily penal, can, by virtue of the Penal Code, be taken only against persons who commit an act in the Netherlands. From this, it has been said that some "concrete activities" in the country are a prerequisite to application of the law.[150] In practice, the law does not appear to have been applied to any other than Dutch nationals, and then only for activities in the Netherlands.[151]

Despite these technical and practical limits, the Dutch law seems to be nearly as broad as the American law in theoretical extraterritorial scope, if not broader. It clearly may apply to conduct abroad by both Dutch and foreign firms, where the Dutch public interest is affected.[152] Not only are effects in the domestic market within this concept, but agreements which inhibit either Dutch exports or imports may also, according to extant administrative interpretation, infringe the public interest,[153] thus giving the Act a "foreign commerce" application. The penal requirement of an "act" in the Netherlands has apparently been broadly interpreted, and while this is a limitation on enforcement, it does not necessarily remove jurisdiction over all of the civil consequences which may attach to an extraterritorial violation.

[148] BUSINESS REGULATION IN THE COMMON MARKET NATIONS (Blake ed. 1969), vol. 1 (Ginsburg ed.), pt. 2, THE NETHERLANDS (by Silbiger) 469.

[149] *Id.* at 470.

[150] *Id.*; INT'L LAW ASS'N, REPORT OF THE FIFTY-FIRST CONFERENCE (TOKYO) 460 (1964).

[151] BUSINESS REGULATION IN THE COMMON MARKET NATIONS, *supra* note 148, at 470-71.

[152] Smit, Belgian and Dutch Antitrust Law, in *Hearings, supra* note 19, at 394.

[153] BUSINESS REGULATION IN THE COMMON MARKET NATIONS, *supra* note 148, at 470.

SUMMARY

All of the American and European laws discussed above have some kind of extraterritorial impact, but the theories and rules underlying their applicability vary a great deal, as does their scope in actual practice. The Sherman Act emerges as the farthest-reaching law. Its express "foreign commerce" clause is unique among these laws and, as it has been interpreted, goes to the limit of, if not somewhat beyond, the domestic effect standard endorsed by the Restatement and adopted by the German law. A majority of the actual American cases have involved facts which would enable the decisions to rest alone upon the interstate commerce test of the Act, but the foreign commerce clause undoubtedly extends the Act in important ways.

The laws of Belgium, France and Germany base whatever extraterritorial application they have upon effects or acts within the nation, rather than upon effect on foreign trade. The German law, which is by far the most comprehensive and severe, is also the most explicit in its assertion of jurisdiction over conduct abroad. The Belgian law, although very limited in prohibitions, appears to be capable of reaching as far territorially as the German law. The scope of the French law is in doubt, with some commentators taking the position that the law reaches conduct abroad producing effects in France, and others contending that acts within France are necessary. In one respect, however, the French law explicitly contemplates extraterritorial impact—*i.e.*, in its application to restraints on imports. The Dutch law's real limits are not clear; the theoretical possibilities seem to range from coverage as broad as that of the Sherman Act to a rather narrow limitation to acts within the country.

The Common Market treaty provisions are limited by a double test—of domestic effect similar to that of German law, and of interstate commerce similar to that of American law. The strict interpretation being given to this test by the Commission in negative clearance proceedings involving export and foreign market restrictions, if continued, promises to circumscribe rather narrowly the applicability of the law to conduct abroad. The Coal and Steel Community provisions have only slight extraterritorial significance.

Taken together, the American and European laws make up a complex pattern of overlapping jurisdictions and substantive rules.

Each of the laws overlaps to some extent with all of the others. Many transactions occur which are subject to two or three of the laws at the same time. It is not only possible, but probably not uncommon, that the same arrangement or transaction at one and the same time would be subject to all of them.

The seriousness of the problems created by this much overlapping cannot be determined in the abstract, but must be analyzed and judged in terms of procedures used and of specific types of transactions. This is the task of the next three chapters.

CHAPTER 3 *Extraterritorial Procedure and Enforcement of the Antitrust Laws of the United States and of the Communities and Member States*

The procedural powers and practices of American and European antitrust enforcement institutions and agencies differ substantially in their extraterritorial application. The scope of procedural extraterritoriality is, of course, of major importance to any evaluation of substantive extraterritoriality. On the one hand, it may give practical breadth to broad substantive rules, as illustrated in such cases as the *Swiss Watch* proceeding discussed in Chapter 6. On the other hand, doubts about the ability of authorities to subpoena evidence located abroad or to issue orders to be carried out abroad may seriously limit otherwise fairly far-reaching substantive provisions. As Section 7 of the Restatement (Second) of Foreign Relations Law of the United Stated says, "A state having jurisdiction to prescribe a rule of law does not necessarily have jurisdiction to enforce it in all cases."

In this chapter the scope of American law is discussed with regard to orders and judgments to be carried out in part abroad, and to the taking of personal jurisdiction over foreign defendants in American antitrust proceedings. Commission personal jurisdiction under the Rome Treaty is also briefly discussed in light of the *Dyestuffs* case. A substantial discussion of Commission investigative powers is also included, although only a little can be said about its extraterritorial investigative power at this time. So little is available on these problems under the national laws of the Member States that only very brief references to the latter are included at the end of the chapter. Chapter 7 discusses issues raised by these procedures under international law.

I. AMERICAN LAW

A. Extraterritorial Discovery Orders and Judgments

1. EFFECT OF INCONSISTENT FOREIGN LAW, IN GENERAL

The principle is well-established in American law that an American court having jurisdiction over a party, whether or not a national of the United States, has the power to order that party to do, or to refrain from doing, acts abroad.[1] The most troublesome question relates to the power of the court to issue such orders when compliance with them may be inconsistent with a party's obligations under foreign law. This question has arisen most frequently at the investigation stage of cases in connection with orders to produce or to disclose the contents of documents or other evidence located abroad. In a few antitrust cases, the problem has also been presented as to final judgments or decrees.

At one time the American rule was said to be that a court in one state could order an act to be done in another state only if the act were not contrary to the law of the state in which it was to be performed.[2]

This approach was illustrated in the decree in the *General Electric* (incandescent lamp) antitrust case.[3] A Netherlands corporation, N.V.

---

[1] ABA ANTITRUST SECTION SUPP. TO ATTY. GEN. NAT. COMM. ANTITRUST REP.: ANTITRUST DEVELOPMENTS 1955-1968, at 52 (1968); RESTATEMENT (SECOND) OF FOREIGN RELATIONS LAW OF THE UNITED STATES § §18, 39 (1965); FUGATE, FOREIGN COMMERCE AND THE ANTITRUST LAWS 76 (1958); Onkelinx, *Conflict of International Jurisdiction: Ordering the Production of Documents in Violation of the Law of the Situs,* 64 NW. U. L. REV. 487, 502 (1969).

[2] RESTATEMENT OF CONFLICT OF LAWS §94 (1934); *cf.* Onkelinx, *supra* note 1; see also Note, *Limitations on the Federal Judicial Power to Compel Acts Violating Foreign Law,* 63 COLUM. L. REV. 1441 (1963); Note, *Subpoena of Documents Located in Foreign Jurisdictions Where Law of Situs Prohibits Removal,* 37 N.Y.U. L. REV. 295 (1962); Note, *Ordering Production of Documents from Abroad in Violation of Foreign Law,* 31 U. CHI. L. REV. 791 (1964); the RESTATEMENT (SECOND) OF CONFLICT OF LAWS §53 (Proposed Official Draft, 1967) pointedly eliminates the foreign illegality qualification contained in Section 94 of the first Restatement: "A state has power to exercise judicial jurisdiction to order a person, who is subject to its judicial jurisdiction, to do an act, or to refrain from doing an act, in another state."

[3] United States v. General Electric Co., 115 F.Supp. 835 (D.N.J. 1953), *supplementing* 82 F.Supp. 753 (D.N.J. 1949).

Philips' Gloeilampenfabrieken (Philips), was adjudged part of a cartel to divide world markets in incandescent lamps. The decree enjoining Philips from further contracting to effectuate that purpose carefully specified, however, that

> Philips shall not be in contempt of this Judgment for doing anything outside of the United States which is required or for not doing anything outside of the United States which is unlawful under the laws of the government, province, country or state in which Philips or any [of its] subsidiaries may be incorporated, chartered or organized or in the territory of which Philips or any such subsidiaries may be doing business.[4]

The court explained the purpose of the "safeguard" provision as an attempt to protect Philips "from being caught between the jaws of this judgment and the operation of laws in foreign countries where it does its business."[5]

In recent years, the American courts have assumed that they have the power to order conduct abroad even though such conduct would violate foreign law.[6] The courts also exercise discretion, however, where necessary to avoid placing a party in a position where he must violate foreign law.[7] These powers, whose use in antitrust cases will be illustrated in the following discussion, were implicitly endorsed by the Supreme Court in *Société Internationale Pour Participations Industrielles et Commerciales, S.A. v. Rogers.*[8] This case constituted one chapter in the complex *Interhandel* litigation, in which the plaintiff, a Swiss holding company, brought suit under the Trading With the Enemy Act for

---

[4]*Id.* at 878.

[5]*Id.* Similarly, in SEC. v. Minas de Artemisa, S.A., 150 F.2d 215 (9th Cir. 1945), a subpoena requiring the production in Arizona of corporate books located in Mexico was modified on the ground that compliance would have required a violation of Mexican law. As modified, the subpoena simply ordered the party to apply to Mexican fiscal authorities for permission to remove the books in question or, in the alternative, to allow the SEC to copy the books in Mexico, thus avoiding a violation of Mexican law.

[6]See RESTATEMENT (SECOND) OF FOREIGN RELATIONS LAW OF THE UNITED STATES §39 (1965): "(1) A state having jurisdiction to prescribe or to enforce a rule of law is not precluded from exercising its jurisdiction solely because such exercise requires a person to engage in conduct subjecting him to liability under the law of another state having jurisdiction with respect to that conduct. * * *"

[7]See *id.* §40; Note, *supra* note 2, at 1491.

[8]357 U.S. 197 (1958).

recovery of assets seized by the United States during World War II. The Government requested an order requiring the plaintiff to make available for inspection and copying a large number of banking records. Not disputing the relevancy of these documents, Interhandel contended that it did not have "control" over them, as their production would have violated the Swiss laws relating to economic espionage and the secrecy of banking records. Concurrently, the Swiss Federal Attorney, deeming that production of the accounts would violate Swiss law, confiscated them. This "confiscation" was essentially an order not to remove the documents. A Special Master found that there was no collusion between Interhandel and the Swiss Government in the "confiscation," and that Interhandel had made good faith efforts to comply with the production order. The District Court confirmed these findings, but nevertheless held that Interhandel had control over the documents, ordered their production and, upon Interhandel's non-compliance, dismissed the complaint.

On appeal, the Supreme Court found no fault with the issuance of the discovery order,[9] thereby accepting the proposition that the District Court had the *power* to issue the order notwithstanding the Swiss laws prohibiting disclosure of the documents. The Court, however, reversed the dismissal of the complaint, holding that, because of the due process clause of the United States Constitution, Rule 37 of the Federal Rules of Civil Procedure should not be construed to authorize dismissal when non-compliance with the order is due to inability, rather than to willfulness or bad faith.[10]

[9] *Id.* at 206.

[10] *Id.* at 212. This due process issue was in large part predicated upon the notion that the petitioner in the case was very much in the position of a defendant; the Court gave no indication of what the result might have been had the discovery order been directed at a plaintiff having none of the characteristics of a defendant.

The procedural setting of the *Interhandel* case differs, of course, from that of the ordinary antitrust case. In *Interhandel,* failure to comply with the court order threatened the party, a nominal plaintiff, only with dismissal, whereas ordinarily the threat accompanying non-compliance would be that of sanctions accompanying a finding of contempt. But just as the Supreme Court in *Interhandel* was able to avoid the constitutional question by interpretation of the Federal Rules of Civil Procedure (due process considerations having played a role), a court considering the sanctions to be imposed for a party's non-compliance with a court order could avail itself of the traditional powers of a court of equity so as to avoid the same constitutional questions. The issue would thus be one of fairness, and one might expect the courts

2. SOURCES OF CONFLICT

Conflict between an American court order and foreign law may arise in a number of ways. The following categories represent the chief types of conflict which have occurred in antitrust situations.

a. Foreign Statutes

Some states, reacting to what has seemed to them to be infringement of their sovereignty by American discovery proceedings in antitrust and regulatory cases, have enacted laws designed to frustrate implementation of extraterritorial orders. The Netherlands has expressly barred compliance with the antitrust laws of other nations.[11] The United Kingdom has prohibited compliance with extraterritorial regulations of other nations or orders for the furnishing of documents or information as to ocean shipping.[12] Ontario and Quebec have prohibited the removal of business documents or reports pursuant to the order of any other jurisdiction.[13]

to manifest no insignificant amount of sympathy with a party subject to the conflicting dictates of two or more jurisdictions.

[11] Section 39 of the Netherlands Economic Competition Act of 1956 states in part: "1. Save in so far as Our Ministers have prescribed an exception or, on request, have granted exemption, it shall be forbidden to comply deliberately with any measures or decisions taken by any other State, which relate to any regulations of competition, dominant positions or conduct restricting competition. * * *" OECD GUIDE TO LEGISLATION ON RESTRICTIVE BUS. PRAC., NETHERLANDS. For background, see BUSINESS REGULATION IN THE COMMON MARKET NATIONS (Blake ed. 1969), vol. 1 (Ginsburg ed), pt. 2, THE NETHERLANDS (by Silbiger) 472. This provision has been applied several times, with permission in most cases denied where a Dutch company was involved and the records or information being sought by American authorities were located in the Netherlands and not available in the United States through other means; *id.* at 473. The Dutch authorities follow a policy of authorizing compliance with requests for information if the data are available in the requesting country; OECD Annual Reports on Developments in the Field of Restrictive Business Practice 30 (June 1969).

[12] Shipping Contracts and Commercial Documents Act of 1964, c. 87, § §1, 2.

[13] Business Records Protection Act, 1947, 11 Geo. 6, c. 10, *as amended,* 14 Geo. 6, c. 7 (1950), 1 Ont. Rev. Stat. c. 44 (1960); Business Concerns Records Act, 6 & 7 Eliz. 2, c. 42 (1958), Que. Rev. Stat. c. 278 (1964). A federal statute prohibiting both removal of records and data pursuant to a foreign court order and compliance with foreign antitrust orders, decrees and judgments has been recommended by the REPORT OF THE TASK FORCE ON THE STRUCTURE OF CANADIAN INDUSTRY, FOREIGN OWNERSHIP AND THE STRUCTURE OF CANADIAN INDUSTRY 408 (1968).

Other nations have general laws which prohibit the furnishing or removal of certain kinds of material.[14]

b. Foreign Court Orders

In one antitrust case, the famous *I.C.I.* litigation, an American decree was overridden by foreign court order. The United States district court held that E. I. duPont de Nemours (duPont) and Imperial Chemical Industries (I.C.I.) had conspired to divide world markets in chemicals and other products and had, in fact, curtailed the import and export trade of the United States.[15] Subsequent to the filing of the suit, and, in the view of the court, with "a studied and continued purpose on the part of ICI and duPont to remove [the] patents from within the scope of any decree which might ultimately be made by [the] court," duPont assigned to I.C.I. its basic British nylon patents.[16] Prior to the suit it had given I.C.I. an exclusive license, and I.C.I. had in turn given an exclusive sublicense for the manufacture of nylon yarn to British Nylon Spinners (B.N.S.), an English corporation in which I.C.I. held a 50% interest.[17]

To undo the attempt to thwart its judgment, the American court ordered that the assignment of British nylon patents by duPont to I.C.I. be cancelled, and that I.C.I. be prohibited from asserting the patents to prevent importation of nylon into Great Britain.[18] Recognizing that the effectiveness of the decree would depend on the comity accorded it by the English courts, the judge nonetheless stated that the possibility that enforcement might be refused ought not to deter him from rendering such a decree.[19] His order by its own terms, however, was not to "operate against I.C.I. for action taken in compliance with any law . . . of any foreign government or instrumentality thereof to which

[14]See arts. 89, 93, Law No. 17, Jan. 30, 1961, of the Republic of Panama, prohibiting the removal of, or the copying of documents for use in, an action outside of Panama in compliance with an order of an authority not of the Republic of Panama; quoted in Application of The Chase Manhattan Bank, 297 F.2d. 611, 612 (2d Cir. 1962); SWISS PENAL CODE arts. 271, 273, [1951] ROLF 12, [1938] ROLF 846, prohibiting certain acts for a foreign state, and furnishing of secret economic information to a foreign official or firm.

[15]United States v. Imperial Chem. Indus., Ltd., 100 F.Supp. 504 (S.D.N.Y. 1951).

[16]105 F.Supp. 215, 230 (S.D.N.Y. 1952) (supplemental opinion on remedies).

[17]*Id.*

[18]*Id.* at 231.

[19]*Id.*

I.C.I. [was at that] time . . . subject, and concerning matters over which, under the law of the United States, such foreign government or instrumentality thereof [had] jurisdiction."[20]

Thereafter, B.N.S. successfully brought suit against I.C.I. in the English courts to enjoin I.C.I.'s compliance with the American decree and to obtain specific performance of I.C.I.'s license agreement. The judge who granted specific performance relied expressly on the saving clause in the American decree, which in his view precluded conflict.[21]

c. Duties under Foreign Private Law

An American court order, while not conflicting with a foreign statute or foreign court order, may still place the party concerned in the position of being required to violate an obligation abroad under private law. This would have been the situation, for example, in the *I.C.I.* case, had the British courts not intervened to prevent the American decree from disrupting the I.C.I.-B.N.S. license agreement.

In the *Holophane* case,[22] an American antitrust decree against parties to an international cartel which had allocated world markets included a provision requiring the American defendant to use "reasonable efforts" to sell its products in England, France and other areas from which it had been excluded by the agreement. Compliance with this order might well have made Holophane liable under foreign law for breach of contract in areas where restrictive agreements are enforceable.[23] The Supreme Court affirmed this "reasonable efforts" provision of the judgment by an

[20]Quoted in British Nylon Spinners, Ltd. v. Imperial Chem. Indus., Ltd., [1955] Ch. 37, [1954] 3 All E. R. 88, 92 (Ch.).

[21]British Nylon Spinners, Ltd. v. Imperial Chem. Indus., Ltd., [1953] Ch. 19, [1952] 2 All E. R. 780 (C.A.) (injunction by lower court against compliance with U.S. decree affirmed; American decree was "intrusion" on British sovereignty); British Nylon Spinners, Ltd. v. Imperial Chem. Indus., Ltd., [1955] Ch. 37, [1954] 3 All E. R. 88 (Ch.) (declaratory judgment granting specific performance of the ICI-BNS license).

[22]United States v. Holophane Co., 119 F.Supp. 114 (findings and conclusions), 1954 Trade Cas. ¶67,679 (judgment) (S.D. Ohio 1954), *aff'd per curiam,* 352 U.S. 903 (1956). A consent decree in United States v. R. Hoe & Co. (S.D.N.Y. 1955), 1955 Trade Cas. ¶68,215, ordered the defendant to promote sales in foreign markets by various steps including instituting a new trademark there and placing advertisements in foreign journals.

[23]The issue of possible violation of foreign law was disputed in the oral argument before the Supreme Court, 25 U.S. L. W. 3141 (Nov. 13, 1956).

equally divided vote,[24] after receiving a letter from the Solicitor General interpreting it as requiring "only such acts as do not affirmatively violate a foreign statute, regulation or ordinance, or the valid judgment of a competent foreign court."[25]

In *United States v. First National City Bank,*[26] the Second Circuit Court of Appeals ordered enforcement of a grand jury subpoena despite the bank's contention that it would be subjected to the risk of suit in Germany for breach of contract. The subpoena required the American parent to produce documents held by its Frankfurt branch relating to transactions of a German customer of the bank being investigated in connection with the quinine cartel.[27] Expert testimony indicated that under German law there are no statutory provisions as to bank secrecy, but that the customer has an implicit contractual right to secrecy, which may be waived or which may be enforced by court order upon the customer's motion. For reasons apparently never explained to the court, the German customer firm did not seek a court order enjoining the bank's compliance with the subpoena, but only threatened to sue for damages in contract or tort and to use its influence within German industrial circles to cause the bank to suffer losses.

The trial court found the bank in contempt for its refusal to comply and the Court of Appeals affirmed. The latter treated the threat of civil liability in Germany as relevant, and rejected the Government's contention that threat of criminal liability alone can serve as a justification for non-compliance, saying that this "would show scant respect for international comity."[28] The court agreed with the trial

[24] 352 U.S. 903 (1956).

[25] Quoted in ABA ANTITRUST SECTION SUPP., *supra* note 1, at 53.

[26] 396 F.2d 897 (1968), noted in 1 J. OF LAW AND POLICY IN INT'L BUS. 162 (1969).

[27] Subsequently, on Oct. 25, 1968, the grand jury returned a Sherman Act indictment charging fifteen American and foreign drug firms, including the German firm, and eight executives with international monopolization and price fixing on quinine and quinidine; conspiracy to defraud the U.S. Government by collusive action in the purchase of a government stockpile was also charged, 5 CCH TRADE REG. REP. ¶45,068 (case 2023); see also Chapter 2, text and note 109.

[28] 396 F.2d at 902. The court quoted with approval §40 of the RESTATEMENT (SECOND) OF FOREIGN RELATIONS LAW OF THE UNITED STATES, as follows:

"Where two states have jurisdiction to prescribe and enforce rules of law and the rules they may prescribe require inconsistent conduct upon the part of a person,

judge, however, that the risk of civil damages under German law was "slight and speculative,"[29] and disallowed the defense on the merits.

d. Conduct Authorized, but not Required, by Foreign Law

It may be useful to point out what has been implicit in the above discussion that, while *requirements* of foreign law may provide a basis for an American court to refrain from ordering inconsistent conduct, mere foreign *approval* or *authorization* of acts sought to be prohibited by the American court will seldom, if ever, compel the court to stand aside. This proposition, of course, is followed whenever an American court penalizes or enjoins conduct abroad which occurs in jurisdictions where such conduct is lawful under local law, as described in Chapter 2.

The distinction was recognized by the Supreme Court in *Continental Ore*.[30] The case involved a private suit for damages for violations of the Sherman Act, alleging that Electro Met of Canada, the wholly-owned Canadian subsidiary of one of the American defendants, had actively conspired with other defendants to exclude the plaintiffs from the Canadian vanadium market. All evidence as to Electro Met's activity was

---

each state is required by international law to consider, in good faith, moderating the exercise of its enforcement jurisdiction, in the light of such factors as

(a) vital national interests of each of the states,
(b) the extent and the nature of the hardship that inconsistent enforcement actions would impose upon the person,
(c) the extent to which the required conduct is to take place in the territory of the other state,
(d) the nationality of the person, and
(e) the extent to which enforcement by action of either state can reasonably be expected to achieve compliance with the rule prescribed by that state."

The factors suggested by the Restatement to assist courts in deciding whether or not to issue such orders highlight the problems inherent in the case of any judicial order prescribing conduct inconsistent with a party's obligations under foreign law. Some of these factors, in particular "vital national interests of each of the states" and "the extent to which enforcement by action of either state can reasonably be expected to achieve compliance with the rule prescribed by that state," involve the exercise of judgment in fields which are perhaps not always within the competence of the judiciary.

[29]396 F.2d at 905. The court indicated that were there a possibility that the Bundesbank would revoke the First National City Bank's license for a violation of bank secrecy, it might view such a sanction as being as serious as a criminal penalty, *id.* at 902.

[30]Continental Ore Co. v. Union Carbide & Carbon Corp., 370 U.S. 690 (1962).

excluded by the trial court on the ground that as a wartime emergency measure the Canadian government had delegated to Electro Met the exclusive and discretionary agency power to purchase and allocate to Canadian industries all vanadium products required by them. The Court of Appeals for the Ninth Circuit affirmed because Electro Met had acted "as an arm of the Canadian Government."[31] The Supreme Court reversed, however, stating: "Respondents are afforded no defense from the fact that Electro Met of Canada, in carrying out the bare act of purchasing vanadium from respondents rather than Continental, was acting in a manner permitted by Canadian law. There is nothing to indicate that such law in any way compelled discriminatory purchasing. . . ."[32]

Similarly, in the *Swiss Watch* case (see Chapter 6 *infra*), both comprehensive regulation of the watch industry and approval of the effects of the Collective Convention by the Swiss Government were held insufficient to convert "a vulnerable private conspiracy into an unassailable system resulting from foreign governmental mandate."[33] The court went on to state that "[i]n the absence of direct foreign governmental action compelling the defendants' activities, a United States court may exercise its jurisdiction as to acts and contracts abroad, if, as in the case at bar, such acts and contracts have a substantial and material effect upon our foreign and domestic commerce."[34] The final decree exempted actions *required* by Swiss law, non-performance of actions *prohibited* by Swiss law and compliance with rules and regulations promulgated by the Swiss Government for export and import of watch parts.[35]

e. *Risk of Foreign Government Opprobrium or Business Loss*

Apart from legal defenses based on conflicting foreign statutes, court orders or private law obligations, parties under extraterritorial American orders may be subjected to practical difficulties arising out of foreign government antagonism to such orders. The court in the *First National City Bank* case, *supra*, stated that it was "noteworthy" that neither the German Government nor the State Department had expressed any view

---

[31] 289 F.2d 86, 94 (9th Cir. 1961).

[32] 370 U.S. at 706-07.

[33] United States v. The Watchmakers of Switzerland Information Center, Inc. (S.D.N.Y. 1962), 1963 Trade Cas. ¶70,600 at 77,457.

[34] *Id.*

[35] 1965 Trade Cas. ¶71,352 at 80,491.

on that case.[36] It is not clear, however, what significance a protest would have had, had it been made.

The same opinion did make clear, however, that threatened business loss will not suffice to avoid the duty to comply with a subpoena. Arguments of hardship based on the German customer's threats to promote a boycott of the bank were met with the observation that protection of American economic interests abroad are the appropriate concern of the same government which sought the subpoena, and also that alleged economic reprisals are of "doubtful legal relevance."[37]

3. ADJUSTMENT OF ORDERS AND DECREES TO MEET PROBLEMS OF CONFLICT WITH FOREIGN LAW

Review of the above antitrust cases shows that the courts have been unwilling explicitly to force a party to choose between the inconsistent requirements of United States and foreign law, where the legal conflict is adequately proven. On the other hand, the presence of political or business objections, as distinguished from legal conflict, has not alone been enough to prevent judicial insistence on compliance. In the following discussion, reference is made to other federal decisions involving these problems, with particular emphasis upon the approach used by the courts to define what kind of conflict is relevant, and if it is present, how to avoid it.

In a grand jury investigation of possible Sherman Act violations in the world-wide arrangements of twenty-one oil companies, very broad

---

[36] 396 F.2d at 904.

[37] *Id.* The court relied upon the holding in United States v. First Nat'l City Bank, 379 U.S. 378 (1965), that a U.S. tax lien against deposits in respondent's Montevideo branch belonging to a Uruguayan corporation against whom a large U.S. tax assessment had been made was protectible by a temporary injunction to freeze the account despite various objections by the bank, including that of threatened business harm abroad. See also dissenting opinion of Harlan, J., *id.* at 402.

Cf. the following exculpatory provision in the oil company consent decrees, *infra* note 40, para. V(C)(2): "Where the combination of the kind referred to in said subsection is participated in by Jersey pursuant to request or official pronouncement of policy of the foreign nation or nations within which the transactions which are the subject of such combination take place, or of any supra-national authority having jurisdiction over such transactions within such nation or nations, and where failure to comply with which request or policy would expose Jersey to the risk of the present or future loss of the particular business in such foreign nation or nations which is the subject of such request or policy."

subpoenas were issued calling for the production of documents located abroad. The district court reserved decision as to the production or inspection of papers which were located in foreign jurisdictions, or which were subject to foreign laws, pending a showing by each affected company of the following:

> (a) A good faith endeavor to gain consent from the foreign sovereign to remove the required documents;
> (b) What, if any, interest the foreign sovereign has in the movant corporation, or in the investigation; and
> (c) Proof of the foreign law.[38]

In a later civil case against some of the oil companies, the Government asked for further production of documents. The court ordered the defendants to make good faith attempts to obtain production of the documents, reserving, however, the question of how to deal with a claim of inability to produce them:

> If the good faith attempt meets with failure and the Government contests defendant's statement that it has, in fact, made a good faith attempt, a hearing on that issue will be scheduled at the request of either the Government or the affected defendant as soon as possible. Based upon the determination made as a result of the hearings, the supplying of the information will be dispensed with, further efforts at the obtaining of the information will be directed, or appropriate disciplinary measures will be taken under Rule 37(a), (b) or (d).[39]

This decision relied on the *Interhandel* litigation, *supra,* and this implied that if the defendants' efforts to produce documents were blocked by foreign law, no sanctions would be imposed for failure to comply with the order. Also, in consent decrees entered in the case, language akin to that of the *General Electric* (incandescent lamp) judgment was used to exempt from the scope of the decrees acts prohibited or required by foreign law.[40]

---

[38] *In re* Investigation of World Arrangements with Relation to the Prod., Transp., Ref. & Distrib. of Petroleum, 13 F.R.D. 280, 288 (D.D.C. 1952). The grand jury ultimately was discharged without returning an indictment, and a civil case was filed, note 39 *infra*; FUGATE, FOREIGN COMMERCE AND THE ANTITRUST LAWS 81 (1958).

[39] United States v. Standard Oil Co. (N.J.), 23 F.R.D. 1, 4-5 (S.D.N.Y. 1958).

[40] Paragraph V(C): "The injunctions provided for in subsection (A) of this Section, as qualified in subsection (B) of this Section, shall not apply in the following cases: (1) Where the combination of the kind referred to in subsection (A) of this

Similarly, in *Montship Lines, Ltd. v. Federal Maritime Board*,[41] the Court of Appeals affirmed an order of the Board requiring certain foreign corporations engaged in shipping between the United States and foreign countries to submit certain reports which were physically located abroad. Several Yugoslav and Dutch steamship lines had asserted that production of the documents would be in violation of their national laws.[42] The court held that, prior to determining whether foreign laws did in fact forbid production of the documents and, if so, what effect this should have upon compliance, the petitioners were to make a good faith attempt to obtain a waiver of the restrictions from their respective governments.

Several relevant Second Circuit decisions in non-antitrust cases may also be noted. *First National City Bank v. Internal Revenue Service*[43] involved a subpoena directing the production in New York of records of a Panamanian corporation which were physically located at the bank's Panamanian branch. The Court of Appeals refused to vacate the subpoena on the ground that the law of Panama which was alleged to prohibit removal of the documents had not been adequately proven. But the court emphasized that had the proof of law been adequate, the subpoena would have been vacated.

In another Second Circuit case, *Ings v. Ferguson*,[44] a New York

Section is participated in by Jersey pursuant to requirement of law of the foreign nation or nations within which the transactions which are the subject of such combination take place, or of any supra-national authority having jurisdiction over such transactions within such foreign nation or nations; * * *," United States v. Standard Oil Co. (N.J.) (S.D.N.Y. 1968), 1969 Trade Cas. ¶72,742; *id.* (Gulf Oil Corp.), 1969 Trade Cas. ¶72,743; *id.* (Texaco, Inc.), 1963 Trade Cas. ¶70,819 (para. VIII [D]). Similar exculpatory provisions were incorporated in United States v. United Fruit Co. (E.D. La. 1958), 1958 Trade Cas. ¶68,941 (para. XII); United States v. American Type Founders Co. (D.N.J. 1958), 1958 Trade Cas. ¶69,065 (para. VIII); United States v. American Smelting & Ref. Co. (S.D.N.Y. 1957), 1957 Trade Cas. ¶68,836 (para. VI).

[41] 295 F.2d 147 (D.C. Cir. 1961). *Cf. In re* Grand Jury Investigation of the Shipping Indus., 186 F.Supp. 298, 321 (D.D.C. 1960); for the protests of foreign governments to the subpoenas issued therein, see INT'L LAW ASS'N, REPORT OF THE FIFTY-FIRST CONFERENCE (TOKYO) 403-06 (1964).

[42] For the Dutch law, see note 11 *supra*. Evidently the Dutch government granted permission as to certain documents involved in this proceeding, BUSINESS REGULATION IN THE COMMON MARKET NATIONS, *supra* note 11, at 473.

[43] 271 F.2d 616 (2d Cir. 1959), *cert. denied*, 361 U.S. 948 (1960).

[44] 282 F.2d 149 (2d Cir. 1960).

district court, in a proceeding ancillary to a Chapter X reorganization in California, ordered the New York agencies of certain Canadian banks to produce records physically located in Canada. The subpoenas were modified by the Court of Appeals on the ground that there was a possibility that compliance would violate the laws of Quebec. The court directed the issuance of letters rogatory, stating that "[w]hether removal of records from Canada is prohibited is a question of Canadian law and is best resolved by Canadian courts."[45] The district court in this case had apparently issued the subpoenas under the impression that Canadian law did not prohibit the production of the documents, for it had already quashed in part subpoenas directing the New York agencies of certain foreign banks to produce documents located in Cuba, upon evidence that compliance would subject the bank's employees in Cuba to criminal penalties.[46]

Finally, in *Application of The Chase Manhattan Bank,*[47] the Court of Appeals approved the modification of a subpoena directing the bank to produce, in violation of Panamanian law, records in possession of its Panama branch. The modified subpoena merely required the bank to cooperate with the United States Government in obtaining the records by applying to Panamanian authorities. The court explained:

> The Government, as well as other litigants, has a real interest in civil and criminal cases in obtaining evidence wherever located. However, we also have an obligation to respect the laws of other sovereign states even though they may differ in economic and legal philosophy from our own. As we recently said in modifying subpoenas *duces tecum* in another case, "upon fundamental principles of international comity, our courts dedicated to the enforcement of our laws should not take such action as may cause a violation of the laws of a friendly neighbor or, at the least, an unnecessary circumvention of its procedures." *Ings v. Ferguson.*[48]

The question of what sanctions, if any, will be imposed upon a party who fails to produce documents on grounds of foreign law violation though ordered to do so is posed in the *Ludlow* litigation. In this case, the discovery issue was raised when certain foreign-flag steamship lines, members of a rate-making conference enjoying immunity from United States antitrust laws, refused to comply with a Federal Maritime Commission subpoena directing the production of documents from

[45]*Id.* at 152.
[46]*In re* Equitable Plan Co., 195 F.Supp. 57 (S.D.N.Y. 1960).
[47]297 F.2d 611 (2d Cir. 1962).
[48]*Id.* at 613.

abroad. The Federal District Court for the Southern District of New York ordered compliance with the subpoena.[49] Upon the continued refusal of the foreign-flag respondents to comply with its order, the Maritime Commission moved for an order adjudging the respondents in civil contempt.

The court found that the respondents were prohibited by foreign law from complying with the Commission order and that the respondents had applied to the relevant foreign authorities for permission to comply with the order, which permission was in each instance refused. On this basis, the court denied the motion to hold respondents in civil contempt, saying that it would not order anyone to violate the laws of another country.[50]

The *Ludlow* matter is not yet settled, for upon the respondents' continued refusal to comply with the subpoena, the Maritime Commission ordered the dissolution of the rate-making conference of which the respondents were members.[51] This order is presently on appeal to the federal courts.

B. Court Jurisdiction over Foreign Defendants in Antitrust Suits

Under American law, in order to acquire personal jurisdiction over a party, a court must meet two basic requirements, both of which may be affected by the defendant's residence or nationality: (1) the action must meet the test of proper venue, *i.e.*, the locality of the court must be the proper one in which to sue under governing statutes; and (2) the

[49] Ludlow Corp. v. deSmedt, 249 F.Supp. 496 (S.D.N.Y. 1966), *aff'd,* 366 F.2d 464 (2d Cir. 1966), *cert. denied,* 385 U.S. 974 (1966).

[50] Federal Maritime Comm'n. v. deSmedt, 268 F.Supp. 972 (S.D.N.Y. 1967). The judge stated: "I cannot, of course, direct and order anybody to violate the orders of his native land and I don't intend to do so, and I don't intend the United States Court to be so presumptuous as to attempt to intrude upon the sovereignty of any foreign nation, irrespective of the consent to transact business here that that foreign government has given to its nationals. If in the exercise of its own wisdom it feels that although authorizing the national to become a member of the Conference it can still deny this government access to documents within its own borders, that is for them to determine and not for this Court. It is a matter to be negotiated through diplomatic channels and not through the judicial process of this Court." *Id.* at 974-75.

[51] J. of Commerce, Sept. 15, 1967, at 1, col. 2.

defendant must be amenable to service of the process of the court and must be properly served.[52]

1. VENUE

Section 12 of the Clayton Act, enacted in 1914, provides that an antitrust suit (by the government or a private party) against a corporation may be brought "not only in the judicial district whereof it is an inhabitant, but also in any district wherein it may be found or transacts business."[53] Also, Section 4, which applies only to damage suits by private plaintiffs or by the United States, provides for venue "in the district in which the defendant resides or is found or has an agent." These provisions must be read in light of a general federal venue provision, Section 1391(d) of the Judicial Code enacted in 1948, providing that an "alien may be sued in any district."[54] This did not explicitly modify the Clayton Act, but it was held by a district court in the *Hoffman Motors* case to apply to an individual alien defendant in an antitrust case, thus putting aside the narrower provisions of Section 4 of the Clayton Act.[55] Apparently, however, no court has as yet based venue on this provision in an antitrust action against an alien *corporate* defendant. In the *Hoffman Motors* case, venue as to the latter type of defendant was based on Section 12, with a finding that the corporation transacted business in the district. No compelling reason is evident for not holding that Section 12, equally with Section 4, is superseded by Section 1391(d).[56] If it is superseded, there is really no venue requirement as to antitrust suits against aliens. As will be pointed out presently, however, the requirements for service of process still impose significant limitations upon the place of the action.

[52] See ABA ANTITRUST SECTION SUPP., *supra* note 1, at 40-45.

[53] 15 U.S.C. §22 (1964). This section apparently applies in criminal as well as civil cases. See FUGATE, FOREIGN COMMERCE AND THE ANTITRUST LAWS §3.4, at 62 (1958).

[54] 28 U.S.C. §1391(d) (1964). See 1 MOORE, FEDERAL PRACTICE ¶0.142[6] at 1508 (2d ed. 1964).

[55] Hoffman Motors Corp. v. Alfa Romeo S.p.A., 244 F.Supp. 70, 83-84 (S.D.N.Y. 1965).

[56] *Cf.* 1 MOORE, *supra* note 54; Pure Oil Co. v. Suarez, 384 U.S. 202 (1966), holding that a special venue provision of a statute similar to §12 is supplemented by §1391(c) of the Judicial Code; Olin Mathieson Chem. Corp. v. Molins Organizations, Ltd., 261 F.Supp. 436, 440-41 (E.D.Va. 1966) (patent infringement suit, citing *Suarez*).

If Section 12 still governs suits against corporations, the *Scophony* case establishes a fairly liberal approach to meeting its requirements.[57] Venue was properly laid as to the parent British Scophony corporation in the Southern District of New York on findings that it "transacted business" there because it actively supervised and intervened in the affairs of American Scophony, a partly-owned subsidiary, and also because it had individual agents who carried out substantial and continuing business activities for it there. The Supreme Court reached this conclusion on the particular facts, and did not hold that foreign corporations are automatically "found" or transacting business wherever an American subsidiary happens to be. Since the facts were not very different from those which would be present in many parent-subsidiary situations, however, the case probably makes it relatively easy to establish venue as to an alien parent with an American subsidiary.

2. SERVICE OF PROCESS

The fact that venue lies in a given district does not automatically make the defendant amenable to service of process in, or from, that district. Aliens are entitled to the constitutional protections of due process of law.[58] Process therefore may not be served on an alien from "any district," in the language of the above statutes, unless the district is one that satisfies constitutional limitations on the acquisition of personal jurisdiction.[59] For constitutional purposes, the defendant must have had sufficient contact with the district to satisfy fundamental tests of fairness in suing him there, although it should be noted also that these tests have become quite liberal.[60]

[57] United States v. Scophony Corp. of America, 333 U.S. 795 (1948); see ABA ANTITRUST SECTION SUPP., *supra* note 1, at 40-42. Amplifying an earlier decision, Eastman Kodak Co. v. Southern Photo Materials Co., 273 U.S. 359 (1927), which itself had taken a liberal approach to Section 12, the Court in *Scophony* said: "[F]or venue purposes, the [*Eastman*] Court sloughed off the highly technical distinctions theretofore glossed upon 'found' for filling that term with particularized meaning, or emptying it, under the translation of 'carrying on business.' In their stead it substituted the practical and broader business conception of engaging in any substantial business operations." *Id.* at 807; 1 MOORE, *supra* note 54, ¶0.144[15] at 1667.

[58] See Japan Gas Lighter Ass'n. v. Ronson Corp., 357 F.Supp. 219, 225 (D.N.J. 1966).

[59] See *id.* at 232-36, for an unusually clear discussion and application of this point.

[60] See McGee v. International Life Ins. Co., 355 U.S. 220 (1957) (suit in California after service of process by mail on Texas corporation met due process

Statutory requirements also must be met. Section 12 of the Clayton Act provides that process in antitrust cases may be served in the district of which the corporation "is an inhabitant, or wherever it may be found." Under this provision, British Scophony was held amenable to the process of the Southern District of New York by virtue of its being "found" in that district, because of its course of conduct there through the American subsidiary and through two individual agents who were active in New York.[61]

In the *Swiss Watch* case, the court held five Swiss corporations subject to process in the Southern District, applying a test of whether there was proof of "continuous local activities" and whether the forum was not "unfairly inconvenient" for them.[62] The court agreed with defendants that where "formal separation" of parent and subsidiary is "scrupulously maintained," it is not enough even that the parent completely dominates a subsidiary's commercial and financial affairs. But, it added, "where the substance of corporate independence is not preserved and the subsidiary acts as an agent of the parent, this corporate separation has been found without significance."[63] Two of the Swiss corporations were held answerable to process because of a jointly-owned subsidiary, which was found to have "no independent business of its own," and to be a "mere adjunct of its parents."[64] Two others, which were subsidiaries of American firms, were reached on the theory that the American parents were acting as agents of their Swiss subsidiaries for purposes of carrying out the Collective Convention which precipitated the suit.[65] Another Swiss corporation was held properly served through an exclusive American distributor, because, on the facts, the latter was so completely dominated as to be a mere agent.[66]

---

requirements where defendant's only contact· with California was an insurance contract made and administered by mail with California insured); International Shoe Co. v. Washington, 326 U.S. 310 (1945); Hanson v. Denckla, 357 U.S. 235 (1958).

[61] 33 U.S. at 818.

[62] United States v. The Watchmakers of Switzerland Information Center, Inc., 133 F.Supp. 40 (S.D.N.Y. 1955).

[63] *Id.* at 45.

[64] *Id.*

[65] *Id.* at 47; also see opinion denying reargument, 134 F.Supp. 710, 712 (S.D.N.Y. 1955).

[66] 133 F.Supp. at 49; for other cases, see ABA ANTITRUST SECTION SUPP., *supra* note 1, at 43-44.

Apart from Section 12, it seems clear that aliens may be served with process under the authority of Rule 4(e) of the Federal Rules of Civil Procedure,[67] as was done in the *Hoffman Motors* case.[68] This rule permits the federal court to follow a state statute or court rule governing service of process in the state in which the federal court sits. Many of the state statutes have "long-arm" provisions,[69] permitting service to be made outside of the state through various means, and Rule 4(i) supplements these methods. Where the alien does not have an agent in the United States or some other instrumentality capable of being construed as an agent, any service attempted will usually have to rely upon this rule. Whether such service is valid will depend upon whether the contacts with the jurisdiction satisfy state law and constitutional requirements.

II. EUROPEAN COMMUNITY LAW

The powers of the Commission under the Rome Treaty with respect to enforcement jurisdiction over activities outside the territory of the Common Market are unsettled.[70] The first case in which such issues were contested, the *Dyestuffs* cartel case (mentioned in Chapter 2), was decided by the Commission in 1969, and at this writing is on appeal to

[67] See 2 MOORE, *supra* note 54, ¶4.32 at 1225.

[68] Hoffman Motors Corp. v. Alfa Romeo S.p.A., 244 F.Supp. 70 (S.D.N.Y. 1965) (service in Italy upon an Italian manufacturer, which had used plaintiff as a franchised dealer in the United States, was upheld under both Rule 4 and Section 12 of the Clayton Act, where accomplished by registered letter to Italy and also by a court-designated Italian attorney); see ABA ANTITRUST SECTION SUPP., *supra* note 1, at 45.

[69] See 2 MOORE, *supra* note 54, §4.41-1[3] at 1291.50.

[70] For discussion prior to the *Dyestuffs* case, see Ellis, *The Extra-Territorial Effect of the Community Anti-Trust Legislation Outside the Member States*, in SEMAINE DE BRUGES, DROIT COMMUNAUTAIRE ET DROIT NATIONAL 362, 374 (1965); Kruithof, *The Application of the Common Market Anti-Trust Provisions to International Restraints of Trade*, 2 C.M.L. REV. 69 (1964); McCoy, *The United States Parent Corporation-European Subsidiary Relationship Under the European Antitrust Regulations*, 3 VA. J. INT'L L. 46 (1963); Nebolsine, *Foreign Enterprises under the European Antitrust Rules*, 38 N.Y.U. L. REV. 479 (1963).

No attempt has been made in this chapter to include separate discussion of enforcement jurisdiction and procedure under the ECSC Treaty; see Kruithof, *supra*, at 83-91.

the Court of Justice.[71] The case dealt with an international cartel whose members were found to include a British firm (I.C.I.), three Swiss firms (Ciba, Geigy and Sandoz) and six Common Market firms.[72] The Commission found that the cartel members had engaged in "concerted practices" leading to fixing of prices on sales in the Common Market in violation of Article 85(1).[73]

Apparently the foreign firms manufactured their products in plants outside the Common Market, and shipped to wholly-owned sales subsidiaries in the Common Market.[74] The foreign parents issued instructions from time to time to the subsidiaries, ordering price increases in accordance with the cartel understandings.[75] In what appears to have been a studied attempt to clarify its jurisdiction over foreign-based firms with Common Market subsidiaries, the Commission held the foreign parents in violation and at the same time stated that it would not find the subsidiaries in violation.[76] The latter were absolved

[71] Dyestuffs Producers, July 24, 1969, CCH COMM. MKT. REP. ¶9314, 8 Comm. Mkt. L. R. Supp. D23.

[72] CCH COMM. MKT. REP. ¶9314, at 8689.

[73] *Id.*

[74] *Id.* at 8691 and 8694.

[75] *Id.* at 8690-91.

[76] In holding the foreign parent firms in violation, the Commission relied on the "effects" doctrine, stating: "This decision is binding on all the enterprises that took part in the concerted practices, irrespective of whether or not they are domiciled within or outside of the Common Market. . . . The rules of competition of the Treaty are . . . applicable to all restrictions of competition that produce within the Common Market effects to which Article 85, paragraph 1, applies. There is therefore no need to examine whether the enterprises that originated such restraints of competition have their head office within or outside of the Community." *Id.* at 8693. As indicated in Chapter 2, this statement does not completely reach the fundamental question of whether Article 85(1) extends to a firm which not only does not have its head office or seat in the Common Market, but also which engages in no conduct, as distinguished from causing effects from outside, in the Common Market in pursuance of the violation. Its conclusion that the Common Market subsidiaries acted under binding orders from their foreign parents would support a conclusion legally that the parents were themselves acting inside the Common Market.

The decision prompted the British Government to file an informal note with the EEC, attacking the decision against I.C.I. as exceeding the "limits fixed by the recognized principles of international law;" N.Y. Times, Nov. 28, 1969, 63. The note stated that the distinction between a parent and its subsidiary must be observed, that the antitrust laws can be applied only to companies that do business in the

on the ground that the price instructions from the parents were "binding" on the subsidiaries, and further that even if they were not, it would have been impossible for the latter not to raise prices in view of the large increases in factory prices imposed upon them by their parent producers.[77]

A. Commission Personal Jurisdiction over Foreign Firms

In the *Dyestuffs* case, the Commission claimed not only substantive jurisdiction over the actions of the foreign parent firms, but also authority to impose penalties upon them, levying fines upon each.[78] It did not seek to serve the required notice of these penalties directly outside the territory of the Common Market, but instead attempted service on the parents through service on the subsidiaries.[79] This was done, it said, on the rationale that the latter were "wholly controlled" by the parents, and were therefore considered to be part of the "sphere of influence" of the parents, making such service appropriate under the *A.L.M.A.* decision of the Court of Justice.[80]

This decision constitutes assertion of personal jurisdiction over alien firms on grounds which appear to be as broad as, if not broader than, those relied upon under American law. It has been pointed out above that under American antitrust decisions, the fact that there is a wholly-owned and controlled domestic subsidiary of the foreign parent in the jurisdiction does not *ipso facto* give jurisdiction over the foreign parent; additional facts are sought showing that corporate separateness is disregarded by the parties, or at least that an agency relationship exists. In the *Dyestuffs* case, the Commission did not expressly find that corporate separateness was ignored, nor that an agency relationship existed. On the other hand, its statement that the parents' price instructions were "binding" on the subsidiaries might support one or both of these theories.

jurisdiction, and that action against a conspiracy must be based upon findings that the conspiracy was planned or carried out within the jurisdiction; CCH COMM. MKT. REP. No. 123, Dec. 9, 1969.

[77] CCH COMM. MKT. REP. ¶9314, at 8691.

[78] *Id.* at 8693-94.

[79] *Id.* at 8694.

[80] A.L.M.A. v. High Authority, 3 Recueil de la Jurisprudence de la Cour 179 (1957).

The decision states that the "enterprises concerned" were "heard."[81] But it does not indicate how compliance was made by the Commission with Article 2(1) of Commission Regulation 99/63, requiring that written notice of the complaint and hearing be given, to be addressed to "each enterprise or association of enterprises or to a common authorized representative designated by them."[82]

It remains to be seen how far the Commission's enforcement jurisdiction will be extended, and whether it will prove to be less than, or co-extensive with, its substantive jurisdiction.[83]

B. Extraterritorial Discovery and Other Orders

Great doubt exists as to whether the Commission would have the power to compel conduct abroad, as distinguished from asserting personal jurisdiction over foreign-based firms to regulate their conduct within the Common Market.[84] The order issued to I.C.I. in the *Dyestuffs*

[81] CCH COMM. MKT. REP. ¶9314, at 8689; according to a statement issued by I.C.I., that company had provided the Commission with information and other assistance in the course of the investigations, but had contended from the outset that the Commission had no jurisdiction over it; Financial Times, Aug. 2, 1969.

[82] CCH COMM. MKT. REP. ¶2635, at 1742.

[83] One writer has predicted that the Commission and Court will conclude that personal jurisdiction extends as far as jurisdiction over the subject matter, Kruithof, *supra* note 70, at 92.

[84] See, *e.g.*, Kruithof, *supra* note 70, at 88 *et seq.*; Ellis, *supra* note 70; Thiesing and van Ackere, Remarks on the Problems of the Extra-Territorial Effect of "Anti-Trust" Law Concerning the European Community, before the Ass'n of the Bar of the City of N.Y., May 8, 1969: "The Commission is entitled to deliver orders for discovery of documents, to require enterprises to furnish data on their structure, to impose fines on them, etc. If the Commission finds it necessary to take one of these measures in respect to an action abroad having a causal relation with an ensuing illegal situation within the Community territory, it might lead to questions about its *jurisdiction to compel conduct abroad*. In any case the Member States of the E.E.C. cannot have delegated to the Community Authorities more powers than they held themselves under international law. Since the dominant principles of the latter (except the trends of the U.S. Government and Courts. . . .) limit the State's jurisdiction to its territory, the efficacy of the measures eventually taken by the Community Authorities would be impaired by their inability to regulate conduct abroad" (ms. for oral remarks, 9; transcript of oral remarks appears in Spring, 1970 issue of the RECORD).

Cf. DERINGER, THE COMPETITION LAW OF THE EUROPEAN ECONOMIC COMMUNITY ¶2207 (1968), stating that the Commission may address "requests for

case to pay a fine was, in a sense, an order to do something abroad; *i.e.,* the payment—if made—normally would have to be accomplished by I.C.I. headquarters in England. There may be a difference between this relatively simple act, however, and a requirement that I.C.I. or another foreign firm deliver documents from abroad, or obey orders seeking to govern aspects of its business conduct abroad. If the Commission has such power, then it is capable of creating as much conflict as has arisen from American court orders of this type, including the decree in the *I.C.I.-du Pont* case.

The *Dyestuffs* decision reveals very little about the Commission's view of its powers to engage in discovery of information located outside the Common Market. It states simply that the "Commission undertook a series of investigations in the six Member States."[85] While this may imply that no investigation outside the Common Market was attempted, it does not necessarily show this. American antitrust investigations which seek evidence located abroad customarily proceed by calling upon an enterprise over which personal jurisdiction is obtained in the United States to produce the information from abroad. This too could be called an investigation "in the United States," in contra-distinction to an attempt to serve a discovery order upon someone abroad.

The following is a description of the Commission's general powers of investigation which, it will be seen, are quite extensive. Thereafter, inferences as to extraterritorial power which might be drawn from this discussion are mentioned.

1. COMMISSION INVESTIGATIVE POWERS, IN GENERAL

Articles 11 through 14 of Regulation 17 set forth the manner in which discovery may be carried out in the enforcement of the Rome Treaty antitrust provisions.[86]

a. Requests for Information

Under Article 11, paragraphs 1-4, the Commission may request information from enterprises and also from the Member States. A copy of a request to an enterprise must be sent "to the competent authority in

information" to firms outside the Common Market and attach assets inside the Common Market by way of penalizing such firms.

[85] CCH COMM. MKT. REP. ¶9314, at 8689.

[86] *Id.* at ¶¶2501, 2511, 2521, 2531; for discussion, see DERINGER, *supra* note 84, at ¶2201-62.

the Member State in the territory of which the principal place of business of the enterprise or the association of enterprises is situated." The request must state its legal basis and purposes, and must recite that sanctions may be imposed if the information supplied is not accurate.

In practice, such requests are frequently made to obtain information about agreements which have been notified to the Commission, and these requests evidently have usually been complied with. Nonetheless, one may legitimately refuse to comply with the request or may comply with it only partially until the Commission, acting under paragraph 5 of Article 11, issues a formal decision requesting the information. This decision must specify what information is desired, fix an appropriate deadline, state the penalties which are applicable in the event of non-compliance, and indicate the right of appeal from the decision to the Court of Justice of the European Communities. Unless it is overruled by the Court of Justice, such a decision is binding on the enterprises in question. Moreover, an appeal to the Court does not suspend the Commission's decision unless the Court specifically orders it suspended.

b. *Investigations by the Commission*

Article 12 of Regulation 17 gives the Commission authority to investigate an entire economic sector whenever "the trend of trade between Member States, price movements, inflexibility of prices or other circumstances" indicate a restraint or distortion of competition within a sector of the economy of the Common Market. Such an investigation must be based on a prior "decision" of the Commission and may not come into effect until after it has been submitted for comment to the Consultative Committee on Cartels and Monopolies, provided for in Article 10 of the regulation. Acting under Article 12, the Commission may require the submission of information and agreements and, in the case of enterprises "whose size suggests that they occupy a dominant position within the Common Market or within a substantial part thereof," may require them to supply information relating to their structure and activities. The Member State or States in which the investigation is to be conducted must be notified.

The Commission's principal investigatory powers are set forth in Article 14, which authorizes the Commission to conduct "all necessary investigations into the affairs of enterprises and associations of enterprises" and particularly empowers the Commission, in conducting such investigations, to examine and copy books and other business documents, to ask for on-the-spot verbal explanations, and to have access to the premises, land and vehicles of the enterprises being investigated. The Commission may carry out such an investigation through its own agents, who must have a written warrant stating the subject and purpose of the investigation and setting forth the penalties which may be inflicted in the event that incomplete books or documents are submitted. The authorities of Member States where the investigation is to be conducted are to be advised, or consulted as required in paragraphs 2 and 4 of Article 14.

In practice, the Commission frequently conducts informal investigations without first making a formal decision to investigate, and also in practice the parties being investigated usually cooperate. To be compulsory, however, an Article 14 investigation must be based on a decision by the Commission stating the subject and purpose of the investigation, the date when it is to begin, the penalties which may be inflicted for non-compliance, and the right to appeal the Commission's decision to the European Court of Justice. Again, an appeal does not stay the investigation unless the Court orders a stay. Each Member State has the right to appoint agents to assist the Commission's agents in conducting an investigation in its territory. Under paragraph 6, if "an enterprise resists an investigation, the Member State concerned shall lend the servants authorized by the Commission the assistance necessary to enable them to carry out their investigation." Hence, if compulsion is required to obtain compliance under Article 14, it is the Member State which is to exercise such compulsion.[87]

c. Member State Investigations and Cooperation

Under Article 13, agents of the Member States, at the request of the Commission, are to carry out investigations which the Commission considers appropriate or has formally decided upon; the criteria of Article 14 govern such investigations.

---

[87]Some of the Member States have adopted special legislation to carry out Section 6 of Article 14: Belgian Royal Decree of Jan. 18, 1966, *Moniteur Belge,* Jan. 22, 1966; German Law of Aug. 17, 1967; *Bundesgesetzblatt,* Aug. 23, 1967; Italian Decree of Sept. 22, 1963, Italian *Gazzetta Ufficiale,* Jan. 11, 1964; Luxembourg Regulations of May 26, 1965, Luxembourg *Journal Officiel,* June 15, 1965. A draft law is still pending in the Netherlands respecting discovery under Section 6 of Article 14. In France, such discovery has been assimilated to provisions in *Ordonnance* No. 45/1484 of June 30, 1945, as amended by *Ordonnance* No. 67-835 of Sept. 28, 1967 (French *Journal Officiel,* Sept. 29, 1967).

Although the Commission in practice has preferred to conduct its own investigations under Article 14, rather than to request Member State investigations under Article 13, the Commission is generally able to count on the cooperation of the national authorities (some of which, reportedly, have on occasion encouraged the Commission to act under Article 14). Their cooperation would be essential if documents were to be seized or if coercion were to be employed; as to documents, Article 14 gives the Commission the power only to review, copy or take extracts; and (as noted above) the power to exercise compulsion under Article 14 is reserved to the Member States.

d. Scope of Discovery

The Commission thus has a broad range of powers available to it in obtaining evidence and making investigations respecting a suspected antitrust infraction. No decided cases have as yet placed limits on these powers.

Under Regulation 17, necessity is evidently the criterion which governs the scope of both a request for information and of an investigation by the Commission. Paragraph 1 of Article 11 states that information requested under that article must be "necessary;" Article 14 authorizes the Commission to conduct "all necessary investigations." According to Jacques Vandamme, a Commission investigations official, "it is generally accepted that the information requested must be more than merely useful for the investigating staff."[88]

In the *Brescia* decision, relating to the investigatory powers of the High Authority of the European Coal and Steel Community, the Court

[88] *Rechtskundig Weekblad* 1630 (April 25, 1965).

Professor W. L. Haardt has observed: "It would have been useful to state in this respect that such authority only exists insofar as it is necessary for the execution of the Commission's cartel policy. This can be inferred from the beginning of the article, but it would have been better to state this more explicitly, since the enterprises should have some safeguards against the useless examination of their books and documents. Nonetheless, a reasonable construction of the first words in the article supports the conclusion that enterprises may raise objections against such a useless taking of information." *Europees Kartelrecht,* Europese Monografieen No. 2, at 139 (1965).

Professor Haardt also points out that an appeal to the Court of Justice "can take several months" and that, meanwhile, "the enterprise will have to admit the officials to its premises and give the required information—which, of course, makes the appeal practically academic."

of Justice indicated that the necessity of the information required by the High Authority must be clearly apparent from the decision of the High Authority demanding the information:[89]

> In this connection, the only consideration which can serve as a criterion is the end sought, and not a statement deduced from the anticipated results, which, unilaterally framed without a known basis, may change as the result of the investigations conducted.

In the light of this decision, Mr. Vandamme concluded that an investigation should be considered as "necessary" if the Commission is in the possession of facts establishing a "presumption" of a violation of Article 85 or 86 of the Rome Treaty. He added:

> A preventative investigation therefore seems impossible in this connection. The existence and the importance of a "presumption" are questions of fact.[90]

When Regulation 17 was in draft form, it was the subject of a report by a committee of the European Parliament, commonly known as the "Deringer Report."[91] Sections 120-22 of this Report made specific recommendations concerning what are now Articles 11 and 14 of Regulation 17. In view of statements in the Report, the final texts of Articles 11 and 14 were modified to require that a formal request for information and a request relating to an investigation must indicate not only the subject matter, but also the legal basis and the purpose of the request.

On the other hand, the Deringer Report made recommendations which were not followed. On the basis of general principles of national law safeguarding persons under investigation, the Report suggested that any person required to supply information should have the right to refuse to testify if professional secrets were involved, and that searches should be subject to the prior authorization of a judge or court. These safeguards, however, do not appear in Articles 11 and 14.

---

[89]*Acciaieria e Tubificio di Brescia v. High Authority,* 6 Recueil de la Jurisprudence de la Cour 151 (1960). (The High Authority has since been merged into a single Commission for the European Communities.)

[90]*Supra* note 88.

[91] Rapport fait au nom de la Commission du Marché Intérieur ayant pour objet la consultation demandée à l'Assemblée Parlementaire Européenne par le Conseil de la Communauté Economique Européenne sur un premier règlement d'application des Articles 85 et 86 du Traité de la C.E.E. (Document 104/1960-61).

The Deringer Report also commented on the provision which was incorporated in Article 14 relating to the "necessary assistance" which national authorities are to provide the Commission, suggesting that the national authorities should assist the Commission only within the framework of national procedural law. Apparently, a representative of the EEC Commission stated to the Parliamentary Committee which prepared the Deringer Report that such an express statement was not necessary, as Article 14 as then drafted should be interpreted in that way. Referring to this statement, the Deringer Report indicated that Articles 11 and 14 can be carried out by national authorities only in conformity with the constitutional rules of the Member States. No reported cases suggest that a conflict has arisen to date between Articles 11 and 14, on the one hand, and national law on the other.

2. EXTRATERRITORIAL DISCOVERY

As the foregoing discussion shows, broad discovery powers under the antitrust provisions of the Rome Treaty are lodged in the Commission by Regulation 17. The Regulation does not state in so many words that these powers may be exercised only as to information located within the territory of the Common Market. May an inference of such a limitation be drawn from the various requirements that the authorities of the Member States be notified or consulted as to investigations to be conducted "in their territory?"

Article 11, dealing with "requests for information," carries a fairly strong implication of territorial limitation by stating that a copy of the request must be sent to the competent authority in "the Member State in the territory of which the principal place of business of the enterprise or the association of enterprises is situated." The implication here is that, to be subject to such a request, a firm must have its "principal place of business" in a Member State, thus ruling out requests to foreign-based firms.[92] If such an implication is warranted, however, it is important to note that the language, "principal place of business," does not appear in Articles 12, 13 or 14, thus supporting the opposite inference as to "investigations," *i.e.,* that they may be made into the affairs of firms whose "principal place of business" is outside the Common Market. This, of course, is a necessary power, for without it the Commission could not

[92] But see DERINGER, *supra* note 84, at ¶2207.

investigate a branch office of a foreign firm located inside the Common Market.

If documents are located within the Common Market, access may be had to them; they may be copied; and oral explanations of them may be required. Suppose, however, that a Common Market-based firm has an office or subsidiary located outside the Common Market, which possesses a document, a copy of which is desired by the Commission. Or suppose the document is outside the Common Market in the possession of a foreign-based firm with a branch or subsidiary in the Common Market. Although the Commission has no power (or right) to send its representatives to conduct an investigation abroad, may it, by virtue of personal jurisdiction over the enterprise, coupled with its Article 14 investigative powers, order a copy of such a document to be produced inside the Common Market? This key question of compelling conduct outside the Common Market in order to force movement of documents from a foreign state into the Common Market does not appear to be capable of resolution by resort to the language of Regulation 17. Ultimately, it appears that the question will have to be settled by court decision, if the Commission is disposed to make a test case.[93]

III. NATIONAL ANTITRUST LAWS IN THE EUROPEAN COMMUNITY

The first three volumes of this series describe enforcement powers and procedures of the antitrust laws of the Member States.[94] Very little can be said at this point on the extraterritorial scope of these powers, and the following brief discussion depends mainly upon references to those volumes with small supplementation from other sources.

A. Belgium

The authorities have extensive investigatory powers, including the taking of testimony, demanding production of documents, searching of

[93] See the views of writers cited in note 70, *supra*. The possibility has been discussed that the Commission might, under Regulation 17, Article 13, ask a Member State to seek to obtain information outside the Common Market through the use of commissions or letters rogatory to foreign courts; see McCoy, *supra* note 70, at 65. This is beyond the scope of the present study.

[94] See Chapter 2, note 131, *supra*, for description of these volumes.

premises and seizing of property.[95] It appears possible that production of documents located outside Belgium might be ordered, but apparently this has not been attempted, and its practicality has been questioned for some situations.[96]

Although private suits may not be filed under the Law of May 27, 1960, under some circumstances the same conduct prohibited by that law may supply the basis for an action for unfair competition, or for tort or contract remedies.[97] In such proceedings, the new Judicial Code may make it possible to compel production of documents or other evidence from abroad.[98]

B. France

Very little application of any kind has been made of the French antitrust laws to foreign firms,[99] although, of course, at least *activities* carried on within France may be attacked. It appears to be unlikely that French jurisdiction would be asserted extraterritorially in any substantial way.

Investigative procedures are generally very broad, insofar as evidence located in France is concerned.[100] But again, there apparently has been little or no effort to use these powers to compel production of evidence located abroad.

C. Germany

For the most part, German enforcement powers, extraterritorially speaking, stand in sharp contrast to the extremely cautious approach of the other Member States. Court and administrative jurisdiction in public proceedings to proceed against foreign parties "is deemed to be

[95] BUSINESS REGULATION IN THE COMMON MARKET NATIONS (Blake ed. 1969), vol. 1 (Ginsburg ed.), pt. 1, BELGIUM (by de Keyser & Suetens) 71.

[96] del Marmol & Fontaine, *Protection Against the Abuse of Economic Power in Belgium: The Law of May 27, 1960*, 109 U.PA. L. REV. 922, 931 (1961).

[97] BUSINESS REGULATION IN THE COMMON MARKET NATIONS, vol. 1, *supra* note 95, at 157.

[98] Judicial Code, Oct. 10, 1967, arts. 877-82.

[99] BUSINESS REGULATION IN THE COMMON MARKET NATIONS (Blake ed. 1969), vol. 2 (B. Blake and Perillo eds.), pt. 1, FRANCE (by Bergsten) 308.

[100] *Id.* at 117-26.

coterminous with the reach of the substantive domestic law."[101] Since German antitrust law expressly applies to activities outside Germany having effects within Germany,[102] a very broad theoretical jurisdiction is thus asserted, backed by rules on how personal jurisdiction is acquired which are more sweeping than American rules.[103]

Insofar as investigations are concerned, formal procedures, including imposition of fines, are limited to German territory.[104] No attempt seems to have been made as yet to use investigative powers within Germany to compel production of documents located outside Germany;[105] but evidently such action, paralleling American practice, is not out of the question.

D. The Netherlands

As pointed out in Chapter 2, Dutch law is not expressly confined in its substantive territorial scope.[106] It is not clear how far it may reach substantively in some situations, nor how extensively enforcement measures could be applied.[107]

One observation may be made with reasonable certainty, however. In view of Section 39, prohibiting compliance with antitrust laws of other nations,[108] it would be rather anomalous if Dutch law were to be enforced extraterritorially. Specifically, it seems quite unlikely that Dutch authorities would seek to compel production of evidence located in another country, or to require other kinds of conduct outside Dutch territory.

[101] BUSINESS REGULATION IN THE COMMON MARKET NATIONS (Blake ed. 1969), vol. 3 (K. Ebb ed.), WEST GERMANY (by Juenger, Markert, Pfeifer & Steckhan) 363.

[102] *Id.* at 354.

[103] *Id.* at 363.

[104] *Id.*

[105] *Id.* at 367, n.71.

[106] Chapter 2, *supra,* at 113.

[107] BUSINESS REGULATION IN THE COMMON MARKET NATIONS (Blake ed. 1969), vol. 1 (Ginsburg ed.), pt. 2, THE NETHERLANDS (by Silbiger) 469.

[108] *Id.* at 472, 511; see also this chapter, *supra* note 11.

CHAPTER **4** *The Nature and Extent of Conflict*
Between American Antitrust Law
and Laws in the Common Market

Chapters 2 and 3 describe the extent to which American antitrust law reaches beyond the borders of the United States, and also indicate the extent to which Common Market antitrust laws appear to have extra-territorial scope. The purpose of the present chapter is to outline how these laws overlap in their application to different types of activities having antitrust significance, and to identify the chief conflict situations which may arise. An analysis of so broad a subject necessarily requires the use of definitions and assumptions, and these are stated immediately below. The reader is invited to omit this discussion if he finds it too abstract, and to begin at Section I on Horizontal Arrangements.

Definitions and Assumptions

1. *Overlap relevant to this study exists not only when two systems of antitrust law coincide, but also when the antitrust law of one sovereignty overlaps general non-antitrust laws of another.* The source of conflict is frequently found in the overlapping of antitrust law and contract law. This was an important feature of the controversy in the *I.C.I.* case, for example, and it was the chief source of conflict between American antitrust law and European law prior to the post-World War II emergence of European antitrust systems. It is still the basic situation as to Italy and Luxembourg, which have no general antitrust laws.

2. *While most cases of overlap result in subjecting a given* firm *to two or more sets of laws simultaneously, relevant overlap is defined here more broadly to encompass situations in which a given* transaction *feels*

148

the impact of two legal systems, even though the individual firms involved are obliged to obey only one of the two systems. This definition is primarily designed to cover problems arising in "third country markets" (outside both the United States and the Common Market), where an American firm may be subject to American law and not to European law, while at the same time a Common Market firm may be subject to European law and not to American law. If the two firms enter into an agreement with each other applicable to the third country market, or even merely compete there, their relationship may be significantly affected if there is conflict between the American and Common Market legal rules.

3. *Private conflict of laws principles are generally not applicable here so as to permit a choice of law to be made.* Antitrust law is public law, and it does not yield to the public or private laws of other nations, nor will the laws of other nations yield to it. In the situations with which this chapter is concerned, both laws are assumed to persist in applying, within the practical limits of their ability to do so.

4. *This study is not concerned with situations in which difficulties exist simply because a given firm must obey different laws in different markets.* Such differences undoubtedly often make business operations more costly, but they are not true conflict situations, and presumably they may be dealt with satisfactorily by carefully following correct legal advice. Our concern is with the situations in which two sets of laws apply simultaneously to the same firm or transaction.

5. *Conflict relevant to this study exists if it appears that a well-informed lawyer would conclude that there is a substantial risk of significant inconsistency in the application of the overlapping laws to his client's activities.* In determining abstractly whether laws conflict in various kinds of transactions, questions arise as to both the scope and the impact of laws in hypothetical situations. If one were to insist upon legal certainty as to the answers to these questions, the focus of the study would be too conservative; conflict would rarely be a sure thing. On the other hand, an assumption that conflict will exist merely because of theoretical possibilities for inconsistent legal interpretation or development would overstate the problem. A "lawyer's judgment" test is therefore used in determining whether conflict exists in a given situation.

6. *Conflict may be classified in three broad categories: immaterial, prohibitive* and *disadvantageous.* In some cases, while substantial differences in law may exist, the conflict may be of interest only to

lawyers and not to their clients. One law may be more stringent than the other, but the practical situation may be such that the firm would not alter its conduct even if the stricter law were not present. For example, price fixing is per se illegal in American law, whereas there is a possibility of obtaining an exemption for a price-fixing arrangement under Article 85(3) of the Rome Treaty. But the firm may not wish to engage in price fixing. Or even if it would like to engage in price fixing, the possibility of obtaining an exemption may be so unlikely under a given set of facts that the theoretical difference in the laws will have no real bearing on the firm's actions. Such conflict is treated as *"immaterial."*

At the other extreme, conflict may be so great as to make a given business function or transaction impossible, and it is therefore *"prohibitive."* Such conflict would exist in its most severe form where the law of one jurisdiction requires something important which the other jurisdiction prohibits, as would have been the case with the conflicting orders of the American and English courts in the *I.C.I.* case had one of the courts (the American) not retreated.[1] Conflict with equally serious practical consequences may exist if the law of one jurisdiction prohibits the firm from doing something which is a matter of real business necessity, and which the other jurisdiction permits. This might occur, for example, if a firm found it impossible to get access to supplies or distribution in a given foreign market without joining a cartel which was lawful under the foreign law, but unlawful under the firm's own law.

The third type of conflict is that which imposes a significant business disadvantage upon the firm without having prohibitive consequences. An example of such *"disadvantageous"* conflict would be where an American firm, because of American law, refrains from using a given distribution method in a foreign market which would result in lower costs, and which is lawfully used by its foreign competitors.

Judgments about how serious such conflicts are and as to what should be done about them would ultimately depend upon a determination of

---

[1] United States v. Imperial Chem. Indus., Ltd., 100 F.Supp. 504 (S.D.N.Y. 1951) (American decision ordering, among other things, that I.C.I. assign British nylon patents to du Pont, and grant immunity in imports); British Nylon Spinners, Ltd. v. Imperial Chem. Indus., Ltd. [1953] Ch. 19, [1952] 2 All E.R. 780 (C.A.) (affirming injunction by lower court against compliance with American decree); British Nylon Spinners, Ltd. v. Imperial Chem. Indus., Ltd., [1955] Ch. 37, [1954] 3 All E.R. 88 (Ch.) (declaratory judgment granting specific performance of license of the patents in question to BNS).

their practical impact.[2] Accordingly, any opinion given here concerning the apparent seriousness of particular kinds of conflict must be subject to the qualification that in the practical world of business variables, alternatives often exist which will enable a firm to avoid even apparently "prohibitive" conflict. It may simply decide to adopt a quite different business approach which avoids the problem entirely. The fact that conflict reduces the firm's business options is itself significant, of course, but evaluation of the actual consequences to firms, to the economies concerned and to world trade is an extremely complex matter largely beyond the capability of this book. A further important variable which cannot be fully dealt with in this discussion is that of the kind of enforcement given to the different laws. The stern nature of American antitrust prosecutions and remedies is not matched in Europe, and this undoubtedly has important consequences in the attitudes and practices of firms acting abroad.

In the discussion, problems of overlap and conflict are examined as to the following different categories of activities: (1) horizontal arrangements; (2) acquisitions and mergers; (3) joint ventures (including restrictive agreements in their operation); (4) distribution and marketing arrangements; (5) transactions involving patents; and (6) restraints resulting from governmental action.

I. HORIZONTAL ARRANGEMENTS

Attention to various types of possible conflict in the laws governing horizontal arrangements is necessary for several reasons: (1) The

---

[2] Some of the observations in this chapter have been influenced by empirical research being carried on currently by the author of this chapter on the impact of antitrust law on American business abroad. This research is incomplete, however, and no attempt is made here to report definitive findings from it. Published sources containing examples of concrete situations in which some sort of conflict with American antitrust law was considered to be present include: Statement of Edward B. Hall, in *Hearings on A Study of the Antitrust Laws Before the Subcomm. on Antitrust and Monopoly of the Sen. Comm. on the Judiciary,* 84th Cong., 1st Sess., pt. 4 (Foreign Trade) 1825-38 (1955); Statement of William Persen, in *Hearings on Foreign Trade and the Antitrust Laws Before the Subcomm. on Antitrust and Monopoly of the Sen. Comm. on the Judiciary,* 88th Cong., 2d Sess., pt. 1, at 45-61 (1964); Statement of Arthur Dean, *id.* at 66-106. See Edwards, *The World of Antitrust,* 4 COLUM. J. OF WORLD BUS. No. 4, at 11 (1969), evaluating these examples.

American anticartel approach is not duplicated uniformly in Europe, and the resulting differences in law may produce difficulties for both American and European firms. Difficulties may be most serious as to certain kinds of cooperative activities of small and medium-sized firms which are being encouraged by the EEC Commission. (2) Special inconsistencies sometimes arise in the overlapping application of American and European laws as to horizontal activities in markets outside the territory of both, *i.e.,* "third country markets." (3) The United States and most of the European entities under study grant exemptions to, or do not reach, export cartels, but do not exempt the cartels of other countries which operate in their import commerce.

In the ensuing discussion, the general approach of the different laws to horizontal agreements is briefly summarized, followed by a discussion of conflicts likely to exist in five different categories of arrangements, for convenience grouped in terms of their relation to American commerce. Other problems of horizontal arrangements are also discussed in later sections of this chapter dealing specifically with joint ventures, marketing arrangements and patents.

A. Applicable Laws

1. AMERICAN LAW

American antitrust law is, of course, known for its strictness in prohibiting substantial restraints of competition produced by agreements, associations or conspiracies among competitors. This strictness has had a major impact upon American participation in the classic forms of international cartels. The cases cited in Chapter 2, as well as other sources, indicate that there has been a significant amount of American firm involvement in international cartels in the past, and that this has been followed by an equally substantial and often painful amount of litigation.[3]

---

[3] A study by Leonard J. Seraphin, International Cartels and the Impact of American Antitrust Law (1968) (unpublished manuscript submitted in the Senior Research Program of Northwestern University School of Law; on deposit in the Law School Library) found published evidence of over seventy international cartels in which one or more American firms participated at some time between 1940 and 1967; *id.* at 12-28. For description of different international cartels, see NEWMAN, CARTEL AND COMBINE (1964); STOCKING & WATKINS, CARTELS IN ACTION (1946); HEXNER, INTERNATIONAL CARTELS (1945); MARLIO, THE ALUMINUM CARTEL (1947); HEXNER, THE INTERNATIONAL STEEL CAR-

The result has certainly been greatly to reduce the number and effectiveness of such cartels.[4]

American per se rules against price fixing, limitation of production, market allocation and boycotts prevent even relatively small combinations lacking market control from using such practices—*i.e.*, in the absence of an exemption which is available for some export associations under the Webb-Pomerene Act, discussed below.

2. EUROPEAN LAWS

a. EEC and ECSC

While the American anti-cartel approach is not uniformly duplicated in Europe, there is less conflict in substantive law than formerly in this area, at least insofar as the EEC is concerned. Article 85(1) of the Rome Treaty on its face is as sweeping a prohibition of the activities typically carried on by international cartels—largely market division, customer allocation, production control and price fixing—as Section 1 of the Sherman Act. The quinine and dyestuffs cases show that the Commission intends to enforce this prohibition strictly,[5] and because of the market dominance normally possessed by the great cartels, there seems little likelihood that Article 85(3) exemptions would often be available to temper enforcement as to them. If an American indictment against American and foreign members of the quinine cartel had been returned prior to 1958, it would have conflicted sharply with European laws. When such an indictment was actually brought in 1968,[6] however, it was merely a counterpart to action already occurring under Common Market antitrust law.

A substantial cleavage between American and Common Market law is becoming increasingly evident, however, with respect to some types of cooperative activity among competitors. As pointed out in Chapter 2, the Commission in 1968 issued a statement which was designed to

TEL (1943); FTC, THE INTERNATIONAL PETROLEUM CARTEL, *Report Submitted to Subcomm. on Monopoly of the Sen. Select Comm. on Small Business*, 82d Cong., 2d Sess. (1952).

[4] See Vernon, *Antitrust and International Business*, HARV. BUS. REV., Sept.-Oct. 1968, at 78, questioning the relevance of antitrust doctrines shaped by the earlier cartel cases, and urging the need for new approaches because of changes in the nature of international business organization and activity.

[5] See Chapter 2, text at notes 109 and 110.

[6] See Chapter 2, text at note 109.

encourage cooperation among small and medium-sized enterprises, "where such co-operation enables them to work more economically and increases their productivity and competitiveness on a larger market." The statement listed a number of different kinds of joint activity considered to be outside the scope of Article 85(1), at least where it does not result in an "appreciable" restraint of competition.[7] These activities would not necessarily violate American law. Some are commonly carried on in the United States, even by large combinations, with little or no challenge— *e.g.,* various forms of exchange of market information; joint advertising; common-quality labels; cooperation in providing business services such as debt-collection and accounting or tax consulting service; and even occasionally joint research and development and joint use of facilities.[8] But American law casts an inherently suspicious eye upon practically any arrangement among competitors, and a small misstep by an association which otherwise has excellent intentions to avoid both per se offenses and substantial restraints of any kind may lead to prosecution.[9] Cooperation is thus negatively treated and is inherently dangerous in the

[7] See Chapter 2, note 105 and text. In November 1969, a Commission press release announced that the Commission was considering three draft regulations (which would have to be adopted by the Council of Ministers to be effective), which are designed further to encourage cooperation among small and medium-sized firms, including: (1) a specification as to the types of "minor agreements" which are not caught by Article 85(1) because they do not appreciably impair trade between Member States; (2) an amendment of Reg. 17, art. 4 to extend the exemption therein from the notification requirement to all research and development agreements and specialization arrangements; and (3) an authorization to issue a group exemption for agreements for standardization, research and development, specialization and joint buying and marketing.

[8] See Turner, *Cooperation Among Competitors,* 61 NW.U.L.REV. 865 (1967); *cf.* Citizen Publishing Co. v. United States, 394 U.S. 131 (1969), disapproving an arrangement between two competing newspapers which involved joint marketing as well as joint use of facilities; United States v. Sealy, Inc., 388 U.S. 350 (1967), invalidating cooperation among mattress manufacturers, where a common trademark was accompanied by price and territory controls.

[9] For discussion of trade association activities under American law, see REPORT OF ATTORNEY GENERAL'S NATIONAL COMMITTEE TO STUDY THE ANTI-TRUST LAWS 18-23 (1955) [hereinafter cited ATTY. GEN. NAT. COMM. ANTITRUST REP.]; LAMB & KITTELLE, TRADE ASSOCIATION LAW AND PRACTICE (1956); OPPENHEIM & WESTON, FEDERAL ANTITRUST LAWS ch. 5 (3d ed. 1968).

United States, whereas it is being encouraged on a rather broad scale by the Commission.

Moreover, the Commission will use the Article 85(3) exemption device on occasion to authorize very substantial restraints which would definitely be beyond the pale under American law, including such things as specialization agreements (*i.e.,* division of fields), production rationalization arrangements (*i.e.,* curtailment of production to increase efficiency), and even restraints on selling and territorial protection where ancillary to schemes to increase efficiency or promote research and development.[10]

As for the European Coal and Steel Community, Article 65 of the Treaty provides a broad prohibition for horizontal activity which restrains competition, but gives the Commission authority to exempt joint buying and selling agreements and specialization agreements, an authority which is liberally exercised.[11]

b. Member States

National European laws do not provide a consistent pattern. Most strict is the German law, Section 1 of which broadly parallels the prohibitions of the Sherman Act and of Article 85.[12] Under this provision, German participants in the international dyestuffs cartel were

[10] See cases discussed in Chapter 2, notes 106-08 and text. See also the Limeburner's case, May 5, 1969, CCH COMM. MKT. REP. ¶9303, where the Commission granted negative clearance to an agreement entered into in 1936, between an association of Portland cement manufacturers and a group of natural cement producers ("limeburners"), under which the latter agreed not to manufacture any cement other than natural cement in return for the promise of the former to pay to them an indemnity of 0.5% of total cement sales of the cement manufacturers; in 1962, after natural cement production had declined to extremely small amounts, the Portland cement manufacturers stopped paying the indemnity; a suit in the Belgian courts was suspended pending Commission action; the Commission found that there was no possibility that the few surviving limeburners could enter the Portland cement business because of the large capital requirements of that industry and accordingly that the agreement could not restrict competition to an "appreciable extent;" *id.* at 8653.

[11] See Chapter 2, note 126.

[12] See BUSINESS REGULATION IN THE COMMON MARKET NATIONS (Blake ed. 1969) vol. 3 (K.Ebb ed.) WEST GERMANY (by Juenger, Markert, Pfeifer & Steckhan) 100; EDWARDS, TRADE REGULATIONS OVERSEAS: THE NATIONAL LAWS 168 (1966).

prosecuted and fined by the German Bundeskartellamt (BKA) even before the Commission acted against these same German firms and against participants from other nations.[13] But the German law has significant loopholes as to several kinds of horizontal arrangements.[14] Thus—subject to various conditions and exceptions—the BKA may give approval to "crisis" cartels designed to control production in cases of declining demand; to "rationalization" cartels which raise efficiency and improve "satisfaction of demand;" to export cartels which promote exports, even though they restrain some domestic competition; to import cartels which face a monopoly on the supplier side; and to "emergency" cartels in "exceptional" situations. Also, exemptions are provided under certain circumstances for cartels which agree upon "conditions" of sale (terms of sale, delivery or payment); upon uniform discounts or rebates; upon "specialization" in products or services produced; upon uniform technical or production standards; upon exports, where domestic competition is not affected; and upon uniform methods of "specification" in bidding.

French law—in particular, Article 59 bis of the Price Ordinance—is also potentially as broad as Section 1 of the Sherman Act.[15] In fact, the Commission Technique des Ententes et des Positions Dominantes has been quite strict in finding violations in price fixing, market division, and other cases. Such findings, however, have usually been offset by the "economic balance sheet" process, which is allowed by Article 59 ter, and prosecutions are seldom instituted.[16] Rationalization, specialization, and emergency ententes are allowed and sometimes encouraged.[17] In 1967, a new law was passed permitting the formation, as a matter of company law, of "economic interest groups." These "EIG's" might further complicate enforcement of free competition rules, although it has been stated that they are not actually in conflict.[18]

[13] See Chapter 2, note 110.

[14] See BUSINESS REGULATION IN THE COMMON MARKET NATIONS, vol. 3, *supra* note 12, at 103 *et seq.*; EDWARDS, *supra* note 12, at 177 *et seq.*

[15] See BUSINESS REGULATION IN THE COMMON MARKET NATIONS (Blake ed. 1969) vol. 2 (B. Blake & Perillo eds.) pt. 1, FRANCE (by Bergsten) 162, 340; EDWARDS, *supra* note 12, at 37.

[16] BUSINESS REGULATION IN THE COMMON MARKET NATIONS, vol. 2, *supra* note 15, at 163.

[17] *Id.* at 195 *et seq.*

[18] DuBois, *French Economic Interest Groups and the Rules of Competition,* 14 ANTITRUST BULL. 667, 683 (1969).

Dutch law is quite lenient to some kinds of horizontal arrangements which would be strictly condemned by American (and often Common Market) law.[19] Agreements which are not intended by the parties to be judicially enforceable are not touched at all, unless they involve positions of economic dominance. Judicially enforceable agreements must be registered, and are tested as to whether they conform to the public interest. Under these tests, price fixing is generally allowed;[20] only agreements found to involve exorbitant prices are interfered with. Market sharing is approached tolerantly.[21] Rationalization, standardization and other forms of cooperation are permitted.[22]

Belgian law, which is limited to control of abuse of market power, follows a policy of "indulgence toward anticompetitive practices with lax enforcement of the few existing legislative controls."[23] Price fixing and market division are rather generally lawful, and even boycotts (treated more harshly under German, French and Dutch law) are permissible if designed to pursue a "legitimate interest" of the group.[24]

Italian law at present apparently does not interfere with horizontal combinations, except where unfair competition is involved, although some scholars have argued that a principle of free competition may be found in the Constitution and Civil Code.[25] Under antitrust legislation which has been proposed, but not yet adopted, certain horizontal agreements would be prohibited, subject to several types of exemption.[26] Under Luxembourg law, horizontal restrictive agreements are generally lawful.[27]

---

[19] BUSINESS REGULATION IN THE COMMON MARKET NATIONS (Blake ed. 1969) vol. 1 (Ginsburg ed.) pt. 2, THE NETHERLANDS (by Silbiger) 345; EDWARDS, *supra* note 12, at 88.

[20] BUSINESS REGULATION IN THE COMMON MARKET NATIONS, vol. 1, *supra* note 19, at 351.

[21] *Id.* at 364.

[22] *Id.* at 381.

[23] BUSINESS REGULATION IN THE COMMON MARKET NATIONS (Blake ed. 1969) vol. 1 (Ginsburg ed.) pt. 1, BELGIUM (by de Keyser & Suetens) 105-06.

[24] *Id.* at 113; EDWARDS, *supra* note 12, at 144.

[25] BUSINESS REGULATION IN THE COMMON MARKET NATIONS (Blake ed. 1969) vol. 2 (B. Blake & Perillo eds.) pt. 2, ITALY (by Amato & Macconi) 506-08.

[26] *Id.* at 510.

[27] BUSINESS REGULATION IN THE COMMON MARKET NATIONS (Blake ed. 1969) vol. 1 (Ginsburg ed.) pt. 3, LUXEMBOURG (by Shalit) 547.

B. Conflict Analysis

1. RESTRAINT OF COMPETITION IN AMERICAN IMPORTS

As pointed out in Chapter 2, American law descends heavily upon horizontal combinations which restrain import competition by preventing it, reducing it, or subjecting it to price fixing, market sharing or other restrictive practices. American firms, acting at home or abroad, which enter into such arrangements are vulnerable to prosecution for per se violations. As *Alcoa, I.C.I., Swiss Watch* and other cases teach,[28] foreign firms engaged in combinations which restrict sales in foreign trade to the United States market may also be caught by the American law, if there is personal jurisdiction and if both an intent to affect American imports and actual effect are shown.

American and European law overlap substantially in these situations, especially when viewed from the position of firms in Europe which are engaged in exporting to the United States and are subject to both sets of laws. Conflict can occur because export cartels organized in the Common Market frequently may engage in restraints aimed at the American market which would be per se offenses under American law, but which would be lawful under both EEC and ECSC law—provided competition is not restrained within the Common Market, or trade between Member States is not affected.[29] The Commission's liberal policy in finding that export combinations do not violate Article 85(1), even when they control not only sales outside the Common Market but also sales within a single Member State, has been noted in Chapter 2.[30] This policy seems likely to encourage the formation of more export groups, and thus to enhance the possibilities of substantial conflict with American law.

If the European cartel applies to sales in interstate trade within the Common Market, however, the impact of Community prohibitions may be similar to that of American law, as in the quinine and dyestuffs cases. This kind of consistency is undermined to some extent by the Commission's liberal attitude toward various forms of cooperation, and is subject to disruption by an Article 85(3) exemption. Such exemption for hardcore restraints by cartels controlling an industry is unlikely, but

---

[28] Citations are not repeated here for cases discussed in Chapters 2 and 3.

[29] For examples, see, in Chapter 2: Dutch Engineers and Contractors Ass'n, text at note 115; and Johs. Rieckermann Kg., note 117.

[30] See the fertilizer joint selling agency cases, Chapter 2, text at note 119.

the *Transocean Marine Paint Ass'n* case illustrates how substantial restraints may be permitted in situations where conflict with American law may easily be encountered. In that case, the Commission exempted an agreement among eighteen medium-size paint manufacturers, including an American firm, which contained provisions, among others, requiring payment of a commission where a member sells paint to a customer located in another member's territory.[31] If this exempt agreement applied to sales in or to the United States, it could be caught in a potentially prohibitive conflict with American law. The agreement was approved by the Commission because it found that it would strengthen the ability of the association members to compete, and would fit Community policy of encouraging smaller firms to cooperate. As applied to American commerce, however, the agreement might be treated, subject to the facts, as an illegal division of territory under the Sherman or Federal Trade Commission Acts, and an American lawsuit could occur against both American and European participants in the association (subject to service of process and venue requirements as to the latter). There would seem to be no easy way out of a direct clash between American and European authorities here, except through American forbearance. The parties could provide that the agreement would not apply to sales to or from the United States, but this would probably make it impossible for the American firm to belong to the association. Other similar types of conflict may confront any American firm, or its European subsidiary, which cooperates with an exempt, or tolerated, European export group.

Europeans also could be made subject to the American law in these situations, either through direct application of the law or indirectly if its application to the American firms concerned defeats the export group's plans. This may seem egregious to them. Indeed, it was this kind of application of American law which precipitated the great international uproar about the *Swiss Watch* case—a case which was designed to free the American market from restraints imposed by the Swiss.[32]

There would seem to be little likelihood of a change of substantive law to eliminate these conflicts; no nation may be expected to go out of its way to exempt foreign cartels operating in its import or domestic markets. The conflict would be reduced if the Europeans were to make

[31] See Chapter 2, note 106.
[32] See Chapter 6.

their laws more strict in their application to export trade, but this is probably unlikely without some kind of mutual action by all of the major trading nations.

The shoe could also be on the other foot. For example, it was reported in 1969 that European steel producers agreed to restrict increases in exports to the United States to a maximum of 5% per year during the next several years at the urging of the State Department, in order to give some protection to the American steel industry, and at the same time head off a drive in Congress for adoption of import quotas on steel. The Commission indicated, in response to a question from a member of the European Parliament, that it could act against this agreement under Article 65 of the ECSC Treaty, if the arrangement were shown to restrict competition in the Common Market.[33] Similarly, German law, and possibly other national laws, might apply.

If European laws were used against this steel agreement, there would be an obvious conflict between European antitrust policy and the American policy represented by the State Department. There would not be any conflict with American antitrust law, however, since the Sherman Act would also apply to such an agreement, and there is no apparent basis for an exemption.

2. RESTRAINT OF COMPETITION IN AMERICAN EXPORTS TO THE COMMON MARKET

In this section, the discussion is limited to restraints in or affecting American exports which are not exempt under the Webb-Pomerene Act (discussed later). American law is quite strict in its prohibition of restrictive export agreements. The *Continental Ore* case shows that the strict approach will apply not only to agreements made in the United States but also to agreements abroad to which an American is a party, under which foreign buyers are induced to restrain American exports by boycotting a given American seller. Under the *Alcoa* doctrine, even a combination acting abroad and composed entirely of foreign buyers could be held to violate American law if it restrained American exports

[33] See Chapter 7, text at note 67; Thiesing, Remarks on the Problems of Extra-Territorial Effect of "Anti-Trust" Law, Concerning the European Community, before the Ass'n of the Bar of the City of N.Y., May 8, 1969 (to be published in the RECORD); Question No. C42, Official Journal of the European Communities, April 2, 1969, at 4 [hereinafter cited E.C.J.O.] .

deliberately and effectively, although substantial practical difficulties might attend enforcement in this instance, not to mention possible problems of international law.[34]

Greater overlap would exist as to restraints in American export trade than as to American imports because of the greater applicability of European laws; restraint of competition in American exports has direct impact on domestic European markets. Thus, EEC law would apply if the particular agreement restrains competition within the Common Market on a multi-state basis. There have been no cases of this exact description as yet, although the *Grosfillex* and *Vitapro* cases implicitly support the proposition. There would appear to be little question about the theoretical applicability of the Rome Treaty provisions to EEC importers in this situation. Exemption under Article 85(3), however, would always be a possibility, as in the *Transocean Marine Paint Ass'n* agreement which involves certain restraints on imports.

Moreover, the Commission's view of its extraterritorial jurisdiction appears to be much like that of the United States, *i.e.*, that it extends to foreign firms located outside the Common Market, including the United States, when effects are felt within the Common Market.[35] A combination of American exporters which restricts prices or reduces the flow of goods in EEC imports presumably could in some cases meet the tests of restraining competition within the Common Market and affecting interstate trade. For example, if American manufacturers of a given machine agreed with American manufacturers of the product made with this machine to limit sales of machines to Common Market processors in order to enable American processors to gain an advantage in sales in the European market, there seems no reason to doubt that Article 85(1) would be offended, and that an Article 85(3) exemption would be unlikely. As indicated in Chapter 3, however, there are very substantial questions as to how much power the Commission has to investigate activities abroad and to take action against firms not located in the Common Market.

ECSC law and the laws of the Member States of the European Communities could also apply to a combination of American exporters or European importers restricting American exports in such a way as also to restrain competition within European markets. But the Commission is

---

[34] See Chapter 2, text at note 82 *et seq.*; also Chapters 3 and 7.
[35] See Chapter 2, text at note 112; Thiesing, *supra* note 33.

required by Article 65(2) of the ECSC Treaty to grant an exemption to a joint buying group which meets tests laid down there.[36] The French and German laws also clearly apply to import restraints, but Section 7 of the German law provides for exemption of import cartels where necessary to deal with a monopoly or cartel on the selling side. Similar exempting results could apparently occur under French, Belgian or Dutch law through administrative discretion, and Belgian law would not apply in any event unless the restraint exercised a dominant influence in the Belgian market. Italian and Luxembourg laws apparently interpose no obstacles. Also, as pointed out in Chapters 2 and 3, application of the national laws to conduct of persons outside the territory of the nation concerned is in any event difficult.

Direct conflict will often be avoided in this overlapping area of American and European law because European law will frequently condemn the arrangement. Conflict will be present, of course, if an exemption under European law is obtained for the restriction. The possibilities for serious conflict are substantial where an exempt European import cartel restrains American exports. If American interests are seriously impinged, or if a private litigant's export ability has been adversely affected, a suit under American law may well occur, provided personal jurisdiction can be obtained over members of the cartel. A suit on such facts may succeed, and the result could be to interfere in a disadvantageous and possibly prohibitive way with conduct which has been expressly made lawful under European law.

As indicated later in this chapter, the mere authorization or exemption of restrictive conduct by a foreign government will not have much effect on an American court.[37] As the court said in the *Swiss Watch* case: "Nonetheless, the fact that the Swiss Government may, as a practical matter, approve of the effects of this private activity cannot convert what is essentially a vulnerable private conspiracy into an unassailable system resulting from foreign governmental mandate."[38] As this statement implies, however, where a foreign government *requires* the

---

[36]*E.g.,* the High Authority of the ECSC in 1955 authorized sixty-four German steel firms to engage in joint importing of American coal. Thiesing, *supra* note 33.

[37]United States v. American Tobacco Co., 221 U.S. 106 (1911); Continental Ore Co. v. Union Carbide & Carbon Corp., 370 U.S. 690, 707 (1962).

[38]United States v. Watchmakers of Switzerland Information Center, Inc., 1963 Trade Cas. ¶ 70,600 at 77, 456-57.

activity in question, an American court is more likely to refrain from issuing a conflicting order.

Insofar as the prospects for resolving such conflicts are concerned, a reasonable amount of self-restraint seems to be about all that one may expect from American authorities. Such self-restraint seems unquestionably to occur at the administrative level; as yet there apparently have been no suits filed by the United States against foreign buying groups. Self-restraint by private litigants is, of course, much less predictable, and once a suit is filed by either the Government or a private plaintiff, forbearance by the American court appears unlikely except in the face of mandatory foreign legal or judicial requirements.

While foreign courts perhaps could reduce conflict by choosing to recognize and give effect to American antitrust decrees, they are not required to do so by any legal principle, and are most unlikely to do so in the absence of some such treaty or international convention as is being considered by the Council of Europe.[39] Conservatism in the issuance of exemptions and a strong enforcement policy against restraints applied to European import trade would be the chief contribution which foreign authorities could make to the avoidance of such conflict situations.

3. RESTRAINTS AFFECTING EXPORT TRADE WITH THIRD COUNTRIES

A special problem exists with respect to American and European export trade with "third country" markets outside the United States and the Common Market. The problem arises both where American and Common Market firms are competing in third country trade, and where such firms enter into agreements restraining competition as to such trade. In these situations, American law will apply to the American firms in the same way as it would apply to exports to buyers in the Common Market. On the other hand, American law would be unlikely to apply to the Europeans concerned, except in unusual situations, because the Europeans would not be engaged in a phase of American foreign commerce.

Great imbalance could result from the fact that the European laws generally would *not* apply to third country situations, for the same reasons that they seldom apply to European export trade with the

---

[39] See summary of proposal of the Legal Committee of the Council of Europe, *infra* in Chapter 7, note 126.

United States in the absence of a showing of domestic effects. As a consequence, American firms may be subjected to a substantial impact from American law in these situations, while the European firms may be free from the burden of any antitrust law, unless the third country has such a law which will apply.

For example, American firms interested in large engineering and construction projects in third countries may encounter handicaps in engaging in some forms of cooperation on these projects which their European competitors are free to use. As the EEC *Dutch Engineers* case shows,[40] consortia to pool capital and personnel and share the costs, risks, and profits of large projects of this nature are lawful under European law, if limited in operation to areas outside the EEC. Moreover, the Commission's policy statement on permissible cooperation indicates that such arrangements may fall outside Article 85(1) even though they affect domestic competition, if the participants would be unable to carry out the job individually.[41] The same statement also reminds firms that an Article 85(3) exemption may still be available, even if Article 85(1) applies.

Consortia of this kind normally require agreement upon prices and allocation of shares in the job, and American law would therefore impose certain risks of violation upon firms forming them, although they may be lawful under some circumstances.[42] If American firms wishing to

[40] Chapter 2, text at note 115.

[41] Chapter 2, note 105.

[42] It is interesting to note that Donald F. Turner, while head of the Antitrust Division, stated to a Senate Committee in 1967 that "antitrust law may permit two or more exporters to use a joint selling agency, delegating to it the authority to determine price and agreeing on shares of what the agency manages to sell, provided it is convincingly shown that joint selling is necessary to produce significant economies essential to the participants competing abroad, that the price and quota arrangements are necessary to the functioning of the joint selling agency, and that the totality of the firms involved is sufficiently small that permitting the combination creates no danger of adverse effects on competition in price or product." *Hearings on International Aspects of Antitrust Before the Subcomm. on Antitrust and Monopoly of the Sen. Comm. on the Judiciary*, 90th Cong., 1st Sess., Review of the Webb-Pomerene Act of 1918, at 127 (1967). See also Turner, *Cooperation Among Competitors*, 61 NW U.L. REV. 865 (1967).

It may also be reasoned, under United States v. Penn-Olin Chem. Co., 378 U.S. 158 (1964), *judgment for defendants after remand*, 246 F.Supp. 917 (D.Del. 1965), *aff'd per curiam*, 389 U.S. 308 (1967), that a joint venture of the nature discussed in

undertake jobs of this sort decide for legal reasons that they must operate unilaterally, and if the costs and risks would be too great for single-firm operation, the imbalance in American and European law would produce prohibitive consequences for Americans.

It should not be assumed that this kind of conflict resulting from unequal impact of two legal systems would invariably be disadvantageous to American firms in competing for foreign business. Under some facts, an American firm acting free of any cartel restraint may have an advantage over European competitors who are required by a cartel agreement to live by various restrictions.[43]

4. RESTRAINTS EXEMPTED BY THE WEBB-POMERENE ACT

In some situations, an exemption under the Webb-Pomerene Act may be available to American firms.[44] The example just discussed might not come within the exemption, however, because the exemption is available for export trade in "goods, wares or merchandise," and might not reach engineering and contracting services. Also, conceivably it might not cover collaborative buying and handling of materials acquired by a consortium outside the United States, because the Act's exemptive scope is limited to American exports.[45] Of course, however, such collaboration might be too remote from American commerce to be reached by the antitrust laws.

Where available, the Webb-Pomerene exemption permits an association of American competitors to fix prices, allocate sales, and carry out other

the text would not violate the Sherman Act or Section 7 of the Clayton Act if the joint venturers had not previously competed in the market concerned and if none of them would have entered the particular market alone.

[43] For an example, see Edwards, *supra* note 2; see also testimony of Rahl, in *Hearings on International Aspects of Antitrust Before the Subcomm. on Antitrust and Monopoly of the Sen. Comm. on the Judiciary*, 89th Cong., 2d Sess., pt. 1, at 370 (1966).

[44] Export Trade Act, April 10, 1918, 15 U.S.C. §61 (1964). For a summary of the Act and details concerning its operation, see FTC, ECONOMIC REPORT ON WEBB-POMERENE ASSOCIATIONS: A 50-YEAR REVIEW (1967); see also *Hearings, supra* note 42; Note, *The Webb-Pomerene Act: Some New Developments in a Quiescent History*, 37 GEO. WASH. L. REV. 341 (1968).

[45] *Cf.* United States v. Concentrated Phosphate Export Ass'n, 393 U.S. 199, 209 (1968), holding that sales to Korea under A.I.D. arrangements were not in "export trade" within the meaning of the exemption, because the transactions were "American, not Korean." See also Chapter 2, note 62.

types of restrictions in export trade, and to function as a joint selling agency.[46] It has been interpreted by the Federal Trade Commission, to whom the agreement must be notified, as not authorizing the inclusion of any foreign firm, nor participation by the association in an international cartel.[47] Statutory provisos state that the association must not cause restraint of competition within the United States, must not restrain the export trade of any domestic competitor, and must not enhance or depress prices within the United States.[48]

While, economically speaking, any restraint of competition in export trade probably affects domestic commerce and prices in the same goods,[49] the provisos have been interpreted to mean some restraint over and above that which is inherent in such association; otherwise the Act would be made nugatory.[50] Acquisition of foreign competitors by an association in order to protect the domestic market has been held illegal by the Commission,[51] and a Justice Department suit has established that the use of an association to stabilize domestic prices by removing surpluses is illegal.[52]

In 1965, there were only 29 active Webb-Pomerene associations, as reported by the FTC.[53] Exports by members of these associations accounted for only 4.2% of total United States exports of goods in that year.[54] Moreover, the exports which actually moved through, or were assisted by, Webb associations have accounted in recent years for only about half the total exports by firms which were members of such associations,[55] so that apparently such "Webb-assisted" exports have been less than 2.5% of total American exports of goods.

[46] See FTC, ECONOMIC REPORT, *supra* note 44, at 15-16.

[47] *Id.* at 19; also United States v. United States Alkali Export Ass'n, 86 F.Supp. 59, 64 *et seq.* (S.D.N.Y. 1949), holding that the exemption did not cover an export association which entered into international cartel arrangements with foreign competitors.

[48] Section 2 of the Export Trade Act, 15 U.S.C. §62.

[49] See testimony of Donald F. Turner, in *Hearings, supra* note 42, at 124.

[50] United States v. Minnesota Mining & Mfg. Co., 92 F.Supp. 947, 965 (D.Mass. 1950).

[51] Export Screw Ass'n of the United States, 43 F.T.C. 980 (1947).

[52] United States v. United States Alakli Export Ass'n, 86 F.Supp. 59 (S.D.N.Y. 1949).

[53] FTC, ECONOMIC REPORT, *supra* note 44, at 23; same data in *Hearings, supra* note 42, at 32.

[54] *Id.*

[55] FTC, ECONOMIC REPORT, *supra* note 44, at 36.

In 1967, the Department of Justice recommended repeal of the exemption because it is little used, sets a bad example for other nations, has harmful domestic consequences in affected industries, is not needed for legitimate cooperative activities, and has often served to permit collaboration by very large, powerful firms, whereas it was intended to aid small exporters.[56]

In situations to which the Webb-Pomerene exemption does apply, the resulting American legal leniency will sometimes overlap with European prohibitions. It has been pointed out above that EEC law will reach an American export combination if its restraint of competition is felt within the Common Market, and if interstate commerce is affected. The first of these two conditions would seem to be met if, for example, the export association fixed prices in what would otherwise be competitive selling in the Common Market. As to interstate commerce, the fairly liberal test followed by the Commission and so far approved in decisions of the Court of Justice indicates that the test will not be hard to meet in such cases.

German law also is applicable to American export associations.[57] It appears to be debatable whether ECSC or French law can apply, but Belgian and Dutch laws probably would if their relatively lenient substantive standards are violated. An American association might seek an exemption or clearance under some of the European laws, but success would appear to be a doubtful prospect at best. Accordingly, overlap and conflict are potentially present in high degree.

The conflict situation presented is the converse of the problem discussed above as to European export cartels which encounter strict American antitrust prohibitions. In one respect, the conflict may be even sharper: the *Alcoa* test gives European firms accused of violating American antitrust law in activities outside the United States the benefit of a double requirement of proof of intent and effect, but those European laws which are applicable to restraints committed by Americans acting outside the Common Market seem to require only proof of an effect within the jurisdiction, without regard to intent.[58]

---

[56] Testimony of Donald F. Turner, Assistant Att'y Gen'l, in *Hearings, supra* note 42, at 125; repeal was also recommended by the Report of the Task Force on Productivity and Competition, appointed by President Nixon, ATTR No. 413, X-1 (June 10, 1969).

[57] See Chapter 2, text at note 142.

[58] *Id.*

At this writing, there has been no sign of an attempt by European governments to enforce their laws against American Webb-Pomerene associations. But the warnings that this may be done have been plain enough.

A serious consequence of the American exemption for export associations. But the warnings that this may be done have been plain invites. Such retaliation is expressly permitted by German law,[59] and is probably permitted by the ECSC and some of the other national laws, and perhaps by EEC law. A case of this kind occurred in Great Britain, where the Restrictive Practices Court held that a British sulphur buying group could justify its restraint of competition under an express "gateway" in the Restrictive Practices Act of 1956 because of the American sulphur export association organized under Webb-Pomerene.[60] Where such counter-cartel formation occurs, American policy generates a costly, if deserved, offset to itself.[61]

Export and import cartel exemptions thus can cause embarrassing and potentially irreconcilable conflicts. Neither side in such a conflict is likely to be inclined to ignore the other's allowance of cartel intrusion into its domestic economy, and the only broad solution therefore appears to lie along the line of multilateral abolition of the exemptions.

II. ACQUISITIONS AND MERGERS

A. Applicable Laws

Trans-national acquisitions and mergers, as well as multi-national joint ventures which are discussed in the next section, are a potential source of great conflict between American and European law. This situation results from the extremely strong anti-merger approach of American law, while European laws in general not only avoid merger prohibitions, but give substantial encouragement to increased merger activity.

[59] Section 7 of the Act against Restraints of Competition permits the BKA to authorize cartels of German importers if they are "faced with no competition or only insignificant competition among the suppliers." OECD, GUIDE TO LEGISLATION ON RESTRICTIVE BUSINESS PRACTICES, Germany; BUSINESS REGULATION IN THE COMMON MARKET NATIONS, vol. 3, *supra* note 12, at 201.

[60] *In re* National Sulphuric Acid Association's Agreement, 4 R.P. 169 (1963).

[61] Theoretically, a counter-European cartel probably violates American antitrust principles against restraint of American exports, although such an application of American law would be the height of irony.

1. AMERICAN LAW

American anti-merger law, as domestically applied, has developed to the point that almost any acquisition or merger between competing firms engaged in interstate commerce and occupying a substantial share of the market must be counted as presenting at least some risk of attack by the Justice Department, the Federal Trade Commission, or private plaintiffs. Under present case law, an acquisition of a competitor by a leading firm may be held illegal even if the combined shares in the relevant market are very small, if the merger occurs in an industry in which there is a significant trend toward increased "concentration," as that term is used in American law.[62] Even in the absence of such a trend, a merger involving a fairly small increase in the acquiring firm's market share may be challenged on various grounds.[63]

Vertical mergers are not quite as vulnerable, but may be held illegal if they significantly raise barriers to entry or impose serious disadvantages upon competitors.[64] Conglomerate mergers are still less vulnerable but are coming under increasing attack. Under present case law, a conglomerate merger may be illegal if it eliminates substantial potential competition or gives rise to significant opportunities to engage in substantially anti-competitive reciprocity practices.[65] New cases may be expected to produce additional doctrines under which conglomerate mergers may be challenged.[66]

The American law may reach acquisitions and mergers involving American and foreign parties, and it could even apply to a merger of

[62] United States v. Von's Grocery Co., 384 U.S. 270 (1966); United States v. Pabst Brewing Co., 384 U.S. 546 (1966); Department of Justice Merger Guidelines, para. 7, 1 CCH TRADE REG. REP. ¶4430 (1968). The term "concentration" in American law is used to refer to the extent to which a small number of firms account for a large share of the market. In European writings, however, the term is often used as a synonym for "merger" as that term is used in American antitrust law (*i.e.,* a "close-knit" combination of firms). See generally JOLIET, MONOPOLIZATION AND ABUSE OF DOMINANT POSITION: A COMPARATIVE STUDY OF THE AMERICAN AND EUROPEAN APPROACHES TO THE CONTROL OF ECONOMIC POWER (1970).

[63] See Department of Justice Merger Guidelines, *supra* note 62.

[64] *Id.,* para. 11.

[65] *Id.,* paras. 17-19.

[66] After publication of the Merger Guidelines, *supra* note 62, a new head of the Antitrust Division took office in 1969, Richard W. McLaren, who greatly increased the attention paid to conglomerate mergers; five major attacks on such mergers were launched by his office in the first eight months of 1969.

foreign firms abroad, under theories explored in Chapter 2. A merger involving one or more foreign firms which compete in the American domestic market may be dealt with as a matter of course under Section 7 of the Clayton Act and under the Sherman Act, and several such cases have been brought.[67] A merger of importers, American or foreign, operating in the United States similarly may be attacked.[68] A merger involving only foreign firms located abroad could theoretically be reached if it were intended to and did affect exports to the United States, although it may be difficult for an American court to obtain effective jurisdiction or to issue a workable decree in such a case.[69]

Mergers involving companies engaging only in American export trade, or in imports of American goods into foreign markets, may be somewhat more difficult to reach under Section 7 of the Clayton Act because of its requirement, discussed in Chapter 2, of a showing of adverse competitive effect "in any section of the country." It is not clear at this writing how

---

[67]United States v. Jos. Schlitz Brewing Co., 253 F.Supp. 129 (N.D.Cal. 1966), *aff'd per curiam,* 385 U.S. 37 (1966) (stock acquisition by American brewer in Canadian brewer affected competition between defendant and American affiliate of Canadian company, and also deterred potential entry of Canadian company into American market); United States v. Aluminium Ltd., 1966 Trade Cas. ¶71,895 (D.N.J. 1966) (consent decree against vertical acquisition of American fabricating assets by Canadian primary aluminum producer); United States v. Standard Oil Co. (N.J.), 253 F.Supp. 196 (D.N.J. 1966) (Acquisition by Standard of American potash company was enjoined because of both horizontal and vertical effects, one of which was effect on potential competition with a Canadian subsidiary of Standard).

Two recent cases against acquisitions of foreign firms by Americans have aroused considerable interest; both rest upon theories that the acquisition eliminates actual or potential competition by the foreign firm in the domestic market: United States v. Gillette Co., 5 CCH Trade Reg. Rep. ¶45,068 (case No. 1988) (D.Mass. 1968) (complaint against Gillette's acquisition of a German producer of electric razors, Braun A.G.); and Litton Indus., Inc., FTC Docket No. 8778 (1969), 3 CCH TRADE REG. REP. ¶¶18,729 and 18,828 (complaint issued April 11, 1969 against Litton's acquisition of German typewriter company, Triumph-Adler).

[68]United States v. Schenley Indus., Inc., 5 CCH Trade Reg. Rep. ¶45,066 (case No. 1897) (pending case against merger of two large American importers of Scotch whiskey).

[69]"Needless to say, there would be jurisdictional and other problems for U.S. enforcement addressed to the merger of two foreign firms. Nonetheless, such a merger could have adverse effects in the U.S. market. For example, they could have competing U.S. subsidiaries or they could be competitors themselves for the U.S. market." Zimmerman, in *Hearings, supra* note 43, at 489.

this requirement will be interpreted. Such domestic effect might conceivably be found where the merger eliminates competition between two American-based exporters on the theory that this competition occurs partly "in" the United States. On a similar theory, the Clayton Act could reach an American exporter's vertical or conglomerate merger with a European firm if the result were illegally to foreclose other American exports or imports,[70] but there is as yet no case law on these problems. The Sherman Act may, of course, apply, although its standards may be more lenient.[71]

Any case attacking a merger on a theory of effect on export commerce may face a difficult problem as to the definition of the relevant geographic market. This problem is discussed later in connection with joint ventures.

2. EUROPEAN LAWS

By and large, European approaches to mergers stand in sharp contrast. In most instances relevant to this study, there would probably be no antitrust law operating within the Common Market which would prohibit a merger.

The Rome Treaty's antitrust provisions do not apply to corporate mergers and acquisitions, according to the Commission, unless an abuse of dominant power is involved. In its Memorandum on Concentration in 1965, the Commission announced a conclusion that Article 85(1) does not reach mergers because of considerations of interpretation, history and policy.[72] This approach was heavily influenced by the Community

---

[70] For discussion of the requirement of effect in a "section of the country," as well as of other requirements of Section 7, including the "engaged in commerce" test and the problem of showing effect on competition where foreign markets are involved, see writings cited in note 3 of Chapter 2.

[71] See United States v. Columbia Steel Co., 334 U.S. 495 (1948), upholding under the Sherman Act rule of reason a large horizontal and vertical acquisition; *cf.* United States v. First Nat'l Bank & Trust Co., 376 U.S. 665 (1964), whose dictum would permit very strict condemnation of horizontal mergers under the Sherman Act. For discussion, see Donovan, *Antitrust Considerations in the Organization and Operation of American Business Abroad,* 9 B.C. IND. & COM. L. REV. 239, 272 *et seq.* (1968); Donovan, *The Legality of Acquisitions and Mergers Involving American and Foreign Corporations under the United States Antitrust Laws—Part I,* 39 S. CAL. L. REV. 526, 535 *et seq.* (1966); Scott & Yablonski, *Transnational Mergers and Joint Ventures Affecting American Exports,* 14 ANTITRUST BULL. 1, 16 *et seq.* (1969).

[72] EEC Commission Memorandum to the Member States on Concentration of Enterprises in the Common Market, Dec. 1, 1965, CCH COMM. MKT. REP. No. 26,

policy of promoting the integration of firms in the Common Market in order to achieve enterprises of larger scale and of multinational composition. The only check on mergers—apart from those which result in restrictive agreements continuing after the merger and to which Article 85(1) could apply—is that provided by Article 86. The Memorandum explains that a firm already having a dominant position might unlawfully "abuse" that position by making an acquisition under certain circumstances. An example given is that of a dominant firm which monopolizes a market through a merger.[73]

While the ECSC Treaty, in contrast to the Rome Treaty, provides for comprehensive control of mergers involving Common Market coal and steel companies, as a practical matter this control imposes only a minimum of restraint upon such mergers. A great many mergers have been approved, even where a strengthening of existing oligopoly has been the result; none have been formally disapproved; and it has been predicted that ECSC policy will soon lead to a market structure in which only six or eight independent groups of steel companies will produce the bulk of Community steel output.[74]

Except for their provisions dealing with dominant economic power, the national laws of Belgium, France and the Netherlands do not

pt. 1 (Mar. 17, 1966) (separate print). The Commission's interpretation of the Treaty provisions was in part expressly contrary to the views of a majority of the group of experts it had appointed to advise it on this question, the latter believing that Article 85 should be applied to mergers ("concentrations") where the firms involved remain legally distinct after the acquisition, though not to true mergers, *id.* at 24; see JOLIET, *supra* note 62; de Jong, in *Hearings on Economic Concentration Outside the United States Before the Subcomm. on Antitrust and Monopoly of the Sen. Comm. on the Judiciary,* 90th Cong., 2d Sess., pt. 7, at 3628 (1968); Markert, *Antitrust Aspects of Mergers in the EEC,* 5 TEX. INT'L L.F. 32, 47 (1969); Mailänder, *Mergers and Acquisitions in the E.E.C.,* 1 N.Y.U.J. of INT'L L. & POL. 19 (1968); Rahl, in *Hearings, supra* note 43, at 384.

[73]Memorandum, *supra* note 72, at 30. Professor de Jong characterizes Europe's approach to mergers as a return to a laissez-faire policy; *supra* note 72.

[74]de Jong, *supra* note 72, at 3627. See Markert, *supra* note 72, at 38-41; EDWARDS, CONTROL OF CARTELS AND MONOPOLIES: AN INTERNATIONAL COMPARISON 269 (1967). See also Mueller, *The Policy of the European Coal and Steel Community Towards Mergers and Agreements by Steel Companies,* 14 ANTITRUST BULL. 413, 444 (1969): "Overall, the Authority appears to favor the restructuring of the ECSC steel sector into a concentrated oligopoly in which no single enterprise commands a dominant position in a major product line."

generally apply to mergers.[75] (It should be noted, however, that under Belgian law, a second offender under the provisions against abuse of economic power may be prohibited from making acquisitions and may be required to divest past acquisitions.[76]) The German law also does not prohibit mergers, but it requires that they be reported to the Bundeskartellamt (BKA) if any one of the following conditions are met: (1) one of the parties controls 20% or more of a market; (2) the combined market share of the parties is 20% or more; or (3) the parties combined exceed a certain size, *viz.*, 10,000 employees, DM 500 million in sales or DM 1,000 million in assets.[77] These provisions apply to mergers involving foreign companies if they affect the German domestic market.[78] The BKA has no power to prohibit a merger, but it may hold a public hearing and require certain information to be produced if it appears that a market-dominating enterprise will be involved.

B. Conflict Analysis

American anti-merger law clearly can reach and prohibit a number of different types of mergers which are lawful under the various European laws. Predictions as to the actual seriousness of the conflicts which may arise from this overlapping depend to some extent upon more than legal

[75] BUSINESS REGULATION IN THE COMMON MARKET NATIONS, vol. 1, *supra* note 23, at 97-98, 138 (Belgium); *id.* at 336, 416 (Netherlands); *id.* at 535 (Luxembourg); BUSINESS REGULATION IN THE COMMON MARKET NATIONS, vol. 2, *supra* note 15, at 149, 260 (France); *id.* at 528 (Italy); Markert, *supra* note 72, at 62-65.

[76] BUSINESS REGULATION IN THE COMMON MARKET NATIONS, vol. 1, *supra* note 23, at 97.

[77] See BUSINESS REGULATION IN THE COMMON MARKET NATIONS, vol. 3, *supra* note 12, at 166, 392; Günther, in *Hearings on Economic Concentration Outside the United States Before the Subcomm. on Antitrust and Monopoly of the Sen. Comm. on the Judiciary,* 90th Cong., 2d Sess., pt. 7, at 3473 (1968); Markert, *supra* note 72, at 56.

Shortly after taking office, Chancellor Willy Brandt, in a speech to the German parliament, called for a strengthened cartel law which would include some control of mergers; N.Y. Times, Oct. 29, 1969.

[78] Dr. Günther, president of the BKA, has provided a breakdown of types of mergers by industry groups reported in the years 1958-67 in *Hearings, supra* note 77, at 3477 and 3820; see also BUSINESS REGULATION IN THE COMMON MARKET NATIONS, vol. 3, *supra* note 12, at 166 *et seq.*, and Markert, *supra* note 72, at 56 for further discussion of reporting requirements.

analysis, however. As will be pointed out below, it appears that in some situations, a clash of underlying policies could produce conflict of very high intensity. In others, however, the legal inconsistency may be misleading; underlying policies may actually be more harmonious than first appears.

1. MERGERS OF EUROPEAN FIRMS

If American law were to seek to prohibit a merger of two European firms which was being promoted by European authorities in the name of building trans-national enterprises of Community size, serious conflict would be inevitable. Such a case is at least possible. For example, two European companies may be engaged in competition in export to the United States of a product as to which the two account for an important share of American domestic supply. Their merger might have a very substantial adverse effect upon competition in the United States. If it were found further that one of the motivating factors in the merger would be to obtain higher prices in the American market through reduced competition, thus satisfying the *Alcoa* doctrine of requiring a showing of intent, all of the substantive legal elements necessary for attack under the Clayton Act would be present.

If one of the firms were American, such an attack would be likely, judging from cases already brought.[79] If the firms were both non-American, attack still would not be unlikely if they were manufacturing in the United States through branches or subsidiaries, or if they were operating distributive facilities there.[80] Would the fact that they were merely exporting to the United States from European plants make an important difference? Theoretically, the difference would not be critical; American law could be applied under familiar principles, although as a practical matter it probably would not be.

If American law is applied to mergers of European firms, however, it is not clear how effective it can be. Even if the court obtains personal jurisdiction over the firms, the problem of decreeing relief will be very difficult. The best remedy for an illegal merger is to prevent it, or break

---

[79] See note 67 *supra*.

[80] A planned merger between two Swiss drug and chemical manufacturers, Ciba and Geigy, was reported to be under study as to American antitrust aspects because both companies had American subsidiaries; Wall St. J., Sept. 5, 1969, at 5; N.Y. Times, Nov. 22, 1969, at 62.

it up. If an American court were to issue such an order to firms whose main assets, headquarters and personnel were in Europe, foreign authorities and courts would in all probability be called upon to employ their power and tactical position to frustrate the order. An international conflict of high intensity would be created, and as in the *I.C.I.* case, it could well be a conflict in which the American court would have to retreat.

Other less drastic forms of relief might be considered. Since the court's appropriate function is only to protect American commerce, it might seek to design a decree which would achieve some of that goal without destroying the entire merger itself. Where the merging firms have American branches or subsidiaries, a divestiture of these assets might be considered as a device to preserve competition in the United States. Severed from their parents, however, some of these subsidiary units might lose much of their value as going enterprises. An attempt could be made to require the merged firm to continue to offer two lines of the product in the United States through competing distributors as a condition of being allowed to operate there. This would be unworkable, however, unless the firm continued to produce two lines at home. Moreover, the order would be relatively valueless unless the court could find some means of forcing competitive pricing at the manufacturing level to continue—a factor which would ordinarily necessitate the very kind of interference with the basic structure of the enterprise which the court would be seeking to avoid.

In summary, it appears that major conflict would be largely unavoidable in the application of American law to a merger of European firms. If the firms manufacture or distribute in the United States, the Government may risk the conflict in some cases. But if they merely export to or import from the United States, it seems unlikely that attack will occur; administrative discretion may be expected to be exercised to avoid it.

2. MERGERS OF AMERICAN AND EUROPEAN FIRMS

Many mergers and acquisitions have occurred with an American and a European firm as the participants. As already pointed out, a few of these have been subjected to attack under American law on the ground that competition in the American domestic or import market has been allegedly restrained.[81] While there have been occasional charges that

---

[81] See note 67 *supra.*

some of the cases have overreached proper limits of American law, there would not seem to be great merit in the contention. There is a rather obvious legitimacy in a nation's efforts to guard its domestic economy against what it considers to be serious interference with its policies on the part of firms participating in that economy, particularly when a chief actor is one of its own nationals.

If the acquiring firm is European and the acquired American, objections to American antitrust action may seem more persuasive, in view of the fact that European nations and the Common Market have not used antitrust laws to inhibit the many American acquisitions of their firms which have occurred.[82] No real legal difference would be involved, however.

In either kind of case, legal conflict is present in the sense that American law is seeking to prohibit what European laws permit, and is exerting a significant impact upon the economy of one or more European nations—an impact which is radically different from that decreed by European laws. For example, in the acquisition of Braun A.G., the German electric razor manufacturer, by Gillette Co., the American safety razor firm, the take-over of Braun's assets in Germany is a matter which is fully subject to control by German law, and is permitted by that

---

[82] The Justice Department asked that a tender offer by the Dutch company, Koninklijke Zout-Organon N.V., for the stock of the American company, International Salt Co., be delayed pending investigation; ATTR No. 430, at A-10 (Oct. 7, 1969). Later, the head of the Antitrust Division, Richard W. McLaren, announced that the acquisition would be allowed, as "K.Z.O. persuaded us that if it did not get International Salt it would not be able to enter the American market;" N.Y. Times, Nov. 22, 1969, at 53, 62.

A large amount of international criticism was reported when the Antitrust Division objected to initial plans of British Petroleum Co. (BP) to merge with Standard Oil Co. of Ohio (Sohio). Earlier, BP had entered the American market by acquisition from Atlantic Richfield Co. of about 9,000 service stations in the East, previously acquired by Atlantic Richfield from Sinclair and sold to BP after the Government attacked that acquisition in United States v. Atlantic Richfield Co., 297 F.Supp. 1075 (S.D.N.Y. 1969). See N.Y. Times, Oct. 7, 1969, at 61; Oct. 9, at 69; Oct. 18, at 71; Wall St. J., Oct. 8, 1969, at 4; Oct. 16, editorial; Chicago Sun-Times, Oct. 13, at 69. Agreement on a consent decree which would provide for divestiture of competing BP or Sohio stations in Ohio and Western Pennsylvania was later announced, Wall St. J., Nov. 18, 1969, at 3; about one-third of the Sohio outlets in Ohio would be divested, perhaps by exchange for stations in other market areas owned by firms wishing to acquire Ohio stations; *id.,* Nov. 19, 1969, at 40.

law.[83] The American suit, if successful, will have a major effect on the German market.

Nonetheless, this kind of conflict is generally less serious than the conflict which can arise in all-European merger cases. What is apparently a major inconsistency in the laws on the surface may prove to present little or no conflict when underlying policy considerations are more fully identified. Actually, American anti-merger law, if applied to prevent take-over of Europeans firms by American companies, may accomplish something very much desired by European policy-makers which they themselves have been unable, or unwilling, to do.

Although the pouring of American capital into Western Europe since World War II has been of great importance in the rebuilding and growth of the European economy, much concern has been expressed by Europeans over the size and strategic importance of the American investment there.[84] A substantial portion of this investment has arisen through acquisitions.[85] European authorities might have impeded this

[83] See note 67 *supra*.

[84] See, *e.g.*, LAYTON, TRANS-ATLANTIC INVESTMENTS (1966); SERVAN-SCHREIBER, THE AMERICAN CHALLENGE (English ed. 1968); McMILLAN & HARRIS, THE AMERICAN TAKE-OVER OF BRITAIN (1968).

Professor de Jong has calculated that direct U.S. investments in EEC countries in 1965 amounted to 5.9% of total gross investments in fixed assets of industrial establishments in the EEC, as compared with 3.5% in 1958; *Hearings, supra* note 72, at 3624, 3822 (App. Table 4); see *id.* at 3627-28 for description of arguments in the "drive for size" (which he criticizes) based on comparisons with the size of American firms.

A study by Charles M. Steinberg, American Industrial Concentration and Acquisition in Western Europe and the Prospect of Prosecution under the Rome Treaty (1967) (unpublished manuscript submitted in the Senior Research Program of Northwestern University School of Law; on deposit in the Law School Library) developed statistics from various sources showing that American-owned firms in 1964 accounted for 12% of total Western European production of non-electrical machinery, 10% of electrical machinery, 8% of chemicals and 12% of transportation equipment (aircraft, automobiles, boats, and trailers); *id.* at 29 *et seq.* In 1968, a newspaper story asserted that in automobiles, American producers controlled 15% of French, 30% of German, and almost 50% of British production; N.Y. Times, Oct. 1, 1968, at 61.

[85] According to the FTC, 16% of the direct investment transactions in Western Europe by U.S. firms from Jan. 1, 1958 to Jan. 31, 1966 were by means of acquisitions; *Hearings, supra* note 43, at 644. In 1966 and 1967, 19.5% and 17%

development; France at times has delayed American acquisitions through controls exercised at the level of administrative discretion. But these countries, including France, have largely refrained from halting American acquisitions. Also, the Commission resisted attempts to induce it to promote a policy of discouraging American acquisition,[86] until its 1969 statement in the Westinghouse matter discussed below.

Two problems arise with any policy of European anti-merger activity aimed at Americans. One is that interference with American acquisitions without corresponding interference with other forms of entry may be damaging to domestic European enterprises and investors if, as a result of anti-merger rules, the American firms decide—as they sometimes might—to enter without an acquisition through internal expansion. The other is that it is difficult for forward-looking European statesmen to adopt measures designed to discriminate against investors from other nations, particularly the most friendly nations. To work against American take-overs, the law would have to be discriminatory; a non-discriminatory anti-merger law, applicable to European as well as American firms, would stand in the way of the very integration of European firms which Common Market policies strongly wish to encourage.

The result heretofore has been a vacuum into which merger activity could easily flow. The trouble for European policymakers has been that, while American firms have quickly taken advantage of the opportunities thus afforded, European firms—especially firms of different nationality—have been notably slow to move in this direction for a variety of reasons.

---

respectively of the increases in value of the total U.S. investment in Europe were accounted for by acquisitions; see Lederer and Cutler, *International Investments of the United States in 1966,* 47 SURVEY OF CURRENT BUSINESS No. 9, at 39, 47-49 (1967); Nelson and Cutler, *The International Investment Position of the United States in 1967,* 48 SURVEY OF CURRENT BUSINESS No. 10, at 19, 28 (Table 8) (1968).

See Günther, in *Hearings, supra* note 77, at 3477 for a list of important U.S.-German mergers.

[86] For discussion, see testimony of Professor Houssiaux, in *Hearings, supra* note 77, at 3606-08. Also see Anthony J. Leitner, the Impact of the Challenge of American Direct Investment in the Common Market on Developing Community Corporate Law (1969) (unpublished manuscript submitted in the Senior Research Program of Northwestern University School of Law; on deposit in the Law School Library).

In October of 1969 the Commission, in replying to a question from a member of the European Parliament, changed its stance. The question, by Mr. Glinne of Belgium, asked for the Commission's attitude toward an announced plan of the American company, Westinghouse, to acquire control of several electrical equipment companies in different Common Market nations. The Commission replied that, while direct foreign investments make an important contribution to the Common Market, they can be "undesirable" in some cases for reasons of Community industrial or competition policy. "In the present case," it said, "we would be justified in asking whether an interpenetration of European firms, which would also help to overcome the present separation of the national markets and would permit real competition on the market under consideration, would not be preferable to a re-organization of the heavy electrical equipment sector under American aegis."[87]

Having thus stated the issue, however, the Commission backed away and said that it was up to the national governments to take the measures necessary to deal with the root difficulties raised by such an investment, and it urged collaboration to that end among the Member States. It promised that it will contribute if its intervention is requested, and that "it will see that competition within the Common Market is not distorted on the market under consideration." But it did not expressly mention Articles 85 or 86 or even state that it was conducting an investigation. Having renounced in the Concentration Memorandum most of its potential legal power to deal with such a situation, it was forced to adopt a largely hortatory role—with only a veiled reminder of its small retained powers to attack those probably rare acquisitions which constitute an

[87]EC Commission Response to Written Question No. 156/69, Oct. 1, 1969; Agence Europe, Oct. 10, 1969; E.C.J.O. No. C 129/1, Oct. 10, 1969; CCH COMM. MKT. REP. ¶9327. The Westinghouse plans called for acquisition of holdings of Baron Edouard-Francois Empain of 52% of the stock of the Belgian electrical equipment company, A.C.E.C., and 61% of the stock of the French company, Jeumont-Schneider; also to be acquired, according to the Written Question, were two other French firms (Merlin-Gérin and Alsthom) and two Italian firms (Marelli and Tossi). See N.Y. Times, Oct. 16, 1969, at 67, and Nov. 9, 1969, §3, at 1, 13.

The Commission has published an economic study of the electronics industry of the Common Market and of American investment therein: L'INDUSTRIE ELECTRONIQUE DES PAYS DE LA COMMUNAUTE ET LES INVESTISSE-MENTS AMERICAINS, Etudes, Serie Industrie No. 1 (1969); see CCH COMM. MKT. REP. ¶9326.

abuse of dominant power,[88] and to enjoin restrictive agreements, if any, which might exist among the parties after the merger.

Under these circumstances, the application of American anti-merger law to some acquisitions by American firms, while superficially conflicting with European pro-merger policies, might often be quite consistent with the underlying reasons for those policies. Increased anti-merger activity abroad by American authorities could help to relieve European authorities of a very difficult dilemma.

In summary, in the merger field, the kind of analysis made concerning the dimensions and seriousness of conflict depends upon whether the question is approached from the point of view of private firms or from the point of view of governments. To the former, the legal conflict will invariably appear to be prohibitive in nature. To the latter, application of American law to all-European mergers will produce great conflict if the firms are not manufacturing or distributing in the United States; and even if they are, some problems may arise. On the other hand, application of American law to prevent American take-over of European firms is likely to be viewed with official approval. Use of American law to prevent European take-over of American firms, however, being contrary to the practice heretofore followed by the Europeans, may continue to be met with disfavor.

There appears to be very little likelihood that European laws will evolve an anti-merger approach in the near future which will significantly reduce the great gap between the American and the European policies. Nor is American anti-merger law likely to go into a retreat; on the

[88] In response, on July 25, 1968, to Written Question No. 93/68 by M. Armengaud, the Commission stated that it was investigating the situation raised by reports (in Agence Europe, April 10, 1968) of: an acquisition by an American automotive parts company, TRW, Inc., of a German company, Friedrich Goetze A.G., said to occupy a "preponderant" position in manufacture of pistons and other parts; another acquisition by TRW in the same sector; an acquisition by International Telephone & Telegraph Corp. of control of the largest German manufacturer of brakes, Alfred Teves; and an acquisition by Borg-Warner Corp. of control of a German clutch firm, Rollkupplungs-GmbH.

Dr. Markert, *supra* note 72, at 51, indicates that up to the time of his article, the Commission had initiated only one actual case against a merger under Article 86, *viz.* the attempted takeover of one French flat glass company, Compagnie de Saint-Gobain, by another, Boussoie-Souchon-Neuvesel—a merger which would have created a monopoly in the German market and a dominant position in the whole Common Market; the takeover bid failed, however.

contrary, it gives every indication of continuing to increase in severity and scope. The merger field must therefore be counted as an important potential source of certain kinds of conflict.

III. CORPORATE JOINT VENTURES

Discussion of joint ventures here is limited to those in which a separate corporation is formed to conduct joint operations for two or more enterprises which own the joint venture company. Most other joint arrangements not involving the establishment of a separate enterprise fall under the heading of horizontal or marketing arrangements, discussed elsewhere in this chapter.

Antitrust legal problems connected with corporate joint ventures are of two different types: (a) those involving effects on competition which result from the *formation* of the joint venture; and (b) those involving competitive consequences of agreements and relationships among the parties as to the *operations* of the joint venture company and of its owners. Applicable laws bearing on these two types are discussed separately below, followed by an analysis of conflict problems presented.

A. Formation of Joint Ventures

1. AMERICAN LAW

In general, American law tests the formation of a joint venture company as to whether the act of forming it eliminates actual or potential competition between the founding firms. Section 7 of the Clayton Act is the primary source of legal control for domestic corporate joint ventures.[89] The Sherman Act also applies, however, and for reasons

---

[89] In United States v. Penn-Olin Chem. Co., 378 U.S. 158 (1964), the Supreme Court held that the issuance to the corporate joint venturers of the stock of a joint venture company formed by them to manufacture and sell sodium chlorate in the southeastern part of the United States constituted a stock acquisition within the scope of Section 7 of the Clayton Act. See generally: Pitofsky, *Joint Ventures under the Antitrust Laws: Some Reflections on the Significance of* Penn-Olin, 82 HARV. L. REV. 1007 (1969); Mead, *Competitive Significance of Joint Ventures,* 12 ANTITRUST BULL. 819 (1967); Berghoff, *Antitrust Aspects of Joint Ventures,* 9 ANTITRUST BULL. 231 (1964); Backman, *Joint Ventures and the Antitrust Laws,* 40 N.Y.U.L. REV. 651 (1965); Backman, Bernstein & Gesell, *Panel, Joint Ventures*

already stated as to mergers may be the only statute which might reach some joint ventures formed to operate in foreign markets.

If the founding firms have been competing with each other as to the same product and geographic market for which the joint venture is formed, the creation of the joint venture will in all probability be treated as adversely affecting that competition for antitrust purposes.[90]

If the firms have not previously been competing, the situation must still be examined to determine whether formation of the joint venture will eliminate "potential competition" as that term has been interpreted in the cases. If, but for the joint venture, both firms probably would have entered the relevant market separately, potential competition between them will be considered to have been eliminated.[91] Moreover, the Supreme Court in *Penn-Olin* held that potential competition would also be adversely affected under Section 7 of the Clayton Act if only one of the joint venturers probably would have entered alone, provided the other would have remained "at the edge of the market, continually threatening to enter,"[92] *i.e.*, as a "significant potential competitor."[93]

---

in the Light of Recent Antitrust Developments, 10 ANTITRUST BULL. 7, 25, 31 (1965); Taubman, *Pennsalt and Entertainment Pepper,* 9 ANTITRUST BULL. 813 (1964).

[90]This is probably subject to the defense developed in merger cases that the joint venture was necessary to prevent one of the firms from failing. The "failing company" defense was given an extremely narrow interpretation by the Supreme Court in Citizen Publishing Co. v. United States, 394 U.S. 131, 136-38 (1969): it must be shown that the allegedly failing firm faced the "grave probability" of failure, that there was no other available purchaser (or joint venturer) and that the prospects of saving the firm through corporate reorganization were "dim or non-existent."

[91]United States v. Penn-Olin Chem. Co., 217 F.Supp. 110, 130 (D. Del. 1963), *rev'd on other grounds,* 378 U.S. 158 (1964), *judgment for defendants on remand,* 246 F.Supp. 917 (D. Del. 1965), *aff'd per curiam,* 389 U.S. 308 (1967).

[92]378 U.S. at 173.

[93]*Id.* at 176. On remand, the trial court found that there was no "reasonable probability" that either firm acting alone would have entered into manufacturing of this product in the southeastern part of the United States; 246 F.Supp. 917, 928, 934.

For discussion of types of situations which may be considered to involve "potential competition" for antitrust purposes, and of problems of proof, see writings, *supra* note 89; also Turner, *Conglomerate Mergers and Section 7 of the Clayton Act,* 78 HARV. L. REV. 1313 (1965); BOCK, MERGERS AND MARKETS: 7 (1969); *cf.* Rahl, *Applicability of the Clayton Act to Potential Competition,* 12 A.B.A. ANTITRUST SECTION REP. 128 (1958).

Application of these principles to international situations would presumably be along the following lines. If the joint venture company is formed to operate in the United States in domestic or import commerce, it will be approached in the same way as the joint venture in the *Penn-Olin* case. Thus, if two firms, one or both of which is foreign, are considering entry into a given field in a given market in the United States through a joint venture for this purpose, they must face the possibility that the venture may be attacked if there is evidence that one would probably have entered alone with the other remaining a significant potential entrant.

For example, in the *Mobay* case, Bayer, a German chemical firm, entered the American market as a producer of isocyanate by formation in 1954 of a joint venture with Monsanto, an American firm.[94] There was evidence that Bayer did not wish or intend to enter into production in the United States without the aid of an American partner.[95] But the Justice Department in 1964 (two months before the Supreme Court opinion in the *Penn-Olin* case) attacked the formation of the joint venture under both the Sherman Act and Section 7. Had the case gone to trial, the Government would have relied upon evidence that Bayer had approached other American chemical firms but that they had declined, giving the antitrust laws as a reason. The Government also claimed evidence that Bayer had abandoned its previously substantial exports to the United States because of the joint venture; that Monsanto had previously planned to enter into major isocyanate production alone; and that Monsanto's abandonment of this plan in favor of the joint venture made it an especially attractive partner for Bayer.[96] A consent decree on the eve of trial forced the sale of Monsanto's interest to Bayer.[97] A Bayer attorney has charged that because of the difficulty foreign manufacturers have in entering into production in the United States, the harsh attitude of the Department of Justice toward joint ventures is

[94] United States v. Monsanto Co., Civ. No. 64-342 (W.D. Pa.), complaint filed April 13, 1964; consent decree entered, March 20, 1967, 1967 Trade Cas. ¶ 72,001.

[95] Bayer Pre-Trial Narrative Statement, filed Feb. 7, 1967. In United States v. E.I. duPont de Nemours & Co., 118 F.Supp. 41,219 (D. Del. 1953), *aff'd*, 351 U.S. 377 (1956), the court sustained a joint venture in the United States between duPont and a French cellophane producer, where duPont lacked the ability to enter the field alone.

[96] Plaintiff's Pretrial Statement of Fact, dated Nov. 30, 1966.

[97] Note 94 *supra*.

calculated to discourage entry by foreign firms.[98] On the other hand, the Government noted that Mobay was the leading firm in a very tightly concentrated industry (Mobay and its leading competitor accounted for 60% or more of sales). Thus, the Government undoubtedly regarded the case as an important step toward achieving a more competitive structure in a rapidly growing industry.[99]

If the joint venture is formed purely for export purposes, some difficulty might attend application of Section 7 of the Clayton Act, but the Sherman Act unquestionably would be applicable, although possibly with different standards.

How will American law operate as to joint venture formation for manufacture abroad? A large number of such joint ventures have been formed by American companies in Europe, usually with a European partner.[100] None of these seem to have been attacked because of elimination of competition inherent in the formation of the joint venture.[101] On the other hand, they cannot automatically be assumed to

---

[98]Unpublished paper by Dr. Dieter Schaub, Assistant General Counsel of Bayer-Leverkusen, at Washington Conference on Trans-Atlantic Investment and the Balance of Payments, sponsored by The Institute for International and Foreign Trade Law, Georgetown Univ., Sept 27, 1968.

[99]Plaintiff's Pretrial Statement of Fact, note 96 *supra.* On April 15, 1964, two days after the complaint in the *Mobay* case, the Government attacked the proposed acquisition of General Foam Corp., a large isocyanate customer, by Allied Chemical Corp., a competitor of Mobay; a consent decree enjoining the acquisition was entered on Jan. 7, 1965; United States v. Allied Chem. Corp., Civil Action No. 64-Civ-1175 (S.D.N.Y.), 1964 Trade Cas. ¶71,311.

[100]FTC figures indicate that 584 direct investment transactions by U.S. firms in Western Europe between Jan. 1, 1958 and Jan. 31, 1966 took the form of joint ventures, constituting 18% of all types of direct investment. 108 joint ventures constituted 28% of the direct investments in Western Europe made by the 50 largest U.S. manufacturing firms in the above period. *Hearings, supra* note 43, at 644-45.

On trans-national and foreign joint ventures generally, see Donovan, *Antitrust Considerations, supra* note 71; Scott and Yablonski, *supra* note 71; Meek & Feltham, *Foreign Sales, Distribution, Licensing and Joint Venture Agreements,* 17 DE PAUL L. REV. 46 (1967); Sproul, *United States Antitrust Laws and Foreign Joint Ventures,* 54 A.B.A.J. 889 (1968); Landon, *Franco-American Joint Ventures in France: Some Problems and Solutions,* 7 HARV. INT'L L. CLUB J. 238 (1966).

[101]*Cf.* discussion of the *Minnesota Mining* case, *infra.* In United States v. Imperial Chem. Indus., Ltd., 100 F.Supp. 504, 557 (S.D.N.Y. 1951), the court held illegal under the Sherman Act the formation by the American and British defendant firms of foreign joint manufacturing enterprises, where the purpose was shown to be to

be beyond the scope of American antitrust law. Just as with mergers, each joint venture must be examined on its facts to determine its effect on competition and its relationship to American commerce.[102]

For example, a joint manufacturing venture established in Europe between an American firm and a European firm would eliminate competition between the two in the American import and domestic markets if the joint venture company were to supply American demand which had previously been supplied by domestic production of the American parent and by exports to the United States by the European parent. The legal situation would be similar to that of the *Mobay* case discussed above. The fact that the plant would be located in Europe instead of in the United States could have important practical effects, but it would not seem to affect the legal analysis. Even if both founders were European, the theoretical analysis would not be altered, except to add the additional question of intent.

If the only effect of forming a joint venture in Europe were an impact on American export trade, however, the application and requirements of American antitrust law would be somewhat more debatable. Suppose that an American firm has been exporting a product to Europe and selling there in competition with a European manufacturer. If these two firms form a joint manufacturing venture abroad with the result that the American firm stops exporting the particular product, an effect on American export trade obviously occurs. The question of whether a sufficient effect on competition is present, however, depends first upon what statute applies. A competitive effect "within a section" of the United States under Section 7 could be considered to be present if the theory is accepted that the competition eliminated was carried on in part where the American firm's U.S. facilities were located. As has been pointed out previously, there is no present case support for this theory.[103]

---

restrain competition. In Phillips Petroleum Co., FTC Dkt. No. C-1088, CCH TRADE REG. REP. ¶ 17,640 (1965-67 Trfr. Binder), the FTC issued a consent order under Section 5 of the FTC Act and Section 7 of the Clayton Act dissolving four joint ventures between Phillips and National Distillers & Chemical Corp., including a foreign joint venture; as to each joint venture company, one of the parties was required to sell its interest to the other; the foreign joint venture, the legal theory of attacking which is not made clear in the report, was a polyethylene plant in Belgium.

[102] See generally Scott & Yablonski, *supra* note 71; Donovan, *Antitrust Considerations, supra* note 71, at 282-302.

[103] See Chapter 2, text at note 3.

Under the Sherman Act, the effect on competition in the export line of commerce would clearly be cognizable. But it is not so clear how the relevant market would be defined for purposes of determining the extent of the competitive effect. In the example given, the relevant market might be defined by: (a) sales of the particular product by U.S.-based firms in export to buyers in the area now to be served by the joint venture; (b) sales by all sellers wherever located (U.S. and foreign) to such buyers; or (c) sales by U.S.-based firms in export to all buyers wherever located. There is no case law on this subject. Professor Brewster suggested that definition "(c)" might be appropriate,[104] and perhaps it is, on the theory that it is largely a matter of indifference to sellers where their exports go. Such a definition would be unacceptable in a domestic case, because the antitrust laws are as concerned with protection of buyers as they are with protection of sellers. On this basis, definition "(b)" would be appropriate. An argument doubtless could be made for definition "(a)" on the ground that it is more realistic than "(c)" and that it properly focuses on United States sellers.

Many American joint ventures abroad probably may be regarded as having no significant anti-competitive effect under any theory, however the market is defined, because they represent entry into foreign markets in which the American firm was not previously competing either by export or by production abroad. The only doubt in this situation is raised by the potential competition theory—if the American firm would have entered the foreign market alone but for the joint venture, with the other party also in the market, *Penn-Olin* of course raises the possibility of American legal attack.

2. EUROPEAN LAWS

The European legal approach to corporate joint venture formation is generally the same as already described for mergers and acquisitions. Neither the Rome Treaty provisions nor the national laws interfere with the formation of a joint venture enterprise in and of itself, as distinguished from problems which may arise in the operation of the joint venture in the form of restrictive operating agreements, or abuse of a dominant position.[105]

[104] BREWSTER, ANTITRUST AND AMERICAN BUSINESS ABROAD 85 (1958).
[105] See EEC Commission Memorandum, *supra* note 72, at 27. On the national laws, see BUSINESS REGULATION IN THE COMMON MARKET NATIONS, vol.

In the European Coal and Steel Community, on the other hand, clearance would be required for formation of a manufacturing or wholesaling joint venture operating within the Common Market.[106]

B. Agreements Concerning Joint Venture Operations

In the operating relationships of the parties to a joint venture, competition may be restricted by horizontal agreements which (1) limit competition between the founders, (2) restrain the freedom of one or more of the founders to compete with the joint venture company, or (3) restrain the freedom of the latter to compete with one or more of the founders. Vertical agreements between a founder and the joint venture company may also present problems.

1. AMERICAN LAW

In general, American law applies to such agreements as if they were made by completely independent parties. In the *Timken* case, the Court rejected an argument that the fact of a joint venture should make a division-of-territory agreement among a founding firm and two joint venture companies reasonable, stating that "common ownership or control of the contracting corporations does not liberate them from the impact of the antitrust laws."[107]

Obviously, the Sherman Act applies with full force to arrangements between founding firms to restrict their competition with each other. The mere use of a corporate joint venture device as part of such an agreement would not alter its essential nature.

More doubt could exist as to the status of agreements between founding firms not to compete with the joint venture company.

1, *supra* note 23, at 140 (Belgium) and at 429 (Netherlands); vol. 2, *supra* note 15, at 266 (France) and at 530 (Italy); vol. 3, *supra* note 12, at 299 (West Germany). In France, in order to gain some protection from business decisions and foreign laws which do not conform to French policy, there has been "pressure on foreign investors, particularly American, to enter into joint ventures with French partners rather than form wholly owned subsidiaries;" vol. 2, *supra*, at 266.

[106] See Chapter 2, text at note 126 *et seq.*

[107] Timken Roller Bearing Co. v. United States, 341 U.S. 593 (1951); the American Timken company formed a joint venture with a British individual, controlling 54% of British Timken and 100% of French Timken. The Court held that the existence of these joint venture arrangements would not justify an agreement among the three Timken companies not to compete in each other's territory; *id.* at 597-98.

Something can be said for the reasonableness of an agreement by one founding firm that it will not jeopardize the other founding firm's investment in this way. For example, suppose that an American manufacturer which has been exporting to the Common Market forms a joint venture company with a European company to manufacture the product in Europe. Under these circumstances, it would be natural for the European company to ask for the American company's agreement that it will not export to customers in the market area of the joint venture company; indeed, the American firm may entertain a wish to restrict the European party in the same way. In the absence of antitrust laws, a mutual agreement of this kind—ancillary to the main agreement to form the joint venture—would probably come into being in most such cases.

Such an agreement to restrain the American firm, however, on its face restricts competition in American exports and would be subject to the Sherman Act. An agreement by the European firm with the American firm that the former would not compete with the joint venture might not come within the Sherman Act if independently made, but if it were viewed as the inducement for a reciprocal restraint of the American firm, it too probably would fall under the Act. In the *Minnesota Mining* case, competing American firms which together owned foreign joint manufacturing venture companies were held to have engaged in an illegal combination when it was found that their export association refrained from export competition with the joint ventures.[108] By agreement among the firms, exports were handled exclusively through a Webb-Pomerene association. The latter association followed the policy of refraining from selling in areas where it was more profitable for the defendants to make sales from the jointly-owned plants. The court indicated that, standing alone, the agreement to export only through the association would be within the statutory exemption, but that the agreement became unlawful when combined with the export association's restrictive export policy. That policy had the same effect as an outright agreement by defendants to restrict their exports, and this was held to place the defendants' agreement outside the scope of the exemption.[109]

[108] United States v. Minnesota Mining & Mfg. Co., 92 F.Supp. 947 (D. Mass. 1950). See Chapter 2, text at note 44 *et seq.*

[109] 92 F.Supp. at 965. For general discussion of the Webb-Pomerene exemption, see text *supra* at note 44.

Would it make a difference if only one founding firm agrees with the joint venture company not to compete with it, and makes no restrictive agreement with the other founding firm? The *Timken* case probably disposes of such agreements. American Timken entered into a joint venture with a British individual pursuant to which control of two foreign joint venture companies was exercised—British Timken and French Timken. The three companies allocated territory among themselves, and the Court held this allocation to be illegal,[110] thus condemning an arrangement in which only one founder of the joint ventures—American Timken—restrained its own freedom to compete with the joint venture companies.

A case for legality might perhaps be made for an agreement which only restricts the joint venture company's freedom to compete with one or more of its founders. Such an agreement may fit into the traditional category of ancillary restraints which recognize the right of a grantor, lender or licensor to obtain assurance from the one to whom he transfers valuable property that the latter will not use the assets in competition with him.[111] The *Timken* case did not discuss this question explicitly. By implication, it may have held that investment in a joint venture does not in itself entitle the investor to require the joint venture company to refrain from competing. But the facts were complicated by the presence of two joint venture firms which were restricted as to competition with each other, and by the restraint placed upon the founder as well. A simple situation, limited to restriction of the joint venture company's competition with one or more of its founders, remains to be considered by the Court.

The additional fact of licensing of a trademark or other industrial property right might in some circumstances provide a separate foundation for a restriction on the joint venture licensee. American Timken had licensed the trademark TIMKEN to the joint venture companies. Its argument that the territorial restraints were reasonable because ancillary to proper treatment of the trademarks was rejected by the Court—but

---

[110]*Supra* note 107.

[111] See Bork, *Ancillary Restraints and the Sherman Act,* 15 A.B.A. ANTITRUST SECTION REP. 211 (1959); Bork, Let's Make Per Se Reasonable, Proceedings of 6th Ann. Corp. Couns. Instit., Northwestern Univ. School of Law, Oct. 1967, at 28, 41. The status of the "ancillary restraints" doctrine under the Sherman Act is uncertain; in United States v. Sealy, Inc., 388 U.S. 350 (1967), the Court brushed aside an argument that price fixing and territorial restraints attached to trademark licensing should be justifiable on this basis, but its rationale was not clear.

not on the ground that such an argument is inadmissible. Rather, the Court relied on the lower court's finding that the trademark provisions were incidental to "the central purpose of allocating trade territories," thus holding that the restraints were not ancillary. The Court also found that the restraints applied to goods which did not bear the trademark. The possibility remains that a truly ancillary territorial restriction attached to a trademark license, or to a transfer of some other valuable right, might escape condemnation.[112]

Vertical agreements, such as requirements contracts, exclusive distribution agreements and resale price agreements, between a founder and the joint venture company present special problems of analysis. If the joint venture company is viewed as analogous either to a wholly-owned subsidiary, or to an entirely independent company, the agreement may be given traditional vertical treatment under American law (see the next section for discussion). Neither analogy is adequate, however. An agreement by one founding company with its joint venture company cannot ignore the fact that the other founding firm also has an interest in the joint venture. To be safe, the agreement must therefore be tested to see how it would fare if it were made directly between the two joint venturers. Its legal nature will then be determined by the particular relationship between them—if the relationship is actually or potentially a competitive one, the agreement should receive horizontal treatment; if not, it may be treated as vertical.

2. EUROPEAN LAWS

In its Concentration Memorandum, the EEC Commission carefully pointed out that agreements which survive joint venture formation are subject to Common Market antitrust rules:

> If, after the concentration process, several independent enterprises continue to exist (e.g., in the case of joint ventures), it will be necessary to examine carefully whether, apart from changes in ownership, the participating enterprises did not enter into agreements or concerted practices within the meaning of Article 85, paragraph 1.[113]

(Also, of course, Article 86 may apply to a joint venture which has, and abuses, a dominant market position.)

---

[112] *Cf.* United States v. Sealy, Inc., 388 U.S. 350 (1967). See discussion in Chapter 5.

[113] EEC Commission Memorandum, *supra* note 72, at 27.

It is not clear, however, how vigorously the prohibitions of Article 85 will be applied to restrictive agreements concerning joint venture operations. While the Commission has not ruled on a case presenting facts similar to those of the *Timken* case, it may be of some significance that, in the *Christiani & Nielsen* case, it gave negative clearance to a division-of-territory agreement between a parent corporation and its subsidiaries in different Common Market countries.[114] The Commission rejected mere "separate legal personality" as a test for whether competition could be restricted by the agreement in the Treaty sense, and instead put the question as "whether it is possible for the subsidiary to take an economic measure independently of the parent company." It found that the subsidiaries were established "for reasons of management," and that the agreement was "only a division of labor within the same economic entity." Accordingly, competition within the family group of corporations was not to be expected, and the agreement therefore did not violate Article 85(1).

There is, of course, a major difference between a joint venture corporation owned by two independent companies, and the wholly-owned subsidiary of a single parent. Antitrust policy may reasonably expect and seek to guard competition between the founding firms of a joint venture. But it is probably not reasonable to expect competition between a founding firm and the joint venture company; indeed, the assumption of *Penn-Olin* is that firms which found a joint venture for a given market will not compete independently in that market. It is thus possible that the Commission will build upon the *Christiani & Nielsen* decision to permit agreement by the founding firms not to compete with the joint venture firm, as well as to permit a reciprocal agreement not to compete by the latter. The contrary doctrine of the *Timken* case is compatible with equally contrary American doctrines regarding parent-subsidiary conspiracy.[115]

The Commission's Notice on permissible cooperation among enterprises in the Common Market may be examined for further clues as to lines of future development in the joint venture area. In this Notice, it will be recalled, the Commission stated that it wishes to encourage cooperation among small and medium-sized enterprises, "where such

---

[114] Christiani & Nielsen N.V., June 18, 1969, CCH COMM. MKT. REP. ¶9308.

[115] See Rahl, *Conspiracy and the Anti-trust Laws,* 44 ILL. L. REV. 743, 762 (1950); ATTY. GEN. NAT. COMM. ANTITRUST REP. 30-36.

co-operation enables them to work more rationally and increase their productivity and competitiveness on a larger market," and where there is no "appreciable restraint" of competition.[116] Even some kinds of cooperation among large enterprises, it said, may be economically justifiable without raising antitrust problems. Specifically, the Commission listed eight broad categories of joint activities which it considers will not "restrict competition" within the meaning of Article 85(1).[117]

None of the specified activities consist of formation of a separate joint venture company coupled with restrictive agreements of the kind discussed above.[118] On the other hand, some of them come close. One is joint research and development work; as to this, the Commission says that for "determining the compatibility of the agreement with the rules of competition, it does not matter what legal form the common research and development work takes." Thus, a joint venture research and development corporation could be formed. The restrictive agreement most likely to arise in such a case would be an agreement that the joint venture will furnish the results of its work only to the founders. The Commission does not directly state that this would be approved, but it indicates that it would be acceptable to have "arrangements binding the enterprises to grant licenses to third parties only by common agreement or by majority decision."[119] It would also be acceptable to have an agreement whereby participating firms will share in the results "in proportion to their participation." But the firms may not restrict their own research activity or agree to manufacture only products developed jointly.[120]

Another approved activity is the joint use of production facilities and

[116]EEC Commission Notice concerning agreements, decisions and concerted practices in co-operation between enterprises, July 23, 1968, CCH COMM. MKT. REP. ¶9248, at 8519, 8520; see Chapter 2, note 105 and text.

[117]*Id.* The categories included certain arrangements for: exchange of market information; cooperation in accounting, credit guarantees, debt-collection and business or tax consulting services; joint research and development; joint use of production facilities and storing and transport equipment; working partnerships for common execution of orders; joint selling and joint after-sales and repair service; use of a common-quality label; and joint advertising. Various conditions, qualifications and limitations are built into the Notice.

[118]See list, *supra.*

[119]EEC Commission Notice, *supra* note 116, at 8522.

[120]*Id.*

of storage and transport equipment. The permissible activity, according to the Commission, is confined to "organizational and technical arrangements for the use of the facilities."[121] There "may be" a restraint of competition, it says, if the firms do not bear the costs themselves, "or if agreements are concluded or concerted practices applied regarding joint production or the sharing out of production or the establishment or running of a joint enterprise."[122] This ambiguous statement perhaps is intended to disapprove of agreements to limit production, or to allocate it in the form of percentages ("sharing out"?). The phrase, "running of a joint enterprise," if taken literally would preclude a joint manufacturing enterprise entirely. It obviously is not intended to mean that, and instead probably was inserted to indicate that agreements concerning the operation of joint venture companies present sufficient opportunities for restraint of competition that the Notice cannot approve them as a class.

A third category of permissible activity which comes very close to that of corporate joint venture activity is that of agreements "having as their sole object the setting up of working partnerships for the common execution of orders, where the participating enterprises do not compete with each other in the work to be done or where each of them by itself is unable to execute the orders."[123] This description seems tailor-made to fit the kind of consortia found in the construction and engineering industries. The language avoids reference to joint venture companies, while permitting "working partnerships." Perhaps the explanation for this distinction is that the formation of a joint venture corporation is a transaction which so clearly—to the Commission—does not come within Article 85 that it need not be mentioned here (although it seems to have been mentioned in the preceding paragraph). Contrariwise, a partnership—depending upon its particular legal nature in the different Member States—has the elements of a loose association to which Article 85(1) might apply, and hence there is need to discuss it.

In another category, the Notice treads on the treacherous ground of approval of joint selling agencies. Such arrangements among non-competitors are said to be outside Article 85(1), because they "cannot restrict competition."[124] Even where competitors are concerned, the

---

[121] *Id.*

[122] *Id.*

[123] *Id.*

[124] *Id.* at 8523. This flat statement may not withstand the pressure of analysis. Some kinds of agreements between non-competitors clearly do restrain competition

Commission states that "[v]ery often joint selling by small or medium-sized enterprises . . . does not entail an appreciable restraint of competition," but that it is "impossible to establish in this Notice any general criteria or to specify what enterprises may be deemed 'small or medium-sized.' "[125] In a series of cases, the Commission has given negative clearance to arrangements for joint venture companies to act as joint selling agents for competing firms in sales within a single Member State where all of the participants are located and in sales outside the Common Market.[126] While these decisions rest largely upon the conclusion that interstate commerce is not affected (because the arrangements carefully avoid having the joint venture operate in sales to other Member States), they show a lenient disposition on the part of the Commission toward joint selling arrangements in general.

It is obviously difficult to find clear guidance in the Notice for predicting the treatment to be accorded the kinds of agreement surrounding corporate joint venture operations discussed earlier in connection with American law. Two significant factors stand out, but they have conflicting implications: (1) the Commission favors joint activities which will increase productivity and efficiency and which will "strengthen" competition; but at the same time, (2) hemmed in by the sweeping character of the prohibitions of Article 85(1), it must be quite cautious in indicating approval of restrictive agreements.[127]

More decisive, of course, is a Commission decision granting exemption under Article 85(3), for here the Commission can approve quite substantial restraints of competition. It has not yet done this in a

in the Treaty sense—*e.g.,* various vertical agreements; see also the *ACEC-Berliet* agreement discussed in the text *infra.* Suppose the non-competitor participants in a joint selling agency agreed that one of the products should not be sold separately from the other product; this would be a tying arrangement which is expressly covered by the language of Article 85(1)(e).

[125]*Id.*

[126]See Chapter 2, text at note 119.

[127]The Notice itself does not constitute a grant of negative clearance under Regulation 17, art. 2 to parties falling within its descriptions. The national courts remain competent to apply the Treaty provisions to the described arrangements until the parties request negative clearance or give notification seeking an Article 85(3) exemption. When the Commission has initiated a negative clearance proceeding, however, the national authorities may no longer act in the particular case; DERINGER, THE COMPETITION LAW OF THE EUROPEAN ECONOMIC COMMUNITY ¶2017 (1968).

corporate joint venture case. But in the *ACEC-Berliet* case,[128] the Commission granted exemption for restraints connected with a joint development arrangement which might well have been accompanied by a corporate joint venture. ACEC, a Belgian electrical equipment firm, has invented an electrical transmission which is especially useful in heavy motor coaches and patents have been applied for. It entered into an agreement with Berliet, a French motor coach manufacturer, providing for joint development of a vehicle embodying this transmission. Under the agreement, if a marketable prototype is developed, the parties are to collaborate in mass production, with ACEC supplying the transmissions and assembling them in Berliet shops. The agreement restricts ACEC's sales of the transmissions, permitting it to sell only to Berliet in France and to sell to only one coach manufacturer in each other Member State except Belgium, where it is not restricted but where there are few potential buyers. Berliet must purchase all electrical transmissions from ACEC.

The Commission said that these restrictions would enable the parties to specialize in research and to concentrate on the tasks for which each is best suited, thus improving the chances of success. The provisions for exclusive dealing between the parties were found to be justified as essential protection for the investment in research and production facilities to be made by both. And the restriction on ACEC's sales to coach manufacturers outside France was squarely based on the proposition that a limit on the number of coach manufacturers is needed in order to achieve a sufficient scale in mass production.[129] There would appear to be no reason why the same theories would not apply if the parties had formed a joint venture corporation to carry on the research and to produce the new vehicles.

This approval by the Commission of an agreement which is frankly intended to restrict entry at the manufacturing level to a small number of Common Market producers on grounds of efficiency may signify that Common Market law in the joint venture area—as well as in the restrictive agreements area generally—will develop along quite different lines from American law. Manufacturing joint ventures necessarily are formed with a given level of output in mind as a basis for efficient,

---

[128]S.A. Ateliers de Constructions Electriques de Charleroi and Société des Automobiles Berliet, July 17, 1968, CCH COMM. MKT. REP. ¶9251.

[129]*Id.* at 8534.

profitable operations. Agreement that the founding firms will not jeopardize this level by competing with the joint venture may seem every bit as reasonable under given circumstances as the restrictions on selling upheld in the *ACEC-Berliet* case. While the latter restrictions are vertical, whereas an agreement not to compete is horizontal, this would not seem material. In substance, both kinds of agreement are designed to restrict competition with the joint venture in order to preserve its market.[130]

Insofar as the national antitrust laws are concerned, a fairly clear pattern of treatment of restrictive agreements in the joint venture setting appears to have emerged only in Germany. There, in general, "only restrictive agreements among the parent enterprises themselves come within the prohibition" of Section 1 of the German law.[131] Agreements among the parents not to compete with the joint venture company have been objected to by the BKA as violations of Section 1 of the Act Against Restraints of Competition. On the other hand, the BKA has held that a joint selling company may be required by its parents not to compete with them, so long as there is no restraint on the freedom of the parents to compete with each other. This was on the theory that the restriction of the joint venture company "was an exercise of corporate rights and outside the reach of section 1."[132]

Only one case involving a joint venture seems to have come before the French Commission Technique des Ententes et des Positions Dominantes.[133] Violations of Article 59 bis of the Price Ordinance were found in a magnesium entente case, in which the parties, among other things, established "sole" joint production and distribution companies.

---

[130] In Alliance de Constructeurs Francais de Machines-Outils, July 17, 1968, CCH COMM. MKT. REP. ¶9249, the Commission gave negative clearance to a corporate joint selling agency of French machine-tool manufacturers each of whom made tools which were different from those of the others; included in the agreement was a provision that the manufacturer-shareholders would not make or sell machines which might compete with machines manufactured by another party; the Commission found that this was necessary to make the joint operation work well, and that it was unlikely under then-market conditions that the manufacturers would want to add other products.

[131] BUSINESS REGULATION IN THE COMMON MARKET NATIONS, vol. 3, *supra* note 12, at 300.

[132] *Id.*

[133] BUSINESS REGULATION IN THE COMMON MARKET NATIONS, vol. 2, *supra* note 15, at 267.

Apparently, the entente had industry control and its restrictive operating agreements were the basis for the finding of violation. In general, the lenient approach of French law toward restrictive arrangements among competitors does not seem likely to interpose frequent obstacles to routine joint venture arrangements.

In Belgium, it has been said that joint venture agreements often include an undertaking by one or both of the joint venturers to "(1) sell exclusively to the joint enterprise, (2) buy all or a substantial part of the joint company's output, (3) license to it patents and trademarks, or (4) divide the market (manufacture or distribution) with the joint enterprise."[134] Such agreements are not illegal insofar as "antitrust law" is concerned unless they constitute an abuse of economic power within the Law of May 27, 1960. Such an abuse could occur, *e.g.,* if the joint venture created a monopoly and exacted unreasonably high prices. In the absence of something approximating that situation, or of independent violation of some other law, however, it does not appear that agreements of the above kind would be disturbed.

In the Netherlands, the Economic Competition Act can apply to restrictive joint venture agreements, but there appear to be no decisions as yet, and the sanctions, if any were imposed, would ordinarily be quite mild.[135]

C. Conflict Analysis

The potential conflict situation in some respects is very much like that pertaining to mergers; in some cases, however, the problems may be more severe.

Insofar as the formation of joint ventures for operation in the United States is concerned, the *Mobay* case demonstrates that American law will apply strictly. Since the permissive climate of Europe does not always prepare European firms fully for the strong legal attack which may occur, the result may sometimes be a rude shock and a good deal of complaining. Some deterrent effect upon foreign investment in the United States may be the result, since some European firms may not wish to risk entry without reliable American partners.

---

[134] BUSINESS REGULATION IN THE COMMON MARKET NATIONS, vol. 1, *supra* note 23, at 141.

[135] BUSINESS REGULATION IN THE COMMON MARKET NATIONS, *supra* note 19, at 429-30.

It does not seem, however, that American law can be expected to discriminate in favor of American-European joint venture combinations of the *Mobay* type; to do so would discriminate *against* all-American ventures, and at the same time would confer an unfair immunity upon an American firm which could line up a European partner. Perhaps all-European joint ventures could be approached more leniently, but this would not solve the problem for European firms which think they need a domestic partner.

With respect to joint ventures formed for operation in the Common Market, a more complex and potentially very serious conflict situation exists. It is probably unlikely that American law would be applied to an all-European joint venture except under unique facts. But as indicated above, there are situations in which formation of foreign-based joint ventures with American participants may well be attacked and disrupted by American law, although no cases of this kind have as yet been filed.

If all the joint venturers are American, it may be that the conflict will not arouse European antagonisms, unless the joint venture is necessary to provide an otherwise unavailable product or service. If one of the joint venturers is European, however, the application of American law will disrupt the plans of European, as well as American, interests. If also the joint venture route has been preferred, or encouraged, by some European national or Community policy, conflict of high intensity may arise. The situation thus differs from that of mergers in that, as pointed out above, European governmental and Community policy may actually favor American antitrust prevention of American acquisitions of European firms.

Restrictive operating agreements, on the face of things, may not present quite as serious a conflict pattern. Rome Treaty law and some of the national laws often parallel American antitrust rules pertaining to the most substantial kinds of restraint. The Commission evidently intends to scrutinize with some care the arrangements which continue after formation of joint ventures.

But it is not at all clear that the Commission would disapprove of the kind of agreement struck down in the *Timken* case. Had the Rome Treaty been in effect at that time and had the parties applied to the Commission for negative clearance for an agreement that French Timken would not compete with its part-owner, American Timken, and with its sister, British Timken, it is quite possible (though at this point speculative) that the Commission would have said that such an intra-enterprise arrangement is only a sensible method of internal management, which should not be touched by antitrust law. German law seems already to have reached this conclusion, and the other European national laws can probably be counted upon to do likewise.

Even the agreement of the founding firm, American Timken, not to compete with the joint venture firms might pass the Commission unchallenged, although apparently it would not fare so well in Germany. It is not inconceivable that a horizontal *Minnesota Mining*-type agreement among otherwise competing joint venturers not to compete with their joint venture company in the Common Market would receive negative clearance. Even if it would not, its chances for an Article 85(3) exemption could be rated fairly high—if this kind of protection seems essential to assure survival of the joint enterprise in the Common Market, if it confers significant benefits on the Common Market economy, and if it and its parents do not dominate the market.

There is little basis for optimism that these areas of potential conflict will work themselves out without positive international action of some sort. Far from harmoniously growing together, American and European law and enforcement policies appear to be diverging in important respects.

IV. DISTRIBUTION AND MARKETING ARRANGEMENTS

Many domestic American antitrust proceedings have involved restraints of competition of a vertical nature in connection with various kinds of marketing and distribution contracts and arrangements. Some of these cases have dealt with the activities of foreign firms in domestic American markets.[136]

Very few vertical restraint cases have been filed, however, as to marketing by American firms in foreign markets, apparently for a number of reasons. Some marketing restraints may have discernible impact only in foreign markets, and American jurisdiction to attack them may well be lacking. As to others, the relation to American foreign commerce may be sufficient to support jurisdiction, but the restraint

---

[136] See Chapter 2, note 63; on the subject of this section generally, see Rahl, *Overseas Distribution, Franchising, and Licensing—Comparison with Domestic Techniques*, 13 ANTITRUST BULL. 193 (1968).

itself may be of equivocal, rather than obvious or per se, illegality. Or it may appear to have too little impact on American interests to warrant intervention by American enforcement agencies. American authorities presumably would be especially reluctant to move in cases where applicable foreign law makes the particular practice explicitly lawful, since foreign resentment over intervention in cases of relatively minor American interest would tend to be relatively great. While these considerations would not ordinarily deter potential private suits, the most frequent potential plaintiffs in such suits would be foreign businessmen, who may be discouraged by the necessity of suing in a distant American court, and who often might be unaware that any cause of action exists.

Consequently, the vertical distribution restraint area does not on its face appear to be one of the most important sources of conflict. Nonetheless, the discussion in Chapter 2 has shown that there are a number of vertical situations abroad in which American law might be applied; and conflict between American and foreign law in transactions in the American market is not infrequent.

It is not possible in the following pages to account for all of the various types of vertical arrangements, nor all of the possible variations in approach to such arrangements by the different sets of laws involved. Attention will be centered upon four major types of vertical problems: individual refusal to deal, compared with boycotts; resale price maintenance agreements; exclusive buying and selling arrangements; and territorial and customer restriction of dealers.

A. Refusal to Deal

1. AMERICAN LAW

Individual refusal to deal on the part of a seller or buyer in an unregulated industry remains, in and of itself, a lawful act under American antitrust law.[137] In certain particular contexts, however,

---

[137]ATTY. GEN. NAT. COMM. ANTITRUST REP. 133-34; Fulda, *Individual Refusals to Deal: When Does Single-Firm Conduct Become Vertical Restraint?* 30 LAW & CONTEMP. PROB. 590 (1965); Barber, *Refusals to Deal Under the Federal Antitrust Laws,* 103 U.PA.L. REV. 847 (1955); Halper, *Individual Refusals to Deal: Customer Selection or Dealer Protection?* 22 A.B.A. ANTITRUST SECTION REP. 49 (1963).

refusal to deal may turn into a violation. If coupled with a specific intent to exclude competition or to acquire a monopoly, it may violate the "attempt" to monopolize prohibition of Section 2 of the Sherman Act or may be an unfair method of competition under Section 5 of the Federal Trade Commission Act. If done for the purpose of coercing dealers to observe announced resale prices, it may—with few additional facts—be treated as creating an illegal combination in restraint of trade under Section 1 of the Sherman Act.[138] If accompanied by a condition that the buyer refrain from buying from a competitor of the seller, it may violate Section 3 of the Clayton Act; and if used to require the buyer to purchase one item in order to obtain another, it may constitute illegal tying under the Sherman Act. Unconnected with facts which integrate it with an independent violation, however, individual refusal to deal is still a relatively safe act. If the facts show an agreement or conspiracy among competitors to refuse to deal, however, the case will ordinarily fall within the strict American rule that "concerted refusals to deal," or boycotts, are per se illegal.[139]

2. EUROPEAN LAWS

Article 85(1) of the EEC Treaty broadly parallels Section 1 of the Sherman Act and requires agreement or its equivalent (an association decision, or a "concerted practice") in order to make out a violation.[140] Consequently, it is clear that individual refusal to deal—if unconnected with circumstances from which some sort of agreement or concert of action can be inferred—will not come within the prohibition. Since the EEC law has neither an unfair trade practices act, nor Clayton Act-type provisions, its application to individual conduct appears to be limited to situations which fall within Article 86, prohibiting abuse of a dominant market position.[141] This prohibition is narrower than Section 2 of the Sherman Act, in that the act of acquiring a dominant position (even if by

[138] See debate by Professors Dam and Pitofsky, *Is the Colgate Doctrine Dead?* 37 A.B.A. ANTITRUST L. J. 772 (1968).

[139] See citations, *supra* note 137; also, Buxbaum, *Boycotts and Restrictive Marketing Arrangements,* 64 MICH.L.REV. 671 (1966); Rahl, *Per Se Rules and Boycotts under the Sherman Act: Some Reflections on the Klor's Case,* 45 VA.L. REV. 1165 (1959); Turner, *The Definition of Agreement Under the Sherman Act: Conscious Parallelism and Refusals to Deal,* 75 HARV. L. REV. 655 (1962).

[140] DERINGER, *supra* note 127, ¶115.

[141] See JOLIET, *supra* note 62.

"specific intent" to do so) is not itself prohibited, nor is retaining and exercising it unlawful; "abuse" of an already-acquired position of dominance is the offense. Such abuse obviously may take the form of individual refusal to deal; for example, Article 86 states that such individual acts as imposition of "unfair trading terms," unequal treatment of trade partners in equivalent transactions and coerced tying practices are to be treated as abuses, thus reaching some particular forms of individual refusal.

As with American law, EEC law may be expected to apply strictly to a concerted refusal to deal or boycott on the part of competitors. No cases handled by the Commission have yet been reported which involved boycotts in their simplest form, but cartels engaging in collective exclusivity arrangements have been required to abandon that practice.[142] In these cases, a group of manufacturers and a group of distributors or dealers have entered into a reciprocal agreement under which the distributors buy only from members of the manufacturer group and the latter sell only to members of the distributor group. Such arrangements are seldom seen today in American cases, but where they have appeared they have been held illegal.[143]

The national laws, except for those of France, take an approach to individual refusal to deal which is roughly similar to that of American and EEC law, although some significant variations appear. Belgium prohibits refusal to deal only when it constitutes an abuse of economic power under the Law of May 27, 1960 or amounts to unfair competition; absence of a valid business purpose is necessary for either.[144] The Netherlands also permits individual refusal to deal for valid business reasons; under a Government order of 1964, however, vertical enforcement of resale prices in certain durable consumer goods is not permissible.[145] Luxembourg prohibits resale price maintenance by a 1965 Decree, and refusal to deal for the purpose of avoiding this

[142] See Chapter 2, note 110 (last par.).

[143] Montague & Co. v. Lowry, 193 U.S. 38 (1904), collective exclusivity among manufacturers and dealers in tiles; Standard Sanitary Mfg. Co. v. United States, 266 U.S. 20 (1912), similar as to enameled ware; NEALE, THE ANTITRUST LAWS OF THE U.S.A. 66 (1962).

[144] BUSINESS REGULATION IN THE COMMON MARKET NATIONS, vol. 1, *supra* note 23, at 138.

[145] BUSINESS REGULATION IN THE COMMON MARKET NATIONS, vol. 1, *supra* note 19, at 413-16.

prohibition is illegal.[146] In general, Germany limits its prohibitions to market-dominating enterprises, but under some circumstances refusal to sell connected with resale price maintenance may be illegal.[147] Refusal to deal is generally lawful in Italy.[148]

The great exception to this European pattern of lenient treatment of individual refusal to deal is France, where Article 37(1) of the Ordinance of June 30, 1945 makes it illegal for any trader:

> a) to refuse to satisfy to the best of his ability and upon the customary trade terms any request for the purchase of goods or the performance of services which has no abnormal character and is made in good faith. . . .[149]

There has been some uncertainty as to whether this prohibition is limited to situations in which the motivation behind a refusal to sell is to maintain prices.[150] Also, various kinds of justification are recognized.[151] The breadth and severity of the prohibition, however, make it unique among the national laws.

Insofar as collective refusals to deal are concerned, Belgian law permits them where used in defense of the "legitimate interests" of the group.[152] In the Netherlands, however, boycotts which exclude persons from access to markets have been "primary targets" of the administration of the antitrust law.[153] Under German law, a horizontal boycott falls under the prohibition of Section 1.[154] French law appears to treat

---

[146] BUSINESS REGULATION IN THE COMMON MARKET NATIONS, vol. 1, *supra* note 27, at 548.

[147] BUSINESS REGULATION IN THE COMMON MARKET NATIONS, vol. 3, *supra* note 12, at 272; Busch, *Vertical Restrictions in German Consumer Goods Industries,* 14 ANTITRUST BULL. 473, 495 (1969).

[148] BUSINESS REGULATION IN THE COMMON MARKET NATIONS, vol. 2, *supra* note 25, at 528.

[149] BUSINESS REGULATION IN THE COMMON MARKET NATIONS, vol. 2, *supra* note 15, at 232.

[150] *Id.* at 233.

[151] *Id.* at 237.

[152] BUSINESS REGULATION IN THE COMMON MARKET NATIONS, vol. 1, *supra* note 23, at 111.

[153] BUSINESS REGULATION IN THE COMMON MARKET NATIONS, vol. 1, *supra* note 19, at 367.

[154] BUSINESS REGULATION IN THE COMMON MARKET NATIONS, vol. 3, *supra* note 12, at 208; Section 26(1) deals with secondary boycotts, *id.* at 209, 394.

such boycotts fairly strictly, subject to some exceptions.[155] In Italy and Luxembourg, principles of unfair competition may apply to some boycotts, but in general they appear to be lawful.[156]

B. Resale Price Maintenance Agreements

1. AMERICAN LAW

Vertical resale price maintenance agreements between a manufacturer (or distributor) and its dealers fall within the general price-fixing rule of American law and are per se illegal in the absence of an exemption.[157] The prohibition extends not only to express contracts, but it has also been applied to invalidate price maintenance systems based upon consignment-agency relations with dealers,[158] and upon refusal to deal.[159] The McGuire Amendment exempts vertical resale price agreements from these prohibitions, as well as enforcement against nonsigners having notice, for branded commodities which are in "free and open competition with commodities of the same general class produced or distributed by others," when such agreements "are lawful as applied to intrastate transactions under any statute, law, or public policy now or hereafter in effect in any State, Territory, or the District of Columbia in

---

[155] BUSINESS REGULATION IN THE COMMON MARKET NATIONS, vol. 2, *supra* note 15, at 184.

[156] BUSINESS REGULATION IN THE COMMON MARKET NATIONS, vol. 2, *supra* note 25, at 514 (Italy), and vol. 1, *supra* note 27, at 547-48 (Luxembourg).

[157] ATTY. GEN. NAT. COMM. ANTITRUST REP. 150; Fulda, *Resale Price Maintenance,* 21 U.CHI.L. REV. 175 (1954); Weston, *Resale Price Maintenance and Market Integration: Fair Trade or Foul Play?* 22 GEO.WASH.L. REV. 658 (1954); NEALE, *supra* note 143, at 340.

[158] Simpson v. Union Oil Co., 377 U.S. 13 (1964); Rahl, *Control of an Agent's Prices: The Simpson Case—A Study in Antitrust Analysis,* 61 NW.U.L. REV. 1 (1966).

[159] The Supreme Court has not held that simple refusal to deal with dealers who do not observe announced resale prices is itself illegal; but its recent decisions have made it easy to find an illegal combination under Section 1 of the Sherman Act, if the manufacturer actively promotes compliance with his resale price program among the dealers and obtains the cooperation of distributors, United States v. Parke, Davis & Co., 362 U.S. 29 (1960); or even if he merely obtains the cooperation of another distributor to replace one who has been cut off until the latter complies, Albrecht v. Herald Co., 390 U.S. 145 (1968); see debate by Dam & Pitofsky, *supra* note 138.

which such resale is to be made, or to which the commodity is to be transported for such resale."[160]

Under this language, a foreign producer making sales in American markets may rely upon the exemption in the same manner as a domestic American producer, *i.e.*, he may enter into resale price maintenance agreements with distributors and dealers for sales in states in which such agreements are lawful as a matter of state law. For other sales, the Sherman and Federal Trade Commission Act prohibitions apply. Currently, about 38 states have valid "Fair Trade" Acts legalizing such agreements.[161] While the Fair Trade Acts also typically contain provisions requiring nonsigners to obey prices set in a valid agreement, such nonsigner control has been held unconstitutional in 22 states.[162] As a result, use of resale price maintenance in the American market requires careful adaptation to a confusing patchwork of varying laws.

Insofar as agreements applying to sales in foreign markets are concerned, while there are no cases in point, it appears that the McGuire exemption will not apply, as its reference to resale in a "State, Territory, or the District of Columbia" undoubtedly refers to American political units and not to foreign states. Legislative history of the amendment and of the predecessor Miller-Tydings Amendment shows that the exemption was originally passed because of a drive for Fair Trade legislation in the states; the idea was to enact federal "enabling" legislation to permit the states to have their own policy in this area, free from federal interference if they so desired.[163] It is not likely that Congress meant to give such discretion as to the applicability of the Sherman Act to foreign

---

[160] The McGuire Amendment of 1952, 66 Stat. 631, is found in the Federal Trade Commission Act, §5(a)(2)-(5); it applies both to the FTC Act and to the Sherman Act, and in effect supersedes the earlier Miller-Tydings Amendment of 1937, 50 Stat. 693, to Section 1 of the Sherman Act.

[161] CCH TRADE REG. REP. ¶6041.

[162] *Id.*

[163] The enacting clause of the McGuire Amendment states that the purpose of the Act is "to protect the rights of States under the United States Constitution to regulate their internal affairs and more particularly to enact statutes . . . which authorize contracts . . . prescribing minimum or stipulated prices. . . ." 66 Stat. 631-32. See citations in note 157 *supra,* and Rahl, *Fair Trade Since the McGuire Amendment,* 1953 MICHIGAN SUMMER INSTITUTE, FEDERAL ANTITRUST LAWS 188, 191.

governments. Also, when referring to foreign countries, the Sherman, Clayton and Federal Trade Commission Acts all use the expression, "foreign nations," rather than "states."[164]

2. EUROPEAN LAWS

The prohibitions of Article 85(1) apply to agreements to control resale prices.[165] The express language reaches agreements to "directly or indirectly fix buying or selling prices or other trading terms," and Article 85(1) clearly reaches vertical as well as horizontal restraints.[166] Not all resale price situations, however, will meet the effect on interstate commerce requirements of the Treaty.[167]

Despite the clear prohibition, the EEC has maintained a languid attitude toward resale price agreements, in that they are exempted from the notification requirement of Regulation 17, art. 4(2). This does not mean that they are not prohibited, but it reflects the view that they are "less of a threat" to development of the Common Market than are notifiable restraints.[168] The technical legal effect of the non-notification rule is that if at some future time a resale price agreement is granted an Article 85(3) exemption (to obtain which a notification would still be necessary), the effective date of the exemption may pre-date the date of the notification, whereas agreements falling within the general notification requirement may be exempted only prospectively from the date of notification.[169] It should also be noted that price restrictions on commercial agents are not regarded as falling within the Article 85(1)

[164] Sherman Act, §§ 1-3; Clayton Act, § 1; Federal Trade Commission Act, §4; Webb Export Trade Associations Act, §1; Wilson Tariff Act, §73 ("foreign country").

[165] DERINGER, *supra* note 127, ¶150; GRAUPNER, THE RULES OF COMPETITION IN THE EUROPEAN ECONOMIC COMMUNITY 16 (1965); LANG, THE COMMON MARKET AND THE COMMON LAW 394 (1966); WOHLFARTH-EVERLING-GLAESNER-SPRUNG, DIE EUROPÄISCHE WIRTSCHAFTSGEMEINSCHAFT, KOMMENTAR ZUM VERTRAG 244 (1960).

[166] In Italy v. EEC Council and Comm'n, CCH COMM. MKT. REP. ¶8048, 5 Comm. Mkt. L. R. 97 (1966), and in Ets. Consten and Grundig-Verkaufs-GmbH v. EEC Comm'n, CCH COMM. MKT. REP. ¶8046, 5 Comm. Mkt. L.R. 418 (1966), the Court of Justice ruled squarely that Article 85(1) applies to vertical as well as to horizontal restraints.

[167] DERINGER, *supra* note 127, ¶151.

[168] *Id.* at ¶2055.

[169] *Id.*

prohibition. In fact, one of the indicia of a true commercial agent, as distinguished from an independent merchant, is that he does not have power to determine prices.[170]

The national laws differ substantially from one another in their treatment of resale price maintenance. In France, both agreements and refusals to sell for resale price maintenance purposes are prohibited outright under Article 37 of the Price Ordinance.[171] Provision is made for some exceptions which may be granted by the Ministry of Economic Affairs, but these have been relatively small in number.[172]

In Germany on the other hand, Section 16 of the antitrust law expressly permits resale price maintenance on branded goods, provided the agreements are notified in writing to the BKA (and placed on a public register), and also provided the goods are in price competition with "similar goods" of other producers or dealers.[173] The BKA has rather broad powers under Section 17 to invalidate a given restriction if it finds that the required conditions are not met, that the resale price maintenance is "being abused," or that it is "likely, in a manner not justified by the economy in general," to increase prices, prevent lowering of prices or restrict production or distribution. Under the last paragraph of Section 17(1), the latter conditions are presumed to obtain if the fixed prices are undercut in a significant number of instances, or if the same product is offered for sale partly at prices much lower than those fixed. The BKA has applied heavy pressure under these provisions. For example, it is now established that resale price maintenance will be held to prevent lower prices in the statutory sense where prices are set on the basis of the customary high margins of specialized dealers, when at the same time a substantial portion of the particular goods are sold through low-margin distributors, such as supermarkets, department stores and discount houses.[174]

[170] EEC Commission Official Notice on Contracts for Exclusive Representation Concluded with Commercial Agents, Dec. 24, 1962, CCH COMM. MKT. REP. ¶2697; DERINGER, *supra* note 127, ¶187.

[171] BUSINESS REGULATION IN THE COMMON MARKET NATIONS, vol. 2, *supra* note 15, at 339.

[172] *Id.* at 225.

[173] BUSINESS REGULATION IN THE COMMON MARKET NATIONS, vol. 3, *supra* note 12, at 252, 387; Busch, *supra* note 147, at 475.

[174] BUSINESS REGULATION IN THE COMMON MARKET NATIONS, vol. 3, *supra* note 12, at 269; OECD ANNUAL REPORTS ON DEVELOPMENTS IN THE FIELD OF RESTRICTIVE BUSINESS PRACTICES 11 (Aug. 1969).

In Belgium, vertical resale price maintenance is generally lawful.[175] The same has been true in the Netherlands, but in 1964, the Government issued an Order nullifying enforcement of collective resale price maintenance arrangements (horizontal resale price control), and went further to nullify vertical resale price controls in certain durable consumer goods industries, including: radios, television sets and phonographs; home electrical appliances; passenger cars; photographic equipment; and phonograph records.[176] In Luxembourg, a Grand-Ducal Decree prohibits resale price maintenance except as to books, newspapers and magazines,[177] while in Italy, resale price agreements are lawful.[178]

In summary, the European Community situation on resale price maintenance is as confused as that prevailing in the United States. The Rome Treaty prohibits resale price maintenance, but the authorities are disinclined to enforce the prohibition. Two of the six Member States prohibit it (France and Luxembourg); one does so in part, but not as to all goods (the Netherlands); one expressly permits it, but subjects it to strict governmental surveillance (Germany); and two generally permit it without serious interference (Belgium and Italy).

C. Exclusive Selling and Buying Arrangements; Tying

Under this heading are included the following broad types of vertical restrictive arrangements: (1) restrictions requiring the seller to sell a given product only to a given buyer, usually in a defined territory (restrictions confining the buyer to the territory in resales are covered in the next section); (2) restrictions obligating the buyer to buy a given product only from a given seller; and (3) tying practices under which a buyer is required to purchase a given product from the seller or a third party in order to obtain another product desired from the seller.

---

[175] BUSINESS REGULATION IN THE COMMON MARKET NATIONS, vol. 1, *supra* note 23, at 128.

[176] *Id.* (Netherlands) at 404. Under an Act of June 1, 1969, these measures against resale price maintenance will expire on June 15, 1972 unless they are made permanent by further statute.

[177] *Id.* (Luxembourg) at 548.

[178] BUSINESS REGULATION IN THE COMMON MARKET NATIONS, vol. 2, *supra* note 25, at 524.

1. AMERICAN LAW

American antitrust rules differ as to these three types, ranging from virtual per se legality to per se illegality. The first—exclusive selling agreements (sometimes called "exclusive franchise," or "exclusive territory" agreements) are generally regarded as reasonable and lawful when not coupled with other more serious restraints such as price control or territorial confinement of the dealer, and in the absence of too much market power in the seller.[179]

Exclusive buying agreements, often called "exclusive dealing" in the United States and frequently taking the form of "requirements contracts," are dealt with under quite different rules. Usually, they are subject to Section 3 of the Clayton Act, which prohibits sales (for use, consumption or resale within the United States or some place within its jurisdiction) on the "condition, agreement or understanding" that the buyer will not deal with a competitor of the seller, where the effect "may be to substantially lessen competition or tend to create a monopoly in any line of commerce." Under this test of "incipient" undue restraint of competition, exclusive buying agreements are unlawful if they "foreclose" competition in a "substantial share of the line of commerce."[180] To have such foreclosure, "the opportunities for other traders to enter into or remain in that market must be significantly limited."[181] This determination is made by defining the relevant market, determining the share preempted by the exclusive contract, and then

[179] Schwing Motor Co. v. Hudson Sales Corp., 138 F.Supp. 899 (D.Md. 1956), *aff'd per curiam,* 239 F.2d 176 (4th Cir. 1956), *cert. denied,* 355 U.S. 823 (1957); Packard Motor Car Co. v. Webster Motor Car Co., 243 F.2d 418 (D.C.Cir. 1957), *cert. denied,* 355 U.S. 822 (1957); United States v. Arnold Schwinn & Co., 388 U.S. 365, 376 (1967); Pollock, *Alternative Distribution Methods After* Schwinn, 63 NW.U.L. REV. 595, 603 (1968).

[180] Standard Oil Co. of California v. United States, 337 U.S. 293, 314 (1949); Tampa Elec. Co. v. Nashville Coal Co., 365 U.S. 320, 327 (1961); Bok, *The Tampa Electric Case and the Problem of Exclusive Arrangements under the Clayton Act,* 1961 S.CT. REV. 267; W. Smith, *Vertical Arrangements in Antitrust Law: Exclusive Dealing Arrangements,* 22 A.B.A. ANTITRUST SECTION REP. 18 (1963); on agreements covering less than full requirements, see Helman, *Partial Requirements Contracts under Section Three of the Clayton Act,* 55 NW.U.L. REV. 288 (1960).

[181] Tampa Elec. Co. v. Nashville Coal Co., 365 U.S. 320, 328 (1961).

determining whether under all the circumstances this preempting eliminates a "substantial volume of competition."[182]

If the seller occupies a dominant position in the market, the contract
will be held illegal,[183] and even requirements contracts covering only a
relatively small percentage of total supply have been invalidated, where
their general use by most sellers in the industry has sealed off markets
from newcomers.[184] On the other hand, the Supreme Court has upheld a
20-year requirements contract for the purchase of coal which was found
to cover about 1% of supply in the relevant market.[185]

It is important to note that, although Section 3's scope is limited to
domestic resale situations, Section 1 of the Sherman Act may also reach
exclusive dealing agreements. Moreover, Section 5 of the Federal Trade
Commission Act may be applied to restrictive practices used in foreign
commerce.[186] The Supreme Court has held not only that the same
practices which are prohibited by the Clayton Act may be held illegal
under the FTC Act, but also that the Commission may go further and
invalidate "incipient" violations of the Clayton Act.[187] Taken literally,
this probably means that the Commission could issue orders against
exclusive buying arrangements used in foreign commerce on very slight
evidence of competitive impact; it has not availed itself of these powers,
however.

The third type listed above—tying—is treated as "per se" unlawful
under the Sherman Act, where the seller's market power in the tying
product or service enables him to impose an "appreciable restraint on
competition" in the tied product or service. The seller's advantage may
be relatively slight, and the restraint is "appreciable" if the dollar volume
of sales affected is substantial even if the market percentage is small.[188]

---

[182]*Id.* at 335.

[183]*Id.* at 334.

[184]Standard Oil Co. of California v. United States, 337 U.S. 293 (1949);
Richfield Oil Corp. v. United States, 343 U.S. 922 (1952) (per curiam); see dissenting
opinion of Justice Frankfurter in FTC v. Motion Picture Advertising Serv. Co., 344
U.S. 392, 398 (1953).

[185]Tampa Elec. Co. v. Nashville Coal Co., 365 U.S. 320 (1961).

[186]See Chapter 2, notes 5 and 9 and text.

[187]*Id.* at notes 6 and 7.

[188]Fortner Enterprises, Inc. v. United States Steel Corp., 394 U.S. 495, 501, 503
(1969) (tying of sale of prefabricated steel houses to availability of credit on
favorable terms; remanded for trial on issue of market power); *cf.* United States v.

Tying is seldom tolerated by the courts even where it is imposed in order to assure the technical quality of supplies or parts used with machines, except where it appears that a requirement that such supplies meet certain specifications is insufficient.[189] The main line of defense against a tying charge must normally be that the two products or services are physically or functionally really only one, so that tying does not exist. The tests on this issue are not fully developed.

A variation of the exclusive dealing and tying cases is represented by Federal Trade Commission proceedings under Section 5 of the FTC Act invalidating the practice of some oil companies who induce service station dealers in their products to buy tires, batteries and accessories ("TBA") from a third company which pays a commission on such purchases to the oil company. The Commission found that oil companies had coerced or exercised dominant power over the service stations, and the Supreme Court affirmed these holdings under a test similar to that used in the tying cases: *i.e.,* that the practice adversely affects competition in a "not insignificant volume of commerce."[190]

Jerrold Electronics Corp., 187 F.Supp. 545 (E.D.Pa. 1960), *aff'd per curiam,* 365 U.S. 567 (1961), allowing tying in a new industry, but holding it unlawful after industry matured. See Bodner, *The Expanded Prohibitions Against Tying Arrangements and Exclusive Dealing: The Search for a Viable Legal Alternative,* 37 A.B.A. ANTITRUST L. J. 759 (1968); Day, *Exclusive Dealing, Tying and Reciprocity—A Reappraisal,* 29 OHIO ST.L.J. 539 (1968); Stedman, *Tying Arrangements,* 22 A.B.A. ANTITRUST SECTION REP. 64 (1963); Turner, *The Validity of Tying Arrangements under the Antitrust Laws,* 72 HARV. L. REV. 50 (1958); Ferguson, *Tying Arrangements and Reciprocity: An Economic Analysis,* 30 LAW & CONTEMP. PROB. 552 (1965); Pearson, *Tying Arrangements and Antitrust Policy,* 60 NW.U.L. REV. 626 (1965); Singer, *Market Power and Tying Arrangements,* 8 ANTITRUST BULL. 653 (1963).

[189] International Business Machines Corp. v. United States, 298 U.S. 131 (1936), holding tying not permissible where specifications would suffice; *cf.* Dehydrating Process Co. v. A. O. Smith Corp., 292 F.2d 653 (1st Cir. 1961), holding tying to be justified in order to assure satisfactory operation of machinery where previous efforts at educating users had failed; also, Susser v. Carvel Corp., 332 F.2d 505 (2d Cir. 1964), *cert. dismissed,* 381 U.S. 125 (1965), upholding tying of ingredients used in franchised soft ice cream operation because of necessity of controlling quality of trademarked goods; similar decision in Carvel Corp. [1965-67 Transfer Binder], CCH TRADE REG. REP. ¶17,298 (FTC 1965).

[190] Atlantic Ref. Co. v. FTC, 381 U.S. 357 (1965); FTC v. Texaco, Inc., 393 U.S. 223 (1968).

A practice which resembles tying in some respects—*i.e.,* "reciprocity," in which one's purchases from a firm are used to promote one's sales to the same firm—is receiving increased attention from enforcement authorities.[191]

2. EUROPEAN LAWS

Under the Rome Treaty, the first two types of restrictions under discussion are treated alike—both have the benefit of the group exemption under Commission Regulation 67/67.[192] This exemption, issued in 1967 upon authorization by the Council, was designed to relieve the Commission of the overwhelming burden of ruling individually upon thousands of notifications of such agreements. The Commission stated that the agreements comply with the requirements of Article 85(3) because they: "generally result in an improvement in distribution;" benefit consumers through such improvements; and will not seriously eliminate competition if "parallel imports" are provided for, *i.e.,* if dealers are not restricted in their freedom to sell into the territory of other dealers in the product.[193] Thus, territorial confinement of the dealers will destroy the exemption. Certain other restrictions are expressly permitted to accompany the authorized exclusive dealing arrangements, however, including, among others, prohibitions against advertising or maintaining a branch or warehouse outside the assigned

---

[191] Presence of the danger of reciprocity was established as a ground of illegality of a merger in FTC v. Consolidated Foods Corp., 380 U.S. 592 (1965); it is under Sherman Act attack as illegal restraint of trade; see *Analysis: The Current Attack on Reciprocity,* ATTR No. 434, B-1 (Nov. 4, 1969); see also Bodner, *supra* note 188; Day, *id.*; Ferguson, *id.*; Flinn, *Reciprocity and Related Topics under the Sherman Act,* 37 A.B.A. ANTITRUST L. J. 156 (1968); G. & R. Hale, *Reciprocity under the Antitrust Laws: A Comment,* 113 U.PA.L. REV. 69 (1964).

[192] 1 CCH COMM. MKT. REP. ¶2727. See Champaud, *The Group Exemptions of E.E.C. Regulation 67/67,* 5 COMM. MKT. L. REV. 23 (1967); Cohen, *The Application of Article 85(3) of the Treaty Establishing the European Economic Community to Exclusive Dealing Agreements,* 54 CORNELL L. REV. 379 (1969); for discussion of procedural problems, see Buxbaum, *The Group Exemption and Exclusive Distributorships in the Common Market—Procedural Technicalities,* 14 ANTITRUST BULL. 499 (1969).

[193] 1 CCH COMM. MKT. REP. ¶2727, at 1820. Under Article 6 of the Regulation, the Commission may withdraw the exemption in a particular case on several grounds including lack of competition from similar products in the market and impossibility of sales in the market by competing manufacturers; *id.* at 1822.

The Nature and Extent of Conflict

territory,[194] and an obligation to buy the seller's full line (a practice called "full line forcing" in the United States and usually treated there like tying).[195]

The group exemption expires in 1972, but is renewable by the Commission. Some confusion has resulted from the fact that under Court of Justice decisions, the applicability of the Article 85(1) prohibition to exclusive dealing agreements is not automatic, but turns upon market analysis tests which are not unlike those used under Section 3 of the Clayton Act, or under the Rule of Reason.[196] Accordingly, to an uncertain extent the exemption purports to exempt some agreements which are not prohibited anyway.[197] The regulation itself says that it is unnecessary to "expressly exclude" such cases.

Tying is expressly covered by Article 85(1), which provides that it is unlawful to:

e) make the conclusion of a contract subject to the acceptance by trade partners of additional goods or services which are not by their nature or by the custom of the trade related to the subject matter of such contract.

An almost identical provision appears in Article 86.[198] Evidently, if the tied product or service is closely "related" to the tying product or service, either functionally or by trade custom, the tying will be lawful, in contrast to American law in which the relationship must be so close

[194] This is called a "location clause" in American parlance; at first, it was regarded as lawful, Boro Hall Corp. v. General Motors Corp., 124 F.2d 822 (2d Cir. 1942); but when the issue arose recently, the Court left it unresolved in United States v. General Motors Corp., 384 U.S. 127 (1966); the "restraint on alienation" rationale of the *Schwinn* case might be used to invalidate it; see text at note 215 *infra*.

[195] *Cf.* Burstein, *A Theory of Full-Line Forcing,* 55 NW.U.L. REV. 62 (1960).

[196] See Société Technique Minière v. Maschinenbau Ulm GmbH, CCH COMM. MKT. REP. ¶8047, 5 Comm. Mkt. L. R. 357 (1966); S.A. Brasserie de Haecht v. Consorts Wilkin-Janssen, CCH COMM. MKT. REP. ¶8053, 7 Comm. Mkt. L. R. 26 (1967).

[197] See JOLIET, THE RULE OF REASON IN ANTITRUST LAW: AMERICAN, GERMAN AND COMMON MARKET LAWS IN COMPARATIVE PERSPECTIVE 175 (1967).

[198] Article 85(1)(e) and Article 86(d); DERINGER, *supra* note 127, ¶159 interprets the Article 85 prohibition as reaching simple vertical two-party tying agreements; *cf.* OBERDORFER, GLEISS & HIRSCH, COMMON MARKET CARTEL LAW ¶72 (1963), who argue that the Article 85(1) language does not prohibit tying itself, but only reaches agreements to impose tying upon third persons.

that the two are really regarded as inseparable. Also in contrast to American cases, in its Official Notice on Patent Licensing Agreements of December 24, 1962, the Commission stated that clauses in patent licenses tying in the purchase of supplies are not prohibited if "they are indispensable for a technically proper utilization of the patent."[199] There have been virtually no reported cases to indicate how broadly or narrowly the Commission and courts will interpret these standards,[200] but it appears that there is some room in the Common Market tests for a more lenient approach to tying than has developed in the United States.

In Belgium, exclusive selling and buying contracts are valid, subject to narrow exceptions.[201] Tying is also lawful, even on the part of a dominant seller, unless it is shown that the primary purpose is to eliminate competitors.[202] In the Netherlands, exclusive dealing agreements are exempt from registration,[203] and tying contracts have not been challenged, although ministerial intervention is authorized in cases of abuse.[204] All three of the types of agreement under discussion are generally lawful in Luxembourg,[205] and in Italy.[206]

In France, exclusive selling arrangements are lawful, with the interesting proviso that official Government interpretation (the Fontanet Circular) and the Cour de Cassation have said that to be valid as against the prohibition of refusal to sell, the buyer must also be bound to

---

[199] 1 CCH COMM. MKT. REP. ¶ 2698 at 1777, para. I, C.

[200] In a press release, March 3, 1966, the Commission stated that it had started proceedings against two French firms which had entered into patent cross-licenses with each other with the right to grant sub-licenses; sub-licensees who bought non-patented supplies from the two licensors paid no royalties; other sub-licensees were required to pay; the parties cancelled the discriminatory royalty provisions; 2 CCH COMM. MKT. REP. ¶ 9093. This agreement in effect was a horizontal arrangement to impose tying upon third persons, and hence within Article 85(1)(e) under either view of its scope, note 198 *supra*.

[201] BUSINESS REGULATION IN THE COMMON MARKET NATIONS, vol. 1, *supra* note 23, at 128.

[202] *Id.* at 136-37.

[203] BUSINESS REGULATION IN THE COMMON MARKET NATIONS, vol. 1, *supra* note 19, at 397.

[204] *Id.* at 413.

[205] BUSINESS REGULATION IN THE COMMON MARKET NATIONS, vol. 1, *supra* note 27, at 548.

[206] BUSINESS REGULATION IN THE COMMON MARKET NATIONS, vol. 2, *supra* note 25, at 526-27.

buy exclusively from the seller.[207] The converse is not required; *i.e.*, a requirements contract need not be matched by an exclusive selling agreement, since there is no prohibition against refusal to buy. Tying, in contrast, is expressly prohibited by Article 37(1)(c), but this is apparently not enforced and has been called a "dead letter."[208]

In Germany, all three types of restrictive agreements are basically lawful because the prohibitory language of the Act does not reach them. Under Section 18, however, the BKA may intervene and invalidate such agreements if it finds either (1) that a restraint impedes access of third parties to the market, or (2) that it has a substantial adverse effect on competition. The BKA has engaged in very little action of this kind, but it has been predicted that its interventions may increase in the future.[209] It should be noted that the BKA has attacked "TBA" arrangements of the same type as those invalidated by the FTC in the United States.[210]

D. Territorial and Customer Restriction of Dealers

1. AMERICAN LAW

After indecisiveness on the matter for most of its history, American antitrust law recently arrived at the result that restrictions as to the territory within which, or the classes of customers to which, distributors may resell goods they have purchased are per se illegal, except possibly in cases of failing firms or newcomers seeking to gain a market foothold. This was the conclusion of the *Schwinn* decision in 1967.[211] The

[207]BUSINESS REGULATION IN THE COMMON MARKET NATIONS, vol. 2, *supra* note 15, at 218.

[208]*Id.* at 230.

[209]BUSINESS REGULATION IN THE COMMON MARKET NATIONS, vol. 3, *supra* note 12, at 249, 252, 270, 271.

[210]*Id.* at 251; see text at note 190 *supra*.

[211]United States v. Arnold, Schwinn & Co., 388 U.S. 365 (1967); the issue of what rule of law to adopt had been left open in the earlier case of White Motor Co. v. United States, 372 U.S. 253 (1963). On *Schwinn*, see McLaren, *Territorial and Customer Restrictions, Consignments, Suggested Resale Prices and Refusals to Deal,* 37 A.B.A. ANTITRUST L. J. 137 (1968); Zimmerman, *Distribution Restrictions after Sealy and Schwinn,* 12 ANTITRUST BULL. 1181 (1967); Orrick, *Marketing Restrictions Imposed to Protect the Integrity of 'Franchise' Distribution Systems,* 36 A.B.A. ANTITRUST L. J. 63 (1967); Pollock, *supra* note 179; Keck, *Alternative Distribution Techniques—Franchising, Consignment, Agency and Licensing,* 13 ANTITRUST BULL. 177 (1968); Comanor, *Vertical Territorial and Customer*

decision placed such restraints largely on the same basis as resale price maintenance agreements, to which they are analogous in that both classes of restraints, though vertically imposed, have substantially the same effect as would horizontal agreements among the dealers themselves. A major distinction remains, however. In the *Simpson* case, the Court held that the Sherman Act may condemn resale price controls even where dealers hold the goods as consignment-agents of the seller rather than as purchasers.[212] But in the *Schwinn* case, without analytically distinguishing *Simpson,* the Court held that the seller may restrict the territory and customers of bona fide consignment-agents.[213] This strange result evidently grew out of the *Schwinn* opinion's rationale that resale restrictions are objectionable because they are "restraints on alienation," a doctrine of very dubious relevance to antitrust law. Under such a rationale, restriction of one holding goods as an agent, rather than as a purchaser, would not be bad, because it is not a restraint on alienation.

Still undecided by the Supreme Court is the status of so-called "area of primary responsibility" agreements. Such arrangements do not prohibit the dealer from selling outside his assigned territory, but they make it his obligation to devote his "best efforts" to exploiting his assigned territory effectively. Enforcement agencies so far have been rather surprisingly tolerant of these agreements.[214]

Restrictions: White Motor and Its Aftermath, 81 HARV. L. REV. 1419 (1968); Pogue, *Vertical Restrictions on Price, Territory and Customers–The Certainty of Uncertainty,* 29 OHIO ST. L. J. 272 (1968). For discussion of the advantages of franchising to antitrust competition policy, see Chadwell & Rhodes, *Antitrust Aspects of Dealer Licensing and Franchising,* 62 NW. U. L. REV. 1 (1967).

[212] Simpson v. Union Oil Co., 377 U.S. 13 (1964); see Rahl, *supra* note 158.

[213] 388 U.S. at 380.

[214] The Antitrust Division has agreed to such arrangements in consent decrees: *e.g.,* United States v. Rudolf Wurlitzer Co. (W.D.N.Y. 1958), 1958 Trade Cas. ¶69,011; United States v. Bostitch, Inc. (D.R.I. 1958), 1958 Trade Cas. ¶69,207; United States v. Philco Corp. (E.D.Pa. 1956), 1956 Trade Cas. ¶68,409; and has strongly advanced their use as a less restrictive alternative: see Stewart, *Exclusive Franchises and Territorial Confinement of Distributors,* 22 A.B.A. ANTITRUST SECTION REP. 33, 41-43 (1963), pointing out that the Government took this position in argument in the *White Motor* case; see also Pollock, *supra* note 179, at 603; Turner, in Panel Discussion, *Orderly Marketing, Franchise and Trademark Licensing: Have They Been Routed by Schwinn and Sealy?* 1968 N.Y. STATE BAR ASS'N ANTITRUST LAW SYMP. 27, at 68; *cf.* Zimmerman, *supra* note 211, at 1187-88; also, de Keyser, *Territorial Restrictions and Export Prohibitions under the*

Also currently in doubt since the *Schwinn* case are "location" clauses, prohibiting the dealer from establishing a branch or other place of business outside his franchised territory,[215] and "profit pass-over" agreements under which a dealer who sells to a customer outside his territory is required to pay a commission, or part of his profit, to the dealer in whose territory the customer is located.[216]

2. EUROPEAN LAWS

In the *Grundig-Consten* case, decided before *Schwinn,* the Commission and Court of Justice adopted an approach to territorial restriction of dealers which, at first glance, appears to be as strict as that of *Schwinn.*[217] Grundig's scheme of confinement of its distributors within national boundaries in the Common Market (Consten had the exclusive franchise for France) obviously affected—in fact, largely prevented— interstate sales on the part of distributors, an effect dramatized by evidence that resale prices in France were much higher than in Germany. Given Grundig's market importance, it was inevitable that competition within the Common Market would be found restrained. Moreover, the Commission denied an Article 85(3) exemption, primarily on the ground that the territorial restraints were not shown to be indispensable to

United States and the Common Market Antitrust Laws, 2 C.M.L. REV. 271 (1964),
The Federal Trade Commission supported use of area-of-primary-responsibility clauses in Sandura Co. v. FTC, 339 F.2d 847, 855 (6th Cir. 1964) and in Snap-On Tools Corp. v. FTC, 321 F.2d 825, 832 (7th Cir. 1963); the distinction from closed territory arrangements was criticized by the court in the latter case.

[215] See note 194 *supra*; also Pollock, *supra* note 179, at 603-05; Zimmerman, *supra* note 211, at 1187-88.

[216] See Pollock, *supra* note 179, at 605; Turner, *supra* note 214; Zimmerman, *supra* note 211, at 1187-88.

[217] Decision of Commission in Grundig Verkaufs-GmbH, Sept. 23, 1964, CCH COMM. MKT. REP. ¶2743; Court of Justice decision in Ets. Consten S.A. and Grundig-Verkaufs-GmbH v. EEC Comm'n, CCH COMM. MKT. REP. ¶8046, 5 Comm. Mkt. L. R. 418 (1966); see de Keyser, *supra* note 214; Deringer, *Exclusive Agency Agreements with Territorial Protection Under the EEC Antitrust Laws,* 10 ANTITRUST BULL. 599 (1965); Fulda, *The First Antitrust Decisions of the Commission of the European Economic Community,* 65 COLUM. L. REV. 625 (1965); Fulda, *The Exclusive Distributor and the Antitrust Laws of the Common Market of Europe and the United States,* 3 TEX. INT'L L. FOR. 209 (1967); Newes, *The European Commission's First Major Antitrust Decision,* 20 BUS. LAW. 431 (1965); Timberg, *The Impact of Antitrust Laws on Multinational Licensing and Franchising Arrangements,* 13 ANTITRUST BULL. 39, 50 (1968).

achieving distribution advantages conceded by the Commission to flow from an exclusive dealing system.[218]

One might conclude that *Grundig-Consten* establishes a virtual per se rule against territorial protection plans which prevent dealer intra-brand competition across Member State lines. Such restraints are peculiarly inimical to the integration of the Common Market, and their existence will defeat allowance of the group exemption for exclusive arrangements under Regulation 67/67.[219]

On the other hand, the Commission is always free to grant an individual exemption under Article 85(3) in light of particular facts. Its policy of promoting cooperation among small and medium-sized firms could on occasion lead it to such a move in the case of smaller manufacturers. Also, the Court of Justice has established in the *Völk* case that territorial confinement of dealers by a manufacturer having a very small market share may even escape the prohibition of Article 85(1).[220]

The Commission has approved the "location" clause in Regulation 67/67,[221] and it granted exemption to a "profit pass-over" agreement in the *Transocean Marine Paint Association* case.[222]

Customer allocation in the strictly vertical sense appears to have received little discussion from the point of view of EEC law. It seems clear that such agreements would fall within the scope of Article 85(1). Their exemptibility under Article 85(3) might be somewhat easier than as to territorial restrictions, however, since some kinds of customer restrictions would not be as obviously contrary to integration of the Common Market as are territorial restraints of the Grundig type. A seller who reserves to himself sales to governmental bodies, for example, may decide to leave all other sales throughout the Common Market to his distributors; if significant efficiencies result for the government purchasers without harm to other consumers, exemption might be forthcoming, since Common Market goals would not seem to be broadly interfered with.

---

[218] CCH COMM. MKT. REP. ¶2743 at 1866.

[219] Art. 3, CCH COMM. MKT. REP. ¶2727.

[220] Völk v. Ets. J. Vervaecke, S.P.R.L. 8 Comm. Mkt. L. R. 273 (1969).

[221] See text at note 194, *supra*.

[222] Chapter 2, text at note 106.

Territorial and customer restrictions of the buyer are frequently used within the Member States. They are not questioned in Belgium,[223] the Netherlands,[224] Luxembourg,[225] or Italy.[226] In France, such restrictions appear actually to be encouraged.[227] In Germany, they also are valid unless and until the BKA intervenes under Section 18, something it has not been inclined to do.[228]

E. Conflict Analysis

Given the variegated approach of the laws under discussion to different types of distribution restrictions, it is a foregone conclusion that there will be some kinds of conflict between the American and the European systems (not to mention conflict between Rome Treaty law and the laws of the Member States). In the following discussion, the possibilities for conflict are analyzed from the viewpoint of distribution in the American market and in European markets. Separate treatment is not given to questions of conflict in third country markets, as the pattern of analysis would be essentially the same as for horizontal restraints discussed above.

1. DISTRIBUTION IN THE UNITED STATES

In the strict sense of this study, conflict as to distribution in the American market may seem relatively infrequent because of the limited extraterritorial application of most of the European laws. Since they seldom purport to control practices carried out in foreign markets, the European laws seldom overlap American laws in American domestic markets. It is possible, however, to discern frequent conflict under the

[223] BUSINESS REGULATION IN THE COMMON MARKET NATIONS, vol. 1, *supra* note 23, at 133, 135.
[224] BUSINESS REGULATION IN THE COMMON MARKET NATIONS, vol. 1, *supra* note 19, at 410, 411.
[225] BUSINESS REGULATION IN THE COMMON MARKET NATIONS, vol. 1, *supra* note 27, at 548.
[226] BUSINESS REGULATION IN THE COMMON MARKET NATIONS, vol. 2, *supra* note 25, at 525, 526.
[227] BUSINESS REGULATION IN THE COMMON MARKET NATIONS, vol. 2, *supra* note 15, at 228, 229.
[228] BUSINESS REGULATION IN THE COMMON MARKET NATIONS, vol. 3, *supra* note 12, at 269, 270.

definition employed in this study in transactions involving export from Europe to the United States. If the exports move from Europe pursuant to contracts containing restrictive provisions which are lawful there and unlawful in the United States, application of American law may cause disadvantageous or prohibitive conflict insofar as the *transaction* is concerned, whether or not it applies to the European party himself. Conflict of this type undoubtedly occurs often.[229]

Sharper conflict is possible in a few situations where European laws apply to extraterritorial conduct causing internal effects in domestic European markets. For example, suppose that a Luxembourg exporter, selling a product which is rather difficult to transport and distribute in overseas markets because of language and technological difficulties, finds an American distributor who is qualified to handle his product, and executes an exclusive dealing agreement with him. Let us assume that the agreement is lawful under American law because there are numerous domestic American suppliers and distributors of competing goods. If the particular distributor is the only qualified one available to handle foreign imports, the agreement may give the Luxembourg firm a European monopoly of the export trade to the United States. Despite typically lenient European attitudes toward agreements of this type, if the consequence should happen to be serious domestic competitive injury to European competitors of the Luxembourg firm, might not European authorities act? In Germany, it appears that the BKA could intervene, if it happens to have jurisdiction over the Luxembourg firm. The EEC might withdraw the group exemption for the agreement. Even France, Belgium and the Netherlands might find some basis for acting. Only Luxembourg itself, and Italy, would seem incapable of proceeding.

European action in the example just given would create a largely "European" problem, as American policy would be relatively indifferent because of the marginal illegality of the agreements concerned.

2. DISTRIBUTION IN THE COMMON MARKET

Many more possibilities for conflict exist as to sales of goods in the Common Market, either exported from the United States or manufactured there.

---

[229] See Chapter 2, note 63.

a. Refusal to Deal

An American exporter who sells in France and refuses to sell to some French dealers because he prefers selective distribution may be operating lawfully in this branch of American foreign commerce and quite unlawfully as far as the French are concerned. This same refusal could be a violation of Article 86 if the American firm has dominant power in the European market, while at the same time it might be entirely lawful under American law.[230]

Conversely, an American refusal to sell which is designed to carry out a resale price maintenance policy in export sales may fall within the scope of American law because it is committed *"in"* American foreign commerce, and it may be substantively illegal under the doctrines of *Parke, Davis* or *Albrecht*. At the same time, it may be lawful under the Rome Treaty and in some Member States (though probably unlawful in France and Luxembourg).

A different kind of conflict, involving both European and American markets, may occur along the lines of the *Sanib* case.[231] Thus, a manufacturer in Europe might refuse to supply necessary raw materials to a finished goods manufacturer who exports to the United States. This probably lawful European distribution restraint might have secondary market consequences in the United States which could make it illegal. For example, if the first manufacturer happened to be competing in the United States with the second, the case might involve illegal monopolization, given the necessary intent or market share.

b. Resale Price Agreements

Use of resale price agreements by an American exporter may be reached by American law, as explained in Chapter 2,[232] and may violate it because of the inapplicability of the McGuire Act exemption. At the same time, the agreements may be lawful in several of the European countries (though not in all), and under present approaches may be ignored by Common Market authorities.

---

[230] See JOLIET, *supra* note 62; statement of Rahl in *Hearings, supra* note 43, at 383.

[231] See Chapter 2, text at note 77.

[232] See *id.*, text at note 68.

Conflict will apparently be uniform and complete if the seller acting in American commerce relies upon the consignment-agency device to control his dealers' selling prices. Such control is likely to be illegal under the *Simpson* case, while its use is not only lawful in Europe, but actually seems required under the EEC Notice on Commercial Agents in order to make the agency bona fide. Prohibitive conflict of the most serious sort lurks here, in that it may be necessary to risk violation of American law in order to have a valid agency, while compliance with American law may destroy the agency.

c. Exclusive Arrangements and Tying

In Chapter 2, it was pointed out how simple exclusive selling and buying contracts, executed by American exporters or even by American firms manufacturing abroad, could in some cases fall within the scope of American law because they restrain or exclude American export or import commerce.[233] Since exclusive selling or franchise agreements are so generally lawful in both the United States and the Common Market, there is little likelihood of conflict as to them. Exclusive buying or requirements contracts, however, present more possibilities for conflict, since they are usually lawful under Common Market laws, but may be attacked under the Sherman or FTC Acts if sufficient "foreclosure" of competition occurs. Even if a given system of requirements contracts covers only a small part of a European market, it might still be illegal under American law if it seriously limits the opportunities of American exporters, as well it might. This is simply the converse of the Luxembourg example given above.

Inability to make such contracts may interfere with ability to compete with European competitors who use them, with possible disadvantageous effects. Also, since European authorities, *e.g.,* the Commission in Regulation 67/67, take the position that such agreements are often positively beneficial to consumers in the Common Market,[234] such an application of American law would conflict not only with private legal rights abroad, but with Community policy. It should be added, however,

[233] *Id.,* text at note 46 *et seq.*
[234] See text at note 193 *supra.*

that there are no reported cases of action of this sort by American enforcement agencies.[235]

Tying contracts present a somewhat similar problem, except that they are less favored by EEC law than requirements contracts. However, an arrangement tying in supplies or parts with the sale or lease of machinery to European users may be lawful under the Rome Treaty's dispensation for such restrictions when they are "by nature" closely related.[236] The same kind of tying may often violate American law.

Similarly, the evolving American disapproval of reciprocity may conflict with European law, where there appears to be no disapproval of the practice.

d. Territorial and Customer Restrictions

Territorial or customer restriction of dealers by American firms selling in Europe may directly restrain sales to the United States if the product can be exported, and must therefore be regarded as likely to activate American enforcement machinery. If the restraint expressly prohibits export to the United States of goods owned by the dealer, the violation is obvious. More innocent-appearing restrictions may be equally illegal— *e.g.,* a restriction to sales in a part of France, or to customers located in the Low countries. If these restrictions prevent export to the United States, they may fall under the *Schwinn* doctrine.

A territorial restraint which precludes sales across Member State lines will probably also violate EEC law under the *Grundig-Consten* case. But if the restraint merely prohibits export from the Common Market, while leaving the dealer free to sell without restraint within the Common Market, the Rome Treaty probably will not reach it.[237]

Customer restrictions present frequent possibilities of conflict, since they are per se illegal under *Schwinn,* but generally lawful under European national laws and are perhaps less obnoxious to EEC law than territorial restrictions. The use of "location" clauses and "profit

---

[235]*Cf.* the *Dymo Industries* case, Chapter 2, text at note 46. Also, it was reported orally to the author that in a suit in Belgium by a Belgian distributor seeking enforcement of an exclusive contract with an American manufacturer, the latter raised a defense based on illegality under the Sherman Act; the result is not known.

[236]See text at note 198 *supra.*

[237]See Chapter 2, text at note 114 *et seq.*

pass-over" agreements, which are lawful in Europe but of doubtful American status, also may one day be a source of conflict.

The best harmonizer for American and EEC law may appear to be the use of the agency relationship, under which—if it is bona fide—territorial and customer control may be lawfully achieved under both sets of laws. A trap for the unwary may exist here, however. As just pointed out in the discussion of conflict in resale price maintenance situations, the EEC regards price control by the principal to be an important indicium of a true agency, whereas such price control may make the whole relationship illegal under American law.

V. PATENTS

Chapter 5 is devoted entirely to discussion of the most substantial problems of conflict pertaining to industrial property, *i.e.,* those associated with territorial restriction growing out of licenses and out of separate national patent and trademark systems. The present discussion is limited to a brief listing and analysis of conflict possibilities as to other principal types of restrictions used in connection with patents. A discussion of problems of trademark and know-how licensing would also be useful, but it would lengthen the present chapter unduly and has had to be omitted.[238]

A. American Law

Three main features of American patent-antitrust jurisprudence may be singled out for comparison with the European laws: (1) the allowance of

---

[238] On foreign trademark licensing, see Kestenbaum, *Enforcement Policy on Foreign Trademark Licensing,* 36 A.B.A. ANTITRUST L. J. 74 (1967); BREWSTER, ANTITRUST AND AMERICAN BUSINESS ABROAD 170 (1958); FUGATE, FOREIGN COMMERCE AND THE ANTITRUST LAWS ch. 9 (1958). On foreign know-how licensing, see Barton, *Limitations on Territory, Field of Use, Quantity and Price in Know-How Agreements with Foreign Companies,* 28 U. PITT. L. REV. 195 (1966); MacDonald, *Know-How Licensing and the Antitrust Laws,* 62 MICH. L. REV. 351 (1964); Maddock, *Know How Licensing under the Antitrust Laws of the United States and the Rome Treaty,* 2 C.M.L. REV. 36 (1964); Stedman, *Legal Problems in the International and Domestic Licensing of Know-How,* 29 A.B.A. ANTITRUST SECTION REP. 247 (1965). Generally, see Timberg, *The Impact of Antitrust Laws on Multinational Licensing and Franchising Arrangements,* 13 ANTITRUST BULL. 39 (1968).

various restrictions on the licensee, as an exception to antitrust rules, subject to very strict limitations and to a continuing attack on the exceptions by the Antitrust Division; (2) the stringent approach to patent pools; and (3) the strong impact of the doctrine of patent misuse.

1. LICENSE RESTRICTIONS

It may sometimes be surprising to Europeans to see how lenient American antitrust law appears to be with respect to some patent license restrictions. Thus, under certain circumstances as a result of the *General Electric* case,[239] patent licensors may control the licensee's selling prices,[240] and other cases permit control of quantity,[241] and field of use.[242] The licensee may also be required to grant back to the licensor rights to improvements in the licensed field, and the leading case found reasonable a requirement of outright assignment of improvements, not merely a license.[243]

On the other hand, license restrictions controlling competition in

[239] United States v. General Electric Co., 272 U.S. 476, 488 (1926).

[240] See Furth, *Price-Restrictive Patent Licenses under the Sherman Act*, 71 HARV. L. REV. 815 (1958); Gibbons, *Price Fixing in Patent Licenses and the Antitrust Laws*, 51 VA. L. REV. 273 (1965); ATTY. GEN. NAT. COMM. ANTITRUST REP. 233 (1955); A.B.A. ANTITRUST SECTION SUPP. TO ATTY. GEN. NAT. COMM. ANTITRUST REP.: ANTITRUST DEVELOPMENTS 1955-1968, at 171 (1968) [hereinafter cited ABA SUPP. TO ATTY. GEN. NAT. COMM. ANTITRUST REP].

[241] See United States v. Aluminum Co. of America, 148 F.Supp. 416, 438 (2d Cir. 1945).

[242] General Talking Pictures Corp. v. Western Electric Co., 304 U.S. 175, 546 (1938), *opinion modified on rehearing*, 305 U.S. 124 (1938); ATTY. GEN. NAT. COMM. ANTITRUST REP. 236 (1955); ABA SUPP. TO ATTY. GEN. NAT. COMM. ANTITRUST REP. 171 (1968); Baxter, *Legal Restrictions on Exploitation of the Patent Monopoly: An Economic Analysis,* 76 YALE L. J. 267 (1966); Gibbons, *Field Restrictions in Patent Transactions: Economic Discrimination and Restraint of Competition,* 66 COLUM. L. REV. 423 (1966); Comment, *Patent Use Restrictions,* 75 HARV. L. REV. 602 (1962); NORDHAUS & JUROW, PATENT-ANTITRUST LAW ch. 5 (1961).

[243] Transparent-Wrap Machine Corp. v. Stokes & Smith Co., 329 U.S. 637 (1947); *cf.* United States v. General Electric Co., 80 F.Supp. 989, 1005-06 (S.D.N.Y. 1948) (Carboloy case), where the court held illegal the use of grant-back requirements on the ground that defendants' dominant position in the industry lent such provisions to abuse; also United States v. General Electric Co., 82 F.Supp. 753, 815-16 (D.N.J. 1949) (incandescent lamp case), similar.

subject-matter which is outside the scope of the patent grant are generally prohibited as constituting an unlawful use of the monopoly of the patent. The classic example is that of tying—particularly of unpatented supplies to the license of a patented process or machine, but also other forms of tying.[244] Package licensing, *i.e.,* the tying of the license of one patent to the license of another, falls under the same ban.[245]

The allowance of price fixing is hemmed in by limitations. Resale prices of the licensee may not be controlled, as the patent right in a given unit is exhausted by the first sale.[246] Price control may extend only to a patented product, and control over unpatented products produced by patented processes or machines is not permitted.[247] Price control has also been struck down where it was part of a cross-license agreement.[248] And in one federal circuit, the court has ruled that it is not permitted where control covers more than one licensee.[249]

There is also a general limitation on otherwise valid restrictions which derives from their origin and purpose. The *General Electric* case rationale was that the licensor should be allowed to impose restrictions which were reasonably designed to protect and assure the reward to which the patentee is said to be entitled.[250] Consequently, restrictions which are found to be intended primarily to control competition among licensees, rather than to secure legitimate protection for the patentee, are struck down even though in form they appear to come within the *General Electric* doctrine.[251]

The Antitrust Division has carried on a sustained effort to invalidate *General Electric.* Twice it has brought the Supreme Court to within an inch of overruling it,[252] and the doctrine's life expectancy is rated as

---

[244] United States v. Loew's, Inc. 371 U.S. 38 (1962); ABA SUPP. TO ATTY. GEN. NAT. COMM. ANTITRUST REP. 173.

[245] *Id.* See also American Securit Co. v. Shatterproof Glass Corp., 268 F.2d 769 (3d Cir. 1959), *cert. denied,* 361 U.S. 902 (1959).

[246] ATTY. GEN. NAT. COMM. ANTITRUST REP. 234.

[247] *Id.*

[248] United States v. Line Material Co., 333 U.S. 287 (1948).

[249] Newburgh Moire Co. v. Superior Moire Co., 237 F.2d 283 (3d Cir. 1956); ABA SUPP. TO ATTY. GEN. NAT. COMM. ANTITRUST REP. 171.

[250] 272 U.S. at 490.

[251] United States v. U.S. Gypsum Co., 333 U.S. 364 (1948).

[252] United States v. Line Material Co., 333 U.S. 287 (1948) and United States v. Huck Mfg. Co., 382 U.S. 197 (1965), in both of which the Court was evenly divided on this issue.

extremely precarious. The Government has also stated an intention to seek rulings which will limit grant-backs to non-exclusive licenses on a mutual basis, prohibit certain types of field-of-use restrictions, and invalidate some restrictions on sales.[253] It does not appear to intend to attack all forms of restrictive licensing. If *General Electric* is overruled, however, much depends upon the rationale which will be involved. By analogy to German and EEC approaches, price fixing could be invalidated as outside the scope of the patent, while certain other restrictions could be viewed as inside, and therefore still allowable. On the other hand, a sweeping denunciation of license restrictions could bring most of them down.

2. PATENT POOLS

Interchanges of patent rights held by two or more patentees which place control of the patents in single hands are not inherently unlawful, and are sometimes of great value in making inventions generally available.[254] If the agreement includes price fixing or other restrictive practices, however, it will in all likelihood be treated as illegal.[255] In the *Hazeltine Research* case, the Court held participation by an American firm in foreign patent pools illegal merely because the pool agreements restricted licenses to firms which would manufacture in the foreign countries concerned and refused import licenses, thereby restraining American export trade.[256]

Moreover, where a patent interchange gives control over an industry, the exercise of this control must be free from unlawful purpose or abuse, or it will be held illegal.[257] Thus, in the *Singer Manufacturing* case,[258] it was held that cross-licensing and assignments of patents among an American, a Swiss and an Italian company were illegal, in part because

[253] See address by Assistant Attorney General McLaren on Patent Licenses and Antitrust Considerations, ATTR No. 413, X-11 (June 10, 1969), 5 CCH TRADE REG. REP. ¶50,246 at 55,503; and address by R. W. Donnem, Antitrust Division Director of Policy Planning, The Antitrust Attack on Restrictive Patent License Provisions, 5 CCH TRADE REG. REP. ¶50,260 (Sept. 25, 1969).

[254] ATTY. GEN. NAT. COMM. ANTITRUST REP. 242.

[255] *Id.* at 246; ABA SUPP. TO ATTY. GEN. NAT. COMM. ANTITRUST REP. 179.

[256] Zenith Radio Corp. v. Hazeltine Research, Inc. 395 U.S. 100, 113 n.8 (1969).

[257] ATTY. GEN. NAT. COMM. ANTITRUST REP. 243.

[258] United States v. Singer Mfg. Co., 374 U.S. 174 (1963).

they were motivated by a plan to enable the American company to exclude Japanese competition from the American market. As the Attorney General's Committee Report indicated, to be safe, a patent pool which has monopoly power over an industry must license all applicants on reasonable, non-discriminatory terms.[259] Even if it lacks monopoly power, it should do the same if the members have given up their power to grant licenses other than through the pool.[260]

3. PATENT MISUSE

The patent misuse doctrine goes beyond statutory antitrust sanctions and, if the patent is being misused, denies to the patentee the right to enforce it in an infringement action.[261] In general, misuse occurs when the patentee extends the monopoly of his patent to obtain some form of control over subject matter which is beyond the scope of the patent.[262] This occurs most obviously where the patent right is used as leverage for tying purposes.[263] It has also been held to occur where the patentee exacts royalties which extend beyond the life of a patent,[264] and even where he merely charges discriminatory royalties, if they injure competition among licensees.[265] The doctrine of contributory infringement, which may permit suit against persons who supply unpatented components for use by a direct infringer, was at one time virtually extinguished by the misuse doctrine in the *Mercoid* case.[266] Congress reinstated it in Section 271(c) and (d) of the Patent Code, but the Court, in the *Aro* cases, has construed these provisions quite narrowly.[267]

The misuse doctrine is still developing in the case law and its ultimate limits cannot presently be determined.

B. European Laws

The Common Market does not appear to treat restrictive practices used in connection with patents as problems of first-rank seriousness. As with

[259] ATTY. GEN. NAT. COMM. ANTITRUST REP. 245.

[260] *Id.*

[261] *Id.* at 250.

[262] ABA SUPP. TO ATTY. GEN. NAT. COMM. ANTITRUST REP. 180.

[263] *E.g.*, Morton Salt Co. v. Suppiger, 314 U.S. 488 (1942).

[264] Brulotte v. Thys Co., 379 U.S. 29 (1964).

[265] La Peyre v. FTC, 366 F.2d 117 (5th Cir. 1966).

[266] Mercoid Corp. v. Mid-Continent Investment Co., 320 U.S. 661 (1944).

[267] Aro Mfg. Co. v. Convertible Top Replacement Co., 365 U.S. 336 (1961); Aro Mfg. Co. v. Convertible Top Replacement Co., 377 U.S. 476 (1964).

vertical resale price maintenance, Article 4(2)(ii) of Regulation 17 exempts from the notification requirement two-party agreements which "impose restraint on the rights of any person acquiring or using industrial property rights" (including not only patents, but also trademarks and know-how). The effect of this seems only to be that if an exemption under Article 85(3) is granted, it may pre-date the application for it.[268] While this may appear to be a somewhat minor distinction from the treatment given to other restraints, it manifests the initial belief that industrial property restraints do not pose as much threat to the development of the Common Market as do other types of restraint.[269]

Further indication that most of the simpler forms of patent license restraints were not initially thought to be of serious concern is provided by the Commission's Official Notice on Patent Licensing Agreements, issued December 24, 1962.[270] This notice undertakes to describe various types of restrictions which are considered not to fall within the prohibition of Article 85(1). The rationale is that restrictions which are "covered by the patent" (*i.e.,* within its scope) "involve only the partial *retention* of the right of prohibition incidental to the patent holder's exclusive right."[271] In other words, the enumerated restrictions, though they take the form of an agreement between patentee and licensee, arise basically from the patent right and not from the agreement; as to them, it is really the patent which restrains competition, not the agreement.[272] A Commission which was greatly concerned about patent restraints might have been less eager to adopt this theory and to disclaim jurisdiction in this manner.

Under the Official Notice, the allowable restrictions on patent licensees include: limitation to less than all of the "methods of exploitation" of the invention (*i.e.,* making, using or selling); limitation of the manufacture of a patented product (presumably restrictions as to the type of product which may be made); limitation of the "application of the patented process to specified fields of technical application" (*i.e.,* limiting the technical field of practice of a process having more than one type of application); limitation of the quantity of the product to be

[268] DERINGER, *supra* note 127 at ¶ 275.
[269] *Id.*
[270] CCH COMM. MKT. REP. ¶ 2698; for a different English translation, see OECD, GUIDE TO LEGISLATION ON RESTRICTIVE BUSINESS PRACTICES, E.E.C., 2 bis, at 3.
[271] CCH COMM. MKT. REP. ¶ 2698 at 1778 (emphasis supplied).
[272] See DERINGER, *supra* note 127 at ¶ 176.

manufactured or the number of times a patented process may be used; limitation to a time shorter than the life of the patent, or to an area less than, or a specific location within, the territorial scope of the patent; and prohibition against assignment or sublicensing of the license.

Also, the Notice permits the licensor to impose standards of quality upon the licensee, or obligations "with respect to the obtaining of supplies of certain products, insofar as they are indispensable for a technically proper utilization of the patent." Thus, tying is permitted if it is essential to the proper use of the invention. Grant-back agreements as to improvements and know-how are permissible, provided that they must not be exclusive, and the licensor must assume similar obligations; accordingly, it appears that assignments-back are not covered—only non-exclusive licenses are allowed. Apart from the grant-back situation, however, exclusive licenses, including agreements excluding the licensor as well as single-licensee agreements, are said to be lawful.

The Notice states that it "does not seem possible to give a general opinion" as to restrictive agreements relating to "joint patents," "reciprocal licenses," and "multiple parallel licenses." Presumably, this reservation was made as to the first and second-named types because they may involve horizontal arrangements among patentees, such as patent pools, creating restraints which are outside the scope of any single patent or group of patents held by a single patentee. In its only reported action against patent license restrictions to date, the Commission started proceedings on a complaint filed by a French chemical manufacturer against two competitors who had entered into a cross-license agreement as to plastics process patents.[273] The agreement provided for royalty-free sublicensing to firms who agreed to buy non-patented products used in the process from the licensors, whereas royalties were required to be paid by sublicensees who patronized other suppliers. Before any decision was made, the parties abandoned the offending conditions.

The third type, "multiple parallel licenses," involves a problem of special concern to the Common Market—licensing under patents on the same invention in different nations, wherein the result may be to carve up the Common Market on national lines (see discussion in Chapter 5).

Notably missing from the list of permissible license restraints is price control, reflecting the conclusion that such a restraint is not within the scope of the patent right. The Notice reflects a sharpness of analysis

[273] Press release, March 3, 1966, CCH COMM. MKT. REP. ¶9093.

concerning the relation of different types of license restrictions to the scope of the patent which is not always seen in discussion of the same problems under American law. Without such analysis, it is easy to conclude that overruling of the *General Electric* case would more or less automatically destroy not only price control, but also limitation of quantity, territory and type or field of manufacture. If thinking is governed by the "scope of the patent" analysis, however, carefully defined instances of the latter restraints could well survive the *General Electric* doctrine, provided the assumption also continues that a patentee may lawfully license less than his entire bundle of rights.

As to restrictions which are not allowable under the Notice, an Article 85(3) exemption may still be available. Moreover, Council Regulation 19/65, which authorized the group exemption already propounded by the Commission for exclusive dealing agreements, also authorizes the Commission to issue a group exemption—not yet done—for industrial property and know-how restrictions.[274]

The German statute, in Section 20, also follows the distinction between restraints which are within, and those which are outside, the scope of the patent, and was obviously the forerunner of the EEC Official Notice. It invalidates patent license restrictions which "go beyond the scope of the right to protection," and at the same time states that restraints as to "type, extent, quantity, territory or period of exercise" do not exceed the scope of the patent.[275] Having adopted this test, however, it then departs from it by granting certain exceptions, including: restrictions on the licensee which are "justified by any interest of the . . . licensor in technically satisfactory exploitation of the protected matter," thereby (as in the EEC) permitting quality control and certain forms of tying; price control (contrary to the EEC); grant-back licenses, provided the licensor has "identical obligations" (as in the EEC); agreements not to contest validity of the patent; and restraints "relating to the regulation of competition in markets outside the area to which this Act applies."

Section 20(3) goes still further and gives the BKA authority to authorize an otherwise prohibited patent license restriction if "the

---

[274] CCH COMM. MKT. REP. ¶2717; see DERINGER, *supra* note 127 at ¶2701.
[275] BUSINESS REGULATION IN THE COMMON MARKET NATIONS, vol. 3, *supra* note 12, at 280, 390; Section 21 extends the application of Section 20 to certain kinds of trade secrets; *id.* at 296.

freedom of economic action of the ... licensee ... is not unfairly restricted, and if competition in the market is not substantially restrained."

Interpretation of these provisions has been fairly substantial.[276] Among other questions, it appears that it is within the scope of the patent to limit the number of products and type produced under a process patent; to restrict the number of customers; and to prohibit the licensee from selling to competitors of the licensor. On the other hand, an agreement by both the licensor and the licensee not to sell would fall under Section 1 of the Act. Prohibitions against competition with the licensor by the licensee through use of competing inventions, and resale controls are not allowed.

The exception for tying clauses appears to be strictly limited to situations in which lesser restraints will be inadequate to assure technically sound working of the invention; however, the BKA sometimes grants exemptions under Section 20(3) for tying which does not meet this test. The price control exception, as in American law, has been interpreted as being available only for patented products.[277]

The German Act applies to foreign as well as German patents. The exception in Section 20(2)(5) for restraints in foreign markets, however, permits extraterritorial restraints as to both types of patents, provided— according to a BKA interpretation—the restriction does not have "an appreciable effect on the domestic market."[278]

Horizontal agreements among patentees will be governed, in general, by the prohibition of Section 1 of the Act. Thus, for example, patent pools are not *ipso facto* illegal, but will become so if coupled with restrictions on competition.[279]

Under the antitrust laws of other Common Market nations, scant attention has been paid to these problems. Belgium permits vertical license restraints generally, and Government intervention is unlikely to occur except in cases of systematic suppression of patents, or where a pool dominates the market and abuses its power.[280] In the Netherlands, vertical restrictions are generally regarded as within the scope of the

[276] See *id.* at 283 *et seq.*
[277] *Id.* at 284-86.
[278] *Id.* at 288.
[279] See *id.* at 294-95.
[280] BUSINESS REGULATION IN THE COMMON MARKET NATIONS, vol. 1, *supra* note 23, at 140.

patent, and it is possible that this will include price restrictions on the licensee, though not on his customers.[281] Tying probably does not come within the scope of the patent, but there has been very little enforcement against tying of any kind.[282] Horizontal restraints may be subjected to control. In France, the Price Ordinance may reach patent restraints, but there has been no significant development of the law as yet.[283]

C. Conflict Analysis

Patent arrangements are an important part of the international trade and investment activity carried on between American and Common Market firms, and there are many opportunities for overlap and conflict to exist with respect to the various legal systems involved. Such situations will probably arise more frequently as to transactions occurring in European markets than in American markets, simply because of the more limited applicability of European laws in foreign markets. There are situations, however, in which restraints imposed in the American market may contravene one or more European laws, and in some cases, European laws may apply more strictly than the American law.

1. LICENSE RESTRICTIONS

Common Market firms which grant licenses under American patents with restrictive provisions may often encounter American prohibitions, *e.g.,* as in the *Chemagro* case.[284] Conflict with European laws in the

---

[281] BUSINESS REGULATION IN THE COMMON MARKET NATIONS, vol. 1, *supra* note 19, at 420-22.

[282] *Id.* at 422.

[283] BUSINESS REGULATION IN THE COMMON MARKET NATIONS, vol. 2, *supra* note 15, at 263.

[284] United States v. Farbenfabriken Bayer A.G. and Chemagro Corp., Civil No. 586-68 (D.D.C.), consent decree entered, Oct. 24, 1969, 1969 Trade Cas. ¶72,918, prohibiting German parent and its American subsidiary from requiring purchasers of patented insecticide to observe resale restrictions as to customers, areas, consumer end use, and the particular formulation or concentration of the product, and also requiring purchasers not to resell outside the United States. It should be noted that these resale restrictions, if applied as to American export commerce to Europe could conceivably restrain competition within the Common Market and within Germany in

sense of this study may be hard to perceive because of the inapplicability of the European laws to foreign markets. But it may exist as to the transaction, and even as to an individual firm.

More obvious conflict can also be hypothesized. Suppose that a European firm holding several corresponding European and American patents on a given process grants licenses to licensees in both markets with tying clauses attached which require purchases of supplies from the patentee. Suppose further that the tying is not essential for the "technically sound" working of the invention, but is granted an exemption under Article 85(3) because it promotes efficiencies and does not dominate competition. The tying clause will at the same time be illegal in the United States and will also constitute misuse, rendering the American patent unenforceable in American courts. This situation will permit European competitors of the patentee to sell the unpatented goods to American licensees. Depending upon the economic facts, the result may be to prevent the European patentee from achieving the efficiencies which were the justification for the Article 85(3) exemption, thus defeating Common Market policy.

Situations in which American firms encounter conflict as to license restrictions used in European markets may be more frequent. Under present law, price control imposed by an American licensor of a product patent upon European manufacturing licensees could—if the goods are exported to the United States—be unlawful under the Rome Treaty and protected under American law (if we make the assumption that the *General Electric* doctrine would apply to a foreign patent). Similarly, an American licensor relying upon the *Trans-Wrap* case,[285] might lawfully exact from a European licensee an obligation to assign back improvements, whereas both EEC law and German law limit legality in such cases to agreements to grant back non-exclusive licenses, provided also that the licensor is mutually bound to do the same thing for the licensee.

The shoe may of course be on the other foot. American law may prohibit the American firm from requiring European licensees to observe various kinds of restrictions which would be lawful under given national laws (*e.g.,* in highly permissive Belgium, Netherlands, Luxembourg, Italy or France), and even lawful under EEC law by virtue of exemp-

violation of laws of the latter jurisdictions, thereby removing the appearance of conflict.

[285] See text at note 243 *supra*.

tions (individual or group) which may be forthcoming under Article 85(3).

2. PATENT CROSS-LICENSING AND POOLS

Some of the best-known American antitrust cases in the foreign commerce area have involved patent interchanges or pools which were held illegal because of their impact on American domestic or foreign commerce. These include such famous examples as the *duPont-I.C.I.* case,[286] in which nylon patents were found to have been interchanged in order to support a division-of-markets arrangement; the *National Lead* case,[287] involving a world cartel in titanium, in which a pool of world patent rights was utilized to divide markets; the *General Electric* incandescent lamp case,[288] in which American companies and a Dutch company were found to have combined to monopolize the industry through patent pooling; the *Singer* case,[289] where American and European companies were found to have interchanged patent rights to give the American company power to exclude Japanese competitors from the American market; and the *Hazeltine Research* case,[290] where it was found that foreign patent pools operating lawfully in Canada, Australia and England restrained American exports and that an American patent holding company violated American law by putting its patents into the pools.

On occasion, cases of this type have produced sharp procedural as well as substantive clashes, as in the conflict of American and English court decrees in the *duPont-I.C.I.* case, and the stern protest of Canada as to American enforcement efforts against the Canadian Electronic Patents pool (the same pool which was later involved in the *Hazeltine Research* case, *supra*).[291]

Were Common Market law the same as English and Canadian law, the patent pool problem would be a continuing source of conflict. But

[286] See Chapter 3, text at note 15 *et seq.*
[287] United States v. National Lead Co., 63 F.Supp. 513 (S.D.N.Y. 1945), *aff'd*, 332 U.S. 319 (1947).
[288] United States v. General Electric Co., 82 F.Supp. 753 (D.N.J. 1949).
[289] United States v. Singer Mfg. Co., 374 U.S. 174 (1963).
[290] Hazeltine Research, Inc. v. Zenith Radio Corp., 239 F.Supp. 51 (N.D.Ill. 1965), *aff'd in part and rev'd in part*, 395 U.S. 100 (1969); opinion of Court of Appeals on remand on other issues, 1969 Trade Cas. ¶72,949.
[291] See Chapter 9, text at note 10 *et seq.*

within the Common Market, there is no clear, present inconsistency with American law. The EEC Official Notice does not offer any comfort for horizontal arrangements among patentees; its dispensations are limited to simple licensor-licensee restrictions, and patent pools will be dealt with under Articles 85(1) and 86. Similarly, German law, and even the other national laws, through their controls of abuse of dominant power, may interpose obstacles to patent pools which exert market control. Actually, however, there has been too little case development in any of these systems to predict how strong these controls will be.

3. PATENT MISUSE

With the exception of the Netherlands, where it may achieve some recognition, the patent misuse doctrine does not appear to be available in the Common Market as an additional sanction against restrictive licensing activities. In any event, since it is indigenous to the patent infringement action, which in turn is strictly limited territorially, the patent misuse doctrine does not itself appear to be a source of genuine conflict.

In conclusion, it is possible to exaggerate the dangers of substantive conflict in the patent area. Over-all, EEC law—insofar as it has developed—is strikingly like American law, with the few exceptions noted in the examples above. German law seems even more like American law. Conflict between American and national laws of the other Member States is always a theoretical possibility, but the most important situations will probably be ones in which EEC law will govern, with inconsistent national laws having to give way.

The greatest chances for conflict lie in the possibility that the presently very similar American and EEC policies may gradually diverge—U.S. law becoming more and more strict under the strong pressure of the Department of Justice, and EEC law emerging as more and more lenient under the relaxed attitude now manifest and under the large exemption possibilities which are within the Commission's control.

VI. RESTRAINTS RESULTING FROM GOVERNMENT ACTION

By way of concluding this chapter's study of types of conflict which may arise in the overlapping of one jurisdiction's antitrust laws with the laws of another, attention must be paid to the conflicts which may arise through government-imposed or government-approved restraints. In general, three types of government action may be identified for purposes of analysis: (1) exemption or authorization of private restraint; (2) compulsion of private restraint; and (3) restraint committed by government-owned enterprise.

As to the first type, this chapter has previously identified a number of kinds of exemption which may be granted, including the various exemptions in the United States and Europe for export cartels, and the important general exemption process contained in Article 85(3) of the Rome Treaty, in Articles 65 and 66 of the ECSC Treaty and in some of the national laws. To this list must be added the availability under American statutes of many kinds of exemptions for regulated industries.[292]

It was concluded in earlier discussion, and it may merely be repeated here, that it is most unlikely that the United States or the Common Market authorities will recognize each others' exemptions to the extent of allowing them to be effective against the home jurisdiction's antitrust laws. Article 90 of the Rome Treaty provides, with a narrow exception for public utilities and fiscal monopolies, that the Member States shall not grant special rights, or maintain measures, which are contrary to Articles 85 and 86. Similarly, it was early established that the American States could not, through the grant of special corporate charters, defeat application of the Sherman Act.[293] While both of these doctrines rest upon internal federal supremacy and are not perfect analogies to the question of the effect to be given to a foreign country's exemptions or authorizations, it would seem unlikely that either the United States or the EEC would accord more force to acts of foreign governments than to the acts of their own constituents. The *Swiss Watch* case, discussed in Chapter 6, is an example of great conflict which arose when the United States refused to recognize the Swiss Government's broad sanctioning of cartel organization and activity in its basic watch industry. While no converse example of EEC attack upon an American exemption has yet arisen, this is probably just a question of time.

As to the second type, *i.e.*, government compulsion, governments of

[292] For a thorough study and listing of American exemptions, see Report of A.B.A. Antitrust Section Committee on Antitrust Exemptions, 33 A.B.A. ANTITRUST L. J. 1-110 (1967); see also ABA SUPP. TO ATTY. GEN. NAT. COMM. ANTITRUST REP. ch. VI.

[293] Northern Securities Co. v. United States, 193 U.S. 197, 332 (1904).

course create a great deal of restraint of competition through direct exercise of their sovereign powers. So long as this takes the form of direct government action, as distinguished from action by an enterprise under government control, it will probably not be disturbed either by American or by Common Market law.[294] If, however, the Government—through legislative, administrative, or judicial action—compels a private enterprise to participate in what amounts to a restraint of competition, what is the effect upon antitrust law?

It is doubtful that American law, under existing authorities, will apply to compulsion by a foreign government. This much is probably still left of the old *American Banana* case,[295] where the Supreme Court held the Sherman Act inapplicable to acts in Central America which damaged the defendant's competitor—acts which the Court said were done by a foreign sovereign, albeit at the instigation of the American defendant. Although international law does not seem to require recognition of such "acts of state,"[296] American courts in antitrust cases continue to accord immunity to such acts. In the *Swiss Watch* decree, for example, the court excepted from its prohibitions actions done, or refrained from, pursuant to requirements of Swiss law.[297] Of related significance also is the Supreme Court's holding, in the *Noerr* case, that the Sherman Act does not apply to activities of private persons which seek to restrain competition by inducing government regulatory action.[298] While this doctrine could be limited to inducement of American state or national government action, there does not seem to be a compelling reason for doing so, and the continued survival of the *American Banana* doctrine supplies a contrary logic.

[294] In Parker v. Brown, 317 U.S. 341 (1943), the Court held the Sherman Act inapplicable to a comprehensive California program of State controls of competition in the raisin industry, even though the program was largely carried out for the State by the producers. For the proposition that the Rome Treaty antitrust provisions do not apply to sovereign action, see DERINGER, *supra* note 127, at ¶827.

[295] American Banana Co. v. United Fruit Co., 213 U.S. 347 (1909).

[296] Section 39(1) of the RESTATEMENT (SECOND) OF FOREIGN RELATIONS LAW OF THE UNITED STATES says that a state is not precluded from exercising jurisdiction "solely because such exercise requires a person to engage in conduct subjecting him to liability under the law of another state having jurisdiction with respect to that conduct." See Chapter 7 *infra*.

[297] See Chapter 6, text at note 40 *et seq.*

[298] Eastern Railroad Presidents Conference v. Noerr Motor Freight, Inc., 365 U.S. 127 (1961).

It is not clear how Common Market law is likely to evolve on this issue, but it is possible that it will not develop in the same way as has American law. Article 90(1) is an explicit command to the Member States not to require conduct which is contrary to the Treaty's antitrust provisions. Both Belgium and the Netherlands have laws which permit the government to require participation in cartels in some situations,[299] but these "compulsory cartels" will probably violate Article 90 if interstate trade is affected. This does not mean that the private firms involved will be guilty, as they may be able to use the fact of government compulsion as a defense. But the compelling government may be found to violate the treaty.[300]

The latter analysis does not necessarily mean that a cartel compelled to act by American law, if there were such a thing, would be held illegal under the Rome Treaty. If illegality must be found in the action of a state itself, this might be difficult to find as to the action of a state which is not a party to the Treaty. But there would be great pressure to reach a contrary result in order to avoid defeat of the Treaty's aims. If foreign cartels can operate with impunity where they are cloaked with some sort of governmental command, they could be very difficult to control. (This same argument, of course, would apply to American law, which has not been put to a real test by foreign compulsory cartels.)

Finally, as to the third type, *i.e.*, government-owned enterprise, Article 90(1) explicitly prohibits "public undertakings" from violating the antitrust rules, with the exception that public utilities and "fiscal monopolies" may avoid these rules if their application would "prejudice the performance of the special duties entrusted to them." The prohibition prevents a Member State from gaining immunity for its publicly-owned manufacturing, mining and processing firms to the disadvantage of privately-owned competitors.[301] There would seem to be little reason for according a greater privilege in the Common Market to foreign publicly-owned enterprises even though the Treaty is silent on the matter.

American law approaches this question, insofar as foreign government-owned enterprise is concerned, in terms of whether the enterprise

[299] See BUSINESS REGULATION IN THE COMMON MARKET NATIONS, vol. 1, *supra* notes 19 and 23, at 115 and 384.

[300] DERINGER, *supra* note 127, at ¶804, n.8.

[301] *Id.* at ¶803.

represents "proprietary" action by the government, in which case the antitrust laws apply, or whether it is "governmental," in which case "sovereign immunity" is recognized.[302]

There are obviously numerous possibilities for conflict in these different kinds of government action situations. Any case in which one government authorizes, compels or commits an act which is contrary to the substantive antitrust law of another would be a case of conflict of a high order. The American and EEC "federal" systems have built-in supremacy principles designed to resolve such conflicts when they occur internally. No such relatively simple devices exist to solve conflicts of this nature between the United States and European governments. Chapters 7, 8 and 9 deal with the international approaches which have been tried so far.

SUMMARY

The nature and extent of conflict between American law and the Community and national laws of the Common Market may briefly be summarized as follows:

Horizontal combinations, in the past, have been the source of most of the conflicts which have appeared in litigated cases. The recent development of cartel controls under the Rome Treaty and some of the national laws has definitely diminished the potential amount of this kind of conflict. On the other hand, the recently growing tolerance, and indeed encouragement, of various kinds of business cooperation in the Common Market is a new trend which will probably restore some of the potentiality of conflict in horizontal cases, other than those involving hard-core restraints by market-dominating combinations.

Export cartels, which are permissible under certain conditions under both American and Common Market laws, are a continuing obvious

---

[302] BREWSTER, ANTITRUST AND AMERICAN BUSINESS ABROAD 61 (1958); FUGATE, FOREIGN COMMERCE AND THE ANTITRUST LAWS 73 (1958); United States v. Deutsches Kalisyndikat Gesellschaft, 31 F.2d 199 (S.D.N.Y. 1929), French-owned company held amenable to antitrust action because not acting in governmental capacity; *cf. In re* Investigation of World Arrangements, 13 F.R.D. 280 (D.D.C. 1952), British Government-controlled company held immune from antitrust process because instrumentality of British Government.

source of potentially prohibitive conflicts. Since the exemptions provided in one way or another by each system authorize a form of illegal cartel-preying upon the antitrust-protected markets of the others, a strong potentiality of attack by someone exists. That no such attack seems yet to have occurred may be due only to an international sense of *in pari delicto*—a most unreliable basis for prediction of future policy. A bad side effect is the allowance for defensive import cartels in Europe, a device which American law does not permit.

Corporate mergers present an area in which the greatest inconsistencies exist between American and European law. Growing difficulties arise from the fact that American law cracks down extremely hard on mergers affecting domestic competition, while European laws and policies not only tolerate, but encourage mergers. One result is a feeling in Europe that American policy somehow discriminates against foreign investors in the United States—a feeling which is actually as much caused by European laxity in the merger area as by American sternness. Another result is that American "merger capital" may be driven into European markets by the stiff American laws operating in the presence of a European legal vacuum, thus intensifying the problem of increasing control of European business by American interests in some sectors. Against this background, analysis of legal conflict is complex. Attacks by American authorities on mergers of European companies, which are possible under American law, would undoubtedly create severe conflict. On the other hand, application of American law to take-over of European firms by Americans, while also theoretically in conflict with European law, might sometimes be harmonious with over-all European policies, although the conflict will be prohibitive to the firms involved.

Joint ventures, insofar as their formation is concerned, receive legal treatment in both the United States and Europe which is very similar to that given to mergers. Consequently, the analysis of conflict is much the same. An important difference exists, however, in that joint ventures involving American and European partners are probably viewed with greater favor under European policies than are American acquisitions of European firms. Hence, reaction to American antitrust attack is likely to be more uniformly intense than as to the latter kind of merger.

Joint venture operating agreements potentially give rise to less sharp differences in approach among the various legal systems involved. American law is quite strict with respect to agreements not to compete among participants in a joint venture, but as to some of the situations likely to exist, European law (at least EEC and German law) is likely to be equally strict. The clearest difference will probably be as to a promise by the joint venture company not to compete with its founders. As a practical matter, even this may not give rise to many real conflict situations, however, since the average joint venture company does not need to be made to promise not to invade its parents' markets. A more important potential area of conflict lies in the prospect of increasingly lenient treatment by the EEC of various kinds of joint activity under the new spirit of cooperation referred to above.

Vertical or distribution restraints have not heretofore been a significant source of conflict in litigated cases involving European markets. There have been a number of cases, however, in which American law has been applied to prohibit various kinds of distribution restraints by European sellers in the American market—often as to restraints which are lawful under European law. Comparison of approaches by the different legal systems to various specific marketing restraints reveals the potentiality of a great many kinds of conflict in both American and European markets, if the laws are actually applied to international transactions. Most productive of difficulty is the existence of complex inconsistency in the various rules pertaining to resale price maintenance and to exclusive buying and tying arrangements. On the other hand, exclusive selling and territorial confinement of dealers are areas in which American and Common Market laws have coincided rather well. Refusals to deal and customer restrictions on dealers seem to fall in between the no-conflict and the high-conflict areas, with much depending upon future legal development.

Patents create many kinds of problems for antitrust law, and vice versa. Examination shows, however, that Common Market and German law have for the most part developed along lines which are very similar to those of American law, and there is no real basis in established case law or principles for describing this as a major source of conflict in the sense of this study (compare the discussion of territorial restraints involving industrial property in Chapter 5). The greatest prospect for conflict probably lies in the possibility that American law—heretofore fairly lenient to vertical patent license restrictions—will become much more strict under continuing Justice Department pressure for changes in the law.

Finally, government action itself is a fairly frequent source of restraint of competition, in the form of exemptions, compulsion of restrictive conduct, or restraint by government enterprises. The exemption or authorization area is by far the greatest source of government-created restraint and is an extremely important source of potential conflict in practically every area of antitrust law discussed in this chapter. Government compulsion of restrictive conduct is probably rather rare, but where it occurs, conflict could be intense. Restraint of competition by government enterprises would not ordinarily create a special kind of conflict, since such enterprises are generally amenable to the antitrust laws of other jurisdictions and normally would be treated there like private enterprises.

5 *Patent and Trademark License Agreements in the Common Market and Antitrust Law — The Problem of Territorial Limitation*

Introduction

The steady growth of Common Market anticartel law since its inception more than a decade ago has given rise to much speculation and some concern as to the possibilities of duplication, overlap and conflict with American antitrust law as it is applied to industrial property transactions. Both bodies of law may be applicable to the same private practices in international trade and licensing transactions—practices which may be characterized as unlawful restraints of trade by the one but not by the other, or practices which both may regard as restrictive but which may be given a special exemption under the terms of the one but not of the other.

International patent and trademark licensing practices merit particular attention because of the prominence of licensing as a method of doing business abroad. Moreover, the extent to which antitrust law, American or foreign, is applicable to practices that are derived from, and traditionally justified as being ancillary to, rights conferred by industrial property law[1] is an extraordinarily complicated and controversial

---

[1] "Industrial property" includes patents, trademarks, and copyrights. A more comprehensive definition is furnished in Article 1(2) of the International Convention for the Protection of International Property: "The protection of industrial property is concerned with patents, utility models, industrial designs, trademarks, service marks, trade names, and indications of source or appellations of origin, and the repression of unfair competition." To label these intangible interests and rights "industrial property" is to analogize them to ordinary personal property, and may make patent and trademark protection under the law sound more immutable and

subject, well worth singling out for comparative study. The Common Market administrators and the European Court of Justice are in the process of fashioning their own approach. Many of their views as to applicability of Community anticartel provisions to licensing practices are closely similar to American enforcement concepts. But the Common Market approach to this problem of applicability diverges occasionally and significantly with respect to some of these practices, especially in the field of allocation of territories.

Trademark and patent licensing and transfers may involve restrictions on territory, field of use, prices, and other restraints, as well as controls over unpatented and branded products (see Chapter 4 for general discussion). This chapter focuses on territorial restrictions, which in turn may take the form of "simple" licensing, multiple licensing, cross-licensing and patent pools.

I. ALLOCATIONS OF NATIONAL TERRITORIES INHERENT IN OR BASED ON INDUSTRIAL PROPERTY RIGHTS

The broad category of allocation of national territories is of particular importance to an economic community, given the basic purpose of a Common Market. Allocation may arise because of the territorial nature of patent and trademark rights, and the concomitant relationship between infringement remedies and the right to impose a ban on imports of trademarked or patented products. A more stringent and far-reaching

sacrosanct than it really is. Compare BLAKE & PITOFSKY, CASES AND MATERIALS ON ANTITRUST LAW 258 (1967): "A word of warning. Those who favor broad protection of the interests of owners of patents, copyrights, trademarks and the like—and correlative de-emphasis of antitrust policy—like to use the term 'industrial property' and draw analogies to traditional property law. This characterization may divert attention from crucial differences between 'industrial' and traditional forms of property. [Industrial property law, unlike traditional property law, prevents others from making or acquiring any number of other such items identical in every feature to the item protected. Industrial property laws provide a right of exclusion as an economic incentive to the publication of creative work (patents, copyrights) or to prevent public confusion and enhance producers' 'responsibility' for their products (trademarks).] This is a kind of 'legal monopoly' which may or may not carry with it substantial economic power but which is quite different from traditional property rights. . . . The law of 'industrial property' comes more frequently into conflict with the antitrust laws."

allocation may result from the insertion in license agreements of clauses expressly prohibiting the licensee from exporting the licensed product directly, or exporting it indirectly through his domestic customers. The former may be called territorial *licensing, i.e.,* the grant of a trademark or patent license for a particular territory—in international terms, for use in a particular country. The latter is the imposition of a territorial *restriction* upon a licensee—*i.e.,* expressly prohibiting a licensee from exporting the product outside the licensed country. These are clearly different types of territorial limitations. Whether the differences merit different antitrust treatment, however, is another matter, and, as suggested below, the American and European views on this question may diverge.

The existence of national trademark and patent systems, with rights that are in the main independent of those enjoyed by holders of corresponding ("parallel") trademarks and patents in other countries, contains a built-in potential for compartmentalizing international trade. Patents and trademarks have separate historical origins and were devised to furnish governmental protection for private interests of a diverse nature. But they have in common the availability of a right (frequently expressed by the courts in terms of relief from unfair competition)[2] to protection against infringement on the part of distributors and users in the national territory. The infringement rights extend, *inter alia*, against those who import the patented or trademarked product from a foreign country, even though it was properly manufactured or affixed with a parallel trademark in the foreign country—*e.g.,* under license from the person asserting the infringement, or under license from a person who has also licensed the complainant, or by the complainant's licensor himself.[3]

---

[2] For example, in United Drug Co. v. Theodore Rectanus Co., 248 U.S. 90, 97 (1918), Mr. Justice Pitney said: "The law of trade-marks is but a part of the broader law of unfair competition. . . ." See also Hanover Star Milling Co. v. Metcalf, 240 U.S. 403, 412-13 (1916); 1 CALLMANN, THE LAW OF UNFAIR COMPETITION, TRADEMARKS AND MONOPOLIES § §4-4.3, 16, 16.1, 16.2 (3d ed. 1967); 3 *id.* at § §67.1, 67.2, and citations in footnotes 23, 24, 32, 33 (3d ed. 1969). For a description of the historical origins and partial convergence of the unfair competition and trademark infringement remedies, see Chafee, *Unfair Competition,* 53 HARV. L. REV. 1289, 1291-1301 (1940).

[3] See EBB, REGULATION AND PROTECTION OF INTERNATIONAL BUSINESS 460-525 (1964).

This protective and restrictionist principle of trademark and patent law has been somewhat eroded, particularly in the area of trademark law, by exceptions unrelated to the free-competition implications of antitrust law. For example, many jurisdictions, including the United States, Germany, and the Netherlands, do not permit the "same person" (a much-worried term) who holds parallel trademarks in two or more countries to bar import of a product trademarked by him or his licensee in one of these other countries.[4] The import-ban privilege of the "same person" holding parallel *patent* rights in more than one country has been challenged far less frequently[5]—at least prior to the adoption of the Treaty of Rome and the establishment of the European Common Market.

In interpretation and enforcement of antitrust laws in the United States, and more recently in Germany and other European countries, administrators and courts have had to cope with the existence of these import-ban privileges, which have been used as the basis for developing additional explicitly contractual supportive restraints of trade that are claimed to be "ancillary" or "reasonably ancillary" to the industrial property rights themselves. American antitrust law has accorded considerable, though by no means overwhelming, deference to these privileges and rights. It has allowed trademark and patent holders or licensees to exercise import-ban privileges under customs law provisions or as part of infringement remedies, so long as the exercise of these privileges has not been clearly linked to an attempt by a horizontal combination to restrain competition.[6]

[4] See the American regulations on imports of trademarked merchandise, 19 C.F.R. §11.14, and Swiss, Dutch and German judicial decisions to this effect cited or reported in EBB, *supra* note 3, at 476-77, 482-95, 503-07.

[5] For a few such early challenges see, *e.g.*, Holiday v. Mattheson, 24 F. 185 (S.D.N.Y. 1885); Dickerson v. Matheson, 57 F. 524 (2d Cir. 1893); Dickerson v. Tinling, 84 F. 192, 195 (8th Cir. 1897); and other materials and comments in EBB, *supra* note 3, at 499-507.

[6] *Compare* A. Bourjois & Co. v. Katzel, 260 U.S. 689 (1923) and United States v. Guerlain, Inc., 155 F.Supp. 77 (S.D.N.Y. 1957), judgment for the Government on a charge of violating §2 of the Sherman Act, vacated by the Supreme Court on the Government's own motion, 358 U.S. 915 (1958), and motion to dismiss the judgment granted, 172 F.Supp. 107 (S.D.N.Y. 1959); *with* United States v. Singer Mfg. Co., 374 U.S. 174 (1963); Timken Roller Bearing Co. v. United States, 341 U.S. 593, 598 (1951); United States v. Bayer Co., 135 F.Supp. 65 (S.D.N.Y. 1955);

The use of industrial property rights as a basis for private territorial restraints in the field of international trade, however, appears to be destined to diminish significantly within the European Common Market as the implications of Articles 85 and 86 of the Treaty of Rome are spelled out by regulations and judicial decisions.[7] To the extent that American and Common Market law may overlap in applicability to distribution arrangements that involve patents or trademarks, a potential source of conflict may be created by disparate development of regulatory law as between the United States and the European Economic Community in these fields.

What follows in the balance of this section and the next three sections of this chapter is preliminary to consideration of this possible overlap or conflict. The final section, Section V, deals in detail with the possibilities of overlap and conflict.

United States v. Holophane Co., 119 F.Supp. 114 (S.D. Ohio 1954); United States v. Imperial Chem. Indus., Ltd., 100 F.Supp. 504, 518 (S.D.N.Y. 1951) and 105 F.Supp. 215 (S.D.N.Y. 1952); United States v. General Electric Co., 82 F.Supp. 753 (D.N.J. 1949).

[7] Treaty Article 85(1) provides in part:

"The following practices shall be prohibited as incompatible with the Common Market: all agreements between undertakings, all decisions by associations of undertakings and all concerted practices which are liable to affect trade between Member States and which are designed to prevent, restrict or distort competition within the Common Market or which have this effect. This shall, in particular, include:

    (a) the direct or indirect fixing of purchase or selling prices or of any other trading conditions;

    (b) the limitation or control of production, markets, technical development or investment;

    (c) market-sharing or the sharing of sources of supply. . . ."

Article 86 provides in part:

"To the extent to which trade between any Member States may be affected thereby, action by one or more enterprises to take improper advantage of a dominant position within the Common Market or within a substantial part of it shall be deemed to be incompatible with the Common Market and shall hereby be prohibited.

Such improper practices may, in particular, consist in:

    (a) the direct or indirect imposition of any inequitable purchase or selling prices or of any other inequitable trading conditions;

    (b) the limitation of production, markets or technical development to the prejudice of consumers. . . ."

(Translation from 1 CCH COMM. MKT. REP. ¶¶ 2005, 2101.)

A. Articles 36 and 222 as Immunizing Exercise of Industrial Property Rights from Articles 85 and 86

At the inception of the Common Market, the vast majority of European commentators held no tenet of faith more firmly than the belief that the new anticartel law that was to emerge under the Treaty of Rome would have no impact upon the territorial distribution restrictions conforming to national boundaries that manufacturers selling in Europe had traditionally imposed upon their trademarked and patented products. Clutching at what today seem increasingly slender reeds, they relied largely upon Articles 36 and 222 of the Treaty, on early announcements of somewhat ambiguous import by the EEC Commission, and on a heavily territorial concept of trademark and patent rights. In light of recent developments—the European Court of Justice decision in the *Grundig-Consten* case in July 1966;[8] Regulation 67/67, issued by the Commission (effective May 1, 1967); and the rationale presented to the Court of Justice by the EEC Commission in the *Parke, Davis* case[9]—the viability of this protectionist, territorialist view is open to serious question in a number of respects.

Article 222 merely provides that "the Treaty shall in no way prejudice the property system in the Member States." Whatever its meaning, it could hardly have been intended by the Treaty-makers to grant to patent or trademark license agreements a blanket immunity from anticartel regulations or decisions to be adopted under Articles 85 and 86. So extensive an exemption for arrangements so frequently linked with restraints of trade could not plausibly be founded on the general statement that "the property system in the Member States" should not be prejudiced by the Treaty. It is conceivable that the term "the property system" is intended to include the trademark and patent systems of the various States, and thereby in some sense and in some

[8] Ets. Consten S.A. and Grundig-Verkaufs-GmbH v. EEC Comm'n, CCH COMM. MKT. REP. ¶8046, 5 Comm. Mkt. L. R. 418 (1966), discussed in Ebb, *The Grundig-Consten Case Revisited: Judicial Harmonization of National Law and Treaty Law in the Common Market,* 115 U. PA. L. REV. 855 (1967). The facts of the case and its relevance to the theme of this chapter are considered in detail in Section IV *infra.*

[9] Parke, Davis & Co. v. Probel Co., CCH COMM. MKT. REP. ¶8054 (the Commission's views on the impact of anticartel law on patent rights appear at 7817-19), 7 Comm. Mkt. L. R. 47 (1968).

manner to protect property rights deemed to be inherent in such legal systems. But an American observer may be forgiven for seeing in Article 222 a limitation on regulatory action by the Commission as great as, but not greater than, that imposed by the Due Process Clause of the Fifth Amendment[10] on the implementation of the Sherman Act.

Actually, those who criticize broad regulation by the Commission in this area rely far more heavily on Article 36, which they regard as more clearly relevant, either explicitly or by virtue of inferences that are more plausibly drawn from its mention of "industrial and commercial property" rights than from Article 222's reference to "property systems."[11] In the Rome Treaty, Article 36 appears in the context of exempting certain measures of the Member States from the ban imposed by Articles 30-34 upon "quantitative restrictions on importation and all measures with equivalent effect" as between Member States. Articles 30-34 deal primarily with quota restrictions and similar measures that had long hampered liberalization of international trade among the Western European countries. Article 36 was added to this part of the Treaty to clarify the scope of this interdiction, by preserving the right of Member States to use local police power to block certain types of imports. Thus, it expressly exempts from the ban restraints which are justified on grounds of public morality,[12] order, and safety; protection of human, animal or plant life; protection of national art, historical and archeological treasures; and "the protection of industrial and commercial property." A concluding caveat provides that such restraints or measures "shall not, however, constitute either a means of arbitrary discrimination or a disguised restriction on trade between Member States."

This proviso to Article 36 makes it clear that governmental protective measures purportedly taken to attain the exempted ends may be invalidated if, upon close scrutiny, they turn out to be only colorable exercises of the exempted powers for illegitimate ends. Use of state police power ostensibly aimed at public health objectives, but really designed to uphold unreasonable restraints on interstate or foreign

---

[10] "No person . . . shall be deprived of . . . property, without due process of law. . . ." U.S. CONST. amend. V.

[11] See, *e.g.*, OBERDORFER, GLEISS & HIRSCH, COMMON MARKET CARTEL LAW ¶49 (1963).

[12] Compare the Twenty-first Amendment to the United States Constitution, which sanctions state regulation over imports of liquor from other states.

commerce in the interest of local enterprise, has been condemned in the United States in a variety of circumstances.[13] Similarly, an extreme national regulation which blocks entry of products from another Member State on grounds of protecting domestic trademark or patent rights and which does so in an "arbitrary" manner, may well fall within the caveat.[14] Moreover and more important, the fact that a State's general grant of import-ban privileges to trademark or patent holders is immunized by Article 36 from the ban on governmentally-imposed quantitative restrictions under Articles 30-34 could hardly be determinative of the legality of certain private restrictive arrangements for the exercise of such privileges which infringe the free competition objectives of Articles 85 and 86.[15] The very presence of the saving clause in Article 36 makes at least noteworthy the absence in Article 85 of a similar savings proviso with respect to private exercises of industrial property rights.

Some commentators, espousing the view that Article 36 governs Articles 85 and 86 as well as Articles 30-34, seem to have ignored the operative terms of Article 36.[16] Other commentators who expressly

[13] See, *e.g.,* Dean Milk Co. v. City of Madison, 340 U.S. 349 (1951) and Minnesota v. Barber, 136 U.S. 313 (1890).

[14] Examples of "arbitrary discrimination" or "disguised restriction on trade" based on these grounds are less common than those based on protection of public health. The Mexican courts' refusal in the 1920's to permit American exporters to Mexico to sue for trademark infringement unless they registered to do business in Mexico is one example. Exporters who were not seeking to rely on trademark protection in Mexico were not required to comply with the "onerous conditions of registration under the Commercial Code." See EBB, *supra* note 3, at 412, and generally, 410-24. Article 2(2) of the International Convention for the Protection of Industrial Property bars the imposition of so burdensome a requirement: "[N]o condition as to the possession of a domicile or establishment in the country where protection is claimed may be required of persons entitled to the benefits of the Union for the enjoyment of any industrial property rights." Reproduced, *id.* at 359.

[15] See VerLoren van Themaat, *Article 36 in Relation to Article 85 and Patent Licensing Agreements,* 1 C.M.L. REV. 428 (1964).

[16] See, *e.g.,* Ehlers, *Export und Re-Import-verbote in Lizenvertragen aus der Sicht des EWG-Kartellrechts,* GRUR. 424-32 (1963); Hepp, *Les Conventions de Licence Exclusive au regard des Règles de Concurrence .e la C.E.E.,* SOCIAAL ECO-NOMISCHE WETGEVING 85 (1964), commented upon in 2 C.M.L. REV. 118 (1964); Maddock, *Know-How Licensing Under the Antitrust Laws of the United States and the Rome Treaty,* 2 C.M.L. REV. 36, 65-66 (1964); and other European writers cited in DERINGER, THE COMPETITION LAW OF THE EUROPEAN ECONOMIC COMMUNITY ¶ 133 nn.12 & 13 (1968).

recognize the special context in which Article 36 stands in the Treaty have nevertheless drawn what appear to be overly-broad implications from its existence.[17] Still others have come close to sensing that the evaluation of Article 36 as predominant is not inevitable.[18] But their sensitivity to the potential impact of anticartel law upon industrial property rights in the Common Market itself is blunted by what may be an over-emphasis on the meaning and implications of Articles 36 and 222, by deep-seated traditional feelings about the "inherent rights" of patentees and trademark holders, and by their arguably excessive reliance on the precedential value of the German anticartel law, which permits patentees to exercise broad territorial restrictions in international trade.[19]

The views of two of the commentaries may be set forth and examined as representative of an influential school of thought on the relationship of Treaty competition law to national patent and trademark law. It would be difficult to have a really meaningful understanding of the evolution of Community law unless the Commission and Court of Justice rulings are considered against the background of the beliefs of those who regard Community regulation of licensing arrangements with some misgivings. *La doctrine* (commentary), moreover, has always been of great importance in the civil law countries of Europe, particularly in the absence of a well-defined body of case law.[20] However, with the

[17]See, *e.g.,* CAMPBELL & THOMPSON, COMMON MARKET LAW 175-76 (1962): "It therefore follows [from the presence of Articles 36 and 222] that the powers for protecting industrial property remain in the hands of the several Governments of the member states *and are not subject to control by the Community. . . .*" (emphasis added).

[18]OBERDORFER, GLEISS & HIRSCH, COMMON MARKET CARTEL LAW ¶49 n.5 (1963): "The cartel laws of all countries respect industrial protective rights in principle, although the courts of the United States have progressively narrowed their scope vis-à-vis the public policy expressed in the antitrust laws."

[19]See Chapter 2 *supra,* at 113.

[20]On the importance of the academic commentators in the civil law countries, where the "unflattering term 'secondary authority' is unknown . . . and virtually defies translation into non-English languages," see SCHLESINGER, COMPARATIVE LAW 187 & n.33 (2d ed. 1959). "[C]ourts in civil law countries show more respect for the scholar's view than is customary in the common law world. Overwhelming disapproval of a rule of case law by the academic commentators often induces a civil law court to reexamine its holding. . . ." *Id.* at 312. See also Rheinstein, *Law Faculties and Law Schools: A Comparison of Legal Education in the United States*

Common Market tribunals, *la jurisprudence* (case law) has undoubtedly acquired greater significance.

The writings of Arved Deringer, in cooperation with a number of European legal scholars from 1962 on, have been consolidated and published in English in 1968, and thus reflect views formulated both before and after the decision of the Court of Justice in the *Grundig-Consten* case in 1966. Deringer begins with a proposition that has become incontrovertible as a result of *Grundig-Consten*: "It is no longer possible to maintain the thesis proposed by Gotzen[21] that because of Articles 36 to 90, industrial property rights do not at all come within the Treaty, or in any event not within Article 85."[22] He proceeds to the familiar comment:

> To the extent that these restrictions [upon the rights of patent licensees] stay within the limits of the industrial property right ("within the scope of the patent"), they do not constitute an improper restraint of competition, but only a legitimate exercise of the industrial property right. This principle, developed in American antitrust law and adopted, among others, in GWB [Gesetz gegen Wettbewerbsbeschränkungen, the German Law against Restraints of Competition], §20, paragraph 1, is also applicable to Article 85(1).

From this he concludes, more debatably, that a patent holder may properly prohibit his licensees' exporting the patented goods to other Member States without violating Article 85(1),[23] so long as the product is protected in the other Member State by patents that give the licensor a right to prohibit distribution of the product in that State. And he further believes that a German patent licensor may impose such an export ban without violating Article 85(1) even with respect to a destination country in which the licensor lacks patent protection, because German

---

and Germany, 1938 WIS. L. REV. 5, 6-7, 10; DAVID & DeVRIES, THE FRENCH LEGAL SYSTEM 27, 115-26 (1958).

[21] [1958] GRUR AUSL. UND INT'L TEIL 224.

[22] DERINGER, *supra* note 16, at ¶133.

[23] What is intended to be covered by a ban on "export" by a licensee? Does such a ban preclude sales by the licensees to local customers who export the product? If so, German anticartel law itself would treat the restriction as illegal (see note 29 *infra*), and it would be equally unlawful under Article 85(1). See discussion of Regulation 67/67 in text at notes 65-67 *infra,* and see Froschmaier, *Progress Toward the Proposed Conventions for a European Patent and for a Trademark,* 6 PAT., T.M. & COPYRT. J. 479, 499 (1963).

patent law regards the "marketing" as commencing in the country in which the merchandise is produced.

This belief appears to be based in large part on reading into Article 85 not only the content of German patent law but also the conclusions of German anticartel law. Section 20(1) of the German Law against Restraints of Competition invalidates agreements concerning the exploitation of patents to the extent they impose upon the licensee any restrictions in his business conduct that go beyond the "scope of the right to protection."[24] Section 20(2)(5), however, expressly provides that the prohibitions of Section 20(1) shall not apply to "obligations of the . . . licensee relating to the regulation of competition in markets outside the area to which this Act applies." For this reason, the Bundeskartellamt (Federal Cartel Office) has interpreted the law as permitting the licensor to ban exports of the product by the licensee even to countries where the licensor lacks patent protection.[25] But the express territorial limitation on the scope of the German anticartel law in this particular field contrasts sharply with the less circumscribed territorial scope of the EEC Treaty anticartel law in the corresponding field.[26] Accordingly, Continental

---

[24] Section 20(1) adds that "restrictions pertaining to the type, extent, quantity, territory or period of exercise . . . shall not be deemed to go beyond its scope."

[25] See DERINGER, *supra* note 16, at ¶134 & n.16. See also Schapiro, *The German Law against Restraints of Competition—Comparative and International Aspects* (pt. 2), 62 COLUM. L. REV. 201, 219-20, 229-30 (1962); Markert, *The Application of German Antitrust Law to International Restraints of Trade,* 7:2 VA. J. INT'L L. 47, 60-61 (1967); BUSINESS REGULATION IN THE COMMON MARKET NATIONS (Blake ed. 1969), vol. 3 (K. Ebb ed.), WEST GERMANY (by Markert, Juenger, Steckhan & Pfeifer) ch. 6. The American antitrust view is considerably more skeptical about the presence and legitimacy of export bans imposed on the licensee. See note 112 *infra.*

[26] *Per contra,* Section 98(2) of the German antitrust statute which provides explicitly for some international or "extraterritorial" application of the Act: "[The Act] shall apply to all restraints of competition which have effect in the area to which this Act applies, even if they result from acts done outside such area." The exemption from the statutory prohibition provided under Section 20(2)(5) for those licensing restrictions that relate solely to the "regulation of competition in markets outside the area to which this Act applies" is thus an exception to the general principle of Section 98(2). The coexistence of two such contrary principles has been an uneasy one which has given rise in practice to some complicated attempts on the part of the Federal Cartel Office to harmonize the foreign-market exemption of 20(2)(5) with the domestic-effect principle of 98(2). See Markert, *supra* note 25, at

commentators may be reading too much of the substance of the former into the latter.[27]

A more extensive and more traditional statement of the relationship between Articles 85 and 86 and industrial property rights under national law of the EEC member countries is given by the authors of a much-cited manual on "Common Market Cartel Law."[28] They acknowledge that there is no "general immunity" from Article 85(1) for license agreements. But they assert that restraints imposed upon a patent licensee by the license agreement which come within the traditional, normal or non-abusive "range of legal protection" enjoyed by a patentee under national patent law are not even "agreements" within the general meaning of that term as used in Article 85—since Article 36 "reserves the matter of industrial property . . . for the legislation of the member states." "Were Article 85(1) to apply to restraints covered by the contents of the licensed protective right, it would mean that this provision would intrude directly into the protected area of industrial property rights. That area, however, is defined by the national laws, from which Article 85(1) must not derogate." From these principles, based on belief in supremacy of Article 36 over Articles 85 and 86, the authors conclude that patent and trademark licensors may impose export prohibitions on their licensees without risk of infringing Article 85(1) whenever the licensor holds a parallel patent or trademark in the banned destination country. This is because "it is not the agreement between licensor and licensee that is the efficient cause for the adverse effect upon interstate trade, but rather the patent [or trademark, or process patent] situation in the several EEC states." They further conclude that:

> If the licensee is prevented by the patent situation from exporting into the other EEC states, so too, of course, are his customers. Therefore, the licensor

60-62, 66. It would appear that this obscurely worded and intricate portion of German anticartel law may prove a somewhat unreliable guide to the interpretation of the less complicated provisions of Community law.

[27]Interestingly, in a subsequently written passage contained in the same Deringer volume, ¶177, note is made of the fact that the Commission and the Federal Cartel Office are critical of licensing restrictions against exports to countries where parallel patents do not exist, and the authors observe, of their earlier statement of views: "Although no decision has been rendered as yet, the view expressed in ¶134, third paragraph, is no longer valid."

[28]OBERDORFER, GLEISS & HIRSCH, COMMON MARKET CARTEL LAW 34-35, 37-38 (1963).

may also obligate the licensee to impose a corresponding export prohibition on the latter's customers. Here, too, it is not the consensual restraint on competition that is the cause of the adverse effect upon interstate trade.

The licensor is not under any legal duty to lift this export prohibition for the licensee (and his customers) by means of granting licenses under his protective rights in the EEC states for the entire Common Market as a unit; that would in effect be a compulsory license and thereby an impermissible interference with the applicable local laws.[29]

It is difficult to see how such conclusions can survive intact in view of the opinion expressed by the Court of Justice in the 1966 *Grundig-Consten* decision that Articles 36 and 222 "do not prevent Community Law from having an influence on the exercise of industrial property rights under domestic law." Reconciliation would be possible if the Court of Justice meant merely that only an exceptional abuse of national industrial property rights would be "influenced" by Treaty law, and such a reconciliation was promptly proposed by some commentators.[30] The view was advanced at the Symposium held by the Free University of Brussels that prohibited abuse or "abusive use" (*abus de droit*) "means a use with the *sole* purpose to jeopardize the Community laws," an interpretation which, as the rapporteur commented, would make the importance of the Court's decision "very restricted indeed."[31]

For reasons indicated hereafter, this denigrating interpretation appears unwarranted, for the Court seems to have intended a much broader meaning. In replying to arguments based on Articles 36 and 222, it stated that the Community competition system, under Article 85(1), "does not permit the use of rights flowing from the trademark law of the different Member States for purposes contrary to the Community cartel

---

[29]*Id.* at 38. It should be noted that despite the permissive attitude of Section 20(2)(5) of the German law toward export prohibitions (text *supra*, 254), an obligation imposed on a licensee *to bar his customers* from exporting the product has been held by the Bundeskartellamt to violate the German anticartel law on the ground that the patent protection is exhausted by the first sale by the licensor. Schapiro, *supra* note 25, at 229-30; GRAUPNER, THE RULES OF COMPETITION IN THE EUROPEAN ECONOMIC COMMUNITY 62 (1965).

[30]See Report, *The Free University of Brussels Symposium on Patents, Trademarks and Antitrust in Europe and America (Nov. 15-16, 1966),* 4 C.M.L. REV. 490-91 (1967).

[31]*Id.* (emphasis added); see also Jeantet, *Esquisse de la jurisprudence de la Cour de Justice des Communautés sur les accords restreignant la concurrence,* 40 JURIS CLASSEUR PERIODIQUE 2029, Section 1, §4 (1966).

law." Whether or not the trademark rights in that case, available under French and other EEC country law, were exercised in a manner abhorrent to or abusive of the national industrial property law was largely irrelevant (at any rate, not an essential ingredient) in the Court's view. Contrary to the view advanced at the Brussels Symposium, the exercise of the right may well be intended for a purpose that would be legitimate within the context of national industrial property law taken in isolation from Community cartel law and, yet, by virtue of its trade-restrictive effect, be held to violate Article 85.

The view of some critics, that any license agreement found by the Commission and Court to violate Article 85(1) is ipso facto an abusive use of industrial property rights, is merely a tautological definition, with no predictive value. Indeed, it is more likely that the Court, rather than its critics, would be inclined to employ—and an examination of its recent opinions shows that it does employ—the "abusive" phraseology. The critics' argument of course is really intended to go beyond this tautology, and to urge that "abuse" for this purpose should mean a use not normally found to be within the scope of the patent or trademark right under traditional interpretations of national law, and perhaps also a use of such rights to support a flagrant cartel arrangement involving horizontal rather than vertical restrictions.

II. REGULATIONS AND OTHER PUBLIC ANNOUNCEMENTS OF EEC AUTHORITIES PRIOR TO THE *GRUNDIG-CONSTEN* DECISION OF 1966

The starting point for the Common Market authorities in spelling out their thinking on the relation between Community antitrust law and national industrial property law was to adopt the rationale that licensing practices that impose restraints greater than, or in addition to, those implicit in the trademark or patent right itself might infringe Article 85(1) or 86—a rationale foreshadowed in one informal document and expressed a few months later in an official announcement. The EEC Commission issued a *Guide Pratique* or Manual for Firms on September 2, 1962, to explain the practical implications of regulations previously adopted.[32] The *Guide* expressed many caveats, particularly with respect

---

[32] Parallel French and English versions appear in CAMPBELL, RESTRICTIVE TRADING AGREEMENTS IN THE COMMON MARKET 160 (1964); also in 1 CCH

to territorial limitations that set one Member State off from another, and with respect to multiple licensing arrangements that involve such restraints. On the permissive side, it noted first that the ban in Article 85(1) "does not, generally speaking, take in restrictions imposed on the licensee which are inherent in the exercise of the protected industrial property right itself, *i.e.,* which stem from the fact that the licensor is exercising his protected right within the limits prescribed or allowed by domestic law."[33] But its very definition of this protected area is fraught with negative implications:

1. Restrictions imposed on the licensee fall within the protected right "where a specified area (within the territory in which the right is valid), a specified time (within the period during which it remains valid) or a specified quantity or value are prescribed for the exercise of that right. These restrictions are not caught by Article 85(1) and therefore require neither notification [under Regulation 17] nor a decision to issue a declaration under Article 85(3)."[34] From the viewpoint of territorial restraints, it should be noted that it is only intranational ("within the territory in which the right is valid")—not international—territorial restrictions that are sanctioned by this explanation.[35]

2. "Restraints which no longer have any real bearing [*rapport réel*] on the exercise of the industrial property right, *i.e.,* which are no longer directly related to its exercise, are not affected" by this statement of non-applicability of the notification requirement and hence fall within

COMM. MKT. REP. ¶2802 (English). The *Guide Pratique* was issued by the Commission's Press Relations Section in an attempt to answer inquiries that had been raised most commonly by firms. Its Foreword explains that the views expressed in it "are without prejudice to any interpretations placed on the Treaty or regulations under decisions handed down by the Commission or the courts in individual cases; no responsibility is taken for the matter contained in this manual." While unofficial, it makes up for its lack of definitiveness by its explicatory character, which furnishes many clues to the kinds of problems with which the Commission is concerned, its general attitudes on the pending issues and its tentative conclusions.

[33] CAMPBELL, *supra* note 32 at 182.

[34] *Id.*

[35] Contrariwise, Newes, in *The European Commission's First Major Antitrust Decision,* 20 BUS. LAW. 431, 437 (1965), construes the same wording as sanctioning *international* restrictions, and then finds the *Grundig-Consten* decision to some extent inconsistent with the position the Commission had taken in its Communique of Dec. 24, 1962.

the latter requirement unless elsewhere exempted.[36] Such notifiable licensing restraints "might exist, for example, where the licensee . . . may not acquire, manufacture or sell any competing product; undertakes not to export to another Member State; [or] undertakes to impose competitive restrictions on his customers."[37]

3. The *Guide Pratique,* in cautioning that the "exact delimitation" of those categories of licensing agreements free from the notification requirement "is not an easy matter and can only be done by examining particular cases," added the caveat: "It will always be necessary to verify that, besides the restrictions contained in the licensing contract proper, there are no agreements or concerted practices among the various licensees, either between themselves or between licensees and licensor, liable to come under Article 85(1). . . ."[38]

The Commission's formal Official Notice on Patent Licensing Agreements of December 24, 1962 in effect recapitulates the points summarized above, but in more authoritative and definitive form. Its general approach is to treat as innocuous those restraints on licensees that are "inherent in the exercise of the protected industrial property right itself." But the only territorial restraints upon the licensee clearly sanctioned, as not covered by the prohibition of Article 85(1), are those relating to "part of the territory covered by the patent or with regard to a particular factory or location of the plant"—in other words, a restraint within a single nation and not coterminous with the national boundaries. The Commission stated that, as of that moment, "a general appraisal does not appear possible for agreements relating," *inter alia,* to "multiple parallel licenses."[39] And the Notice said that a decision was "to be made

---

[36] Quoted in CAMPBELL, *supra* note 32, at 182.

[37] *Id.* at 184.

[38] *Id.*

[39] See Chapter 4 *supra* at 229; 1 CCH COMM. MKT. REP. ¶2698; CAMPBELL, *supra* note 32, at 134. The phrase, "multiple parallel licenses," was not defined in the announcement, but it refers to the grant to licensees in more than one Member State of a license under patents taken out by the same patentee on the same product (or process) in the different Member States concerned. Compare the definition given by VerLoren van Themaat, then Director General of the Competition Department, EEC Commission, in NEW YORK STATE BAR ASS'N, ANTITRUST LAW SYMPOSIUM 52 (1963): "exploitation of identical inventions, protected under patents of different nationality by separate firms."

later" on the question of the applicability of Article 85(1) to contractual clauses relating to multiple parallel licenses and "to agreements relating to the exploitation of other industrial property rights"[40] (that is, trademark rights, and know-how agreements).[41] Comments by EEC officials left no doubt that these questions were reserved for subsequent decision because the Commission thought it would be particularly difficult to reconcile "the monopoly-oriented patent law and the competition-directed antitrust law" and because, in the case of multiple parallel licenses, "eventual restrictive effects on competition [result] less from the legal monopoly granted by patent law than from the agreements themselves."[42] While the Commission expressed its general attitude of treating as innocuous licensing restraints "inherent" in industrial property rights, it was in effect saying that it deems restraints involved in multiple parallel licensing of patents (as well as in joint ownership of patents, and reciprocal licenses) to be less intrinsic, less essential than such "inherent" restraints. This is not, it will be observed, an assertion that multiple parallel patent licensing is an abuse of the patent right as such, or an abnormality within the context of patent law considered by itself. It conveys, rather, the thought that these forms of exercising industrial property rights are particularly likely to come into conflict with the Common Market trade liberalization objectives of Articles 85 and 86 and may not be defensible on the "inherent restraint" theory.

The revolutionary implications of this view, breaking away from condemnation under Treaty law only of manifest abuses of industrial property rights as judged from the viewpoint of trademark or patent law itself, have perhaps become more apparent with the handing down of the *Grundig-Consten* decision and the promulgation of Regulation 67/67. But the reaction among some traditionalists has been one of strong skepticism if not virtual disbelief: *E.g.,* the patent license "constitutes essentially an enlargement in the scope of competition and must be regarded as legitimate under Art. 85(1). Accordingly it could only be in

---

[40] 1 CCH COMM. MKT. REP. ¶2698 at 1778; CAMPBELL, *supra* note 32, at 134.

[41] VerLoren van Themaat, *Current Antitrust Developments in the European Common Market and the Relation Thereto of Industrial Property Rights,* 6 PAT., T.M. & COPYRT. J. 432, 443 (1963).

[42] *Id.* at 440, 443.

an accidental manner, by the presence of clauses that are adventitious and entirely unrelated to the license properly speaking that a contract of this sort could fall within the prohibitions of the European law."[43] With this concept in mind, the same commentators observe: "The Commission's reservation of its position as to reciprocal and multiple parallel licenses is difficult to understand. Neither the one nor the other, as such, appears to us to infringe Article 85(1). It is the content of the contracts which is significant."[44] The *Grundig-Consten* decision and its aftermath have furnished ample ground for this uneasiness on the part of the European commentators.

III. THE *GRUNDIG-CONSTEN* DECISION AND TERRITORIAL RIGHTS OF TRADEMARK HOLDERS WITHIN THE COMMON MARKET

The story of the *Grundig-Consten* case and of the rulings by the EEC Commission and the European Court of Justice has been told elsewhere and need not be reviewed in the same detail here.[45] In essence, the Commission, in a decision sustained with minor qualifications by the Court, held invalid under Article 85(1) an exclusive distributorship system set up within the Common Market area by the German consumer electronics firm, Grundig, with extensive, or "absolute," protection assured for each national market allocated by Grundig to each of the distributors. The case involved a rather elaborate set of protectionist devices: (a) nationally-delineated exclusive distributorships; (b) parceling out to national distributors territorially-defined rights in a trademark supplemental to "GRUNDIG" and common to a multi-country market; (c) a formal agreement on Grundig's rights to retrieve the supplemental mark if and when a distributorship terminated; and (d) commitments by distributors not to re-export. Whether or not each and every circumstance actually present was an indispensable prerequisite to the ruling of invalidity is a question that underlies any attempt to evaluate the long-run significance of the decision.

[43] BRAUN, GLEISS & HIRSCH, DROIT DES ENTENTES DE LA COMMUNAUTE ECONOMIQUE EUROPEENNE 111-12 (1967). The translation is the author's.

[44]*Id.* at 125.

[45] See, *e.g.*, Ebb, *supra* note 8, at 855, and Chapter 4 *supra*, note 217.

For our purposes, it is important to consider whether or not the case is, as some have suggested, merely a minor episode with an extraordinary set of facts—facts so unusual as to convert an ordinarily legitimate use of a trademark right into an abuse under national trademark law and then, derivatively, into a violation of Treaty law. If so, it would be a ruling of relatively slight and transitory significance. Alternatively, the ruling can be construed as treating the Community anticartel objective as overriding the legitimacy that a distributorship arrangement would otherwise enjoy under national trademark law, considered by itself. If that interpretation is correct, *Grundig-Consten* has really signalled a major development in the relationship between European anticartel law and territorial restrictions related to the exercise of trademark rights, and industrial property rights generally. One European writer emphasizes the cautious, conservative aspects of the Court's statement "that the EEC Commission's order enjoining Consten to refrain from using the national trademark rights to prevent parallel imports leaves these rights untouched and limits their exercise only insofar as necessary to enforce the prohibition of Article 85(1)." But, aware of those aspects that are not so conservative, he adds: "It is nevertheless impossible now to anticipate the legal consequences that the Court of Justice's interpretation will have on the application of Article 85 to industrial property rights."[46]

The facts, in greater detail, were that in 1957, Grundig's sales company, Grundig-Verkaufs-GmbH, entered into a contract with Etablissements Consten designating the latter as exclusive distributor in France for Grundig's German products—radios, tape recorders, dictating machines and television sets. Grundig agreed not to sell, directly *or indirectly,* to other persons in the territory ceded to Consten. To strengthen that undertaking, it imposed an export prohibition on its German distributors as well as its distributors in other Common Market countries.[47] Some of the German distributors, nevertheless, sold the

---

[46]DERINGER, *supra* note 16, at ¶176.

[47]The linkage of the export prohibition with the Grundig-Consten distributorship is cited in the Court's opinion. German sources have commented that Grundig had in fact imposed such restrictions on distributors for many years before entering into its agreement with Consten, implying that the pre-existing status of one of the factors thus linked weakens the restrictiveness of the distributorship arrangement. The master plan, in other words, was not created in one fell swoop. For reasons suggested in the text below, this discrepancy in description constitutes a minor difference in detail rather than any impairment of a major prerequisite finding.

products to an unauthorized, or "parallel," French importer, UNEF, which in turn sold to French retailers at prices lower than those charged by Consten, to the detriment of Consten and Consten's customers.

The territorial allocations had been further strengthened by reliance on trademark allocations and import-ban privileges available under the trademark and unfair competition law of the Member States. Grundig maintained trademark registrations in each of the EEC countries, holding the GRUNDIG mark in its own name. It also held a companion or "supplemental" mark, GINT ("Grundig International") in Germany, but assigned the corresponding GINT mark in each of the other Member countries to the sole national distributor as a further protection against "parallel" imports by others. Grundig had registered GINT in France in Consten's name, with the understanding that at the termination of the exclusive agreement Consten would reassign the mark to Grundig or allow it to expire. GINT, as well as GRUNDIG, was affixed to all appliances manufactured by Grundig, including those sold in Germany, and, the EEC Commission found, "was introduced by Grundig shortly after it lost a decision in the Netherlands, in December 1956, against a parallel importer."[48]

A French trial court held UNEF liable in damages to Consten for unfair competition (finding it unnecessary to give judgment in a related trademark infringement suit) because of willful disregard of the "sole agency" agreement of which UNEF had knowledge. The Paris Court of Appeal, however, suspended judgment pending a decision of the Commission, a request for such a decision having been made by UNEF. The Commission proceeded to rule that the Grundig-Consten agreement violated Article 85(1). It regarded the distributorship agreement as conferring "absolute" territorial protection, designed to prevent parallel im-

---

[48] Ets. Consten and Grundig-Verkaufs-GmbH, CCH COMM. MKT. REP. ¶ 2743 at 1861, 3 Comm. Mkt. L. R. 489, 492 (1964). The Netherlands Hoge Raad (Supreme Court) had ruled at that time that a Dutch importer-distributor licensed under the GRUNDIG trademark could not ban imports of the Grundig products by others, on the national-law ground that the trademark owner—Grundig—had exhausted its rights to control the distribution of the product once it had put the trademarked products into commerce. Grundig v. Prins, [1962] N.J. No. 242 (1956). To avoid this result without relinquishing its tight grip on its primary housemark, the Grundig enterprise adopted the policy of registering the additional mark GINT in the Netherlands (and correspondingly in each of the other countries to which it exported) in the name of the exclusive distributor.

ports into the French market from other Member States. The exemptive provisions of Article 85(3) were held inapplicable, the Commission having concluded that any generalized economic benefits resulting from the Grundig arrangements were independent of those restrictive provisions that established the territorial protection.[49]

To keep open the possibility of imports into France by persons other than the exclusive distributor, the Commission enjoined Grundig and Consten "from making more difficult or from hampering parallel imports of Grundig products into France by any means whatsoever, including the use for this purpose of the GINT trademark."[50] This does not mean, of course, that the GINT registration is invalidated or that Consten would be barred from using the GINT trademark against the sale of products not originating in the Grundig factories and falsely labelled "GINT."[51]

The fact that the device of employing a supplementary trademark to be owned by the national distributor had been conceived to bolster the distributor's absolute territorial protection under the national law, rather than to serve the essential trademark purpose of designating the origin of the goods (the GRUNDIG trademark being sufficient for that purpose), was cited by the Commission and the Court as evidence that the

---

[49] Article 85(3) provides:

"The provisions of paragraph 1 may, however, be declared inapplicable in the case of:

—any agreement or type of agreement between undertakings,

—any decision or type of decision by associations of undertakings, and

—any concerted practice or type of concerted practice which helps to improve the production or distribution of goods or to promote technical or economic progress, while allowing consumers a fair share of the resulting profit and which does not:

    (a) subject the concerns in question to any restrictions which are not indispensable to the achievement of the above objectives;

    (b) enable such concerns to eliminate competition in respect of a substantial part of the goods concerned."

(Translation from 1 CCH COMM. MKT. REP. ¶2051.)

The Commission evaluated the highly-protected sole-agency agreements here as impeding, if not preventing, the integration of the national markets into the Common Market, citing the fact that Grundig products sold in France at prices 20% higher than German prices, after deducting customs duties and taxes from the French prices.

[50] Ets. Consten and Grundig-Verkaufs-GmbH, CCH COMM. MKT. REP. ¶2743 at 1868-69, 3 Comm. Mkt. L. R. 489, 504 (1964).

[51] *Id.*

agreement providing for Consten's use of the mark was primarily a restrictive agreement. Moreover, the restriction took the form of partitioning the Common Market along national boundary lines.

Notwithstanding the interest shown by the Commission and Court in the fact that the GINT trademark was a supplemental device, was its existence really the crucial element in the case? If Grundig had been willing to assign the GRUNDIG mark itself to each national distributor, would the arrangement then have been deemed compatible with Article 85(1)? Presumably not. The supplementary trademark agreement in *Grundig-Consten* really imposed on the contracting parties no express restriction as such relevant to Article 85(1). It simply made available *a* trademark which *could* then be used, at Consten's discretion, as an additional means of protecting itself against competition from abroad—a potential effect which itself flowed from rights conferred by trademark law.[52]

The regulatory approach of the EEC Commission seems to be broad and realistic rather than formalistic. It is based on the general principle that, in the case of exclusive distribution agreements carving out national territories for different distributors, the national-law import-ban privileges of persons sharing trademark rights with the manufacturer should be deemed curtailed by Article 85. Would this curtailment of the national-law privileges of the trademark holder be required by the Commission even in the absence of a *formal* trademark agreement containing reversionary rights to the sales arm of the manufacturing enterprise, such as was present here? Or would the curtailment be required if the exclusive distribution arrangements did not expressly exact from other purchasers of the products an undertaking not to export? The implication of what has been suggested above as the general principle of the ruling appears to be that, even if these factors were absent, the Commission would regard Consten's trademark rights in France as necessarily limited by Article 85.[53]

[52] See Deringer, *Exclusive Agency Agreements with Territorial Protection under the EEC Antitrust Laws,* 10 ANTITRUST BULL. 599, 601-02 (1965).

[53] Indeed, in the exercise of its power to make regulations to enforce Article 85, the Commission now seems to have no doubt that the mere existence of such trademark arrangements, if used to bolster absolute territorial protection for exclusive distributorships, infringes Article 85. Regulation No. 67/67, issued by the Commission, effective May 1, 1967, grants to certain exclusive distribution

Did anything turn on the existence of the supplemental agreement which provided for the restoration of the GINT mark to Grundig or for its cancellation on the termination of Consten's exclusive distributorship? This emphasized the relationship of the trademark to the system of absolute territorial protection, but it is difficult to see why or how the absence of an agreement that is notable more for its explicitness than for the mere fact of its existence would have induced the Commission to rule differently than it did and to sanction Consten's use of the GINT mark as an import barrier. Nevertheless, the extensive arguments presented by the parties and by the Advocate General in his conclusions before the Court indicate that these persons did regard the supplemental agreement as a key element in the case. The agreement was deemed by them to bear either on the establishment of a violation of Article 85(1), or on the justification (vis-à-vis Articles 36 and 222) for the Commission's injunction barring the use of the GINT mark to curb parallel imports.

The supplemental agreement was also cited by the Court of Justice both as additional evidence of the restrictive purpose of the overall arrangement and as showing overt action by the parties beyond the scope of operation of French law.[54] However, it may be doubted that the Court treated the formal document itself as more than a symbol or makeweight. The Commission and Court might well have appraised even a *simple* transfer or cession to Consten of the French trademark right in GINT as sufficient to constitute a "concerted practice" by the parties, or an agreement in itself, or a component of an overall restrictive "agreement" or "concerted practice" within the meaning of Article 85(1), and hence improper to the extent used to bar parallel imports.[55] The Commission might have regarded a trademark transfer in such

---

agreements exemption from the anticartel provisions of Article 85(1) until December 31, 1972. But, as explained in greater detail in the next section of this chapter, the exemption is inapplicable if the contracting parties exercise industrial property rights to block free movement within the Common Market of the products covered by the agreement. The presence or absence of a supplemental trademark, or of a trademark reversionary right agreement, or of commitments not to export does not appear to be indispensable to a finding that the parties are exercising trademark rights in the proscribed manner.

[54] CCH COMM. MKT. REP. ¶8046 at 7654, 5 Comm. Mkt. L. R. 418, 475-76 (1966).

[55] Recall Deringer's critical evaluation of the decision, in text at note 52 *supra*.

circumstances as being subject to a tacit reversionary interest on Grundig's part. But even if it assumed that no reversionary interest in GINT had been retained, and that Grundig regarded *that* mark as expendable if the distributorship came to an end, the territorially restrictive impact of the arrangement would not have been diminished. The existence of Grundig's reversionary interest highlights the fact that Consten was not acquiring the GINT mark for a purpose genuinely independent from the objective of serving Grundig's distribution system. While the existence of the supplemental agreement makes that point quite neatly, it is a point that could have been established without difficulty on the basis of the rest of the arrangements and their *modus operandi*.

It is notable that the Court, in approving the Commission's finding of an Article 85 infringement, spoke simply of the re-export undertakings plus "Consten's registration in France of the GINT trademark, which Grundig affixes to all of its products"—rather than specifying the supplemental trademark agreement—as "designed to fortify the agreement's [*i.e.*, the basic exclusive distribution agreement's] built-in protection against parallel imports with the protection arising out of industrial property law."[56]

The Commission's subsequent ruling in the *Sperry Rand Italia S.p.A.* case confirmed this analysis of the real meaning of *Grundig-Consten* and fulfilled the expectations set forth above.[57] The transfer of Italian trademarks for electric razors by an American parent to an Italian subsidiary was relied upon by the latter in the Milan courts in an attempt to ban, under trademark and unfair competition doctrines, parallel imports of Remington razors from other Common Market countries. No "supplemental agreement" appears to have been in existence. Nevertheless, the agreement in question, *"as interpreted and applied by the parties,"*[58] was found by the Commission to justify "reservations" as to the compatibility of the agreement with Article 85; and the Italian

[56]CCH COMM. MKT. REP. ¶8046 at 7653, 5 Comm. Mkt. L. R. 418, 475 (1966). The supplemental agreement is mentioned by the Court at this part in its opinion only as the agreement whereby Consten was enabled to register the GINT trademark (Grundig having been the initial owner of that mark by virtue of its international registration under the Madrid Arrangement). *Id.* at 7654, 5 Comm. Mkt. L. R. at 475.

[57]EC Commission Press Release, June 11, 1969, CCH COMM. MKT. REP. ¶9307.

[58]*Id.* (emphasis added).

subsidiary agreed to discontinue its attempts to use its trademark rights to prevent parallel imports of authentic Remington razors.

Thus, it appears that the factors essential to the determination of invalidity in *Grundig-Consten* were at most: (a) an exclusive distribution network with (or perhaps even without) export-ban undertakings by the various national distributors; (b) the peculiarly strong French doctrine of unfair competition with respect to third parties who have notice of an exclusive distribution arrangement; and (c) the inherent import-restrictive potential of the mark under French trademark law (a potential which all parties assumed to be present).

Moreover, given the import-ban capability of trademark ownership under the national trademark and unfair competition law of France and other Member States, export prohibitions imposed on German buyers and the various national distributors add an element of convenience rather than of indispensability to the territorial allocations. Thus, it seems proper to read *Grundig-Consten,* particularly after *Sperry Rand Italia,* as meaning that Article 85(1) is infringed by the combination of a network of exclusive distributorships, each confined to a national territory, and an allocation of the respective national trademarks, even in the absence of explicit re-export ban undertakings, as well as the absence of a written undertaking to restore the trademark. Certainly if the Commission finds that a distributorship-trademark arrangement of this type implies a set of commitments not to re-export, and if, by combining the explicit with the tacit agreements, it concludes that the arrangement provides "absolute" territorial protection, the Court could hardly hold such fact-finding unwarranted. The negative implication of Regulation 67/67 (discussed *infra*) is that the Commission would probably find that this kind of trade-restrictive conduct violates Article 85(1), and that the Regulation would not accord such conduct automatic "class" exemption under Article 85(3). *Sperry Rand Italia* seems to confirm this analysis.

If this reasoning is correct, an effective system of multiple parallel trademark licensing or transfer arrangements within the Common Market, headed by a single manufacturer within one Member State (or in a non-Member State) and embracing exclusive distributor-licensees in other Member States, should no longer be feasible. The scope of the national import-ban privilege of the trademark holder who has consented, by license or assignment, to the use of his mark in other Member States, or who has received rights in another's mark by such means, has become greatly circumscribed under Treaty law. Recently, the

Commission expressly sanctioned, under Article 85(3), the agreement of eighteen medium-sized members of a marine paint manufacturers association to use a common set of trademarks and to refrain from exporting into each other's national market during a five-year transitional period. But the Commission noted that the national trademark registrations of the commonly-held marks by themselves could no longer be used to exclude "imports from other Member States of the Transocean products manufactured by other members" because of EEC anticartel doctrine, pursuant to the *Grundig-Consten* ban on "the abusive exercise of the national trademark rights to frustrate the effectiveness of the Community law on restrictive agreements."[59]

It is significant that, following the Court of Justice decision in the *Grundig-Consten* case, Grundig revised its agreements with its exclusive distributors to conform with the principle laid down in the Commission's ruling, and informed the Commission that it will no longer prevent any German dealer from selling Grundig equipment to dealers or other persons in other Member States of the Common Market.[60] Presumably this means that neither Grundig nor its distributors will henceforth assert any import-ban privilege in the other Member States with respect to any "genuine" GRUNDIG or GRUNDIG/GINT brand products. Actually, even as early as the latter part of 1966, Grundig had conceded in a Belgian court the right of a parallel importer to bring GRUNDIG-branded radio products into Belgium and sell them there under that

[59] Transocean Marine Paint Ass'n, 6 Comm. Mkt. L. R. Supp. D9, D19 (1967). In an article written shortly after the Commission's decision in *Grundig-Consten,* the view was expressed that the Commission had not "as yet determined whether . . . an exclusive licensee in a certain country may enjoin the use of the licensed trademark on goods imported into his country by a licensee in another country." The hope was also expressed that the anticartel view would follow the national trademark-law view that "each country grants to the proprietor of a trademark separate trademark rights which are territorial in character, and where the proprietor grants a license under his trademark in one country he does so under the separate trademark rights granted him in that country. He should not be deemed, therefore, to have granted an authorization to use his trademark in all other countries." Ladas, *Problems of Licensing Abroad,* 56 T.M. REP. 484, 521 (1966). As indicated by the *Transocean* case, the course of events during the past three years has resulted in the Commission's adoption of views largely antithetical to these.

[60] EEC Bulletin No. 9/10, 2 CCH COMM. MKT. REP. ¶9212 (1967). Another manufacturer of electrical equipment informed the Commission that it had revised its marketing agreements to conform to the conditions laid down in Regulation 67/67.

trademark. It had claimed, however, that Belgian unfair competition principles should still be deemed applicable to bar the parallel importer from using in its sales circulars the pictorial or composite trademark in which the name GRUNDIG is outlined by an oval on an oblong block. In rejecting this complaint, the Belgian court had noted that the composite mark appeared on the imported product, thus implying the manufacturer's consent to having the goods for sale "by appropriate description, *i.e.,* reproduction of the trademark."[61] The legitimacy of the import and sale having been established by the Court of Justice decision in *Grundig-Consten,* the Belgian court refused to apply a stringent view of unfair competition law to circumscribe the effectiveness of that decision.

There is a theoretical possibility that Grundig (and other manufacturers in similar fashion) could establish its own sales subsidiary in each of the Common Market countries as the exclusive national distributor, holding title to its primary trademark, GRUNDIG.[62] Such a distribution arrangement might be consistent with Article 85(1), which some have urged (albeit against strong opposition) does not ban restrictive agreements between parent and subsidiary companies,[63] even though the sales subsidiaries use their trademark rights to ban "parallel" imports. And national courts might enforce trademark import-control privileges in such circumstances. But such a network would fall far short of a system composed mainly of independent distributors, and could make no use of

[61] Grundig Werke GmbH and J.N.J. Sieverding N.V. v. P.V.B.A. Common Market Import & Trade Co., 7 C.M.L. REP. 97, 100 (1968).

[62] Grundig reportedly acquired a majority equity in the Consten firm, which was renamed "Grundig-France." Le Monde, Mar. 17, 1967, at 2. It is said to have a subsidiary company in Italy as well.

[63] It has been argued that the wording of Article 85(1), which bans restrictive agreements between "enterprises" and "associations of enterprises," does not interdict agreements between parent and subsidiary because those companies constitute merely a single enterprise. See OBERDORFER, GLEISS & HIRSCH, COMMON MARKET CARTEL LAW ¶¶ 1, 2, 21 (1963). The Commission's staff has indicated an intention to use an "intra-enterprise conspiracy" doctrine. See VerLoren van Themaat, *supra* note 39, at 53. See generally GRAUPNER, *supra* note 29, at 11; Duwel, *Signification du Mot "Enterprise" dans le sens de l'article 85 du Traite C.E.E., à propos d'accords entre sociétés mères et filiales entre elles,* 2 REVUE TRIMESTRIELLE DE DROIT EUROPEEN 400 (1966); Schapiro, *The German Law Against Restraints of Competition—Comparative and International Aspects* (pt. 1), 62 COLUM. L. REV. 1, 11 (1962).

commitments by German or other dealers to refrain from exporting the branded commodity from within the Common Market.

Some recent developments in Community legal thinking bearing on parent-subsidiary arrangements under Article 85 should be noted. The net effect of superficially conflicting rulings seems to be to cast doubt even on the feasibility of a rigid allocation of Member States as among a manufacturer and its own sales subsidiaries, if the allocation is based on trademark import-control privileges. In one case, the Commission ruled that a division of markets between a parent company and its wholly-owned subsidiary was "only a division of labor within the same economic entity" and hence not restrictive of competition within the Common Market.[64] However, the Commission's antipathy to the use of trademark-supported import bans within the Common Market is so strong that it has applied the *Grundig-Consten* result even to arrangements involving a parent company in one country and a wholly-owned subsidiary in another.[65] This is not wholly surprising since the market division sought to be imposed by an import ban under trademark or unfair competition doctrines is directed against third parties in the market (notably, parallel importers), and thus, under the rationale of Regulation 67/67, is against the interests of the consumers.

IV. THE STATUS OF TERRITORIAL RESTRICTIONS IN MULTIPLE PARALLEL PATENT LICENSING ARRANGEMENTS IN THE COMMON MARKET AFTER THE *GRUNDIG-CONSTEN* DECISION

We have seen that, early in the history of the implementing regulations and announcements under the Treaty of Rome, doubt was cast on the legitimacy of interstate trade restrictions imposed on the movement of products manufactured under multiple patent licensing arrangements within the Common Market. The effective suspension of national

[64] Negative clearance granted in Christiani & Nielsen, June 18, 1969, CCH COMM. MKT. REP. ¶9308, on ground that Danish parent and Dutch subsidiary are integrated managerially and financially and are not natural competitive units.

[65] See *Scott Paper,* text *infra* at notes 77 and 78, and *Sperry Rand Italia,* text *supra* at note 57.

import-ban privileges with respect to trademark holders, caused by the *Grundig-Consten* decision, has inevitably deepened the doubts as to the present status of such privileges on the part of patent holders within the Common Market. Mr. Ellis has posed the question pointedly: "Let us suppose that Grundig was the manufacturer of a patented article and that, in addition to appointing Consten its exclusive distributor in France, it assigned to Consten its French patent rights and permitted Consten to register the pertinent patent in Consten's own name with the French patent authorities. Would the Commission feel able to brush aside the patents in order to unify the six national markets of the EEC into one Common Market. . . . ?"[66] Language in Regulation 67/67 and the views of the Commission as revealed in the argument in the *Parke, Davis* case before the European Court of Justice suggest that Article 85(1) may indeed be applied to outlaw the interstate territorial restraints imposed under patent licenses to much the same extent, if not in precisely the same manner, as it has been applied to such restraints based on trademark licensing.

Regulation 67/67 itself may cover export and import trade restraints based on patent, as well as on trademark licensing. The regulation furnishes a group exemption under Article 85(3) for certain types of exclusive dealing agreements that comply with stated conditions. While it is thus aimed primarily at exclusive dealing agreements, rather than at licensing arrangements as such, it is explicitly concerned with the use of industrial property rights in a manner ancillary to exclusive distributorships. In general, as the Commission explains in the preamble to the regulation, exclusive territorial dealerships organized along national territorial lines (in contrast to agreements merely dividing up one Member State) are regarded as likely to violate Article 85(1). Since such agreements may nevertheless have beneficial effects, as where an improvement in distribution costs is passed on to consumers in the form of lower retail prices, broad exemptions for certain categories of these agreements are provided for in the regulation, under the authority of Article 85(3). But, as a prerequisite to any such class exemption, "parallel imports must be provided for, in order that consumers may share in the advantages resulting from the exclusive dealership. Industrial property rights and other rights cannot therefore be allowed to be

[66] Ellis, *The Legality of Exclusive Distributorships under Common Market Antitrust Laws,* 9 ANTITRUST BULL. 775, 783 (1964).

misused so as to create absolute territorial protection."[67] This explanation in the preamble is implemented by Article 3(b) which withholds the exemption when "contracting parties make it difficult for middlemen and consumers to obtain the products under contract from other dealers in the Common Market, particularly when the contracting parties exercise industrial property rights to prevent dealers or consumers from obtaining in other areas of the Common Market supplies of the products under contract properly marked and marketed, or from selling them in the contract territory."

"Industrial property rights," as that term has been uniformly used in Commission announcements, include patent, copyright, industrial design and know-how rights as well as trademarks. Thus, the regulation apparently withholds its group exemption from exclusive distributorships whose territorial restraints are bolstered by use of import-ban privileges of holders of multiple parallel patent licenses (or of the patents themselves).

To the extent that Mr. Ellis, quoted at the outset of this section, is inquiring whether the French patent infringement remedy could be utilized as against imports of the products from the other Member States to bolster the exclusive distributorship without violating Article 85(1), Regulation 67/67 furnishes one clue to the answer: the group exemption it provides would not be available in such circumstances. The same answer should apply whether the original German patentee assigns its French patent rights to another, or grants a license to another under its French patents (although, procedurally, the "vindication" of the patent right via an infringement suit will usually be carried out by the patentee on behalf of itself and its licensee, as in the *Parke, Davis* case discussed below). This answer should also apply whether the licensor has granted a non-exclusive license in France coupled with an undertaking to impose an export prohibition on customers, or has granted an exclusive license under a French patent without such undertaking but with reliance on threats of infringement suits to bar parallel imports.[68]

[67] 1 CCH COMM. MKT. REP. ¶ 2727 at 1820, 1967 Journal Officiel des Communautés Européennes 849 (1967) [hereinafter cited E.C.J.O.].

[68] Oberdorfer, Gleiss & Hirsch, writing before the issuance of Regulation 67/67, in COMMON MARKET CARTEL LAW ¶ 63 (1963), reached a contrary conclusion on the basis of their general view of the relationship between national patent rights and Treaty cartel law.

Nothing has appeared thus far in the handful of Common Market patent or know-how cases that involve territorial restrictions of any type to suggest that the Commission and the Court of Justice would deal more leniently with import bans based on multiple parallel patent licenses than with those based on trademarks. Examination of these cases reveals, moreover (to consider another issue implicit in this study), that the Commission would not rigidly confine the impact of Community cartel law to licensing restraints that arise and exist completely within the boundaries of the Common Market.

(a) In the case of Harbison-Walker Refractories Co. of Pittsburgh (licensor) and Basref N.V. of the Netherlands (licensee), an American company gave an exclusive license under a fifteen-year agreement to a Dutch company to use its technical know-how for the manufacture of basic refractory products in Holland. On February 15, 1967, the Commission announced its intention to find the agreement to be consistent with Article 85(1).[69] The license and the exclusivity related only to the use of the secret know-how in manufacturing in Holland. No export limitations were imposed on the licensee, and the licensor gave no commitment to bar imports into Holland of his own product or the product of other licensees, whether by himself, other licensees, or their customers. Since Basref was licensed only to use secret rather than patented technology, no question was raised as to its ability under patent law to bar imports from other Common Market countries (or the United States) of products embodying the technology. Apparently to satisfy itself that the license agreement imposed no export prohibition on the licensee, the Commission is reported to have required the parties, in April 1965, to answer a "detailed questionnaire that requested submission of information . . . on the sales patterns of the products across EEC borders."[70] The inquiry is said to have elicited the information that most of the licensee's sales were indeed outside Holland.[71]

The fact that this inquiry was made gives rise to the inference that the Commission might have found an infringement of Article 85(1) if the license agreement, even though emanating from outside the Common Market, had imposed a restriction curtailing the flow of trade in the

[69] 2 CCH COMM. MKT. REP. ¶9155, 1967 E.C.J.O. 418 (1967).
[70] BUSINESS INT'L, Feb. 24, 1967, at 59.
[71] *Id.* Presumably this means there was a free flow of the Dutch company's products throughout the Common Market.

relevant product as among the EEC countries. The point, while inferential, is by no means a minor one for those interested in the anticartel status of license agreements running between one country within and one outside the Common Market. The Commission has stated that agreements originating outside the Common Market but affecting trade and competition within it can violate Article 85(1).[72] But two of the Commission's early grants of negative clearance were for agreements between Member State producers and "third-country" enterprises prohibiting the latter from exporting to the Common Market. These may have conveyed the misleading impression that any exclusive distribution or patent or trademark license agreement entered into by two such parties was *ipso facto* outside the scope of Article 85(1). In both,[73] the Commission relied on particular circumstances to conclude that the non-competition agreements were unlikely to affect competition or interstate trade within the Community.[74] There is room for questioning the adequacy of the Commission's finding,[75] but it is worth noting, in any event, that neither case involved a restrictive license imposed by a third-country licensor upon a Member State licensee. Also, in neither case was a Member State licensee barred from exporting its products to other EEC countries.[76]

[72] Statement on the Quinine Cartel, 2 CCH COMM. MKT. REP. ¶9180 at 8385, 1967 E.C.J.O. 2153, 2154 (1967); in the quinine cartel case, six Member State firm participants were found guilty and fined a total of $500,000 for fixing prices, limiting production and agreeing to refrain from exporting to each others' home markets; N.V. Nederlandse Combinatie voor Chemische Industrie, July 16, 1969, CCH COMM. MKT. REP. ¶9313. Shortly thereafter, the Commission found that ten European dyestuffs manufacturers, including Imperial Chemical Industries, Ltd. of Great Britain and three Swiss chemical companies, had violated Article 85 by fixing prices; fines totalling $490,000 were imposed. Badische-Anilin- und Soda-Fabrik A.G., July 24, 1969, CCH COMM. MKT. REP. ¶9314. See Chapters 2 and 3 *supra*, where these cases and the general problem of extraterritorial application of the Rome Treaty provisions are discussed.

[73] Grosfillex Co., CCH COMM. MKT. REP. ¶2412.37, 3 Comm. Mkt. L. R. 237, 1964 E.C.J.O. 915 (1964); S.A. Nicholas Frères, CCH COMM. MKT. REP. ¶2412.46, 3 Comm. Mkt. L. R. 505, 1964 E.C.J.O. 2287 (1964).

[74] *Id.* See Weiser, quoting interview with members of the Commission staff, in *Patent and Antitrust Development and Prospects of the European Economic Community*, 8 IDEA 1, 4-5 (1964).

[75] See, *e.g.*, EBB, *supra* note 3, at 676-78; DERINGER, *supra* note 16, at 40 n.19 (1968).

[76] In one of these cases, for example, the French company, Nicholas Frères, sold to Vitapro (U.K.) Ltd., an English company, various patents, trademarks and designs

(b) This impression as to possible applicability of Article 85(1) is borne out, although with an interesting modification in ultimate result, by a recent announcement of the Commission on the validity of know-how and trademark licenses granted by the American firm, Scott Paper Company, to a wholly-owned subsidary in Belgium and to an Italian company in which it holds a half interest.[77] The licenses grant manufacturing and sales rights for special paper products made with Scott know-how, and on which Scott requires its trademarks to be affixed. The Italian company may manufacture and sell in Italy, France and Germany—but not in the Benelux nations; the Belgian company has corresponding rights in Benelux, France and Germany—but not in Italy. The Commission has announced that it intends, by exercising its Article 85(3) authority, to permit the American licensor to restrain each of its licensees from selling goods bearing its trademarks outside the licensee's respective territory. But, the "enterprises concerned" have given assurances that if the goods have been resold by the licensee to a wholesaler, they will not prevent the wholesaler from selling anywhere within the Common Market, not even by invoking trademark rights. This decision preserves the multiple trademark registrations as possible import barriers

to enable it to manufacture and sell cosmetic products for the hair from the "Vitapointe" range of products, using the "Vitapointe" trademark, for distribution within certain specified countries *outside* the Common Market. The facts that the French and English companies are unrelated entities, that each manufactures the trademarked product, and that, as the Commission found, the products compete with many similar preparations within the Common Market were also highly relevant to the Commission's determination. See note 93 *infra,* and contrast *Vitapro* with the *Timken* and *Holophane* sets of facts discussed in the text *infra.*

In the other case, *Grosfillex,* a French manufacturer entered into an exclusive representation agreement providing for the sale of its plastic household products by a Swiss merchant. A non-competition covenant undertaken by the Swiss company was construed by the Commission as barring re-export of the French product into the Common Market. Since the Commission assumed such trade would be impracticable because of the double burden of crossing and recrossing the tariff barriers between the Common Market and Switzerland, it deemed the covenant incapable of affecting competition within the Common Market. License arrangements emanating from outside the Common Market and binding trademark transferees or patent licensees to distribution of a product solely within their national territory may well be regarded in a very different light by the Commission.

[77] Commission Announcement No. C 110, 1968 E.C.J.O., 2 CCH COMM. MKT. REP. ¶9263 (1968).

against the licensees themselves,[78] but only by virtue of an exercise of the Commission's exemptive discretion, based on the special facts of the case. Thus, the decision indicates that the trademark arrangement, even as among these related licensees and though emanating from a licensor outside the Market, falls within Article 85(1). Moreover, the exemptive authority will not be used to enable the licensor to require its licensees to impose export bans upon their customers.

(c) The Netherlands Supreme Court (Hoge Raad), in *Constructa Werke GmbH v. de Geus en Uitdenbogerd*,[79] sustained a trial court's refusal to issue an injunction to bar imports of a patented product because of its belief in the substantiality of the defendant's defense, which was based on the anticartel provisions of the Treaty. The plaintiff sought unsuccessfully to prohibit sale in Holland of products embodying an invention on which it held both Dutch and German patents, the products having been manufactured and sold in Germany under its German patent. The patented products consisted of servicing equipment which was attached to fully automatic washing machines. They had been purchased in Germany by a distributor, who had undertaken not to export them to Holland, but had permitted their export in violation of the contract. In a summary proceeding in the Supreme Court, the respondent, de Geus, argued that the plaintiff's attempted reliance on its patent rights in this situation constituted a contravention of Article 86 of the Treaty, in that it was an improper exploitation of its dominant position affecting interstate trade. The Supreme Court held that there was sufficient probable merit in this defense to warrant refusal to issue the sweeping injunction sought. Since no preliminary ruling on the Article 86 defense was sought from the European Court of Justice, there has been no full-fledged review of the issue on its merits.

(d) The *Parke, Davis* case,[80] with rulings by the Hague Court of Appeal and the European Court of Justice in 1967 and 1968, has

---

[78] Even so, under the trademark law of such countries as the Netherlands, as previously noted in considering the Grundig and GINT trademark arrangements, if the American company has retained title to the national marks, it may not be able to assert an import-ban right under claim of trademark infringement.

[79] 4 Comm. Mkt. L. R. 17 (1964).

[80] Parke, Davis & Co. v. Probel Co., CCH COMM. MKT. REP. ¶8054, 7 Comm. Mkt. L. R. 47 (1968).

intensified speculation on the inter-relation between patent rights and Treaty competition law. It has done so despite the fact that the case itself, while raising a question of the permissible scope of the import-ban rights connected with a patent infringement action, did not directly involve multiple parallel patent licensing or transfers. The arguments submitted to the Court of Justice by the EEC Commission and the French, Dutch and German Governments, even more than the arguments of the parties themselves, extend far beyond the immediate issue in the case and spell out or forecast their views on the broader questions. These arguments foreshadow the same kind of clash between the Commission and Member State governmental authorities on the patent-Treaty law relation as occurred in the *Grundig-Consten* case as to trademarks.[81]

The Hague Court of Appeal sustained Parke, Davis' claim that two Dutch distributors of imported chloramphenicol were infringing Dutch process patents on this pharmaceutical product held by the American company. The defendants had imported the chloramphenicol from Carlo Erba, a major Italian pharmaceutical company, which manufactured the product in Italy and exported it to Holland without authorization or license from Parke, Davis.[82] Under Article 14 of the Italian Patents Act, no product or process patent may be issued for pharmaceuticals, and accordingly the production of the drug in Italy, although unlicensed by Parke, Davis, was proper under Italian law. As the American company (which licenses certain Dutch companies and which pressed the infringement suit to protect its licensees' interests, as well as its own) explained:

> The Italian pharmaceutical industry does not bear the considerable costs connected with developing new products. It simply studies the inventions patented in other countries and published in the patent registers, applies them to its own purposes, without payment or sanctions, and freely puts the products so manufactured on the market in its own country. The countries of

[81] The French, German and Italian Governments had submitted briefs and oral argument in *Grundig-Consten.*

[82] A claim made by Centrafarm, one of the defendants, that there was a "direct or indirect existence of an agreement" between Parke, Davis and Carlo Erba permitting the latter to sell the product freely in the Netherlands was found by the Hague tribunal to lack substantiation. Thus, a subsequent claim made in the Court of Justice by Centrafarm that the Italian company manufactured chloramphenicol "under a license granted by Parke, Davis" was ignored by that court. See CCH COMM. MKT. REP. ¶8054 at 7817.

western Europe have been flooded with these Italian products, which infringe the patents issued in those countries, and this compels the patentees to bring numerous patent infringement suits to protect their rights against this illegal importation.[83]

The Hague Court had made at least a preliminary finding, as an essential ingredient of the case, that Carlo Erba's chloramphenicol was produced by use of the same process as that protected in Holland by one of the Dutch patents owned by Parke, Davis. Other chloramphenicol, the importation of which into Holland was claimed to infringe the American company's Dutch patents, originated from other unlicensed sources in Hungary, which apparently—unlike Italy—furnishes either product or process patent protection for pharmaceuticals.

It does not appear from the record that Parke, Davis holds the relevant patents in Hungary. Accordingly, the Dutch court assumed that import of the Hungarian products into Holland constituted an infringement of the Dutch patents that could not have been justified under any theory, and issued an injunction as to products from that source. As to Italian-made products, however, it requested the Court of Justice to rule on the question whether the use of an injunction to ban imports of chloramphenicol originating in another Member State violates Article 85(1) or 86 of the Rome Treaty. Given the context of the case, the question necessarily refers to products originating legitimately—*i.e.,* within the terms of the local patent law of the country where produced—in the other Member States.

The precise issue to be decided was a narrow one, although the argument of the parties and the intervenors dealt with broader issues which may arise in future cases. As to the instant case, Parke, Davis accurately noted that the much-mooted and controversial problem of application of Treaty competition law to imports of products produced lawfully within the Common Market under multiple parallel patents owned by a single patentee "is not within the scope of the questions submitted by the Court at The Hague with respect to Article 85, paragraph 1, of the EEC Treaty" because it had no "agreement" with Carlo Erba, and engaged in no "concerted practices" with it.[84]

The Commission concurred in this estimate of the question before the Court, noting that the Dutch patent protection was not being used as

[83] *Id.* at 7812-13.
[84] *Id.* at 7813.

part of a plan to "share out and partition the markets, where patent protection already exists." On the contrary, the Commission agreed that the Dutch patent was being used to serve its main purpose, which is to guarantee that the patent holder can exploit its monopoly by preventing entry of products for which, because of the lack of patent protection under Italian law, it had not derived any monopoly profit. It assumed similarly that neither Article 85(1) nor 86 would be violated if the Dutch patent right were used to bar imports of products manufactured in "one of the Member States" by a company holding a patent or license there, unless the holder of the Dutch patent had been able to derive compensation in the other State from the patent on such products. The latter situation would occur if the company in the other State, after manufacturing the product there but before the import of the product into Holland, had "*lawfully* put [it] into circulation" in "one of the Member States" (other than Holland) where Parke, Davis had a patent.[85]

[85] *Id.* at 7819. Emphasis added—the implication being that Parke, Davis in that instance would have made and sold it in the other country or would have collected a royalty upon the manufacture in the original country or upon importation of the product into an intermediate Member State. It is noteworthy that the *Parke, Davis* case involved Dutch process patents. In the United States, unlike the Netherlands (and Britain, see Von Heyden v. Neustadt, 14 Ch. D. 230 [1880], in EBB, *supra* note 3, at 512; Pfizer Corp. v. Ministry of Health, [1965] Pat. Cas. 261, 303-04, 309-11, 319 [H.L.]; and see Lynfield, *Infringement in Great Britain by Importation of Transformed Products,* 9 IDEA 577 [1965-66]), a process patentee has no rights in the sale or use by others of a product made according to his process within the United States. Such sale or use, unlike the case of a product subject to a "product patent," does not constitute an infringement and no remedy is available. Thus the import-ban privilege of a patentee in the United States cannot be rooted in a process patent here. Legislation has been suggested that would amend the Patent Code by defining infringement to include unauthorized importation into the United States of products made by a process which, if practiced in the United States, would constitute an infringement of a United States patent; but the proposal was "quietly dropped." H.R. Rep. No. 9133, 81st Cong., 2d Sess. §231(b) (1950), discussed in DeLio & Worth, *A Review of Protection of Patent Interests from Unfair Methods of Competition in Importation,* 39 J. PAT. OFF. SOC'Y 282, 306 (1957). See also EBB, *supra* note 3, at 514-19. (The bill was introduced again in 1967, was endorsed by the Patent, Trademark and Copyright Section of the ABA, disapproved by the Antitrust Section, and again failed to be enacted.) On the other hand, the United States, unlike many countries, grants patents for chemical products. Other countries usually, but not always (recall Italy), "grant patents for processes of making the chemical substance and in some instances the claim for the process confers protection on the product when produced by that same process." *Id.* at 524 (referring to the Netherlands as coming within this latter category).

Agreeing with that analysis, the Court of Justice held that Articles 85(1) and 86 would permit the exercise of rights against infringement under national patent law to prohibit entry into the country of products coming from another Member State which does not grant patents conferring exclusive rights to manufacture and sell that product. Such a situation involves no restrictive agreements entered into by the patent holder as the key element in the import restriction, and the patent (with the exclusive rights to which it gives rise) "viewed by itself and apart from any agreement of which it might be the subject" is simply a bundle of rights that "results from a legal status granted by a State for products meeting certain criteria."[86]

Significantly, however, in apparent response to the extensive argument presented by the intervenors concerning multiple parallel patent licensing arrangements, the Court warned that the provisions of Article 85(1) could be applicable if the utilization of one or more patents by enterprises acting in concert were to result in a situation falling within the agreement concept of the article. The potential significance of the Court's dictum is highlighted by the views on parallel licensing put forward by the Commission during the argument. The essence of the latter's position was that "patent law must be governed by the same principle as that already recognized by the Court for trademark law"—namely, that the Court should not permit national patent rights, particularly the import-ban privileges connected with them, to restrain interstate commerce within the Common Market, any more than it permitted such restraints through the use of trademark rights in the *Grundig-Consten* case.[87]

This does not argue that import-ban privileges, as an aspect of patent infringement actions, should be abolished. But it does imply an extensive curtailment of the privilege where the patent holder has already received a reasonable reward for the invention and cost of developing the product whose interstate movement he seeks to limit. Within each national territory, patent law recognizes, as a general principle, that rights of the patent holder to protection of his patent monopoly become exhausted

---

[86]CCH COMMON MKT. REP. ¶8054 at 7825. The same conclusion would prevail, presumably, if the Italian manufacturer were acting under an Italian patent which had been granted entirely independently of Parke, Davis. The Article 85 problem, when it does appear, would arise out of agreements by persons like Parke, Davis and by their activities or those of their licensees.

[87]*Id.* at 7818.

once the patented product has been put into circulation legitimately.[88] The patent holder, in this situation, has received his reasonable reward either in the form of profit when he himself has manufactured and sold the product in that country, or in the form of royalties when the product has been manufactured by a licensee. Thereafter, competition by buyers of the patented product cannot be impaired by the patent holder or by his licensee under claim of right derived from the patent.

Previously, in international trade, however, this principle has been applied in a manner that emphasizes the "territoriality" of the national patent of the country of import and regards as irrelevant the fact that compensation has been received by the patent holder or his licensee in the country where the product was manufactured or first put into circulation. With the creation of a single Common Market under the Treaty of Rome, however, the Commission now asserts that the territoriality principle should be deemed to have been modified by Article 85(1) and/or 86, at least to the extent of removing the ability to bar imports from another Member State if the patentee has already received a reward from the manufacture or sale of the product in that State:

> There is no reason why the profit, whatever it is, would not be the same in the Common Market as that obtained previously within the framework of partitioned markets. . . . National and Community measures, such as the reduction of customs duties on substitute products, have such an influence on the market situation that the previous monopolistic position of patent holders and licensees would change anyway. An enterprise which, on the basis of parallel patents, has granted licenses in various Member States and was using its rights under such patents to prevent trade in the patented products between the Member States concerned, could violate paragraph 1 of Article 85. The same would be true if a patent holder were to agree with its licensees to use its right under the patent in the same way, or if the licensees themselves were to make use of the import prohibition based on patent law.[89]

[88] See, *e.g.*, Adams v. Burke, 84 U.S. 453 (1873). On this ground courts have invalidated limitations as to resale prices and tying clauses. But certain limitations have been held justified as being reasonably designed to protect the patentee—*e.g.*, certain types of restriction of the field of use made of the patented product after it has passed into the hands of a purchaser. See General Talking Pictures Corp. v Western Electric Co., 305 U.S. 124 (1938); REPORT OF THE ATTORNEY GENERAL'S NATIONAL COMMITTEE TO STUDY THE ANTITRUST LAWS, 240-41 (1955) [hereinafter cited as ATTY. GEN. NAT. COMM. ANTITRUST REP.] ; Chapter 4 *supra* at 224.

[89] Commission analysis of the questions submitted in the *Parke, Davis* case, CCH COMM. MKT. REP. ¶8054 at 7818 (1968).

And even in the absence of any network of licensing or other agreements that might serve as a basis for finding a violation of Article 85(1), a patentee who makes use of parallel patents and occupies a dominant position in the Common Market with little competition from other patented or unpatented products might be held to violate Article 86.

These views of the Commission, it may be noted, were anticipated in more detail in a frequently-cited article by two staff members of the Commission's General Directorate for Competition, Drs. Norbert Koch and Franz Froschmaier.[90] The article, perhaps more clearly than the summary of the Commission's Brief as published in the Court of Justice opinion in *Parke, Davis,* explains that the theory of "consumption" (or exhaustion) of the patent right advocated by the authors, and presumably now by the Commission, "discards the fictional independence of parallel patents in the context of the field of competition . . . when the patents belong to the same person."[91] This rationale is admittedly based on striking "a balance between the inventor's reward and the protection of competition" under Treaty law, and thus breaks away sharply from concepts that had been developed by "jurisprudence dominated by the patent protectionist viewpoint."

Under these views, a licensor could not exact an export prohibition undertaking from his licensee. Moreover, in the interest of consistency and effective enforcement of the Treaty law, even in the absence of such restrictions imposed upon the licensee, the licensor should not be able to achieve much the same restraint on international trade by being allowed to assert his infringement rights so as to bar imports of the licensee's product.[92] If, however, the patentee completely transfers ownership of

---

[90] Koch & Froschmaier, *The Doctrine of Territoriality in Patent Law and the European Common Market,* 9 IDEA 343 (1965), originally published in German in GRUR AUSL. UND INT'L TEIL, 121-27 (1965).

[91] *Id.* at 356.

[92] *Id.* at 349-51. Note, however, that the Commission is apparently prepared, as indicated by its preliminary decision in the *Scott Paper Co.* case, discussed *supra,* to permit a know-how licensor (and thus presumably also a patent licensor in a similar case) to impose an export ban on his licensee within the Common Market, by use of its Article 85(3) authority, though apparently not prepared to permit imposition of the export ban on the licensee's customers. Compare Froschmaier, *supra* note 23, at 498-99: the draft European Patent Convention would permit the holder of a European Patent to give a license to a French firm to use the patent only within the territory of France. If the French firm produces the product in France but sells it in Italy, this act would constitute patent infringement by the French licensee. However, a purchaser in France could freely import the product into Italy without infringing

one of several parallel patents to an independent person, its "legal and economic life" for purposes of the theory of consumption and anticartel law must then be treated as separate from that of the patents remaining in the possession of the transferor.[93]

A. Impact of European Trademark and Patent Conventions

Whether or not the Common Market countries will agree to put into effect within the foreseeable future either a European Trademark Convention or a European Patent Convention, both of which now exist in draft form, is conjectural. The Draft Conventions, in establishing supranational trademarks and patents, even though national industrial property rights would be perpetuated as alternative methods of protection, foreshadow a major shift from well-established legal procedures and concepts. Resistance to the substantial amount of technical change involved inevitably results from major political cross-currents which have checked the pace of new integration moves that call for action by the EC Council or national legislatures. Such political forces may exercise influence which is disproportionate to the difficulties that remain to be resolved. The Patent Convention, moreover, may be set aside for a lengthy period while a number of countries are pressing for the adoption of a more universal and less supranational Patent Cooperation Treaty.[94] Nevertheless, the Common Market authorities

the patent, and the French company making its sale in such circumstances would not have infringed any legitimate portion of its license agreement.

[93] Otherwise, as the authors note, the further extension of the theory of exhaustion of patent rights that would be required "would amount to anticipating a common patent of the Member States such as is contemplated by a Draft Convention on a European Patent Act." Koch & Froschmaier, *supra* note 90, at 356. Compare the Commission's negative clearance in the *Vitapro* case, discussed *supra*, where a French manufacturer and trademark holder had sold outright to an English manufacturing firm its trademark registrations outside the Common Market. These trademarks would thus be affixed to the product of an enterprise that is completely independent from the French company.

[94] A draft of this Treaty was prepared by "BIRPI" (Bureaux Internationaux Réunis pour la Protection de la Propriété Intellectuelle [United International Bureau for the Protection of Intellectual Property], Geneva) as a result of an American-sponsored resolution enacted by the Executive Committee of the Paris Union. See Note, *Toward the Establishment of an International Patent: Progress and Problems*, 7:2 VA. J. INT'L L. 163 (1967); O'Brien, *A Realistic Appraisal of the Draft Patent*

have repeatedly expressed their intent to pursue their long-held objective of establishing a European Patent and a European Trademark by Common Market conventions as rapidly as practicable,[95] although the Council discussions have disclosed that "many problems, technical as well as political, remain to be solved before agreement on this subject could be arrived at."[96]

Speculative though the achievement of this goal may be, it is so intrinsic to the development of a genuine economic community that the ultimate adoption of these Conventions by the Member States may be assumed as a concomitant to further growth of the Common Market beyond the status of a mere customs union. Any evaluation of the future of territorial restrictions ancillary to trademark and patent licensing within the Common Market, and as between the United States and the Common Market, should accordingly give some consideration to the present content and potential impact of the Draft Conventions. This is particularly the case because the impetus to set up a European Patent and a European Trademark derives to a great extent from the Commission's desire to root out whatever territorial barriers to free movement of products within the Common Market may be implicit in national industrial property rights and may somehow survive the anti-partitioning effect of Articles 85 and 86.[97]

The Draft Convention relating to a European Patent Law was prepared by a committee of experts, representative of the Member States (a

---

Cooperation Treaty, 11 IDEA 159, 162, 166-70 (1967); Weiser, *Patent and Antitrust Developments in the European Economic Community—A Sequel,* 10 IDEA 1, 4-5 (1966).

[95] See Weiser, *supra,* at 3-4.

[96] Council reply to written question No. 105, 2 CCH COMM. MKT. REP. ¶9145 at 8314, 1967 E.C.J.O. 113 (1967). An Inter-Governmental Conference for the Establishment of a European System for the Grant of Patents was held in Brussels in May 1969, with representatives from seventeen European countries (seven from EFTA, six from the Common Market, and from Greece, Turkey, Ireland and Spain). A "patent rights" study group of experts from Britain, Sweden, Switzerland, the Netherlands, Germany and France was set up, and was scheduled to hold Convention drafting sessions in Luxembourg in July, October, and November 1969, with a plenary session to be held early in 1970; press release from the Inter-Governmental Conference, May 21, 1969, No. BR/3/69, CCH COMM. MKT. REP. ¶9304; EFTA Reporter, July 11, 1969, at 2.

[97] See VerLoren van Themaat, *supra* note 41, at 443; Froschmaier, *supra* note 23, at 483-87.

Working Group of the Coordinating Committee of the EEC Commission), pursuant to the directives contained in a protocol that had been formally approved by the Governments of the Member States. It was published in 1962 to enable the Governments and the Commission to elicit opinions of interested groups in Member States, international organizations and "third party states." A complete draft of a European Trademark Convention was prepared in 1964 by a similar Working Party established by the Coordinating Committee of the Commission. It has not yet been published because of the delay encountered by the proposed European Patent Law, but has been extensively described by commentators.[98] Both proposed laws provide for the establishment of supranational industrial property rights, whose territorial base is that of the Common Market rather than that of each Member State.

Thus, Article 2(2) of the Patent Convention provides that "European patents" shall have a "unitary" character in that "they shall have effect on the territory of all Contracting States and may only be assigned or permitted to lapse in respect of the whole of this territory."[99] Article 29 permits the European Patent to be licensed, not only for the whole of the Convention territory, but also for any part of such territory. But there was a split of opinion within the drafting group as to the rights of those licensed for part of the Convention territory, paralleling a split of opinion as to the patentee's rights after he had marketed the product in one of the Member States. As to the latter, Article 20(a) reflects the views of the majority, who would treat the patentee's legal monopoly on the making, using, selling and importing (*and the derivative exclusionary rights of his licensees*) as exhausted throughout the Convention territory once the patentee has marketed his product in one of the States. Correspondingly, the majority's version of the licensing provision, Article 29(2), would treat the rights attached to the patent as exhausted once the licensee has lawfully put the patented article on the market,

[98] See, *e.g.,* Ladas, *Recent Trademark Developments in Foreign Countries,* 55 T.M. REP. 689, 699-703 (1965).

[99] 2 CCH COMM. MKT. REP. ¶ 5507 at 4623 (1962). This contrasts with the territorial divisibility of a United States patent. Articles 18 and 208 provide, more precisely, that the territorial scope of the European patent shall be over the whole of the territories designated by the Contracting States upon signing or ratifying the Convention. Article 25, another supplementary provision, states that a "European patent may not be assigned except in its entirety and for the whole of the territories in which it is effective."

regardless of any clauses of the license providing for territorial limitation. The minority wing of the drafting group would treat the holder of a European patent as entitled to the same rights as would be conferred by a national patent granted in each Member State, and apparently (as a matter of patent law) would allow effect to be given to territorial limitation clauses in patent license agreements. The Commission has clearly aligned itself with the majority view.[100]

Would the principles of the Patent Convention—even assuming that the patent rights exhaustion principles favored by the Commission were adopted—curtail the patentee's or licensee's import-ban privileges more than the Commission has proposed be done by administrative and judicial action under Articles 85 and 86? To be sure, a holder of a European Patent could assign his patent only in its entirety, and could not transfer it with respect to only one Member State or less than the whole Common Market. In the absence of the Convention, a patent holder can trasfer his patent for a single Member State to a completely independent person, and in that event, as previously noted, the "legal and economic life" of each patent for purposes of the theory of consumption and anticartel law would be treated quite separately from that of the patents remaining in the transferor's possession. But this is a narrow difference in light of the fact that the European patentee under the Convention could license use of his patent to licensees in one or more Member States.[101] If the Commission's views, expounded in its brief in the *Parke, Davis* case, as to the present applicability of Articles 85 and 86 to multiple parallel patent licensing arrangements ultimately receive judicial approval, it is not clear that any significant anticartel objectives would then be attained by adoption of the Convention.

The same reasoning appears applicable to the proposed European Trademark Convention. As in the case of its patent counterpart, the drafters were divided on the question whether the rights obtained by registration of a European mark should be those granted by the

[100] Froschmaier, *supra* note 23, at 497-99.

[101] Froschmaier comments that territorial licensing was provided for because it was thought to be justified by "economic necessities," and explains that an "eventual application" of Article 85 was reserved. *Id.* at 498. It should be noted that "territorial *licensing*"—*i.e.,* giving a patent license for manufacture and sale in a particular country—is not synonymous with a "territorial *restriction*" imposed upon a licensee—*i.e.,* expressly prohibiting a licensee from exporting the product outside the licensed territory.

trademark law of each of the Member countries, or those defined by the Convention on a supranational basis. The majority is said to have favored the latter, and correspondingly to have espoused the view that the trademark holder's rights should be deemed exhausted when properly marked products had been placed in circulation, inside or outside the Common Market, by the owner of the European mark, or by agreement with him, or by any person who is "economically connected or acting in agreement" with him. As in the case of the European Patent, the European Trademark could be assigned only for the entire Common Market area, and no territorial restrictions would be permitted to be included in license agreements.[102]

V. CONFLICT BETWEEN AMERICAN AND COMMON MARKET ANTITRUST PRINCIPLES

A. Conflict Arising with Respect to "Unilateral" License Arrangements

The process of implementing Articles 85 and 86 inevitably creates pressure for removing or limiting traditional territorial restraints on the interstate movement of goods subject to trademark and patent licensing within the Common Market. American antitrust law, in contrast, has sanctioned the import-ban privileges of trademark and patent holders and their licensees in international transactions so long as the license agreements are not themselves instruments of a horizontal conspiracy to restrain trade.[103] Thus, it would be permissible under American standards for Parke, Davis (in the absence of any element of horizontal combination) to enter into multiple parallel trademark and patent licensing agreements throughout the Common Market, based on the assumption and expectation that each holder of a trademark or patent license within a Member State could legitimately bar imports of the trademarked or patented product emanating from licensees in the other Member States. But Article 85, as construed by Regulation 67/67, by one view of the implications of *Grundig,* and by the dictum in *Transocean Marine Paint Association* and the ruling in *Sperry Rand*

---

[102] Ladas, *supra* note 98, at 701-02; Froschmaier, *supra* note 23, at 503-04.
[103] See note 6 *supra* and adjacent text.

Italia, makes it unlawful for a manufacturer and a derivative trademark holder to use trademark rights as a means of barring imports of the "genuine" trademarked product from other Member States. And the Commission's views in *Parke, Davis,* if ultimately endorsed and implemented, would curb the rights of a patent holder or his licensee in similar fashion.

Could these legal disparities create a true case of conflict? The classic illustrations of conflict concerning territorial restraints and industrial property rights as between American and European antitrust views, and as between American antitrust decrees and European courts, have involved very different situations. American decisions, as in the *I.C.I.-B.N.S.,*[104] *Timken,*[105] and *Holophane* cases,[106] have characterized certain types of trademark arrangements in European countries which affect American foreign commerce as unlawful, and have treated them as subject to reformation by American judicial action. By contrast, in the hypothetical case posed by the Commission in its argument on the *Parke, Davis* case, *supra*, import-ban privileges based on certain licensing arrangements involving two or more European countries would be deemed lawful under American standards, but unlawful under Community pronouncements. For example, an American patentee's licensing of European companies under counterpart European patents would give rise to import protection which is proper under American law. This protectionism would have been legitimate in the European countries under their own antitrust principles prior to Treaty law and Regulation 67/67, but has probably ceased to be valid in intra-Community trade as a result of those developments. Under American antitrust law, an American trademark owner could transfer its marks in EEC countries to a network of independent exclusive national distributors, and each distributor could exercise its rights under its Member State's trademark, customs regulations or unfair competition doctrines to bar parallel imports of the genuine trademarked product from the other Member

[104] United States v. Imperial Chem. Indus., Ltd., 105 F.Supp. 215 (S.D.N.Y. 1952); British Nylon Spinners, Ltd. v. Imperial Chem. Indus., Ltd., [1952] 2 ALL E.R. 780 (C.A.).

[105] United States v. Timken Roller Bearing Co., 83 F.Supp. 284 (N.D. Ohio 1949), *aff'd in part,* 341 U.S. 593 (1951).

[106] United States v. Holophane Co., 119 F.Supp. 114 (S.D. Ohio 1954), *aff'd per curiam,* 350 U.S. 814 (1955).

States or from "third countries," including the United States—so long, at any rate, as none of the distributors had been actual or potential competitors of the American enterprise. But the rationale of *Grundig-Consten* and the terms of Regulation 67/67 will prevent the authorized distributors from barring such imports if the products are shipped from other Member States, and the Commission has ruled accordingly in the recent *Sperry Rand Italia* case.

Thus, the American and Common Market views on the validity of exercise of such traditional Balkanizing attributes by patent licensees and trademark transferees would be different. But each legal view would prevail in its own "proper" territory, and it is difficult to foresee any clash here between the two legal systems caused by any extraterritorial application of the American law.

Indeed, such diversity of views as to the propriety of import-ban privileges for trademark holders could be found as between the United States and European countries even before the emergence of a body of anticartel law under Article 85. There was then a divergence of views on the level of the doctrines of trademark law itself. For example, the Swiss courts, in the *SABA*[107] and *Philips*[108] cases, asserted that under local trademark and unfair competition law a Swiss trademark holder who acts simply as a distributor for a product imported from abroad cannot bar parallel imports of the "genuine" product by others in Switzerland. American law permits such an import ban to be exercised even though the American trademark holder is a mere importer-distributor,[109] and denies the right only if the "same person" holds the like-sounding trademark abroad as well as in the United States.[110] Yet the fact that

---

[107]SABA Radio-, Televisions- & Elektro A.G. v. Eschenmoser, 84(IV) Entscheidungen des Schweizerischen Bundesgerichtes, Amtliche Sammlung [BGE] 119, 48 Die Praxis des Bundesgerichts [DPB] 44 (Cour de Cassation Pénale, 1958), in EBB, *supra* note 3, at 490-94.

[108]Philips A.G. v. Radio Import GmbH, 86(II) BGE 270, 49 DPB 517 (Bundesgericht 1960).

[109]See, *e.g.,* A. Bourjois & Co. v. Katzel, 260 U.S. 689 (1923).

[110]Reg. 19, C.F.R. §11.14. Up to 1959, the Regulation was more restrictive, and denied the privilege where the foreign and American trademarks were owned by "related companies." A related company, for this purpose, was defined by a footnote to the Regulation as meaning "any person, partnership, association, or corporation which legitimately controls, or is controlled by, the registrant . . . in respect to the nature and quality of the goods in connection with which the mark is used." This broad view of related companies and correspondingly narrow view of the import ban

the import-control privilege of a Swiss trademark holder is more limited (*i.e.*, more rarely available) than that of his American counterpart has created no dramatic difficulties obstructing the grant of trademark licenses by Americans to Swiss distributors.

The Common Market situation poses a problem of similar magnitude. But the grant of a trademark plus an explicit undertaking intended to support an import ban capability within the European Community would also violate Common market anticartel law, and hence might involve quasi-penal sanctions, rather than simply infringing local trademark or unfair competition principles. In effect, American holders of trademark rights will be unable to assure those to whom they transfer their European trademark rights of any ability to restrain imports of validly trademarked products from other sources within the Common Market. The European trademark transferee may still be able to exercise rights to block direct imports of the product from outside the Common Market. But even in that sector, there is no guarantee that national trademark or patent law of Member States would preserve such import-ban privileges intact vis-à-vis "third" countries once those privileges have been abolished, or virtually abolished, as against products legitimately put on the market elsewhere within the Community.[111]

If the transoceanic patent licensing or trademark transfer operation were accompanied by agreements expressly purporting to bolster or to take the place of protectionism formerly derived from Member State trademark, patent and unfair competition laws, would conflict be more likely? Such agreements might take various forms: They might be undertakings by each party not to export the patented or trademarked products to the national territory of the others nor to permit "parallel"

privilege was used as the basis for a major proceeding brought by the Justice Department in the 1950's against allegedly restrictive practices in the import of foreign perfumes; United States v. Guerlain, Inc., 155 F.Supp. 77 (S.D.N.Y. 1957), *judgment vacated and dismissed with prejudice,* 358 U.S. 915 (1958). The Government, having won its antitrust suit in the trial court against a group of American importers, developed qualms about its interpretation of the trademark and related customs law provisions involved in the case, and when the decision was appealed to the Supreme Court moved to have the judgments vacated and the cases dismissed. It sought clarifying legislation from Congress in the 1959-60 session, an effort that was unsuccessful and not further pursued, and simultaneously amended the basic Regulation to reflect its changed view of the present state of the law. See EBB, *supra* note 3, at 467-482.

[111] For speculation on this point, see Ebb, *supra* note 8, at 884-88.

exports by their customers. Alternatively, they could take the form of agreements that Member-State trademark transferees who are manufacturers would always affix the key trademark to their product in the hope that national trademark law, by supplying import-ban privileges, will confine distribution to each national territory (or to a designated group of Member States—*e.g.*, Belgium, the Netherlands and Luxembourg). The presence of such contractual arrangements leaves open the possibility (albeit extreme improbability) that an American court might enjoin a rebellious European party from breaching its undertaking by distributing to other Member States, while Community anticartel law would bar its adhering to any such commitments by bringing restrictive pressure upon its customers or upon parallel importers. In all likelihood, American courts would not order specific enforcement of ancillary export- or import-ban agreements, nor grant damages for non-performance of any such implied or explicit agreements, even if the owner of the European trademarks or patents were an American company and the European defendants were subject to the jurisdiction of the American courts. Even prior to the existence of European anticartel law, American courts showed no enthusiasm for decreeing specific performance of restrictive arrangements affecting United States foreign commerce, nor for awarding damages for breach of such agreements.[112] In such circumstances mutually supportive action is more likely than conflict between American and EEC Member-State authorities and courts.[113]

[112] See, *e.g.*, Foundry Services, Inc. v. Beneflux Corp., 206 F.2d 214 (2d Cir. 1953) and United States v. Bayer Co., 135 F.Supp. 65 (S.D.N.Y. 1955). Brownell v. Ketcham Wire & Mfg. Co., 211 F.2d 121 (9th Cir. 1954), which runs counter to this tendency, has been criticized. ATTY. GEN. NAT. COMM. ANTITRUST REP. 237 n.55. See also American Optical Co. v. New Jersey Optical Co., 58 F.Supp. 601 (D. Mass. 1944) and FUGATE, FOREIGN COMMERCE AND THE ANTITRUST LAWS 200-02 (1958). Such agreements might well be found to violate American antitrust law too. The very presence of supplemental export-prohibition agreements, though arguably "merely ancillary" to trademark or patent licensing privileges, might be deemed by American courts to constitute presumptive evidence of an unreasonable private restraint violating Section 1 of the Sherman Act. See BREWSTER, ANTITRUST AND AMERICAN BUSINESS ABROAD 145-47 (1958); FUGATE, *supra*, at 232.

[113] *Compare* Fugate, *The Common Market and the United States Antitrust Laws,* 38 N.Y.U.L. REV. 458, 469 (1963) and Ass't Attorney General Turner's testimony in *Hearings on Prices of Quinine and Quinidine Before the Subcomm. on Antitrust and Monopoly of the Sen. Comm. on the Judiciary,* 90th Cong., 1st Sess. 235 (1967), reprinted in 1968 Supp. to EBB, *supra* note 3, at 35-37, *with* Oral Argument

B. Conflict Concerning Cooperative Use of Industrial Property: Concurrent Trademark Use Commitments, Cross-Licensing and Patent Pools

The "unilateral" trademark and patent licensing and transfer arrangements dealt with in the preceding subsection involve primarily a transfer or license of an industrial property right flowing in one direction, from the original owner to his transferee or licensee. Such complications as exist in those arrangements are caused either by the presence of multiple parallel recipients, or by supplemental export-ban undertakings by the licensees or transferees. An additional level of complication arises when licensing involves an exchange of industrial property rights between two or more participants, or a joint conferring of such rights upon another entity, as in patent pools. These arrangements may be motivated by bona fide commercial and manufacturing reasons, by a desire to achieve restrictive practices in a veiled form, or by an admixture of both. On this complicated level, it is likely that Common Market law may be more permissive than American antitrust law, thus creating a possibility of conflict.

1. CONCURRENT TRADEMARK USE COMMITMENTS

Where competing manufacturers agree to use the same trademark on their products in particular fields, one effect of their agreement may be to restrain competition, although their motivation and intent may have been directed at very different, legitimate objectives. Wartime or revolutionary expropriations may sever one portion of a multinational enterprise from the rest, and result in the transfer of key trademarks to the hands of others in the expropriating countries, thereby creating disputes over the right of the original owners at least to the concurrent use of their old trademarks in such territories,[114] and use in third-

in the *Holophane* case before the Supreme Court in 1956, EBB, *supra* note 3, at 603-06. In the case of the quinine cartel, American and Commission action against EEC participants occurred almost simultaneously; a member of the Commission stated that its investigation had been prompted by the U.S. Senate hearings and had been carried out in collaboration with the Department of Justice, N.Y. Times, July 25, 1969, at 72. For further description of this case, see Chapter 2 *supra*, at 100.

[114] See, *e.g.*, the lengthy and persistent attempts by the German pharmaceutical house to export its products to the United Kingdom under some form of the Bayer trademark, the English registration of which is now owned by an American-con-

country export markets.[115] Or, the passage of ownership of an overseas subsidiary to new shareholders in the ordinary course of commercial developments may cast doubt on the right of the original multinational company to retrieve its beneficial ownership of the overseas trademarks, in order to permit it to export its products under those marks to the foreign country.[116] Judicial decisions establishing rights to some sort of concurrent use of such marks in the same territory, or private agreements resolving the disputes in similar manner, may result in the two competing companies using the same mark in the same country or countries. Such compromises and overlapping of trademark use—*e.g.,* two "Bayer" lines of pharmaceutical products, or two "Zeiss" lines of optical products—may foster greater competition than would be the case if only one party were allowed to use the mark. Whatever trade restriction may result from concurrency based on such compromises will probably be negligible,[117] and it is not this kind of situation in the simple form presented that gives rise to American or European antitrust problems.

Nevertheless, the situation could be availed of as a pretext and used as the basis for an international cartel arrangement. Private arrangements, entered into by the German and American Bayer pharmaceutical enterprises after World War I expropriations, were subsequently found by the American courts not merely to have resolved disputes as to the right to use the trademark in particular countries, but also to have established a territorial division of large portions of the world as between the two corporate empires. Trademark (and patent) rights in certain territories were transferred by each to the other in order to concentrate these rights and corresponding marketing rights in the hands of one or the other of

trolled English company. Sterling-Winthrop Group, Ltd. v. Farbenfabriken Bayer A.G., [1966] Pat. Cas. 477, No. 18 (Ch.).

[115] See, *e.g.,* the *Mumm Champagne* cases, illustrated by Société Vinicole de Champagne v. Mumm Champagne & Importation Co., 10 F.Supp. 289 (S.D.N.Y. 1935), *aff'd per curiam,* 143 F.2d 240 (2d Cir. 1944), Browne-Vintners Co. v. National D. & C. Corp., 151 F.Supp. 595 (S.D.N.Y. 1957), and other similar controversies summarized and discussed in EBB, *supra* note 3, at 439-60.

[116] See Columbia Nastri & Carta Carbone v. Columbia Ribbon & Carbon Mfg. Co., 367 F.2d 308 (2d Cir. 1966), and related Italian litigation, discussed in Ebb, *Current Problems of American Companies that Permit Use of their Corporate Name and Trademark Overseas,* 1968 SYMPOSIUM ON PRIVATE INVESTORS ABROAD 321 (1968), reprinted in 59 T.M. REP. 344 (1969).

[117] See the reasoning of the British court on this point in the British *Bayer* case, *supra* note 114, at 484-86.

the parties for each country (and a newly-created, jointly-owned company operating in several British Commonwealth countries). These arrangements abused trademark rights and unreasonably restrained American foreign commerce, thus violating Section 1 of the Sherman Act.[118] The Continental European market, including the six Common Market countries, was reserved as the exclusive territory of the German enterprise, which in turn agreed to use its best efforts to prevent others from exporting its Bayer-marked products to the United States, Canada, Cuba, the United Kingdom, Australia and South Africa. A 1941 consent decree enjoined the American Bayer company from combining with the German company to restrain shipment or sale to the United States or to withdraw from or refrain from entering any foreign market.

Would an agreement like the one enjoined affect trade or competition between the EEC Member States? If France were reserved for the American Bayer products and the other Member States were allocated to I. G. Farbenindustrie A.G., Article 85(1) would be clearly infringed. But all six of the countries were in fact treated as a bloc in the agreement. The fact that the entire Common Market had been reserved for the German company's products precluded American competition within the Common Market. And the fact that the German Bayer products were subject to a ban against export from the Member States to the United States and other "third countries" prevented Common Market competition against these third country areas. Could these factors be said to be "liable to affect trade between Member States" and to "prevent, restrict or distort competition within the Common Market"? The terminology of Article 85(1) sounds inherently more limited in applicability than, in a different geographical context, the Sherman Act's reference to "commerce among the several States, *or with foreign nations.*" And, as pointed out in Chapter 2 and also above,[119] the EEC Commission has shown that it is much less concerned about certain trade restrictions running between the Common Market and third country areas than about those that apply expressly as among the Member States.

Nevertheless in the case put, the substantial distortion in the flow of imports into the Common Market and among its constituent members caused by American Bayer's grant of absolute territorial protection to that Market, as well as by the outsider's imposition of a ban on exports

---

[118] United States v. Bayer Co., 135 F.Supp. 65 (S.D.N.Y. 1955).
[119] Discussed in note 76 *supra* and in Chapter 2 *supra* at 103-06.

from the Common Market to third country areas, would have a far greater potential for distorting competition among the Member States than was likely in the cases already decided. The primary objective of the Treaty cartel law is to dismantle trade-restrictive barriers among the EEC countries considered vis-à-vis one another, and the Commission has been tolerant of the concentration of industry through mergers within the Common Market to permit more effective competition between Community and third-country enterprise. But these objectives and attitudes would not be consistent with the sanctioning of cartels between American or British industry and Common Market firms. An international cartel agreement of the type involved in the *Bayer* litigation could be shown to affect trade and competition within the Common Market, and Article 85(1) could accordingly be deemed applicable.[120] If it were so regarded, it is doubtful that the Commission would exercise its exemptive powers under Article 85(3) to permit the perpetuation of the cartel.

The hypothetical variant of the Bayer arrangements whereby compulsory concurrent use of the same trademark would be coupled with an allocation of the French market to one company and the German to another was actually exemplified by the Timken roller bearing cartel.[121] The American Timken company licensed British, French and German companies to make, use and sell roller bearings under its patents, and the licenses continued after the expiration of the patents. Trademark rights to the word, TIMKEN, were transferred to the French and German companies and licensed to the British, and each one of the three agreed

---

[120]Consider the implications of the Commission's finding that the British company, ICI, and three Swiss companies had violated Article 85 by their participation with Member State manufacturers of dyestuffs in a price-fixing agreement; see note 72 *supra* and discussion in Chapters 2 and 3. For a variety of speculative commentary on these issues, see, *e.g.,* GRAUPNER, *supra* note 29, at 37-47, 126-31; OBERDORFER, GLEISS & HIRSCH, COMMON MARKET CARTEL LAW ¶¶23, 29-31, EEckman, *L'Application de l'article 85 du Traité de Rome aux ententes étrangères a la C.E.E. mais causant des restrictions à la concurrence a l'intérieur du Marché Commun* in 54 REVUE CRITIQUE DE DROIT INTERNATIONAL PRIVE 499 (1965); Kruithof, *The Application of the Common Market Anti-Trust Provisions to International Restraints of Trade,* 2C.M.L. REV. 69, 72-76 (1964).

[121]The *Scott Paper* case, discussed *supra* at 276, is distinguishable in this respect since, by contrast, the trade-restrictive intent and effect of the *Timken* arrangement overshadowed and indeed displaced any legitimate purpose of the licenses.

not to manufacture or sell bearings except under the trademark. Each agreed also to sell only within its own territory, which in each case included the country of incorporation of the trademark-rights recipient.[122] When the German company discontinued its business in 1934, British Timken took over its territory, so that France and Germany remained compartmentalized markets under the trademark and related agreements. The American court found the division of world markets effectuated by these and other means to constitute a violation of Section 1 of the Sherman Act.[123] It ruled that the trade restrictions could not be justified as merely ancillary to the transfers of the trademarks, and enjoined their continuance.

Were this case to come before the Commission today,[124] the latter would presumably regard the cartel as clearly affecting interstate trade in violation of Article 85(1).[125] This would eliminate any possibility that might otherwise be thought to exist that a French or German court

[122] United States v. Timken Roller Bearing Co., 83 F.Supp. 284, 290-95 (N.D. Ohio 1949).

[123] *Id., aff'd in part,* 341 U.S. 593 (1951).

[124] *Cf.* Chapter 4 *supra* at 198.

[125] For speculation on the probable attitude of the EEC Commission and courts in the Common Market toward another cartel that bolstered territorial protection by compulsory use of the same trademark by actual or potential competitors, see comments on United States v. Holophane Co., 119 F.Supp. 114 (S.D. Ohio 1954), *aff'd per curiam,* 350 U.S. 814 (1955), in Ebb, *supra* note 8, at 888. La Société Anonyme Française was allocated three countries which are now within the Common Market: France, Belgium and Italy; Holophane Ltd.'s territory included the United Kingdom, Germany and The Netherlands. Each company imposed on its customers and dealers contractual obligations not to export products purchased from it to the territories of the others. The trial court's decree required, *inter alia,* that the American defendant use reasonable efforts to compete in the "territories" of the others, using a new trademark if necessary. Since competing within these countries and failure to use the "Holophane" trademark would violate the outstanding patent and trademark agreements, the defendant argued in the Supreme Court that compliance with the decree would subject it to suits for damages overseas. But four of the eight Justices ruled in favor of the Government on the appeal, apparently believing it likely that the foreign courts, in the event of any such suits, would give effect to a plea of impossibility, or that the American court would revise its decree if a foreign court indicated that the contracts were still enforceable. See Chapter 3 *supra* at 123-24; EBB, *supra* note 3, at 603-06. There would appear to be less risk now that any serious conflict would arise in a Member State court between such an American decree and the law of the Member state.

would seek to counter the American injunction by providing import-ban protection or other judicial assistance to the holders of the French and German TIMKEN trademark registrations. Moreover, the Commission would be unlikely to find grounds for granting an exemption to this cartel under Article 85(3), since the cartel enabled its participants "to eliminate competition in respect of a substantial part of the goods concerned."

Conflict is more likely to arise, of course, where the Commission under Article 85(3) sanctions an agreement among potential competitors who manufacture and sell in different national territories to engage in concurrent use of a trademark, coupled with prohibitions on exports of the trademarked product to territories reserved to other parties to the agreement. Such a case was presented by the exemption granted by the Commission in its decision concerning the *Transocean Marine Paint Association.* The Association comprises eighteen medium-sized producers of marine paint in eighteen different countries, including five of the six Member States and the United States.[126] Each member binds itself to market its marine paints under the same trademark, which is registered in each country in the name of the member established there, the members being authorized to add to it their own tradename or mark. At the Commission's insistence, a provision completely prohibiting export of both Transocean and other marine paints to another member's territory except with that member's approval was modified to authorize exports of Transocean paints on payment of a commission to the other member. Exports of other marine paints were permitted on payment of a commission and subject to the other member's agreement as well, with the proviso that such agreement should always be given unless the interests of the Association would be harmed thereby. The Commission found that the agreement restrained interstate trade under Article 85(1) because of the restrictions outlined above, as well as because of others not enumerated here. But it granted an exemption under Article 85(3) because it found that the agreement contributes to improving the distribution of the products by an association of medium-sized companies which, by themselves, would be unable to undertake the investments and risks required to create their own distribution networks in a large number of countries. Larger marine paint manufacturers are

[126] June 27, 1967, CCH COMM. MKT. REP. ¶9188, 6 Comm. Mkt. L. R. Supp. D9 (1967); see also discussion in Chapter 2 *supra* at 99.

present in all of the major countries, so that the agreement does not eradicate competition but permits more effective competition by the smaller companies—a support that the Commission regarded as justified for a limited transitional "launching period" (running to December 31, 1972). It regarded the concurrent use of the same-sounding trademark as a useful adjunct to the eighteen-country distribution system, and noted its understanding that members who were established in the Common Market could not use their trademark rights to hinder imports of Transocean products from other Member States.

In a somewhat comparable domestic network of territorially restricted manufacturers of "Sealy products," the Supreme Court of the United States held features of territorial exclusivity coupled with horizontal agreement on resale prices to constitute an "aggregation of trade restraints" unlawful under Section 1 of the Sherman Act, although it did not seem to regard unified quality control as itself anti-competitive.[127] It is conceivable that the Justice Department might be sufficiently concerned about American participation in even so weak a cartel as the Transocean Marine Paint Association to seek an injunction against further participation by the American member. Presumably, the political delicacy of such enforcement action would be carefully considered by the State and Justice Departments as a preliminary matter, in view of the Article 85(3) exemption that has been accorded to the cartel to the extent that it affects interstate commerce in the Common Market. This factor by itself might dissuade the Justice Department from moving at all against the American particpant (or, for that matter, against any European or other foreign participants over whom, fortuitously, it might be able to obtain personal jurisdiction), although an Article 85(3) exemption is not the kind of mandatory foreign governmental action that American authorities have recognized as an effective barrier against American regulatory action.[128]

If an American antitrust suit were indeed instituted and were successful, the terms of the *Holophane* decree give some indication of the kind of enforcement action that might be decreed in the circumstances of this case. At worst, the American member might be required to sever its ties with the Association and to attempt to compete in the other countries, without use of the Transocean trademark. The risk of

[127] United States v. Sealy, Inc., 388 U.S. 350 (1967).
[128] See Chapters 3 at 125, and 4 at 237.

undergoing suit in foreign countries for damages for breach of contract would appear to be no greater because of the existence of the Article 85(3) waiver than the risk that the Holophane company was forced to assume in an earlier day. The major effect of the Article 85(3) action would appear to be a reduction in the likelihood that American enforcement agencies and courts will take any action in these circumstances. Discretionary determinants may be: the extent to which American participation is essential to the effective existence and development of the distribution system which the Common Market authorities seek to foster; the substantiality of competition via the manufacture and sale of rival brands in American interstate and foreign commerce; and the extent to which the American participant occupies a dominant position in that market.

2. COOPERATIVE USE OF PATENTS AND PATENT LICENSES AND ALLOCATION OF TERRITORIES

More pervasive and more significant than concurrent use of the same trademark by international competitors are various types of cooperative use or "reciprocal exchange" of patents and patent licensing, notably cross-licensing and patent pools. These bilateral or multilateral arrangements frequently are indispensable to the effective utilization of one or more patents with complementary patents, or are desirable to resolve bona fide patent controversies as to priority rights, infringement, etc. On the other hand, such arrangements, particularly those which are exclusive and entered into by dominant international competitors, may have as the primary objective or result the dividing up of various portions of the world market between the participants by allocation of territories, by price and sales quota restrictions within "common" territories, or by product exclusivity or restraints on field of use. Under American antitrust views, territorial and other restraints achieved in this manner would be unlawful.[129] In the *National Lead* case,[130] for example, the

---

[129]See generally ATTY GEN. NAT. COMM. ANTITRUST REP. 84-86, 242-47; BREWSTER, ANTITRUST AND AMERICAN BUSINESS ABROAD 140-44, 154-57 (1958); FUGATE, *supra* note 112, at 211-19; Timberg, *International Patent and Trademark Licenses and Interchanges: The United States Approach*, in 2 CARTEL AND MONOPOLY IN MODERN LAW 751, 761-64 (1961).

[130]United States v. National Lead Co., 63 F.Supp. 513 (S.D.N.Y. 1945), *aff'd*, 332 U.S. 319 (1947).

court held unlawful a network of cross-licensing agreements that walled off the United States market, so that no titanium products were imported from abroad, and U.S. titanium exports were restricted to the rest of the Western Hemisphere. From the Common Market viewpoint, it is especially noteworthy that in addition to this and other territorial allocations of markets, subsidiary agreements regulated production, sales quotas and prices within certain European countries, including France, Germany and Italy.

One of the most dramatic confrontations between judicial enforcement of the American antitrust laws and European court protection of vested contract and property rights arose over an American decree seeking to regulate ownership and use of British and British Commonwealth patent rights acquired by a British company under the umbrella of a restrictive cross-licensing agreement between dominant American and British producers in the nylon field: the ICI-duPont-British Nylon Spinners arrangements.[131] But, if the observations in the preceding section on cooperative use of trademark rights for cartel objectives are sound, cross-licensing of patents by dominant American and Common Market manufacturers should not engender similar judicial clashes between American and Common Market courts.

Whether or not Community authorities and courts will regard a cross-licensing foundation for a horizontal cartel as violating Article 85(1) will depend upon whether they discern a distortion and restraint of interstate competition within the Common Market over and beyond a restriction between the United States and the Common Market. Cross-licensing arrangements between dominant competitors have traditionally included supplementary restrictive agreements as to territorial allocation, prices, and sales quotas among key European manufacturers operating in the same or different European countries. If these continue, they will be exposed to attack under Community anticartel law. The Court of Justice decision in the *Grundig-Consten* case indicates that the Commission might be constrained to isolate and enjoin only the strictly interstate restraints. If so, there would continue to be room for disagreement between American and Community courts concerning

---

[131] See the American decree, United States v. Imperial Chem. Indus., Ltd., 105 F.Supp. 215 (S.D.N.Y. 1952), and the British reaction, British Nylon Spinners, Ltd. v. Imperial Chem. Indus., Ltd., [1952] 2 All E.R. 780 (C.A.); see also Chapter 3 *supra* at 122-23.

those aspects of restrictive cross-licensing agreements which bear directly on foreign trade between the United States and the Common Market, but only indirectly on trade within the Common Market. On the other hand, as a practical matter, a cartel system predicated on absolute territorial protection for some states coupled with fool-proof industry self-regulation of prices and sales quotas in others would have great difficulty surviving an attack by Common Market authorities on its Community interstate aspects and by American courts on its domestic and international aspects.[132]

Cartel agreements concluded under the umbrella of a very restrictive Euro-American cross-license arrangement between dominant producers may appear to be confined to individual countries, when regarded in isolation from other affiliated single-country cartel agreements and without regard to the overall Euro-American or world-wide division of the market. When examined as a package, however, the price and sales quotas agreed upon for application in one Common Market country may well turn out, in such circumstances, to be dependent on the existence of the other related single-country cartel agreements. The tacit if not explicit assumption is that the participants in the various agreements understand that each such agreement is to be respected by those participating in the other-country arrangements. The agreements described in the *National Lead* case illustrate this point.[133] The *Grundig-Consten* decisions illustrate the further point that Common Market authorities will evaluate single-country cartel agreements in their total Common Market context, including the existence of other parallel arrangements in other Member States. As noted in our earlier consideration of the EEC *Guide Pratique* and the Commission's formal Notice on Patent Licensing Agreements of December 24, 1962, the Commission has repeatedly emphasized the necessity for examining license agreements on a case-by-case basis in the full context of related agreements or concerted practices among the various licensees, and has also emphasized the need for close scrutiny of the possible restrictive effect of "reciprocal

---

[132] See the quinine cartel case, *supra* notes 72 and 113.

[133] Compare similar "home territory" and "common territory" divisions of the world market in other cross-license arrangements: United States v. General Electric Co., 82 F.Supp. 753, 827-47 (D.N.J. 1949) (incandescent lamp case); United States v. Imperial Chem. Indus., Ltd., 100 F.Supp. 504, 513-48 (S.D.N.Y. 1951).

licenses" as well as multiple parallel licensing and joint ownership of patents.

Where patent pooling and cross-licensing result in substantial restraints on competition, they are suspect, since such restraints are thought by Commission officials to result more from the existence of the license or patent-transfer agreements than from the legal monopoly granted by patent law.[134] In some cases, moreover, a major cross-licensing pact between dominant American and European producers in an industry may be supplemented by a multiple parallel licensing agreement blanketing some or all of the Common Market countries, under the aegis of the dominant American or European producer as the licensor. In the *duPont-ICI* case, duPont was allocated Germany, France and Italy as its exclusive territory for the manufacture and sale of coated textiles, paints and varnishes, and correspondingly held exclusive patent licensing rights from ICI for those countries.[135] ICI presumably held the Benelux countries as its exclusive territory. If this arrangement were in effect today and if products were manufactured under these patents in any of the Common Market countries, attempts by ICI or duPont or one of their subsidiaries to exercise import-ban privileges under their exclusive patent licenses to restrict the free flow of these products throughout the Common Market would probably be deemed to violate Article 85(1), or, alternatively, to be ineffective because of an application of the Commission's newly-developing views of the status of multiple parallel patent licensing within the European Community.

Is it likely that the Commission, while recognizing the restrictive effect of a Euro-American cross-licensing arrangement between dominant

[134] See VerLoren van Themaat, *supra* note 41, at 443-44. Compare the similar attitude of the Federal Cartel Office of Germany, where cross-licensing between domestic and foreign enterprises involves a great number of patents: "It is difficult to ascertain to what degree such an agreement is void under [Section 20(1) of the German cartel law] or to what degree it represents only a large number of independent license agreements. The actual effects of such license agreements can be similar to those of a cartel." Quoted from Weiser, *Recent EEC Antitrust Activity Relating to Exclusive Distributorships and Trademarks,* 9 IDEA 35, 45 (1965). See also Buxbaum, *Restrictions Inherent in the Patent Monopoly: A Comparative Critique,* 113 U. PA. L. REV. 633, 649 n.70, 652, 661 (1965).

[135] United States v. Imperial Chem. Indus., Ltd., 100 F.Supp. 504, 537 (S.D.N.Y. 1951).

producers operating in effect largely on an exclusive basis might nevertheless find sufficiently redeeming factors to justify an Article 85(3) exemption? Consider the duPont-ICI cross-licensing arrangement with respect to nylon, which was "wholly a duPont development from beginning to end."[136] The American company had originated the nylon technology. Thus, the patent and secret process licensing agreement covering that product might readily be construed in a present-day context as contributing to the improvement of the production or distribution of nylon products or promoting technical or economic progress concerning the nylon industry in the Common Market, as well as in Britain. On the other hand, this contribution to the technological progress of the Community would seem to have been accomplished by an arrangement that enabled the participating enterprises to eliminate competition with respect to a substantial proportion of the goods concerned, thus violating the prerequisite condition of Article 85(3)(b).

It is not difficult to imagine a situation in which a cross-licensing arrangement might restrain American foreign commerce in a manner offensive to the Sherman Act and yet be deemed either not to restrain interstate competition in the Common Market, or alternatively, to warrant exemption under Article 85(3). A series of bilateral cross-licenses of world-wide scope were entered into by three major producers of household zigzag sewing machines equipped with a patented multiple cam zigzag mechanism. The participants were Singer Manufacturing Company of the United States, Fritz Gegauf A.G. of Switzerland, Arnaldo Vigorelli S.p.A. of Italy. There were Singer-Gegauf, Singer-Vigorelli, and Gegauf-Vigorelli cross-licenses. The Supreme Court construed these cross-licenses, which were followed by an assignment of Gegauf's American patent to Singer, in the full setting of the negotiations among the parties. Against this background, it held them to be motivated primarily by the common purpose of suppressing competition within the United States from imports of Japanese sewing machines, and only secondarily by the desire to resolve conflicts over priority of invention among the parties. Accordingly, it ruled that the arrangement violated Section 1 of the Sherman Act.[137] Common Market authorities might well be less perturbed by the existence and implementation of the cross-licenses and the patent assignment. A major impact of the

[136]*Id.* at 552.
[137]United States v. Singer Mfg. Co., 374 U.S. 174 (1963).

arrangement, as one of the concomitants of barring American imports of Japanese sewing machines, would have been to increase the opportunity for substituting exports of European machines (especially from Germany and Italy, within the Community). The United States was importing 1,100,000 Japanese sewing machines in 1959, but only 100,000 from Europe at that time. Community officials have indicated from time to time their desire to strengthen the ability of Member-State enterprises, especially small or medium-sized enterprise, to compete effectively against major producers outside the Common Market.[138]

On close scrutiny, however, it is difficult to see how the actual decision in *Singer* could really evoke conflicting action on the part of the Common Market administrative and judicial tribunals. Although the Supreme Court's judgment indicated a general condemnation of the world-wide cross-licensing coupled with the assignment of Gegauf's American patent to Singer,[139] the implementing decree simply enjoined Singer from "adhering to any contract, combination or conspiracy . . . to use any patent rights to prevent or restrict the importation into the United States of any machine-carried multiple cam zigzag sewing machines, or to prevent their use or sale within the United States."[140] Correspondingly, Singer was required to make its five American patents available to all comers on reasonable non-discriminatory royalty terms.

Unlike the directive in the *duPont—ICI-BNS* case, the *Singer* decree concentrates on barring the use of the American patent arrangements to exclude imports of Japanese machines, and does not purport to operate on the European aspects of the cross-licenses.[141] The Justice Department was not asserting that the cross-licensing resulted in a territorial allocation of the European market to Gegauf, Vigorelli and their

---

[138] See, *e.g.*, Commission Notice on Restrictive Business Agreements, CCH COMM. MKT. REP. ¶9248 at 8517, 7 Comm. Mkt. L. R. Supp. D5 (1968). Recall the Commission's decision concerning the Transocean Marine Paint Association, discussed in the text at note 123 *supra*, and see Waelbroeck, *Cooperation Agreements and Competition Policy in the EEC*, 1 N.Y.U.J. INT'L L. & POL. 5 (1968).

[139] 374 U.S. 174, 177, 180, 190 n.7 (1963).

[140] Final judgment in Civil Action No. 154-108, S.D.N.Y., filed July 2, 1964.

[141] United States v. Singer Mfg. Co., 231 F.Supp. 240, 1964 Trade Cas. ¶71,133 (S.D.N.Y. 1964). The district court judge commented during the trial that Singer, by its cross-licenses with European manufacturers, "did not limit or restrict their market," and "did not interfere with the United States commerce *by way of exports.*" Record in the Supreme Court, vol. 1, at 197 (emphasis added).

European licensees. Unlike *duPont-ICI-BNS,* the vice here lay in the impact of the arrangements on Japanese imports to the United States rather than in any claimed reservation and allocation of the United States and Western Europe as "home territories" to the respective cross-license participants—although the concerted practice helped to bar Japanese imports from the European countries as well. And as to *that* restrictive effect, the American antitrust laws were not directly involved and American authorities presumably did not regard any resultant curb on Japanese imports to Europe as sufficiently related to the restraint on imports to the United States to warrant an attempt at breaking up the cross-licensing of the European patents.

The concentration of patents in a pooling arrangement, where one or more of the patent owners or a separate entity has the right to license others under the pooled patents,[142] may be manipulated in such fashion as to reduce or eliminate competition. A foreign patent pool that precludes the participants from issuing a license that would permit the import from the United States of a product allegedly covered by the pool, and which confines package licensing to local manufacture, cuts off American competition and restrains American foreign commerce. Injunctive decrees have been granted by our courts, at the instance of the Justice Department and of private litigants under the Sherman Act, to require American participants and their subsidiary companies to refrain from continued membership in such a preclusive pool and to refrain from enforcing or claiming any rights under such a plan that would directly or indirectly restrict American manufacturers from exporting their products to the foreign country.[143] Since these decrees have an impact on the rights of foreign participants in foreign contractual arrangements, the risk of conflict with foreign courts is far greater than

[142] ATTY. GEN. NAT. COMM. ANTITRUST REP. 242 (1955).

[143] See the consent decrees entered against Westinghouse Electric Corporation, General Electric Company, and N.V. Philips' Gloeilampenfabrieken, in United States v. General Electric (S.D.N.Y.) 1962 Trade Cas. ¶¶ 70,342, 70,428, 70,546, involving the radio and television patent pool and licensing agency, Canadian Radio Patents Ltd. See also Zenith Radio Corp. v. Hazeltine Research, Inc., 395 U.S. 100 (1969), upholding district court findings with respect to Hazeltine's participation in a Canadian patent pool that blocked the import into Canada by Zenith of radio and television apparatus made in the United States. The Supreme Court held that sufficient evidence of injury to Zenith's business had been shown to warrant damages and an injunction.

in the *Singer* case. The *Canadian Electronic Patents* case involving just such a situation has evoked strong dissent from Canadians.[144]

If patent pools of a similarly exclusionary nature, *i.e.*, barring imports from countries, were established in Member States of the Community, they would clearly violate Article 85(1) to the extent they prevented the free movement of products within the Common Market. The very existence of the Common Market, even in the absence of a European Patent Convention, suggests that exclusionary national patent pools within a Member State will be modified at least to avoid exclusion of imports from other Member States. Alternatively, such national pools might be converted to Community-wide concentrations; whether or not such new aggregations of patents could be used, consistently with Article 85(1), to bar imports from outside the Common Market is subject to speculation. Whether or not an American decree, seeking to prevent such a pool from barring imports from the United States, would create a significant conflict with the contract law of a Member State, would depend in part, though not wholly, on the validity of such a Community-wide exclusionary pool under Common Market cartel law. In any event, against the background of Community cartel law, there appears less likelihood of clash between American decrees in this field and Community law or national contract law than of clash between decrees thus far issued as to radio and television patent pools and the laws of Canada, England and Australia.

---

[144] See, *e.g.*, the views of the Canadian Minister of Justice and Attorney General, Hon. E. Davie Fulton: "Our specific objections to an action such as this are threefold: That it is concerned not so much with strict compliance with United States laws in the United States as it is concerned with actions in Canada of Canadian companies which actions are in accord with Canadian laws and Canadian commercial policy; that compliance with the decree sought may bring these companies in Canada into conflict with Canadian laws and/or policy; and thirdly that the only way effect could be given to such a decree is if American directors of U.S. companies could give instructions to directors of Canadian companies to do something in Canada which is not in accord with Canadian business or commercial policy but is dictated by American policy. Nothing could more clearly illustrate the objectionably extraterritorial effect of the action taken." NEW YORK STATE BAR ASS'N, ANTITRUST LAW SYMPOSIUM 39 (1959). The REPORT OF THE TASK FORCE ON THE STRUCTURE OF CANADIAN INDUSTRY, FOREIGN OWNERSHIP AND THE STRUCTURE OF CANADIAN INDUSTRY 409 (1968) recommended that Canada enact legislation to prohibit Canadian compliance with foreign antitrust orders, decrees or judgments; see Chapter 9 *infra*.

C. Possible Long-Run Mitigation through Patent and Trademark Conventions

One long-run solution for whatever conflict may ultimately develop between American and Common Market competition law concerning territorial restrictions tied to Euro-American patent and trademark licensing is implicit in the very provisions of the draft European Patent and Trademark Conventions. While a single Patent and single Trademark covering the entire Common Market area have been deemed indispensable to a full-fledged economic community, those who have worked with these concepts have simultaneously contemplated the possibility that third-party countries, not members of the Community, might nevertheless participate in it for industrial property rights purposes only.

Article 211 of the Draft Patent Convention permits accession by any adherent to the International ("Paris") Convention for the Protection of Industrial Property, a group including virtually all of the industrialized nations of the world, subject to unanimous approval of its application by an Administrative Council, although part of the Study Group suggested that accession be restricted to "European countries." A looser association with the Patent Convention, by virtue of a special agreement concluded with the Contracting States, is provided as an alternative by Article 212.[145] It was frequently speculated, at the time the Convention was published, that the United Kingdom and at least some of the Continental European countries not in the Common Market would be interested in adhering to the Patent and Trademark Conventions.[146]

---

[145] See Froschmaier, *supra* note 23, at 500-02, 505-08. A related question, only peripherally germane to our present inquiry, is whether or not nationals of non-EEC countries should be entitled to obtain a European Patent or Trademark (the "accessibility" question). See *id.* at 499-500; Ladas, *Common Market Patent and Trademark Treaties Open or Closed,* 51 T.M. REP. 1203 (1961); Bucknam, *Access to the European Patent System,* 7 IDEA 427 (1963); Armengaud, *Political Aspects of Accessibility to the European Patent,* 7 IDEA 314 (1963); Jecies, *Non-Accessibility of Proposed Common Market Patents of Third Party Nationals and its Effect on U.S. Convention Rights,* 9 IDEA 61 (1965), and other articles cited therein.

[146] See, *e.g.,* Tookey, *Current Developments in Industrial Property Rights in Great Britain,* 6 PAT., T.M. & COPYRT. J. 451, 464 (1963), citing patent and trademark liaison groups set up in the Board of Trade; and Tookey, "Patents and Antitrust Law," in *Comparative Aspects of Antitrust Law in the United States, the United Kingdom and the European Economic Community,* INT'L & COMP. L.Q. Supp. Pub. No. 6, 141-45 (1963) (Geoffrey W. Tookey, Q.C., was President of the

Recent developments indicate a likelihood that the arrangement will be Europeanized very broadly.[147] While the American patent and trademark bar has not as yet evinced any perceptible interest in American accession, it should be recognized that such association or adherence would be permitted, that separate licensing for different portions of the territory of the Contracting Parties remains possible under the Convention despite the curtailment of ancillary territorial restraints, and that partial adherence through the loose association principle of Article 212 is available as an alternative to full accession.[148] Americans may very properly wish to study the European Conventions in operation, when and if they go into effect, before considering seriously the possibility of American adherence or association. The existence of these possibilities suggests one long-run overriding technique that might ultimately contribute to resolution of some of the problems of conflict that may arise under the headings of American antitrust and EEC anticartel law.

CONCLUSION

The limits imposed by Community cartel law on the traditional doctrine of territoriality in national trademark and patent law and on territorial license restrictions are in part explicit and firmly established and in part speculative and slowly emerging. This discussion, moreover, does not exhaust the range of licensing restrictions that will come within the ambit of Community law. Common Market cartel law sets limits on other licensing restrictions, such as price restraints and requirements for tie-in purchases of unpatented materials.[149]

The types of territorial restraint discussed above, however, are of greatest importance in considering American licensing relationships with enterprises in the Common Market and possible overlap or conflict of

British Group of the Int'l Ass'n for the Protection of Industrial Property and Chairman of the Board of Trade Liaison Group dealing with European Patent Proposals); Spencer, *A European Patent: A New Solution to an Old and Vexing Problem*, 48 A.B.A.J. 747, 748 (1962).

[147] See note 96 *supra*.

[148] Dr. Froschmaier has suggested that the elastic concept of association would provide a better basis than adherence for United States participation in a European Patent. See quotation in Weiser, *Patent and Antitrust Development and Prospects of the European Economic Community*, 8 IDEA 1, 8-11 (1964).

[149] See Chapter 4 *supra* at 228.

European and American antitrust law. Analysis of past conflict, real or potential, between American antitrust decrees and European contract and industrial property rights in the new context of Community cartel law suggests that the likelihood of sharp conflict between the two bodies of antitrust law will be reduced in this setting. The possibility of a new kind of conflict—between American antitrust requirements and Community exemptive action under Article 85(3)—exists, but, for reasons indicated in this analysis, the actual likelihood of such conflict seems remote. To the extent the possibility is a real one, it is equally likely that American antitrust decrees may be shaped to avoid head-on conflict with exemptive action by the Commission. The growth of international cooperation on antitrust matters through the Organization for Economic Cooperation and Development, discussed in Chapter 9, should facilitate the synchronization of American and Community regulation of restrictive licensing as well as other restrictive business practices.

CHAPTER 6 *The Swiss Watch Case*

Introduction

. The lengthy antitrust proceedings against the Swiss jeweled watch industry and American companies involved in it provide a typical example of conflicts which can arise when one country applies antitrust proscriptions to the conduct of foreign nationals in a foreign country. In the annals of American antitrust law, the case is unique, however, in that the complaint attacked a scheme of agreements governing a whole foreign industry—one which for twenty-five years had been actively supported by a foreign government.

A further unique feature of the case is the active part which the Swiss Government played in the American proceedings. The Government vigorously protested the case at its inception, and appeared at the end of the trial in the District Court as *amicus curiae* to present arguments based on foreign law and international law. During later hearings on the final judgment, a senior Swiss Government official testified regarding the impact of injunctive provisions proposed by the Department of Justice. After the final judgment had been rendered, the Swiss Government requested the State Department to arrange direct negotiations with the Department of Justice for modifications which would explicitly recognize its sovereign rights. At the hearing on these modifications, the Swiss Government again appeared as *amicus curiae.* It was made clear in the final stages that, if the issues between the two governments were not satisfactorily disposed of through negotiations or appeal, a case against the United States would be presented to the World Court at The Hague.

Notwithstanding the active interest and strong position thus taken by the Swiss Government, the case was treated by the court substantially as an ordinary antitrust proceeding involving per se violations of the Sherman Act resulting from a comprehensive conspiracy on the part of a foreign industry. The concerns of the Swiss Government were not accepted as justifying these violations because the violations were not a result of compulsion by a foreign government.

Important conflicts between the antitrust system of the United States and the Swiss system of government-supported private regulation were thus revealed. The treatment these conflicts received raises major issues regarding policies to be adopted for dealing with such issues in the future. One question is whether conflicts of this nature can adequately be resolved in an adversary proceeding before a national court. Another is whether more consideration should be given, within the substance of national antitrust law—here the Sherman Act—to the validity of the challenged practices within the context of the public order of a foreign state and to the support given to them by a foreign government. The types of antitrust offenses found to have been committed, *i.e.,* collective refusals to deal, limitations on production, allocations of markets, boycotts and blacklists, are hardly novel as American cases go. But the conduct constituting these offenses was committed by foreign nationals in a foreign country and was a fundamental part of the structure of an entire industry which was vital to that country's welfare.

In the following discussion, the proceedings are reviewed, including a brief summary of the complaint, of the District Court's decision, and of the Final Judgment. The practical significance of the case is then discussed from the point of view of industry structures in both Switzerland and the United States, with particular reference to government support for the industry agreements in Switzerland and to protective tariffs in the United States. The chapter concludes with a review of questions arising from the conflicts relating to subject-matter jurisdiction and foreign government intervention.

The voluminous transcript of record of the proceedings before the district court and the reports of the court's actions are the source of all factual material presented here, except where otherwise indicated. Because the transcript is unpublished, specific citations to it have not been made.

I. SUMMARY OF THE CASE

A. Outline of the Proceedings

The complaint in this case was filed in the Southern District of New York on October 19, 1954 against the following: the Swiss Federation of Watch Manufacturing Associations (FH); a Swiss holding company controlling manufacturers of watch parts (Ebauches); the Watchmakers of Switzerland Information Center, Inc. in New York (Wosic); their advertising agency, Foote, Cone & Belding, Inc.; two Swiss manufacturers (Eterna A.G. and Montres Rolex S.A.) and their American subsidiaries; three important American corporations which manufactured or at one time had manufactured in both the United States and Switzerland (Bulova, Benrus and Gruen) and the Swiss subsidiary of one of them (Gruen S.A.); eleven other American corporations engaged in distributing Swiss watches in the United States and the Swiss subsidiary of one of them (Wittnauer); and the American Watch Association. In addition, a Swiss association of watch part manufacturers (UBAH), a Swiss holding company in which the Swiss Government was a major shareholder (ASUAG), eighteen Swiss manufacturers of Swiss brand-named watches imported by American defendants, and seven American importers of repair parts were named as "co-conspirators."

Early in 1955, FH, Ebauches, Eterna A.G., Gruen S.A. and Wittnauer moved to dismiss the case as against them for lack of personal jurisdiction. These motions were all denied by District Judge Walsh in July of 1955, and rearguments were denied in the following September.[1]

---

[1] United States v. Watchmakers of Switzerland Information Center, Inc., 133 F.Supp. 40, *reargument denied,* 134 F.Supp. 710 (S.D.N.Y. 1955). For other comment on various aspects of the *Swiss Watch* case, see ABA ANTITRUST SECTION SUPPLEMENT TO REPORT OF ATTORNEY GENERAL'S NATIONAL COMMITTEE TO STUDY THE ANTITRUST LAWS: ANTITRUST DEVELOPMENTS 1955-1968, at 42-45, 47-50 (1968); INT'L LAW ASS'N, REPORT OF FIFTY-FIRST CONFERENCE, TOKYO (1964) 321-22 (remarks by Swiss member), 410-13 (A. J. Riedweg), 575-77 (by G. W. Haight); see *id.* at 565-92 for compilation of official protests and reactions of foreign governments to other United States antitrust cases, compiled by G. W. Haight; INT'L LAW ASS'N, REPORT OF FIFTY-SECOND CONFERENCE, HELSINKI (1966), 67-74 (by G. W. Haight); Timberg, *Extraterritorial Jurisdiction under the Sherman Act,* 11 RECORD 101, 108-10, 116-17 (1956); Note, *Limitations on the Federal Judicial Power to Compel*

The case was voluntarily dismissed by the Government as against Montres Rolex S.A.

During the following four years, the District Court sustained some objections to interrogatories and requests for admissions, dismissed others, and otherwise dealt with pre-trial discovery proceedings.[2] Numerous conferences were held between the Government and defendants, and a number of hearings were held before Judge Cashin with a view to disposing of the case by consent decrees. In 1959 and 1960, such decrees were signed by the American Watch Association, the advertising firm, and eleven American corporate defendants.[3] Although extensive discussions were conducted in Switzerland among the Swiss defendants, efforts to conclude further consent decrees failed. The case accordingly went to trial in November of 1960 against FH, Ebauches, Wosic, Bulova, Benrus, Eterna A.G., Gruen, Gruen S.A., Longines-Wittnauer, and Wittnauer. The trial lasted from November 14 to November 30, 1960, and from February 8 to May 17, 1961. Further hearings were held in December 1961. The District Court rendered its opinion on December 20, 1962, together with 247 findings of fact and 46 conclusions of law.[4] During 1963, hearings were conducted and arguments held, with written briefs, on the form of Final Judgment. The Judgment was entered on January 22, 1964.[5]

Following entry of the Final Judgment, and while appeals to the Supreme Court were pending, the Swiss and United States Governments held private discussions regarding its provisions. The result of these discussions was a hearing on December 17, 1964, at which all of the defendants remaining in the case acquiesced and concurred in proposed changes in the Final Judgment offered by the United States. The Swiss Government appeared as *amicus curiae* and urged that the plaintiff's motion be granted. The United States Department of Justice stated that the Department of State had indicated that a resolution of the litigation

---

Acts Violating Foreign Law, 63 COLUM. L. REV. 1441, 1448-52, 1488-89 (1963); Note, *Extraterritorial Antitrust—Jurisdiction over Nationals—Inapplicability of Decree Abroad where Law of the Territorial Sovereign Acts in Violation of the Laws of the National Sovereign,* 7 HARV. INT'L L. CLUB J. 328 (1966).

[2] 1959 Trade Cas. ¶¶69,314, 69,516, 69,550, 69,571; 1960 Trade Cas. ¶¶69,654, 69,668, 69,669, 69,680, 69,732, 69,769; 1961 Trade Cas. ¶69,988.

[3] 1960 Trade Cas. ¶69,655.

[4] 1963 Trade Cas. ¶70,600.

[5] Not reported.

on a basis consistent with both the antitrust laws and the basic objectives of the Final Judgment "would be advantageous from the standpoint of American foreign policy."

The Final Judgment was modified accordingly on January 7, 1965.[6] The defendants consented to the modifications and to a dismissal of their joint appeal. Rights to appeal from the modified Judgment were waived, and the case came to an end after more than ten years of litigation.

B. Allegations of the Complaint

The complaint charged that, beginning on or about April 1, 1931 and continuing thereafter up to and including the date of the filing of the complaint, the defendants and co-conspirators had engaged in an unlawful combination and conspiracy in unreasonable restraint of interstate and foreign trade and commerce of the United States in violation of Section 1 of the Sherman Act and Section 73 of the Wilson Tariff Act. The trade and commerce involved were described as the manufacture, importation, exportation and distribution of jeweled watches and of component parts and repair parts thereof. As used in the complaint, the term "watches" referred to (a) a jeweled watch designed to be worn or carried and containing a jeweled lever escapement utilizing a minimum of seven jewel bearings, and (b) the movement of a jeweled watch consisting of the entire mechanism, including the dial and hands, but excluding the case and crystal. The term "ébauches" was used to mean all the parts making up a movement other than regulating parts, mainspring, hands and dial. The term "component parts" referred to the watch case, dial, hands and all parts contained in the movement, including the ébauches, plate, escapement, balance wheels, hairsprings, mainsprings and jewel bearings utilized in the manufacture or assembly of the watch. References to "watch manufacturer" included companies which produced some or all of their own component parts and also to companies which only assembled parts.

It was noted that 95% of the watches, component parts and repair parts imported into the United States were purchased from concerns located in Switzerland. In 1953, total sales of watches in the United States amounted to about 12 million units valued at wholesale in excess

[6] 1965 Trade Cas. ¶ 71,352.

of 225 million dollars, of which approximately 20% were manufactured in the United States and approximately 75% were imported from Switzerland. Imports from Switzerland in that year totalled approximately 10 million units; total exports from the United States amounted to approximately 200,000 units.

The Swiss industry consisted for the most part of medium-sized and small enterprises divided into three categories: companies manufacturing component parts for both manufacture and repair purposes, companies purchasing component parts which they assembled into watches, and companies producing brand-named watches and also manufacturing some of their own component parts for both manufacture and repair purposes.

The defendant Swiss Federation, referred to as "FH", was composed of six regional organizations (known as "Sections") comprising more than 450 manufacturers and assemblers of watches. The Swiss defendant company, Ebauches, owned the stock of most of the companies producing "ébauches" for manufacture and repair purposes. The co-conspirator Swiss association known as UBAH comprised regional organizations consisting of more than 500 firms which manufactured watch components and repair parts other than ébauches. Substantially all of the firms comprising the Swiss watch industry were members of one of these three organizations. In addition, the co-conspirator Swiss holding company "ASUAG" (called "Superholding" in the complaint) and the Swiss Watch Chamber played import roles in regulating the industry. The former, which was owned by the watch industry, Swiss banks and the Swiss Government, controlled various manufacturers of component parts. The latter, comprising members appointed by FH, Ebauches and UBAH, supervised exports of the industry.

The complaint charged that on or about April 1, 1931, FH, Ebauches and UBAH, acting on behalf of themselves and their members, executed an agreement for the comprehensive regulation of the industry. This was known as the "Collective Convention." As amended and modified, it provided in substance that: (a) all Swiss watch firms which were signatories to the Convention were required to deal only with each other in the purchase and sale of ébauches and other component parts and in the resale of component parts to others (except that non-members of foreign firms which had purchased such components prior to 1931 might continue purchases on condition that they observed Convention terms and did not resell them); (b) watches and repair parts produced in Switzerland might be sold to any person in the United States, except that specified types of watches had to be exported as completed watches and not as movements, movements could not be exported unless accompanied by both dial and hands, and repair parts could be used only for repair purposes and could be sold by FH, Ebauches and UBAH solely for the repair or replacement of products manufactured by them; (c) all signatory firms and their foreign affiliates agreed not to establish manufacturing facilities outside Switzerland or to give any assistance to any foreign firm located outside Switzerland; (d) prices and terms of sale were to be fixed by agreement; and (e) FH, Ebauches and UBAH were responsible for enforcement.

The unlawful combination and conspiracy charged in the complaint was alleged to have consisted of a continuing agreement and concert of action: (a) to prevent, discontinue or curtail the manufacture of watches and component parts within the United States; (b) to eliminate the importation of component parts from Switzerland (except under special circumstances); (c) to eliminate the importation of watches and component parts from all countries other than Switzerland; (d) to eliminate United States exports of American-produced component parts from the United States to the rest of the world; (e) to allocate foreign markets and eliminate United States watch exports to non-allocated areas; (f) to establish minimum prices for watches and maximum prices for repair parts, and to police and enforce such prices for products imported into and sold within the United States; and (g) to regulate the distribution in the United States of watches, component parts and repair parts imported from Switzerland. Violations were to be discouraged and punished by fines, blacklisting and boycotting.

It was alleged that, pursuant to this combination, conspiracy and concert of action: the defendants and co-conspirators had adhered to and effectuated the Collective Convention; Benrus, Wittnauer, Eterna and others had agreed not to manufacture in the United States or to provide any assistance therefor; Gruen Ohio and Bulova had agreed to restrict and curtail their manufacturing operations in the United States and to refrain from reselling component parts and from importing watches and component parts from countries other than Switzerland; many of the defendants had entered into market-allocation agreements and other restrictions on their freedom to deal in watches and component parts, including exclusive distribution agreements; and numerous other unlawful acts had been committed.

The Government asked that the defendants be perpetually enjoined from participating in, maintaining or carrying out the combination and conspiracy, and from importing any Swiss watches subject to unlawful restrictions, and it also requested that other steps be taken to sever relationships with the Swiss watch industry insofar as these unreasonably restrained the trade and commerce of the United States.

In describing this proceeding in New York City on October 25, 1954,[7] Assistant Attorney General Barnes said that the objective of the suit was "to free our domestic watch industry from practices which curtail domestic production and restrict the importation and exportation of watches." The case had been severely criticized by the Swiss watch industry, he said, on the ground that the suit was designed to attack the internal operations of the industry in Switzerland, thereby attempting to give to the United States antitrust laws an extraterritorial application. The Department of Justice, however, he said, disclaimed any such objective:

> No invasion of Swiss sovereignty or "concerted attack" on the Swiss watch industry can reasonably be inferred from this action. All of the defendants, a majority of whom are American companies, are private parties operating in the United States and of necessity bound by American laws. The Swiss defendants, in the opinion of the Department of Justice, have subjected themselves to American jurisdiction through their own activities in the United States and through the activities of their agents or wholly-owned subsidiaries incorporated in the United States. If this opinion be erroneous, it will be simple for any defendant who is not doing business in the United States to avoid any liability.[8]

The restraints charged, he added, related "solely to United States importation, exportation, and domestic trade in jeweled watches, component parts, and repair parts thereof." While certain of the practices arose out of basic agreements among members of the Swiss watch industry, the suit was concerned with these agreements only insofar as they affected "the manufacture and sale of watches in the United States and the export-import trade of American watch firms." All of the private agreements alleged in the complaint concerned such clearly United States commerce problems as the extent of watch manufacture permitted within the United States, the extent to which United States

---

[7] Address on Current Antitrust Problems and Policies, before the Metropolitan Economic Ass'n, New York City, Oct. 25, 1954 (mimeo).
    [8] *Id.*

businessmen could import watches from countries other than Switzerland, the extent to which Swiss-produced watch parts could be exported from the United States to countries other than Switzerland, the designation of large areas of the world in which United States businessmen were not to be permitted to sell Swiss-produced watches which they had bought and received in the United States, the fixing and policing of minimum prices for watches sold within the United States, and the fixing and policing of maximum prices for watch parts sold there. The suit was designed to guarantee free access to the American market by all companies, foreign and domestic, and to prevent the imposition of restraints by agreements of private parties.

Prior to filing the suit, Barnes said, consultations had been held with representatives of the Swiss Government for the specific purpose of clarifying the issues involved. Swiss officials were advised of "the limited scope of the proposed complaint" and it was "carefully pointed out that the suit was not directed against operations of the Swiss watch industry in Switzerland." It was made clear that the action "dealt only with practices affecting the domestic and foreign commerce of the United States."[9]

C. The District Court's Decision of December 1962

Much of the Government's case, although not all of it, was sustained by the court. The defendants, FH, Ebauches, Benrus, Bulova, Longines-Wittnauer, Wittnauer, Gruen S.A., Gruen Ohio, and Eterna A.G. were all found to have entered into a combination and conspiracy to eliminate competition in the American manufacture, import, export and sale of watches, watch parts and watchmaking machinery. Most of those—FH, Ebauches, Benrus, Bulova, Wittnauer, and Gruen S.A.—were held to have voluntarily entered into industry-wide agreements, known as Collective Conventions, "in order to prevent the development and growth of competitive watch industries in countries other than Switzerland, and particularly in the United States."[10] Longines-Wittnauer and Gruen Ohio were found to have known and approved of the execution of the Collective Conventions by their respective Swiss subsidiaries and to have adhered to the provisions of the Conventions; to have known and

[9] *Id.*
[10] 1963 Trade Cas. ¶70,600 at 77,453 (concl. X).

approved of the FH membership of their respective subsidiaries; and to have agreed and adhered to FH regulations applicable to the sale of Swiss watches in the United States. The defendant Wosic, however, was found to have had no part in adopting or adhering to the Collective Conventions, in the negotiation, execution or performance of other unlawful contracts, in limiting exports from Switzerland, or in restraining manufacture in the United States. The complaint was accordingly dismissed as to it for failure of proof.[11]

1. EFFECT OF RESTRAINTS ON U.S. COMMERCE

The court concluded that the Collective Conventions were intended to and did "affect and relate to the activities of United States companies and to the manufacture of watches and watch parts in the United States, the United States import and export of watches, watch parts and watchmaking machines, and the sale, use and distribution of watches, watch parts and watchmaking machines in the United States."[12] The findings and some of the evidence on these issues may be summarized as follows:

a. Restraints on Manufacturing in the United States

Under the 1949 Collective Convention, signatories were bound not to establish production facilities abroad or to develop pre-existing facilities, and not to assist foreign manufacturing in any way. As every signatory was made responsible for the acts of its affiliates and branches, including parent companies, these restrictions effectively reached the activities in the United States of American companies affiliated with Swiss enterprises.[13] Of the more than 1,000 signatories to the Convention, four—Bulova, Benrus, Gruen and Longines-Wittnauer—were owned or controlled by American firms, and the first three engaged in watch manufacturing in the United States at some time relevant to the case.

Bulova, for many years the largest manufacturer of watches in Switzerland, had been the largest customer of both Ebauches and UBAH, and in 1927 Ebauches had undertaken to furnish parts for a small American plant. In return, Bulova agreed to limit its manufacturing operations in the United States to a production of 48,000 units a year

[11]*Id.* at 77,452, 77,453 (concl. VII, VIII).
[12]*Id.* at 77,453 (concl. XV).
[13]*Id.* at 77,426 and 77,427 (findings 82, 83).

and to purchase all of its hair spring, escapement, ébauches and balance wheel requirements for its Swiss production from Ebauches.

In 1933, the 1927 arrangements were succeeded by an agreement with ASUAG, which had been formed with the active participation and support of the Swiss Government. The agreement continued the limitation of 48,000 watches a year, subject to Bulova's agreeing to keep its American manufacture of watch movements secondary to its Swiss manufacture of such movements.[14]

In 1935, ASUAG was concerned about Bulova's rapid growth in the United States, and the agreement was modified so as to limit Bulova's watch production there to one-third of its imports of Swiss watches. In the following year a further agreement was entered into under which ASUAG undertook to supply parts for Bulova's operations in the United States in the average quantities delivered during the years, 1934 to 1935, and in the same advantageous state of manufacture as before. In return, the Swiss branch of Bulova agreed to sign the Collective Convention and not to expand its manufacture of ébauches, escapements and balance wheels.[15]

After World War II, a new agreement was concluded, this time with FH, Ebauches and UBAH. Pursuant to this, Bulova agreed to limit its manufacture of watches in the United States in any one year to not more than the number of watches and movements which it imported from Switzerland, so long as its total United States production for any three-year period did not exceed two-thirds of its Swiss imports during that time. It also agreed not to manufacture watch jewels in the United States, not to manufacture watch movements outside the United States and Switzerland, not to purchase any kinds of watch movements or watch parts from countries other than Switzerland, not to engage in the United States in the sale of watch parts either purchased by it from Switzerland or manufactured by it in the United States, and to deal exclusively in watches of its own manufacture and watches produced in Switzerland. In return, the Swiss organizations agreed that Bulova's Swiss branch, Bulova Bienne, could ship watch parts to Bulova in the United States for the latter's manufacturing operations there, provided that the number of parts did not exceed the number of watches which Bulova was permitted to manufacture in the United States. Bulova Bienne was

[14] *Id.* at 77,436 (findings 148, 149).
[15] *Id.* at 77,436 and 77,437 (findings 150-54).

bound by the Collective Convention and its membership could be cancelled if Bulova in the United States acted contrary to the Conventional obligations of the Bienne branch.[16]

The District Court indicated, although it did not so find explicitly, that this last arrangement had resulted in a reduction in Bulova's operations in the United States. It noted a decrease in production from 785,357 units in 1949 to 423,685 in 1954 and that the ratio of Bulova's United States production to Swiss imports fell from 56.5% in 1949 to 35.7% in 1954. In every one of these six years Bulova's United States production was below the figure permitted by the contract.[17]

There was extensive checking by the Swiss on Bulova's operations in the United States to insure compliance with the agreement and with the Collective Convention. Warnings were issued from time to time regarding the manufacture of jeweled bearings in the United States and regarding operations in Canada, the purchase of alarm watches in Germany, and the furnishing of technical assistance by the Bienne branch.[18]

Benrus had become a member of FH in 1929; it was then producing watches in Switzerland for sale in the United States. In 1936, it acquired the Waterbury Clock Company, which had previously had a right to obtain parts from UBAH. The acquisition was considered to be a breach of the Collective Convention and UBAH's shipments of parts accordingly ceased. Benrus asked the United States Government to intervene on its behalf with the Swiss Government to help it obtain a permit to purchase Swiss watch parts. The result was a directive by the Swiss Government to FH, Ebauches and UBAH to relax the Collective Convention prohibition against exporting watch parts and to permit Benrus to import from Switzerland into the United States approximately 175,000 sets of parts without any restrictions attached to them.[19]

During the Second World War, the Waterbury plant ceased producing watches, being devoted wholly to war production. By 1945, much of its machinery had become obsolete, and substantial rehabilitation would have been required if the plant were to be used for watch manufacture. In these circumstances, an agreement was made with ASUAG in July 1945 pursuant to which Benrus agreed to terminate manufacture of

[16]*Id.* at 77,437 and 77,438 (findings 156-60).
[17]*Id.* at 77,438 (finding 161).
[18]*Id.* at 77,439 (findings 164-68).
[19]*Id.* at 77,440 (finding 173).

watches in the United States, to liquidate the Waterbury plant in such a way that it could not be used by any other person for the manufacture of watches, to renounce its license to import watch parts into the United States, to confine its manufacturing operations in the United States solely to the production of watch cases and bracelets, and to become exclusively a manufacturer of Swiss watches. In return, Benrus was accorded an increase in its Swiss dollar quota, which governed the number of Swiss watches it could ship to the United States. The contract was cancelled in 1954, but, according to the District Court, this was only after Benrus had learned of the Department of Justice investigation of the watch industry.[20]

Gruen did not attempt to manufacture in the United States until 1940 when it applied to the Swiss industry to obtain watch parts for manufacturing purposes there. This application was denied. However, Gruen obtained the support of the United States Government in an appeal to the Swiss Government. Gruen then affirmed its willingness to accept the same restrictions on its manufacture of watches in the United States as had been accepted by other American companies. In 1941, the Swiss Government granted its request and directed the industry to permit Gruen to purchase Swiss watch parts and to fix the conditions for exportation. This directive was vigorously protested by the industry, but as a result of further Swiss Government pressure it was agreed in 1943 that Gruen could purchase 300,000 watches annually from its Swiss subsidiary (Gruen S.A.) and could obtain the watch parts it needed for manufacture in the United States, provided that these were obtained exclusively from Switzerland and provided that it did not manufacture in the United States more than 20% of the watches imported by it from Switzerland and in no event more than 75,000 watches. It appears that manufacture in the United States never reached either the figure of 20% nor the maximum of 75,000 watches.[21] After 1953, its watch business dropped substantially until domestic manufacture was eventually abandoned and Gruen confined its watch activities to imports from Switzerland.

b. Restraints on Imports into the United States

The District Court found that from 1946 through 1954, 95% of all

[20] *Id.* at 77,440 and 77,441 (findings 174-78).
[21] *Id.* at 77,441 and 77,442 (findings 179-83).

jeweled-lever watches imported into the United States were imported from Switzerland. In 1953, imports of such watches totalled 10,020,000, as compared with 7,431,000 units in 1948.[22] Nevertheless, the District Court concluded that imports into the United States had been unreasonably restrained.

The court was particularly concerned with restrictions on export from Switzerland of watchmaking machinery. It held that an agreement entered into in July 1946 by FH, Ebauches, UBAH and others with Swiss watchmaking machinery manufacturers and the Swiss Watch Chamber was a part of the conspiracy to prevent machinery exports to manufacturers in the United States and in other countries, and that it imposed unreasonable restrictions on manufacture in the United States and on imports into the United States. Further, it held that refusals to export certain types of watchmaking machinery, except on a lease basis, and the restrictive provisions of the leases also imposed unreasonable restrictions on manufacture in the United States, on imports into the United States and on the sale of watch parts in the United States.[23]

These restrictions were, however, the result of Swiss governmental controls and policy. Prior to 1939, there were no barriers to machinery exports, but between 1939 and 1946, the Swiss Government imposed an absolute embargo. After the war, concessions were made to the British industry pursuant to an agreement in 1946 between the Swiss and British governments, under which machinery was made available to British watchmaking firms on a restricted lease basis.[24] Thereafter, machinery was also leased to American manufacturers, and some machines were sold outright for Korean War purposes to the United States Army and Navy for defense purposes, on assurances that the machines would

[22] *Id.* at 77,425 (findings 70, 71).

[23] *Id.* at 77,433-34, 77,453-54 (findings 128-34, concl. XX-XXII). A separate civil proceeding under the Sherman Act was instituted in December 1955 against FH, Wosic, Bulova, Hamilton, Elgin and others alleging that the defendants had conspired with Swiss manufacturers of watchmaking machinery to restrict the manufacture, importation, use, lease, purchase and sale of watchmaking machinery in the United States (Civil Action No. 105-210, filed Dec. 2, 1955, S.D.N.Y.). This action was held in abeyance until the "main case" was disposed of, when it was dismissed by agreement among the parties "with prejudice," the Government being apparently satisfied that the Final Judgment in the "main case" provided all the relief required on this aspect.

[24] *Id.* at 77,429-32 (findings 102-16).

remain the property of the United States Government, or that there was no intent to sell them to the watch industry.

The District Court found that certain "cartel agreements" between FH, Ebauches and UBAH, on the one hand, and members of the British, French and German watch industries respectively, on the other hand, had been entered into by the Swiss organizations in "furtherance of their conspiracy" to prevent the growth of competitive manufacture in the United States and elsewhere. By these agreements, foreign industry members were prohibited from purchasing watch parts from any persons other than signatories of the Collective Convention and from selling watch parts which they purchased or which they produced themselves. These agreements, the court found, imposed unreasonable restrictions on manufacture in the United States, on imports of watch parts into the United States, and on exports therefrom.[25]

There was substantial contrary evidence before the court on these "cartel agreements." The Swiss defendants pointed out that the agreements had not been entered into for the purpose of restricting trade with the United States, but in order to increase Switzerland's share of the markets involved in the face of threatened restrictions by way of boycott or embargo. The conditions exacted in return were designed to prevent indirect violations of Swiss laws prohibiting exports through purchases of Swiss parts by a foreign firm not on the approved list of UBAH foreign customers.

The British contract had been entered into upon the insistence of the British Government, which had threatened denial of access to British Commonwealth raw materials and import quota reductions for Swiss watches. The agreement had been opposed by both the Swiss watch industry and Swiss labor. Both governments participated in its negotiation and ratified it. It assured to the Swiss an increase in the British import quota, and the British obtained leases of watchmaking machinery and watch parts other than ébauches not exceeding 15% by value of Swiss shipments of watches and movements to the United Kingdom. British purchasers were required to use the Swiss parts in their own manufacture and not to resell them.

Both the Swiss and French Governments participated in negotiations in 1946 and 1951. The objective again was to obtain an increase in the import quota for Swiss watches and movements, and in return, the Swiss

[25] *Id.* at 77,435-36, 77,454 (findings 138-45, concl. XXIII).

agreed to supply French manufacturers with ébauches and other parts, but not machinery. The provisions preventing resale were, according to the Swiss defendants, adopted for the same reasons as in the case of the British agreement and were not directed at American watchmaking firms. As the approximately 100 French manufacturers of parts other than ébauches were not parties to the agreement, they were free to sell parts to American purchasers. For many years before the agreement they had exported parts to the United States and they continued to do so thereafter.

There was no evidence that a German industry-wide agreement had ever been entered into. During the period from 1946 through 1950, Ebauches had sold parts to purchasers in Germany subject to restrictions similar to those contained in the British and French agreements. Again, there were no provisions, however, restricting manufacturers of either ébauches or of other parts from selling to American purchasers.[26]

c. Restraints on Exports from the United States

Under the Collective Convention, the signatories were bound to purchase all their requirements of ébauches and watch parts from the parties designated in the Convention, thus excluding all purchases from the outside. Exceptions could be granted when the parts concerned were not manufactured by subsidiaries of Ebauches or members of UBAH, or could not be provided by Conventional suppliers in sufficient quantities. The evidence in the case indicated four situations in which proposals to except parts manufactured in the United States were considered. In two such instances the parts were permitted to be imported freely into Switzerland; on one occasion the application was denied; and on one occasion import was permitted subject to conditions.[27]

All of the restrictions on exports from the United States were caught up under the District Court's sweeping condemnations of the provisions in the Collective Convention prohibiting dealings in watch products manufactured by persons other than signatories, and by the general conclusion that the defendants' agreements limiting exports of watches and watch parts from the United States were illegal under Section 1 of the Sherman Act.[28]

[26] Brief on Behalf of the Swiss Defendants, Sept. 15, 1961, at 32-36.
[27] 1963 Trade Cas. ¶70,600 at 77,433-45 (findings 188-99).
[28] *Id.* at 77,453-55 (concl. XV, XVIII, XXV and XXIX).

d. Exclusive Distribution Agreements

The court also found that Longines-Wittnauer and Eterna (N.Y.) each had entered into agreements with certain Swiss manufacturers to act as exclusive distributors, and that these agreements contained provisions which imposed unreasonable restrictions upon United States imports and exports of watches. Longines-Wittnauer had agreements with several manufacturers in which it agreed not to sell or distribute movements or watches produced by any other watch manufacturer without obtaining the consent of its supplier; the latter agreed to take steps to prevent the importation into the United States of watches produced by the same supplier and sold to other countries; and Longines-Wittnauer agreed not to export or permit its customers to export watches and movements of its supplier outside Longines' territory.

Eterna (N.Y.) had an exclusive distribution agreement with Eterna A.G. which prohibited the export from the United States, or the sale for export, of watches produced by Eterna A.G., and the distributor agreed not to deal in watches produced by any other manufacturer without the supplier's consent. The same provisions were contained in the contracts made by Eterna A.G. with distributors in other countries.

The court found that the Longines-Wittnauer agreements "were designed for the sole purpose of protecting Longines-Wittnauer from price competition in the United States, were executed in furtherance of the defendants' conspiracy and were intended by the parties to and did impose unreasonable restrictions upon the United States import and export of watches." It also found that the provisions prohibiting Longines-Wittnauer and Eterna from dealing in any watches other than those of their suppliers were designed to further the conspiracy to eliminate the sale of non-Swiss watches in the United States and imposed unreasonable restrictions on United States imports. Similarly, the provisions in the distribution agreements of Eterna A.G. restricting exports were designed to further the conspiracy and imposed unreasonable restrictions on United States imports and exports. All of these agreements were accordingly held to be illegal.

The court rejected arguments by Longines-Wittnauer that the agreements were not related to the Collective Convention, or to any overall conspiracy; that it was not barred from handling other watches; and that there was no proof of any anti-competitive effect flowing from these agreements.[29]

[29]*Id.* at 77,445, 77,454-55 (findings 200-03, concl. XXVII-XXX).

e. Blacklists and Boycotts

The court found that the Collective Convention did not provide for the blacklisting of customers of signatories, but that since at least 1938 and continuing through 1954, FH members had agreed, as a condition of their continued membership in FH, not to deal with any person who was blacklisted by FH in accordance with its blacklist regulations. Under Swiss law, if the means were not disproportionate to the ends and if the interests of the boycotters deserved protection, blacklists, boycotts and group refusals to deal were lawful and enforceable.

The purpose of the FH blacklisting was to compel dealers in Swiss watches anywhere in the world (including the United States) to conform their conduct in the sale of Swiss watches to FH regulations. The system was designed to prevent losses to FH members, particularly small firms, resulting from the refusal or inability of customers, Swiss or foreign, to accept or pay for watches which had been ordered and delivered. The blacklists were regularly furnished to the Department of Public Economy of the Federal Government (DEP).

Dealers in Swiss watches who violated FH regulations and were accordingly blacklisted were prohibited from purchasing any watches of certain types or any watch parts for such watches. The blacklisting of a company extended to all of its affiliates. All FH blacklists were required to be observed not only by FH members but also by all foreign representatives, branches, affiliates and customers, wherever located. During the period from 1946 through 1954, at least 69 United States companies engaged in the sale of Swiss watches in the United States were blacklisted. An indeterminate number were threatened.

Although instances were cited of Bulova, Benrus, Gruen, Longines-Wittnauer and Eterna being involved in the boycotting of price-cutters and other blacklisted firms, the District Court found that on the whole the American defendants frequently disregarded the FH lists in deciding with whom to deal. Some American customers continued to receive shipments of Swiss watches and movements from FH members even after their names had been placed on the list, and some violators were not even put on the list. Therefore, although the blacklists were binding on the American defendants and were circulated in the United States, "the practical effect of the blacklist was considerably diminished by the laxity with which it was obeyed and enforced in the United States." Nevertheless, the court concluded that the defendants did boycott and blacklist United States companies selling watches in the United States which did not comply with FH regulations and it held such action to be illegal. The court added: "The illegality of defendants' action cannot be cured by a showing that compliance with the black list was not always rigidly enforced."[30]

The Government did not sustain its burden of proving that the defendants had established minimum sales prices or price levels below which Swiss watches were not to be sold in the United States.[31] It also failed to prove that the defendants had established uniform guarantees to be offered on the sale of Swiss watches in the United States,[32] or that the defendants had adhered to any agreements in fixing their own guarantees or in regulating watch advertising in the United States. And it failed to prove its charges relating to repair parts programs in the United States.[33] The defendants were, however, held to have boycotted and blacklisted United States companies selling Swiss watches in the United States which did not comply with FH regulations,[34] although the practical effect of the blacklist, the court found, was considerably diminished by the laxity with which it was obeyed and enforced in the United States.

The court concluded that the combination was "directed towards the United States," that it "substantially affected United States trade and commerce," and that "many of the acts of defendants in furtherance of the conspiracy took place in the United States."[35] The court also held that the illegal agreements and actions were "not required by any Swiss law," and that they were illegal "notwithstanding that some of the conspirators are foreign nationals, that some of the agreements were entered into in a foreign country or that the acts of defendants were lawful in such foreign country."[36]

2. DISCUSSION OF LEGAL ISSUES

Apart from the specific findings of fact and conclusions of law, there was only a small amount of discussion by the court of the important

---

[30] *Id.* at 77,447-48, 77,455, 77,456 (findings 217-24, concl. XXXIII and XLII).

[31] *Id.* at 77,455 (concl. XXXI).

[32] *Id.* (concl. XXXII).

[33] *Id.* (concl. XXXIV).

[34] *Id.* (concl. XXXIII).

[35] *Id.* (concl. XXXV).

[36] *Id.* at 77,456 (concl. XLIII). In support, the court cited the *Continental Ore, Timken, Thomsen, Pacific & Arctic, Alcoa,* and *General Electric* (incandescent lamp) cases; see discussion in Chapter 2 *supra* at 67-75.

legal issues involved. In reply to a contention that it should not assume jurisdiction over the activities of the defendants "because American antitrust laws cannot be applied to acts of sovereign governments," the court said:

> If, of course, the defendants' activities had been required by Swiss law, this court could indeed do nothing. An American court would have under such circumstances no right to condemn the governmental activity of another sovereign nation. In the present case, however, the defendants' activities were not required by the laws of Switzerland. They were agreements formulated privately without compulsion on the part of the Swiss Government. It is clear that these private agreements were then recognized as facts of economic and industrial life by that nation's government. Nonetheless, the fact that the Swiss Government may, as a practical matter, approve of the effects of this private activity cannot convert what is essentially a vulnerable private conspiracy into an unassailable system resulting from foreign governmental mandate. In the absence of direct foreign governmental action compelling the defendants' activities, a United States court may exercise its jurisdiction as to acts and contracts abroad, if, as in the case at bar, such acts and contracts have a substantial and material effect upon our foreign and domestic commerce.[37]

It stated that arguments of business necessity and foreign trade conditions could not grant immunity under the antitrust laws. Further, it should not be assumed that a judgment of the court would violate rights of Swiss citizens under the United States Constitution, would be contary to treaty obligations of the United States, or would violate the sovereignty of the Swiss Confederation. All such claims, the court said, were "entirely premature" and presupposed that the judge intended to permit the issuance of a decree which would have such a drastic effect. Such a presupposition, it said, was erroneous.[38]

In dealing with an argument that the restrictions of the Collective Conventions were "not directed at the United States watch industry," it said:

> The United States watch industry was the Swiss watch industry's biggest competitor, and the restrictions of the Convention have obviously had a crippling effect in this country, and were so intended.
>
> The only question suggested here is whether the acts of the defendants have affected United States trade and commerce and, if so, whether they have restrained such trade and commerce. It is obvious from the facts that they have.

[37] *Id.* at 77,456-57.
[38] *Id.* at 77,457.

The American defendants' arguments of so-called economic necessity as a justification for their behavior are also unavailing. If such arguments were accepted by the courts, the American antitrust laws would become a "dead letter."[39]

Finding no merit in the other arguments advanced by the defendants, it directed that a decree be submitted in accordance with its findings and conclusions, or in the alternative, that the court and parties work out a decree together.

D. The Initial and Modified Final Judgments

More than a year elapsed before the initial Final Judgment was entered on January 22, 1964, and almost another year elapsed before the judgment was modified and appeals to the Supreme Court were withdrawn. One reason for the delay between the findings and the initial judgment, according to the Department of Justice, was the fact that months of discussion between the Department of Justice and the Swiss defendants were spent over drafts of the judgment, designed to make sure that the Government would not be "going beyond the absolute essentialities of what we think is necessary relief." The Department stated that it wished to make sure that it "understood what the Swiss problems were" and that they "were not unwittingly imposing restrictions of any kind on purely Swiss internal matters."

1. COURT HEARINGS ON PROPOSALS FOR FINAL JUDGMENT: 1963

Notwithstanding the long negotiations referred to above, there were still many points of disagreement between a proposed final judgment submitted by the Government in September of 1963 and one proposed by the Swiss defendants. Pursuant to the district court's directive, hearings were held on these points in November of that year.

In its proposals, the Government sought to reach not only FH but also its six Sections, which were separate entities and had not been parties to the action or before the court. It also sought to cover not only jeweled-lever watches but also pin-lever, electric and electronic watches as well. It wished to extend the reach of the decree to the removal of restrictions on manufacture by Bulova, Benrus and Gruen not only in the

[39]*Id.*

United States, but anywhere in the world outside Switzerland. It sought to enjoin FH and Ebauches from enforcing, performing or renewing (insofar as applicable to United States commerce) every provision of the Collective Convention which restricted any other defendant "or any signatory" from producing watches, movements or parts anywhere in the world outside Switzerland; from furnishing aid to any person engaged anywhere in the world outside Switzerland in producing, importing, exporting, selling or distributing watches, movements or parts; from selling or exporting such items anywhere to any person not a signatory; or from acquiring such items anywhere from any non-signatory. Further, it proposed to enjoin membership on boards and committees taking actions contrary to or inconsistent with any of the terms of the judgment, or omitting to take action, "where such omission would be contrary to or inconsistent with any of such terms," and to order FH to prohibit each member of a Section from engaging in prohibited activities and to provide in its by-laws for the punishment of members who violated obligations imposed on FH.

In opposition to these proposals, the General Secretary of FH, George Matthey, testified regarding the structure of FH, its relations with the Sections and the 520 members of the Sections, the powers of members and of the FH General Assembly, and the constitution of the arbitral and appeals tribunals. He mentioned that in 1960, a consent decree in the case had been proposed by the management of FH, but that it was rejected because it was opposed by all six Sections.

A Swiss lawyer and professor, Conrad Fehr, testified regarding practice before the arbitral tribunal, the independence of the FH Sections from FH, the non-enforceability in Switzerland of foreign penal laws, and the infringement of Swiss sovereignty inhering in provisions in the judgment proposed by the Department of Justice that would require FH to punish its members.

The Secretary General of the Swiss Government's Department of Economic and Political Affairs, Dr. Karl Huber, testified regarding the relationship and close coordination between the Swiss Government and the watch industry, the guidance and assistance provided by industry experts, the importance to the Government of having industry personnel on government committees and boards, and the extent of governmental controls over quality standards, exports, and the licensing of manufacture. Dr. Huber was one of the five Government members on the board of ASUAG and was a member of its executive committee. He said that it was "extremely rare" for a Swiss Government official of his rank to testify in court, and in a foreign court it was "exceptionally rare." His Government, however, felt so strongly about the situation that it directed him to be a witness in this case. As he put it:

When the Swiss Government and the Federal Council became aware of the opinions of this court, it was found absolutely necessary in the public interest of Switzerland that the court receive an explanation by one of the highest officials of the government as regards the implementation of Swiss law in certain special cases, in particular within the framework of the Swiss watch industry, and in particular as to the watch statute. . . .

An aspect of major concern to the Swiss Government, he said, was the procedure for giving effect to the new Watch Statute of 1961. This statute involved the establishment of industry committees, some of which were to advise the Government and make recommendations to it, but one of which was to exercise "executive functions" in connection with quality controls in the industry. Although the Government had the power in the statute to implement its provisions itself, it preferred to delegate these functions to private bodies. As noted above, he stressed the Swiss tradition that matters such as this

should in all possible cases be entrusted to a private organization which in most cases is as well equipped as the state may be to implement such a statute as the watch statute. This is the Swiss system.

The Government was also, he testified, concerned with the maintenance of export controls under the new statute. For this purpose, it had established an advisory committee which would be asked to give its opinions on applications for export licenses. One of the criteria established by the Federal Council for the granting of export licenses was whether the foreign buyer would use the exported parts in its own operations, or would in effect act as a "turntable" passing such parts on to others. In order to prevent this, the Swiss had proposed a provision in the Final Judgment that would permit limiting exports to bona fide manufacturers or assemblers in the United States. The Swiss Government, he said, had "a vital interest" in having this proposal adopted by the court.

Dr. Huber also testified that restrictions on imports were "of great interest to Switzerland" and the maintenance of restrictions by the industry was "one of the constitutional conditions which the industry must fulfill if it wishes to be entitled to special protection."

The Swiss proposals were rejected by the Department of Justice and the court seemed unwilling to make any concession beyond limiting the judgment to jeweled-lever watches. Accordingly, its Final Judgment was entered, in January of 1962, largely as proposed by the Government. As a result, the Swiss defendants filed notice of appeal to the Supreme Court.

2. SWISS GOVERNMENT INTERVENTION AND THE MODIFIED JUDGMENT: 1964-65

Following entry of the Final Judgment, the Swiss Government requested the State Department to ask the Department of Justice to discuss with Swiss watch representatives the difficulties which their industry had with the judgment. After some dozen conferences, the Department advised the District Court that they could not go along with what was proposed because of inconsistencies with the antitrust laws "and the antitrust objectives of this case." Following these discussions, the Department of Justice was again advised by way of the State Department that the Swiss Government wished to discuss the matter directly with the Department and for this purpose had retained counsel in Washington. At the request of the State Department, a further series of discussions accordingly took place. Modifications in the Final Judgment were eventually agreed upon between the two Governments, and the agreed proposals were submitted to the District Court on December 17, 1964.

At the hearing on these modifications, the Justice Department representative referred to the interest of the State Department in settling the case without further litigation, if that could be done within the framework of the antitrust laws. He also referred to the desire of the Antitrust Division to terminate the litigation without any appeal to the Supreme Court, adding that there had been "some talk with respect to trying to take the case to the International Court of Justice." The Antitrust Division was satisfied, he said, that, if the proposed changes were made by the court, the case would still have achieved its basic antitrust objectives. The court also heard counsel for the Swiss Government as *amicus curiae,* whose only concern, he said, was to call attention to various provisions of the initial judgment which, it was felt, held or carried with them

the potential threat of intruding upon the sovereignty of Switzerland and vital concerns of the Swiss Confederation with respect to the maintenance of its watch industry as a vibrant part of its total economy. . . . Our concern throughout has been only with respect to possible interpretation of the Judgment that might be construed to impinge upon Swiss sovereignty and Swiss concern for its domestic watch industry.

Despite earlier efforts of the Swiss defendants to avoid interference with Swiss sovereignty, it was argued that such interference was imminent, and that the sovereign rights of the Swiss Confederation were apparently being disregarded.

The agreed proposals, the Swiss counsel said, represented an "accommodation of legitimate antitrust interests in . . . protecting American foreign and domestic commerce" to the interest of the Swiss Government "in protecting from its points of view its own domestic economy." Acceptance of the proposals would eliminate further appeals and avoid confronting the Swiss Confederation with "the embarrassing question of taking even perhaps a judgment of our Supreme Court to the International Court of Justice." It would mean termination of the long litigation on the basis of preserving the "heart and core" of the judgment, at the same time permitting the Swiss to "exercise their own sovereignty with respect to the heart and core of their economy, the Swiss watch industry."

In the Modified Final Judgment of February 3, 1965, the United States, as plaintiff in the action, gave formal recognition to the sovereignty of the Swiss Confederation and to its right to regulate its commerce and its watch industry.[40] The court retained from the original judgment a provision, which it enlarged, that nothing should be deemed to prohibit "any defendant, FH member or any other person in Switzerland" from doing certain things, as follows (paragraphs 1, 2, 5 and 6 were in the original judgment, and paragraphs 3 and 4 were new):

(1) Performing any act in Switzerland which is required of it under the law of Switzerland;

(2) Refraining from any act in Switzerland which is illegal under the law of Switzerland;

(3) Taking any joint or individual action, consistent with the applicable law of the nation where the party taking such action is domiciled, to comply with conditions for the export of watch parts from Switzerland established by valid ordinances, or rules and regulations promulgated thereunder, of the Swiss Government;

[40] 1965 Trade Cas. ¶71,352 at 80,491 (Revision of Section XI to add a new subsection, [L]).

(4) Taking any joint or individual action required by the scheme of regulation of the Swiss watch industry based on Article 31 bis of the Swiss Constitution, with respect to imports of watch parts into Switzerland other than from U.S. companies;

(5) Advocating the enactment of laws, decrees or regulations or urging upon any Swiss governmental body, department, agency or official the taking of any official action;

(6) Furnishing to the Swiss Government or any body, department, agency or official thereof, its independent advice or opinion when requested to do so.

And at the end of this section dealing with exclusions it added a provision that nothing should be deemed to:

(K) Limit or circumscribe the sovereign right and power of the Government of the Swiss Confederation or any agency thereof, or specifically the sovereign right and power of the Government of the Swiss Confederation or any agency thereof to control or regulate its domestic or foreign commerce or to make and apply regulations with respect to the watch-making industry or any part thereof.[41]

The Modified Judgment, however, also retained many prohibitions which, in the absence of intervention by the Swiss Government, would reach far into the domestic operations of the Swiss industry. On the other hand, the United States, while obtaining sweeping injunctions against FH and Ebauches, failed in its efforts to have the judgment apply specifically to the FH Sections.

Apart from the recognition given to overriding powers of the Swiss Government, the changes made in the initial Final Judgment do not appear to have altered the substance of provisions requiring FH and Ebauches to cancel, terminate, withdraw from or otherwise render inapplicable to United States imports and exports, and to production, sale and distribution within the United States, the terms of the Collective Convention and of the contracts between the Swiss Watch Chamber, FH and others with British, French and German watch organizations. It was stated that the Swiss Government had filed a memorandum with the court setting forth its reasons why these provisions presented problems for it. Although several provisions were deleted in the Modified Final Judgment, new paragraphs were inserted which enjoined FH and Ebauches in general terms from enforcing, performing or renewing these

---

[41] *Id.* at 80,491-92 (Revision of Section XI to delete Subsection [C], and to change Subsection [E]).

provisions of the Collective Convention and other contracts, or from entering into, performing, adhering to or renewing, in whole or in part, directly or indirectly, any provisions so enjoined.[42] In commenting on these changes, the representative of the Department of Justice said that it was the view of the Antitrust Division that, as revised, the modified version contained in substance what the District Court had originally ordered.

Section IV of the Modified Final Judgment still operated to sweep away contractual restrictions on imports into the United States of watches, movements, parts and machinery, on exports from the United States of such items, and on their production, sale or distribution within the United States. It also enjoined any renewal of any such provision. In the case of the Swiss contractual arrangements with Bulova, Gruen and Benrus, broad provisions were retained relating to manufacturing which the Swiss defendants were unsuccessful in having geographically confined. Not only did they reach restrictions on United States imports and exports, but they also prohibited restrictions on the manufacture by these companies of watches, movements and parts any place in the world outside Switzerland without reference to effects on United States trade and commerce.

Further points of major concern to the Swiss Government in the initial judgment had been prohibitions relating to membership in, and contributions to, industry associations and committees which took action contrary to or inconsistent with the judgment. It considered that its nationals should be entitled to engage in these activities under the Swiss scheme of industry regulations. In finally accepting the deletion of these prohibitions, the Department of Justice advised the court that it did not believe that their absence would detract from the basic antitrust objectives of the case. The judgment would still enjoin restrictions on production, and it said that there was still "adequate injunctive relief to prevent private restrictions on imports into and exports from the United States of watches, watch parts and watch machinery."

The Department also agreed, as quoted above, to permit joint or individual action, consistent with the applicable law of its domicile, "to comply with conditions for the export of watch parts from Switzerland established by valid ordinances, or rules and regulations promulgated thereunder, of the Swiss Government." Export controls relating to parts

[42] *Id.* at 80,491 (Revision of Sections IV [C] and [D] and Section VIII).

and machinery could thus continue. The Judgment also permitted joint or individual actions in import controls required by the scheme of regulation of the Swiss watch industry based on the Swiss Constitution.

In the compliance provision relating to the production of records in the possession of or under the control of Swiss defendants, the Modified Final Judgment provided that no one would be required to bring to the United States any books or other records or copies when such action was prohibited by the law of Switzerland, if the defendant in question had exercised good faith efforts to obtain permission to bring them, and such permission had not been secured. The Swiss Government wished to have this exemption expressed, and the Department of Justice acquiesced, pointing out that the provision, which originated in the *Interhandel* case,[43] was "perfectly acceptable" and did not present any problem.

Finally, it was agreed that, if FH and Ebauches should decide to withdraw from operations in the United States, and if they satisfied the court that they were no longer within the jurisdiction, the court might cancel the provision that they maintain in the jurisdiction a representative authorized to accept service.

Having concluded that these modifications did not "affect the crucial objectives sought to be achieved in the Final Judgment heretofore filed," but that they mainly related "to peripheral areas of the Judgment which might have been construed to have bearing upon the sovereignty of the Swiss Confederation,"[44] the District Court modified the Judgment accordingly on January 7, 1965. In doing so, it pointed out that these modifications would

> prevent any situation from arising such as has occurred in other litigation in the past when there was believed to be a possible conflict between a decree of a United States court and the sovereignty of a foreign nation.[45]

II. THE STRUCTURE OF THE INDUSTRY AND THE ORIGINS OF THE JURISDICTIONAL CONFLICTS

The conduct attacked in this extraordinary case occurred mainly in a foreign country. The agreements were made there, and it was there that

[43] See Chapter 3 *supra* at 119-20.
[44] 1965 Trade Cas. ¶ 71,352 at 80,492-93.
[45] *Id.* at 80,493. The judge cited the *I.C.I.* cases, discussed in Chapter 3 *supra* at 122.

they were carried out. Admittedly, restraining effects were produced on commerce within the United States and on American exports and imports. But the agreements were an integral part of the legal, economic and political order of the country where they were established and operated. It was really that order which was in issue.

Because the United States sought to reach and dissipate these collective arrangements the district court was confronted with issues that transcended the relatively simpler questions of legality under the Sherman Act. What would have been largely per se offenses, as applied to the protection of American interests in American domestic economic contexts, were defended by foreign interests as reasonable in relation to foreign economies. The clash of interests thus arising, and the consequences of applying American law and American judicial orders to foreign economic and legal structures and institutions, required consideration of many factors—economic, social and political, as well as legal. This necessity is indicated by the following summary of data presented to the court and for the most part included in its Findings of Fact.[46]

A. The Swiss Watch Industry

Throughout the period under review, the Swiss watch industry was the largest producer of watches in the world. Although its share of total world production declined from 67.5% in 1946 to 53.4% in 1954, its output rose from 21 million units in 1946 to 31 million in 1954. Before the war, the industry's exports of finished movements and watches had risen from 17 million in 1926 to 20.7 million in 1929, declined to 8 million in 1932, reached 24 million in 1937, and had then fallen off to 15 million in 1940.[47]

The industry was wholly self-sufficient in the production of both watch parts and watchmaking machinery, and was of immense importance to the Swiss economy. As was said by counsel for the Swiss Government at the final hearing on the Modified Final Judgment:

[T]he Swiss watch industry is the very heart and core of the entire Swiss economy . . . it constitutes better than 25% of the entire gross national

[46] 1963 Trade Cas. ¶ 70,600 at 77,417.
[47] *Id.* at 77, 423, 77, 424 (findings 61, 63, 64); U.S. Tariff Commission Report, "Watches, Watch Movements, and Watch Parts," T.C. Rep. No. 177, June 1966, at 102 (Table 1).

production of Switzerland . . . 95% of the production . . . is exported, and it constitutes more than half of all Switzerland's exports.

Unlike the watch industry in the United States, that in Switzerland was composed of a large number of small companies and other units specializing in the manufacture of particular parts or classes of parts or in the assembly of parts into completed watches. Only a relatively few watch manufacturers produced their own watch parts and none of these manufactured all of their watch parts requirements. In 1955, there were over 2,800 separate firms employing over 66,000 workers. Nearly 50% of all the workers were employed in firms of 100 persons or less, and 20% were in firms (more than 2,200) comprising only 1 to 20 workers. Most of the diversity was in the production of separate parts where 80% of the units each employed not more than 20 people.[48]

In the manufacture of ébauches and regulating parts (escapements, balance wheels and hairsprings), larger units were employed. In this area there were only 68 firms employing nearly 10,000 workers and only 18 of these employed 81% of the total. Assemblers did not themselves manufacture parts, but purchased them from specialized factories. In this branch small enterprises predominated, with 943 firms or 82% of the total employing no more than 1 to 20 workers.[49]

The United States was the largest single export market for Swiss watches. The industry also exported watch parts and watchmaking machinery. While the total number of jeweled-lever watches exported by Switzerland increased by 240% from 1938 to 1953, the volume of Swiss exports of jeweled-lever watches to the United States during the same period increased by 460% and the value of these exports by over 1,000%.[50]

During the antitrust proceedings, it was pointed out by the Swiss defendants that American manufacturers had been severely handicapped by labor costs, which ran two to three times as high as those in Switzerland. As these costs accounted for 80% to 85% of the cost of manufacturing a jeweled-lever watch, both in the United States and in Switzerland, the disadvantage was apparent. Nor were the Swiss wage

---

[48]Message of the Federal Council of the Swiss Confederation to the Federal Assembly, dated Dec. 16, 1960, 112-II FEUILLE FEDERALE [F.F.] 1489, Tables I and II (Dec. 29, 1960).

[49]*Id.* Tables III and IV.

[50]1963 Trade Cas. ¶ 70,600 at 77,424 (finding 64).

scales depressed. Wage rates in Switzerland were as high or higher than in any watchmaking country other than the United States.[51]

The horizontal, highly-decentralized organization of the Swiss industry, consisting of hundreds of small individual firms specializing in the production of individual component parts, which were assembled by specialized firms, contrasted strikingly with the vertical structure of the American industry. The former resulted in lower unit costs when production was at a relatively low level and permitted much greater flexibility in a fluctuating industry than the more rigid structure in the United States. The latter required a higher level of output in order to achieve lower unit costs. Finally, the Swiss possessed a large central pool of skilled labor, historical pride in watchmaking transmitted from father to son, and specialized training schools. None of these existed in the United States.[52]

The Swiss industry's organization, which was in effect when the suit was brought in 1954, had its origin in the economic depression in Switzerland of 1921 and 1922. At that time, production and employment were reduced to levels substantially below those which prevailed during and immediately following the First World War. The Swiss Government responded to the distress of the watchmakers by providing financial assistance in the amount of 9.5 million francs. In 1923, the Swiss Watch Chamber, a government organization, brought together representatives of regional employer organizations to form an association of nine regional Sections, each composed of individual Swiss firms engaged in the manufacture or assembly of jeweled-lever watches and movements. This was the Fédération Suisse des Associations de Fabricants d'Horlogerie, referred to throughout as "FH." In 1926, Ebauches S.A. was established as a holding company to secure ownership of the stock of eighteen firms specializing in the manufacture of ébauches. In 1927, Groups of some 500 producers of hair springs, balance wheels, escapements and other regulating and component parts were bound together in the association known as UBAH (Union des Branches Annexes de l'Horlogerie). In December of 1928, FH, Ebauches and UBAH entered into agreements with each other to enforce minimum prices for their respective products and to prevent the export of ébauches and unassembled movements known as "chablons."[53]

[51] Brief on Behalf of the Swiss Defendants, Sept. 15, 1961, at 42.

[52] *Id.* at 42, 43.

[53] Message of the Federal Council of the Swiss Confederation to the Federal Assembly, dated Sept. 11, 1931, at 6-30, 83-II F.F. 193 (Sept. 16, 1931).

Despite recovery of the industry to the 1919 level by 1929, the export of "chablons," designated "chablonnage," continued to be a major problem, in addition to tariff barriers abroad (*e.g.,* the high United States tariffs of 1930), and decreases in purchasing power and demand. As various "dissident" firms remained outside the scope of the industry's arrangements, foreign buyers were able to obtain regulating parts without great difficulty not only for repair purposes but also for the assembly of new movements. Large orders came from foreign manufacturers of watch cases for ébauches and chablons, as less-skilled workmen abroad could, with these combinations, complete the assembly of watches behind the protective tariffs in their countries. Parts were also exported in greater numbers. The employment problem was acute. From a total of 48,378 workers in the industry in 1929, the number fell to 24,733 in 1934. Approximately one-quarter of the workers were unemployed. So desperate was the situation in 1931 that 56,000 persons signed a public petition to the Government requesting it to take emergency action to save the industry. The Message of the Federal Council to the Assembly in 1931 stated that it was "the duty of the Confederation to come to the aid of the watch industry" and support its efforts to overcome the crisis and guarantee its future. It was pointed out in this 1931 Message:

> The watch industry is the most important source and, for many localities, the only source of revenue of our people of the Jura. The establishment of new industries in that region would meet with major difficulties. Industries necessitating the use of heavy raw materials and producing very weighty merchandise could not exist in these valleys remote from major traffic arteries. This is one more reason for exerting every possible effort to maintain what is established and nurtured in the region and for not allowing an industry to disappear which has so far supported an entire population, which regards the projected plan as the only means of escaping dire straits.[54]

After the industry had been told by the Federal Government that it was up to it to initiate recovery measures, extensive negotiations among the various segments of the industry and their bankers led to agreements in 1931 replacing earlier arrangements which had proved ineffective and had lapsed. The main problem was to organize the industry, stop the export of chablons and manufacturing parts and build up the manufac-

[54]*Id.* at 42. See also Message of the Federal Council of the Swiss Confederation to the Federal Assembly, dated Oct. 6, 1950, at 11-18, 23-25, 102-III F.F. 57 (Oct. 12, 1950).

turing processes within the country. For this purpose, ASUAG (Société Générale de l'Horlogerie de Suisse) was formed as a superholding company for the purpose of buying up "dissidents" and controlling manufacturers of ébauches and essential parts. It acquired control of Ebauches S.A. and important UBAH groups.

The scheme was approved by the Assembly of the Federal Government and authority was given for the investment of six million francs in the capital of ASUAG and for an interest-free loan in the amount of 7,500,000 francs. This gave the Swiss Government a three-eighths share in the capital and the right to nominate five directors out of a total of thirty. Five-sixteenths of the remaining capital was subscribed to by a syndicate of Swiss banks, and five-sixteenths by FH, Ebauches and UBAH.[55]

This effort in 1931 failed to eliminate chablonnage, because it was then unable to control through Ebauches every one of the firms specializing in the production of ébauches and regulating parts, and also because there were then no prohibitions on the establishment of new firms. As a result, the Swiss Government again took action. By a statute enacted in October of 1933, entitled "Measures of Economic Defense Against Foreign Countries," the Federal Assembly authorized the Federal Council to issue decrees for the protection of various Swiss industries, including the watch industry. In March of 1934, the Federal Council prohibited the export of chablons, ébauches and separate parts without a permit issued either by the Swiss Watch Chamber or by "FIDHOR" (Le Fiduciaire Horlogerie Suisse), an independent public accounting and auditing corporation organized for the purpose of investigating compliance by watch firms with the Conventions and rulings of the industry's organizations. Moreover, unless otherwise directed by the Department of Public Economy of the Federal Government (DEP), such export permits would be granted solely for deliveries conforming to the Collective Conventions.

As a corollary measure, the same decree provided that the creation, expansion or conversion of any watchmaking enterprises, including factories for producing ébauches and regulating parts, would be lawful only if permitted by the Department of Public Economy of the Swiss Government. It was specified that no permit for any such enterprise

[55] Message of the Federal Council, *supra* note 54, at 18-22, 30-33.

could be issued if such a change would in any way prejudice the interests of the watch industry.[56]

In March of 1936, when the basic agreements between FH, Ebauches and UBAH and their respective members were amended, the Swiss Federal Council authorized the DEP to declare minimum price lists negotiated by FH, Ebauches and UBAH binding on all watchmaking enterprises. It also prohibited non-signatories to the Convention from selling their products on conditions more favorable than those established by the signatories. In December of 1937, the Federal Council combined into a single statute all of the measures taken by the Swiss Government with respect to the watchmaking industry; it also added repair parts to the products whose export was prohibited without a permit. In December of 1939, the 1937 decree was renewed, and dies, tools and other special equipment were added to the lists of products requiring export permits. The system of manufacturing and export permits remained in force throughout the Second World War. By the end of 1940, "dissenting" firms had apparently lost interest in view of the export regulations and the enforcement of minimum prices. With further financial assistance from the Government, ASUAG was also able to purchase all factories which it did not already control and which manufactured jeweled-lever watches, ébauches and regulating parts.[57]

The industry agreements were renewed from time to time, and the provisions of the 1939 decree of the Federal Council were extended by decrees in 1942, 1945 and 1948 and remained continuously in effect until the end of 1951. In that year new economic clauses of the Swiss Constitution became effective. These empowered the Government, "when the common interest warrants," to adopt measures to safeguard major branches of the economy "whose existence is threatened." In order to benefit from such measures, the industry concerned had to establish that it had taken measures to help itself. The Federal Council Message to the Federal Assembly of December 1960 said that it was clear from the legislative history of these constitutional provisions that the self-help measures of the watch industry were considered a typical case of application of this provision. These measures were embodied in the Collective Conventions, which are reviewed in the next section.[58]

[56]*Id.* at 24-27, 33-38.
[57]Message of the Federal Council, *supra* note 48, at 16-24.
[58]*Id.* at 20.

B. The Collective Conventions and Government Controls[59]

Apart from governmental regulation under legislative measures and from controls exercised by FH, Ebauches, UBAH and ASUAG, the principal mechanism for organizing the industry and maintaining its restrictive features was the series of agreements known in each case as "The Collective Convention of the Swiss Watch Industry." As noted above, the agreements of 1931 were replaced in 1936 by "a single detailed joint agreement." This was in turn followed by successive Conventions, the latest of which prior to the institution of the proceedings was dated April 1, 1949. It was this instrument which constituted the basis of the complaint.[60]

A dominant feature of the 1949 Convention was the principle of "trade reciprocity," pursuant to which the members of the FH Sections were required to purchase solely from Ebauches and UBAH members the ébauches and watch parts which they did not produce themselves. Ebauches was bound to purchase only from UBAH members the parts which it did not produce itself; and the members of UBAH undertook to purchase parts solely from other members of UBAH. Ebauches could in turn sell ébauches in Switzerland only to members of FH Sections, and UBAH could sell parts in Switzerland only to other UBAH members, to Ebauches and to members of FH Sections. The parties also undertook to deal only in finished products, ébauches and parts manufactured in accordance with the terms of the Convention.[61]

Apart from these reciprocal exclusive dealing arrangements, the Convention bound the signatories not to engage directly or indirectly in any horological business transactions outside the Convention or outside Switzerland, or to be in any manner interested in any such transaction. These restrictions were aimed particularly at any form of assistance to a non-Conventional or foreign manufacturer or dealer in, watches, ébauches or watch parts, or to any other non-Conventional or foreign firms which dealt in a manner contrary to the Convention in watches, ébauches or watch parts manufactured under the Convention. There were also prohibitions against the sale or export of watchmaking

[59]*Id.* at 21-44.
[60]1963 Trade Cas. ¶70,600 at 77,425-26 (finding 76).
[61]*Id.* at 77,426-27 (finding 82).

machines and tools, and against the direct or indirect acquisition by any person of foreign nationality of any interest in any Swiss watch enterprise.[62]

Strict limitations were imposed on sales and exports of parts for manufacturing purposes. FH members agreed that the watch parts which they purchased or manufactured would be used solely for their own manufacturing purposes and would not be sold by them except for the repair of their own finished products; Ebauches and UBAH agreed to export certain products solely to certain specially designated watch manufacturers located outside Switzerland who agreed not to resell such parts and to adhere to other provisions of the Convention. Certain parts could never be offered for sale or export. These included parts which were not in a specified state of manufacture, chablons, parts making up escapements, and unfinished escapements.

Broad restrictions on the sale of repair parts were included, and on dealings with companies outside Switzerland which dealt in watches or watch parts produced by persons who were not parties to the Convention. Sales prices of watches and movements were fixed in accordance with FH regulations for the stabilization of prices. Deliveries of watches and watch parts would be suspended to purchasers who violated the Convention. Each signatory agreed that the provisions of the Convention applied to the conduct of each of its branches, parents or affiliates located in countries outside Switzerland and that violation of the Convention by foreign affiliates would subject Convention membership to cancellation.[63]

It was agreed that the Convention should be interpreted, modified, administered, and enforced by a body called the Délégations Réunis (DR), composed of three members appointed by Ebauches, three by UBAH, six by FH, and a President who had no connection with the industry and was chosen by the three organizations. The principal powers of the DR were to interpret, grant exceptions to, and modify the Collective Convention, except where FH, Ebauches or UBAH objected. The DR could penalize breaches of the Convention by cancelling it as to the violator, by cancelling existing contracts which violated the Convention, and by imposing fines. It was also empowered to expel a firm from membership for acts of a foreign affiliate. The District Court

[62] *Id.*
[63] *Id.* at 77,426-27 (findings 82, 83).

found that during the years prior to 1954 the DR had never exercised this last power, although there were references to the possibility of its doing so.[64]

All final decisions of the DR, except decisions modifying the Collective Convention, could be appealed to an Arbitral Tribunal composed of three professional judges selected by the courts of three of the Swiss watchmaking cantons from among their members, together with three judges from the watchmaking industry selected by the three professional judges. Each proceeding brought before the Tribunal was heard by a panel of five judges, including the three professional judges and two of the industry judges. All proceedings were governed by the code of civil procedure for the canton of Berne. All decisions had the same legal effect and were enforceable in the same manner as judgments of the Swiss cantonal courts, and all were reviewable by the Supreme Court of Berne.[65]

This private Conventional system of the industry was part of a broader system of regulation and control by the Federal Government, without which it would have been ineffective. The two segments of the system were essentially complementary and interacting, so much so that it was believed that abandonment of the exercise of public power in relation to the industry and a return to "pure and simple free trade" would seriously prejudice the existence of the industry. This view was held not only by the leading watch trade organizations, both employer and employee, but also by federal departments and the Federal Council. As stated in the 1950 Message of the Federal Council to the Federal Assembly, a return to "absolute and untrammeled freedom" would have presented very great dangers.[66]

Both the private and the public aspects of the system were reviewed in detail in this Message and in a later Message on the same subject in 1960. It was pointed out in the earlier communication that, if the legislation of October 1933 "concerning measures of economic defense abroad" were not extended in accordance with the new economic provisions of the Constitution, they could no longer serve as the basis of watch trade legislation beyond that date. If the entire system were to disappear, "a new dissidence would make its appearance forthwith." Plants for making

---

[64] *Id.* at 77,427 (findings 84-86).
[65] *Id.* at 77,427-28 (findings 88, 89).
[66] Message of the Federal Council, *supra* note 54, at 45-50.

watches and ébauches, balance wheels, escapements and other loose parts could be set up freely outside the Convention system, and the system would be in danger of collapse, "or at least of losing its effectiveness." There would be a rebirth of "chablonnage." Dissident watchmaking enterprises would engage in cut-throat underbidding, watch quality would suffer, and this would bring discredit to the entire national output and have a highly adverse effect on wages. There would be a risk of a return to "the sorry procession of bankruptcies, insolvencies and failures." Manufacturers of separate parts would be tempted to fill big orders for foreign competitors and watchmakers might finally leave the Convention associations. Thus, the Message said, "the success achieved by a quarter century of strenuous efforts would have been irremediably compromised."[67]

Consideration was also given in 1950 to new legislation which would be confined to maintaining the system of export permits without any control over the establishment of new enterprises. Here again the Federal Council foresaw that this would mean "sapping the foundations of the organization set up at the cost of long and arduous endeavors," and chablonnage and price-cutting "would celebrate new triumphs." The decision was, therefore, taken to buttress and complement the Conventional system of the industry itself by appropriate federal legislation. This extended the system of requiring permits not only for exports but also for the establishment of new enterprises or the extension of existing enterprises.[68]

In the 1960 Message to the Federal Assembly, regarding which there was Swiss Government testimony at the hearings on the Final Judgment, it was said that the private regulations of the 1949 Collective Convention had been attacked both within the industry and from the outside. A critical study of the industry's competitive conditions had been published by the DEP in 1959. Criticism was mainly directed at the system of manufacturing permits. It was also pointed out that export controls retarded the development of certain separate parts factories and encouraged dynamic enterprises in other countries.

In proposing a new statute, which became effective in 1961, these criticisms were taken into account. The general structure of the industry was also reviewed in relation to competitive developments in other

[67]*Id.* at 45-50, 65-68; Message of the Federal Council, *supra* note 48, at 44-48.
[68]Message of the Federal Council, *supra* note 54, at 53-57.

countries. Consideration was given to the question of continuing, on the one hand, the small business units or craft structure "for political, social and demographic reasons," and on the other, the encouragement of concentrations and mass production. There were thus, in both 1950 (before the antitrust suit was brought), and again in 1960 (after it had been brought), thorough reviews, both public and private, of the industry structure and of its restrictive aspects.[69]

The statute adopted in 1961 and the ordinances issued pursuant to it by the Federal Council maintained a system of export controls over watches, watch movements, chablons, ébauches, bridges, plates, pinions, regulating parts (escapements, balance wheels and hair springs), watch jewels, mainsprings and other parts, dies and tools of all kinds required in the manufacture of ébauches and parts, blueprints, drawings, assembling and finishing apparatus, and watchmaking machinery. The issuance of permits was entrusted to the Swiss Watch Chamber. Controls were also continued on an interim basis over the opening of new enterprises, the reopening of those closed for more than two years, and the transformation of existing enterprises. Elaborate technical controls were established over quality under the supervision of a commission appointed by DEP after consultation with the organizations concerned.

All of this was explained in some detail to the District Court by an official of the DEP during the hearings on the Final Judgment.

C. The American Watch Industry

At the time suit was brought in 1954, the main watch-producing countries in the world were Switzerland, the United States, Germany, Russia, France, the United Kingdom and Japan. Switzerland had by far the largest production, accounting in 1954 for 53.4% of the total. The United States was second with 12.1%; the Soviet Union and West Germany were tied for third with 10.3% each; France and the United Kingdom followed with 5.2% each; and Japan ended the list with 3.5%.[70]

From 1946 to 1954, the Swiss share of world production had declined from 67.5% to 53.4%, although Swiss total output had increased from 21 million to 31 million units. The United States' share, with a steady

[69] Message of the Federal Council, *supra* note 48, at 34-62.
[70] 1963 Trade Cas. ¶ 70,600 at 77,423 (finding 61).

production of 7 million units during this period, also fell from 22.5% to 12.1%. The Soviet Union, on the other hand, increased its production from 500,000 units in 1946 to 6 million in 1954; West Germany, from 1 million units to 6 million during the same period; France and the United Kingdom, from 500,000 units and 600,000 units respectively to 3 million each; and Japan, from 500,000 to 2 million.

Perhaps more significant were the increases during the next ten years while the suit was pending, from 1954 to 1964. During this period, Switzerland increased its production from 31 million units to 48 million; the Soviet Union, from 6 million to 26 million; Japan, from 2 million to 13 million; and the United States, from 7 million to 12 million. Increases by West Germany, France and the United Kingdom were less significant.[71]

In the United States, there had at one time been as many as sixty manufacturers, but by 1933 the number manufacturing in the United States had fallen to only three, Hamilton, Elgin and Waltham. In that year, as noted above, Bulova, an American-owned firm with a plant in Switzerland, made an agreement with the Swiss industry by which it obtained Swiss parts for manufacturing in the United States. A few years later, Benrus, also an American firm with a Swiss manufacturing branch, acquired the Waterbury Clock Company and, with an allocation of Swiss parts, entered the field of jeweled-lever watch production in the United States. Benrus abandoned watch manufacture in the United States during the war, however, and did not resume it. Both Bulova and Benrus continued to manufacture in Switzerland.[72]

During the 1946-54 period, the main producers of jeweled-lever watches in the United States were Bulova, Elgin, Hamilton and Waltham. In 1948, Gruen, another United States company with a Swiss manufacturing subsidiary, arranged with the Swiss for watch parts to enable it to start manufacturing jeweled-lever watches in the United States. Its Swiss subsidiary continued to manufacture in Switzerland. At the time suit was brought there were thus five American producers of jeweled-lever watches, two of them also manufacturing in Switzerland. Gruen's production in the United States never was significant, however, and it

[71] U.S. Tariff Commission Report, *supra* note 47.

[72] Brief on Behalf of the Swiss Defendants, Sept. 15, 1961, at 40, 41; 1963 Trade Cas. ¶ 70,600 at 77,438-41 (findings 160, 173, 175, 176).

ceased producing watches in the United States soon after the suit was begun.[73]

Production of jeweled-lever watches in the United States increased from a low point of 463,000 units in 1933 to a high of 3,162,000 in 1951. After that date, production fluctuated between 2,433,000 units in 1952 and 947,000 in 1958. By 1959 it was up to 1,614,000. Total production of all watch movements in the United States amounted to 11,559,000 units in 1951, 7,396,000 units in 1954, and 11,334,000 units in 1959.[74]

From 1931 to 1954, imports of jeweled-lever watch movements containing two or more jewels rose from an average of 730,000 units in the 1931-35 period to 7,431,000 units in 1948, and 10,020,000 in 1953.[75] While United States production in 1931 had accounted for 52% of the jeweled-lever watches sold in the United States, it declined to 38% in 1940, to 24% in 1950, and to 19% in 1954.[76]

From 1946 through 1954, 95% of all jeweled-lever watches imported into the United States were imported from Switzerland.[77] Of the approximately 200 importers of Swiss watches, Bulova, Benrus and Gruen, as mentioned above, maintained manufacturing facilities in Switzerland, either through branches or a subsidiary, and the American company, Longines-Wittnauer, had a subsidiary there which assembled watches. Other United States importers were associated with Swiss manufacturers, either as subsidiary companies, such as Eterna, distributing watches in the United States, or as independent exclusive distributors.

During the 1931-35 period, United States production of jeweled watches averaged 781,000 units per year as compared with jeweled watch imports of 730,000 units per year. By 1953, the corresponding amounts were 2,365,000 units containing domestic movements and 10,020,000 imported units.[78] While, therefore, imports were slightly

[73] 1963 Trade Cas. ¶ 70,600 at 77,441-42 (findings 179-183).

[74] U.S. Tariff Commission Report, "Watch Movements" (July 1956) 39 (Table 8); U.S. Tariff Commission Report, "Watch Movements," T.C. Rep. No. 150, March 1965, at 48 (Table 4).

[75] U.S. Tariff Commission Report, "Watch Movements" (July 1956) 33 (Table 4).

[76] 1963 Trade Cas. ¶ 70,600 at 77,425 (finding 70).

[77] *Id.*

[78] *Id.* at 77,425 (finding 71).

behind American-made products in the United States market in the early 1930's, they were more than three times ahead in 1953. As President Truman pointed out in rejecting a tariff increase in 1952, consumption of watches in the United States had quadrupled in the sixteen years during which tariff concessions had been in effect. In that period, a mass demand for watches had been developed, both for relatively inexpensive watches and for those of high quality and expensive casing.[79]

Swiss imports had had much to do with developing this demand, and in selling the American public on wrist watches for men and small watches for women. With greatly increased consumption, merchandising methods had radically changed. Department store, mail order and drug store sales had become more important, and mark-ups were smaller. While importers had obtained the largest share in the increased consumption, domestic producers had also benefited.[80]

A major problem of the domestic industry, however, was the high labor-cost factor. In 1954, labor costs averaged 80% or more of the total cost of producing watches. The average number of employees producing jeweled-lever watches in that year was 4,199, and their average hourly wage was $1.90, exclusive of social security, pensions and other fringe benefits. In relation to the Swiss, labor costs in the United States were two to three times as high.[81]

Total sales of all United States-produced watches and watch movements amounted to $66 million in 1954, as compared with $38.8 million for imports.[82] In the case of manufacturers of jeweled-lever watches, the ratio of profits to net worth before taxes for Elgin, Hamilton and Waltham was 15.8%.[83] President Truman pointed out that profits of jeweled watch manufacturers before taxes averaged 12% of their net worth, from which he concluded that the industry was hardly suffering serious injury.[84]

[79] U.S. Tariff Commission Report, "Watches, Watch Movements, Watch Parts, and Watchcases," T.C. Rep. No. 176, 2d Series, June 14, 1952, at 77, 78.

[80] *Id.* at 39, 55-64, 78.

[81] *Id.* at 11; U.S. Tariff Commission Report, "Watch Movements" (July 1957) 39 (Table 13).

[82] U.S. Tariff Commission Report, "Watch Movements" (March 1965) 49 (Table 6).

[83] U.S. Tariff Commission Report, "Watch Movements" (July 1956) 46 (Table 15).

[84] U.S. Tariff Commission Report, *supra* note 79, at 78.

With only four major domestic producers of jeweled-lever watches, the American industry was thus strikingly simple as compared with the large number of small producers in Switzerland. The American companies were large, vertically integrated enterprises. They produced their own parts (except for what they imported under Swiss quotas for domestic manufacture) and assembled these into complete watches. At the time of the suit, there were no companies in the United States which produced watch parts (other than cases) and watchmaking machinery for resale. The industry was capable of producing its own watchmaking machines, but because of the excessive cost of doing so, it purchased its requirements of such machines from Switzerland, when they were available for export. It initiated many technological developments in advance of the Swiss industry, including the unbreakable mainspring, balance wheels unaffected by temperature changes, electric and electronic watches, and the use of assembly line techniques in watch production.[85]

After 1954, three of the domestic jeweled-lever watch producers (Bulova, Elgin and Hamilton) and two pin-lever watch producers (General Time and U.S. Time) purchased or expanded facilities for producing watch movements in foreign countries. By 1965, Bulova had two plants in Switzerland and Elgin had one; General Time had one in Scotland; Hamilton had one in Switzerland and controlled one in Japan; and U.S. Time owned one in England, one in France, two in Scotland, and one in West Germany.[86]

D. The American Watch Tariffs

In the competitive struggle between the American and Swiss industries for the American watch market, an important factor was the American tariff. The relevant rates were imposed by paragraph 367 of the Tariff Act of 1930. These constituted one of the major problems for the Swiss industry at that time and contributed to the organization of the industrial combinations which the complaint alleged originated the unlawful "conspiracy."[87]

In 1936, however, a Reciprocal Trade Agreement between the United

---

[85] 1963 Trade Cas. ¶70,600 at 77,424 (findings 65, 67).

[86] U.S. Tariff Commission Report, "Watch Movements" (March 1965) 21.

[87] Message of the Federal Council, *supra* note 53, at 8.

States and Switzerland was concluded which provided for substantial reductions in the watch tariffs in return for reductions in Swiss tariffs on such American exports as lard, prunes and office machines.[88] Thereafter, watch movement imports from Switzerland substantially increased. In 1950, the Agreement was amended to include an "escape clause," which permitted the United States to raise tariffs where imports were causing or threatening to cause serious injury in the United States.[89] Legislative authority for such action was later provided in Section 7 of the Trade Agreements Extension Act of 1951.[90]

In February 1951, Elgin and Hamilton filed an application with the Tariff Commission for an investigation with respect to jeweled watches and watch movements containing seven or more, but not more than seventeen, jewels, and parts thereof. The application was subsequently endorsed by the trustees in reorganization of the Waltham Watch Company. An investigation was undertaken by the Commission in March as requested, but on the Commission's own motion it was extended to cover the whole range of articles dutiable under paragraph 367 of the 1930 Tariff Act. Public hearings were held in May 1951.

Based on the report of this investigation the Commission found that no serious injury or threat thereof existed by reason of importation of articles not affected by the 1936 Trade Agreement (*e.g.*, jeweled-lever watches containing more than seventeen jewels) or by reason of imports of certain other articles. However, it found with reference to reductions affected by the Trade Agreement in the duties imposed on other jeweled-lever movements that these were being imported in such increased quantities as to threaten serious injury to the domestic industries producing like or directly competitive products. In order to prevent this threat from materializing, it was found necessary that the reduced rates be increased for an indefinite period by 50%, but in no case to exceed the rates originally imposed under the 1930 Tariff Act.

This recommendation of the Tariff Commission was, however, rejected by President Truman in August 1952.[91] He noted the substantial increases in the consumption of watches since the 1936 Trade

----

[88] 49 Stat. 3927, E.A.S. No. 90 (Jan. 9, 1936).

[89] [1951] 1 U.S.T. 453, T.I.A.S. 2188 (Oct. 13, 1950).

[90] 65 Stat. 72, 74, 19 U.S.C. §§1360-67 (1964); §7 *repealed*, 76 Stat. 882 (1962).

[91] U.S. Tariff Commission Report, *supra* note 79.

Agreement and the initiatives taken by the American importers of Swiss watch movements in their merchandising. Further, he noted that domestic producers had benefited from the increased demand, that they had been employing more workers than ever before, and that their profits were at a satisfactory level. The only threat of injury which the Commission had found was based on the fact that domestic jeweled watch production had not kept pace with the expansion of imports, so that the industry enjoyed a smaller share of the larger market, and that the domestic industry had shifted from the production of watches with seventeen jewels or less to producing watches with more than seventeen jewels. In neither of these facts could he find any injury, or threat of injury, to the industry. There were, moreover, "cogent reasons of an international character" which argued against acceptance of the recommendation. The escape clauses had been included in the international tariff agreements largely because they were desired by the United States. Considerable skepticism had been expressed, however, regarding the use that might be made of them. Apprehension abroad concerning United States trade policy had been heightened by various events. He said:

> The impact which the tariff increase now proposed would have on Swiss-American relations would be extremely serious. United States imports from Switzerland in 1951 totalled only $131 million of which over 50 percent were watches. Thus, tariff action on watches would strike at Switzerland's most important export to us, affecting adversely an industry tailored in large part to the United States market and employing one out of every ten industrial workers in the country. In addition, the industry is concentrated in a part of Switzerland where there is relatively little other industry and the possibilities for transfer of employment small.[92]

Finally, he mentioned that during 1951, Swiss imports from the United States had totaled over $216 million and comprised a long and varied list of commodities, such as wheat, cotton, tobacco, automobiles, machinery, office appliances and pharmaceuticals. Exports to Switzerland were almost double our imports from them, and the Swiss market was one of the very few that remained free of restrictions against dollar imports. If in these circumstances the United States should erect new barriers against Swiss watches, we would be erecting barriers against our own exports: "More than that, we would be striking a heavy blow at our

[92] *Id.* at 79.

whole effort to increase international trade and permit friendly nations to earn their own dollars and pay their own way in the world."[93]

This action was reversed two years later, however, after a new administration had taken over. It was then found, with two Commissioners who had dissented in 1952 again dissenting, that increased imports had caused serious injury to the domestic industry. Increases in the duties by 50% for an indefinite period were again recommended, but not to exceed the 1930 Act rates. This time, President Eisenhower accepted the recommendation and the higher rates went into effect in July 1954.[94]

In his statement in October 1954 relating to the antitrust proceeding, Assistant Attorney General Barnes said that the tariff increases in July had not been coordinated with the filing of the suit in October, but were rather the result of independent determination. The two actions were nevertheless, he said, "consistent in their ultimate objectives."[95] In the antitrust complaint, it was stated that expansion of the domestic watch industry was important to the economic development and national defense of the United States.

The tariff increases did not alter the tariffs on watch movements having more than seventeen jewels; the 1930 rate of $10.75 for such movements had not been changed by the 1936 agreement. In the case of movements having more than one but not more than seventeen jewels, the 1930 tariffs were restored in many respects, and in others, the 1954 rates were set between the 1930 and 1936 agreement rates. Thus, a movement of over 1.0 but not over 1.2 inches in width paid a duty in 1930 of $1.55. This was reduced to 90¢ by the 1936 agreement. In 1954, the rate was raised to $1.35. In addition, if the movement contained more than seven jewels, but not more than seventeen, it paid a tariff of 15¢ in 1930 for each jewel in excess of seven. This per-jewel rate was decreased to 9¢ by the 1936 agreement. In 1954, it was increased to 13½¢.[96]

The increased tariffs did not stem the tide of Swiss imports. In a proceeding in December 1964 on a complaint by Elgin and Hamilton, in

[93] *Id.* at 79, 80.

[94] U.S. Tariff Commission Report, "Watches, Movements, and Parts (1954)" (May 1954).

[95] *Supra* note 7.

[96] U.S. Tariff Commission Report, "Watch Movements" (March 1965) 13, 14, 44-46 (Tables 1 and 2).

which a combination, or unfair methods of competition, having the effect of restraining or monopolizing United States trade in jeweled-lever watches, movements and parts was charged, the Tariff Commission noted that imports of all watch movements from Switzerland had increased from 9,380,000 units in 1954 to 12,123,000 in 1964. During this same period, domestic production had increased from 7,183,000 to 11,970,000. While there had thus been a greater increase in domestic production, Swiss imports had not declined, but had risen by nearly 30%. The Commission reviewed developments since the bringing of the action by the Justice Department and the changes which had taken place in the Swiss industry and in world trade, and reported to the President in June 1966 that the charges were then without foundation.[97]

III. SOME QUESTIONS RAISED

The history of the *Swiss Watch* case prompts three major questions. Similar questions are likely to appear in some form in most other antitrust cases brought by the United States or by other nations, where foreign nationals acting in foreign countries are involved: (1) What effect should have been given to the fact that the agreements under attack were largely made and carried out in Switzerland, by Swiss nationals, under arrangements which were integrated with Swiss legislation and governmental controls? (2) How should the American administrative choice to bring an antitrust action have been balanced with other considerations of American policy, including international relations and tariff policy? (3) Why were the conflicts not avoided, or dealt with, at the level of international treaties and institutions?

A. Application of American Law to Foreign Nationals for Lawful Acts Abroad

The court in the *Swiss Watch* case followed the American antitrust case law, as described in Chapters 2 to 4, and gave no weight to the fact that the case involved foreign nationals, foreign industries, foreign markets and foreign governmental approval. The issue was sharply raised by the Swiss defendants, as stated in their reply brief:

[97] U. S. Tariff Commission Report, *supra* note 47.

The fundamental issue in this complex and important case—the ultimate decision in which is bound to shape the law for years to come—is simply the applicability of the American antitrust laws: whether a United States court has power under the Sherman Act (or the Wilson Tariff Act) to penalize or control acts of Swiss nationals, in Switzerland, performed within the framework of encompassing Swiss legislation and Swiss governmental policy.

Buttressed by various findings that the defendants had intentionally restrained American domestic and foreign commerce, the court's brief opinion held the activities illegal despite the foreign elements and contacts present. The opinion seemed to misconceive the position of the defendants, for it stated that they claimed that the case was an attempt to apply American law to the "acts of sovereign governments." Agreeing that this would be a defense if proved, the court found that "the defendants' activities were not required by the laws of Switzerland," but were "agreements formulated privately without compulsion on the part of the Swiss Government," although "recognized as facts of economic and industrial life" by that government. "The fact that the Swiss Government may, as a practical matter, approve of the effects of this private activity," it said, "cannot convert what is essentially a vulnerable private conspiracy into an unassailable system resulting from foreign governmental mandate."[98]

But the Swiss defendants were not contending that their acts in every situation had been compelled by their government. Instead they were seeking to have the American antitrust process take into account the foreign political, social and economic policies and circumstances which were, to them, the fabric of the case. The court's failure to deal with these issues revealed an unwillingness to grasp and apply the flexibility which is possible under the Sherman Act. Thus, it could have heeded the admonition in *Alcoa* to have regard to "limitations customarily observed by nations upon the exercise of their powers"—a process of self-limitation now described in Section 40 of the Restatement (Second) of Foreign Relations Law of the United States (see Chapter 7 *infra*). In doing this, it might well have concluded that the Sherman Act should not be applied at all to acts performed abroad by foreign nationals when those acts are so fully integrated with foreign governmental policy and law as were the acts of the Swiss watch industry.

[98] 1963 Trade Cas. ¶70,600 at 77,456-57.

Instead, most of the particular activities involved were treated as ordinary domestic per se offenses. No factual inquiry into their reasonableness was made. Agreements which Bulova, Benrus and Gruen Ohio (American nationals) found necessary in order to obtain imports of Swiss watch parts were held illegal without balancing their adverse effects against the beneficial effects on competition resulting from the fact that some Swiss watch parts were thus enabled to enter the country. So also, Swiss refusals to supply parts and machinery were condemned without taking any account of either official policies and controls in Switzerland, or of the profound interest of the Swiss industry in preventing migration to other countries and assistance to rival industries abroad.

Similarly, the Sherman Act conspiracy concept was employed in mechanical fashion without recognizing the apparent incongruity of applying this concept to long-standing industrial charters operating abroad in accordance with foreign law and with the active participation of a foreign government. The findings of intentional restraint of American commerce, legally necessitated by the *Alcoa* doctrine applicable to conduct of foreigners abroad, were made without accounting for the fact that the Swiss system was directed primarily at Switzerland—to preserve the industry there—rather than specifically against the United States or other affected foreign countries.

In view of the extensive submissions of the Swiss Government, it is surprising that the court treated the case as one falling wholly within the domestic ambit of the Sherman Act, without regard either for principles of conflict of laws or of international law. In its opinion, it dismissed the claims of invasion of the sovereignty of the Swiss Confederation as "entirely premature," but its decree demonstrated that these fears were by no means unfounded. The subsequent modification of the decree, which deferred to the "sovereign right and power" of the Swiss Government, did give effect to the "limitations customarily observed by nations" upon their powers, but only because the State and Justice Departments and the defendants agreed that it should be done.

B. The Decision to Proceed

Even if American antitrust doctrine is fairly inflexible, the administrative decision to initiate a proceeding of this kind is a matter of governmental choice. The desire to bring the case to break up what appeared on the evidence introduced to be serious interference with the maintenance of the American domestic watch industry, is spread on the record. But it does not appear what other factors were taken into account, or whether the decision to bring the case was balanced at all with other policies and information. Specifically, it is not clear what, if any, attempt was made at the administrative level to harmonize this case with American policies in the fields of international relations and tariffs.

There may have been a lack of coordination between the Department of Justice and the State Department. The head of the Antitrust Division stated that "consultations were held with representatives of the Swiss Government for the specific purpose of clarifying the issues," and that they were advised "of the limited scope of the proposed complaint."[99] It was "carefully pointed out" to them, he said, that the suit was "not directed against operations of the Swiss watch industry in Switzerland," and that "the proposed antitrust action dealt only with practices affecting the domestic and foreign commerce of the United States."

In fact, however, the case *was* directed against operations of the Swiss watch industry in Switzerland. Even agreements made by the Swiss with the British, French and German industries were attacked because they provided for exclusive purchases from the Swiss, thus "excluding" American exports, and because they restricted exports of Swiss parts to the United States. Two of the main units of the Swiss industry were made parties defendant, and the other two (including the holding company in which the Swiss Government held the largest share) were named as "co-conspirators." The Department of Justice pressed for a stringent decree despite the pleas of Swiss Government representatives, and it was only after the Swiss Government formally intervened with the State Department that Justice receded and recommended changes to the court which the Swiss Government had long urged. The drawbacks of an adversary proceeding in the presence of conflict with a foreign government are made quite apparent by this case.

Further, actions taken by the White House on tariffs raise serious doubts about the consistency of American policies applied to foreign trade in watches. Only two years before the suit, President Truman had reported to Congress that "the weight of evidence does not support the claim that our domestic watch industry has been seriously injured, or

[99] *Supra* note 7.

that there is a threat of serious injury" from imports. Production in the United States was evidently not suffering noticeably at the time from competition with the Swiss. Since the war there had been a substantial increase in the total consumption of both domestic jeweled-lever watches and pin-lever watches. Although the domestic industry had not kept pace with the expansion of imports, President Truman found that it was "prospering by all of the customary standards of levels of production, profits, wages and employment."

Even if the evidence were strong that domestic production was shackled by the Swiss restrictions, should antitrust weapons have been employed on the theory of removing restrictions on imports at the same time that tariffs were being increased by President Eisenhower in order to stop imports? The tariff increase went into effect almost simultaneously with the filing of the suit. There was certainly some kind of lack of coordination at the administrative level in those two decisions.

C. Decisions at the International Level

At the time this suit was brought, there was in effect a treaty between the United States and Switzerland, signed in 1931, which provided that:

> Every dispute arising between the Contracting Parties, of whatever nature it may be, shall, when ordinary diplomatic procedures have failed, be submitted to arbitration or to conciliation, as the Contracting Parties may at the time decide.* * *
>
> The Contracting Parties bind themselves to submit to arbitration every difference which may have arisen or may arise between them by virtue of a claim of right which is juridical in its nature provided that it has not been possible to adjust such difference by diplomacy and it has not in fact been adjusted as a result of reference to the Permanent Commission of Conciliation. . . .[100]

Since the Swiss Government protested the suit, it is not clear why its differences with the United States were not submitted for settlement under this treaty. Or did the United States Government take the position that the difference concerned subject matter which was within its domestic jurisdiction and hence excluded by the terms of the treaty?

Perhaps this controversy was affected by the Swiss claim to the shares

---

[100] Arbitration and Conciliation Treaty with Switzerland, Feb. 16, 1931, arts. I and V, 47 Stat. 1983, T.S. No. 844 (proclaimed May 25, 1932).

of General Aniline and Film Corporation, which had been vested in the United States under the Trading with the Enemy Act and which the Swiss contended should be transferred to them pursuant to a treaty providing for the unblocking of Swiss assets in the United States. In the course of this dispute, the United States was pressed to submit it for determination by arbitration or conciliation under the 1931 treaty. Both claims were rejected by the United States and the matter was referred to the World Court in 1957. There in 1959 in the *Interhandel* case, the United States' preliminary objections were upheld on the ground that the Swiss had not exhausted their local remedies in the United States. [101]

The Swiss Government may have concluded when the *Swiss Watch* case was filed that the questions of local remedies and arbitration in the *Interhandel* case should first be presented to the World Court before any question of American antitrust jurisdiction was raised there. When it lost in *Interhandel* in 1959, it may then have decided that no choice remained but to defer taking the antitrust issues in the watch case to the World Court until a final judgment had been entered in the district court and an appeal to the Supreme Court had been concluded.

State Department testimony before a Senate subcommittee in 1966 indicates that greater efforts may be made in the future to avoid some of the problems of the *Swiss Watch* case. It was stated that we are "increasingly notifying other governments of U.S. antitrust activities affecting their interests." [102] In such notifications the problems and procedures are explained "to the extent our antitrust authorities find permissible." Meetings of the OECD Committee of Experts on Restrictive Business Practices (described in Chapter 9) provide an opportunity for discussions relating to conflicts and other controversies. In the Senate hearings, the State Department spokesman singled out the *Swiss Watch* case as an example of what could be done. He said that "consultation between the Department of Justice and representatives of a foreign government, arranged and encouraged by the Department of State, resulted in an amicable solution" of the troublesome issues involved. The Swiss Government, he continued, had felt that the Judgment "intruded on its sovereignty and adversely affected its interests." It requested a

[101] Interhandel Case, [1959] I.C.J. 6.

[102] Assistant Secretary of State Solomon, in *Hearings on International Aspects of Antitrust Before the Subcomm. on Antitrust and Monopoly of the Sen. Comm. on the Judiciary,* 89th Cong., 2d Sess., pt. 1, at 454 (1966).

conference with the Department of Justice, conversations were arranged, and these took place over a period of several months. The outcome was the modified judgment which the Swiss Government was satisfied "did not affect its sovereign rights."[103]

In future antitrust cases involving important international issues, if diplomatic negotiation does not succeed in resolving conflict, it is to be hoped that some form of impartial adjudication will be resorted to. Certainly every effort should be made to avoid disposing of such problems in domestic judicial proceedings like those of the *Swiss Watch* case, involving years of costly and acrimonious litigation.

[103] *Id.*

CHAPTER 7

The Limits Under International Law of National Jurisdiction to Regulate the Conduct of International Trade

Introduction

Extraterritorial application of antitrust laws inevitably presents conflicts and disputes. They arise not only because two or more differing sets of rules become applicable to particular conduct, but because two or more sovereign states claim jurisdiction to prescribe the governing rules. The more nations expand their foreign trade and become dependent upon its flow and balance, the greater becomes their interest in controlling and regulating that flow—or in defending established positions. Thus, conflicting regulatory measures derive largely from conflicting economic policies or interests of the countries involved. It is not surprising, therefore, that strong protests have been aroused by the application of the American antitrust laws to nationals of other countries who may not share either the objectives or the benefits of the highly regulatory features of those laws. The protests have ranged from diplomatic representations to retaliatory legislation, not to mention the flood of criticism from unofficial sources. All such protests stem from the idea that a state is sovereign within its own territory and that no foreign state may properly intervene in matters of exclusively domestic concern.

Resolution of disputes among states is a problem of international law, whether the disputes concern extraterritorial application of antitrust laws or other application of domestic (municipal) law to aliens or to conduct abroad. And resolution or avoidance of such disputes is essential to the full and free flow and development of international trade in the world today. However, not only are the existing methods and techniques for settlement of disputes in the antitrust area inadequate, but the rules to be applied are themselves the subject of dispute. To what extent may one state properly regulate trade within another state? The experts do not agree.

As a matter of its own domestic law a sovereign state's power to act within its own borders is limited only by constitutional or other self-imposed restraints. In the antitrust area those limitations in most states either do not exist or have been largely eroded through the process of increasing governmental regulation of business activities.[1] In the United States, the outer limits imposed by due process requirements on the jurisdiction of the States of the United States to regulate conduct within other States of the Union have been set by a line of cases decided by the Supreme Court.[2] That Court has not, however, in recent years considered the limits imposed on municipal jurisdiction by international law. Indeed, insofar as has been ascertained, no international

---

[1] The "reach" or "extraterritorial application" of antitrust laws, as a matter of municipal law, is considered in Chapters 2 and 3 *supra*.

[2] In the United States during recent years the constitutional and legislative limitations on municipal jurisdiction to deal with business affairs have been largely eroded. In International Shoe Co. v. Washington, 326 U.S. 310, 316 (1945) the Court stated: "[D]ue process requires only that in order to subject a defendant to a judgment *in personam,* if he be not present within the territory of the forum, he have certain minimum contacts with it such that the maintenance of the suit does not offend 'traditional notions of fair play and substantial justice.' "

In Hanson v. Denckla, 357 U.S. 235, 251 (1958), the Court added: "[I]t is a mistake to assume that this trend heralds the eventual demise of all restrictions on the personal jurisdiction of state courts. . . . Those restrictions are more than a guarantee of immunity from inconvenient or distant litigation. They are a consequence of territorial limitations on the power of the respective States. However minimal the burden of defending in a foreign tribunal, a defendant may not be called upon to do so unless he has had the 'minimal contacts' with that State that are a prerequisite to its exercise of power over him."

The contacts with the forum state required to support judicial jurisdiction under the due process clause have become minimal indeed. Examples of the trend toward expanded jurisdiction are found in the so-called "single act" and "long-arm statutes" and the revised Federal Rules of Civil Procedure. See, *e.g.,* N.Y. Civ. Prac. L. R. §§302, 313 (McKinney 1963); Notes of the Advisory Committee on Civil Rules accompanying the preliminary Draft of Proposed Amendments to Rules of Civil Procedure for the United States District Courts, 1 U.S. Code Cong. & Admin. News 1375, 1380-85, 87th Cong., 1st Sess. (1961) (Rule 4(f)). For further discussion, see Chapter 3 *supra*.

tribunal—nor even any national tribunal outside the United States—has had occasion to pass upon that question, since the *British Nylon Spinners* case in 1952.[3] The paucity of court decisions on the subject, however, has been more than offset by the enormous volume of writings by experts and others on every aspect of state jurisdiction under international law and from every point of view.[4] Notwithstanding the sharp conflicts of opinion and wide differences in national interests involved, it is the purpose of this chapter to consider what limits international law places upon a state in the application of its restrictive trade practices legislation to conduct abroad. Applicable principles of international law will be stated, as well as the pros and cons of rules that are in dispute.

I. THE ROLE OF INTERNATIONAL LAW

International law comprises those rules of law and principles that govern the relations between states, between states and international organizations, and between states and nationals of other states.[5] It is a

[3] British Nylon Spinners, Ltd. v. Imperial Chem. Indus., Ltd., [1953] Ch. 19 (C.A.) (interlocutory appeal).

[4] See Bibliographies, INT'L LAW ASS'N, REPORT OF THE FIFTY-FIRST CONFERENCE (TOKYO) (1964) [hereinafter referred to as TOKYO REPORT] 483-91 (Annex B, covering Continental European materials), 492-510 (Annex C, covering Anglo-American materials).

[5] "International law is the standard of conduct, at a given time, for states and other entities subject thereto. It comprises the rights, privileges, powers, and immunities of states and entities invoking its provisions, as well as the correlative fundamental duties, absence of rights, liabilities and disabilities." 1 WHITEMAN, DIGEST OF INTERNATIONAL LAW 1 (1963).

"International law has been defined as those rules for international conduct which have met general acceptance among the community of nations. It reflects and records those accommodations which, over centuries, states have found it in their interest to make. It rests upon the common consent of civilized communities. It is not to be found in any code. It is made up of precedent, judicial decisions, treaties, arbitrations, international conventions, the opinions of learned writers in the field, and a myriad of other acts and things, which represent in the aggregate those rules which enlightened nations and their people accept as being appropriate to govern international conduct. It is constantly changing, and expanding, as modern science shrinks the world and brings its peoples into ever closer contact. . . ." Phleger, *Some Recent Developments in International Law of Interest to the United States,* 30 DEP'T STATE BULL. 196 (1954).

system of jurisprudence that impedes encroachments in international affairs and induces self-restraint by states. It derives from the customs, practices and other precedents generally accepted by nations in their dealings one with the other (customary or general international law), and the treaties and conventions from time to time negotiated between and among states (conventional international law).[6] It is the only law generally accepted as applicable in dealings among nations and thus regulates a vast flow of international commerce and innumerable transnational affairs. It is not only the law applied by international tribunals, but in some states, as in the United States, it is also the "law of the land,"[7] to be applied, or respected, by national courts when relevant to a controversy involving an alien or a foreign government.

[6] Article 38 of the Statute of the International Court of Justice provides:

"1. The Court, whose function is to decide in accordance with international law such disputes as are submitted to it, shall apply:

   (a) international conventions, whether general or particular, establishing rules expressly recognized by the contesting states;
   (b) international custom, as evidence of a general practice accepted as law;
   (c) the general principles of law recognized by civilized nations;
   (d) subject to the provisions of Article 59, judicial decisions and teachings of the most highly qualified publicists of the various nations, as subsidiary means for the determination of rules of law.

2. This provision shall not prejudice the power of the court to decide a case *ex aequo et bono,* if the parties agree thereto."

[7] Following the English tradition, it has been accepted generally that customary international law is a part of the law to be applied by United States courts. The position was unequivocal in *The Paquete Habana* in 1900, when the Supreme Court stated: "International law is part of our law, and must be ascertained and administered by the courts of justice of appropriate jurisdiction, as often as questions of right depending upon it are duly presented for their determination." 175 U.S. 677, 700. That is not to say, of course, that in national courts international law does not yield to domestic law; it does indeed, as in the case of an Act of Congress clearly inconsistent with it. See The Over the Top, 5 F.2d 838, 842 (D. Conn. 1925); Sprout, *Theories as to the Applicability of International Law in the Federal Courts of the United States,* 26(1) AM. J. INT'L L. 280 (1932); Dickinson, *The Law of Nations as Part of the National Law of the United States,* 101 U. PA. L. REV. 26, 792 (1952, 1953); ERADES & GOULD, THE RELATION BETWEEN INTER-NATIONAL LAW AND MUNICIPAL LAW IN THE NETHERLANDS AND IN THE UNITED STATES (1961). *Cf.* Banco Nacional de Cuba v. Sabbatino, 376 U.S. 398 (1964) wherein the Court refused to apply international law, invoking a "principle of decision" (the "act of state doctrine") to remove the issue from its judicial competence. The Court did, however, note: "[I]t is, of course, true that United

Within its own territory a state is virtually supreme, and international law places few restraints upon the exercise of its authority. Absent a treaty of limitation, a state may admit or expel aliens at pleasure; it may, within limits, discriminate against aliens, prohibiting their ownership of land or their participation in businesses or other activities; it may admit, tax or exclude imports; it may prohibit exports or attach conditions on the use or destination of exported goods; and it may order compliance by aliens with substantially all rules and procedures imposed upon its own nationals. Under international law, however, a state is required to conform to certain minimum standards of conduct toward aliens regardless of how it treats its own nationals.[8]

The great deference accorded a state with respect to its conduct within its own territory is a recognition of the exclusiveness of a state's own sovereignty. Similarly, any infraction of a state's sovereignty by another state, or assumption or usurpation of extraterritorial authority, without permission of the affected state, not only provokes domestic outrage but may also constitute a breach of international law. Thus, in large measure, international law resolves into mutual restraints and

---

States courts apply international law as a part of our own in appropriate circumstances. . . ." *Id.* at 423. See also Burdell v. Canadian Pacific Airlines, Ltd., No. 66 L 10799 (Circuit Court, Cook County, Ill., Nov. 7, 1968), reproduced in 8 INT'L LEGAL MATERIALS 83 (1969), in which the court held that "the venue provisions and damage limitation provisions of the Warsaw Convention Treaty are unconstitutional, as applied to this case; that such provisions deny to the plaintiffs due process and equal protection of law guaranteed to them by their Constitution." *Id.* at 107.

[8] "(1) Conduct attributable to a state and causing injury to an alien is wrongful under international law if it

    (a) departs from the international standard of justice, or

    (b) constitutes a violation of an international agreement.

(2) The international standard of justice specified . . . is the standard required for the treatment of aliens by

    (a) the applicable principles of international law as established by inter-
        national custom, judicial and arbitral decisions, and other recognized
        sources or, in the absence of such applicable principles,

    (b) analogous principles of justice generally recognized by states that have
        reasonably developed legal systems."

RESTATEMENT (SECOND) OF FOREIGN RELATIONS LAW OF THE UNITED STATES §165 (1965) [hereinafter referred to as RESTATEMENT].

Not all states subscribe to the above rule. Some maintain that an alien is not entitled to a higher standard of justice than a national.

accommodations among nations by which they live and let live according to their own respective forms and standards. In the main, the restraints are effective, notwithstanding the absence of an international court having unrestricted compulsory jurisdiction,[9] because nations and people normally prefer to abide by generally accepted rules of conduct. Fortunately, mutual self-interest, if not morality, brings about an accommodation or settlement of conflicts in most cases.

The development of customary international law is at best a slow evolution, a process of achieving a "consensus" among nations establishing a course of conduct that most will follow. Such a process is obviously inadequate to meet the enormous demands and conflicting forces of a world that within half a century has emerged from steam to atomic power, has gone from ship lanes to airways and from cables to satellites with instantaneous worldwide communication—hence the flood of treaties and multinational conventions to meet the onrush of present-day problems and business complexities.[10] Absent a treaty, however, and until states can reach agreement to establish conventional international

[9] By the Connally Amendment's reservation to United States acceptance of the compulsory jurisdiction of the International Court of Justice, the United States retained the right to self-judge whether the matter in issue is "essentially within the domestic jurisdiction of the United States" and therefore not within the jurisdiction of the Court. The reservation also gives reciprocal rights to other nations vis-à-vis the United States. See United States Declaration, signed Aug. 14, 1946, 15 DEP'T STATE BULL. 452 (1946). The result of this Amendment is that the United States need not submit to the International Court for determination of important questions of international law in disputes to which it is a party. See note 123 *infra.*

[10] See, *e.g.,*: the Convention for the Unification of Certain Rules Relating to International Transportation by Air; the Convention on Fishing and Conservation of Living Resources on the High Seas; the Convention on the Settlement of Investment Disputes between States and Nationals of Other States; the General Agreement of the International Monetary Fund; the General Agreement on Tariffs and Trade; the Geneva Convention on the Continental Shelf; the General Inter-American Convention for Trademark and Commercial Protection; the Convention on the Intergovernmental Maritime Consultative Organization; the International Consultative Convention for the Protection of Industrial Property (Paris Union Convention); the Restrictive Business Practices Draft Convention; and the numerous bilateral treaties of friendship, commerce and navigation, listed in the publication of the Department of State, Office of the Legal Adviser, Treaty Affairs Staff, entitled TREATIES IN FORCE (1969) (Publication No. 8432). See generally, EBB, REGULATION AND PROTECTION OF INTERNATIONAL BUSINESS (1964); STEIN & HAY, LAW AND INSTITUTIONS IN THE ATLANTIC AREA (1967).

law,[11] customary international law provides the only restraint upon the conduct of nations in the area of our present concern.

II. JURISDICTION

Under international law the competence of a state to prescribe or enforce rules of law is measured by its "jurisdiction."[12] Thus, if a state acts with respect to persons, things or events beyond the scope of its jurisdiction, the act, as a matter of international law, is not only a nullity and may be ignored, but any state injured thereby (or having nationals so

[11]Except for the work of the European Communities, efforts to achieve agreement among nations in the area of antitrust and restrictive trade practices have been singularly unsuccessful. See Chapters 8 and 9.

[12] "'Jurisdiction' . . . means the capacity of a state under international law to prescribe or to enforce a rule of law." RESTATEMENT §6. "A state does not have jurisdiction to enforce a rule of law prescribed by it unless it has jurisdiction to prescribe the rule." *Id.* §7(2).

The concept of jurisdiction under international law comprises two basic elements: (1) prescriptive or legislative jurisdiction and (2) enforcement jurisdiction. Judicial jurisdiction may be either prescriptive or enforcement depending on its function. However, the "problem of jurisdiction only arises *in matters not exclusively of domestic concern.* . . . It is only when there is some foreign element, when the State purports to affect or reach persons of foreign nationality, domicile or residence or facts which happen abroad that the problem of international law, whether public or private and, in particular, the problem of international jurisdiction makes its appearance." Mann, *The Doctrine of Jurisdiction in International Law,* 111 HAGUE ACADEMY RECUEIL DES COURS 1, 14 (1964) (emphasis added).

"Jurisdiction" under international law is not coterminous with "jurisdiction" under municipal law. For the purpose of the domestic rules of conflict of laws, "jurisdiction" is concerned with the contacts which a state must have with a person, thing or occurrence in order to affect legal interests. In the United States the rules are dictated by the due process and full faith and credit clauses of the Constitution. Thus, as a matter of United States municipal law, jurisdiction is defined as the power of a state to "create or affect legal interests" which it may do "whenever its contacts with a person, thing or occurrence are sufficient to make such action reasonable." RESTATEMENT (SECOND) OF CONFLICT OF LAWS §42(1) (Tent. Draft No. 3, 1956).

On the other hand, under international law "jurisdiction" is concerned with the competence of the state prescribing the rule or asserting jurisdiction, not solely with the recognition that should be given to the prescription or action in the courts of another state.

injured) has a claim for redress. The limits of a state's jurisdiction under international law are not, generally speaking, laid down by any charter or convention, but are established by the customs and practices generally accepted by states. Views of states (and of authorities within states) differ, however, as to limits of permissible jurisdiction according to the political or economic ends to be served. Thus lesser states may well cherish the sanctity of their territorial integrity with a fervor not shared by larger or more aggressive powers fully able to fend for themselves.

The authority of a state to exert its will on others finds its ultimate limit in notions of sovereignty, not only of the acting state, but also of those states which would be affected by an act in excess of jurisdiction. In one sense, "jurisdiction" is a measure of the *limits* within which one state may prescribe and enforce rules of law without violating or infringing the sovereignty of another state. In a more positive sense, jurisdiction is a "manifestation of state sovereignty," an expression of the inherent power to govern.[13]

The principal basis of jurisdiction is, of course, territorial and, as noted, in the absence of a treaty of limitation a state has practically complete and exclusive authority over persons, things and events within its borders.[14] This principle is "everywhere regarded as of primary

[13] "Jurisdiction is a manifestation of State sovereignty; and the classical function and purpose of traditional international law has, after all, been to set limits to the lawful exercise of State power, to the end that Sovereign States might live together without strife." Jennings, *The Limits of State Jurisdiction*, 32 NORDISK TIDSKRIFT FOR INTERNATIONAL RET 209 (1962).

[14] "Probably the most basic and ubiquitous function of international law is to prevent or minimize friction between states by delimiting the sphere of their authority. Where does the authority of one state end and that of another state begin? In the absence of a commonly accepted answer to this question, officials of two or more states might attempt to exercise their powers at the same place and time. The consequent confusion and conflicts not only would give rise to friction and breaches of the peace between otherwise friendly states, but would impose additional and probably prohibitive risks on economic and other private activity. The universally accepted principle that with some exceptions a state has the exclusive right to exercise governmental authority within its territory and that consequently the officials of one state may not exercise such authority within the territory of another state without the consent of the latter thus serves to facilitate private activities as well as friendly relations between states." LISSITZYN, INTERNATIONAL LAW TODAY AND TOMORROW 13 (1965).

importance and of fundamental character."[15] Qualifications and exceptions to absolute, exclusive territorial jurisdiction have been developed over the years, however, to meet the needs of the international community. Under these exceptions a state may support its claim to jurisdiction on the "nationality principle" over persons who are its nationals wherever they might be; on the "protective principle" with respect to acts threatening the state's security (*e.g.,* counterfeiting or falsification of official documents); on the "universality principle" dealing with acts so contrary to international public policy that any state may punish them (*e.g.,* piracy); or on the "passive personality principle" concerning acts abroad harmful to nationals of the claimant state. These "permissive rules" for extraterritorial applications of municipal law are discussed more fully below. As will be seen, they are not uniformly accepted.

A. Territorial Principle of Jurisdiction

The principle of exclusiveness of territorial jurisdiction under international law was read, early and emphatically, into American law by Chief Justice John Marshall. In *The Schooner Exchange v. McFaddon* he wrote:

> The jurisdiction of the nation within its own territory is necessarily exclusive and absolute. It is susceptible of no limitation not imposed by itself. Any restriction upon it, deriving validity from an external source, would imply a diminution of its sovereignty to the extent of the restriction, and an investment of that sovereignty to the same extent in that power which could impose such restriction.
>
> All exceptions, therefore, to the full and complete power of a nation within its own territories, must be traced up to the consent of the nation itself. They can flow from no other legitimate source.
>
> This consent may be either express or implied. . . .
>
> The world being composed of distinct sovereignties, possessing equal rights and equal independence, whose mutual benefit is promoted by intercourse with each other, and by an interchange of those good offices which humanity dictates and its wants require, all sovereigns have consented to a relaxation in practice, in cases under certain peculiar circumstances, of that absolute and complete jurisdiction within their respective territories which sovereignty confers.

[15] Research in International Law under the Auspices of The Faculty of the Harvard Law School, *Draft Convention on Jurisdiction with Respect to Crime,* 29 AM. J. INT'L L. (SUPP.) 435, 445 (1935) [hereinafter cited as *Harvard Draft*].

This consent may, in some instances, be tested by common usage, and by common opinion, growing out of that usage.[16]

Marshall's opinion, when written, was consistent not only with the established principles of international law, but with the basic political philosophy of American statesmen and jurists of the time. The United States was then an "emerging nation," most zealous in defending its sovereignty and jurisdiction against encroachments by the established powers.[17]

Although the traditional concept of the territorial principle of jurisdiction has been eroded in the United States over the years, at least as a matter of municipal law, a broad consensus elsewhere adheres to that concept.[18] A report submitted at the Tokyo Conference of the International Law Association (1964) stated:

> A State possesses exclusive jurisdiction over a defined territory, including the persons within that territory. International law recognizes that supreme control of the territory and accepts the exclusive jurisdiction of a State over its territory as the first and basic principle of jurisdiction under international law. As a corollary to such territorial jurisdiction, international law recognizes the right of a State to be free from intervention by other States in its territory and subjects any intervening State to liability to the injured State, except in cases where a State's sovereignty is limited by treaty or by customary principles well established by international law (permissive rules).[19]

---

[16] 11 U.S. (7 Cranch) 116, 136 (1812). Despite the broad language quoted above, however, the Court in fact held that the jurisdiction of the United States to hear a claim of title to a foreign warship is limited by the customary international law of "sovereign immunity."

[17] Almost a century after *The Schooner Exchange*, Mr. Justice Holmes commented: "[T]he general and almost universal rule is that the character of an act as lawful or unlawful must be determined wholly by the law of the country where the act is done. . . . For another jurisdiction, if it should happen to lay hold of the actor, to treat him according to its own notions rather than those of the place where he did the acts, not only would be unjust, but would be an interference with the authority of another sovereign, contrary to the comity of nations, which the other state concerned justly might resent. . . .

"The foregoing considerations would lead in case of doubt to a construction of any statute as intended to be confined in its operation and effect to the territorial limits over which the lawmaker has general and legitimate power. . . ." American Banana Co. v. United Fruit Co., 213 U.S. 347, 356-57 (1909).

[18] See discussion *infra* under "Jurisdiction Based on Territorial Effects."

[19] TOKYO REPORT 362 (Dr. A. Riedweg, Rapporteur).

In the famous *Lotus* case, the Permanent Court of International Justice stated the principle as follows:

> The first and foremost restriction imposed by international law upon a State is that—failing the existence of a permissive rule to the contrary—it may not exercise its power in any form in the territory of another State. In this sense jurisdiction is certainly territorial; it cannot be exercised by a State outside its territory except by virtue of a permissive rule derived from international custom or from a convention.[20]

The doctrine of exclusive territorial jurisdiction is most vigorous in the domain of public law. In private controversies between citizens of different states, questions of jurisdiction relate principally to the fairness of subjecting a party to the authority of the court.[21] The presence of foreign elements in the case will be reflected in the application of the forum's "choice of law" rules to select either the local law or the law of a foreign state as the more appropriate law to be applied in the resolution of all or part of the controversy, or in the application of the rule of "forum non conveniens" under which the forum will decline jurisdiction altogether. In cases involving public regulatory laws, and especially in penal cases, the only law which will be applied is that of the forum. The courts of one state will not enforce the penal laws of another state,[22] and there is no rule of "forum non conveniens." The

---

[20] Case of the S.S. "Lotus," [1927] P.C.I.J., ser. A, No. 10, at 18-19).

[21] See notes 2 and 12 *supra.*

[22] "There is no principle better settled than that the penal laws of a country have no extraterritorial force. Each state may, it is true, provide for the punishment of its own citizens for acts committed by them outside of its territory. . . .To say, however, that the penal laws of a country can bind foreigners and regulate their conduct, either in their own or in any other foreign country, is to assert a jurisdiction over such countries and to impair their independence. . . . There being then no principle of international law which justifies such a pretension, any assertion of it must rest, as an exception to the rule, either upon the general concurrence of nations or upon express conventions." Instructions of Secretary of State Bayard to the American chargé in Mexico, Nov. 1, 1887, in connection with the so-called *Cutting* incident, 2 MOORE, A DIGEST OF INTERNATIONAL LAW 236 (1906). In that incident, an American citizen was prosecuted and convicted in a Mexican court of libel against a Mexican national, although the alleged defamatory remarks had been printed exclusively in a newspaper published in El Paso, Texas. The prosecution was based on a part of the Mexican Penal Code which provided that "penal offenses committed in a foreign country by a Mexican against Mexicans or foreigners, or by a foreigner against Mexicans, may be punished in the Republic." The defendant, Cutting, was

jurisdictional issue, therefore, concerns the propriety of subjecting the parties to the state's own conception of public order, and of exacting penalties for its violation. Restrictive trade practice laws frequently contain penal provisions, as do the United States Sherman Act and the antitrust provisions of the Wilson Tariff Act.[23]

1. OBJECTIVE TERRITORIALITY

The territorial principle of jurisdiction is not so rigid as to require that all acts constituting a crime occur within the prescribing state's territory. Yet, by hypothesis, it may be said that to support jurisdiction based on territorial sovereignty, some acts or events constituting an essential element of the offense must have occurred within the territory. On the other hand, the mere fact that conduct takes place outside the territory does not bar a state from dealing with it. In the classical textbook example: *X* in State *A* shoots *Y* in State *B*; State *B* has jurisdiction to prosecute and punish for the crime commenced in State *A* but consummated in State *B*.[24] As stated in the Tokyo Report:

> As far as the territoriality principle is concerned, it must immediately be recorded that the concept of territoriality has been expanded in case law to

eventually released after the incident had provoked strong protest from the United States Government.

[23] Section 1 of the Sherman Act provides: "Every contract, combination in the form of trust or otherwise, or conspiracy, in restraint of trade or commerce among the several States, or with foreign nations, is hereby declared to be illegal * * * Every person who shall make any [such] contract or engage in any [such] combination or conspiracy . . . shall be deemed guilty of a misdemeanor. . . ." 15 U.S.C. §1 (1964). Violations of the Sherman Act are thus crimes, and may be prosecuted as such for fines and imprisonment; the Government may bring a civil action for equitable relief as an alternative, or it may use both actions. Damage suits, in which damages are trebled where the plaintiff is a private person, may be brought by injured parties. The antitrust prohibitions of the Clayton and Federal Trade Commission Acts are enforced only by civil or administrative proceedings. Most of the American antitrust cases with extraterritorial features have been civil suits under the Sherman Act; see Chapter 2 *supra*.

For a definition of crime for the purposes of international law, see *Harvard Draft* art. 1(c) and Comment at 469-70.

[24] "The setting in motion outside of a State of a force which produces as a direct consequence an injurious effect therein, justifies the territorial sovereign in prosecuting the actor when he enters its domain." 1 HYDE, INTERNATIONAL LAW 798 (2d rev. ed. 1945).

mean "objective territoriality"; that is to say, when part of a criminal act has taken place on the territory of a State, that State is deemed to have jurisdiction over the whole of the criminal act. This objective territoriality doctrine comes particularly into play in the case of delicts which are not completed until an effect has occurred. It is obvious that too broad an interpretation of the objective territoriality principle could ultimately lead to the assumption of jurisdiction by a State over acts committed outside its territory but of which a very remote effect might be felt within its territory. This would then no longer be a matter of territorial application of law, even allowing for a broad interpretation of "territory," but would mean that the objective territoriality principle had led to extra-territorial application of law.[25]

The Harvard Draft provides in Article 3:

A State has jurisdiction with respect to any crime committed in whole or in part within its territory.
This jurisdiction extends to
(a) Any participation outside its territory in a crime committed in whole or in part within its territory;
(b) Any attempt outside its territory to commit a crime in whole or in part within its territory.

The commentary to Article 3 states:

The modern formula, incorporated in this article, recognizes that there is territorial jurisdiction of any crime which is committed in whole or in part within the territory. A crime is committed "in whole" within the territory when every essential constituent element is consummated within the territory; it is committed "in part" within the territory when any essential constituent element is consummated there. If it is committed either "in whole or in part" within the territory, there is territorial jurisdiction.[26]

The thrust of the Harvard Draft and of the Tokyo Report is that to support jurisdiction as objectively territorial some *"essential constituent element"* of the criminal conduct must have occurred within the territory.[27] An "essential constituent element" is something necessary to

---

[25] TOKYO REPORT 369.

[26] *Harvard Draft* at 495.

[27] "Generally accepted and often applied is the objective territorial principle, according to which jurisdiction is founded when any essential constituent element of a crime is consummated on state territory." BROWNLIE, PRINCIPLES OF PUBLIC INTERNATIONAL LAW 263 (1966).

"In order to justify the criminal prosecution by a State of an alien on account of an act committed and consummated by him in a place outside of its territory or of

the completion of the crime, *i.e.*, without which the crime would not be legally proscribed. Mere consequential or remote effects within the territory which are not themselves essential ingredients of the offense are not determinative.

In the *Lotus* case, the Permanent Court of International Justice considered at length the scope and application of the objective territorial principle of criminal jurisdiction.[28] The case has become a classic and is perhaps the major authority on fundamental aspects of criminal jurisdiction under international law. A French vessel, *Lotus,* collided with and sank a Turkish vessel, *Boz-Kourt,* on the high seas, drowning a number of persons on board the Turkish ship. Turkey instituted criminal proceedings against the officer of the watch on the *Lotus* under a law providing for punishment of any foreigner who "commits an offense abroad to the prejudice of Turkey or of a Turkish subject." The officer was convicted, and France raised the contention in the Permanent Court of International Justice that principles of international law prevented such criminal proceedings. Although Turkey had prosecuted the French officer under a law based on the nationality of the victims, rather than on the theory that the offense had been committed on Turkish territory, a majority of the Court sustained Turkey's right to proceed on the basis of the territorial principle, stating that

> the courts of many countries, even of countries which have given their criminal legislation a strictly territorial character, interpret criminal law in the sense that offences, the authors of which at the moment of commission are in the territory of another State, are nevertheless to be regarded as having been committed in the national territory, if one of the constituent elements of the offence, and more especially its effects have taken place there.[29]

a place fairly to be assimilated thereto, such as one of its own vessels on the high seas, it needs to be established that there is a close and definite connection between that act and the prosecutor, and one which is commonly acknowledged to excuse the exercise of jurisdiction. There are few situations where the requisite connection is deemed to exist." 1 HYDE, *supra* note 24, at 804. In support of the last sentence Hyde cites Mr. Justice Story in *The Apollon,* 22 U.S. (9 Wheat.) 362, 370 (1824): "The laws of no nation can justly extend beyond its own territories, except so far as regards its own citizens. They can have no force to control the sovereignty or rights of any other nation, within its own jurisdiction. And however general and comprehensive the phrases used in municipal laws may be, they must always be restricted in construction, to places and persons, upon whom the Legislature have authority and jurisdiction."

[28] Case of the S.S. "Lotus," [1927] P.C.I.J., ser. A, No. 10.
[29] *Id.* at 23.

and that

> the offence produced its effects on the Turkish vessel and consequently in a place assimilated to Turkish territory in which the application of Turkish criminal law cannot be challenged, even in regard to offences committed there by foreigners.[30]

The decision predicating Turkey's jurisdiction on an assimilation of the Turkish vessel to Turkish territory has been severely criticized and superseded by treaty.[31] The reasoning of the Court, however, in finding jurisdiction "if one of the constituent elements of the offense, and more especially its effects have taken place" in the national territory, has been the occasion for, if not the source of, a controversy of profound significance concerning jurisdiction under international law. Unfortunately, the Court failed to explain precisely what could be included within the "effects" of an offense as a basis for "territorial" jurisdiction. The Court noted, however, that in the context in which it was speaking it did not know of any cases "in which governments have protested against the fact that the criminal law of some country contained a rule to this effect or that the courts of a country construed their criminal law in this sense."[32]

Apart from the relatively recent cases involving application of the United States antitrust laws, judicial decisions both prior to and following *Lotus* have been largely limited to situations involving a sharply defined effect of a concrete nature, such as homicide, fraud, smuggling or entry of goods or carriers. In these cases, the jurisdictional "effect" has clearly been an essential ingredient of the crime without which the offense would not have occurred.

It is important to distinguish between effects which are "essential constituent elements" of criminal conduct and those which are not. Logically, it cannot be said that a crime has been committed "in part"

---

[30] *Id.*

[31] See, *e.g.*, Mann, *supra* note 12, at 33-36. Article 11 of the Convention on the High Seas of April 29, 1958, supersedes the holding in the *Lotus* case regarding the territorial status of the vessel. It provides that no criminal or disciplinary proceedings may be instituted against the master or other persons in the service of a ship, in any case involving a collision or other incident of navigation on the high seas, except before the judicial or administrative authorities either of the flag state or of the state of which such person is a national. See RESTATEMENT §30, Reporters' Note at 89.

[32] [1927] P.C.I.J., ser. A, No. 10, at 23.

within the territory unless something occurred there or conduct abroad "took effect" therein. The *Lotus* court presumably had no intention of departing from the traditional approach; on the facts of the case, the "effects" in question were the direct and immediate result of the impact on the Turkish ship (which was deemed to be Turkish territory) of a physical force (the French ship) set in motion outside Turkish territory, and the death of persons aboard the Turkish ship was an "essential constituent element" of the alleged crime.

As Professor Jennings has stated:

> The majority judgment in the *Lotus* case, which was decided on the objective test of territoriality, says that many countries regard offences as having been committed in their national territory "if one of the constituent elements of the offence, and more especially its effects, have taken place there."[33] Later in the judgment it is made clear that by "effects" is here meant those effects which are a constituent element in the crime, for the court says the negligence on the French ship and the effect felt on the Turkish ship were "legally and entirely inseparable, so much so that their separation renders the offence non-existent"[34].[35]

Strassheim v. Daily[36] is probably the leading American case to consider the problem in other than an antitrust context. As in the *Lotus* case, the Court's statement of the rule in *Strassheim* (per Mr. Justice Holmes), taken alone and broadly construed, could support jurisdiction in a wide variety of situations:

> Acts done outside a jurisdiction, but intended to produce and producing detrimental effects within it, justify a State in punishing the cause of the harm as if he had been present at the effect, if the State should succeed in getting him within its power.[37]

[33] *Id.*

[34] *Id.* at 30.

[35] Jennings, *Extraterritorial Jurisdiction and the United States Antitrust Laws*, 33 BRIT. Y.B. INT'L L. 146, 159-60 (1957).

[36] 221 U.S. 280 (1911).

[37] *Id.* at 285. Judge John Bassett Moore in his dissent in *Lotus* stated the principle of "constructive presence," as follows: "[I]t appears to be now universally admitted that, where a crime is committed in the territorial jurisdiction of one State as the direct result of the act of a person at the time corporeally present in another State, international law, by reason of the principle of constructive presence of the offender at the place where his act took effect, does not forbid the prosecution of the offender by the former State, should he come within its territorial jurisdiction." [1927] P.C.I.J., ser. A, No. 10, at 73.

Thus, the test suggested is "intent" and production of "detrimental effects . . . as if he had been present at the effect"—so-called constructive presence.[38] But the facts, involving bribery of an official of the State of Michigan and obtaining money from Michigan under false pretenses, indicate that an extension of the jurisdictional base was unnecessary, since as the Court pointed out, "material steps" in the scheme were taken in the forum state.[39]

While *Strassheim* dealt with the question of jurisdiction as between two states of the United States, it is frequently cited as authority for the objective territorial principle of jurisdiction in international contexts.[40] Following *Strassheim,* in *Ford v. United States,*[41] the Supreme Court applied the principle to give the United States jurisdiction where the crime was "carried on partly in and partly outside this country."[42] Canadian nationals had been arrested on a British vessel outside the three-mile limit of the United States and charged with conspiracy to violate the prohibition and revenue laws of the United States. Although defendants had at all times during the alleged conspiracy been physically outside the United States, personal jurisdiction over them for purposes of their arrest was upheld on the basis of a treaty with Great Britain providing for the seizure of vessels suspected of engaging in smuggling alcoholic beverages into the United States.[43] Defendants argued,

[38] 221 U.S. at 285.

[39] Defendant was present in Michigan on several occasions during the negotiations leading up to the criminal act itself, although he was absent at the time the crime was completed. In the Court's opinion, however, "[t]he criminal need not do within the State every act necessary to complete the crime. If he does there an overt act which is and is intended to be a material step toward accomplishing the crime, and then absents himself from the State and does the rest elsewhere, he becomes a fugitive from justice, when the crime is complete, if not before. . . . [I]n this case offering the bid and receiving the acceptance were material steps in the scheme, they were taken in Michigan, and they were established in their character of guilty acts when the plot was carried to the end. . . ." *Id.* at 285.

[40] See, *e.g.,* United States v. Pizzarusso, 388 F.2d 8, 10-11 (2d Cir. 1968).

[41] 273 U.S. 593 (1927).

[42] *Id.* at 624.

[43] Convention with Great Britain on the Prevention of Smuggling of Intoxicating Liquors, Jan. 23, 1924, 43 Stat. 1761 (1924), T.S. No. 685 (effective May 22, 1944). The Court concluded that: "The treaty did not change the territorial jurisdiction of the United States to try offenses against the importation laws. That remained exactly as it was. . . . If the persons on board could not have been convicted before the treaty, they can not be convicted now." 273 U.S. at 610.

however, that even if subject to the jurisdiction of the court under the treaty, they had committed no offense against the United States, since "they were corporeally at all times during the alleged conspiracy out of the jurisdiction of the United States." The Court rejected this argument on the ground that overt acts necessary to the offense were committed within the jurisdiction of the United States, and the conspiracy was intended to be and was partly carried out in the United States.[44] The Court relied on John Bassett Moore's opinion as Assistant Secretary of State in connection with the *Cutting* incident:

> The principle that a man who outside of a country wilfully puts in motion a force to take effect in it is answerable at the place where the evil is done, is recognized in the criminal jurisprudence of all countries. And the methods which modern invention has furnished for the performance of criminal acts in that manner has made this principle one of constantly growing importance and of increasing frequency of application.[45]

More recently, in *Armement Deppe, S.A. v. United States,*[46] the Court of Appeals for the Fifth Circuit held that foreign-flag shipping lines are subject to the provisions of Section 14b of the Shipping Act of 1916,[47] prohibiting certain so-called dual-rate contracts covering transportation in foreign commerce to American ports. It was contended that, notwithstanding that the contracts covered the shipment of goods into the United States, the latter did not have jurisdiction to legislate with respect to the terms in question because they were entered into abroad between foreign shippers and foreign carriers. The court had "no difficulty" in holding, however, that Congress has authority to regulate such contracts,

> inasmuch as the contracts are to be used, employed, and carried out in American foreign commerce in the delivery of goods to American ports. Consummation of the contracts is, therefore, by acts which are ultimately performed in the United States—thus making them subject to the laws of this nation. The only logical conclusion fairly to be reached is that foreign-owned ships which use our American ports must comply with the laws of the United States in connection with shipping contracts . . . [covering goods brought into the United States].[48]

[44] *Id.* at 624.
[45] *Id.* at 622-23; see MOORE, *supra* note 22, at 244.
[46] 399 F.2d 794 (5th Cir. 1968).
[47] 46 U.S.C. §813(a) (1964).
[48] 399 F.2d at 798-99.

In summary, there is general agreement among the authorities that under the objective territorial principle State *B* has jurisdiction to prosecute and punish for a crime effectuated within its borders as a result of a force put in motion in State *A*, where there is some sort of "physical intrusion" into the territory of State *B*. Extensions of the principle to jurisdiction based on effects alone, however, are not uniformly accepted and have prompted wide differences of opinion and strong protests, as hereinafter noted.

2. JURISDICTION BASED ON TERRITORIAL EFFECTS

The step from "acts" (partly in and partly outside the territory) to economic "effects" within the territory (unaccompanied by "acts" within the territory) as a jurisdictional base was taken for the United States in the *Alcoa* case in 1945.[49] While the step may have been presaged by earlier decisions,[50] *Alcoa* was the first antitrust case to assert jurisdiction over acts abroad solely on the ground that those acts produced "economic" effects within the United States. In all prior United States antitrust cases, some act essential to effectuate the restraint had taken place within the country and the defendants included United States corporations.

In *Alcoa,* Judge Learned Hand construed the American antitrust laws as proscribing restrictive agreements wherever entered into or consummated, "if they were intended to affect imports [into the United States] and did affect them,"[51] notwithstanding the fact that no American party was involved in this phase of the case and no act took place in the United States. He wrote:[52]

[W]e are concerned only with whether Congress chose to attach liability to the conduct outside the United States of persons not in allegiance to it. That being so, the only question open is whether Congress intended to impose the liability, and whether our own Constitution permitted it to do so: as a court of the United States, we cannot look beyond our own law. Nevertheless, it is quite true that we are not to read general words, such as those in this Act, without regard to the limitations customarily observed by nations upon the

[49] United States v. Aluminum Co. of America, 148 F.2d 416 (2d Cir. 1945) (on certification and transfer from the United States Supreme Court for failure of a quorum of qualified justices).

[50] See cases prior to *Alcoa* discussed in Chapters 2 and 3 *supra.*

[51] 148 F.2d at 444.

[52] *Id.* at 443-44 (emphasis added in quotation following in text).

exercise of their powers; limitations which generally correspond to those fixed by the "Conflict of Laws." We should not impute to Congress an intent to punish all whom its courts can catch, for conduct which has no consequences within the United States. American Banana Co. v. United Fruit Co., 213 U.S. 347, 357 * * *; United States v. Bowman, 260 U.S. 94, 98 * * *; Blackmer v. United States, 284 U.S. 421, 437 * * *; *on the other hand, it is settled law—as "Limited" itself agrees [*53*]—that any state may impose liabilities, even upon*

[continued on next page]

53 Aluminium Limited did, indeed, make broad and sweeping concessions as to the extraterritorial application of the United States antitrust laws to acts abroad which produced "a direct and important effect" in the United States. It argued, however, that no such effect had been proved. Relevant portions of "Limited's" briefs before the District Court and before the Court of Appeals are set forth below.

Briefs before the District Court:

"The antitrust laws of the United States are designed to protect the interstate and foreign commerce of this country. They do not purport and could not purport to compel a standard of business conduct for the rest of the world. Because of this, agreements and understandings entered into abroad by foreign corporations are entirely beyond the scope and power of our laws unless they have so important and direct an impact upon the interstate or foreign commerce of this country that they may be truly said to be principally concerned with the United States market and therefore appropriately subject to regulation by our courts. Not only is this a general principle of International law recognized by our courts (*Underhill vs. Hernandez*, 168 U.S. 250 (1897)) but the principle has been given specific application to our antitrust laws. *American Banana Co. vs. United Fruit Co.*, 213 U.S. 347 (1909)." Brief for Defendants at 89-90, United States v. Aluminum Co. of America, 44 F.Supp. 97 (S.D.N.Y. 1941).

"When the decisions are put together the principle stands out in bold outline. *Our laws, including the antitrust laws, are territorial in the sense that they do not include acts abroad unless those acts have a direct and important effect here.* If the acts abroad do have such an effect here, and particularly if that effect was intended, then they are subject to our laws. In the *Banana* case the throttling of competitive production was too far removed from the United States market; in the *American Tobacco* case, however, the agreements were concerned entirely with a division of the British and United States markets, including the United States export market; and finally, in the *Sisal* case, the monopoly abroad was merely the springboard for the monopoly in the United States. . . .

"We point out, therefore, that the Government must concede the application of this underlying principle,—*unless the foreign acts, combinations or agreements are shown to have had a direct and substantial effect upon United States commerce in aluminum, they do not come within the jurisdictional scope of this case.* We turn then to an application of this principle to the evidence." *Id.* at 94 (emphasis added).

"The Government asserts that we rely almost entirely upon *American Banana*

persons not within its allegiance, for conduct outside its borders that has consequences within its borders which the state reprehends; and these liabilities other states will ordinarily recognize. Strassheim v. Daily, 221 U.S. 280, 284, 285 * * *; Lamar v. United States, 240 U.S. 60, 65, 66 * * *; Ford v. United States, 273 U.S. 593, 620, 621 * * *; Restatement of Conflict of Laws §65. * * *

Both agreements would clearly have been unlawful, had they been made within the United States; and it follows from what we have just said that both were unlawful, though made abroad, if they were intended to affect imports and did affect them. . . .

Although Judge Hand termed this view "settled law," *Alcoa* actually represented a fundamental departure from prior holdings of American courts. Its most important feature was the extension of the traditional

Co. vs. United Fruit Co., 213 U.S. 347 (1909). If that case be interpreted to mean that any act done outside of the United States is immune from the antitrust laws, we do not place our reliance upon it. *We rely upon the proposition that a direct and substantial effect upon United States commerce must be shown* in order to invoke the antitrust laws, and that proposition is not dependent upon any considerations of extra-territoriality." Reply Brief for Defendants at 37 (emphasis added).

Brief before the Court of Appeals:

"The appellant seems to assume that it is enough to state that such an outside agreement as this 'could not fail to affect' the United States market or, at best, that it is enough to show an incidental and speculative effect on United States commerce.

"No such flagrantly extraterritorial application has ever been given the Sherman Act. All the cases cited (Govt. Brief 311-2) go no farther than to support a contention that an agreement among foreign companies would be illegal if it were directed toward protecting someone's domestic market from undue competition from abroad, and directly and materially affected the United States market. But having failed to show that Limited was acting on behalf of Alcoa or for Alcoa's protection, the appellant is left with the issue whether the Alliance agreement, entered into among Canadian, English, French, Swiss, and German producers, directed as it was toward markets outside the United States, was within the Sherman Act by virtue of any incidental effect (if, indeed, there were more than a theoretical effect) on the United States market. No case has been found supporting such an application of the Act." Brief for Appellees at 83, United States v. Aluminum Co. of America, 148 F.2d 416 (2d Cir. 1945).

"The cases applying the Sherman Act to foreign companies agreeing abroad have done so only under circumstances where not only were the effects here direct, immediate and important but where the agreements were aimed particularly at the United States market. The Act does not and could not purport to compel a standard of business conduct for the rest of the world; it is 'directed only to the protection of

application of the objective territorial principle of jurisdiction to economic effects of wholly foreign conduct of a type which other nations generally did not recognize as a crime or even as a tort.[54]

It has been suggested that the extension may even include economic effects of foreign conduct constituting little more than remote consequential damage.[55] Judge Hand did require, however, that the proscribed

American interests,' *United States vs. Associated Press,* 52 F.Supp. 362, 374 (S.D.N.Y. 1943). *The test is whether the combination directly and materially affects our commerce. United States vs. Hamburg-Amerikanische P.F.A.G.,* 200 Fed. 806, 807 (S.D.N.Y. 1911)." *Id.* at 84-85 (emphasis added). . . .

"The principles of territoriality rest not alone on comity of nations or even on the dictates of international law: They also rest on the practical question of effectiveness. 'A threat that depends upon the choice of the party affected to bring himself within that power hardly would be called law in the ordinary sense.' This was one of the considerations which 'would lead in a case of doubt to a construction of any statute as intended to be confined in its operation and effect to the territorial limits over which the lawmaker has general and legitimate power.' *American Banana Co. vs. United Fruit Co., supra,* at 357. Practicality dictates the construction here argued for. . . ." *Id.* at 89-90 (emphasis added).

[54] Professor Jennings has recently stated that the application of the objective territorial principle "to a trade arrangement made between aliens abroad which has repercussions on United States imports or exports . . . becomes no longer a fulfilment, but a reversal, of the principle of territoriality." This explains, he says, "the controversy which has long dogged the judgment of . . . [Judge Hand in *Alcoa*], a decision no doubt right on the merits but highly controversial in its reasoning. From the proposition that 'it is settled law that any State may impose liabilities, even upon persons not within its allegiance, for conduct outside its borders that has consequences within its borders'; the Judge felt able to say of the agreements in question: [quoting last paragraph of excerpt from Judge Hand's opinion set forth in the text at note 52 *supra.*] But of course the fact is that there can be very little in the way of significant commercial activity that does *not* have repercussions upon United States trade. The principle of territoriality has at this point become void of real content and has become a mere way of talking whilst exercising *extra*territorial jurisdiction." Jennings, *General Course of International Law,* 1968 PROCEEDINGS OF THE HAGUE ACADEMY OF INTERNATIONAL LAW 519, 520.

[55] Jennings, *supra* note 35, at 159.

It should be noted that neither the briefs of Aluminium Limited (see note 53 *supra*) nor Judge Hand's opinion included any reference to standard sources or authorities on international law, other than *American Banana* and other prior United States Supreme Court cases.

conduct abroad be *"intended"* to produce effects upon imports into the
United States, and that it actually produce those effects. The significance
of this expansive treatment of the territorial principle is perhaps less in
the result reached on the particular facts,[56] than in the potential
applicability of the decision to virtually *any* intended manifestation of
foreign conduct.[57]

Viewed as a statement on international law, the *Alcoa* doctrine has been
subjected to a vast amount of criticism by both American,[58] and foreign
writers.[59] Nevertheless, it was the main support for the controversial rule
of the Restatement (Second) of Foreign Relations Law of the United

[56]The decision might have been justified on other grounds. Specifically,
Aluminium Limited, the Canadian affiliate of Alcoa, bought and sold aluminum
products in the United States. It maintained business offices in New York City, and,
at the time of the suit, most of its stock was owned by Americans. Some
commentators have found in these additional "American elements," a satisfactory
basis for the court's rejecting the necessity for acts within the United States. See
BREWSTER, ANTITRUST AND AMERICAN BUSINESS ABROAD 72-73 (1958);
Note, *Extraterritorial Application of the Antitrust Laws,* 69 HARV. L. REV. 1452,
1456 (1956); TOKYO REPORT 378.

[57]Presumably, *de minimis* "effects" might still be an insufficient basis even after
Alcoa, but the forum would determine the sufficiency of the "effects" principally on
the basis of the state's own interest in the matter. 148 F.2d at 443-44.

[58]See, *e.g.,* Haight, *International Law and Extraterritorial Application of the Anti-
trust Laws,* 63 YALE L. J. 639 (1954); Raymond, *A New Look at the Jurisdiction in
Alcoa,* 61 AM. J. INT'L L. 558 (1967); Whitney, *Sources of Conflict Between
International Law and the Antitrust Laws,* 63 YALE L. J. 655 (1954). *Contra,*
Timberg, *Extraterritorial Jurisdiction under the Sherman Act,* 11 RECORD 101
(1956); *cf.* Brewster, *Extraterritorial Effects of the U.S. Antitrust Laws: "An
Appraisal,"* 11 ABA ANTITRUST SECTION REP. 65, 69 (1957), concluding that
international law "is not very helpful" in providing guidelines for antitrust; and
Miller, *Extraterritorial Effects of Trade Regulation,* 111 U. PA. L. REV. 1092, 1111
(1963), similar.

[59]See, *e.g.,* Jennings, *supra* note 35; Mann, *supra* note 12, at 100-06;
Kahn-Freund, *Extraterritorial Application of Antitrust Laws,* ABA SECTION OF
INT'L & COMP. L. 1957 PROCEEDINGS 33; Verzijl, *The Controversy Regarding
the So-called Extraterritorial Effect of the American Anti-trust Laws,* 8 NEDER-
LANDS TIJDSCHRIFT VOOR INTERNATIONAAL RECHT 3 (1961); TOKYO
REPORT 370-84 (Riedweg, Rapporteur). *Cf.,* Report to the Consultative Assembly
of the Council of Europe by the Legal Committee (deGrailly, Rapporteur), The
Extra-Territorial Application of Anti-Trust Legislation, Doc. 2023 (Jan. 25, 1966).

States, which provides:

§18. *Jurisdiction to Prescribe with Respect to Effect within Territory*

> A state has jurisdiction to prescribe a rule of law attaching legal consequences to conduct that occurs outside its territory and causes an effect within its territory, if either
>
> (a) the conduct and its effect are generally recognized as constituent elements of a crime or tort under the law of states that have reasonably developed legal systems, or
>
> (b) (i) the conduct and its effect are constituent elements of activity to which the rule applies; (ii) the effect within the territory is substantial; (iii) it occurs as a direct and foreseeable result of the conduct outside the territory; and (iv) the rule is not inconsistent with the principles of justice generally recognized by states that have reasonably developed legal systems.

Not all states having reasonably developed legal systems subscribe to the principle of antitrust jurisdiction expounded by Judge Hand and set forth in the Restatement.[60] The Restatement does, however, attempt to

[60] A European Advisory Committee, composed of Lord McNair (Chairman) and Professors Francois, Rousseau, Seidl-Hohenveldern and D.H.N. Johnson (Reporter and Secretary), was appointed by the American Law Institute in 1958 to advise on certain sections of the then pending draft of the Restatement. The portion of its report dealing with extraterritorial jurisdiction is reprinted in the TOKYO REPORT at 537. While certain recommendations of the Committee were adopted, its recommendations relating to the scope of extraterritorial jurisdiction were not.

The draft Section on jurisdiction submitted to the Committee was as follows:

"A State has jurisdiction to prescribe rules attaching legal consequences to conduct, including rules relating to property, status or other interests, with respect to conduct occurring:

(a) in its territory;

(b) partly within and partly outside its territory;

(c) entirely outside its territory if the conduct has, or is intended to have, effects within its territory which have a reasonably close relationship to the conduct."*Id.*

In its report on this Section, the European Advisory Committee said:

"We propose here a major change, the first major change we have so far proposed. This is that paragraph (c) should be deleted. . . .

"The principal reason is simply one of logic. We do not see how a State's jurisdiction to prescribe rules relating to conduct outside its territory—assuming such jurisdiction exists—can be said to be 'jurisdiction based on territory.' . . .

"To make our position absolutely plain, we would say that we agree with the sentence in the commentary . . . to the effect that 'The mere fact that the conduct

circumscribe *Alcoa* with what might be regarded as safeguards, in that it requires, as prerequisites to the application of the *Alcoa* rule (1) that both conduct and effect be "constituent" elements of the offense; (2) that the effect be "substantial," (3) that it be a "direct and foreseeable" result of the conduct,[61] and (4) that the rule be "consistent" with

takes place partly or completely outside of the territory does not bar the State from dealing with it.' But we do not agree with the sentence which immediately precedes this one, namely, the sentence which reads 'A State may, when there is sufficient relationship between its territory and conduct occurring outside of it, *treat such conduct on the same basis as conduct occurring in its territory.*' The words *in italics* seem to us to be illogical and tend to make more difficult a sound classification of the various bases of jurisdiction.

. . . .

"... We wish to make it plain that this recommendation is not connected with any view we may have formed as to the proper limits for the extra-territorial application of the United States anti-trust laws. . . . But, even if we should hold the view that in no instance has the application of the United States anti-trust laws exceeded the proper limits, fixed by international law, we should still recommend the suppression of paragraph (c) for the reason which we have already mentioned, namely, that the exercise of jurisdiction over conduct occurring entirely outside the territory could not constitute a form of jurisdiction based on territory.

"It will be noticed that our recommendation in regard to section 8 would bring that section very much into line with article 3 of the Harvard Draft Convention on Jurisdiction with Respect to Crime, (1935). Indeed, we find ourselves in agreement with that article and its underlying reasoning. . . .

"Where we seem to differ from the reporters of Tentative Draft No. 2 is in drawing a distinction—which is also drawn by the reporters of the Harvard Research Draft—between the 'essential constituent elements' of criminal conduct on the one hand and its mere 'effects' on the other hand. In our view, the exercise of 'Jurisdiction based on Territory' is not justified in cases where all that has occurred within the territory is the effects of certain conduct and not at least part of the conduct itself." *Id.* at 538-39.

[61] Judge Hand's requirement of "intent" as a necessary element for U.S. jurisdiction over conduct abroad has been changed in the Restatement from *mens rea* to "direct and foreseeable result." Thus, the Restatement avoids the difficult, if not untenable, position of basing jurisdiction on an alien's state of mind abroad; *cf.* Chapter 2 *supra* at note 84, inquiring whether the Restatement test is broader than *Alcoa* in this respect, although it is perhaps somewhat narrower in another respect, *i.e., Alcoa* allows jurisdiction to be based on effects on foreign commerce (imports), while the Restatement requires effects *within* the country (see Chapter 2, note 16).

The REPORT OF THE ATTORNEY GENERAL'S NATIONAL COMMITTEE TO STUDY THE ANTITRUST LAWS (1955) states, at 76:

"We believe that conspiracies between foreign competitors alone should come

generally recognized principles of justice.[62] These limitations, however, do not meet the objection that Section 18 broadly sanctions an attempt by one state to require citizens of a foreign state to obey in their own country rules of law of a state to which they owe no allegiance and

within the Sherman Act only where they are intended to, and actually do, result in substantial anticompetitive effects on our foreign commerce. The 'international complications likely to arise' from any contrary view convince us, as they did the Court in *Alcoa* 'that Congress certainly did not intend the Act to cover' such arrangements when they have no restrictive purpose and effect on our commerce."

A Supplement to that Report published by the American Bar Association in 1968 rationalizes that "intent" means "direct and foreseeable": "An apparent difference between this [Section 18(b) of the Restatement] and the guideline [in the 1955 Report quoted above] is that clause (b) (iii) of the Restatement requires that the anticompetitive effects be a 'direct and foreseeable result' of the extraterritorial conduct, whereas the guideline requires that the effects were 'intended' by those causing them. However, when the meaning of 'intent' as used in the guideline is examined, the two requirements appear to be essentially identical.

"The *Alcoa* and *General Electric* cases from which the guideline was derived both clearly indicate that 'intent' does not mean the specific intent to accomplish the result of monopoly or restraint of trade. The element of intent is established if the actor should have known that its conduct would have the forbidden effects and the conduct itself was deliberate. There are numerous cases not involving extraterritorial conduct which hold that intent means deliberately engaging in conduct the natural and probable consequences [sic] of which is restraint of trade or monopoly." ABA ANTITRUST SECTION SUPPLEMENT TO THE REPORT OF THE ATTORNEY GENERAL'S NATIONAL COMMITTEE TO STUDY THE ANTITRUST LAWS: ANTITRUST DEVELOPMENTS 1955-1968, at 49 (1968).

[62] *Cf.* the article by Professor Metzger, who criticizes the final version of Section 18 because of the insertion of these limitations, which—with the exception of the "constituent elements" formula in par. (b)(i)—he says, "are unsupported by the authorities." Metzger, *The Restatement of the Foreign Relations Law of the United States: Bases and Conflicts of Jurisdiction,* 41 N.Y.U.L. REV. 7, 15 (1966).

Comment f of Section 18 specifically notes that "[t]he fact that a substantial number of states with reasonably developed legal systems do not recognize certain conduct and its effects as constituent elements of crimes or torts does not prevent a state which chooses to do so from prescribing rules which make such conduct and its effects constituent elements of activity which is either criminal, tortious, or subject to regulation." Nor would a particular rule be deemed inconsistent with "generally recognized principles of justice" by virtue of the fact that "most states with reasonably developed legal systems [do not] . . . have a similar rule;" RESTATE-MENT §18, comment g.

which may be significantly different from the law of their own state.[63] While the factors enumerated by the Restatement may well be reasonably prerequisite to a state's justifiably prescribing rules to govern foreign conduct, they nonetheless fail adequately to define limits of jurisdiction which are acceptable under theretofore established principles of international law as interpreted by most leading commercial nations.[64]

The Restatement tempers its statement of jurisdiction under Section 18 with rules of forebearance, which must be read in conjunction with Section 18 for the full impact of the Restatement rule.[65] The primary

---

[63] Professor Jennings has expressed the view that Section 18 recognizes "that the effects notion needs considerable qualification to make it consistent with the principles of international law." He further states that, although the section "is by no means free from difficulty, not least in introducing a question of causation into the equation," it "does appear to go a long way towards accepting the principle stated so clearly by the European Advisory Committee" under Lord McNair's chairmanship (see note 60 *supra*) that "the exercise of jurisdiction based on territory is not justified in cases where all that has occurred within the territory is the effects of certain conduct and not at least part of the conduct itself." Jennings, *General Course of International Law,* 1968 PROCEEDINGS OF THE HAGUE ACADEMY OF INTERNATIONAL LAW 521.

[64] As noted in Chapter 2, Section 98(2) of the German antitrust law expressly asserts jurisdiction over conduct abroad having effects in Germany, *id.* at 111; also, the EC Commission has stated that it will rely upon the "effects" concept, *id.* at 102. It is possible that the Belgian and Dutch laws embody the same concept in some respects, but this is not made express and may be disputed, *id.* at 109 and 113. See also Hug, *The Applicability of the Provisions of the European Community Treaties against Restraints of Competition to Restraints of Competition Caused in Non-Member States, but Affecting the Common Market,* in 2 CARTEL AND MONOPOLY IN MODERN LAW 639, 651 (1961).

[65] It is important that Section 18 be read in the light of Part IV of the Restatement as well as Section 40. Even though a state has jurisdiction under the rule in Section 18 with respect to a specified extraterritorial act of an alien, it is not only required by the rule in Section 40 "to consider, in good faith, moderating the exercise of its enforcement jurisdiction," but, *regardless of the outcome of such consideration,* it is precluded by the rules in Part IV from taking enforcement action which, as a matter of procedure or substance, would violate the international standard of justice specified in Section 165(1)(b)—just as it would be precluded if the alien's offense had been committed entirely within the territory. In other words, the existence of jurisdiction is not enough under the Restatement; it must be exercised in a manner consistent with international law.

question, however, is whether under international law a state may validly assume jurisdiction over conduct by aliens abroad solely because of "effects," even though it limits the relevant effects to ones which it determines are "constituent elements" of the offense proscribed. Only if a state does have jurisdiction does it become pertinent to consider whether or not to abstain from its exercise. That a state or its courts render wise or considerate judgments is not itself a basis for jurisdiction under international law, at least not jurisdiction based on any variation of the territorial principle.

Application of the Restatement jurisdictional rule on a wide scale would produce potentially staggering conflicts. The *Alcoa* opinion itself recognized this in a passage which, while it was addressed more to statutory construction than to international law, is equally cogent as to the latter:

> There may be agreements made beyond our borders not intended to affect imports, which do affect them, or which affect exports. Almost any limitation of the supply of goods in Europe, for example, or in South America, may have repercussions in the United States if there is trade between the two. Yet when one considers the international complications likely to arise from an effort in this country to treat such agreements as unlawful, it is safe to assume that Congress certainly did not intend the Act to cover them. . . .[66]

For example, European steelmakers recently agreed voluntarily to limit their steel exports to the United States.[67] They were responding to complaints of their American counterparts against rising imports of steel from Europe, and sought by voluntary action to forestall Congressional imposition of import quotas. The arrangements could easily produce a substantial, well-intentioned and foreseeable effect on United States imports. Would those facts give a United States court jurisdiction over the European enterprises involved and over their respective officers and agents for possible violations of the Sherman and Wilson Tariff Acts? If

[66]148 F.2d at 443.

[67]Steel producers in the European Coal and Steel Community, as well as Japanese steel companies, announced that they would voluntarily limit exports to the United States to a maximum increase of 5% per year during each of the next three years, beginning with 1969. The United States Department of State participated in working out the arrangement, negotiating directly with the foreign steel companies rather than with their governments; Wall Street Journal, Nov. 20, 1968, at 9, col. 1; New York Times, Dec. 6, 1968, at 69, col. 4; *id.*, Jan. 8, 1969, at 63, col. 2; Steel Facts, Feb.-March, 1969, at 2.

so, the American court could enjoin the arrangement and even order the flow of European steel into United States "foreign commerce." Section 18 of the Restatement would give the American court that jurisdiction, but could the court properly punish those foreign participants that it might catch? Conversely, could the United States make it a crime for persons abroad to engage in a conspiracy or boycott in their own countries against the purchase of American-made automobiles under a "Buy French" or "Buy German" program?

If the United States does have jurisdiction under Section 18 of the Restatement in such cases, then so do other states if they discern "effects" within their borders. It would also follow that other states feeling effects of conduct in the United States would have jurisdiction to prescribe rules for that conduct. If the shoe were on the other foot, would not the United States deny the jurisdiction of "Tobago" to regulate the conduct of American business in the United States, assuming, of course, that their courts could catch a vacationing culprit?[68] There is no consensus among nations that local effects of foreign conduct in trade or commerce give all nations who feel the effects jurisdiction to prescribe rules for that conduct, subject only to self-imposed forebearance and the limitations mentioned in Section 18.[69]

B. Nonterritorial Bases of Jurisdiction

International law does recognize the right of a state to prescribe and enforce rules of law in respect of persons and conduct abroad, regardless

[68] "Can the island of Tobago pass a law to bind the rights of the whole world? Would the world submit to such an assumed jurisdiction?" Lord Ellenborough, C.J., in Buchanan v. Rucker, 9 East 192, 194, 103 Eng. Rep. 546, 547 (K.B. 1808).

[69] "[T]here is no territorial jurisdiction, or any jurisdiction, to order a foreigner abroad to act abroad in order to cause an effect within the state. If the order is obeyed, the fact that the action abroad causes an effect within the state's territory does not retroactively provide a territorial jurisdiction for ordering the action originally, otherwise jurisdiction which was lacking could be acquired merely by the state's own act of legislating. If this could be done, 'jurisdiction' in international law would become meaningless. * * * We clearly have the jurisdiction and the right, as the territorial sovereign, to forbid the taking of a human life within our territory, or the importation into it of forbidden merchandise, or the perpetration of a fraud here; but we have no jurisdiction or right to order a foreigner abroad to ship to us or to buy from us, and hence we have no jurisdiction or right to penalize him for the negative effect of his failing to do so." Raymond, *supra* note 58, at 563-65.

of effects in the territory, in well-defined, limited situations. In such cases, jurisdiction is based on one of three generally accepted theories which are treated as exceptions to the exclusiveness of the territorial principle of jurisdiction, and are commonly referred to as "permissive" rules. They are (a) the nationality principle, (b) the protective principle, and (c) the universality principle. In addition, some states claim a fourth principle: the passive personality principle.

1. NATIONALITY PRINCIPLE

Apart from the territorial principle of jurisdiction, the nationality principle defines the most important and far-reaching basis of jurisdiction recognized in international law. According to this principle, a state has jurisdiction over its nationals wherever they may be, or wherever they do business.

Section 30 of the Restatement states:

(1) A state has jurisdiction to prescribe a rule of law
   (a) attaching legal consequences to conduct of a national of the state wherever the conduct occurs or
   (b) as to the status of a national or as to an interest of a national, wherever the thing or other subject-matter to which the interest relates is located.[70]

The term, "national," as used in this Section, includes a corporation organized under the laws of the claiming state.[71] Foreign corporations which are owned or controlled by nationals of the claiming state are not "nationals" of that state, but may be effectively regulated by it through its jurisdiction over the controlling interests.[72]

---

[70] Comment *b* to Section 30 of the Restatement states: "The fact that a state has jurisdiction under the rule stated in Subsection (1) does not mean that it is permitted by international law to direct a national to engage in activities without regard to harmful consequences to another state."

[71] Section 27 of the Restatement: "A corporation or other private legal entity has the nationality of the state which creates it."

[72] Comment *d* to Section 27 of the Restatement states: "When the nationality of a corporation is different from the nationality of the persons (individual or corporate) who own or control it, the state of the nationality of such persons has jurisdiction to prescribe, and to enforce in its territory, rules of law governing their conduct. It is thus in a position to control the conduct of the corporation even though it does not have jurisdiction to prescribe rules directly applicable to the corporation."

While common law countries have not asserted the nationality principle to the extent that civil law countries have relied on it for extraterritorial authority,[73] the United States has exercised jurisdiction over its nationals abroad in numerous situations.[74] Under the Federal Rules of Criminal Procedure, for example, a United States citizen outside the country may be subpoenaed to return to the United States and appear as a witness;[75] acts of treason outside the United States are punishable;[76] the Internal Revenue Code applies to citizens wherever resident unless specifically exempted;[77] United States corporations having foreign branches and subsidiaries abroad must respond to antitrust grand jury subpoenas covering documents located abroad, unless excused,[78] as mentioned below; and the Lanham Act has extraterritorial effects on the conduct of United States nationals abroad.[79]

[73] See BISHOP, INTERNATIONAL LAW 343 (1953); Jennings, *supra* note 35, at 153; Mann, *supra* note 12, at 88 *et seq.*

[74] See, *e.g.,* Steele v. Bulova Watch Co., 344 U.S. 280 (1952); Skiriotes v. Florida, 313 U.S. 69 (1941); Blackmer v. United States, 284 U.S. 421 (1932); Cook v. Tait, 265 U.S. 47 (1924); United States v. Bowman, 260 U.S. 94 (1922). See generally *Harvard Draft,* Articles and Comment, 519-39. But see Mann, *supra* note 12, at 88 ("in the United States . . . [the nationality principle] has been adopted only seldom and only in specific cases").

[75] Fed. R. Crim. P. 17(e)(2); *cf.* Fed. R. Civ. P. 45(e)(2); see Blackmer v. United States, 284 U.S. 421 (1932); but see United States v. Thompson, 319 F.2d 665 (2d Cir. 1963). In *Blackmer,* while the Court was principally concerned with the constitutionality of the procedure, Chief Justice Hughes, speaking on behalf of the Court, noted: "The mere giving of such notice to the citizen in the foreign country of the requirement of his government that he shall return is in no sense an invasion of any right of the foreign government; and the citizen has no standing to invoke any such supposed right." 284 U.S. at 439.

[76] 18 U.S.C. §2381 (1964), provides: "Whoever, owing allegiance to the United States, levies war against them or adheres to their enemies, giving them aid . . . within the United States or elsewhere, is guilty of treason. . . ."

[77] See Int. Rev. Code of 1954 § §911, 2001.

[78] See generally discussion in Chapter 3 of extraterritorial discovery orders.

[79] Steele v. Bulova Watch Co., 344 U.S. 280 (1952); Ramirez & Feraud Chili Co. v. Las Palmas Food Co., 146 F.Supp. 594 (S.D. Cal. 1956), *aff'd,* 245 F.2d 874 (9th Cir. 1957), *cert. denied,* 355 U.S. 927 (1958); *cf.* Vanity Fair Mills, Inc. v. T. Eaton Co., 234 F.2d 633 (2d Cir. 1956), *cert. denied,* 352 U.S. 871 (1956). But see FALK, THE ROLE OF DOMESTIC COURTS IN THE INTERNATIONAL LEGAL ORDER 33 n.37 (1964).

The Sherman Act does not by its terms make any distinction between nationals and aliens but applies to conduct of any "person" involving "restraint of trade or commerce among the several States [of the United States], or with foreign nations." Thus, to the extent that the Act validly applies to the conduct of aliens, it is based exclusively on the territorial principle, and to the extent that it applies to similar conduct of nationals, it also has a valid territorial basis. Insofar as nationals are concerned, however, the nationality principle supplies an additional basis for jurisdiction. To the extent that "trade or commerce . . . with foreign nations" within the meaning of the Act may include commerce conducted by American nationals entirely outside of United States territory, the application of the Act is based exclusively on the nationality principle.[80]

The nationality principle is probably nowhere more significant than in areas of fiscal concern and regulation of transactions in international trade.[81] For example, in the *First National City Bank* case,[82] the U.S.

[80] In Pacific Seafarers, Inc. v. Pacific Far East Line, Inc., 404 F.2d 804 (D.C. Cir. 1968), the court held the Sherman Act applicable to a combination of American shipping lines which allegedly destroyed another American line's business in carrying A.I.D.-financed cargo between Taiwan and South Vietnam. This business was held to be in American foreign commerce because it was limited to American-flag carriers as a result of A.I.D. regulations and policies.

While head of the Antitrust Division, Professor Turner stated: "There is usually no question but that the Sherman Act forbids American corporations to enter into agreements that significantly affect American markets whether those agreements are entered into at home or abroad . . . .

"When the Sherman Act applies to the foreign activities of an American company, there is no problem in obtaining jurisdiction over the American company. Nor is there any problem with venue or service of process . . . .

"To sum up, we have adequate legal authority to bring and to prosecute suits against American companies participating in foreign activities which are intended to affect, and which do affect, American markets directly. But the international aspects of such suits may, nonetheless, create complications that require the cooperation of the State Department and foreign countries to resolve. . . ." Statement of Donald F. Turner, in *Hearings on Prices of Quinine and Quinidine Before the Subcomm. on Antitrust and Monopoly of the Sen. Comm. on the Judiciary,* 90th Cong., 1st Sess., pt. 2, at 234-35 (1967).

[81] See, *e.g.,* the United States Foreign Direct Investment Regulations regulating investments by U.S. nationals in foreign enterprises (CCH BALANCE OF PAYMENTS REP. ¶505 [1968]) and the United Kingdom Exchange Control Act of 1947 (10 & 11 Geo. 6, c. 14) under which the U.K. Treasury controls fiscal transactions of its nationals and of their foreign subsidiaries.

[82] United States v. First National City Bank, 396 F.2d 897 (2d Cir. 1968).

Court of Appeals for the Second Circuit upheld an antitrust grand jury subpoena requiring First National City to produce documents in the possession of its branch in Germany pertaining to a depositor under investigation, notwithstanding the argument that civil liability under German law and business losses might be incurred thereby.[83] The court stated:

> The basic legal question confronting us is not a total stranger to this Court. With the growing interdependence of world trade and the increased mobility of persons and companies, the need arises not infrequently, whether related to civil or criminal proceedings, for the production of evidence located in foreign jurisdictions. It is no longer open to doubt that a federal court has the power to require the production of documents located in foreign countries if the court has *in personam* jurisdiction of the person in possession or control of the material.[84]

There is serious doubt as to whether "*in personam* jurisdiction of the person in possession or control of the material" is sufficient if that person is an alien and is not charged with any violation of law. The court, however, was

> called upon [only] to decide whether a domestic bank may refuse to comply with a valid Grand Jury subpoena duces tecum requiring the production of documents in the possession of a foreign branch of the bank on the ground that compliance would subject it to civil liability under the law of the foreign state.[85]

It seems appropriate, therefore, to treat the holding as being grounded on the principle of nationality.

It is often asserted that the nationality principle should be applied with the limitation that a state has no jurisdiction to order its nationals abroad to commit acts which are forbidden by the law of the country where committed, or to refrain from acts required by the latter.[86] This

---

[83]*Id.* at 904.

[84]*Id.* at 900.

[85]*Id.* at 898.

[86]Professor F. A. Mann has suggested that certain limitations should be recognized: "If Utopia were to enjoin all Utopians to drive on the left wherever they may be, a Utopian motorist driving in Holland would be breaking either Utopian or Dutch law. If Ruritania should prohibit all its nationals from doing business with certain countries and if such a discriminatory practice were a criminal offense in Holland, the Dutch branch of a Ruritanian corporation could not help committing an

view of a state's jurisdictional prerogative fails to take account of the fact that the citizen who is called upon by the laws of the country of his nationality to act in a manner contrary to some foreign law can avoid the difficulty by keeping out of a country whose laws are in conflict with those of his own. While such an alternative may appear harsh, it is a result which respects the national interests of each state, rather than forcing one to yield before the other.[87]

2. PROTECTIVE PRINCIPLE

According to the Restatement:

(1) A state has jurisdiction to prescribe a rule of law attaching legal consequences to conduct outside its territory that threatens its security as a state or the operation of its governmental functions, provided the conduct is generally recognized as a crime under the law of states that have reasonably developed legal systems.

(2) Conduct referred to in Subsection (1) includes in particular the counterfeiting of the state's seals and currency, and the falsification of its official documents.[88]

offense under either law. Accordingly, Oppenheim is fully justified in stating that 'a State is prevented from requiring such acts from its citizens abroad as are forbidden to them by the Municipal Law of the land in which they reside, and from ordering them not to commit such acts as they are bound to commit according to the Municipal Law of the land in which they reside.' " Mann, *supra* note 12, at 90 (footnote omitted).

[87]There is authority to the effect that a United States court cannot require an alien defendant to violate foreign law. See, *e.g.*, Federal Maritime Comm'n v. deSmedt, 268 F.Supp. 972, 974-75 (S.D.N.Y. 1967) ("I cannot, of course, direct and order anybody to violate the orders of his native land. . . ."); United States v. The Watchmakers of Switzerland Information Center, Inc., 1963 Trade Cas. ¶70,600 at 77,456 (S.D.N.Y. 1962) ("If, of course, the defendants' activities had been required by Swiss law this court could indeed do nothing. An American court would have under such circumstances no right to condemn the governmental activity of another sovereign nation."); *cf.* American Banana Co. v. United Fruit Co., 213 U.S. 347, 359 (1909) ("A conspiracy in this country to do acts in another jurisdiction does not draw to itself those acts and make them unlawful, if they are permitted by the local law.") The language of the *American Banana* case quoted above has, however, been treated by later cases "as having been overruled *sub silentio* to the extent that it purports to insulate from the antitrust laws conduct abroad having substantial anticompetitive effects in this country." ABA ANTITRUST SECTION SUPPLE-MENT, *supra* note 61, at 49-50 n.52.

[88]RESTATEMENT §33.

Under this principle, an alien may be prosecuted by an offended state for conduct wholly outside its borders whether or not the conduct was lawful at the place where it occurred. There need by no "effects" within the territory of the offended state,[89] nor any connection between the conduct abroad and any activity within that state. Obviously this principle is capable of abuse, as Professor Mann has pointed out:

> [I]t is clear that States must make a reasonable and just assessment of acts which so much affect their interests as to make it proper to impose punishment for them irrespective of the identity of place and person. It would be abusive if a State invoked the protective principle without due regard to the importance of the offence. In all cases, here as elsewhere, the standard is supplied solely by international law, *i.e.* by the general practice of civilised States.[90]

The protective principle can, of course, easily produce friction among states, for what one might consider an essential liberty to be enjoyed as of right by its citizens, another might consider inherently prejudicial to its national interests. Article 7 of the Harvard Draft sets forth the protective principle, but with a proviso limiting such jurisdiction to cases in which "the act or omission which constitutes the crime was not committed in exercise of a liberty guaranteed the alien by the law of the place where it

[89] Judge Medina in United States v. Pizzarusso, 388 F.2d 8, 10-11 (2d Cir. 1968) stated the principle as follows: "[T]he objective territorial principle is quite distinct from the protective theory. Under the latter, all the elements of the crime occur in the foreign country and jurisdiction exists because these actions have a 'potentially adverse effect' upon security or governmental functions, Restatement (Second) Foreign Relations Law, Comment to Section 33 at p. 93, and there need not be any actual effect in the country as would be required under the objective territorial principle. Courts have often failed to perceive this distinction. Thus, the Ninth Circuit, in upholding a conviction under a factual situation similar to the one in the instant case, relied on the protective theory, but still felt constrained to say that jurisdiction rested partially on the adverse effect produced as a result of the alien's entry into the United States. The Ninth Circuit also cited *Strassheim* and *Aluminum Company of America* as support for its decision. With all due deference to our brothers of the Ninth Circuit, however, we think this reliance is unwarranted. A violation of 18 U.S.C. Section 1546 is complete at the time the alien perjures himself in the foreign country. It may be possible that the particular criminal sanctions of Section 1546 will never be enforced unless the defendant enters the country, but entry is not an element of the statutory offense. *Were the statute re-drafted and entry made a part of the crime we would then be presented with a clear case of jurisdiction under the objective territorial principle.*" (emphasis added)

[90] Mann, *supra* note 12, at 94 (footnote omitted).

was committed."[91] A similar limitation is provided in Section 33 of the Restatement, with the explanation that the limitation "prevents a state from basing an extension of its jurisdiction on the rule. . . ."[92]

The possibility that the protective principle might be utilized to justify extraterritorial application of antitrust laws was considered in a comment to Section 32 of Tentative Draft No. 2 of the Restatement. It was noted there that the protective principle might be considered to be "most nearly descri[ptive], of all bases of jurisdiction," of the approach of the Department of Justice in bringing antitrust actions (i) involving per se violations of the Sherman Act by conduct abroad having only "slight economic effects" within the United States, and (ii) against members of foreign cartels "contrary to the philosophy of the American antitrust laws but not having direct, or measurable, or intended economic effects within the United States."[93] Tentative Draft No. 2 rejected such an application of the protective principle, however,

> because (a) the protective principle is not universally or even commonly accepted as authorizing a state to legislate against possible frustration by foreigners from abroad of its political, economic, or social policies where there are no reasonably close relationships between the conduct and effects within its territory; (b) *if extended so far as to explain jurisdiction in antitrust proceedings of the sort described above, the protective principle could equally be extended in other instances, possibly objectionable to United States interests, in which a state might like to enforce, whenever it could catch a defendant, general agreement with its views on matters of political, economic, or social organization.* Like the doctrine of public policy in the Conflict of Laws, the protective principle in its broader aspect is "an unruly horse," the problem being that once a state gets astride it, it might have difficulty saying where the doctrine might take it.[94]

The European Advisory Committee, appointed by the American Law Institute to advise on Tentative Draft No. 2,[95] reached the same conclusion as expressed in Tentative Draft No. 2, stating:

[91] *Harvard Draft* 543.
[92] RESTATEMENT §33, comment *d*.
[93] RESTATEMENT OF THE FOREIGN RELATIONS LAW OF THE UNITED STATES §32, comment *b* at 94 (Tent. Draft No. 2, 1958).
[94] *Id.* at 94 (emphasis added).
[95] See note 60 *supra*.

[T]he protective principle does not, in our opinion, ordinarily apply to the protection by a State of its economic policies, such as policies regarding the control of imports or restrictive trade practices.[96]

On the other hand, the European Advisory Committee did not categorically reject the protective principle, and advised:

We can see no reason why a State shall lose the jurisdiction referred to in article 7 of the Harvard Draft merely because the law of another State on whose territory these acts are committed permit the perpetrators to do them.
. . . .

Whether . . . jurisdiction may be exercised under the protective principle will depend, in our view, on whether the acts committed by aliens outside the territory of the State are or are not "against its security, territorial integrity or political independence."

We admit that expressions such as "security," "territorial integrity" and "political independence" are somewhat vague and difficult to define precisely. Nevertheless they are in general use in international law and appear in the Charter of the United Nations and other international treaties.

. . . [T]he possible abuse of a principle is no argument against the validity of the principle itself. . . . [S]tates are not the sole judges of whether acts committed outside their territory are committed against their security, territorial integrity or political independence. In the last resort, like the exercise of the right on self-defence itself, that is a matter for objective determination by international law. . . .

A burden of proof certainly rests upon a State seeking to exercise jurisdiction under the protective principle to show (a) that the exercise of that jurisdiction really is necessary for the protection of the State, and (b) that the jurisdiction which it is necessary to exercise cannot validly be based on any other principle. In the case of counterfeiting currency, plots against the government and so on, that burden is easily discharged on the basis of common consent. . . . The protective principle cannot . . . be invoked to justify the application of the United States antitrust laws in the manner illustrated by some of the decisions referred to in the commentaries. . . . We can, however, conceive of circumstances in which a powerful group of manufacturers or producers or traders might deliberately conspire to deprive a State of some commodity vital to its military defence. And we can imagine that, in such circumstances, a State would be justified in invoking the protective principle so as to safeguard its security, territorial integrity and political independence by

[96] A.L.I., FINAL REPORT OF THE EUROPEAN ADVISORY COMMITTEE ON TENTATIVE DRAFT NO. 2, RESTATEMENT OF FOREIGN RELATIONS LAW OF THE UNITED STATES (JURISDICTION) 30 (1961) (privately submitted unpublished draft).

enforcing rules of conduct against such a combination, should any of its perpetrators come within the jurisdiction of that State.[97]

Whether or not the policy underlying the American antitrust laws is so fundamentally tied to the national interest that the protective principle could be used to justify prosecution of aliens whose conduct abroad violates those laws, the protective principle has not been invoked *eo nomine* for this purpose.[98] Indeed, to apply the protective principle as a basis for the extraterritorial application of antitrust laws would be releasing a most "unruly horse," a danger the United States has long recognized. If every state could determine for itself what protective measures were necessary, and could punish every alien it might catch who infringed those measures, the international community would be far more chaotic than it is.

3. THE UNIVERSALITY PRINCIPLE

The Restatement, the Harvard Draft and most states recognize extraterritorial jurisdiction over aliens based on the proposition that the suppression of certain crimes is permissible "as a matter of international public policy."[99] Piracy is the prime example of a crime, the suppression of which is of universal interest. In addition, certain other crimes are universally, or almost universally, condemned, such as traffic in women and children, traffic in narcotics, etc. However, the Restatement commentary notes that

> universal interest in the suppression of slavery and these other crimes has not as yet been carried to the point of recognizing, either in customary law or in international agreements, the principle of universal jurisdiction that obtains in the instance of piracy.[100]

As states become more aware of their interdependence in the

---

[97]*Id.* at 27-30.

[98] In the *Alcoa* case, the court adverted to the possibility that Congress might have intended the Sherman Act to apply to an alien conspiracy intended to affect, but not actually affecting, U.S. commerce, but it apparently assumed that jurisdiction for such an application of the law would be based on the territorial, rather than the protective principle; *cf.* 148 F.2d at 443-44.

[99]BROWNLIE, PRINCIPLES OF PUBLIC INTERNATIONAL LAW 265 (1966); see RESTATEMENT §34; *Harvard Draft* arts. 9, 10; Jennings, *supra* note 35, at 156; Mann, *supra* note 12, at 95.

[100]RESTATEMENT §34, Reporters' Note No. 2 at 97.

community of nations, the list of crimes of universal interest may grow. War crimes and genocide, for example, might now be included in the list of crimes of universal interest. Antitrust violation, however, quite clearly is not yet a crime of such interest.

4. PASSIVE PERSONALITY PRINCIPLE

A number of states have asserted jurisdiction over offenses committed against their nationals abroad, regardless of the nature of the "offense" or the nationality of the offender. This principle is generally considered to be the least justifiable of all grounds asserted as bases for extraterritorial jurisdiction, and supplies no support for extraterritorial antitrust application. It is rejected by the Harvard Draft,[101] as well as the Restatement, which provides:

> A state does not have jurisdiction to prescribe a rule of law attaching legal consequences to conduct of an alien outside its territory merely on the ground that the conduct affects one of its nationals.[102]

The diversity of opinion concerning the acceptability of the passive personality principle was responsible, for example, for the heated diplomatic exchange between the United States and Mexico in the landmark *Cutting* incident in which a Mexican court had exercised jurisdiction over an American citizen who had published remarks in a Texas newspaper allegedly defamatory of a Mexican national.[103] The principle was at issue again in the *Lotus* case, and provoked a rather hostile comment from Judge Moore, the American judge:

> What, we may ask, is this system? In substance, it means that the citizen of one country, when he visits another country, takes with him for his "protection" the law of his own country and subjects those with whom he comes into contact to the operation of that law. In this way an inhabitant of a great commercial city, in which foreigners congregate, may in the course of an hour unconsciously fall under the operation of a number of foreign criminal codes. This is by no means a fanciful supposition; it is merely an illustration of what is daily occurring, if the "protective" principle is admissible. It is evident that this claim is at variance not only with the principle of the exclusive jurisdiction of a State over its own territory, but also with the equally

---

[101] *Harvard Draft* art. 10, Comment at 578-85.
[102] RESTATEMENT §30(2).
[103] [1887] FOREIGN REL. U.S. 751, 757; 2 MOORE, DIGEST OF INTERNATIONAL LAW 228-42 (1906).

well-settled principle that a person visiting a foreign country, far from radiating for his protection the jurisdiction of his own country, falls under the dominion of the local law and, except so far as his government may diplomatically intervene in case of a denial of justice, must look to that law for his protection.[104]

III. CONFLICTS AS TO JURISDICTION

As has been seen, even the traditional and generally accepted principles of jurisdiction result in overlapping or concurrent jurisdiction of two or more states. Consequently, conflicts and possibilities of double jeopardy arise in the exercise of such jurisdiction by the respective states. Additional conflicts arise as the result of claims by states of jurisdiction which is contested by other states.

The two types of conflict are entirely different. Conflicts in the exercise of concurrent jurisdiction present questions of priority or paramount interest. On the other hand, conflicts as to the existence of jurisdiction raise basic questions of international law, *i.e.*, whether the prescribing state has the authority (competence) to make the rules in question. Such conflicts usually arise when a state asserts jurisdiction with respect to conduct occurring in the territory of another state. The respective types of conflicts will be dealt with separately here.

A. Conflicts in the Exercise of Concurrent Jurisdiction

International law has not as yet evolved definitive rules of priorities among applicable laws in most situations where the laws of two or more states are applicable to the same criminal conduct.[105] In such cases, if a state has jurisdiction it may, generally speaking, exercise jurisdiction notwithstanding that another state also has jurisdiction.[106] According to

---

[104]Case of the S.S. "Lotus," [1927] P.C.I.J., ser. A, No. 10, at 92 (Moore, J., dissenting). The majority, although determining that Turkey had jurisdiction on the basis of the territorial principle, declined to pass upon the applicability of the passive personality principle as urged by the French government. *Id.* at 23. See text at notes 28-35 *supra*.

[105]See RESTATEMENT § §44-62.

[106]"[P]ublic international law has not yet developed to the point of controlling the choice that a particular state may make in most cases between its own law and

the Restatement, a state may even exercise its jurisdiction when doing so may subject a person to civil or criminal liability in another state also having jurisdiction.[107] The existence of concurrent jurisdiction to prescribe rules, however, does not give a state authority to enforce its orders in the territory of another state, as explained below.

Accommodation of generally recognized concurrent jurisdiction in most kinds of criminal matters has not heretofore presented insurmountable problems under international law. Conflicts in such cases rarely involve disagreement about the social or political ends to be served—the crimes being generally recognized as contrary to the norms of most, if not all, nations concerned. Questions as to which state shall punish can usually be dealt with by the forum state as a practical matter by

that of another state also having jurisdiction to prescribe. . . ." RESTATEMENT §37, Reporters' Note, No. 1, at 107.

The Harvard Draft attempted to lay down a rule of *non bis in idem.* In Article 13 it proposed:

"In exercising jurisdiction under this Convention, no State shall prosecute or punish an alien after it is proved that the alien has been prosecuted in another State for a crime requiring proof of substantially the same acts or omissions and has been acquitted on the merits, or has been convicted and has undergone the penalty imposed, or, having been convicted, has been paroled or pardoned." *Harvard Draft* 602.

The commentary to that article, however, recognized that "[t]he adoption of the principle formulated in the present article will be a legislative measure." *Id.* at 615.

[107]"A state having jurisdiction to prescribe or to enforce a rule of law is not precluded from exercising its jurisdiction solely because such exercise requires a person to engage in conduct subjecting him to liability under the law of another state having jurisdiction with respect to that conduct." RESTATEMENT §39(1).

The Harvard Draft reached a somewhat different conclusion and proposed in Article 14:

"In exercising jurisdiction under this Convention, no State shall prosecute or punish an alien for an act or omission which was required of that alien by the law of the place where the alien was at the time of the act or omission." *Harvard Draft* 616. The commentary recognized: "There are few precedents for the text of this article, either in national legislation or in treaties or the resolutions of international bodies. . . . The principle of *non bis in idem,* incorporated in Article 13, *supra,* is based upon an underlying concept of fairness and justice which is not wholly unlike the idea underlying the present article. The individual should not suffer, through no fault of his own, because one State punished what another State requires. . . . The article is included, therefore, as legislation so eminently desirable and just that it can hardly fail to commend itself to the favorable consideration of States." *Id.*

application of the simple rules of fair play incorporated in most legal systems.

In some other areas of like policy interests, states have concluded treaties or conventions to fix the rules for exercise of concurrent jurisdiction, *e.g.,* the numerous bilateral tax treaties for the avoidance of double taxation, status of forces agreements, fisheries conventions, and the like.

Extraterritorial Enforcement. Even where concurrent jurisdiction to prescribe rules is recognized, such jurisdiction does not give a state the right to engage in "extraterritorial enforcement" of its rules in the territory of another state. "Extraterritorial enforcement" is generally regarded as a violation of international law, except in certain limited situations—such as enforcement action on a vessel of one state in the territorial waters of another—unless the territorial state consents.[108] The scope of such consent, or the question whether it has been granted by implication, may leave room for controversy.

A different problem is presented by enforcement action taken *within* a state's territory to impose legal consequences in the territory on conduct outside the territory that has effects within it, as in *Alcoa.* Such action may raise questions as to the validity of the state's claim of jurisdiction to prescribe the rule governing extraterritorial conduct that it is seeking to enforce, but it does not raise any issue regarding the validity of extraterritorial enforcement as such. (See heading B below.)

Problems as to extraterritorial enforcement are most likely to arise in the situation where one state, having unquestioned jurisdiction on the basis of nationality to prescribe rules governing the extraterritorial conduct of its nationals, takes enforcement action in its own territory to compel conduct in foreign territory that is inconsistent with the laws of the foreign state. For example, can the United States validly compel an American corporation engaged in business in a European country to conduct that business in a manner contrary to the other nation's laws, or punish it for failure to do so? Both nations have jurisdiction to prescribe rules governing the conduct involved; the question is whether both can enforce their rules, and if not, which prevails.

The Restatement offers no satisfactory answer. It states that the mere fact of inconsistency does not preclude inconsistent enforcement by two

[108] See RESTATEMENT §44.

states having jurisdiction to prescribe,[109] but that each state must consider the effects of such enforcement in the light of specified factors.[110] If either basis of jurisdiction is to prevail automatically over the other, it should clearly be the territorial basis, and many writers have urged that this should be the rule. It seems doubtful that international law has developed, or should develop, to this point, but it may be urged with good reason that there is a strong presumption in favor of territorial jurisdiction (subject always to the rules in Part IV of the Restatement regarding state responsibility for injuries to aliens), and it is to be regretted that the Restatement does not recognize this.

The case for presumptive supremacy of territorial jurisdiction is even stronger when it is an alien, rather than a national of the forum state, who is faced with the dilemma of obeying the forum state's law, or that of his own country. Such a situation would exist, for example, if a court in the United States, having unquestioned jurisdiction to enforce American antitrust laws against a European corporation with respect to its conduct in the United States, were to seek as an aid to such enforcement to compel the production of evidence from abroad, or to require or prohibit other conduct abroad, in violation of the laws of the state where the conduct would occur. Again, the Restatement gives no clear answer, but it does suggest that a state "will be less likely" to compel an alien to violate the laws of his own country than to compel a United States national to violate the same laws.[111]

The trend of American court practice seems to be to order production of documents from abroad or to issue injunctions governing conduct abroad—whether by United States nationals or aliens that are before the court—unless such actions have been proscribed by positive foreign law.[112] Thus, in the *I.C.I.* case, the judgment included provisions governing the British corporate defendant's ownership and use of British patent rights. Enforcement of these provisions was abandoned by the court only after British courts enjoined compliance with them. In the *Holophane* case, the district court unqualifiedly ordered the American

---

[109] RESTATEMENT §39(1), note 107 *supra*.

[110] RESTATEMENT §40, see text *infra*.

[111] RESTATEMENT §40, Comment *c*.

[112] See Chapter 3 for discussion of American cases involving extraterritorial discovery orders and judgments; also Chapter 6 for detailed discussion of the judgment in the *Swiss Watch* case.

defendant affirmatively to use "reasonable efforts" to compete in foreign markets in violation of contract obligations which were lawful in the foreign countries concerned. This order was subsequently tempered by a letter from the Solicitor General to the Supreme Court interpreting the order as requiring only acts which do not violate a "foreign statute, regulation or ordinance, or the valid judgment of a competent foreign court." The Supreme Court then affirmed the order by an equally divided court.

In the *Swiss Watch* case, the court issued a sweeping injunction covering conduct of both Swiss and American defendants abroad. The decree was finally modified to provide exemption for acts required by Swiss law and for failure to act where action would be illegal under Swiss law.

American court orders to produce documents located in foreign countries have produced protests from foreign governments and some foreign statutes prohibiting compliance with such orders. In the absence of a clear foreign legal barrier, however, American courts continue to issue extraterritorial discovery orders.[113]

B. Conflicts in Claims to Jurisdiction to Prescribe

As noted above, conflicts among nations in their claims of jurisdiction to prescribe rules of law governing conduct in a particular territory present problems of a different order from those involved where concurrent jurisdiction is accepted by the states concerned. In the case of conflict as to jurisdiction to prescribe, the question is not one of priorities as to who should exercise power, but whether the right to exercise power exists at all under international law. Where claims of jurisdiction are based upon the mere intent of a person abroad, or upon domestic effects of lawful foreign conduct, the claiming state usually cannot be said to have the "permission," express or implied, of other

[113] A preliminary report by the Legal Committee of the Council of Europe's Consultative Assembly in 1966 stated that the claim of American case law of a right to exercise "coercive" extraterritorial jurisdiction "is contested by all European States." The report distinguished such enforcement activity from the right to prescribe extraterritorial antitrust rules, which it says is a right supported by the objective territorial principle. Report to the Consultative Assembly, *supra* note 59, at 8, 11-12, 14.

states. Moreover, the social and political ends to be served by the prescribed rules may not be reciprocated by the other state—indeed, they may be exactly contrary to its domestic social, economic and political policy.

Extraterritorial measures adopted by the United States during recent years, and particularly by its courts in antitrust matters, have frequently been received abroad with disfavor. On the other hand, as stated by Professor Baxter:

> The economic strength of the [United States], the degree and sophistication of regulation of business activity by the government and the world-wide involvement of the country make it inevitable that the impact of the law and economy of the United States should be felt abroad.[114]

It may be that the export of American antitrust policy is in the best interests of the recipient states. Nevertheless, American extraterritorial antitrust regulation and enforcement have met with great opposition abroad, not only on grounds of economic policy, but of national sovereignty, and may even have involved violations of international law. The result has been a tide of protests and some reprisals.[115] At the very least, these diplomatic and other protests indicate some question as to the existence of the consensus essential for reliance upon the relevant permissive principle of international law.

If not accepted as protestations of violation of international law, these protests have at least served to restrain extraterritorial application of American law. As stated by Professor Baxter:

> [A]ccommodation has been reached between the State asserting jurisdiction and the State resisting jurisdiction through a process of diplomatic negotiation coupled with the willingness of courts and administrative agencies to hold their hand when natural or juridical persons are exposed to conflicting orders from two different systems of municipal law. The withdrawal by the United States

[114]Baxter, "Settlement of Disputes," in INT'L LAW ASS'N, REPORT OF THE COMMITTEE ON EXTRA-TERRITORIAL APPLICATION OF RESTRICTIVE TRADE LEGISLATION, pt. III, at 42 (Buenos Aires Conference, 1968).

[115]See Chapters 3, 6 and 9. For compilations and summaries of protests, see BREWSTER, *supra* note 56, at 46; TOKYO REPORT 565-92; NATIONAL SECURITY AND FOREIGN POLICY IN THE APPLICATION OF AMERICAN ANTITRUST LAWS TO COMMERCE WITH FOREIGN NATIONS 12-15 (1957), a preliminary report by the Special Committee on Antitrust Laws and Foreign Trade of the Association of the Bar of the City of New York.

from the advanced positions which it had proposed to occupy or had actually occupied in these cases was brought about through the enactment of municipal law by the aggrieved States, through diplomatic protests, through pressures from the foreign persons affected and from sympathizers within the United States.[116]

IV. ALTERNATIVES FOR SETTLEMENT OF CONFLICTS

A wide variety of means and methods have been suggested for settlement or avoidance of disputes and conflicts arising from the extraterritorial application of national antitrust rules and other regulatory measures affecting foreign trade. These range from the elimination of conflicts by harmonization of national substantive laws, to the doctrine that in the absence of positive laws to the contrary in the foreign state concerned any state may enact and enforce rules anywhere regarding restraints affecting its foreign trade.[117] Although many nations now have some kind of law dealing with antitrust problems, these laws vary a great deal in both substance and procedure, and it seems most unlikely that a world-wide common accord will be achieved in the foreseeable future either on the merits of particular antitrust laws or policies or upon enforcement measures affecting the flow of international trade. Similarly, uninhibited enforcement abroad of divergent rules or policies is extremely unlikely to bring about either common policy or a rule of law. It is also clear that there is no consensus as to the method most likely to succeed in the settlement of the present disputes and conflicts.

In the main, however, insofar as international law is concerned, the available alternatives are well-defined, and may be stated as follows:

(A) Adherence to generally accepted principles of customary international law until changed by a genuine consensus, or by treaty or other conventional law. (Traditional International Law Approach)

(B) Acceptance of the jurisdiction of the International Court of Justice or another international tribunal, having authority to adjudicate such disputes in accordance with principles of international law or under

[116]Baxter, *supra* note 114, at 43-44.

[117]See "A Preliminary Examination of Possible Lines of Approach," in TOKYO REPORT 544 (Professor Covey T. Oliver, Rapporteur).

rules written into its statute, notwithstanding that determinations may involve issues claimed by some states to be within their "domestic jurisdiction." (International Adjudication)

(C) Assertion of extraterritorial jurisdiction, limited by self-judging rules of restraint to moderate the exercise of enforcement jurisdiction. (The Restatement Rule)

A. Traditional International Law Approach

The evolutionary processes of customary international law are ill-adapted to the formulation of rules to govern the conduct of international trade among competing states with divergent economic and political philosophies. Even within the United States, with its highly developed judicial system and one court of last resort, the evolution of domestic antitrust rules is not without disputes and conflicts.

Although each nation-state, as well as the EEC, has its own ultimate legislative or judicial authority for the resolution of conflicts and disputes within its own jurisdiction, including those relating to antitrust, the community of nations does not as yet possess any such ultimate authority, except to the limited extent that the jurisdiction of the International Court of Justice may be recognized. Development of customary international law, therefore, remains largely dependent upon the process of achieving common accord, or consensus, among states— something virtually impossible to accomplish in economic affairs without negotiation and express agreement. Accordingly, as already noted, states have turned to bilateral and multilateral treaties or conventions to fix the rules for dealing with economic matters of international concern. Because of widely differing views and economic polices, past efforts to achieve international agreement in the area of antitrust have been singularly unsuccessful, with the outstanding exception of the European Communities.[118]

Even though customary international law may be incapable of adequately providing new rules to meet the new economic complexities in a rapidly changing world, it does not follow that established rules and principles should be disregarded without the consent of states affected.

---

[118] See Chapter 8 *infra* and Chapters 1 and 2 *supra;* Note, *The United Nations Draft Convention on Restrictive Business Practices,* 4 INT'L & COMP. L. Q. 129 (1955); TOKYO REPORT 473-82.

Unilateral attempts to extend or modify accepted rules without the concurrence of affected states, however meritorious, do not solve the problem; rather, they are a prime source of the conflicts and disputes with which this book is concerned.

Section 18(b) of the Restatement is regarded by many as such a unilateral attempt to extend or modify heretofore generally accepted rules or principles of international law.[119] There is undoubtedly great merit in the objective sought to be achieved by that section, and there is no question that it fairly states the view of the American antitrust enforcement authorities and a number of United States courts.[120] On the other hand, its approach has been accepted by only a handful of other nations and has been largely rejected by writers outside the United States.[121] Consequently, the disputes and conflicts engendered by the kind of extraterritorial jurisdiction stated in Section 18(b) could most readily be resolved by nonassertion of such jurisdiction. In view of the disputes that are otherwise certain to arise, it is to be hoped that such jurisdiction will not be indiscriminately asserted.

B. International Adjudication

Controversial jurisdictional issues such as those raised by Section 18(b) of the Restatement, or similar jurisdictional claims of other states,

---

[119]See text at notes 59-69 *supra.* In summarizing its extensive comments on the proposed draft of the Restatement, the International Law Committee of the Association of the Bar of the City of New York concluded as follows: "With respect to the 'extraterritorial jurisdiction' aspects of the Restatement, the Committee agrees with the rule stated in §18(a) to the effect that a state has prescriptive jurisdiction over external conduct producing an effect inside such state where the conduct and its effect are generally recognized as constituent elements of a crime under the laws of states that have reasonably developed legal systems. §18(b), however, departs from hitherto accepted principles of international law by declaring that a state's prescriptive jurisdiction also extends to conduct outside its territory where that conduct and its domestic effect are not generally recognized as constituent elements of a crime or tort under the laws of states that have reasonably developed legal systems. §18(b) does not restate existing international law and should be deleted." Association of the Bar of the City of New York, International Law Committee, Report on Certain Aspects of the Proposed Restatement of the Foreign Relations Law of the United States 2-3 (May 22, 1962).

[120]See Chapter 2 *supra.*

[121]See notes 58-60 and 64 *supra.*

should certainly be decided impartially on an international basis rather than unilaterally. It has been the policy of the United States, however, not to permit matters to be adjudicated or arbitrated by an international tribunal except under specific and tightly-drawn terms of reference. If not by the Statute itself,[122] then by the Connally reservation,[123] the International Court of Justice is precluded from adjudicating antitrust disputes involving the United States, unless the latter consents.

Conceivably, the United States will one day consent to international arbitration or adjudication of such jurisdictional issues, either through special treaties or by parallel national declarations under Article 36 of the Statute of the International Court, whereby states may agree to such third-party determinations. It is also possible that other states, as well as the European Communities, may exercise extraterritorial jurisdiction under their antitrust laws in a manner that might precipitate a proceeding before the International Court.

The participation of the United States in any general plan for adjudication or arbitration of jurisdictional disputes in the area of antitrust regulation would require a major alteration in national policy.

[122] I.C.J. Stat., art. 36.

[123] See note 9 *supra.* The Connally Amendment applies to "disputes with regard to matters which are essentially within the domestic jurisdiction of the United States of America *as determined by the United States of America.*" (emphasis added) United States Declaration signed Aug. 14, 1946, first proviso (b), 15 DEP'T STATE BULL. 452, 453 (1946). The eight words *underscored* comprise the Connally Amendment.

The position of the United States under the Connally Amendment was stated in a letter dated May 13, 1960 from Eric Hager, Agent of the United States, to the Registrar of the International Court of Justice requesting that the proceedings in the Case Concerning the Aerial Incident of 27 July 1955 (United States v. Bulgaria), [1960] I.C.J. 146, be discontinued and the case removed from the Court's Lists:

"As it was declared by the United States to this Court in the Interhandel Case (Switzerland v. United States), when the United States had made a determination under reservation (*b*) ['domestic jurisdiction . . . as determined by the United States of America'] that a particular matter is essentially within its domestic jurisdiction, that determination is not subject to review or approval by any tribunal, and it operates to remove definitively from the jurisdiction of the Court the matter which it determines. A determination under reservation (*b*) that a matter is essentially domestic constitutes an absolute bar to jurisdiction irrespective of the propriety or arbitrariness of the determination." I.C.J. PLEADINGS, AERIAL INCIDENT OF 27 JULY 1955 (UNITED STATES V. BULGARIA) 677 (1959).

Until such a major shift can occur, the general position of the United States should not preclude resort to settlement of specific questions by special provision for arbitration or adjudication.

While it appears unlikely that a general plan for adjudication or arbitration of these disputes on a broad international basis will be adopted soon,[124] groups of nations having common economic goals, such as the EC and EFTA, may develop regional solutions. Such a solution has been suggested and is under consideration by the Legal Committee of the Council of Europe.[125] It has proposed a convention to establish uniform rules of extraterritorial jurisdiction and enforcement accepted by all contracting countries, thereby avoiding conflicts by conceding jurisdiction.[126] The proposal presupposes the harmonization of rival or competing national economic policies of the states concerned, an object that might be achieved by some groups of nations.[127]

[124] See Chapter 8 for a review of past efforts at international agreements to solve these problems.

[125] Report to the Consultative Assembly of the Council of Europe, by the Legal Committee (deGrailly, Rapporteur), The Extra-Territorial Application of Anti-Trust Legislation, Doc. 2023 (Jan. 25, 1966). (The report was noted by the Assembly and the committee was instructed to continue to study the question and to report its final conclusions.)

[126] The report states that it is not "considered appropriate that there should be any extra-territorial enforcement procedure unless by virtue of a special convention. It is therefore suggested that by convention States should agree to recognise: (i) that the courts of a State in whose territory restrictive trading practices are to be performed or to produce their effect have jurisdiction to entertain proceedings in relation to such practices; this is a mainly declaratory statement; (ii) that for the impounding of goods there may be a coercive procedure with extraterritorial effects, subject to reciprocity; (iii) that such an agreed procedure should enable the courts of the State having jurisdiction to issue subpoenas to obtain documents: it is suggested that, under the Convention, letters of request should issue from the court having jurisdiction to the court where the documents are located, and that the court receiving such requests shall be obliged to ensure compliance with such request by the persons concerned, by making an order against such persons which in the event of non-compliance shall render such persons subject to penalty and/or imprisonment according to their own municipal law; (iv) that the same procedure should also enable the court receiving a request to such effect from the court of the State having jurisdiction to grant injunctions in accordance with the municipal law of the person against whom such an injunction is sought, in order to uphold the effect of orders made by the court having jurisdiction (in accordance with (i) above)." Report to the Consultative Assembly, *supra* note 125, at 15-16.

[127] But see Markert, *Recent Developments in International Antitrust Cooperation,* 13 ANTITRUST BULL. 355 (1968); the author points out that "it seems

C. The Restatement Rule

The broad assertion of jurisdiction by Section 18(b) made it necessary to establish rules of forbearance to brake excessive application of extraterritorial power. (The same brake, of course, could also apply in cases of generally accepted concurrent jurisdiction.) Accordingly, the Restatement, in Section 40, provides:

> Where two states have jurisdiction to prescribe and enforce rules of law and the rules they may prescribe require inconsistent conduct upon the part of a person, each state is required by international law to consider, in good faith, moderating the exercise of its enforcement jurisdiction, in the light of such factors as
>
> (a) vital national interests of each of the states,
>
> (b) the extent and the nature of the hardship that inconsistent enforcement actions would impose upon the person,
>
> (c) the extent to which the required conduct is to take place in the territory of the other state,
>
> (d) the nationality of the person, and
>
> (e) the extent to which enforcement by action of either state can reasonably be expected to achieve compliance with the rule prescribed by that state.

The Comments on Section 40 add:

> It is clear that if each state having a basis of jurisdiction were in every case to exercise its jurisdiction without considering the interests of another state also having jurisdiction, disputes between states and hardship to persons would often arise. That such disputes and hardship do not arise more frequently is due to compliance with the principles reflected in the rule stated in this Section.

doubtful that rules based on the effect of a particular agreement or practice could achieve harmony, for international restrictive business practices frequently have effects in several countries, each of which would then have jurisdiction and could apply its own law." The author adds that "the proposal raises political problems which are perhaps even more difficult. In the brief debate by the Consultative Assembly on January 27, 1966, the Swedish Delegate Bowman said that it was difficult to conceive that countries such as Sweden and Switzerland, with 'liberal' antitrust laws, would enforce foreign court or administrative orders against their citizens. Indeed, it seems probable that, without further harmonization of the antitrust laws involved and abolition of the exemptions for export restrictions, formal and legally binding international antitrust arrangements that imply recognition of foreign extra-territorial antitrust action and an obligation to give legal assistance to foreign courts and authorities are premature. . . ." *Id.* at 365-66.

As used in this Section "vital national interest" means an interest such as national security or general welfare to which a state attaches overriding importance. The concept of vital national interest is to be distinguished from the protective principle as a basis of jurisdiction. . . . Vital national interest is not itself a basis of jurisdiction but is a factor favoring the exercise of jurisdiction, even though it interferes with such exercise by another state.

Section 40 assumes the existence of concurrent jurisdiction, and sets forth rules of comity, rather than of law.

There is substantial merit in urging forbearance on the part of each government concerned with international antitrust problems, as this undoubtedly would be helpful in reducing conflict to the extent that action is withheld out of concern for interests of other nations.[128] On the other hand, the idea of balancing "vital national interests" of other nations by a national court is likely to seem somewhat presumptuous to the foreign state concerned, notwithstanding the qualifications of the judges. "Self-judging" is not likely to elicit enthusiasm from those who

---

[128] This may be the post-*Swiss Watch* approach of the Department of Justice. In 1967, Donald F. Turner, then Assistant Attorney General in Charge of the Antitrust Division, testified: "The Restatement says that U.S. courts have jurisdiction over acts and agreements, even though made abroad, which directly and substantially affect the foreign commerce of the United States.

"However, this does not mean that the Department of Justice always will push this rule to its outermost limits. Too broad an application of the rule may raise a serious risk of creating conflicts with foreign laws and foreign economic interests— conflicts that might, in some situations, better be resolved through diplomatic negotiation. For this reason, in deciding whether to apply the Sherman Act to foreign activity, it may be necessary also to rely upon a careful resolution of possibly conflicting foreign and domestic legal and economic interests.

"Serious problems would be raised, for example, by invoking the Sherman Act when foreign law requires firms within its jurisdiction to act in a way that American law would prohibit, such as compelling the firms within its borders to engage in the very type of price fixing that American law would forbid. Even if foreign law does not specifically require conduct that violates the Sherman Act, conflicts in policy are possible. Thus, in the *Swiss Watch* case, the Department of Justice, at the instance of the Department of State, met with representatives of the Swiss Government for a period of several months and worked out a satisfactory modification of the final judgment which took into consideration the views of the Swiss Government concerning recognition of Swiss sovereignty and jurisdiction over its own trade." *Hearings on Prices of Quinine and Quinidine Before the Subcomm. on Antitrust and Monopoly of the Sen. Comm. on the Judiciary,* 90th Cong., 1st Sess., pt. 2, at 236 (1967).

are judged to be wrong—especially since what is involved falls outside the area of generally accepted crimes and torts.

CONCLUSION

Disputes and conflicts in the extraterritorial application of antitrust laws are essentially matters of jurisdiction, revolving around claims by one state of the right to prescribe or enforce rules covering conduct in another state. Restraint in the assertion of such claims avoids, or at least minimizes, the problem.

If the United States, or any other state, follows a policy of ordering action abroad by aliens, or in some cases by its own nationals, without the consent of the affected foreign state or states, disputes and conflicts are likely. The most appropriate course under international law for the United States, or any other state maintaining such a policy, is either to obtain the consent of the affected foreign state, or to agree to some form of international adjudication. Reliance upon Sections 18(b) and 40 of the Restatement clearly will not suffice.

CHAPTER **8** *International Organizations*
and Treaties in Antitrust

The most important efforts to deal with restrictive business practices through international agreements have occurred in the years since World War II. A few of these efforts have succeeded, but most have failed. Some have been the world-wide efforts of many nations; others have been the work of smaller groups. Of those that have succeeded, only the European Communities have developed a really supranational and comprehensive approach; the others largely are modest arrangements for consultation and exchange of information.

Part I below is devoted to a description of the efforts made by already existing international organizations, all of which have failed. Any study of means of resolving conflicts between the antitrust laws of different nations must, of course, try to be enlightened by the experience of efforts which have foundered, as well as of those which have succeeded. The successful efforts of the European Communities have been treated at length in previous chapters, and will be discussed only briefly in Part II of this chapter. Also described there are the restrictive practice provisions of the Stockholm Convention creating the European Free Trade Association (EFTA). Chapter 9 discusses the informational arrangements now in force.

Prior to World War II an antitrust problem with serious foreign implications was very likely to arise in the context either of an

417

international cartel,[1] or of a patent pool.[2] Excess capacity—or the threat of it—seems to have been in the background of many of these arrangements.[3] The international cartel problem was considered in a number of studies at the time. The League of Nations showed interest in the possibility of international regulation, but the World Economic Conference, held under the League's auspices in 1927, concluded that, owing to differences in national policy, international rules would not be practicable. The Conference considered, nevertheless, that the League, in cooperation with national governments, might provide some means of supervision over cartels and cartel-like agreements.[4]

The Economic Commission of the League of Nations then requested a group of lawyers and a group of industrial experts to study the legal and economic aspects of the regulatory problems. The lawyers, for their part, took the view that state supervision of international cartels was both desirable and feasible, and that means could be devised to harmonize to an appreciable degree existing systems of supervision. The group of industrial experts, in contrast, concluded that international cartels had a number of advantages and required no further regulation.[5] The Economic Commission never committed itself to either position.

[1] See generally, U.N. ECONOMIC & SOCIAL COUNCIL, RESTRICTIVE BUSINESS PRACTICES: REPORT ON RESTRICTIVE BUSINESS PRACTICES IN INTERNATIONAL TRADE, Official Records: 19 U.N. ECOSOC, Supp. 3A, U.N. Doc. E/2675 (1955); STOCKING & WATKINS, CARTELS IN ACTION (1946); HEXNER, INTERNATIONAL CARTELS (1945). For a good current discussion, see Vernon, *Antitrust and International Business,* 46 HARV. BUS. REV. 78 (Sept.-Oct. 1968).

[2] Antitrust cases involving patent pools going back to pre-World War II include United States v. General Electric Co., 82 F.Supp. 753 (D.N.J. 1949); United States v. United States Alkali Export Ass'n, 86 F.Supp. 59 (S.D.N.Y. 1949); United States v. Imperial Chem. Indus., Ltd., 100 F.Supp. 504 (S.D.N.Y. 1951).

[3] Excess capacity evidently was behind many of the arrangements considered—for example, in United States v. Aluminum Co. of America, 148 F.2d 416 (2d Cir. 1945).

[4] Günther, *The Problems Involved in Regulating International Restraints of Competition by Means of Public International Law,* in 2 CARTEL AND MONOPOLY IN MODERN LAW 581-82 (1961).

[5] *Id.* at 582-83. As Dr. Günther notes, the economic experts chosen were almost inevitably committed to a position in favor of cartels by virtue of their background. The experts were Antonio St. Benni (Italy); Clemens Lammers (Germany), Chief of the Cartel Division of the German Industries Association; Louis Marlio (France), President of the International Aluminum Cartel; and Aloys Meyer (Luxembourg), President of the International Steel Cartel; *id.* at 582 & n.6.

Since World War II, the international cartel problem appears to have diminished somewhat in importance because of fundamental changes in the way international trade is organized and conducted,[6] and other factors have arisen to motivate attempts at obtaining international controls. In any consideration of motivation, however, it is important to note that the problem of restrictive practices has rarely been the dominant force behind such international efforts as have occurred. Rather, that problem has been only a part, though often an important part, of some broader international approach.

The post-War attempts are set forth below largely in chronological order, because in that way the process of development can be seen and the influences of earlier efforts on later ones can be appraised. The Havana Charter came first. Its key chapter was taken over nearly word for word by the ECOSOC Ad Hoc Committee on Restrictive Business Practices. Meanwhile a Draft Convention was developed in the Council of Europe, but was abandoned in favor of the ECOSOC approach. The 1960 Decision of GATT is a watered-down version of the ECOSOC consultation procedure. The EEC text itself reflects some of the features of the Council of Europe draft, and the debt of the EFTA text to the EEC is clear.

I. ATTEMPTS BY EXISTING INTERNATIONAL ORGANIZATIONS TO DEAL WITH RESTRICTIVE PRACTICES

A. The Havana Charter: 1948

The first major international conference on trade after World War II was held in 1947 at Geneva. This conference resulted in the General Agreement on Tariffs and Trade (GATT), opened for acceptance in October, 1947.[7] Initiated by the United States, one of its purposes was to create an International Trade Organization (ITO) as an agency of the United Nations, pledged to freer trade. This purpose was implemented at Havana, when on March 24, 1948, representatives of fifty-three nations finally approved a Charter for ITO.[8]

[6] For a discussion of the evolution of international operations of a modern corporation along functional lines, see Rose, *The Rewarding Strategies of Multinationalism,* 78 FORTUNE 100 (Sept. 15, 1968).

[7] 55 U.N.T.S. 187 (1950); see DAM, THE GATT: LAW AND INTERNATIONAL ECONOMIC ORGANIZATION (1969); JACKSON, WORLD TRADE AND THE LAW OF GATT (1969).

[8] The text of the Charter is in U.S. DEP'T OF STATE, HAVANA CHARTER FOR AN INTERNATIONAL TRADE ORGANIZATION, Publication 3206, COMMERCIAL POLICY SERIES 114 (1948).

In due course, it became apparent that, even though the United States had been instrumental in bringing about the conference,[9] it would not ratify the Havana Charter.[10] The negative American position sufficed to discourage other countries from ratifying it, and it never went into effect. The Charter remains, nonetheless, an important chapter in the evolution of international efforts to deal with restrictive trade practices. Virtually all subsequent post-World War II efforts have, to some degree, been influenced by it.

The terms of the Charter encompass the whole field of trade and employment. Restrictive business practices, of both private and public commercial enterprises, are taken up in Chapter V. The focus is on practices of such commercial enterprises as possess, individually or collectively, effective control of trade in one or more products among a number of countries.[11] Practices covered are those "affecting international trade which restrain competition, limit access to markets, or foster monopolistic control whenever such practices have harmful effects on the expansion of production or trade and interfere with the achievement of any of the other objectives" of the Charter.[12]

The Charter does not provide for a catalog of specifically illegal arrangements, but it does set down a list of specific practices which shall be subject to investigation upon complaint to the Organization (ITO). These are:

(a) fixing prices, terms or conditions to be observed in dealing with others in the purchase, sale or lease of any product;
(b) excluding enterprises from, or allocating or dividing, any territorial market or field of business activity, or allocating customers, or fixing sales quotas or purchase quotas;

---

[9] See Renouf, *The Abortive Charter for an International Trade Organization,* 29 CAN. BAR REV. 53, 55 (1951).

[10] A resolution calling for approval was introduced in Congress and hearings were conducted by the House Foreign Affairs Committee. The Committee did not act on the resolution. See *Hearings on H.R.J.Res. 236 Providing for Membership and Participation by the United States in the ITO Before the House Comm. on Foreign Affairs,* 81st Cong., 2d Sess. 1 (1950). The Executive Branch did not resubmit the ITO to Congress, 23 DEP'T STATE BULL. 977 (1950). See also, Jackson, *The General Agreement on Tariffs and Trade in United States Domestic Law,* 66 MICH. L. REV. 250, 252 n.13 (1967).

[11] Art. 46, para. 2(b) and (c).

[12] Art. 46, para. 1.

(c) discriminating against particular enterprises;

(d) limiting production or fixing production quotas;

(e) preventing by agreement the development or application of technology or invention whether patented or unpatented;

(f) extending the use of rights under patents, trade marks or copyrights granted by any Member to matters which, according to its laws and regulations, are not within the scope of such grants, or to products or conditions of production, use or sale which are likewise not the subjects of such grants.[13]

This list may be expanded by a majority vote of two-thirds of the Members of ITO, who may thereby declare "any similar practices" to be "restrictive business practices."[14] Certain services, as well as trade in products, are referred to,[15] and certain individual contracts are excepted.[16]

The Charter is addressed to Member States, and it confers no rights or obligations on individual enterprises. Each Member State is obligated to "take all possible measures by legislation or otherwise, in accordance with its constitution or system of law and economic organization, to ensure, within its jurisdiction, that private and public commercial enterprises do not engage" in restrictive business practices having harmful effects as referred to above, and it "shall assist the Organization in preventing these practices."[17] This appears to lay an affirmative obligation on Member States to "prevent" harmful restrictive business practices, rather than simply waiting to respond in case of complaint by another Member. But there could easily be more bark than bite to any

[13] Art. 46, para. 2.

[14] Art. 46, para. 2(g).

[15] Where a Member apprehends that a restrictive business practice may have harmful effects on a service so that its interests are likely to be seriously prejudiced, it may submit a statement to the Member whose enterprises, private or public, are engaged in such practices. The Member addressed shall afford adequate opportunities for consultation with a view to effecting a satisfactory adjustment, Art. 53, para. 2. If the matter is not adjusted, it may be referred to the Organization, which may transfer it to any intergovernmental organization which may be available or, should the Members request, make recommendations itself—by virtue of its inherent functions, Art. 53, para. 3.

[16] An exception would be recognized for individual contracts between two parties, such as buyer and seller, lessor and lessee, principal and agent—so long as such contracts do not restrain competition, limit access to markets or foster monopolistic control, Art. 54, para. 2(a).

[17] Art. 50, para. 1.

such obligation, since a Member is under no obligation to treat international restrictive business practices under the same standards, if any, as it would apply to domestic restraints.[18] Also, inasmuch as a Member is permitted to take action by legislation "or otherwise," it might content itself with the use of mere admonitions in place of enforcement.

Any affected Member wishing to complain that a practice exists "which has or is about to have" a harmful effect may call for consultation or investigation.[19] Where a public enterprise acting independently of any other enterprise is alleged to be engaging in a restrictive business practice, consultation is to precede investigation.[20]

Investigatory procedure is provided for, but with due reservation of the sovereign rights of the Members.[21] An obligation to cooperate with the Organization's investigations is tempered, first, by a reference again to each Member's own institutions, and, second, by the proviso that a Member need only "take in the particular case the action it considers appropriate having regard to its obligations under this Chapter."[22]

[18] Art. 54, para. 1.

[19] Arts. 47 and 48.

[20] Art. 46, para. 1.

[21] If the complaint does not involve a practice automatically requiring investigation, the Organization might ask Members for supplementary information—"for example, information from commercial enterprises within their jurisdiction," Art. 48, para. 3. The obligation to provide information contains the proviso that: "any Member, on notification to the Organization, may withhold information which the Member considers is not essential to the Organization in conducting an adequate investigation and which, if disclosed, would substantially damage the legitimate interests of a commercial enterprise," Art. 50, para. 3. And a general provision of the Charter provides exceptions for the essential security interests of the Members, Art. 99. Similar concern is reflected in the reservation appearing in the provisions calling for a report by the Organization of the decision reached, "the reasons therefor and any measures recommended to the Members concerned"—but should a Member so request, "the Organization shall not ... disclose confidential information furnished by that Member, which if disclosed would substantially damage the legitimate business interests of a commercial enterprise," Art. 48, para. 9.

However, the Organization shall afford "reasonable opportunity to be heard" on a complaint by "any Member, and any person, enterprise or organization on whose behalf the complaint has been made, as well as the commercial enterprises alleged to have engaged in the practice complained of . . . ," Art. 48, para. 4.

[22] Art. 50, para. 4.

Should the Organization conclude that some restrictive business practice has had, or is about to have the requisite harmful effect, it "shall request each Member concerned to take every possible remedial action, and may also recommend to the Members concerned remedial measures to be carried out in accordance with their respective laws and procedures."[23]

The Charter relies entirely on the goodwill of the Members to enforce the general policy set forth and the Organization's recommendations. Publicity attaching to publication of a report and recommendation is the only sanction available to the Organization itself. Each Member is to report fully any action taken by it, independently or in concert with other Members, to comply with the requests and carry out the recommendations of the Organization, and when no action has been taken, to inform the Organization of the reasons therefor.[24] It is also required that the Organization report to all Members and make public the remedial action taken by the Members concerned in any particular case,[25] but in the event of failure on the part of any Member to take action, the only obligation is to discuss the matter further with the Organization if so requested, and the Charter is silent as to publicity in such event.[26]

Either on its own initiative or at the request of a Member or an intergovernmental organization, the Organization is authorized to conduct studies concerning general aspects of restrictive business practices affecting international trade, conventions, laws, procedures relating to commercial matters in general and registration of restrictive business agreements. It is also empowered to make recommendations to Members concerning such conventions, laws and procedures as might be relevant to their obligations under Chapter V. The Organization may convene conferences of Members to discuss restrictive business practices affecting international trade.[27]

[23] Art. 48, para. 7. The jurisdiction of Members to enforce their own laws is carefully preserved: "No act or omission to act on the part of the Organization shall preclude any Member from enforcing any national statute or decree directed towards preventing monopoly or restraint of trade," Art. 52.

[24] Art. 50, para. 5.

[25] Art. 48, para. 10.

[26] Art. 50, para. 5.

[27] Art. 49.

The simple fact that representatives of so many countries with different political and economic backgrounds were able to draft such a comprehensive and detailed proposal makes the Havana Charter a considerable technical triumph. Why, then, did it fail to receive the necessary ratifications? (Only one nation, Liberia, ratified without qualification.) As already stated, the principal reason for failure, ironically, was lack of support by the United States, source of so much of the initiative for a Charter. Its abandonment by the United States has been attributed to concern solely with the tariff provisions of the Charter.[28] This may be an oversimplification, however, since considerable opposition was expressed to the antitrust regulatory concepts embodied in the Charter.[29]

One whose official capacity as legal adviser permitted close observation of the work of the Conference has offered several suggestions as to how ratification might have been made more likely.[30] He suggests that it may have been a mistake to aim in the first instance at such a complete code; an agreement which came closer to a statement of general principles and created an instrumentality to work out particular applications over a period of time could have been written more quickly, would have given less cause for opposition, and would have allowed less time for the opposition to mobilize.

A second tactical error, the same observer suggests, may have been to separate consideration of rules for restrictive business practices from arrangements—already worked out when the Havana Conference met—to reduce tariffs and quotas.[31] Had both subjects been taken up at the same time, those opposed to antitrust regulation in any form might have been willing to make concessions in return for other benefits.

[28]Contrast Renouf, *supra* note 9, at 60, with views of various members of the Attorney General's Committee, REPORT OF THE ATTORNEY GENERAL'S NATIONAL COMMITTEE TO STUDY THE ANTITRUST LAWS 98-108 (1955) [hereinafter cited as ATTY. GEN. NAT. COMM. ANTITRUST REP.].

[29]See ATTY. GEN. NAT. COMM. ANTITRUST REP. 105-08. Though the opposition here expressed was a reply to a kind word offered on behalf of the Draft Articles of Agreement proposed by the ECOSOC Ad Hoc Committee on Restrictive Business Practices, the fact that those Articles derived substantially from Chapter V of the Havana Charter invites the conclusion that opposition to the later version would equally have been directed to the earlier.

[30]See Renouf, *supra* note 9. Mr. Renouf was legal advisor to the Havana Trade Conference and to the Contracting Parties to the General Agreement.

[31]*Id.* at 58-60.

Unlike the World Economic Conference of 1927 sponsored by the League of Nations, the Havana Conference invited only representatives of the Governments involved. Private groups were permitted to circulate their views but had no role in the closed deliberations of the working committees. This also may have been a mistake.[32] Participation by representatives of a more diverse constituency might have forestalled later opposition.

The apathy displayed by nearly every prospective signatory suggests that almost no country at the time was persuaded that antitrust regulation should be a matter of international concern.

B. United Nations Economic and Social Council: (ECOSOC): 1951-1955

The next important effort to deal with restrictive business practices on a multinational basis was the world-wide effort of the United Nations Economic and Social Council (ECOSOC). On September 13, 1951, a resolution was approved urging, in part, that Member States take

> appropriate measures and cooperate with one another to prevent, on the part of private or public commercial enterprises, business practices affecting international trade which restrain competition, limit access to markets or foster monopolistic control, whenever such practices have harmful effects on the expansion of production or trade, on the economic development of under-developed areas, or on standards of living.[33]

In the same resolution, the Council established an Ad Hoc Committee made up of representatives of ten countries, and directed that it be guided by the principles of the Havana Charter and submit proposals for an international agreement to implement those principles.[34]

The Committee's report, submitted on March 30, 1953, proposed draft articles of agreement based on Chapter V of the Havana Charter.[35]

[32]*Id.* at 60-61.

[33]REPORT OF THE AD HOC COMMITTEE ON RESTRICTIVE BUSINESS PRACTICES, Annex I, U.N. Economic and Social Council Res. 375 (XIII), Item 1, Official Records: 16 U.N. ECOSOC Supp. 11, at 12, U.N. Doc. E/2380, E/AC. 37/3 (1953).

[34]*Id.,* Items 2 and 3. The ten countries were Belgium, Canada, France, India, Mexico, Pakistan, Sweden, the United Kingdom, the United States and Uruguay.

[35]*Id.,* Annex II. We do not review the details of this ECOSOC draft in the text because of its similarity to the Havana Charter. Reviews and comparisons of the two

The draft exhibits many of the weaknesses of its model. The standards by which practices would be tested for harmful effects are, in both cases, often extremely loose. And, in both cases, a Member's obligation to follow a recommendation is circumscribed in accordance with the Member's constitution or system of law and economic organization. Both drafts sketch general goals, provide for a consensus and recommendations and permit Members, in their own fashion, to raise standards for dealing with restrictive business practices.

In several respects, the ECOSOC draft broke new ground, however. Elaborate safeguards were provided to avoid giving currency to improper complaints. Provision was also made for establishing an international agency carefully engineered to permit expert economic and political judgment to be brought to bear on a given practice.

The draft was first discussed at the sixteenth Session of ECOSOC in July 1953. It developed, however, that the Council could not reach general agreement. It was further discussed at the nineteenth Session in May 1955 at which time the views of the governments were considered. Because of continuing disagreement it was decided not to pursue the matter for the time being.[36] The Council did recommend to Members, however, that they keep the Secretary-General informed of developments in the field of national cartel law so that this information might then be communicated to other Members. It was hoped that this exchange would contribute to the evolution of legal standards.[37]

The draft aroused an extraordinary amount of opposition. The Attorney General's National Committee to Study the Antitrust Laws, by a narrow majority, declined to take any position as to whether the draft should be supported by the United States.[38] Ultimately, the United States withdrew its support.[39]

documents will be found in Günther, *supra* note 4, at 584-89 and in RESTRICTIVE BUSINESS PRACTICES, GATT (prepared by Professor J. L'HUILLIER) 69-75 (Havana Charter), 76-80 (ECOSOC draft) (1959) [hereinafter cited as L'HUILLIER]. See also the comments of Hellwig, Rapporteur of the Committee on Economic Questions, Council of Europe Consultative Assembly, Official Report of the Fourteenth Sitting: EUR. CONSULT. ASS. DEB., 6TH SESS., at 332-36 (Sept. 15, 1954).

[36] Günther, *supra* note 4, at 586-89.

[37] *Id.* at 589.

[38] ATTY. GEN. NAT. COMM. ANTITRUST REP. 98-99.

[39] This is discussed in Timberg, *Restrictive Practices: The Case for an International Agreement,* 6 CARTEL 2 (1956).

Why was this venture not more successful? In retrosprect, the failure of the U.N. effort, as with the Havana Charter, appears to reflect the lack of widespread enthusiasm for international antitrust regulation at the time. In addition, the variety of national approaches to the problem precluded, it was apparently felt, effective international regulation, and only invited disagreement about standards and conflicting reactions to recommendations. The United States itself ultimately seems to have concluded that it would be preferable to seek standardization and coordination of national laws rather than to expect a solution based on public international law.[40]

During this period international cooperation was evolving new concepts and new institutions on other, quite different levels—most spectacularly, as events turned out, in regional terms.

C. Council of Europe: 1949-1955

The third important effort was the undertaking by the Council of Europe to deal with international cartels in the European area. This work began in 1949 and, for the most part, lapsed in 1955 at about the same time as the demise of ECOSOC's effort.

As pointed out in Chapter 1, World War II created strong sentiments in Europe for economic and political cooperation. Political expression of those sentiments took form in the Council of Europe, established by statute signed in London on May 5, 1949 and ratified by ten nations.[41] The preamble recites that the signatories believe that "there is need of a closer unity between all like-minded countries of Europe" and that "it is necessary forthwith to create an organisation which will bring European States into closer association." The aim of the Council is stated to be "to achieve a greater unity between its Members for the purpose of safeguarding and realizing the ideals and principles which are their

[40]Günther, *supra* note 4, at 588.

[41]See ROBERTSON, THE COUNCIL OF EUROPE: ITS STRUCTURE, FUNCTIONS AND ACHIEVEMENTS 1 (2d ed. 1961). The statute is reproduced in *id.* App. I at 257-66.

The original ratifying members were: Belgium, Denmark, France, Ireland, Italy, Luxembourg, Netherlands, Norway, Sweden and the United Kingdom. Subsequent accessions raised membership to eighteen; see Chapter 1 at 8-9.

common heritage and facilitating their economic and social progress"—
this aim to be pursued through the organs of the Council by "discussion
of questions of common concern and by agreements and common action
in economic, social, cultural, scientific, legal and administrative matters
and in the maintenance and further realisation of human rights and
fundamental freedom."[42]

How these aims are to be realized is left to the Council, which has
three principal organs: the Secretariat, the Committee of Ministers and
the Consultative Assembly. Each Member has one representative on the
Committee of Ministers. The Consultative Assembly is made up of
representatives from each Member in a number bearing some proportion
to the Member's population, but not less than three. This minimum
figure is designed to permit all major political parties of a Member to be
represented, and is possibly the most novel aspect of the Council. It is
intended to give each representative to the Assembly a European rather
than a national character.[43]

The Council from its inception has proposed conventions on a variety
of topics, including restraints on competition. At its first session in 1949,
the Consultative Assembly requested the Committee of Ministers to draw
up a convention for the control of international cartels.[44] The
Committee first referred this recommendation to the Organization for
European Economic Cooperation (OEEC). Later it consulted with the
Interim Commission of the International Trade Organization (ICITO)
with a view to undertaking a study of this problem in its European
context.[45] The result was a draft European Convention for the Control
of International Cartels, prepared by the Secretariat and submitted for
comment to all Member Governments in March 1951 and to the
Consultative Assembly shortly thereafter.[46]

---

[42] Ch. 1, Art. I(a), (b).

[43] Ch. V, Arts. 25 and 26. See ROBERTSON, *supra* note 41, at 41-44; Robertson,
The Council of Europe, 1949-1953, 3 INT'L & COMP. L. Q. 235, 240 (1954).

[44] ROBERTSON, *supra* note 41, at 117.

[45] *Id.* at 118.

[46] *Id.* The provisions of this draft are stated in L'HUILLIER, *supra* note 35, at
81-86, and in Günther, *supra* note 4, at 593-95. See also the summary, REPORT OF
THE DEP'T OF STATE TO THE SUBCOMM. ON MONOPOLY OF THE SEN.
SELECT COMM. ON SMALL BUSINESS, FOREIGN LEGISLATION CONCERN-
ING MONOPOLY AND CARTEL PRACTICES, 82d Cong., 2d Sess. 174-76 (Sub-
comm. Print No. 5, 1952) [hereinafter cited as REPORT OF DEP'T OF STATE].

One of the principal innovations of this Convention is the requirement that "all restrictive practices concluded between commercial enterprises within the jurisdiction of two or more High Contracting Parties shall be registered, that is, 'any combination, agreement or other arrangement between private or public commercial enterprises which involves or is likely to involve restrictive practices.' "[47] Registration is with a European cartel board created by the Convention.[48]

The general objective of the Convention, as stated in the Secretariat's memorandum accompanying the draft, is the control of restrictive business practices, rather than their complete suppression. The memorandum states, "In the control of cartels it is . . . necessary to find a solution which will, on the one hand, discourage restrictive practices which place profits before the public interest but, on the other hand, permit practices involving restriction that is necessary for survival."[49] To illustrate the latter, the memorandum refers to a situation where world supply of a commodity exceeds world demand. In that context it is stated that restrictions on production might be in the public interest: otherwise competition might lead to bankruptcy and unemployment.[50]

Like the Havana and ECOSOC texts before it, the Council's draft does not prohibit any restrictive business practices *per se.* It defines restrictive practices as those (1) which affect trade between Member States, and (2) which "restrain competition, limit access to markets or foster monopolistic control," listing, in almost the exact words of the Havana Charter, various types of practices as lying within this part of the definition.[51]

The draft also draws a distinction between "restrictive practices" and "harmful practices." "Harmful practices" are those which "have or are about to have, harmful effects on the expansion of production or trade necessary to maintain a high standard of living and of employment." A practice is not "harmful" unless the enterprise in question, either by itself or in combination with others, possesses effective control of the trade in one or more products between two or more Member countries.[52]

[47] L'HUILLIER, *supra* note 35, at 84.

[48] For the details, see *id.* at 84-85.

[49] Quoted in REPORT OF DEP'T OF STATE, *supra* note 46, at 175.

[50] *Id.*

[51] *Id.* For Havana Charter provisions, see text at notes 11-27 *supra.*

[52] *Id.*

The registration requirement is designed to make it easier to investigate the effect of a particular agreement—which the cartel board could do on its own motion or in response to a complaint.[53] Failure to register a registrable agreement would trigger an important sanction: it would raise a presumption that the agreement is "harmful," thus reversing the usual burden of proof.[54]

In a significant innovation, the draft provides that complaints may be lodged not only by Member States but also by any affected private party, whether person, enterprise or organization. Complaints directed against a public enterprise, however, may be lodged only by a Member State.[55]

After, but only after, there has been an investigation, the consultation procedure may be invoked. This is a departure from the procedure contemplated by the Havana and ECOSOC texts. Insistence that an impartial body establish the facts before any consultation takes place indicates, it has been suggested, an intention to treat harmful practices with greater severity than would have been the case under earlier draft Conventions.[56]

After an investigation is completed, the Commission is to hold a hearing at which it seeks to propose a settlement of the complaint to which all parties might subscribe. Whatever the outcome, a public report is to be made of the Commission's conclusions and recommendations.[57]

Under the draft, each Member obligates itself to encourage registration of agreements and to cooperate in specified respects. And in much the same terms and with the same provisos, each Member agrees "to take all possible measures, by legislation or otherwise, in accordance with its constitution or system of law and economic organization, to insure, within its jurisdiction, that private and public commercial enterprises do not engage in harmful practices."[58]

If no settlement can be reached or if a recommendation addressed to a Member by the Commission with a view to terminating the harmful

---

[53] L'HUILLIER, *supra* note 35, at 84-85, para. 299.

[54] *Id.* at 84, para. 299.

[55] *Id.* at 83, paras. 293-94.

[56] *Id.* at 84, para. 297.

[57] This procedure is described in REPORT OF DEP'T OF STATE, *supra* note 46, at 175-76.

[58] *Id.*

effects of a practice is not implemented, complainants would have a novel recourse to a European Court.[59] The Court, however, is the European Court provided for in the Convention for the Protection of Human Rights and Fundamental Freedoms, and a distinguished commentator has questioned its competence and impartiality in this field.[60]

This draft encountered, in its turn, a great deal of criticism. Some argued that the proposed procedure was too complex, and some feared that national sovereignty would be badly infringed.[61] Several Member Governments, noting that ECOSOC had started work in the same field, argued that a world-wide agreement would be preferable to a European convention, and concluded that it would be better to await the results of ECOSOC's work.[62] This proved to be the basis of the Committee of Ministers' action, and it instructed the Secretariat General to keep in touch with ECOSOC and to report in due course.[63]

The Report of the ECOSOC Ad Hoc Committee on Restrictive Business Practices was, as we have seen, first published in July 1953.[64] It was then submitted for comment to the Council of Europe, where the Committee of Ministers referred it to the Assembly. On September 23, 1954, the Assembly without debate adopted Opinion No. 10.[65] This Opinion described the ECOSOC report as containing "those minimum standards of any agreement in this field to which a large number of countries could agree," and proposed that GATT undertake further work in the field.[66]

The Council of Europe draft convention thus lapsed. As indicated in Chapter 7, however, a proposal for dealing with problems of extraterritorial enforcement of European national antitrust laws was advanced by the Legal Committee in a report to the Consultative Assembly in 1965, and is under study.

[59] See L'HUILLIER, *supra* note 35, at 86, para. 304.
[60] *Id.*
[61] Günther, *supra* note 4, at 594.
[62] *Id.*
[63] ROBERTSON, *supra* note 41, at 118.
[64] See text at note 33 *supra.*
[65] ROBERTSON, *supra* note 41, at 118.
[66] *Id.* Günther, *supra* note 4, at 594; L'HUILLIER, *supra* note 35, at 81, paras. 284-85.

D. GATT: 1954-1960

Prompted by the suggestion made during the deliberations of the Council of Europe and of ECOSOC that international control of restrictive business practices might be entrusted to GATT, that organization took up the matter at the Conference called to consider revising the General Agreement late in 1954. The German Government, and the Danish, Norwegian and Swedish Governments acting together, suggested that GATT use the ECOSOC draft articles as a starting point and initiate discussions of international means of controlling restrictive business practices, with an eye to undertaking such a role.[67]

After consideration of various methods of proceeding, the Contracting Parties eventually instructed the GATT Secretariat in 1957 to collect and analyze prevalent restrictive business practices, including any proposals for intergovernmental control of the harmful effects of such practices in international trade.[68] Professor J. L'Huillier of the University of Geneva was retained to make the study, and his memorandum, "Restrictive Business Practices," was submitted to the GATT Members in November 1958.[69]

On November 5, 1958, the GATT Members adopted a resolution recognizing that the activities of international cartels and trusts might hamper the expansion of world trade and of economic development in individual countries, and that international cooperation was needed to deal effectively with harmful restrictive business practices in international trade. A group was then appointed to study these problems and to make recommendations as to steps to be taken to deal with such restrictive practices.[70]

The group was able to agree that GATT should have some role in regulating restrictive business practices in international trade, but there was disagreement on the appropriate steps. As a consequence, the group was only able to suggest that the Contracting Parties should encourage direct consultations between themselves with a view to eliminating the harmful effects of particular restrictive practices.[71] It was also agreed

[67]Günther, *supra* note 4, at 579, 589-91; L'HUILLIER, *supra* note 35, at 97, paras. 342-43.

[68]Günther, *supra* note 4, at 591; L'HUILLIER, *supra* note 35, at 98, para. 350.

[69]This important study was published by GATT in May 1959.

[70]This resolution is summarized in Günther, *supra* note 4, at 591.

[71]*Id;* generally, see JACKSON, *supra* note 7 at 522 *et seq.*

that a group of experts should be designated, but there was a sharp difference over their functions.

The minority, including France and the Scandinavian Members, wished the experts to have discretionary power to take part in consultation between the Contracting Parties and to contribute a judgment as to the effects of the practice at issue. The majority wished the group of experts to make a more general study of the experience gained from consultations, and to report to the Contracting Parties on the nature and effect of international restrictive practices as developed by reports on individual disputes.[72]

This effort resulted in the Decision of November 18, 1960 of the Contracting Parties. The Preamble of the Decision recognizes that restrictive practices "may hamper the expansion of world trade and the economic development in individual countries and thereby frustrate the benefits of tariff reduction and removal of [quota] restrictions or may otherwise interfere with the objects" of GATT, and that international cooperation is needed. But it retreats immediately, with the words that "in present circumstances it would not be practicable for the Contracting Parties to undertake any form of control of such practices or to provide for investigation."[73]

The Decision offers the recommendation

> that at the request of any contracting party a contracting party should enter into consultations on such practices on a bilateral or a multilateral basis as appropriate. The party addressed should accord sympathetic consideration to and should afford adequate opportunity for consultations with the requesting party, with a view to reaching mutually satisfactory conclusions, and if it agrees that such harmful effects are present it should take such measures as it deems appropriate to eliminate these effects.[74]

If consultations take place, the Secretariat is to be advised of the nature of the complaint and the outcome, and is to transmit this information to all the Contracting Parties.[75] There is evidently no obligation to

---

[72] *Id.* at 591-92.

[73] Preamble, 9th Supp. B.I.S.D. 28.

[74] This language first appears in the Report by the Contracting Parties to GATT on June 2, 1960, L/1015, 9th Supp. B.I.S.D. 170, 173-74 (1961). The resolution proposed was adopted by the Contracting Parties, as noted, on November 18, 1960, 9th Supp. B.I.S.D. 28-29.

[75] *Id.* at 29, paras. (a), (b) and (c).

consult—only the recommendation that this be done. No special institutions or enforcement machinery are established, and the Decision makes no attempt to define the "business practices which restrict competition" which are to be dealt with.[76]

As the Kennedy Round of tariff reductions testifies,[77] GATT is capable of bringing about a very high degree of international cooperation. In view of the clear relation between obstacles to international trade which take the form of tariffs and quotas, and those in the form of restrictive business practices, GATT is probably the most logical instrumentality for international control of restrictive business practices. Yet GATT's first effort in this direction was markedly hesitant and indecisive.

E. Organization for European Economic Cooperation (OEEC): 1949; and the Organization for Economic Cooperation and Development (OECD): 1960

As pointed out in Chapter 1, in June 1947, Secretary of State Marshall used the occasion of an honorary degree at Harvard to outline proposals for the financing of European reconstruction by the United States—what came to be called the "Marshall Plan."[78] As a result, the Organization for European Economic Cooperation was formed on April 16, 1949. Though its aims were stated in broad terms—to permit economic cooperation, increase production, raise employment levels, reduce trade barriers, stabilize currencies and promote full convertibility—it served primarily as the institution through which the Marshall Plan was carried out.

Intergovernmental, rather than supranational, in concept, the OEEC had a Council to which each Member sent a representative. The

[76] Preamble, 9th Supp. B.I.S.D. 28.

[77] See generally OFFICE OF SPECIAL REPRESENTATIVE FOR TRADE NEGOTIATIONS, REPORT ON UNITED STATES NEGOTIATIONS, GATT 1964-1967 Conference (Vol. I: General Summary); *Hearings on the Foreign Policy Aspects of the Kennedy Round Before the Subcomm. on Foreign Economic Policy of the House Comm. on Foreign Affairs*, 89th Cong., 2d Sess. (1966); *id.*, 90th Cong., 1st Sess. (1967); Rehm, *Development in the Law and Institutions of International Economic Relations—The Kennedy Round of Trade Negotiations*, 62 AM. J. INT'L L. 403 (1968); DEP'T OF COMMERCE, KENNEDY ROUND REVIEWED (Nov. 20, 1967).

[78] N.Y. Times, June 6, 1947, at 2, col. 3.

experience in OEEC showed the participating governments the value of an international approach to economic problems and encouraged them to establish a more permanent institution in 1960—the Organization for Economic Cooperation and Development.

The important work in the field of restrictive business practices of OECD and of its predecessor OEEC—largely of an informational nature—is reviewed in the next chapter.

II. REGIONAL EUROPEAN ORGANIZATIONS

A. The European Communities

The first successful post-World War II experiment in attacking anti-competitive conditions on a supranational basis was the European Coal and Steel Community (ECSC), created by the Treaty of Paris signed on April 18, 1951, by Belgium, France, Germany, Italy, Luxembourg and the Netherlands.[79] Encouraged by the success of ECSC, the Member Countries established at Rome on March 25, 1957, two further Communities: the European Economic Community (EEC),[80] and the European Atomic Energy Community (Euratom).[81]

Chapter 1 reviews the legal and political bases for these important efforts at economic integration and points to the revolutionary development of the "supranational" form of institutional organization of these Communities. The provisions of the ECSC and EEC treaties dealing with restrictive practices are reviewed in Chapters 1 through 5, and their extraterritorial features are discussed in Chapters 2 and 3. These organizations are briefly mentioned here in order to emphasize their importance as a different kind of approach to international agreement in the control of restrictive business practices.

Where earlier and other efforts had failed or lapsed, ECSC and EEC have succeeded, and have earned in a short span of years an enduring and effective place in the legal control of national economies. A cardinal feature that gives to the Communities their "supranational" quality and that provides an essential adhesive is that Community antitrust law applies directly to private persons in the Member States and is supreme

[79] 261 U.N.T.S. 140 (1957).
[80] 298 U.N.T.S. 3 (1958).
[81] 298 U.N.T.S. 167 (1958).

over national laws of those states. This is a characteristic of a federal system, and whatever difficulties may arise in accommodating the two systems of law that necessarily exist side by side are capable of resolution within the legal structure of the Community. The result is a much more effective system for approaching international restrictive practices than any other yet designed.

B. The European Free Trade Association (EFTA)

When it became apparent that the EEC would become a reality, other European countries began to think in terms of establishing a free trade area. This was accomplished at the Stockholm Convention, which in 1959 established the European Free Trade Association composed of Austria, Denmark, Norway, Portugal, Sweden, Switzerland and the United Kingdom. Liechtenstein and Finland are also included through special arrangements.[82]

The Stockholm Convention was primarily directed at removing tariffs and quotas which Members had previously enforced against the trade of other Members. In this respect the Convention has been successful—reductions in tariffs and quotas among the Six of the EEC have been generally matched by reductions among the "Outer Seven" of EFTA.[83]

The Convention also deals with the problems of state subsidies, dumping, and competition. With respect to competition, Article 15 of the Convention provides:

1. Member States recognize that the following practices are incompatible with this convention insofar as they frustrate the benefits expected from the removal or absence of duties and quantitative restrictions on trade between Member States:
    (a) agreements between enterprises, decisions by associations of enterprises and concerted practices between enterprises which have as their object or result the prevention, restriction or distortion of competition within the Area of the Association;
    (b) actions by which one or more enterprises take unfair advantage of a dominant position within the Area of the Association or a substantial part of it.[84]

[82] 370 U.N.T.S. 3 (1960). A brief summary of EFTA is in 1 CCH COMM. MKT. REP. ¶110.

[83] 1 CCH COMM. MKT. REP. ¶110.02-.03.

[84] 370 U.N.T.S. 15 (1960).

Though this language clearly reflects the influence of Articles 85 and 86 of the Rome Treaty, the similarities between EFTA and EEC provisions are greatly outweighed by the very different approaches adopted by the two European groups to carrying out this policy. On the one hand, EEC Council Regulation 17, adopted to enforce Articles 85 and 86 of the Treaty of Rome, provides a detailed system of enforcement. The Stockholm Convention, however, provides little more than a statement of principle that competition is a fit subject for consultation among the members and for the expression of grievances.[85] Neither national law nor any private right or duty is altered.

The EFTA test is aimed at restrictive practices which, as stated in Article 15, para. 1, quoted above, "frustrate the benefits expected from the removal or absence of duties and quantitative restrictions on trade between Member States." The concept of "benefits" embraces not only increases in value and quantity of trade between EFTA Countries, but also other advantages, set out in Article 2, to be derived from cooperation between Member States.

Perhaps the fundamental difference between the Rome Treaty and the EFTA Convention arises in the nature of the obligations incurred by the Members. Where the Rome Treaty provides a system of legal prohibition of restrictive practices and abuses of dominant positions, the EFTA Convention regards these things as "incompatible with this convention," but not thereby prohibited.

III. SUMMATION AND ASSESSMENT

The foregoing review of post-World War II efforts to arrive at an international approach to restrictive business practices in international trade shows clearly enough that this kind of regulation has few friends who value it for its own sake. It has invariably been swept along as a part of some far grander design, and has shared the momentum of some far more ambitious plan. It has contributed little momentum of its own.

The first of these efforts was the world-wide effort of the Havana Charter which was designed to deal with the whole range of trade and employment. It failed for reasons largely unrelated to restrictive

[85] See *id.*, at 22-23, especially art. 31 on General Consultations and Complaint Procedures.

practices, yet it provided a constant point of reference on this and other subjects in the attempts that followed. Soon thereafter the United Nations ventured into this area on a similar world-wide basis through ECOSOC. Though modeled on the Havana Charter in important features, the ECOSOC draft stepped into new areas in its elaborate procedures with respect to complaints and in the broad powers conferred on the proposed Organization. It, too, lapsed.

The concurrent work of the Council of Europe was, as the name implies, on a regional basis. While its grandiose objectives ranged over the whole field of economic, social, cultural, scientific, legal and administrative matters with the goal of the "maintenance and further realization of human rights and fundamental freedoms," its work in the field of restrictive practices was modest and largely confined to proposals for the control of international cartels. The draft convention that it put forward included registration requirements and elaborate procedural steps in the handling of complaints. But its proposals foundered with those of ECOSOC and were soon put aside in the years of the far-reaching movements that produced ECSC and EEC.

The record continues with GATT taking up, with little effect, where ECOSOC had dropped out, and ends with the informal arrangements for consultation and exchange of information between governments finally concluded under the auspices of OECD, discussed in Chapter 9.

During these years the decisive roles were played by the economic and political pressures that brought about the creation of the European Communities. Apart from these European supranational systems of control, there is little evidence that during these years the governments of the world regarded international restrictive business practices as of sufficient moment to warrant conventions devoted to that subject.

If there are lessons for the future in the multitude of conferences and drafts that marked the post-World War II years, they may be found in comparisons that can readily be made between procedure by convention and by community.

Procedure by convention is an agreement between governments and necessarily has the disadvantage of the dispersion of the centers of authority. There are as many centers of decision as there are contracting parties. And there are as many methods of implementing the convention as there are national legislatures of the contracting parties. The community form, on the other hand, being supranational, is its own source of power, and like the national governments themselves operates directly upon the companies and individuals within its area. In the EEC, for example, Commission decisions are binding directly on enterprises and individuals and its orders, fines and penalties must be enforced by national governments without question. Under a convention, by contrast, there can be only reliance on the willingness of nations to enforce the obligations of the convention within their own territories.

The conventions resort to very broad phrases to define restrictive practices without clear or ascertainable standards, in contrast to the provisions made by the EEC for detailed definition through regulations and decisions. In several conventions, the criterion is whether a given practice is compatible with the objectives of the convention. This invites consideration of all kinds of factors and is an invitation to non-enforcement.

A striking contrast between the conventions and communities is that conventions usually contain blanket exemptions of government enterprises, whereas the communities—and EFTA, as well—subject all enterprises, whatever the system of ownership or administration, to the same competitive rules.

Further, intergovernmental conventions look to the member states to attack restrictive practices in international trade through their own processes. The conventions do not obligate the contracting parties to adopt enabling legislation or to modify existing "inadequate" legislation, although the Havana and ECOSOC texts come close to specifically calling for new legislation.

The convention procedure thus requires each contracting party of its own accord to attack restrictive practices affecting international trade. This raises very difficult questions. Is it enough if a state merely responds to a complaint from another Member State? The Havana/ECOSOC and Council of Europe Conventions specify that Member States should prevent restrictive business practices from occurring. EFTA condemns practices "incompatible with the Convention." If a state is under a duty to pursue "illegal" practices on its own initiative, this presupposes adequate investigation procedures. If a state is obliged to intervene only after another state has complained, it becomes that much more complicated to investigate restrictive business practices and to prove their illegality.

These inherent weaknesses stem from provisions in all texts that, to a greater or lesser degree, leave the sovereignty of member states intact. The communities, on the other hand, achieve effectiveness by compromising the sovereignty of the members.

CHAPTER 9

American and International
Consultation, Notification and
Cooperation Arrangements

The main thrust of antitrust enforcement, particularly as far as the United States and the European Common Market are concerned, has been along administrative and adjudicatory lines. Informal consultation procedures, however, have also played a role on the multinational scene. This chapter will set forth some of the more important types of consultation procedures which have been used or proposed, together with a short appraisal of their significance and efficacy.

First to be considered will be consultation procedures accompanying United States enforcement activity. These include internal consultations between the Department of Justice and the State Department, the cooperative arrangement between the United States and Canada, and the provisions on consultation in a large number of Treaties of Friendship, Commerce and Navigation. Procedures instituted or recommended by various international bodies will then be discussed.

I. CONSULTATION PROCEDURES OF THE UNITED STATES

A. Justice-State Department Consultation Procedures

An informal liaison procedure has been in operation for a number of years between the Departments of Justice and State.[1] This procedure is designed to implement the OECD program of multinational consultation described below, and bilateral consultations such as the United States-Canadian interchange also described below, and to coordinate antitrust

[1] The procedure is described briefly by government officials in *Hearings on International Aspects of Antitrust Before the Subcomm. on Antitrust and Monopoly of the Sen. Comm. on the Judiciary,* 89th Cong., 2d Sess., pt. 1, at 452, 493 (1966).

440

with foreign policy considerations. Under it, the Justice Department consults with the State Department's International Business Practices Division on all antitrust matters which appear to have foreign relations or foreign policy implications. In addition to advising the Justice Department on the bearing of proposed investigations and proceedings on the foreign relations and foreign policy of the United States, the State Department supplies it with information concerning the foreign aspects of such proceedings as to which State or its offices abroad have particular knowledge.

Whenever it is felt that consultations with foreign governments are called for, representatives of the Justice and State Departments may consult with officials of any foreign government whose interests may be affected by some investigation or proceeding pending in the Justice Department. Such consultations have been carried on with several foreign governments, including Canada.

The Department of Justice has established a Foreign Commerce Section in the Antitrust Division in order to conduct the foregoing liaison with the State Department and with foreign governments, as well as to implement the Justice Department's participation in the OECD Committee of Experts on Restrictive Business Practices, described below.

B. The Canadian-United States Consultation and Cooperation Procedure

Perhaps the best example of provision for continuing consultation and cooperation between two national antitrust authorities is an arrangement which has developed between Canada and the United States. This arrangement began in 1959 with an informal understanding between cabinet officers of the two nations, and in 1969 it was renewed and expanded in scope. Its origin lay in problems which have been described in a Canadian report in 1968 on foreign ownership of Canadian industry, prepared for the Privy Council Office by a task force headed by Professor Melville H. Watkins.

The Report states that:

> The overall level of foreign ownership in Canada is significantly higher than that for any other economically developed country and higher than for most of the underdeveloped countries.[2]

[2] REPORT OF THE TASK FORCE ON THE STRUCTURE OF CANADIAN INDUSTRY, FOREIGN OWNERSHIP AND THE STRUCTURE OF CANADIAN INDUSTRY 300 (1968) [hereinafter cited as the WATKINS REPORT].

This foreign investment is "overwhelmingly from the United States," which in 1964 accounted for $12,901 million out of $15,889 million total book value of non-resident owned direct investment in Canadian industry, or about four-fifths of the aggregate foreign ownership and control.[3] Ownership and control by American interests is particularly heavy in certain industries, amounting in 1963 to 97% of the capital employed in the manufacture of automobiles and parts, 90% in rubber, 54% in chemicals and 66% in electrical apparatus.[4]

This United States domination of much of Canadian industry is objected to in the Report on two main grounds: (1) it vests the focus of corporate decision-making in the American parent firm rather than in its Canadian subsidiary or branch;[5] and (2) it subjects the Canadian subsidiary or branch to the overlapping and divergent demands of a "higher peak" of sovereignty, the United States Government, to the detriment of national interests represented by the weaker sovereign, the Canadian Government.[6]

According to the Report:

> The successful intrusion of foreign law constitutes a direct erosion of the sovereignty of the host country insofar as the legal capacity of the latter to make decisions is challenged or suspended. Insofar as subsidiaries become instruments of policy of the home country rather than the host country, the capacity of the latter to effect decisions, *i.e.*, its political independence, is directly reduced.[7]

This extraterritorial extension of United States law into the areas of Canadian sovereignty has manifested itself not only in the field of antitrust law, but also in the curtailment of the freedom of Canadian firms to export to Communist countries, and in restrictions imposed on Canadian firms on behalf of United States balance-of-payments policy.[8] Hence the Watkins Report urges that, in the name of Canada's sovereignty, "positive steps be taken to block the intrusion into Canada of United States law and policy applicable to American-owned subsidiaries" with respect to these subjects.[9]

[3]*Id.* at 301.
[4]*Id.* at 11.
[5]*Id.* at 187 *et seq.*
[6]*Id.* at 312-13.
[7]*Id.* at 311.
[8]*Id.* at 312-22.
[9]*Id.* at 407.

Because of the interpenetration of the United States and Canadian markets—despite the presence of tariff barriers, businessmen often refer to the United States and Canada as a "common market"—American antitrust enforcement has had greater impact on Canadian companies (and hence on the Government of Canada) than on those of any other foreign country. A grand jury subpoena issued in connection with an investigation into newsprint supply so aroused Canada's provincial governments that first Ontario and later Quebec passed special legislation providing that records may not be removed pursuant to the order of a foreign court without prior governmental approval. And the Canadian Government addressed a formal note to the United States expressing irritation at this intrusion into Canadian affairs by the United States.[10]

The initial Canadian-United States consultation procedure grew out of official Canadian resentment resulting from the *Canadian Electronic Patents* case. The complaint in this case, filed by the United States in November 1958, alleged that General Electric Company, Westinghouse Electric Corporation and N.V. Philips' Gloeilampenfabrieken of Holland had conspired to restrain foreign commerce of the United States in violation of Section 1 of the Sherman Act.[11] Named as co-conspirators were the Canadian subsidiaries and affiliates of the defendants, a Canadian patent licensing organization known as Canadian Radio Patents Limited (CRPL), other foreign companies, and several additional United States companies, including Hazeltine Corporation, North American Philips Company, Radio Corporation of America (and the latter's Canadian subsidiary, RCA Victor Company Limited) and the Western Electric Company. CRPL, the patent licensing organization, had been organized by, and was owned in equal shares by, the Canadian

[10] See Chapter 3 at 121 for reference to the statutes. The episode is described in BREWSTER, ANTITRUST AND AMERICAN BUSINESS ABROAD 49 (1958). Extracts from published material may be found in INT'L LAW ASS'N, REPORT OF THE FIFTY-FIRST CONFERENCE (TOYKO) 565-92 (1964): extracts from the Memorandum dated May 26, 1947 of the Canadian Embassy in Washington to the U.S. State Department; debate in the House of Commons, Province of Quebec, on October 27, 1947, etc. Many of these documents will be found as exhibits to *Hearings Before the Subcomm. on Study of Monopoly Power of the House Comm. on the Judiciary,* 81st Cong., 2d Sess., ser. 14, pt. 6-B, Exhibits N2A-N2I (1950).

[11] Complaint, United States v. General Electric Co., Civil No. 140-157, filed Nov. 24, 1958 (S.D. N.Y.).

subsidiaries and affiliates of GE, Westinghouse, Philips, Western Electric, and an English company, The English Electric Company Limited.

The complaint alleged that the defendants, through their Canadian subsidiaries and affiliates, had entered into agreements under which they gave to CRPL the exclusive right to grant licenses under their Canadian patents applicable to radio and television home receivers, and that these patents were being licensed by CRPL under a standard form which required the licensee to manufacture only in Canada and to refrain from importing from the United States. The complaint also alleged that, in furtherance of the conspiracy, CRPL had refused to grant licenses for the importation of radio and television home receivers from the United States into Canada, and had threatened to institute and had instituted patent infringement suits against dealers undertaking to sell such U.S.-made receivers in Canada.

According to the complaint, the conspiracy had the effect of unreasonably restraining trade between the United States and Canada in radio and television apparatus; had virtually closed the Canadian market to United States manufacturers and exporters; had compelled United States companies which would otherwise have exported such apparatus to Canada to manufacture in Canada; and had deprived United States purchasers "of the benefits which would otherwise have resulted from increased production of such apparatus in the United States."

The issuance of the complaint was criticized by the Canadian authorities as an attempt to interfere with the operations of corporate entities created under and subject to Canadian law and to thwart the provisions of the Canadian statute dealing with the administration and utilization of Canadian patents.[12] The policy of the Canadian statute was stated to be not only to encourage inventions but to cause such inventions to be worked on a commercial scale in Canada.[13] The statute did not require the creation of a restrictive patent pool, but it did provide that a patent could be made subject to compulsory licensing or even revocation, if it were not being practiced in Canada on a commercial scale by the patentee or his licensees, or if such working of the patent were being prevented or hindered by importation from abroad

[12] See Financial Post, Toronto, vol. LII, No. 50, Dec. 13, 1958.
[13] Canadian Patent Act, Can. Rev. Stat. c. 203 (1952) *as amended,* 1953-54 c. 19, 1953-54, c. 40, s. 15; §67(3).

by the patentee or his licensees.[14] While many of the patents controlled by CRPL were being adequately utilized in that country, there was evidently serious concern on the part of the defendant companies that the relief sought by the Justice Department—the grant of broad import licenses on apparatus manufactured in the United States—might place the patents in jeopardy.

On the other hand, the United States Justice Department regarded the complaint as directed against export restraints by American corporations. According to Wilbur L. Fugate, Chief of the Foreign Commerce Section of the Antitrust Division of the Department of Justice:

> The complaint asserted that these companies directed their Canadian subsidiaries to participate in a Canadian Patent Pool and to put into the pool the patents corresponding to those held by the parent companies in the United States, with the purpose of keeping out the export of radios and TVs from the United States.[15]

Thus, the case could be regarded as an exercise of the sovereign power of the United States over its own nationals and over export trade emanating from within its borders.

It was in these circumstances that Canada's Minister of Justice and Attorney General, Hon. E. Davie Fulton, spoke to a meeting of the Antitrust Section of the New York State Bar Association in January 1959, where he attacked the *Canadian Electronic Patents* case as an inroad on Canadian sovereignty and urged restraint by the U.S. authorities

> ... in seeking from the courts, or applying, measures that interfere directly, substantially and deliberately with matters that are essentially matters of Canadian commerce within Canada.[16]

Fulton stressed the predicament of the international businessman, directing attention to the "increasingly lugubrious position of the poor director":

---

[14]*Id.* § § 67(2)(b) and 68(a) and (b).

[15]*Application of Antitrust Laws of the United States to International Trade—A Government Lawyer's View,* 13 PRAC. LAW. 27, 29 (1967).

[16]NEW YORK STATE BAR ASS'N, ANTITRUST LAW SYMPOSIUM 39, 49 (1959).

> Increasingly he would be stretched and shackled, as it were, over the international boundary, with Washington putting lighted splinters under his toenails and Ottawa tearing off his fingernails.[17]

The crux of his complaint was as to the practical, rather than international legal, problems created for Canada by such action on the part of the United States:

> . . . I do not put the issue upon the restricted and somewhat inconstant basis of international law. Even were it to turn out that, in coming to bear upon persons within the United States in order to bring about these results outside the United States, the antitrust cases could be supported upon some theory or view of public international law, that nevertheless would not be a practical solution to a practical problem.
>
> The situation, as it strikes us, can be put in this way: that these cases reach into affairs that we regard as relating to our own sovereignty. These cases involve on the part of the United States more interference, and apparent assertion of a right to interfere, in commercial projects in Canada than is fitting or acceptable between two friendly but independent countries.[18]

The *Canadian Electronic Patents* litigation was eventually settled by the entry of separate consent decrees agreed to by General Electric, Westinghouse and Philips respectively, under which each was enjoined from participating in any agreement which restricts any United States manufacturer from exporting home radio or television sets to Canada or from causing or consenting to any action of their foreign subsidiaries to restrict such importation.[19]

It also left as a legacy an informal agreement, worked out in 1959 by Fulton and William P. Rogers, then Attorney General of the United States, called the "Antitrust Notification and Consultation Procedure." The agreement was later described to a Senate committee, as follows:

---

[17]*Id.*

[18]*Id.* at 47.

[19]United States v. General Electric Co., Final Judgment, para. IV(A), (B), 1962 Trade Cas. ¶70,546 (S.D.N.Y. 1962); identical consent judgments were entered against Westinghouse and Philips, 1962 Trade Cas. ¶¶70,428 and 70,342. A subsequent case growing out of the same patent pool is Zenith Radio Corp. v. Hazeltine Research, Inc., 395 U.S. 100 (1969); on a counterclaim for damages and an injunction on behalf of Zenith against Hazeltine, the Court upheld the trial court's findings of violation of the Sherman Act as to restraints of exports to Canada, and remanded to the Court of Appeals for further proceedings on certain issues; see 418 F. 2d 21 (7th Cir. 1969), *cert. granted,* March 16, 1970.

The present understanding between the two countries is essentially as follows: Each country in enforcing its own antitrust or anticombines laws consults the other when it appears that the interests of the other country will be affected by such enforcement. The object of such consultations is to explore ways and means of avoiding situations which could give rise to objection or misunderstanding in the other country. While such consultations are designed to eliminate friction and to find a common approach to antitrust problems affecting both countries, it is understood that each country reserves the right and responsibility to take such action as it considers appropriate and necessary to enforce its own laws. The consultations do not give one country a veto over the actions of the [other] country. Nor does the fact that consultation has taken place necessarily imply approval of whatever action may be taken.

The arrangement is termed a Notification and Consultation Procedure for the reason that the circumstances or time schedule may permit not consultation but only notification prior to the institution of an antitrust action. The normal course, however, is that each country notifies the other prior to the institution of an antitrust suit which involves the interests or the nationals of the other country and permits time for consultation concerning the contemplated suit. While not required by the understanding, notification is given during the investigative phase whenever possible. In all cases each Government keeps the other informed of significant developments in negotiations with the parties and in litigation.

Further, each Department of Justice refers to the other complaints it has received that would be more appropriately handled by the other. In addition, each keeps the other informed of developments in its own country regarding general antitrust policy of common interest to antitrust officials.

A prerequisite of this Procedure is that the communications between the two governments will not be disclosed to any of the companies involved. Moreover, even the fact that there are consultations on a particular case is normally not publicized.[20]

The procedure initiated by this agreement has promoted greater harmony between Canadian and American antitrust authorities.[21] In November 1969, a Joint Statement was issued by Canadian Consumer and Corporate Affairs Minister Ron Basford and U.S. Attorney General John N. Mitchell.[22] The Statement said that the procedure had been the

[20]*Hearings on International Aspects of Antitrust Before the Subcomm. on Antitrust and Monopoly of the Sen. Comm. on the Judiciary,* 89th Cong., 2d Sess. 453-54 (1966).

[21]*Cf.* the WATKINS REPORT, at 333-35, concluding that the arrangement reduces tensions, but does not strike at the source of the difficulty, and recommending passage of laws similar to those in Ontario, Quebec and the Netherlands (see Chapter 3 at 121).

[22]U.S. Department of Justice Press Release, Nov. 3, 1969 (mimeo.).

forerunner of the cooperative procedure developed in 1967 by OECD, described below,[23] and that the OECD procedure (which calls for cooperation as well as notification) had in turn strengthened the Canadian-U.S. understanding.

Accordingly, in line with the OECD approach, the Statement announced a new stage in antitrust enforcement relations between the two countries, as follows:

> The two Cabinet members expressed the view that, in this time of expanding international trade, with special problems being posed by the multinational corporation, and when most industrial countries have enacted anti-monopoly laws, international cooperation in the antitrust area is essential for carrying out antitrust policy and to avoid conflicts in enforcement.
>
> In addition therefore to continuing the notification and consultation procedure in accordance with the 1959 understanding, the two Cabinet members agreed that the OECD recommendation of 1967 should be actively implemented as between Canada and the U.S. in relation to restrictive business practices in international trade. Notification and consultation will continue under both arrangements. Each country will, insofar as its national laws and legitimate interests permit, provide the other with information in its possession of activities or situations, affecting international trade, that the other requires in order to consider whether there has been a breach of its restrictive business practices laws.
>
> A primary concern would be cartel and other restrictive agreements and restrictive business practices of multi-national corporations affecting international trade. The enforcement agencies of the two countries, each within its own jurisdiction, will where possible coordinate the enforcement of the respective laws against such restrictive business practices.[24]

The Statement concluded by noting that a "close relationship has developed" between the enforcement agencies of the two countries, and that it is intended that more regular and frequent meetings will take place in the future.[25] In this instance, conflict seems to have generated not only a solution, but a move toward positive international cooperation.

C. "Restrictive Business Practices" Clauses in Treaties of Friendship, Commerce and Navigation

During and after World War II, the State Department endorsed antitrust as one of the important features of the foreign economic policy

---

[23] *Infra,* 455.

[24] Press Release, *supra* note 22 at 4-5.

[25] *Id.* at 5.

of the United States. Pursuant to this policy, there was inserted in various Treaties of Friendship, Commerce and Navigation (otherwise known as "FC&N Treaties") negotiated by the Department a clause whereby the United States and the foreign country agree to consult with respect to restrictive business practices in international trade and to take appropriate measures to eliminate the harmful effects of such practices.

This "restrictive business practices" clause first appears in the FC&N Treaty with Italy in 1948. It reads:

> The two High Contracting Parties agree that business practices which restrain competition, limit access to markets or foster monopolistic control, and which are engaged in or made effective by one or more private or public commercial enterprises or by combination, agreement or other arrangement among public or private commercial enterprises may have harmful effects upon the commerce between their respective territories. Accordingly, each High Contracting Party agrees upon the request of the other High Contracting Party to consult with respect to any such practices and to take such measures as it deems appropriate with a view to eliminating such harmful effects.[26]

Similar consultation clauses will be found in FC&N Treaties with nine other countries: Ireland (1950), Denmark (1951), Israel (1951), Greece (1951), Japan (1953), Germany (1956),[27] Korea (1956), Nicaragua (1956) and Pakistan (1959).

In practice, however, the consultation provided for in the restrictive business practices clause of the treaties has not proved to be an effective instrument for resolving international restrictive business practice disputes and relieving the tensions connected with national antitrust enforcement on the international scene. To be of major value in this connection, such consultations should be invoked before an investigation or lawsuit is instituted, and not after the event, as in the *Oldham* case and the *Grand Jury Investigation of the Shipping Industry,* discussed below. These clauses did, however, provide some precedent for development of the informal consultation procedure between the United States and Canada discussed above.

[26] Treaty of Friendship, Commerce and Navigation with the Italian Republic, Feb. 2, 1948, art. XVIII, para. 3, 63 Stat. 2255, 2282 (1949), T.I.A.S. No. 1965 (effective July 26, 1949).

[27] The FC&N Treaty concluded with Germany in 1956 contains a change in language of the first sentence of the above-quoted text: "Accordingly, each Government agrees upon the request of the other Government to consult with respect to any such practices and to take such measures, *not precluded by its legislation,* as it deems appropriate with a view to eliminating such harmful effect." (emphasis added) The italicized language merely reflects the fact that no signatory of

The restrictive business practices consultation clause is not present in the FC&N Treaties with the following countries: the Netherlands (1956), Ethiopia (1951), Iran (1955), Muscat and Oman (1958), Belgium (1961), Viet-Nam (1961), Luxembourg (1962), Togo (1966), Thailand (1966). In the case of the Netherlands, the explanation (never officially given) for the omission of the clause is that it was unacceptable to the Netherlands Government, doubtless because of the latter's traditional sensitivity in this area. At the time the treaty was being negotiated, the prominent Dutch company, N.V. Philips' Gloeilampenfabrieken, was being investigated by the Justice Department.

While the consultation provided for in the "restrictive business practices" clauses was intended by the State Department as a supplement to the existing judicial machinery for United States antitrust enforcement, parties involved in antitrust proceedings have on at least two occasions contended, unsuccessfully, that it was a substitute for such judicial enforcement. In *United States v. R. P. Oldham Co.,*[28] the Government had secured indictments against five United States corporations engaged in importing Japanese wire nails for resale on the West Coast of the United States, three officers of these companies, and an American subsidiary of a Japanese exporter. A number of Japanese firms were named as co-conspirators but not as defendants. The indictment alleged an elaborate allocation of customers in violation of Section 1 of the Sherman Act and Section 73 of the Wilson Tariff Act.

In a motion to dismiss the indictment, the defendants urged that the "restrictive business practices" clause of the FC&N Treaty of 1953 between the United States and Japan provided the exclusive remedy available to the United States in reaching the conspiracy charged in the indictment. But the District Court disagreed, holding that the clause "was intended to supplement the antitrust laws, not replace them."[29] It

---

an FC&N Treaty is obligated to take antitrust measures forbidden by its own laws—a proviso implicit in those treaties which do not contain the new language. Treaty of Friendship, Commerce & Navigation with the Federal Republic of Germany, Oct. 29, 1954, art. XVIII, para. 1, [1956] 7(2) U.S.T. 1839, T.I.A.S. No. 3593 (effective July 14, 1956).

[28] 152 F.Supp. 818 (N.D. Cal. 1957).

[29] *Id.* at 823; the court stated: ". . . The language of this Article is permissive rather than mandatory. If it had been intended that the Article should operate as a pro tanto revocation of the anti-trust laws, the Article could easily have been so

held further that even if the clause were intended to provide the exclusive remedy for antitrust violations, American importers and the wholly-owned American subsidiary of the Japanese company would have no standing to invoke it, as "the Treaty was not intended to exempt nationals from the sanctions of their own country's laws."[30]

Also *In the Matter of Grand Jury Investigation of the Shipping Industry,*[31] which resulted from a Congressional investigation in the late 1950's, grand jury subpoenas were issued to over 150 shipping companies. Japanese shipping lines moved to quash them on the theory that production of the papers would violate the restrictive business practices clause in the FC&N Treaty between the United States and Japan. The District Court noted that the Japanese ambassador had objected to the State Department, but had not based his objection specifically on the Treaty provision; instead his objections were directed against the production of documents located in Japan. The State Department had forwarded this communication to the District Court without comment,[32] but had indicated the willingness of the Justice Department to discuss specific problems of compliance. Referring to a State Department letter to the Senate Committee on Foreign Relations citing the *Oldham* decision, the court saw no Treaty violation.[33]

II. PROPOSALS AND ARRANGEMENTS FOR INTERNATIONAL CONSULTATION, NOTIFICATION AND EXCHANGE

A. Articles 2, 4 and 8 of the Draft Convention of the United Nations Ad Hoc Committee on Restrictive Business Practices

The substantive provisions of the draft convention prepared by the United Nations Ad Hoc Committee on Restrictive Business Practices and submitted to the Economic and Social Council (ECOSOC) on March 30, 1953, follow, with some minor changes, Chapter V of the 1948

---

worded. The tenor of the entire Treaty is *equal* treatment to nationals of the other party, not *better* treatment." *Id.*

[30] *Id.*

[31] 186 F.Supp. 298 (D.D.C. 1960).

[32] *Id.* at 320.

[33] *Id.*

Havana Charter for an International Trade Organization. This draft convention, which was not adopted, is discussed in Chapter 8.

There are three procedures in the Convention involving consultation, as follows:

1. Article 4 authorizes the proposed international agency, the Organization, to conduct and publish studies, on its own initiative or at the request of any U.N. Member country or organ or of any other intergovernmental body or agency, relating to—

> (i) general aspects of restrictive business practices affecting international trade;
> (ii) conventions, laws and procedures concerning, for example, incorporation, company registration, investments, securities, prices, markets, fair trade practices, trade marks, copyrights, patents and the exchange and development of technology insofar as they are relevant to restrictive business practices affecting international trade; and
> (iii) the registration of restrictive business agreements and other arrangements affecting international trade.[34]

In connection with such studies, the Organization may request information from Member countries, make recommendations to Member countries, and arrange for conferences of Member countries to discuss any matters relating to restrictive business practices affecting international trade.[35]

2. Under Article 2 of the draft convention, any Member country which considers itself harmed by a restrictive business practice may consult other Member countries directly or request the Organization to arrange for such consultations, with the view to reaching mutually satisfactory conclusions. Such consultations may take place regardless of whether the Organization is conducting or intends to conduct an investigation procedure of the type described in Article 3, except in the case of a public commercial enterprise acting independently. In the case of such public commercial enterprises, the investigation procedure may be resorted to only after the affected complaining Member country has employed the consultation procedure set forth in Article 2.[36] This

---

[34] REPORT OF THE AD HOC COMMITTEE ON RESTRICTIVE BUSINESS PRACTICES, ANNEX II, DRAFT ARTICLES OF AGREEMENTS, art. 4, Official Records: 16 U.N. ECOSOC Supp. 11, at 14, U.N. Doc. E/2380, E/AC. 37/3 (1953).
[35] *Id.*
[36] Arts. 2 and 3, *id.* at 13.

exception may have been motivated by the pragmatic consideration that prior resort to consultation procedure might facilitate adjustment of disputes and thereby make the investigative procedure unnecessary.

3. On the subject of restrictive practices relating to services, the Ad Hoc Committee recognized the need for special procedures. Article 8 provides that services such as transportation, telecommunications, insurance and the commercial service of banks are substantial elements of international trade, and that restrictive business practices with respect to such services might have harmful effects on that trade. However, the Committee felt that the Organization could play only a limited role in this area. Hence, it provided that, before any matter relating to services was referred to the Organization, a Member country which considered that its interests were adversely affected by a restrictive business practice of a public or private enterprise of another country, might submit a written statement explaining the situation to the other country. Countries receiving such a statement were obligated to give sympathetic consideration to the statement and to such proposals as might be made by the affected country, and to "afford adequate opportunities for consultation, with a view of effecting a satisfactory adjustment." Only if, after consultation, no adjustment could be effected, would the matter in question be referred to the Organization. The Organization would either transfer the matter to the appropriate intergovernmental body or agency or, if no such body or agency existed, make recommendations itself and promote international agreement with respect to measures designed to remedy the situation.[37]

B. The GATT Activity on Restrictive Business Practices

The work of GATT is discussed in Chapter 8 and we note here only that this work never came to effective fruition. GATT's final effort in the restrictive practice field was its Decision of November 18, 1960, making the modest recommendation that the Members should, at the request of a Member, consult with each other with a view to the elimination of the harmful effects of particular restrictive practices. The Decision imposed no obligation to consult, and in fact, no consultations have taken place pursuant to it.

[37] Art. 8, *id.* at 15.

C. OEEC and OECD Informational and Cooperative Procedures

The most important current instrumentality for minimizing the friction surrounding the international application of antitrust laws is the Committee of Experts on Restrictive Business Practices of the Organization for Economic Cooperation and Development (OECD). OECD, whose origin and functions have been previously described,[38] is a treaty organization of nineteen European countries, together with Canada, Japan and the United States. The Committee of Experts is composed of delegations from each of the governments of the Member countries. Although the European Communities are not themselves Members, their own constituent nations are all Members, and representatives of the Commission's staff attend the meetings.

The OECD committee grew out of a predecessor committee, the Group of Experts on Restrictive Business Practices, established in 1953 by the European Productivity Agency of the Organization for European Economic Cooperation (OEEC). This group consisted of officials of Member countries in charge of carrying out national policies on restrictive business practices. They served as a forum for a broad exchange of information on the subject of restrictive business practices, an exchange which was considered useful by Member countries of the OEEC that were contemplating the adoption of novel or amendatory legislation on the matter of restrictive business practices.

The most important contribution of the OEEC Group of Experts was the initiation of the multi-volume looseleaf Guide to Legislation on Restrictive Business Practices, the revision and continuing publication of which is being maintained under the auspices of the successor OECD Committee of Experts. The Guide includes relevant legislation currently in force in Austria, Belgium, Canada, Denmark, France, Germany, Ireland, Italy, Japan, Norway, the Netherlands, Portugal, Spain, Sweden, Switzerland, the United Kingdom, the United States, the European Coal and Steel Community, and the European Economic Community. It is kept up-to-date by supplements, including amendments, new legislation and other information concerning the laws of Member countries. Monographs were also prepared for the OEEC Group of Experts by

---

[38] See Chapter 1, at 3-5; also see this chapter, *supra* at 447-48 for discussion of relationship between Canadian-American antitrust cooperation and OECD.

outside consultants on the subjects of resale price maintenance and freedom of entry.[39]

The successor Committee of Experts on Restrictive Business Practices of OECD, established in 1961, meets two times yearly, and its subcommittees may meet more often. The American delegation to the Committee has included representatives of the Antitrust Division of the Justice Department, of the State and Commerce Departments, and of the Federal Trade Commission.[40] The Committee's terms of reference include the following:

> To review developments in the field of restrictive business practices both in individual countries and in international or regional organisations, such as new legislation, or application of existing legislation;
> To examine and compare laws relating to competition in individual countries and the basic principles underlying them and to study particular problems arising from the nature or application of such laws;
> To examine particular problems arising from the existence of monopolies and restrictive business practices;
> To promote the standardisation of terminology concerning restrictive business practices;
> To develop agreed definitions of specific restrictive business practices which may have an adverse effect on international trade and, on the basis of such definitions, review developments in this field.[41]

The Committee has prepared a comparative summary of the restrictive business practice laws of Europe and North America (1964), a glossary of terms relating to restrictive practices (1965), and studies of information agreements (1967) refusal to sell (1969), and control of market power (1970).

On October 10, 1967, the Council of the OECD adopted a recommendation developed by the Committee of Experts, on "Cooperation Between Member Countries on Restrictive Business Practices Affecting International Trade."[42] This recommendation for closer co-

[39] GAMMELGARD, RESALE PRICE MAINTENANCE, OEEC Proj. No. 238 (1958); MUNTHE, FREEDOM OF ENTRY INTO INDUSTRY AND TRADE, OEEC Proj. No. 259 (1958).

[40] The work of the OECD Group of Experts and the predecessor OEEC group is described in the testimony of Acting Assistant Attorney General Zimmerman and Assistant Secretary of State Solomon, *Hearings, supra* note 20, at 455, 494 (1966).

[41] OECD Observer, No. 6, Oct. 1963.

[42] OECD Doc. (C) (67) 53 (Final); reprinted in Appendix to Markert, *Developments in International Antitrust Cooperation*, 13 ANTITRUST BULL. 355, 370-72

operation between Member governments has such far-reaching implications both for national antitrust policy development and enforcement and for the businesses that may be affected that it is quoted here in full:

RECOMMENDATION OF THE COUNCIL OF OECD CONCERNING CO-OPERATION BETWEEN MEMBER COUNTRIES ON RESTRICTIVE BUSINESS PRACTICES AFFECTING INTERNATIONAL TRADE

Adopted by the Council at its 149th Meeting on 5th October, 1967 (*)

The Council,

Having regard to Article 5(b) of the Convention on the Organisation for Economic Co-Operation and Development of 14th December, 1960;

Having regard to the Resolution of the Council of 5th December, 1961, concerning Action in the Field [of] Restrictive Business Practices and the Establishment of a Committee of Experts [OECD/C(61)47(Final)];

Having regard to the Report by the Committee of Experts on Restrictive Business Practices concerning Co-operation Between Member Countries on Restrictive Business Practices Affecting International Trade [C(67)53];

Recognising that the diminution of free competition through restrictive business practices may have an adverse effect on achievement of the trade-expansion and economic-growth aims of Member countries as set out in Article 1 of the Convention;

Recognising that closer co-operation between Member countries is needed in this field but that the present powers of the authorities of Member countries to co-operate are limited to various degrees;

Recognising, moreover, that the unilateral application of national legislation, in cases where business operations in other countries are involved, raises questions as to the respective spheres of sovereignty of the countries concerned;

Considering therefore that a closer co-operation between Member countries in the form of consultations, exchanges of information and co-ordination of efforts on a fully voluntary basis should be encouraged, it being understood that such co-operation should not in any way be construed to affect the legal positions of Member countries with regard to such questions of sovereignty, and in particular the extra-territorial application of laws concerning restrictive business practices, as may arise;

I.–Recommends to the Governments of Member countries

(*) The Delegate for Switzerland abstained.

(1968); also in *Hearings on International Aspects of Antitrust Before the Subcomm. on Antitrust and Monopoly of the Senate Comm. on the Judiciary,* 90th Cong., 1st Sess. 75 (1967).

1. (a) That in so far as their laws permit, when Member countries undertake under their restrictive business practices laws an investigation or a proceeding involving important interests of another Member country, they should notify such Member country in a manner and at a time deemed appropriate. Notification should, where appropriate, take place in advance in order to enable the proceeding Member country, while retaining full freedom of ultimate decision, to take account of such views as the other Member country may wish to express and of such remedial action as the other Member country may find it feasible to take under its own laws to deal with the restrictive business practice.

(b) That where two or more Member countries proceed against a restrictive business practice in international trade, they should endeavour to co-ordinate their action in so far as appropriate and practicable under national laws.

2. To supply each other with any information on restrictive business practices in international trade which their laws and legitimate interests permit them to disclose.

3. To co-operate in developing or applying mutually beneficial methods of dealing with restrictive business practices in international trade.

II.–Instructs the Committee of Experts on Restrictive Business Practices to keep under review developments connected with the present Recommendation and to examine periodically the progress made in this field.

The purpose of advance notification of an antitrust investigation or proceeding to countries having important interests that will be affected is thus to enable the proceeding Member country "to take account of such views as the other Member country may wish to express and of such remedial action as the other Member country may find it feasible to take under its own laws to deal with the restrictive business practice."[43] This is only a recommendation to the governments, however, and then only insofar as the laws of the proceeding country permit, "full freedom of ultimate decision" being retained with respect to the investigation or proceeding.

The recommendation for coordination of national action where two or more Member countries proceed against restrictive business practices in international trade (I. 1.(b) of the Council's Recommendation) represents an effort to harmonize and strengthen national approaches to international antitrust problems. Such coordination, however, is to take place only "in so far as appropriate and practicable under national laws," raising the troublesome question whether the national antitrust authori-

[43] *Id.* para. I(a), at 372.

ties have the power or discretion to accommodate their respective national antitrust enforcement policies to the stronger or weaker policies, as the case may be, of the other countries involved.

The Council's recommendation for the exchange of information on restrictive business practices in international trade is limited to information which the "laws and legitimate interests" of the Member countries "permit them to disclose." Much of the information that is furnished to national antitrust agencies is supplied on a confidential basis, and different national governments may have differing views on whether legitimate business interests permit the disclosure of business information supplied to them.[44] Hence, it seems that national governments will probably make unequal contributions to the pool of information available to the Committee of Experts.

There are no explicit limitations on the recommendation that Member countries cooperate as to mutually beneficial methods of dealing with restrictive business practices in international trade. However, it must be assumed that differing national policies on competition, on the relationship of government and business, and on the concept of national sovereignty, as well as differing procedures for antitrust enforcement and other similar factors will play a significant role in determining the extent to which cooperation will take place.

The implementation of the recommendation will take time, and further analysis of its implications for international business and for national antitrust policy will have to await the development of specific procedures by the Committee of Experts. It is in order, however, to take note of the specific interest of the United States antitrust authorities in the development of the machinery contemplated by the recommendation. At the hearings held by the Subcommittee on Antitrust and Monopoly of the Senate Judiciary Committee on International Aspects of Antitrust, the Chairman, Senator Philip A. Hart, suggested the establishment of an investigative office or clearing house, under the aegis of the OECD, for the purpose of dealing with cartel and monopoly problems and developments.[45] Edwin M. Zimmerman, at that time First

---

[44] See Markert, *supra* note 42, at 361 n.13. See also McAllister, *Current Developments in United States Antitrust Law and Restrictive Business Practice Law in Western Europe,* 1968 SYMPOSIUM ON PRIVATE INVESTORS ABROAD 109, 127-35.

[45] Statement of Sen. Hart, *Hearings, supra* note 20, at 462-63.

Assistant and later Assistant Attorney General in charge of the Antitrust Division, expressed agreement that some sort of clearing house for foreign merger activities by United States firms would be worthwhile.[46] Assistant Secretary of State Anthony M. Solomon said that he would look into the possibilities of such an agency. After reviewing the failure of international efforts to achieve greater harmony in antitrust legislation, Mr. Solomon stated:

> [t]he answer, at least for the near future, may be a "system" of informal cooperation among as many governments as feasible, perhaps patterned on the United States-Canadian procedure, operating under the aegis of, and regularly reviewed in, a multi-lateral organization such as the OECD. Its basic objectives would be to deal with cartel or monopoly problems and foreign-relations problems as well.[47]

Mr. Solomon pointed out that, through informal cooperation, the OECD countries would be able to see more clearly the ways in which national legislation should be supplemented or revised to facilitate effective intergovernmental cooperation and to lessen disparities of national legislation and regulations that complicate legitimate and wholesome international business.[48] The system of cooperation envisaged by the OECD Council's Recommendation of October 5, 1967 is of the type envisaged by Mr. Solomon.

CONCLUSION

It is difficult to measure the cumulative impact of the foregoing machinery on the reduction of the potential for international friction and controversy in the administration of antitrust laws. Under the OECD program, individual countries retain, on the one hand, "full freedom of ultimate decision" to initiate antitrust investigations and proceedings and, on the other, their legal position with regard to questions of national sovereignty and the extraterritorial application of laws concerning restrictive business practices. Moreover, countries are limited to supplying each other only with the information "their laws and

---

[46] Zimmerman, *id.* at 496.
[47] Solomon, *id.* at 457.
[48] *Id.* at 458.

legitimate interests permit them to disclose." To the extent that these considerations enter into both informal bilateral consultation procedures and the multinational system of international cooperation contemplated by the OECD Council's Recommendation of October 5, 1967, progress will necessarily be slow in removing or reducing through this means the potential for international friction in antitrust law.

INDEX

Index